9-11: THE ULTIMATE TRUTH

Books by **Laura Knight Jadczyk**

Amazing Grace – An
Autobiography of the Soul

The Secret History of the World

**The High Strangeness of
Dimensions, Densities, and the
Process of Alien Abduction**

The Wave – Books 1-4

911: The Ultimate Truth

Laura Knight-Jadczyk

With
Signs of The Times Editors
Scott Ogrin
Joe Quinn
Henri Sy

Preface by
Pentagon Strike Creator
Darren Williams

Red Pill Press
2005

First Edition
Copyright 2002-2005, Laura Knight- Jadczyk
Research Sponsored by Quantum Future Group, Inc.
P. O. Box 241, Rescue, CA 95672
ISBN 0-9764064-7-0
Portions of this book were published in 2002 as *The Occult Significance of 9-11*

Printed in Canada

Table of Contents

Acknowledgements

We are indebted to the many people around the world who have been working on uncovering the truth about 9/11. We draw from their work in the first part of this book. In particular, we would like to acknowledge the work of Thierry Meyssan and his team at Réseau Voltaire for the books *9/11 The Big Lie* (*L'Effroyable imposture*) and *Pentagate* and the work of the fine folks at www.physics911.net.

In the days following September 11, 2001, as we pondered the question "Qui bono", or "who benefits?", the answer that began to emerge as the obvious solution was "Israel". Nevertheless, we assumed the facts on the ground described by the mainstream media were pretty much what had happened in logistical, physical terms. It was only after reading *9/11 The Big Lie* that we saw that there was a mountain of evidence to indicate that the official story did not stand up to careful forensic scrutiny either in the hard data or in the naming of the culprits.

We would also like to recommend David Ray Griffin's *The New Pearl Harbor* as an introduction to a critical analysis of what really happened on September 11, 2001. Griffin holds a carefully circumspect position in his analysis of the flaws in the official story, yet by piling up point after point where the official story collapses against the facts, he leads his readers to the inescapable conclusion that there must have been state sponsorship of the attacks. However, having taken the case that far, Griffin makes no accusations nor any attempt to speculate on what might really have happened that day. It is an excellent primer for those who still accept the fairy tale told by the mainstream American media.

We would also like to acknowledge the work of Gerard Holmgren, Dave McGowan, Killtown for his Pentalawn pages, and The Center For Cooperative Research.

Finally, and most important of all, we would like to thank Andrew M. Lobaczewski for his amazing work and timely input.

Preface

Darren Williams

Typing "9-11 conspiracy" into a popular internet search engine returns over 200,000 hits, just one indication that the events of September 11th, 2001 are some of the most controversial in recent history.

The Signs of the Times *Pentagon Strike Presentation* was created following two-and-a-half years of research into the events of 9/11. The attack on the Pentagon was selected as the subject of the presentation due to the overwhelming evidence contradicting the "official story" presented by the United States Government and subsequently promulgated worldwide by mainstream media organisations.

Drawing on her exhaustive research into the events of 9/11, in addition to over 30 years of research covering a multitude of fields, Laura Knight-Jadczyk and Signs of the Times' *9-11:The Ultimate Truth* presents an in-depth and often shocking expose of the how and the why of the 9/11 attacks and the implications they hold for the entire human race.

9-11:The Ultimate Truth begins with a detailed examination of the evidence for each of the events of 9/11 in turn, focusing on the Pentagon attack in particular, and presents a convincing hypothesis of what really happened to each of the flights on that day. For the first time ever, the authors reveal the possibility of an Israeli double-cross that saw the Neo-con plans take an unexpected and dramatic turn of events as the day unfolded.

Laura's narrative then leads the reader from the events of 9/11 into a labyrinth of Counter Intelligence cover-ups, Mind Programming, Ethnic Specific Weapons and Jewish and Christian "end times" prophecy, until we are brought face to face with "the most dangerous idea in the world". What at first might appear to the reader as intriguing, yet seemingly discontinuous threads, Laura skilfully weaves into a millennia-long panorama that will startle the reader in its implications.

In any given situation, our ability to effect real change in our lives, and therefore on our planet, is limited only by our ability to recognise truth from lies. In essence, the question, "what can anyone do?" can only be answered if one has a sufficiently objective knowledge base. It is in this respect, at a time when the world population is perched on the edge of an abyss, that the truth unveiled in Laura Knight-Jadczyk and Signs of the Times' *9-11:The Ultimate Truth* may yet earn itself a place in history as one of the most important books ever written.

It is indeed a testament to the ability and resolute will of the authors, and the quality of the analysis presented, that what was once consigned to the realm of "conspiracy" and subjective theory now exists as part of the visible reality.

This inspirational work holds enormous potential for the future of the human race. Whether or not that potential is realised will be determined by the choices made by each and every individual who reads and sincerely considers its message.

Darren Williams *is the author of the Flash animation* Pentagon Strike, *the powerful exposé of the problems of the official story of what happened that day at the headquarters of the US military.* Pentagon Strike *has been seen by at least 500 million people around the world. It can be found at www.pentagonstrike.co.uk.*

Introduction

"It must be remembered that the first job of any conspiracy, whether it be in politics, crime or within a business office, is to convince everyone else that no conspiracy exists. The conspirators' success will be determined largely by their ability to do this." [Gary Allen, *None Dare Call It Conspiracy*]

The truth about 9/11 is obviously of central importance.

We're incessantly reminded by prominent politicians and voices in the mass media that "September 11th changed everything".

9/11 has become the defining event of the new century, used to justify an unprecedented surge in militaristic and repressive policies within the USA and elsewhere.

Yet despite the evident significance of 9/11, there has been an astonishing lack of informed discussion in the mainstream media about what really took place on that fateful day.

Many anomalies and suspicious leads in the official story, curiosities which the mass media often helped put into the public domain in the first place, have not been followed up or given the attention they clearly merit. The obvious question: "why is the US Administration so averse to a transparent public inquiry?" has scarcely been asked.

Indeed, the western mass media's reluctance to question the official version of 9/11 critically - and the key role played by elements of the media in actively propagating this unlikely story - calls for explanation in its own right. Any objective investigation of 9/11 must account for the extraordinary phenomenon of gross media bias and apparent blindness." [Physics 9-11 net[1]]

Within hours of the September 11, 2001 attack, the blame was being laid at the doorstep of Osama bin Laden's cave in the mountains of Afghanistan. We were told 19 Arab men, mostly Saudi nationals, were the hijackers, and for some obscure reason, Saudi National Hijackers being the culprits justified the 2003 invasion and occupation of Iraq.

Believing the "official story," many, if not most, United States citizens believe that Saddam Hussein was responsible for 9/11, despite the fact that there has *never been any evidence* of a link between Osama bin Laden and Hussein, while there is a mountain of evidence that there was no love lost between the secular Saddam and the religious zealot bin Laden.

---

[1] http://www.physics911.net/index.htm

Furthermore, there has *never been any proof* offered that any of the 19 men accused of the hijackings were even on the planes that day, not to mention the fact that a number of them have been reported to have been elsewhere on that day, and *some of them are actually still alive* according to mainstream news reports.

The Bush administration provided no proof that Saddam Hussein had weapons of mass destruction that he was preparing to use against the U.S., or might *prepare* to use against the U.S., or might *think* about creating in order to prepare to use against the U.S. We now know, to the contrary, that he had no weapons of mass destruction, nor did he have the means of creating them due to years of international sanctions that had already reduced Iraq to a state of military and economic vulnerability.

We confront a strange problem: If so many people believe a story for which there is not only *no* evidence, but in fact, the real evidence points in a different direction, why is this so? How can so many people be wrong? We will present a scientific study that will answer this question in this book.

In the spring of 2002, after the publication of Thierry Meyssan's book, *9-11 The Big Lie*, many readers of our website[2] deluged us with emails asking what we thought about the evidence that a Boeing 757 did *not* hit the Pentagon.

Up to that moment in time, there was no question in our minds that the physical events of 9-11 happened exactly as described by the media and the Bush Administration. Of course, we had certain ideas as to *who* might be behind those events, but the important point is that we did not question the "facts on the ground" - the physical logistics - of the event.

Certainly, because this was our belief, we began to search for data with something of a bias. I[3] was quite certain that the "no-Boeing" theory was a psy-ops[4] program designed to set up people who were asking "whodunnit" so that when the "proof of the Boeing" hitting the Pentagon was finally unveiled, everyone who suspected an "inside job" would look completely stupid and all related conspiracy theories would be thoroughly squashed. In that way, all other questions - mainly *Qui Bono* - would be silenced. In fact, I expected such a revelation any day as the "No Boeing" theory raced around the globe via the internet and Meyssan's book became a best seller. I began to wonder what was really going on when the "big revelation designed to make everybody look stupid and stop asking questions" never happened. Could it be possible that there was *no* proof that a Boeing 757 hit the Pentagon?

---

[2] http://www.signs-of-the-times.org
[3] Laura Knight-Jadczyk
[4] Intelligence organization operations to convey selected information and indicators to audiences to influence their thinking, emotions and behavior.

I also must admit that I did not consider it within the realm of possibility that such a "switch" could have been perpetrated upon the American public, *much less the media*. [5]Surely no criminal element within our own government would be crazy enough to fake a Terrorist attack on the Pentagon and try to pass it off as a Boeing and expect to get away with it! What a lunatic idea! And yet, as I continued to dig through the piles of information, both pro and con, it was beginning to look as though that was exactly what had happened.

But that idea was so crazy, so impossible, so unbelievable that - like most other average people - I wanted to resist it tooth and nail. And certainly there *seemed* to be many good reasons to resist such an idea the main one being that how could such a theorized "conspiracy" actually exist?

The term "conspiracy theory" has been tootled for a number of years in such a way that the mere pronouncing of the words acts to turn off the thinking capacities of the average citizen of Western nations. The "conspiracy theory" of history has been dismissed repeatedly and pejoratively by US politicians and the media.

I find that to be curious. And when I am curious, I go looking for an answer. The first thing I thought about was the fact that the word "conspiracy" evokes such a strong reaction in all of us - me included - nobody wants to be branded as a "conspiracy theorist". It just isn't "acceptable". It's "un-scientific" or it's evidence of mental instability. Right?

In fact, I think that the very reading of the word even produces certain physiological reactions: a slight acceleration of the heartbeat, and perhaps a quick glance around to make sure that no one is watching while you simply read the word silently.

I asked myself *why* the word evokes such an instantaneous emotional reaction. Have *you* ever wondered why it stimulates such a strong "recoil"? After all, it is only a word. It only describes the idea of people in "high places" thinking about things and doing things that manipulate other people to produce benefits for themselves. The act of conspiring is an ancient and well documented part of history. In the Bible, the sons of Jacob conspired to sell their brother into slavery. They actually wanted to kill him, but one brother would have none of that, so the plan changed. Brutus et al conspired to do in Julius Caesar. The instigators of the

---

[5] I admit to being somewhat naïve. I knew the media could be "swayed" this way or that by government or corporate influence, but I was not yet ready to think that it could be as completely controlled as has been demonstrated since 9/11. I do want to mention that I have a friend who is a program director for a major radio station in the US. He visited us one evening in late 2000 and said that he was concerned that "something was up." He had noted that nearly all the radio stations in the US were being bought up by a single company and all the programs were going to be "canned."

American Revolution were conspirators. In 1934, Irénée du Pont and William S. Knudsen (president of General Motors) conspired with friends of the Morgan Bank to effect a coup d'etat against Franklin D. Roosevelt. They had a mercenary army of terrorists and the only reason they were undone was because they approached Gen. Smedley Butler to lead the coup. Butler didn't like Roosevelt's "New Deal," was, however, a decent human being. He immediately informed on the conspirators. Roosevelt knew that arresting the conspirators would create a worse crisis in the midst of the depression, so instead he decided to leak the story to the press which downplayed it as a "ridiculous rumor." However, knowing that they were unmasked, the plotters left the country. Congress appointed a special commission to investigate the matter, but we can surmise that powerful pressure was put on the committee to not come up with the truth. The congressional committee dragged the process out for four years and finally issued a report for "restricted circulation" only. The report stated that "certain persons made an attempt to establish a fascist organization in this county" and added that the committee "was able to verify all the pertinent statements made by General Butler."[6]

Journalist Jim Marrs writes:

> The fact that this attempted overthrow of the government is not mentioned in history texts illustrates the deficiency of this nation's public education in such matters, thanks to a mass media more concerned with "Mickey Mouse" topics than investigative news. It is ironic that today the Disney empire includes many news media organizations.

> In the preface to their book *Fifty Greatest Conspiracies of All Time*, authors Jonathan Vankin and John Whalen point out "The 'Disney' version of history could just as easily be called the '*New York Times* version' or the 'TV news version' or the 'college textbook version.' The main resistance to conspiracy theories comes not from the people on the street, but from the media, academia, and government - people who manage the national and global economy of information."[7]

The New York Times version has recently been openly exposed for the Disney-esque nature of its reporting; reporter Judith Miller spent 85 days in jail and the assistant to the Vice President, I. Scooter Libby was indicted for "lying" about "leaking" the identity of CIA agent, Valerie Plame. Considered in light of the above situation that Roosevelt found himself in, one has to wonder exactly what is really behind the current "Plamegate" scandal.

Richard M. Dolan studied at Alfred University and Oxford University before completing his graduate work in history at the University of Rochester, where he was a finalist for a Rhodes scholarship studying U.S.

---

[6] Higham, Charles, (1983): Trading with the Enemy: An Expose of the Nazi-American Money Plot 1933-1949; Delacorte Press, NY, p. 99

[7] Marrs, Jim, (1997), Alien Agenda; Harper Collins, NY, p. 570-571

Cold War strategy, Soviet history and culture, and international diplomacy. (The same subjects Condoleezza Rice is supposed to be an "expert" on). He has written about "conspiracy" in the following way:

"The very label [conspiracy] serves as an automatic dismissal, as though no one ever acts in secret. Let us bring some perspective and common sense to this issue.

The United States comprises large organizations - corporations, bureaucracies, "interest groups", and the like - which are conspiratorial by nature. That is, they are hierarchical, their important decisions are made in secret by a few key decision-makers, and they are not above lying about their activities. Such is the nature of organizational behavior. "Conspiracy", in this key sense, is a way of life around the globe.

Within the world's military and intelligence apparatuses, this tendency is magnified to the greatest extreme. During the 1940s, [...] the military and its scientists developed the world's most awesome weapons in complete secrecy... [...]

Anyone who has lived in a repressive society knows that official manipulation of the truth occurs daily. But societies have their many and their few. In all times and all places, *it is the few who rule*, and the few who exert dominant influence over what we may call *official culture*. [...] All elites take care to manipulate public information to maintain existing structures of power. It's an old game.

America is nominally a republic and free society, but in reality an empire and oligarchy, vaguely aware of its own oppression, within and without. I have used the term "national security state" to describe its structures of power. It is a convenient way to express the military and intelligence communities, as well as the worlds that feed upon them, such as defense contractors and other underground, nebulous entities. *Its fundamental traits are secrecy, wealth, independence, power, and duplicity.*

Nearly *everything of significance* undertaken by America's military and intelligence community in the past half-century has *occurred in secrecy*. The undertaking to build an atomic weapon, better known as the Manhattan Project, remains the great model for all subsequent activities. For more than two years, *not a single member of Congress even knew about it* although its final cost exceeded two billion dollars.

During and after the Second World War, other important projects, such as the development of biological weapons, the importation of Nazi scientists, terminal mind-control experiments, nationwide interception of mail and cable transmissions of an unwitting populace, *infiltration of the media and universities*, secret coups, secret wars, and assassinations all took place far *removed not only from the American public, but from most members of Congress* and a few Presidents. Indeed, several of the most powerful intelligence agencies were themselves established in secrecy, unknown by the public or Congress for many years.

Since the 1940s, the US Defense and Intelligence establishment has had more money at its disposal than most nations. In addition to official dollars, much of the money is undocumented. From its beginning, the CIA was engaged in a variety of off-the-record "business" activities that generated large sums of cash. The connections of the CIA with global organized crime (and thus de facto with the international narcotics trade) has been well established and documented for many years. - Much of the original money to run the American intelligence community came from very wealthy and established American families, who have long maintained an interest in funding national security operations important to their interests.

In theory, civilian oversight exists over the US national security establishment. The President is the military commander-in-chief. Congress has official oversight over the CIA. The FBI must answer to the Justice Department. In practice, little of this applies. One reason has to do with secrecy. [...]

A chilling example of such independence occurred during the 1950s, when President Eisenhower effectively lost control of the US nuclear arsenal. The situation deteriorated so much that during his final two years in office, Eisenhower asked repeatedly for an audience with the head of Strategic Air Command to learn what America's nuclear retaliatory plan was. What he finally learned in 1960, his final year in office, horrified him: half of the Northern Hemisphere would be obliterated.

If a revered military hero such as Eisenhower could not control America's nuclear arsenal, nor get a straight answer from the Pentagon, how on earth could Presidents Truman, Kennedy, Johnson, or Nixon regarding comparable matters?

Secrecy, wealth and independence add up to power. Through the years, the national security state has gained access to the world's most sophisticated technology, sealed off millions of acres of land from public access or scrutiny, acquired unlimited snooping ability within US borders and beyond, conducted overt or clandestine actions against other nations, and prosecuted wars without serious media scrutiny. Domestically, it maintains influence over elected officials and communities hoping for some of the billions of defense dollars.

Deception is the key element of warfare, and *when winning is all that matters, the conventional morality held by ordinary people becomes an impediment.* When taken together, the examples of official duplicity form a nearly single totality. They include such choice morsels as the phony war crisis of 1948, the fabricated missile gap claimed by the air force during the 1950s, the carefully managed events leading to the Gulf of Tonkin resolution... [...]

The secrecy stems from a pervasive and fundamental element of life in our world, that *those who are at the top of the heap will always take whatever steps are necessary* to maintain the status quo.

[S]keptics often ask, "Do you really think the government could hide [anything] for so long"? The question itself reflects ignorance of the reality that *secrecy is a way of life in the National Security State.* Actually though, the answer is yes, and no.

Yes, in that cover-ups are standard operating procedure, frequently unknown to the public for decades, becoming public knowledge by a mere roll of the dice. But also no, in that ... information has leaked out from the very beginning. It is impossible to shut the lid completely. *The key lies in neutralizing and discrediting unwelcome information, sometimes through official denial, other times through proxies in the media.*

[E]vidence [of conspiracy] derived from a grass roots level is unlikely to survive its inevitable conflict with official culture. And acknowledgement about the reality of [conspiracies] will only occur when the official culture deems it worthwhile or necessary to make it.[8]

Indeed, the very fact that this is one of many books presenting the case for government involvement in 9/11 is clear evidence that this particular conspiracy has certainly *not* succeeded. The problem lies in the fact that the conspirators have key people in positions of power that enable them to continue to act as they please without fear of repercussions. If you control the military, most of the media, and the judiciary, there isn't much that ordinary people - who just want to live their lives with as little pain as possible - are going to risk to oppose you.

Now, think about the word "conspiracy" one more time and allow me to emphasize the key point: *From a historical point of view, the ONLY reality is that of conspiracy.* Remember: Secrecy, wealth and independence add up to power... Deception is the key element of warfare, (the tool of power elites), and *when winning is all that matters, the conventional morality held by ordinary people becomes an impediment.* Secrecy stems from a pervasive and fundamental element of life in our world, that *those who are at the top of the heap will always take whatever steps are necessary to maintain the status quo, i.e. their position of power and their drive to get what they want.*

And how do they do that? By "official culture". Exactly how this works is one of the subjects we are going to cover in this book.

I recently had an exchange with Robin Ramsay, Editor of *Lobster magazine*. The context of the exchange was related to one of his recent "Konspiracy Korner" pieces published in *Fortean Times*, one of my favorite magazines. He wrote:

"...there is widespread agreement on the pro-conspiracy side that whatever struck the Pentagon, it was not Flight 77."

Ramsay then informs the reader of *Fortean Times* that Christopher Kelly from the US Armed Forces Institute of Pathology (sic) has stated that "What some experts have called 'the most comprehensive forensic investigation in US history ended on November 16 with the identification of 184 of the 189 who died in the terrorist attack on the Pentagon."

---

[8] Richard Dolan, *UFOs and the National Security State*, Revised Edition, Hampton Roads, 2002.

Ramsay dismisses the "conspiracy theorists" by saying "Of course, it must be faked, say many conspiracy buffs. And yes, it's possible that there is no Christopher Kelly; or that he is a stooge for 'the conspirators; or that dcmilitery.com is so in thrall that it is willing to run a fabricated report. But none of this is likely."

The most troubling fact of all is that the Official Version gleaned from the news reports and information released by government officials does not stand up to even the most cursory scrutiny. Contrary to the claims of Christopher Kelly, there never was a complete "forensic analysis." Well, let me correct that: very probably there was a "forensic analysis," but there was no *forensic investigation* prior to that analysis!

After writing a rather long email to Robin Ramsay that included a lot of chunks of material from our research and the research of others, Mr. Ramsay wrote back:

> Ultimately it comes down to how you see the world. The kind of conspiracy you are describing, or implying, is inconceivable to me: too big, too complex, too likely to go wrong or be discovered, ever to be mounted. What you are describing ... is vastly much bigger - and more complex and more dangerous - than any known mind control/psy ops project. And there is no evidence for it. [...]

> Those - like you - who argue for a U.S. state conspiracy are proposing a massive, multi-agency conspiracy of a kind which has never been seen before. All the U.S. state agencies hate each other and barely co-operate, engage in endless turf wars. The kind of inter-agency operation you are proposing simply has never existed in peace time. It is inconceivable to me that such a group could be got together. And this is probably the main reason that the official U.S. state organisations and politicians have never taken the conspiracy theories seriously. They know how the U.S. state operates and thus dismiss this idea at the outset. (And the official inquiry into 9-11 is full of examples of the hostility between state agencies.) In reality, when the planes hit the towers a large slice of the U.S. military and intelligence bodies immediately thought of Bin Laden. And they have never had a good reason to change their minds - not least because Bin Laden and his various cohorts have admitted - boasted of - doing it."[9]

And there is the rub: undoubtedly, Robin Ramsay's remarks are "on target" all things being considered to be equal. But this is where we encounter the problem: based on close and careful scientific observation, all things are *not* equal. More than that, there is the mountain of evidence - much of it circumstantial but so compelling that it would be accepted in a court of law - that there *is* such a gigantic conspiracy, and that the "power elite" - individuals who may be completely unknown to us since the highest level movers and shakers in the political and corporate world may

---

[9] Robin Ramsay, correspondence with one of the authors, LKJ.

only be their "pawns" - are somehow, at the top of the heap, controlling everything beneath them including the governments of various countries.

Boy, does that ever sound crazy! But before you reject such an idea out of hand, let me explain my remark that "all things are not equal". In this book, we are going to present scientific research that demonstrates how it is possible for such a conspiracy to exist in our reality based on little known "natural laws". This research was done in secret by scientists experiencing such a reality in Eastern Europe before, during, and after World War II. The story of this group of scientists and their research has never been publicly revealed though certainly, individuals among the Neocons were aware of it and suppressed it. Let me explain briefly, though the full account is published elsewhere.[10]

In the late Spring - early Summer of 2001, our website was attacked by a couple of Jewish individuals who accused us of anti-Semitism and began an active campaign of slander and defamation, claiming that Ark[11] was a "cold war nuke scientist" and the astonishing accusation that we were involved in Satanic Nazi Magic because of our association with an individual who had insinuated himself into our lives and work without telling us that this was what he was involved in! When we began to examine the issue, we realized that we could not be associated with such activities because it was diametrically opposed to our own work, and even, in our opinion, dangerous. We let the individual in question know that we could not continue this association as long as he was involved in that sort of thing and basically gave him the choice of continuing to work with us, in which case he would have to publicly distance himself from such activity, or if he felt that this was his true "calling," then we could have no further dealings with him. No hard feelings, bifurcation of paths.

His reaction to this was shocking, to say the least. He began to publicly "attack" our work, our website, our group, our personal lives, reputations, etc, in a way that was so bizarre as to challenge our ability to understand it. Initially, this entire incident appeared to be just a couple of individuals who didn't like our view of reality, but as time passed, and the obsessive attacks continued, even to the point of threatening our lives, we realized that this was something more than just a disgruntled individual. These were people with an agenda, with a view of reality that was so foreign to our own "live and let live" policy that we were hard pressed to understand it.

None of our life experiences up to that point in time could account for the behavior of this individual. None of the normal rules of dealing with a conflict seemed to apply. It was as though we had encountered a different species of human being who appeared to be human like everyone else,

---

[10] http://www.cassiopaea.org/cass/happydance.htm
[11] Preofessor Arkadiusz Jadczyk, husband of Laura Knight-Jadczyk

who could speak and write like a human being, could convince people that
he was human, but, based on our factual knowledge of the actual events in
question, we could see that either his awareness of reality was completely
alien, or he was consciously lying in ways and to an extent that had never
seen before. That, in itself, seemed entirely inhuman; that someone could
have such a well-constructed façade that bore no relation to what was
inside him. At least a dozen people knew the actual facts and knew that
what was being said by this person was so twisted as to bear no relation to
reality. And yet, his façade was complete: he could declare his version
with such convincing sincerity that those of us who knew the facts actually
began to question our own sanity. It was this latter effect that alerted us to
the fact that something truly unusual was going on and we knew we
needed to find out what it was.

As we continued to observe this dynamic, we saw how this individual
accumulated a "following" that believed his version of events - even after
we had produce multiple "testimonies" and even documentary evidence
that he was lying - in a way that was baffling and even frightening. It
certainly could be thought that it was a "conspiracy" between this
individual and the Jewish thought police who started the whole thing - it
sure looked like we had been "set up" - but we were certain that it was not;
at least not in the ordinary sense of the word. It was more like what
happens when the fat floating on the top of a bowl of soup begins to clump
together following some laws of nature. The individuals involved probably
did, once they had accreted as a group around this "spellbinder", begin to
actively conspire to commit acts of psychological and even physical
violence against us, but what initiated the accretion was the phenomenon
that fascinated us: their ideology presented as paramoralisms.[12] It was as
though, by announcing a certain mindset, or worldview, individuals began
to "gather around" a "standard" that held resonance for them.

And so, thankfully, we had this experience in the months prior to,
during, and following 9/11 which revealed for us in microcosm exactly the
same types of events we began to observe in the US political arena. It was
clear that the events of 9/11 were a shock that allowed similar individuals
to "spellbind" the American public. Curiously, the individual who was at
the root of the attacks on us sent out a post to a rather extensive mailing
list right after 9/11 declaring:

> ...on September 11th, ... The ringing voice of The Goddess was finally heard
> at last! Sekhmet...

That was completely nutty, in our opinion, and certainly this group,
though they were obviously exulting in the events of 9/11, had nothing "in

---

[12] Insinuation enclosed in moral slogans wherein the "moral" criteria used are just an "ad
hoc" invention and often, even reversals of accepted moralisms.

common" with any individuals involved in high level conspiracies, we thought.

But that was where we were wrong. They did have something in common. But we didn't know it then, and it was to be a full two years of hard work by dozens of members of our research group before we began to get a glimmer, to begin to perceive the theoretical basis for how and why such conspiracies can and obviously do, exist. But certainly, they do not exist or operate in the way we might ordinarily suspect.

Again, this information is crucial to understand how it is truly possible for such a conspiracy to exist in our reality based on little known "natural laws". So, we begin the first section of this book with a discussion of the *scientific basis* for "conspiracy".

Political Ponerology

A science on the nature of evil adjusted for political purposes[13]

The word "psychopath" generally evokes images of the barely restrained - yet surprisingly urbane - Dr. Hannibal Lecter of "Silence of the Lambs" fame. I will admit that this was the image that came to my mind whenever I heard the word. But I was wrong, and I was to learn this lesson quite painfully by direct experience as described above. The exact details are chronicled elsewhere[14]; what is important is that this experience was probably one of the most painful and *instructive* episodes of my life and it enabled me to overcome a block in my awareness of the world around me and those who inhabit it.

Regarding blocks to awareness, I need to state for the record that I have spent 30 years studying psychology, history, culture, religion, myth and the so-called paranormal. I also have worked for many years with hypnotherapy - which gave me a very good mechanical knowledge of how the mind/brain of the human being operates at very deep levels. But even with all of that background, I was still operating with certain beliefs firmly in place that were shattered by my research into psychopathy. I realized that there was a certain set of ideas that I held about human beings that were sacrosanct. I even wrote about this once in the following way:

> ...my work has shown me that the vast majority of people want to do good,
> to experience good things, think good thoughts, and make decisions with
> good results. And they try with all their might to do so! With the majority of
> people having this internal desire, why the Hell isn't it happening?

I was naïve, I admit. There were many things I did not know that I have learned since I penned those words. But even at that time I was aware of how our own minds can be used to deceive us. Here, I want to relate a

---

[13] A discussion based on the work of Andrej Lobaczewski, Ph.D.

[14] http://www.cassiopaea.com/archive/most1a.htm

story which is paraphrased from the description of an experiment undertaken by Hugh Lynn Cayce and described in his book *Venture Inward*.[15] I later made my own experiments which flesh out the details:

A subject was told under hypnosis that when he was awakened he would be unable to see a third man in the room who, it was suggested to him, would have *become invisible*. All the "proper" suggestions to make this "true" were given, such as "you will *not* see so- and-so", etc... When the subject was awakened, lo and behold! the suggestions did *not* work.

Why? Because *they went against his belief system*. He did *not* believe that a person could become invisible.

So, another trial was made. The subject was hypnotized again and was told that the third man was *leaving the room*... that he had been called away on urgent business, and the scene of him getting on his coat and hat was described to the subject under hypnosis... loud footsteps were produced, the door was opened and shut to provide "sound effects", and then the subject was brought out of the trance.

Guess what happened?

He was *unable to see* the Third Man.

Why? Because his perceptions were modified *according to his beliefs*. Certain "censors" in his brain were activated in a manner that was acceptable to his *ego survival instincts*.

The ways and means that we ensure survival of the ego is established pretty early in life by our parental and societal programming. This conditioning determines what *is* or is *not* possible; what we are "allowed" to believe in order to be accepted. We learn this, first, by learning what pleases our parents, and, then, later we modify our belief based on what pleases our society - our peers.. This is "transference". We transfer our desire/need to please our parents to our society, to our religious leaders, and *even to our government*.

To return to our story, the Third Man went about the room picking things up and setting them down and doing all sorts of things to test the subject's awareness of his presence, and the subject became utterly hysterical at this "anomalous" activity! He could see objects moving through the air, doors opening and closing, but he could *not* see the *source* because *he did not believe* that there was another man in the room.

So, what are the implications of this factor of human consciousness? (By the way, this is also the reason why most therapy to stop bad habits does not work - they attempt to operate against a "belief system" that is imprinted in the subconscious that this or that habit is essential to survival.)

---

[15] http://www.amazon.com/exec/obidos/tg/detail/-/0876043546/qid=1130183627/sr=1-2/ref=sr_1_2/103-3216640-8035850?v=glance&s=books

One of the first things we might observe is that everyone has a different set of beliefs based upon their social and familial conditioning, and that these beliefs determine how much of the *objective* reality anyone is able to access.

Realities, objective, subjective, or otherwise, are a touchy subject. Suffice it to say that years of work inside the minds of all kinds of people has taught me that we almost *never* perceive reality as it truly IS.

In the above story, the *objective* reality *is what it is: there was a third man in the room* even if the subject did not believe there was. In this story, there is clearly a *big part* of that reality that is inaccessible to the subject due to a *perception censor* which was activated by the suggestions of the hypnotist. That is to say, the subject had a strong belief, based upon his *choice* as to who or what to believe. In this case, he chose to believe the hypnotist. That put an immediate limit on what he was able to understand via his actual observations.

Now, what beliefs did I hold that made me a victim of a psychopath? The first and most obvious one is that I truly believed that deep inside, all people are basically "good" and that they *"want to do good, to experience good things, think good thoughts, and make decisions with good results. And they try with all their might to do so..."*

As it happens, this is not true as I - and everyone involved in our working group - learned to our sorrow, as they say. In order to come to some understanding of exactly what kind of human being could do the things that were done to me (and others close to me), and why they might be motivated - even driven - to behave this way, we began to research the psychology literature for clues because we needed to understand for our own peace of mind.

If there is a psychological theory that can explain vicious and harmful behavior, it helps very much for the victim of such acts to have this information so that they do not have to spend all their time feeling hurt or angry. And certainly, if there is a psychological theory that helps a person to find what kind of words or deeds can bridge the chasm between people, to heal misunderstandings, that is also a worthy goal. It was from such a perspective that we began our extensive work on the subject of narcissism and psychopathy.[16]

Of course, we didn't start out with such a "diagnosis" or label for what we were witnessing. We started out with observations and searched the literature for clues, for profiles, for anything that would help us to understand the inner world of a human being - actually a group of human beings - who seemed to be utterly depraved and unlike anything we had ever encountered before.

---

[16] http://www.cassiopaea.com/cassiopaea/psychopath.htm

As we proceeded through this project, we realized that what we were learning was very important to everyone because as the data was assembled, we saw that the clues, the profiles, revealed that the issues we were facing were faced by everyone at one time or another, to one extent or another. We also began to realize that the profiles that emerged also describe rather accurately many individuals who seek positions of power in fields of authority, most particularly politics and commerce. That's really not so surprising an idea, but it honestly hadn't occurred to us until we saw the patterns and recognized them in the behaviors of numerous historical figures, and lately including George W. Bush and members of his administration.

Current day statistics tell us that there are more psychologically sick people than healthy ones. If you take a sampling of individuals in any given field, you are likely to find that a significant number of them display pathological symptoms to one extent or another. Politics is no exception, and by its very nature, would tend to attract more of the pathological "dominator types" than other fields. That is only logical, and we began to realize that it was not only logical, it was horrifyingly accurate; horrifying because pathology among people in power can have disastrous effects on all of the people under the control of such pathological individuals. And so, we decided to write about this subject and publish it on the Internet.

As the material went up, letters from our readers began to come in thanking us for putting a name to what was happening to them in their personal lives as well as helping them to understand what was happening in a world that seems to have gone completely mad. We began to think that it was an epidemic and in a certain sense, we were right; just not in the way we thought. If an individual with a highly contagious illness works in a job that puts them in contact with the public, an epidemic is the result. In the same way, if an individual in a position of political power is a psychopath, he or she can create an epidemic of psychopathology in people who are not, essentially, psychopathic. Our ideas along this line were soon to receive confirmation from an unexpected source. I received an email from a Polish psychologist who wrote as follows:

Dears Ladies and Gentlemen.

I have got your Special Research Project on psychopathy by my computer.

You are doing a most important and valuable work for the future of nations.[…]

I am a very aged clinical psychologist. Forty years ago I took part in a secret investigation of the real nature and psychopathology of the macro social phenomenon called "Communism". The other researchers were the scientists of the previous generation who are now passed away.

The profound study of the nature psychopathy, which played the essential and inspirational part in this macro social psychopathologic phenomenon, and distinguishing it from other mental anomalies, appeared to be the necessary preparation for understanding the entire nature of the phenomenon.

The large part of the work, you are doing now, was done in those times. ...

I am able to provide you with a most valuable scientific document, useful for your purposes. It is my book "POLITICAL PONEROLOGY – A science on the nature of evil adjusted for political purposes". You may also find copy of this book in the Library of Congress and in some university and public libraries in the USA.

Be so kind and contact me so that I may mail a copy to you.

Very truly yours!

Andrew M. £obaczewski

I promptly wrote a reply. A couple of weeks later the manuscript arrived in the mail. Most of what follows in this first section is extracted from the scientific studies of Andrew M. £obaczewski, by permission, with no apologies from me for such extensive quoting. This work is so important that I believe that every normal human being ought to read it for their own safety and mental hygiene.

From the Author's Foreword:

In presenting my honored readers with this volume, which I generally worked on during the early hours before leaving to make a difficult living, I would first like to apologize for the defects which are the result of anomalous circumstances such as the absence of a proper laboratory. I readily admit that these lacunae should be filled, time-consuming as that may be, because the facts on which this book are based are urgently needed. Through no fault of the author's, these data have come too late.

The reader is entitled to an explanation of the long history and circumstances under which this work was compiled. This is the third time I have treated the same subject. I threw the first manuscript into a central-heating furnace, having been warned just in time about an official search, which took place minutes later. I sent the second draft to a Church dignitary at the Vatican by means of an American tourist and was absolutely unable to obtain any kind of information about the fate of the parcel once it left with him.

This ... history ... made work on the third version even more laborious. Prior paragraphs and former phrases from one or both first drafts haunt the writer's mind and make proper planning of the content more difficult.

The two first drafts were written in very convoluted language for the benefit of specialists with the necessary background, particularly in the field of psychopathology. The irretrievable disappearance of the second version also included the overwhelming majority of statistical data and facts which would have been so valuable and conclusive for specialists. Several analyses of individual cases were also lost.

The present version contains only such statistical data which had been memorized due to frequent use, or which could be reconstructed with satisfactory precision. [...] I also nurse the hope that this work may reach a wider audience and make available some useful scientific data which may serve as a basis for comprehension of the contemporary world and its history. It may also make it easier for readers to understand themselves, their neighbors, and other nations.

Who produced the knowledge and performed the work summarized within the pages of this book? It is a joint endeavor containing not only my efforts, but also representing the work of many researchers...

The author worked in Poland far away from active political and cultural centers for many years. That is where I undertook a series of detailed tests and observations which were to be combined within the resulting generalisations in order to produce an overall introduction for an understanding of the macro-social phenomenon surrounding us. The name of the person expected to effect this synthesis was a secret, as was understandable and necessary given the time and the situation. I would very occasionally receive anonymous summaries of the results of tests from Poland and Hungary. A few data were published, as it raised no suspicions that a specialized work was being compiled, and these data could still be located today.

The expected synthesis of this work did not occur. All my contacts became inoperative as a result of the secret arrests of researchers in the early sixties. The remaining scientific data in my possession were very incomplete, albeit priceless in value. It took many years of lonely work to weld these fragments into a coherent whole, filling the lacunae with my own experience and research.

My research on essential psychopathy and its exceptional role in the macro-social phenomenon was conducted concurrently with or shortly after that of others. Their conclusions reached me later and confirmed my own. The most characteristic item in my work is the general concept for a new scientific discipline named "ponerology."[...]

As the author of the final work, I hereby express my deep respect for all those who initiated the research and continued to conduct it at the risk of their careers, health and lives. I pay homage to those who paid the price through suffering or death. May this work constitute some compensation for their sacrifices...

New York, N.Y. August 1984 [17]

I understood that I was holding the condensation of a very important work and that the man who had written it had suffered a great deal to assemble that information for the benefit of others. The manuscript had been translated at the University of New York in 1985, and I wondered why it had not been published.

As I continued to read the manuscript, the answer became apparent. Dr. Lobaczewski explains about his sojourn in the United States where he

---

[17] Lobaczewski, Andrew M., Political *Ponerology : A science on the nature of evil adjusted for political purposes.*, author's manuscript, translated into English in 1985 by Alexandra Chciuk-Celt Ph.D., University of New York, NY.

reassembled and wrote down his research after having escaped from Poland via Austria before Solidarity brought the downfall of communism:

> Fifteen years passed, fraught with political occurrences. The world changed essentially due to the natural laws of the phenomenon described in this book, and due to the efforts of people of good will. Nonetheless, the world as yet is not restored to good health; and *the remainders of the great disease are still very active and threatening a reoccurrence of the illness.* Such is the result of a great effort completed without the support of the objective knowledge about the very nature of the phenomenon. [...]

> The author was recognised as the bearer of this "dangerous" science only in Austria, by a "friendly" physician who turned out to be a "red" agent. The communist groups in New York were then set up to organize a "counter action." It was terrible to learn how the system of conscious and unconscious pawns worked. Worst were the people who credulously trusted their conscious "friends" and performed the insinuated activities with patriotic zeal. The author was refused assistance and had to save his life by working as a welder. My health collapsed, and two years were lost. It appeared that I was not the first who came to America bringing similar knowledge and, once there, treated in a similar way.

> In spite of all these circumstances, the book was written on time, but no one would publish it. The work was described as "very informative" but for psychological editors, it contained too much politics and for political editors, it contained too much psychology, or simply "the editorial deadline has just closed." Gradually, it became clear that the book did not pass the insider's inspection.[...]

> The scientific value which may serve the future remains, and further investigations may yield a new understanding of human problems with progress toward universal peace. This was the reason I labored to retype, on my computer, the whole already fading manuscript. It is here presented as it was written in 1983-84 in New York, USA. So let it be a document of good science and dangerous labor. The author's desire is to hand this work into the hands of scholars in the hope they will take his burden over and progress with the theoretical research in ponerology - and put it in praxis for the good of people and nations.

> Poland - June, 1998 [18]

Dr. Lobaczewski left the United States and returned to Poland before September 11, 2001. But his remarks were prophetic:

> Nonetheless, the world as yet is not restored to good health; and the remainders of the great disease are still very active and threatening a reoccurrence of the illness.

What "dangerous science was Dr. Lobaczewski carrying with him when he escaped from communist Poland?

---

[18] Lobaczewski, Andrew M., Political *Ponerology : A science on the nature of evil adjusted for political purposes.*, author's manuscript, translated into English in 1985 by Alexandra Chciuk-Celt Ph.D., University of New York, NY.

He calls it "Ponerology" which the dictionary defines: *n.* division of theology dealing with evil; theological doctrine of wickedness or evil; from the Greek: poneros -> evil'.

But Dr. Lobaczewski was not proposing a "theological" study, but rather a scientific study of what we can plainly call Evil. The problem is, our materialist scientific culture does not readily admit that evil actually exists, per se. Yes, "evil" plays a part in religious discourse, but even there it is given short shrift as an "error" or a "rebellion" that will be corrected at some point in the future, which is discussed in another theological division: eschatology, which is concerned with the final events in history of the world, the ultimate fate of humanity.

There are quite a number of modern psychologists who are actually beginning to move in the direction of what Dr. Lobaczewski said had already been done behind the Iron Curtain many years ago. I have a stack of their books on my desk. Some of them seem to be falling back into the religious perspective simply because they have no other scientific ground on which to stand. I think that is counterproductive. As George K. Simon, Jr., writes in his book *In Sheep's Clothing*:

> ...[W]e've been pre-programmed to believe that people only exhibit problem behaviors when they're "troubled" inside or anxious about something. We've also been taught that people aggress only when they're attacked in some way. So, even when our gut tells us that somebody is attacking us and for no good reason, we don't readily accept the notion. We usually start to wonder what's bothering the person so badly "underneath it all" that's making them act in such a disturbing way. We may even wonder what we may have said or done that "threatened" them. We almost never think that they might be fighting simply to get something, have their way, or gain the upper hand. So, instead of seeing them as merely fighting, we view them as primarily hurting in some way.
>
> Not only do we often have trouble recognizing the ways people aggress us, but we also have difficulty discerning the distinctly aggressive character of some personalities. The legacy of Sigmund Freud's work has a lot to do with this. Freud's theories (and the theories of others who built upon his work) heavily influenced the psychology of personality for a long time. Elements of the classical theories of personality found their way into many disciplines other than psychology as well as into many of our social institutions and enterprises. The basic tenets of these theories and their hallmark construct, neurosis, have become fairly well etched in the public consciousness.
>
> Psychodynamic theories of personality tend to view everyone, at least to some degree, as *neurotic*. Neurotic individuals are overly inhibited people who suffer unreasonable fear (anxiety), guilt and shame when it comes to securing their basic wants and needs. The *malignant impact of overgeneralizing Freud's observations* about a small group of overly inhibited individuals into a broad set of assumptions about the causes of psychological ill-health in everyone *cannot be overstated*.[...]

Therapists whose training overly indoctrinated them in the theory of neurosis, may "frame" problems presented them incorrectly. They may, for example, assume that a person, who all their life has aggressively pursued independence and demonstrated little affinity for others, must necessarily be "compensating" for a "fear" of intimacy. In other words, they will view a hardened fighter as a terrified runner, thus misperceiving the core reality of the situation.[...]

We need a completely different theoretical framework if we are to truly understand, deal with, and treat the kinds of people who fight too much as opposed to those who cower or "run" too much.[19]

The problem is, of course, that when you read all the books about such people as Dr. Simon is describing, you discover that "treatment" really means treating the victims because such aggressors almost never seek help.

Getting back to Dr. Lobaczewski: I wrote to ask for more details as to why this important work was generally unknown. He replied by mail:

[...] Years ago the publication of the book in the US was killed by Mr. Zbigniew Brzezinski in a very cunning way. What was his motivation, I may only guess. Was it his own private strategy, or did he act as an insider of the "great system" as he surely is? How many billions of dollars and how many human lives the lack of this science has cost the world. [...]

As for who else was involved in this work: in those times, such work could only be done in full secrecy. During the German occupation, we learned to never ask for names though it was well known among us that this was an international communication among some scientists. I can tell you that one Hungarian scientist was killed because of his work on this project, and in Poland, professor Stephan Blachowski died mysteriously while working on these investigations. It is a certainty that professor Kasimir Dabrowski[20] was active in the study, being an expert on psychopathy. He escaped to the US and in New York, became an object of harassment as I had been. He went to Canada and worked at the university in Edmonton.

It is in this context of Dr. Lobaczewski's work that we finally found the mechanism for how and why "grand conspiracies" can and DO exist, but not necessarily in the way any of us ever imagined. They exist as a phenomenon of Nature and as such a phenomenon, deserve close and careful study.

---

[19] Simon, Georg K., Jr, Ph.D., 1996, *In Sheep's Clothing*, A.J. Christopher & Co, AR

[20] Kasimir Dabrowski's development theories have particular applicability to understanding the life experiences of HSPs - Highly Sensitive People. The theory identifies inborn "overexcitabilities" (OEs) that can facilitate the achievement of higher levels of development via "positive disintegration", potentially leading individuals to develop higher levels of self-awareness and self-actualization. Dabrowski theory provides a hopeful way of understanding what can be painful and overwhelming experiences. See: http://www.hsperson.com/pages/hsp.htm

Pathocracy

As a youth, I read a book about a naturalist wandering through the Amazon-basin wilderness. At some moment a small animal fell from a tree onto the nape of his neck, clawing his skin painfully and sucking his blood. The biologist cautiously removed it - without anger, since that was its form of feeding - and proceeded to study it carefully. This story stubbornly stuck in my mind during those very difficult times when a vampire fell onto our necks, sucking the blood of an unhappy nation.

The attitude of a naturalist - who attempts to track the nature of macro-social phenomena in spite of all adversity - insured a certain intellectual distance and better psychological hygiene, also slightly increasing the feeling of safety and furnishing a premonition that this very method may help find a certain creative solution. This required controlling the natural, moralizing reflexes of revulsion and other painful emotions this phenomenon provokes in any normal person when it deprives him of his joy of life and personal safety, ruining his own future and that of his nation. *Scientific curiosity becomes a loyal ally during such times.*

May the reader please imagine a very large hall in some old Gothic university building. Many of us gathered there early in our studies in order to listen to the lectures of outstanding philosophers. We were herded back there the year before graduation in order to listen to the indoctrination lectures which recently have been introduced. Someone nobody knew appeared behind the lectern and informed us that he would now be the professor. His speech was fluent, but there was nothing scientific about it: he failed to distinguish between scientific and everyday concepts and treated borderline imaginings as though it were wisdom that could not be doubted. For ninety minutes each week, he flooded us with naïve, presumptuous paralogistics and a pathological view of human reality. We were treated with contempt and poorly controlled hatred. Since fun poking could entail dreadful consequences, we had to listen attentively and with the utmost gravity.

The grapevine soon discovered this person's origins. He had come from a Cracow suburb and attended high school, although no one knew if he graduated. Anyway, this was the first time he had crossed university portals - as a professor, at that! [...]

After such mind-torture, it took a long time for someone to break the silence. We studied ourselves, since we felt something strange had taken over our minds and something valuable was leaking away irretrievably. The world of psychological reality and moral values seemed suspended like in a chilly fog. Our human feeling and student solidarity lost their meaning, as did patriotism and our old established criteria. So we asked each other: "Are you going through this too?" Each of us experienced this worry about his on personality and future in his own way. Some of us answered the questions with silence. The depth of these experiences turned out to be different for each individual.

We thus wondered how to protect ourselves from the results of this "indoctrination." Teresa D. made the first suggestion: Let's spend a weekend in the mountains. It worked. Pleasant company, a bit of joking, then exhaustion followed by deep sleep in a shelter, and our human personalities returned, albeit with a certain remnant. Time also proved to create a kind of psychological immunity, although not with everyone. Analysing the psychopathic characteristics of the "professor's" personality proved another excellent way of protecting one's own psychological hygiene.

You can just imagine our worry, disappointment, and surprise when some colleagues we knew well suddenly began to change their world-view; their thought-patterns furthermore reminded us of the "professor's" chatter. Their feelings, which had just recently been friendly, became noticeably cooler, although not yet hostile. Benevolent or critical student arguments bounced right off of them. They gave the impression of possessing some secret knowledge; we were only their former colleagues, still believing what those professors of old had taught us. We had to be careful of what we said to them.

Our former colleagues soon joined the Party. Who were they? What social groups did they come from? What kind of students and people were they? How and why did they change so much in less than a year? Why did neither I nor a majority of my fellow students succumb to this phenomenon and process? Many such questions fluttered through our heads then. Those times, questions, and attitudes gave rise to the idea that this phenomenon could be objectively understood, an idea whose greater meaning crystallized with time. Many of us participated in the initial observations and reflections, but most crumbled away in the face of material or academic problems. Only a few remained; so the author of this book may be the last of the Mohicans.

It was relatively easy to determine the environments and origin of the people who succumbed to this process, which I then called "transpersonification". They came from all social groups, including aristocratic and fervently religious families, and caused a break in our student solidarity in the order of some 6 %. The remaining majority suffered varying degrees of personality disintegration which gave rise to individual efforts in searching for the values necessary to find ourselves again; the results were varied and sometimes creative.

Even then, we had no doubts as to the pathological nature of this "transpersonification" process, which ran similar but not identical in all cases. The duration of the results of this phenomenon also varied. Some of these people later became zealots. Others later took advantage of various circumstances to withdraw and reestablish their lost links to the society of normal people. They were replaced. The only constant value of the new social system was the magic number of 6 %.

We tried to evaluate the talent level of those colleagues who had succumbed to this personality-transformation process, and reached the conclusion that on average, it was slightly lower than the average of the student population. Their lesser resistance obviously resided in other bio-psychological features which were most probably qualitatively heterogeneous.

I had to study subjects bordering on psychology and psychopathology in order to answer the questions arising from our observations; scientific neglect in these areas proved an obstacle difficult to overcome. At the same time, *someone guided by special knowledge apparently vacated the libraries of anything we could have found on the topic.*

Analysing these occurrences now in hindsight, we could say that the "professor" was dangling bait over our heads, based on psychopaths' specific psychological knowledge. He knew in advance that he would fish out amenable individuals, but the limited numbers disappointed him. The transpersonification process generally took hold whenever an individual's instinctive substratum was marked by pallor or some deficits. To a lesser extent, it also worked among people who manifested other deficiencies, also the state provoked within them was partially impermanent, being largely the result of psychopathological induction.

This knowledge about the existence of susceptible individuals and how to work on them will continue being a tool for world conquest as long as it remains the secret of such "professors." When it becomes skillfully popularized science, it will help nations develop immunity. But none of us knew this at the time.

Nevertheless, we must admit that in demonstrating the properties of pathocracy in such a way as to force us into in-depth experience, the professor helped us understand the nature of the phenomenon in a larger scope than many a true scientific researcher participating in this work in one way or another.

The Hysteroidal Cycle[21]

Three ancient systems coincided to form our Western Civilization: Greek philosophy, Roman imperial and legal ideas, and Christianity. The culture that we have inherited from these influences, consolidated by time and effort of later generations, is quite limited when dealing with aspects of psychology and spiritual life. It is stiffly anchored in materiality and law.

Such a state of affairs has had a serious negative effect on our ability to comprehend reality, especially that reality that concerns human beings and society.

With the imposition of Christianity, Europeans became unwilling to really study reality, (i.e. subordinating their intellects to facts), preferring instead to attempt to impose on Nature their subjective ideational schemes. Not until modern times, thanks to the hard sciences which undertake to study facts by their very nature, as well as the willingness to study the apperception of the

---

[21] Dr. Lobaczewski's manuscript is quite dense due to the academic language. I have slightly edited some of the quoted sections that I am including in this volume so that it will be easier to read by the layperson (including myself).

philosophical heritage of other cultures, has there been any clarification of our world of concepts. [22]

Greek culture included a rich mythological "imagination" that was, apparently, developed in direct contact with nature. These conditions saw the birth of a literary tradition and philosophical reflections searching for essential content and criteria of values. The Greek heritage was rich and individual and primeval.

Rome was too vital and practical to reflect on the thoughts of the Greeks. They appropriated them, and subjugated them to administrative needs and judicial developments with "practical priorities". They thus used the "idea" of philosophy as a means of developing the thinking process that could then be useful for the discharge of administrative functions and the exercise of political options.

In any imperial civilization, the complex problems of human nature are troublesome and only complicate the legal regulations of public affairs and administrative functions. This led to the Roman tendency to dismiss such individualistic human considerations in favor of developing a concept of human personality that was simple enough to serve the purposes of law. Roman citizens could have personal attitudes and follow their goals only within the framework set by "fate" and legal principles having little to do with real, human, psychological properties.

Thus, cognitive psychology was diverted and left barren when Rome conquered Greece. This led to moral recession at both the individual and public levels.

Through Judaism, nascent Christianity claimed strong ties with the ancient cultures of the Middle East, including their philosophical and psychological ideas. This lead to a school of thought characterized by one's relationships to other people: one's neighbor. Understanding, forgiveness, and love opened the door to a psychological cognition which, often supported by charismatic phenomena, bore abundant fruit in the first three centuries of its existence.

One could thus expect Christianity to help develop the art of human understanding to a higher level than the older cultures and religions. One could hope that such knowledge would protect future generations from the dangers of speculative thought divorced from that psychological and profound reality which can only be comprehended through sincere respect for other human beings in all their shapes and sizes, and with all their differences honored and respected.

But that is not what happened.

In the second half of the fourth century, things went terribly wrong for Christianity.

---

[22] What is troubling is to note that, just at the point in time when a quantum leap in progress along this line was possible and gaining energy every day, an event such as 9/11 took place, setting human progress back hundreds, if not thousands of years.

Christianity adapted the Greek heritage of thought and language of philosophical concepts to its purposes. The Christian church appropriated Roman organizational forms and adapted to existing social institutions. As a result, Christianity inherited Roman habits of legal thinking, including its indifference to human nature and its variety. These two items were linked together so firmly and permanently that later generations forgot just how strange they were to each other. Roman influence deprived Christianity of its primeval psychological knowledge.

A civilization thus arose with a serious deficiency in the area which is supposed to protect societies from various kinds of evil, and we are the inheritors of this defect. This civilization developed formulations in the area of law - national, civil, and canon - which were conceived for *invented* beings, not human beings, and which gave short shrift to the total contents of the human personality and the *great psychological differences between individual members of the species Homo sapiens*. For many centuries, any understanding of certain psychological anomalies found among individuals was out of the question - even though such anomalies cause disaster.

Thus, *Western Civilization is insufficiently resistant to evil, which originates beyond the easily accessible areas of human consciousness* and takes advantage of the great gap between formal or legal thought and psychological reality.

In a civilization deficient in psychological cognition, individuals with dreams of imposing their power upon their environment and their society are not recognized as being fundamentally different, and they all too easily find a ready response in individuals with insufficiently developed consciousnesses.[…]

The better our understanding of the causality of the human personality, the stronger the impression becomes that humanity is part of nature and society and there is really very little evidence for real "freedom of action". Human beings have a tendency to repress from their consciousness any associations indicating a causative conditioning of their world-view and behavior, though a good psychologist or psychiatrist can quickly track their life and discover the causes that condition them with only a relatively small selection of facts.

The natural psychological, societal, and moral world-view is a product of man's developmental process within a society, under the constant influence of his innate traits. No person can develop without being influenced by other people and their personalities, or by the values imbued by his civilization and his moral and religious traditions. That his why his world-view can be neither universal nor true.

It is thus significant that the main values of this human world-view of nature indicate basic similarities in spite of great spans of time, race, and civilization. It is thus suggested that the "human world view" derives from the nature of our species and the natural experience of human societies which have achieved a certain necessary level of civilization. Refinements based on literary values or philosophical and moral reflections do indicate some differences, but generally speaking, they tend to bring together the natural conceptual language of various civilizations and eras.

People with a "humanistic" education may have the impression that they have achieved wisdom, but here we approach a problem; we must ask the following question: *Even if the natural world-view has been refined, does it mirror reality with sufficient reliability? Or does it only mirror our species' perception? To what extent can we depend upon it as a basis for decision making in the individual, societal, and political spheres of life?*

Experience teaches us, first of all, that this natural world-view has permanent and characteristic *tendencies toward deformation dictated by our instinctive and emotional features*. Secondly, our work exposes us to many phenomena that cannot be understood and described by natural language alone.

Considering the most important reality deforming tendency, we notice that those *emotional features* which are a natural component of the human personality *are never completely appropriate to the reality* being experienced. This results both from our instinct and from our conditioning of upbringing. This is why *the best traditions of philosophical and religious thought have counseled subduing the emotions in order to achieve a more accurate view of reality*.

Another problem is the fact that our natural world-view is generally characterized by *a tendency to endow our opinions with moral judgments*, often so negative as to represent outrage. This appeals to tendencies which are deeply rooted in human nature and social customs.

We often meet with sensible people endowed with a well-developed natural world-view as regards psychological, societal, and moral aspects, frequently refined via literary influences, religious deliberations, and philosophical reflections. Such persons have *a pronounced tendency to overrate the values of their world-view*. They do not take into account the fact that their system can be also erroneous since it is insufficiently objective.

Let us call such an attitude the *egotism of the natural world-view*. To date, it has been the least pernicious type of egotism, being merely an overestimation of that method of comprehension containing the eternal values of human experience.

Today, however, the world is being jeopardized by a phenomenon that cannot be understood and described by means of such a natural conceptual language; this kind of egotism thus becomes a dangerous factor stifling the possibility of some counteractive measures. *Developing and popularizing the objective psychological world-view could thus significantly expand the scope of dealing with evil via sensible action and pinpointed countermeasures.*

Ever since ancient times, philosophers and religious thinkers representing various attitudes in different cultures have been searching for the truth as regards moral values, attempting to find criteria for what is right, what constitutes good advice. They described the virtues of human character and suggested these be acquired. They created a heritage ... which contains centuries of experience and reflections. In spite of the obvious differences among attitudes, the similarity or complementality of the conclusions reached by famous ancients are striking, even though they worked in widely divergent times and places. After all, whatever is valuable is conditioned and caused by the laws of nature acting upon the personalities of both individual human beings and collective societies.

It is equally thought-provoking, however, to see how relatively little has been said about the opposite side of the coin; *the nature, causes, and genesis of evil.* These matters are usually cloaked behind the above generalized conclusions with a certain amount of secrecy. Such a state of affairs can be partially ascribed to the social conditions and historical circumstances under which these thinkers worked. Their modus operandi may have been dictated at least in part by personal fate, inherited traditions, or even prudishness. After all, justice and virtue are the opposites of force and perversity, the same applies to truthfulness vs. lies, similarly like health is the opposite of an illness.

The character and genesis of evil thus remained hidden in discreet shadows, leaving it to playwrights to deal with the subject in their highly expressive language, but that did not reach the primeval source of the phenomena. *A certain cognitive space thus remains uninvestigated, a thicket of moral questions which resists understanding and philosophical generalizations.* [...]

Ever since human societies and civilizations have existed on our planet, people have longed for happy times full of tranquility and justice, which would allow every man to herd his sheep in peace, search for green valleys, plow his fields, and build houses or palaces. Human beings desire peace so that they can accumulate benefits and enjoy them or to enjoy the benefits accumulated by their parents. They want to observe their children grow up, do a little traveling, create something for future generations to remember them by, and so on.

From time immemorial, man has dreamed of a life in which his efforts to accumulate benefits can be punctuated by rest during which time he enjoys those benefits. He learned how to domesticate animals in order to accumulate more benefits, and when that no longer met his needs, he learned to enslave other human beings simply because he was more powerful and could do it.

Dreams of a happy life of "more accumulated benefits" to be enjoyed, and more leisure time in which to enjoy them, thus gave rise to force over others, a force which depraves the mind of its user. That is why man's dreams of happiness have not come true throughout history: the hedonistic[23] view of "happiness" contains the seeds of misery. Hedonism, the pursuit of the accumulation of benefits for the sole purpose of self-enjoyment, feeds the eternal cycle where good times lead to bad times.

During good times, people lose sight of the need for thinking, introspection, knowledge of others, and an understanding of life. When things are "good," people ask themselves whether it is worth it to ponder human nature and flaws in the personality (one's own, or that of another). In good times, entire generations can grow up with no understanding of the creative meaning of suffering since they have never experienced it themselves. When all the joys

---

[23] Hedonism can be reduced to the idea that "pleasure is the highest good".

of life are there for the taking, mental effort to understand science and the laws of nature - to acquire knowledge that may not be directly related to accumulating stuff - seems like pointless labor. Being "healthy minded," and positive - a good sport with never a discouraging word - is seen as a good thing, and anyone who predicts dire consequences as the result of such insouciance is labeled a wet-blanket or a killjoy.

Perception of the truth about reality, especially a real understanding of human nature in all it's ranges and permutations, ceases to be a virtue to be acquired. Thoughtful doubters are "meddlers" who can't leave well enough alone. "Don't fix it if it ain't broke." This attitude leads to an impoverishment of psychological knowledge including the capacity to differentiate the properties of human nature and personality, and the ability to mold healthy minds creatively.

The cult of power thus supplants the mental and moral values so essential for maintaining peace by peaceful means. A nation's enrichment or involution as regards its psychological world-view could be considered an indicator of whether its future be good or bad.

During good times, the search for the meaning of life, the truth of our reality, becomes uncomfortable because it reveals inconvenient factors. Unconscious elimination of data which are, or appear to be, inexpedient, begins to be habitual, a custom accepted by entire societies. The result is that *any thought processes based on such truncated information cannot bring correct conclusions*. This then leads to substitution of convenient lies to the self to replace uncomfortable truths thereby approaching the boundaries of phenomena which should be viewed as psychopathological.

The facts are that "good times" for one group of people have been historically rooted in some injustice to other groups of people. In such a society, where all the hidden truths lurk below the surface like an iceberg, disaster is just around the corner.

It is clear that America has experienced a long period of "good times" for most of its existence, (no matter how many people they had to oppress or kill to do so), but particularly so during the 50 years preceding September 11, 2001. During that 50 years, several generations of children were born, and the ones that were born at the beginning of that time, who have never known "bad times," are now at an age where they want to "enjoy" the benefits they have accumulated. Unfortunately, it doesn't look like that is going to happen; 9/11 has changed everything so profoundly that it looks like there will be no enjoyment by anyone for a very, very long time.

How could this happen?

The answer is that a few generation's worth of "good times" results in the above described *societal deficits* regarding psychological skills and moral criticism. Long periods of preoccupation with the self and "accumulating benefits" for the self, diminish the ability to accurately read the environment and other people. But the situation is more serious than just a generalized weakness of a society that could be "toughened up" with a little "hard times". Lobaczewski writes:

> The psychological features of each such crisis are unique to the culture and the time, but one common denominator that exists at the beginning of all such "bad times" is an *exacerbation of society's hysterical condition.*[24] The emotionalism dominating in individual, collective, and political life, combined with the subconscious selection and substitution of data in reasoning, lead to individual and national egotism. The mania for taking offense at the drop of a hat provokes constant retaliation, taking advantage of hyperirritability and hypocriticality on the part of others. It is this feature, *this hystericization of society, that enables pathological plotters, snake charmers, and other primitive deviants to act as essential factors in the processes of the origination of evil on a macro-social scale.*

Who, exactly, are the "pathological plotters," and what can motivate such individuals during times that are generally understood by others as "good?" If times are "good," why does anyone want to plot and generate evil?

Well, certainly, the current US administration has come up with an answer: "They hate us because of our freedoms." This is a prime example of "selection and substitution of data in reasoning" which is willingly and gladly accepted as an explanation by the public because of their *deficits of psychological skills* and moral criticism.

> Present-day philosophers developing meta-ethics are trying to press forward in their understanding, and as they slip and slide along the elastic space leading to an analysis of the language of ethics, they contribute toward eliminating some imperfections and habits of natural conceptual language. Penetrating this ever-mysterious nucleus, however, is highly tempting to a scientist.[...]

> If physicians behaved like ethicists and failed to study diseases because they were only interested in studying questions of health, there would be no such thing as modern medicine. [...] Physicians were correct in their emphasis on studying disease above all in order to discover the causes and biological properties of illnesses, and then to understand the pathodynamics of their courses. A comprehension of the nature of a disease, and the course it runs, after all, enables the proper curative means to be elaborated and employed.[...]

---

[24] Here, Dr. Lobaczewski is referring to a precise psychological term. The hysterical person, or "histrionic personality disorder", is described: People with a histrionic personality conspicuously seek attention, are dramatic and excessively emotional, and are overly concerned with appearance. Their lively, expressive manner results in easily established but often superficial and transient relationships. Their expression of emotions often seems exaggerated, childish, and contrived to evoke sympathy or attention (often erotic or sexual) from others. People with a histrionic personality are prone to sexually provocative behavior or to sexualizing nonsexual relationships. However, they may not really want a sexual relationship; rather, their seductive behavior often masks their wish to be dependent and protected. Some people with a histrionic personality also are hypochondriacal and exaggerate their physical problems to get the attention they need.(Merck)

The question thus arises: could some analogous modus operandi not be used to study the causes and genesis of other kinds of evil scourging human individuals, families, societies? Experience has taught the author that evil is similar to disease in nature, although possibly more complex and elusive to our understanding. [...]

Parallel to the traditional approach, problems commonly perceived to be moral may also be treated on the basis of data provided by biology, medicine, and psychology, as the factors of this kind are simultaneously present in the question as a whole. Experience teaches us that a comprehension of the essence and genesis of evil generally make use of data from these areas. [...]

Philosophical thought may have engendered all the scientific disciplines, but the latter did not mature until they became independent, based on detailed data and a relationship to other disciplines supplying such data.

Encouraged by the often "coincidental" discovery of these naturalistic aspects of evil, the author initiated the methodology of medicine; a clinical psychologist and medical co-worker by profession, he had such tendencies anyway. As is the case with physicians and disease, he took the risks of close contact with evil and suffered the consequences. His purpose was to ascertain the possibilities of understanding the nature of evil, its etiological factors and to track its pathodynamics.[...]

A new discipline thus arose: *Ponerology*. The process of the genesis of evil was called, correspondingly, "ponerogenesis." [...]

Considerable moral, intellectual, and practical advantages can be gleaned from an understanding of the genesis of Evil thanks to the objectivity required to study it dispassionately. The human heritage of ethics is *not destroyed* by taking such an approach: *it is actually strengthened* because *the scientific method can be utilized to confirm the basic values of moral teachings*.

Understanding the nature of macro-social pathology helps us to find a healthy attitude and thus *protects our minds from being controlled or poisoned by the diseased contents and influence of their propaganda*.

We can only conquer this huge, contagious social cancer if we comprehend its essence and its etiological causes.

Such an understanding of the nature of the phenomena leads to the logical conclusion that *the measures for healing and reordering the world today should be completely different from the ones heretofore used for solving international conflicts*. It is also true that, merely having the knowledge and awareness of the phenomena of the genesis of macro-social Evil can begin healing individual humans and help their minds regain harmony. [...]

Lobaczewski discusses the fact that "bad times," seem to have a historical "purpose". It seems that suffering during times of crisis lead to mental activity aimed at solving or ending the suffering. The bitterness of loss invariably leads to a regeneration of values and empathy. He writes:

When bad times arrive and people are overwhelmed by an excess of evil,
they must gather all their physical and mental strength to fight for existence
and protect human reason. The search for some way out of difficulties and
dangers rekindles long-buried powers or discretion. Such people have the
initial tendency to rely on force in order to counteract the threat; they may,
for instance, become "trigger happy" or dependent upon armies. Slowly and
laboriously, however, they discover the advantages conferred by mental
effort; improved understanding of psychological situations in particular,
better differentiation of human characters and personalities, and finally,
comprehension of one's adversaries. During such times, virtues which
former generations relegated to literary motifs regain their real and useful
substance and become prized for their value. A wise person capable of
furnishing sound advice is highly respected.

It seems that there have been many such "bad times" in the course of
human history, and it was during such times that the great systems of
ethics were developed. Unfortunately, during "good times," nobody wants
to hear about it. They want to "enjoy" things, to have pleasure and
pleasant experiences, and so any literature that relates to such times is lost,
forgotten, suppressed, or otherwise ignored. This leads to further debasing
of the intellectual currency and opens the gap for bad times to come once
again.

If a collection were to be made of all the books that describe the horrors of
wars, the cruelties of revolutions, and the bloody deeds of political leaders
and systems, most people would avoid such a library. In such a library,
ancient works would be found alongside books by contemporary historians
and reporters. The documentary evidence on German extermination and
concentration camps, complete with dry statistical data, describing the well-
organized "labor" of the destruction of human life, would be seen to use a
properly calm language, and would provide the basis for acknowledging the
nature of Evil.

The autobiography of Rudolf Hess, the commander of camps in Osweicim
(Auschwitz) and Brzezinka, (Birkenau) is *a classic example of how an
intelligent psychopath thinks and feels.*

Our library of death would include works on philosophy discussing the
social and moral aspects of the genesis of Evil, while using history to
partially justify the blood-drenched "solutions".

The library would show to the alert reader a sort of evolution from primitive
attitudes, that it is alright to enslave and murder vanquished peoples, to the
present day moralizing which declares that such behavior is barbaric and
worthy of condemnation.

However, such a library would be missing one crucial tome: *there would not
be a single work offering a sufficient explanation of the causes and
processes whereby such historical dramas originate, of how and why human
beings periodically degenerate into bloodthirsty madness.*

The old questions would remain unanswered: what made this happen? Does
everyone carry the seeds of crime within, or only some of us? No matter how

faithful to the events, nor how psychologically accurate the books that are available may be, they cannot answer those questions nor can they fully explain the origin of Evil.

Thus, humanity is at a great disadvantage because *without a fully scientific explanation of the origins of Evil, there is no possibility of the development of sufficiently effective principles for counteracting Evil.*

The best literary description of a disease cannot produce an understanding of its essential etiology, and can thus furnish no principles for treatment. In the same way, descriptions of historical tragedies are incapable of elaborating effective measures for counteracting the genesis, existence, or spread of Evil.

In using natural language to discuss psychological, social and moral concepts, we find that we can only produce an approximation, which leads to a nagging suspicion of helplessness.

Our ordinary system of concepts are not invested with the necessary factual content - scientific observations about Evil - which would permit comprehension of the quality of the many factors (particularly the psychological ones) which are active before and during the birth of inhumanly cruel times.

Nevertheless, the authors of some of the books that we would find in our Library of Evil took great care to infuse their words with the proper precision *as though they were hoping that someone, at some time, would use their records to explain what they, themselves, could not explain* even in the best literary language.

Most human beings are horrified by such literature. *Hedonistic societies have the strong tendency to encourage escape into ignorance or naive doctrines.* Some people even feel contempt for the suffering of others.

It is true that, in tracking the behavioral mechanisms of the genesis of Evil, *one must keep both abhorrence and fear under control*, submit to a passion for science, and develop the calm outlook needed in natural history.

This book aims to take the reader by the hand into a world *beyond the concepts and imaginings he has trusted and used since childhood*. This is necessary due to the problems our world presently faces, things we can no longer ignore, or ignore only at the peril of all humanity. We must realize that we cannot possibly distinguish the path to nuclear catastrophe from the path to creative dedication unless we step beyond the subjective world of well-known concepts, and *we must also realize that this subjective world was chosen for us by powerful forces against which our nostalgia for homey, human ideas about warmth and safety is no match.*

Moral evil and psychobiological evil are interlinked via so many causal relationship and mutual influences that they can only be separated by means of abstraction. However, *the ability to distinguish them qualitatively protects us from moralizing interpretations* that so easily can poison the human mind in an insidious way.

Macro-social phenomena of Evil, which constitute the most important object of this book, *appear to be subjected to the same laws of nature operating within human beings on individual or small-group levels.* The role of persons with various psychological defects and anomalies of a clinically low level appear to be a perennial characteristic of such phenomena.

In the macro-social phenomenon where Evil runs rampant, "Pathocracy," a certain hereditary anomaly isolated as "essential psychopathy" is catalytically and causatively essential for the genesis and survival of such a State.[...] [25]

This last remark is the key to "grand conspiracies" that Robin Ramsay and others believe cannot exist. Dr. Lobaczewski discusses the kinds of individuals that form a "Pathocracy", or "psychopathic government", and further, he elaborates details about psychopaths based on his studies and the studies of those with whom he was associated, that have never been openly discussed as far as I can tell after reading many thousands of pages of material on the subject generated here in the West. Dr. Lobaczewski, on the other hand, undertook his studies "in the belly of the beast", so to say, with live "specimens". The value of such a study cannot be overstated.

Dr. Lobaczewski tells us that out of his sample of 5000 psychotic, neurotic, and healthy patients, there were 384 that had behaved in a manner that seriously harmed others. His sampling was from a broad range of society, professions, and represented a cross-section of moral, social and political views. After administering a variety of tests, (medical and psychological), and taking detailed histories, both from the patients and those associated with them, he concluded that only about 15 percent of them did not exhibit any psychopathological factors. In other words, there were pathological factors involved in 85 percent of cases of "evildoers", which leads to the hypothesis that if a particular pathology did not exist in that individual, the individual would not have "gone bad". This is represented in the work of many scholars who suggest that evil in this world results from a kind of web of "mutual conditioning", a web of interlocking structures where one kind of evil feeds and opens doors for another.

Such a description of the "origin of evil" is generally accepted today, and is often acknowledged by courts and public opinion. "He was abused as a child, and thus only knows how to abuse others." Or, "he was brain damaged at birth and has a brain lesion that causes him to act that way." Or "he is mentally retarded; he doesn't know right from wrong." That's the Freudian influence that has prevented us from seeing what we need to see about individuals whose fundamental existence is based on getting power over others.

Every person assimilates psychological characteristics throughout his or her life, but particularly during childhood. This can be via mental

---

[25] Lobaczewski, Andrew M., Political *Ponerology : A science on the nature of evil adjusted for political purposes.*, author's manuscript, translated into English in 1985 by Alexandra Chciuk-Celt Ph.D., University of New York, NY.

resonance, identification, imitation, and other means of communication. This assimilation is what *builds a person's personality and world-view*. If these types of influences are contaminated by pathological factors and malformations within those who interact closely with the individual in question, the development of that person may be likewise deformed: unable to correctly understand himself or others or normal human relations and morals, and he or she will commit evil acts with no feeling (or a poor awareness) of being deformed relative to the rest of society. In such cases, our society rightly asks: can he or she be to blame for what they do not know?

> Such "ponerogenic" processes as this are part of a complex network of causation which frequently contains feedback relationships. Sometimes, cause and effect are widely separated in time which makes it difficult to track. Ponerology should thus study the role of pathological factors in the origins of evil since conscious control and monitoring at a scientific, social and individual level could effectively disarm these processes and protect individuals and society.

For instance, in the course of psychotherapy, the patient can learn about the influences from some deformed person in his life who exhibited psychopathological characteristics and then, painful though it may be, the patient can develop the ability to liberate himself from the results of these influences, to improve his ability to understand himself, and to overcome his internal and interpersonal difficulties so as to avoid mistakes which hurt himself and others.

But we are still left wondering about the 15 percent of 384 people who hurt others and in whom there were no pathological factors found in their medical or psychological background. That is 1.15 percent of the total population of 5000 patients. Lobaczewski suggests that there may have been failures in the testing process. In other words, there might be pathologies, but they were not evident via the tests available at the time. We will return to them further on. For now, let's just consider the fact that pathological processes have historically had a profound influence upon human society at large due to the fact that many individuals with deformed characters have played outstanding roles in the formation of social constructs. It is helpful to have some background on this. Dr. Lobaczewski writes:

> Brain tissue is very limited in its regenerative ability. If it is damaged and the change subsequently heals, a process of rehabilitation takes place thanks to which the neighboring healthy tissue takes over the function of the damaged portion. This substitution is never quite perfect thus some deficits as regards skill and proper psychological processes can be detected, even in cases of very small damage, by using the appropriate tests. [...]

> As regards pathological factors of ponerogenic processes, *perinatal or early-infant damages have more active results than damages which occur later*.

> In societies with highly developed medical care, we find among the lower grades of elementary schools that *5 to 7 percent of the children have suffered brain tissue lesions* which cause certain academic or behavioral difficulties.[...][26]

This is actually a frightening figure. If we realize that an even higher percentage of the previous generations have suffered brain tissue lesions during a time when there was no highly developed perinatal and neonatal medical care, not to mention the damage that may be suffered among those populations today where such care is still primitive, we can understand that much of our own culture has been shaped by people with brain damage and we are faced with dealing with a world in which brain damaged individuals have an important influence on the social constructs! Keep in mind that if your grandfather suffered perinatal or neonatal brain damage, it affected how he raised one of your parents, which affects how that parent raised you!

> Epilepsy constitutes the oldest known results of such lesions; it is observed in relatively small numbers of persons suffering such damage. Researchers in these matters are more or less unanimous in believing that Julius Caesar and then later Napoleon Bonaparte had epileptic seizures. The extent to which these ailments had a negative effect upon their characters and historical decision making, or played a ponerogenic role, can be the subject of a separate study. In most cases, however, epilepsy is an *evident ailment*, which limits its role as a ponerogenic factor.[27]

> In a much larger part of the bearers of brain tissue damage, the negative deformation of their characters grows in the course of time. It takes on various mental pictures depending on the properties and localizations of the damage, their time of origin, and also the life conditions of the individual after their occurrence. We will call character disorders resulting from such pathology "Characteropathies."

> Some characteropathies play an outstanding role as pathological agents in the processes of the genesis of evil *on a large social scale*. [...]

> A relatively well-documented example of such an influence of a characteropathic personality on a macro-social scale is the last German emperor, Wilhelm II. He was subjected to brain trauma at birth. During and after his entire reign, his physical and psychological handicap was hidden from public knowledge. The motor abilities of the upper left portion of his body were handicapped. As a boy, he had difficulty learning grammar, geometry, and drawing, which constitutes *the typical triad of academic difficulties caused by minor brain lesions*. He developed a personality with infantilistic features and insufficient control over his emotions, and also a somewhat paranoid way of thinking which easily sidestepped the heart of some important issues in the process of dodging problems.

---

[26] Lobaczewski, op. cit.

[27] In other words, because epilepsy is so evident, people who have it generally do not achieve positions of power. They are known to be sick, and often their sickness is so severe that they are limited in their activities.

Militaristic poses and a general's uniform overcompensated for his feelings of inferiority and effectively cloaked his shortcomings. Politically, his insufficient control of emotions and factors of personal rancor came into view. The old Iron Chancellor had to go, that cunning and ruthless politician who had been loyal to the monarchy and built up Prussian power. After all, he was too knowledgeable about the prince's defects and had worked against his coronation. A similar fate met other overly critical people, who were replaced by persons with lesser brains, more subservience, and sometimes, discreet psychological deviations. Negative selection took place.

Notice this last term: "negative selection took place". That is to say, a defective head of state selected his staff, his government, based on his own pathologically damaged worldview. I'm sure the reader can perceive how dangerous such a situation can be to the people governed by such a "negatively selected" cabal. The important thing to consider here is what effect this had on the social constructs under the rule of such individuals. Lobaczewski explains:

The experience of people with such anomalies grows out of the normal human world to which they belong by nature. Thus, their different way of thinking, their emotional violence, and their egotism find relatively easy entry into other people's minds and are perceived within the categories of the natural world-view. *Such behavior on the part of persons with such character disorders traumatizes the minds and feelings of normal people, gradually diminishing their ability to use their common sense.* In spite of their resistance, *people become used to the rigid habits of pathological thinking and experiencing.* In young people, as a result, the personality suffers abnormal development leading to its malformation. They thus represent pathological ponerogenic factors which, by their covert activity, easily engenders new phases in the eternal genesis of evil, opening the door to a later activation of other factors which thereupon take over the main role. [...]

[In the case of the effect of Wilhelm II], *many Germans were progressively deprived of their ability to use their common sense* because of the impingement of psychological material of the characteropathic type, as the common people are prone to identify with the emperor...

A new generation grew up with *deformities as regards feeling and understanding moral, psychological, social and political realities.* It is extremely typical that in many German families containing a member who was psychologically not quite normal, it became a matter of honor (even excusing nefarious conduct) to hide this fact from public opinion - and even the awareness of close friends and relatives. Large portions of *society ingested psychopathological material, together with that unrealistic way of thinking* wherein slogans take on the power of arguments and real data are subjected to subconscious selection.

This occurred during a time when a wave of hysteria was growing throughout Europe, including a tendency for emotions to dominate and for human behavior to contain an element of histrionics. [...] This progressively took over three empires and other countries on the mainland.

To what extent did Wilhelm II contribute to this, along with two other emperors whose minds also did not take in the actual facts of history and government? To what extent were they themselves influenced by an intensification of hysteria during their reigns? That would make an interesting topic of discussion among historians and ponerologists.

International tensions increased; Archduke Ferdinand was assassinated in Sarajevo. However, neither the Kaiser nor any other governmental authority in his country possessed reason. (Due to the aforementioned negative selection process.) What came into play was Wilhelm's emotional attitude and the stereotypes of thought and action inherited from the past. War broke out. General war plans prepared earlier, which had lost their topicality under the new conditions, unfolded more like military maneuvers. Even those historians familiar with the genesis and character of the Prussian state, including its ideological tradition of bloody expansionism, intuit that these situations contained some activity of an uncomprehended fatality which eludes an analysis in terms of historical causality.

Many thoughtful persons keep asking the same anxious question: how could the German nation have chosen for a Fuehrer a clownish psychopath who made no bones about his pathological vision of superman rule? Under his leadership, Germany then unleashed a second war, criminal and politically absurd. *During the second half of this war, highly trained army officers honorably performed the inhuman orders, senseless from the political and military point of view, issued by a man whose psychological state corresponded to the routine criteria for being forcibly committed to psychiatric hospitalization.*

Any attempt to explain the things that occurred during the first half of our century by means of categories generally accepted in historical thought leaves behind a nagging feeling of inadequacy. Only a ponerological approach can compensate for this deficit in our comprehension, as it does justice to the role of various pathological factors in the genesis of evil at every social level.

Fed for generations on *pathologically altered psychological material*, the German nation fell into a state comparable to what we see in certain individuals raised by persons who are both characteropathic and hysterical. Psychologists know from experience how often such people then let themselves commit acts which seriously hurt others. […]

The Germans inflicted and suffered enormous pain during the first World War; they thus felt no substantial guilt and even thought they had been wronged, as *they were behaving in accordance with their customary habit without being aware of its pathological causes.* The need for this state to be clothed in heroic garb after a war in order to avoid bitter disintegration became all too common. A mysterious craving arose, as if the social organism had … become addicted to some drug. That was the hunger of pathologically modified psychological material, a phenomenon known to psychotherapeutic experience. This hunger could only be satisfied by another personality and system of government, both similarly pathological.

A characteropathic personality opened the door for leadership by a psychopathic individual. [28]

What is interesting at this point in Lobaczewski's discourse is his indication that this pattern repeats itself again and again in history: a pathologically brain-damaged individual creates circumstances that condition the public in a certain way, and this, then, opens the door for the psychopath to come to power. As I read this, I thought back to the last 45 or 50 years of history in America and realized that the "cold war", the nuclear threat, the assassination of JFK, the antics of Nixon, Johnson, Reagan, Clinton, the manipulation of Americans via the media, were just such characteropathic conditionings that opened the door for the Neocons and their nominal puppet, George W. Bush, who can certainly be described as "a clownish psychopath who makes no bones about his pathological vision of super-American rule". We can even see in the cabal that is assembled around George W. Bush, the same "negative selection" of advisors and cabinet officials as Lobaczewski described were assembled around Kaiser Wilhelm.

So, we begin to understand just how important this "science of evil adjusted for political purposes" may be and how much understanding we, as a society, lack. In order to understand exactly how an entire society, even an entire nation, can become a Pathocracy, we need to understand a little bit about the types of individuals that make up the core of such a "conspiracy". Lobaczewski discusses the most frequent characteropathies and their relation to brain lesions giving examples.

Paranoidal character disorders: It is characteristic of paranoid behavior for people to be capable of relatively correct reasoning and discussion as long as the conversation involves minor differences of opinions. This stops abruptly when the partner's arguments begin to undermine their overvalued ideas, crush their long-held stereotypes of reasoning, or force them to accept a conclusion they had subconsciously rejected before. Such a stimulus unleashes upon the partner a torrent of pseudo-logical, largely para-moralistic, often insulting utterances which always contain some degree of suggestion.

Utterances like these inspire aversion among cultivated and logical people, but they enslave less critical minds, e.g. people with other kinds of psychological deficiencies, who were earlier the objects of the egotistical influence of individuals with character disorders, and in particular a large part of the young. [...]

We know today that the psychological mechanism of paranoid phenomena is twofold: one is caused by damage to the brain tissue, the other is functional or behavioral.[...]

In persons free of brain-tissue lesions, such phenomena most frequently occur as a result of being reared by people with paranoidal characteropathia,

---

[28] Lobaczewski, op. cit.

along with the psychological terror of their childhood. Such psychological material is then assimilated creating the rigid stereotypes of abnormal experiencing. This makes it difficult for thought and world-view to develop normally, and the terror-blocked contents become transformed into permanent functional congestive centers.[…]

Frontal characteropathy: The frontal areas of the cerebral cortex (10A and B acc. to the Brodmann division) are virtually present in no creature except man; they are composed of the phylogenetically youngest nervous tissue. Their cyto-architecture is similar to the much older visual projection areas on the opposite pole of the brain. This suggests some functional similarity. […] As described by researchers (Luria et al.), the functions of these areas - thought-process acceleration and coordination - seem to result from this basic function.

Damage to this area … has been significantly reduced due to improved medical care for pregnant women and newborns. The spectacular ponerogenic role which results from character disorders caused by this can thus be considered somewhat characteristic of past generations and primitive cultures.

Brain cortex damage in these areas selectively impairs the above mentioned function without impairing memory, associative capacity, or in particular such instinct-based feelings and functions as for instance the ability to intuit a psychological situation. The general intelligence of an individual is thus not greatly reduced. […]

The pathological character of such people, generally containing a component of hysteria, develops through the years. The non-damaged psychological functions become overdeveloped to compensate, which means that instinctive and affective reactions predominate. Relatively vital people become belligerent, risk-happy, and brutal in both word and deed. Persons with an innate talent for intuiting psychological situations tend to take advantage of this gift in an egotistical and ruthless fashion. In the thought process of such people, a short cut way develops which bypasses the handicapped function, thus leading from associations directly to words, deeds, and decisions which are not subject to any dissuasion. Such individuals interpret their talent for intuiting situations and making split-second oversimplified decisions as a sign of their superiority compared to normal people, who need to think for long time, experiencing self-doubt and conflicting motivations. The fate of such creatures does not deserve to be pondered long.

Such "Stalinistic characters" traumatize and actively spellbind others, and their influence finds it exceptionally easy to bypass the controls of common sense. A large proportion of people tends to credit such individuals with special powers, thereby succumbing to their egotistic beliefs. If a parent manifests such a defect, no matter how minimal, all the children in the family evidence anomalies in personality development.

The author studied an entire generation of older, educated, people wherein the source of such influence was the eldest sister who suffered perinatal damage of frontal centers. From early childhood, her four younger brothers assimilated pathologically altered psychological material, including their sister's growing component of hysteria. They retained well into their sixties the deformities of personality and world-view, as well as hysterical features thus caused, whose intensity diminished in proportion to the greater difference in age. Subconscious selection of information made it impossible for them to apprehend any critical comments regarding their sister's character, also these were capable of offending family honor. The brothers accepted as real their sister's pathological delusions and complaints about her "bad" husband (who was actually a decent person) and her son, in whom she found a scapegoat to avenge her failures. They thereby participated in a world of vengeful emotions, considering their sister a completely normal person whom they were prepared to defend - by the most unsavory methods, if need be - against any suggestions of her abnormality. They thought normal woman were insipid and naive, good for nothing but sexual conquest. Not one among the brothers ever created a healthy family or developed even average wisdom of life.

The character development of these people also included many other factors dependent upon the time and place in which they were reared: the turn of the century, with a patriotic Polish father and German mother who obeyed contemporary custom by formally accepting her husband's nationality, but who still remained an advocate of the militarism and accepting of the intensified hysteria which covered Europe at the time. That was the Europe of the three Emperors: The concept of "honor" sanctified triumph. Staring at someone too long was sufficient pretext for a duel. These brothers were thus raised to be valiant duelist full of saber-scars; however, the slashes they inflicted upon their opponents were more frequent and much worse.[...]

[All other considerations of time and place aside] if the sister had not suffered brain damage and the pathological factor had not existed the evil [these men] sowed too liberally during their lives would either not have existed at all, or else been reduced to a scope conditioned by more remote pathological factors. [...]

Comparative considerations also led the author to conclude that Iosif Vissarionovich Dzhugashvili, also known as Stalin, should be included in the list of this particular ponerogenic characteropathy, which developed against the backdrop of perinatal damage to his brain's prefrontal fields. Literature and news about him abounds in indications: brutal, charismatic snake-charming; issuing of irrevocable decisions; inhuman ruthlessness, pathologic revengefulness directed at anyone who got in his way; and egotistical belief in his own genius on the part of a person whose mind was in fact average. This state explains as well his psychological dependence on a psychopath like Beria. Some photographs reveal the typical deformation of his forehead which appears in people who suffered very early damage to the areas mentioned above. [...]

Drug induced characteropathies: During the last few decades, medicine has begun using a series of drugs with serious side effects: they attack the nervous system, leaving permanent damage behind. These generally discrete handicaps sometimes give rise to personality changes which are often very harmful socially. Streptomycin proved a very dangerous drug; as a result, some countries have limited its use, whereas others have taken it off the list of drugs whose use is permitted.

The cytostatic[29] drugs used in treating neoplastic diseases often attack the phylogenetically oldest brain tissue, the primary carrier of our instinctive substratum and basic feelings. Persons treated with such drugs progressively tend to lose their emotional color and their ability to intuit a psychological situation. They retain their intellectual functions but become praise-craving egocentrics, easily ruled by people who know how to take advantage of this. They become indifferent to other people's feelings and the harm they are inflicting upon them; any criticism of their own person or behavior is repaid with a vengeance. Such a change of character in a person who until recently enjoyed respect on the part of his environment or community, which perseveres in human minds, becomes a pathological phenomenon causing often tragic results.[…]

Similar to the above in psychological picture, such results may be caused by endogenous toxins or viruses. When sometimes the mumps proceeds with a brain reaction, it leaves in its wake a discrete pallor or flatness of feelings and a slight decrease in mental efficiency. Similar phenomena are witnessed after a difficult bout with diphtheria. Finally polio also attacks the brain [..] People with leg paresis rarely manifest these effects, but those with paresis of the neck and/or shoulders must count themselves lucky if they do not. In addition to affective pallor, persons manifesting these effects usually evidence an inability to comprehend the crux of a matter and naïveté. […]

Character anomalies developing as a result of brain-tissue damage behave like insidious ponerogenic factors. As a result of the above-described features, [ponerogenic influences] easily anchor in human minds, traumatizing our psyches, impoverishing and deforming our thoughts and feelings, and limiting individuals' and societies' ability to use common sense and recognize a psychological or moral situation. This opens the door to other pathological characters who most frequently carry some inherited psychological deviations. They then push the characteropathic individuals into the shadows and proceed with their ponerogenic work. That is why various types of characteropathies participate in the initial periods of the genesis of evil, both on the macro social scale and on the individual scale of human families.

An improved social system of the future should thus protect individuals and societies by preventing persons with the above deviations, or the characteristics to be discussed below, from any social functions wherein the fate of other people would depend upon their behavior. This of course applies primarily to top governmental positions. Such questions should be decided by an appropriate institution composed of people with a reputation for wisdom and with medical and psychological training. The features of brain-tissue lesions and their character disorder results are much easier to detect than some inherited anomalies. Thus, stifling ponerogenic process by

---

[29] Used to treat cancers.

removing these factors from the process of the synthesis of evil is effective during the early phases of such genesis, and much easier in practice.

Inherited Deviations

Science already protects societies from the results of some physiological anomalies which are accompanied by certain psychological weaknesses. The tragic role played by hereditary hemophilia among European royalty is well known. Responsible people nowadays are anxious not to allow a carrier of such a gene to become queen. Any society lavishing so much care upon individuals with blood-coagulation insufficiency would protest if a man with this anomaly were appointed to a high office. This behavior model should be extended to many other inherited anomalies.

Daltonists, men with an impaired ability to distinguish red and green colors from grey are now barred from professions in which this impairment might cause a catastrophe. We also know that this anomaly is accompanied by a decrease in esthetic experience, emotions, and the feeling of being linked to a society of people who can see colors normally. Industrial psychologists are thus cautious whether such a person should be entrusted with work involving a dependence upon man's autonomic sense of responsibility, as workers' safety is contingent upon this sense.

It was discovered long ago that this anomaly is inherited by means of a gene located on the X chromosome and tracking the transmission through many generations does not meet with difficulty. Genetics have similarly studied inheritance of many other features of human organisms, but they paid scant attention to the anomalies interesting us. Many features of human character have a hereditary basis in genes located in the same X chromosome; although it is not a rule. Something similar could apply to the majority of psychological anomalies discussed below. [...]

Severe problems are caused by the XYY karyotype which produces men who are tall, strong, and emotionally violent... but their number and role in ponerogenic processes is very small.[30]

Much more numerous are those psychological deviations which play a correspondingly greater role as pathological factors involving ponerological processes; they are most probably transmitted through normal hereditary ways. However, this realm of genetics is faced with manifold biological and psychological difficulties. [31]

Lobaczewski next describes a number of inherited psychological pathologies such as Schizoidal psychopathy - now referred to as "schizotypal personality disorder" - about which he says:

Carriers of this anomaly are hypersensitive and distrustful, but they pay little attention to the feelings of others, tend to assume extreme positions, and are

---

[30] This is due primarily to the fact that they are early identied as violent and anti-social, and commit overt criminal acts which results in their being removed from society.

[31] Lobaczewski, op. cit.

eager to retaliate for minor offenses. Sometimes they are eccentric and odd. Their poor sense of psychological situation and reality leads them to superimpose erroneous, pejorative interpretations upon other people's intentions. They easily become involved in activities which are ostensibly moral, but which actually inflict damage upon themselves and others. Their impoverished psychological world-view makes them typically pessimistic. [...] When they become wrapped up in situations of serious stress, their failings cause them to collapse easily. ...The schizoids frequently fall into reactive psychotic states so similar in appearance to schizophrenia that they lead to misdiagnoses.

If the emotional pressure on them is minimized, they are able to develop proper speculative reasoning, but they tend to consider themselves intellectually superior to "ordinary" people.

The quantitative frequency of this anomaly varies among races. *It is low among Blacks, and highest among Jews.* Observation suggests that it is autosomally hereditary.

A schizoid's ponerological activity should be evaluated in two aspects. On the small scale, such people cause their families trouble, easily turn into tools of intrigue in the hands of clever individuals, and generally do a poor job of raising the younger generation. [...]

However, their ponerogenic role can take on macro social proportions if their attitude toward human reality and their tendency to invent great doctrines are put to paper and duplicated in large editions.

In spite of their typical deficits, or even an openly Schizoidal declaration, their readers do not realize what the authors' characters are like, and tend to interpret such works in a way that corresponds to their own nature. The minds of normal people tend toward corrective interpretation thanks to the participation of their own richer psychological world-view. However, many readers reject such works with moral disgust but without being aware of the specific cause. An analysis of the role played by Karl Marx's works easily reveals all the above mentioned types of apperception and the social reactions which engendered separations among people.[32]

Essential Psychopathy.

We now come to the most important pathology: psychopathy. Psychopathy is not, as many people think, so easy to recognize. The problem is that the term "psychopath" has come to be usually applied by the public (due to the influence of the media) to overtly and obviously mad-dog murderers. There is also some confusion regarding psychopathy vis a vis "antisocial personality disorder".

Nice words, aren't they? They sound so clean and clinical; just a person who is "anti-social". It almost suggests a hermit who never bothers

---

[32] Lobaczewski, op. cit.

anybody. But nothing could be further from the truth. Robert Hare, the current American guru on psychopathy, writes about this problem of terminology as follows:

> Traditionally, affective and interpersonal traits such as egocentricity, deceit, shallow affect, manipulativeness, selfishness, and lack of empathy, guilt or remorse, have played a central role in the conceptualization and diagnosis of psychopathy (Cleckley; Hare 1993; in press); Widiger and Corbitt). In 1980 this tradition was broken with the publication of *DSM-III*. Psychopathy-renamed antisocial personality disorder- was now defined by persistent violations of social norms, including lying, stealing, truancy, inconsistent work behavior and traffic arrests.

> Among the reasons given for this dramatic shift away from the use of clinical inferences were that personality traits are difficult to measure reliably, and that it is easier to agree on the behaviors that typify a disorder than on the reasons why they occur. The result was a diagnostic category with good reliability but dubious validity, a category that lacked congruence with other, well-established conceptions of psychopathy. […]

> The problems with *DSM-III* and its 1987 revision *(DSM-III-R)* were widely discussed in the clinical and research literature (Widiger and Corbitt). Much of the debate concerned the absence of personality traits in the diagnosis of ASPD, an omission that allowed antisocial individuals with completely different personalities, attitudes and motivations to share the same diagnosis. At the same time, there was mounting evidence that the criteria for ASPD defined a disorder that was more artifactual than "real" (Livesley and Schroeder). […]

> Most psychopaths (with the exception of those who somehow manage to plow their way through life without coming into formal or prolonged contact with the criminal justice system) meet the criteria for ASPD, *but most individuals with ASPD are not psychopaths.* […]

> The differences between psychopathy and ASPD are further highlighted by recent laboratory research involving the processing and use of linguistic and emotional information. Psychopaths differ dramatically from non-psychopaths in their performance of a variety of cognitive and affective tasks. Compared with normal individuals, for example, psychopaths are less able to process or use the deep semantic meanings of language and to appreciate the emotional significance of events or experiences (Larbig and others; Patrick; Williamson and others). […]

> Things become even more problematic when we consider that the *DSM-IV* text description of ASPD (which it says is also known as psychopathy) contains many references to traditional features of psychopathy. […]

> The failure to differentiate between psychopathy and ASPD can have serious consequences for clinicians and for society. For example, most jurisdictions consider psychopathy to be an aggravating rather than a mitigating factor in determining criminal responsibility. In some states an offender convicted of first-degree murder and diagnosed as a psychopath is likely to receive the death penalty on the grounds that psychopaths are cold-blooded,

remorseless, untreatable and almost certain to re-offend. But many of the killers on death row were, and continue to be, mistakenly referred to as psychopaths on the basis of *DSM-III, DSM-III-R or DSM-IV* criteria for ASPD (Meloy). We don't know how many of these inhabitants of death row actually exhibit the personality structure of the psychopath, or how many merely meet the criteria for ASPD, a disorder that applies to the majority of criminals and that has only tenuous implications for treatability and the likelihood of violent reoffending. If a diagnosis of psychopathy has consequences for the death penalty- or for any other severe disposition, such as an indeterminate sentence or a civil commitment- clinicians making the diagnosis should make certain they do not confuse ASPD with psychopathy. [...]

Diagnostic confusion about the two disorders has the potential for harming psychiatric patients and society as well.

In my book, *Without Conscience*, I argued that we live in a "camouflage society," a society in which some psychopathic traits- egocentricity, lack of concern for others, superficiality, style over substance, being "cool," manipulativeness, and so forth- increasingly are tolerated and even valued. With respect to the topic of this article, it is easy to see how both psychopaths and those with ASPD could blend in readily with groups holding antisocial or criminal values. It is more difficult to envisage how those with ASPD could hide out among more prosocial segments of society. Yet *psychopaths have little difficulty infiltrating the domains of business, politics, law enforcement, government, academia and other social structures* (Babiak). *It is the egocentric, cold-blooded and remorseless psychopaths who blend into all aspects of society and have such devastating impacts on people around them* who send chills down the spines of law enforcement officers. [33]

Regarding essential psychopathy, Lobaczewski tells us:

Let us characterise another heredity-transmitted anomaly whose *role in ponerogenic processes on any social scale appears exceptionally great.* We should underscore that the need to isolate this phenomenon and examine it in detail became most evident to those researchers who were interested in the *macro social scale of genesis of evil* because they have witnessed it. I acknowledge my debt to Kasimir Dabrowski in doing this and calling this anomaly an "essential psychopathy."

Biologically speaking, the phenomenon is similar to color-blindness and occurs with similar frequency,(slightly above .5 percent) except that, unlike color-blindness, it affects both sexes.

Here, Lobaczewski suggests a particular low frequency of occurrence of psychopathy which reminds us again of the 1.15 percent of Lobaczewski's total population that did not demonstrate any overtly identifiable pathology except that they performed actions that bring harm to other people for no explainable reason. If we consider what Dr. Hare has written

---

[33] Hare, Robert, Ph.D., February 1996, "Psychopathy and Antisocial Personality Disorder: A Case of Diagnostic Confusion"; *Psychiatric Times*, Volume XIII, Issue 2.

above, that psychopaths *have little difficulty infiltrating the domains of business, politics, law enforcement, government, academia and other social structures* [they] *blend into all aspects of society.* we must ask the question: is it possible that Lobaczewski's 1.15 percent of unidentified "evildoers" were this type of psychopath? As he pointed out, it could very well have been the diagnostic criteria that was lacking, and had he utilized Hare's psychopathy check-list, this group might very well have been identified as psychopaths. The point I wish to make is the number of psychopathic individuals likely to be found in any given cross-section sampling of society may be much higher than we suspect. Lobaczewski suggests that the occurrence of psychopathy is about the same as color-blindness: .5 percent. But if you add that figure to the 1.15 percent that he couldn't identify, the actual number may be closer to 1.65 percent.

Here I ought to mention that Harvard psychologist Martha Stout claims that 4 percent of "ordinary people" (one in 25) often have an *"undetected mental disorder, the chief symptom of which is that the person possesses no conscience. He or she has no ability whatsoever to feel shame, guilt, or remorse... They can do literally anything at all and feel absolutely no guilt."*[34] That just happens to fit right in with Hare's description of psychopathy, though we are obviously dealing with an entire spectrum of manifestation, not to mention the difference between pathologies that are mechanical, i.e. brain damage, and pathologies that are inherited. If we add Stout's figure of 4 percent of undetected, "ordinary" people, to Lobaczewski's .5 percent, and include the 1.5 percent of people who had done harm to others with no evident pathology, we then have a figure of 5.65 percent - almost 6 percent of the population. Remember what Lobaczewski wrote about the influence of "indoctrination" on his peers?

> It was relatively easy to determine the environments and origin of the people who succumbed to this process, which I then called "transpersonification". They came from all social groups, including aristocratic and fervently religious families, and caused a break in our student solidarity in the order of some 6 %. [...]
>
> Even then, we had no doubts as to the pathological nature of this "transpersonification" process, which ran similar but not identical in all cases. The duration of the results of this phenomenon also varied. Some of these people later became zealots. Others later took advantage of various circumstances to withdraw and reestablish their lost links to the society of normal people. They were replaced. The only constant value of the new social system was the magic number of 6 %.

This is an interesting thing, this coincidence of numbers. I have no explanation for it because we are certainly talking about many factors and not a single pathology. Continuing with Lobaczewski's ponerological view of psychopathy:

---

[34] Stout, Marth, Ph.D. 2005, *The Sociopath Next Door*, Broadway Books, NY

Its intensity also varies in scope from a level barely perceptive to an experienced observer to obvious pathological deficiency. Like color-blindness, this anomaly also *appears to represent a deficit in stimulus transformation*, albeit occurring *not on the sensory but on instinctive level.* Psychiatrists of the old school used to call such individuals "Daltonists of human feelings and socio-moral values."

The psychological picture shows clear deficits among men only; among women it is generally toned down, as by the effect of the second normal allele. This suggests that the anomaly is also inherited via the X chromosome but through a semi-dominating gene. However, the author was unable to confirm this by excluding inheritance from father to son.

Analysis of the different experiential manner demonstrated by these individuals caused us to conclude that their instinctive substratum is also defective, containing certain gaps and lacking the natural syntonic[35] responses commonly evidenced by members of the species Homo sapiens. [...]

Our natural world of concepts then strikes such persons as a nearly incomprehensible convention with no justification in their own psychological experience. They think that normal human customs and principles of decency are a foreign convention invented and imposed by someone else ("probably by priests") silly, onerous, sometimes even ridiculous. At the same time, however, *they easily perceive the deficiencies and weaknesses of our natural language of psychological and moral concepts* in a manner somewhat reminiscent of the attitude of a contemporary psychologist - except in caricature.

The average intelligence of individuals with the above mentioned deviation, especially if measured via commonly used tests, is somewhat lower than that of normal people, albeit similarly variegated. However, this group does not contain instances of the highest intelligence, *nor do we find technical or craftsmanship talents among them.* The most gifted members of this kind may thus achieve accomplishments in those sciences which *do not require humanistic worldview or practical skills.* Whenever we attempt to construct special tests to measure "life wisdom" or "socio-moral imagination", even if the difficulties of psychometric evaluation are taken into account, individuals of this type indicate a deficit disproportionate to their personal IQ.

In spite of their deficiencies as regards normal psychological and moral knowledge, *they develop and then have at their disposal a knowledge of their own*, something *lacked* by people with a natural worldview.

They learn to *recognize each other in a crowd as early as childhood*, and they develop an awareness of the existence of other individuals similar to them.

---

[35] From the Greek word "Syntony," to "bring into balance".

They also *become conscious of being different* from the world of those other people surrounding them. They view us from a certain distance, lake a paraspecific variety.

Natural human reactions - which often fail to elicit interest because they are considered self-evident - strike psychopaths as strange and therefore interesting, even comical. They therefore *observe us, deriving conclusions*, forming their different world of concepts.

They become *experts in our weaknesses* and sometimes effect heartless experiments upon us. ... Neither a normal person nor our natural worldview can perceive or properly evaluate the existence of this world of different concepts.

A researcher into such phenomena can glean a similar deviant knowledge through long-term studies of the personalities of such people, using it with some difficulty, like a foreign language. ... [The psychopath] will never be able to incorporate the worldview of a normal person, although they often try to do so all their lives. The product of their efforts is only a role and a mask behind which they hide their deviant reality.

Another myth and role - albeit containing a grain of truth - would be the psychopath's brilliant mind or psychological genius; some of them actually believe in this and attempt to insinuate this belief to others. In speaking of the mask of psychological normality worn by such individuals (and by similar deviants to a lesser extent), we should mention the book *The Mask of Sanity*; the author, Hervey Cleckley, made this very phenomenon the crux of his reflections:

> Let us remember that his typical behavior defeats what appear to be his own aims. Is it not he himself who is most deeply deceived by his apparent normality? Although he deliberately cheats others and is *quite conscious of his lies*, he appears unable to distinguish adequately between his own pseudointentions, pseudoremorse, pseudolove, and the genuine responses of a normal person. His *monumental lack of insight indicates how little he appreciates the nature of his disorder*. When others fail to accept immediately his "word of honor as a gentleman," his amazement, I believe, is often genuine. The term genuine is used here not to qualify the psychopath's intentions but to qualify his amazement. *His subjective experience is so bleached of deep emotion that he is invincibly ignorant of what life means to others.*
>
> His awareness of hypocrisy's opposite is so insubstantially theoretical that it becomes questionable if what we chiefly mean by hypocrisy should be attributed to him. *Having no major values himself, can he be said to realize adequately the nature and quality of the outrages his conduct inflicts upon others?* A young child who has no impressive memory of severe pain may have been told by his mother it is wrong to cut off the dog's tail. Knowing it is wrong he may proceed with the operation. We need not totally absolve him of responsibility if we say he realized less what he did than an adult who, in full appreciation of physical agony, so uses a knife. Can a person experience the deeper levels of sorrow without considerable knowledge of happiness? Can he achieve evil intention in

the full sense without real awareness of evil's opposite? I have no final answer to these questions.[36]

All researchers into psychopathy underline three qualities primarily with regard to this most typical variety: The absence of a sense of guilt for antisocial actions, the inability to love truly, and the *tendency to be garrulous* in a way which easily deviates from reality.

A neurotic patient is generally taciturn and has trouble explaining what hurts him most. [...] These patients are capable of decent and enduring love, although they have difficulty expressing it or achieving their dreams. A psychopath's behavior constitutes the antipode of such phenomena and difficulties.

Our first contact [with the psychopath] is characterized by a *talkative stream which flows with ease* and avoids truly important matters with equal ease if they are uncomfortable for the talker. His train of thought also avoids those matter of human feelings and values whose representation is absent in the psychopathic world view. [...] From the logical point of view, the flow of thought is ostensibly correct...

[Psychopaths] are virtually unfamiliar with the enduring emotions of love for another person... it constitutes a fairy-tale from that "other" human world. [For the psychopath] love is an ephemeral phenomenon aimed at sexual adventure. However [the psychopath] is able to play the lover's role well enough for their partners to accept it in good faith. [Moral teachings] also strike them as a similar fairy-tale good only for children and those different "others."[...]

The world of normal people whom they hurt is incomprehensible and hostile to them. [...] [Life to the psychopath] is the pursuit of its immediate attractions, pleasure and power. They meet with failure along this road, along with force and condemnation from the society of those other incomprehensible people.[37]

It should be emphasized that psychopaths are quite often interesting - even exciting! They exude a captivating energy that keeps their listeners on the edge of their seats. Even if some part of the normal person is shocked or repelled by what the psychopath says, they are like the mouse hypnotized by the torturing cat. Even if they have the chance to run away, they don't. Many Psychopaths "make their living" by using charm, deceit, and manipulation to gain the confidence of their victims. Many of them can be found in white collar professions where they are aided in their evil by the fact that most people expect certain classes of people to be trustworthy because of their social or professional credentials. Lawyers, doctors, teachers, politicians, psychiatrists and psychologists, generally do not have to earn our trust because they have it by virtue of their positions. But the fact is: psychopaths are found in such lofty spheres also!

---

[36] Cleckley, Hervey, *The Mask of Sanity*
[37] Lobaczewski, op. cit.

At the same time, psychopaths are good impostors. *They have absolutely no hesitation about forging and brazenly using impressive credentials to adopt professional roles that bring prestige and power.* They pick professions in which the requisite skills are easy to fake, the jargon is easy to learn, and the credentials are unlikely to be thoroughly checked. *Psychopaths find it extremely easy to pose as financial consultants, ministers, psychological counsellors and psychologists.* And that's a scary thought.

Psychopaths make their way by conning people into doing things for them; obtaining money for them, prestige, power, *or even standing up for them when others try to expose them.* But that is their claim to fame. That's what they do. And they do it very well. What's more, the job is very easy because *most people are gullible with an unshakable belief in the inherent goodness of man* which, I should add, has been programmed into normal people by psychopaths.[38]

Returning to the work of Lobaczewski, he next gives us the most important clues as to how and why a truly global conspiracy can and does exist on our planet though it certainly isn't a conspiracy in the normally accepted sense of the word. You could even say that such conspiracies arise simply as a natural result of the opposition between normal people and deviants. In a certain sense, understanding the view the psychopath has of "normal people," that they are "other" and even "foreign," helps us to realize how such conspiracies can be so "secret" - though that is not the precise word we would like to use. Lobaczewski describes it in the following way:

> In any society in this world, psychopathic individuals and some of the other deviants create a ponerogenically active network of common collusions, *partially estranged from the community of normal people.* Some inspirational role of the essential psychopathy in this network also appears to be a common phenomenon.
>
> They are aware of being different as they obtain their life experience and become familiar with different ways of fighting for their goals. Their world is forever divided into "us and them" - their world with its own laws and customs and that other foreign world full of presumptuous ideas and customs in light of which they are condemned morally.
>
> Their "sense of honor" bids them cheat and revile that other human world and its values. In contradiction to the customs of normal people, they feel non-fulfillment of their promises or obligations is customary behavior.
>
> *They also learn how their personalities can have traumatizing effects on the personalities of those normal people, and how to take advantage of this root of terror for purposes of reaching their goals.*

---

[38] Special thanks to Wendy Koenigsmann for this synopsis of the psychopathic traits. Her website is a source of inestimable value to the researcher: http://www.geocities.com/lycium7/psychopathy.html

This *dichotomy of worlds is permanent* and does not disappear even if they succeed in realizing their dreams of gaining power over the society of normal people. This proves that the separation is biologically conditioned.

In such people a dream emerges like some youthful Utopia of a "happy" world and a social system which would not reject them or force them to submit to laws and customs whose meaning is incomprehensible to them. They dream of a world in which their simple and radical way of experiencing and perceiving reality would dominate, where *they* would, of course, be assured safety and prosperity. Those "others" - different, but also more technically skillful - should be put to work to achieve this goal. "We," after all, will create a new government, one of justice. They are prepared to fight and suffer for the sake of such a brave new world, and also of course, to inflict suffering upon others. Such a vision justifies killing people whose suffering does not move them to compassion because "they" are not quite conspecific.[39]

And there it is. Lobaczewski has said outright that psychopaths - from a certain perspective - are a different type of human being, a type that is aware of its difference from childhood. Put this together with his statement that such individuals *recognize their own kind*, and consider normal people as completely "other", and we can begin to understand why and how conspiracies can and do exist among such individuals. They do, indeed, collect together, with similar worldviews, like fat floating on a bowl of soup. When one of them begins to rant, others like them - or those with brain damage that makes them susceptible - "rally round the flag", so to say. Thus it is, when Robin Ramsay writes:

> Ultimately it comes down to how you see the world. The kind of conspiracy you are describing, or implying, is inconceivable to me: too big, too complex, too likely to go wrong or be discovered, ever to be mounted. What you are describing ... is vastly much bigger - and more complex and more dangerous - than any known mind control/psy ops project. And there is no evidence for it.[40]

He may be viewing the world without full knowledge and awareness of psychopaths and their ponerogenic networks.

Speaking of networks, we need to take a closer look at how psychopaths affect other human beings whom they use to create the basis for their rule in macro-social dynamics. This highlights the fact that the lack of psychological knowledge among the general public, not to mention the general neurosis of most people, make them vulnerable to such predators.

> Subordinating a normal person to psychologically abnormal individuals *has a deforming effect on his personality*: it engenders trauma and neurosis. This is accomplished in a manner which generally evades sufficient conscious controls. Such a situation then deprives the person of his natural rights to practice his own mental hygiene, *develop a sufficiently autonomous*

---

[39] Lobaczewski, op. cit.
[40] Robin Ramsay, private correspondence with one of the authors.

personality, and utilize his common sense. In the light of natural law, it thus constitutes a kind of illegality which can appear in any social scale although it is not mentioned in any code of law.[41]

Psychologist George Simon discusses what he refers to as "Covert-aggressive personalities" which, upon reading his book, reveal themselves to be members of the psychopathy spectrum. He writes:

> Aggressive personalities don't like anyone pushing them to do what they don't want to do or stopping them from doing what they want to do. "No" is never an answer they accept.

> [In some cases], if they can see some benefit in self-restraint, they may internalize inhibitions [and become covertly aggressive].

> By refraining from any overt acts of hostility towards others, they manage to convince themselves and others they're not the ruthless people they are.[42] They may observe the letter of a law but violate its spirit with ease. They may exhibit behavioral constraint when it's in their best interest, but they resist truly submitting themselves to any higher authority or set of principles. [They are] striving primarily to conceal their true intentions and aggressive agendas from others. They may behave with civility and propriety when they're closely scrutinized or vulnerable. But when they believe they're immune from detection or retribution, it's an entirely different story. [...]

> Dealing with covert-aggressive personalities is like getting whiplash. Often, you really don't know what's hit you until long after the damage is done. ...

> Covert-aggressives are often so expert at exploiting the weaknesses and emotional insecurities of others that almost anyone can be duped...

> Covert-aggressives exploit situations in which they are well aware of the vulnerability of their prey. They are often very selective about the kinds of people with whom they will associate or work. They are particularly adept at finding and keeping others in a one-down position. They relish being in positions of power over others. It's my experience that how a person uses power is the most reliable test of their character...[43]

Now, just imagine that the almost 2 in 25 people mentioned by Martha Stout: *The Sociopath Next Door,* being the very ones who seek and achieve positions of power and authority in just about any field of endeavour where power can be had, and you begin to understand how truly damaging this can be to an entire society. Imagine school teachers with power over your children who are "covert-aggressives". Imagine doctors, psychologists, "ministers of the faith"[44] and politicians in such positions.

---

[41] Lobaczewski, op. cit.

[42] This echoes exactly what Cleckley said about psychopaths, quoted above.

[43] Simon, George, op. cit.

[44] George Simon relates a case of a Christian minister in his book. It is a fascinating study of how Christianity is used to achieve power over others, subordinating them to psychologically aberrant ideas and thus, deforming their personalities.

With this understanding, we begin to get an even better idea of how psychopaths can conspire and actually pull it off: in a society where evil is not studied or understood, they easily "rise to the top" and proceed to condition normal people to accept their dominance, to accept their lies without question. As noted at the beginning of this section:

> Long periods of preoccupation with the self and "accumulating benefits" for the self, diminish the ability to accurately read the environment and other people. [...]It is this feature, *this hystericization of society, that enables pathological plotters, snake charmers, and other primitive deviants to act as essential factors in the processes of the origination of evil on a macro-social scale.*

We see exactly this pattern of social development in the United States over the past 50 to 60 years or even more. The fact is, many people who may have been born "normal" have become what might be termed "secondary psychopaths" or characteropaths due to the influence of psychopathy on American culture from many fields - including science, medicine, psychology, law, etc - where they are conscious of what they are doing to "normal" people! Lobaczewski continues with his discussion of the effect of psychopaths on normal individuals:

> We have already discussed the nature of some pathological personalities - characteropathies - that may be "created" by an individual's exposure to a person with a severe character deformation. *Essential psychopathy has exceptionally intense effects in this manner.* Something mysterious gnaws into the personality of an individual at the mercy of the psychopath, and it is fought like a demon. His emotions become chilled, his sense of psychological reality is stifled. This leads to decriterialization of thought and *a feeling of helplessness culminating in depressive reactions* which can be so severe that psychiatrists sometimes misdiagnose them as a manic-depressive psychosis. Many people evidently also rebel much earlier and start searching for some way to liberate themselves from such an influence.
>
> A social structure dominated by normal people and their conceptual world easily appears to the psychopath as a "system of force and oppression". If it happens that true injustice does, in fact, exist in that given society, pathological feelings of unfairness and suggestive statements can resonate among those who have truly been treated unfairly. Revolutionary doctrines may then find approval among both groups although their motivations will actually be quite different.
>
> The presence of pathogenic bacteria in our environment is a common phenomenon; however, it is not the single decisive factor as regards whether an individual or a society becomes ill. Similarly, psychopathological factors alone do not decide about the spread of evil. [...][45]

---

[45] Lobaczewski, op. cit.

Other Psychopathies

We can also include within psychopathic categories a somewhat indeterminate number of anomalies with a hereditary substratum...

We also meet difficult individuals with a tendency to behave in a manner hurtful to other people, for whom tests do not indicate existing damage to brain tissue and there is no indication of abnormal child-rearing background. The fact that such cases are repeated within families would suggest a hereditary substratum.[...]

Such people also attempt to mask their different world of experience and play a role of normal people to varying degrees... These people participate in the genesis of evil in very different ways, whether taking part openly or, to a lesser extent, when they have managed to adapt to proper ways of living. These psychopathies and related phenomena may, quantitatively speaking, be summarily estimated at two or three times the number of cases of essential psychopathy, i.e. at less than two per cent of the population.

This type of person finds it easier to adjust to social life. The lesser cases in particular adapt to the demands of the society of normal people, taking advantage of its understanding for the arts and other areas with similar traditions. Their literary creativity is often disturbing if conceived in ideational categories alone; they insinuate to their readers that their world of concepts and experiences is self-evident, also it actually contains characteristic deformities.

The most frequently indicated and known type is the *asthenic psychopath* which appears in every conceivable intensity, from barely perceptible to an obvious pathologic deficiency. These people, asthenic and hypersensitive, do not indicate the same glaring deficit in moral feeling and ability to sense a psychological situation as it appears in essential psychopathy. They are somewhat idealistic and tend to have superficial pangs of conscience as a result of their faulty behavior. On the average, they are also less intelligent than normal people, and their mind avoids consistency and accuracy in reasoning. Their psychological worldview is clearly falsified, so their options about people can never be trusted. A kind of mask cloaks the world of their personal aspirations which is at variance with the official ones demanded by a situation. Their behavior towards people who do not notice their faults is urbane, even friendly. However, the same people manifest a pre-emptive hostility and aggression against persons with a talent for psychology or proper knowledge in this area.

They are relatively less vital sexually and therefore amenable to accept celibacy; that is why some Catholic monks and priests often represent lesser or minor cases of this anomaly. They are the chief factor which inspired the anti-psychological attitude traditional in Church thinking.

The more severe cases are more brutally anti-psychological and contemptuous of normal people; they tend to be active in the processes of the genesis of evil on a larger scale. Their dreams do not lack a certain idealism similar to the ideas of normal people. They would like to reform the world to their liking but are unable to foresee more far-reaching implications and results. Spiced by deviance, their visions may influence naïve rebels of people who have in fact suffered injustice. Existing social injustice may look like a justification for a radicalized world-view and the assimilation of such visions.

The following is an example of the thought-pattern of a person who seems a typical and severe case of asthenic psychopathy:

> *"If I had to start life all over again, I'd do exactly the same: it's organic necessity, nor the dictates of duty. I have one thing which keeps me going and bids me be serene even when things are so very sad. That is an unshakable faith in people. Conditions will change and evil will cease to reign, and man will be a brother to man, not a wolf as is the case today. My forbearance derives not from my fancy, but rather from my clear vision of the cause which give rise to evil."*

Those words were written in prison on December 15, 1913 by Felix Dzierzhynski, (1877-1926), who is best known as the first head of the Soviet "Cheka", or Soviet security police, the forerunner of the KGB. Spreading fear in a time of chaos, the Cheka was the perfect instrument for Stalin's ruthless consolidation of power. Dzierzhynski made Robespierre look like a pansy, being responsible for the murder of literally millions of people.

If the time ever comes when "conditions will change" and "evil will no longer rule," it could be because progress in the study of pathological phenomena and their ponerogenic role will make it possible for societies to quietly accept the existence of these phenomena and comprehend them as categories of nature. The vision of a new, just structure of society can then be realized within the framework and under the control of normal people. Having reconciled ourselves to the fact that psychopaths are different and have a limited capacity for social adjustment, we should create a system of permanent protection for them within the framework of reason and proper knowledge.

Here it should be noted that psychologically normal people constitute both the great statistical majority of human type beings and thus, as Lobaczewski points out, according to natural law, should be the ones to set the pace; moral law is derived from their nature. Power should be in the hands of normal people.

For our purposes, we should also draw attention to psychopathic types with deviant features: these were isolated relatively long ago by Brzezicki and accepted by E. Kretschmer[46] as characteristic of Eastern Europe in

---

[46] Ernst Kretschmer: German psychiatrist, born October 8, 1888, Wüstenrot near Heilbronn, Württemberg; died February 8, 1964, Tübingen. emembered for his correlation of build and physical constitution with personality characteristics and mental illness. He studied both philosophy and medicine at the University of Tübingen, where he remained as assistant in the neurological clinic after completing his studies in 1913. The next year he published his dissertation on manic-depressive delusions, anticipating his later work in mental illness. He studied hysteria while a military physician during World War I. After the

particular. Skirtoids are vital, egotistical, and thick-skinned individuals who make good soldiers because of their endurance and psychological resistance. In peacetime, however, they are incapable of understanding life's subtler matters or rearing the younger generation prudently. They are happy in primitive surroundings; a comfortable environment easily causes hysterization for them. They prove rigidly conservative in all areas and supportive of governments that rule with a heavy hand.

Kretschmer was of the opinion that this anomaly was a biodynamic phenomenon caused by the crossing of two widely removed ethnic groups which is frequent in that area of Europe. If that were the case, North America should be full of skirtoids. This anomaly should be taken into consideration if we wish to understand the history of Russia, as well as Poland to a lesser extent.[...]

The above characterizations are selected examples of pathological factors which participate in ponerogenic processes. [...] The current state of knowledge in this area is nevertheless still insufficient to produce practical solutions to many human problems, particularly those on an individual and family scale. [...]

Some outstanding psychopathologists, convinced that developing a calm and sufficient view of human reality is impossible without psychopathological findings, are therefore unfortunately right, a conclusion difficult to accept by people who believe they attained a mature world-view without such burdensome studies. The defenders of the natural world-view have tradition, belles-lettres, even philosophy on their side. They do not realize that during present times, their manner of comprehending life's questions renders the battle with evil more problematic. [...]

In attempting closer observation of these psychological processes and phenomena which lead one man or one nation to hurt another, let us select phenomena as characteristic as possible. We shall again become convinced that the participation of various pathological factors in these processes is the rule, not the exception.[...]

[O]ur social, psychological, and moral concepts, as well as our natural forms of reaction, are not adequate for every situation with which life confronts us.

---

war, Kretschmer returned to Tübingen as a lecturer and began writing books containing his psychological theories. His best known work, *Körperbau und Charakter* (1921), advanced the theory that certain mental disorders were more common among people of specific physical types. In 1933 Krestchmer resigned as president of the German society of Psychotherapy in protest against the Nazi takeover of the government. But unlike other prominent German psychologists he remained in Germany during World War II. After the war Kretschmer returned to Tübingen and remained there as professor of psychiatry and director of the neurological clinic until 1959. Kretschmer posited three chief constitutional groups: the tall, thin astenic type; the more muscular athletic type, and the rotund pyknic type. He suggested that the lanky asthenics and to a lesser degree the athletic types, were more prone to schizophrenia, while the pyknic types were more likely to develop manic-depressive disorders. Kretschmer further developed new methods of psychotherapy and hypnosis, and studied compulsive criminality, recommending adequate provision be made for the psychiatric treatment of prisoners.

We generally wind up hurting someone if we engage our naturally concepts and reactive archetypes in situations which seem to be appropriate to our imaginings although they are, in fact, essentially different. As a rule, such different situations … occur because some pathological factor difficult to understand has entered the picture. The practical value of our natural world-view generally ends where psychopathology begins.

Familiarity with this common weakness of human nature and the normal person's "naiveté" is part of the specific knowledge we find in many psychopathic individuals. Spellbinders of various schools attempt to provoke such para-appropriate reactions from other people in the name of their specific goals, or in the service of their reigning ideologies. That hard-to-understand pathological factor is located within the spellbinder himself.

We call egotism the attitude, subconsciously conditioned as a rule, thanks to which we attribute excessive value to our instinctive reflex, early acquired imaginings and habits, and individual world-view. …An egotist measures other people by his own yardstick, treating his concepts and experient9ial manner as objective criteria. He would like to force other people to feel and think very much the same way he does. Egotist nations have the subconscious goal of teaching or forcing other nations to think in their own categories, which makes them incapable of understanding other people and nations or becoming familiar with the values of their cultures.

Proper child rearing (and self-rearing) always aims at de-egotizing thereby opening the mind. […]

The kind of excessive egotism which hampers the development of human values and leads to misjudgment and terrorization of others well deserves the title "King of human faults." Difficulties, disputes, serious problems, and neurotic reactions sprout up around such an egotist like mushrooms after a rain. Egotist nations start wasting money and effort in order to achieve goals derived from their erroneous reasoning and overly emotional reactions. Their inability to acknowledge other nations' values and dissimilitudes, derived from other cultural traditions, leads to conflict and war. […]

If we analyze development of excessively egotistical personalities, we find some non-pathological causes, such as having been raised in a constricted and overly routine environment or by the persons less intelligent than the child. However, the main reason is contamination, through psychological induction, by excessively egotistical or hysterical persons who developed this characteristic under the influence of various pathological causes. …

Many people with various hereditary deviations and acquired defects develop pathological egotism. For such people, forcing others in their environment, whole social groups, and, if possible, entire nations to feel and think like themselves becomes an internal necessity, a ruling concept. Some issue a normal person would not take seriously becomes an often lifelong goal for them, the object of effort, sacrifices, and cunning psychological strategy. Pathological egotism derives from repressing from one's field of consciousness any objectionable self-critical associations referring to one's own nature or normality. Dramatic questions such as "who is abnormal here, me or this world of people who feel and think differently?" are answered in the world's disfavor. Such egotism is always linked to a dissimulative attitude, with a Cleckley mask or some other pathological quality being hidden from consciousness, both one's own and that of other people. [...]

The importance of the contribution of this kind of egotism to the genesis of evil thus hardly needs elaboration. It is a primarily societal resource, egotizing or traumatizing others, which in turn causes further difficulties. Pathological egotism is a constant component of variegated states wherein someone who appears to be normal (although he is in fact not quite so_ is driven by motivations or battles for goals a normal person considers unrealistic or unlikely. The average person asks: "What could he expect to gain by that?" Environmental opinion, however, interprets such a situation in accordance with "common sense" and is prone to accept a "more likely" version of occurrence. Such interpretation often results in human tragedy. We should thus always remember that the law principle of *cui prodest*[47] becomes illusory whenever some pathological factor enters the picture. [...]

Spellbinders

In order to comprehend ponerogenic paths, especially those acting in a wider social context, let us observe the roles and personalities of individuals we shall call "spellbinders" who are highly active in this area in spite of their statistically negligible number. They are generally the carriers of various pathological factors, some characteropathies, and some inherited anomalies....

Spellbinders are characterized by pathological egotism. Such a person is forced by some internal causes to make an early choice between two possibilities: the first is forcing other people to think and experience things in a manner similar to his own; the second is a feeling of being lonely and different, a pathological misfit in social life. Sometimes the choice is either snake-charming or suicide.

Triumphant repression of self-critical or unpleasant concepts from the field of consciousness gradually gives rise to [conversive thinking. i.e.   , paramoralism.]

Paramoralisms

The conviction that moral values exist but that some actions violate moral rules is so common and ancient a phenomenon that it seems to have some substratum at man's instinctive endowment level, and is not just a representation of centuries of experience, culture, religions, and socialization. Thus, any insinuation enclosed in a "moral slogan" is always suggestive even if the "moral" criteria used are just an ad hoc invention. Any act can thus be proved to be immoral or moral by means of using

---

[47] Who "advances".

"paramoralisms" through active suggestion and people who will succumb to this manipulation are plentiful.

In searching for an example of an evil act whose negative value would not elicit doubt in any social situation, ethics scholars frequently mention child abuse. However, psychologists often meet with paramoral affirmations of such behavior in their practice.

Lobaczewski earlier gave the example of the woman with prefrontal-field damage who was sadistically abusive to her child, but was supported in her abuse of the child by her brothers who were totally under her influence and convinced of her "exceptionally high moral qualifications". Particularly heinous examples of this type of thing often occur in a religious context where children have been beaten to death to "get the devil out". It is always done to "save their souls", and that is an example of "paramoralism" used in a conversive way.

Paramoralistic statements and suggestions so often accompany various kinds of evil that they seem quite irreplaceable. Unfortunately, it has become a frequent phenomenon for individuals, oppressive groups, or patho-political systems to invent ever-new moral criteria for someone's convenience. Such suggestions deprive people of their moral reasoning and deform its development in children. Paramoralism factories have been founded worldwide, and a ponerologist finds it hard to believe that they are managed by psychologically normal people.

The conversive features in the genesis of paramoralisms seem to prove they are derived from mostly subconscious rejection (and repression from the field of consciousness) of something completely different which we call the "voice of conscience." ... Like all conversive phenomena, the tendency to use paramoralisms is psychologically contagious.

Returning to the subject of Spellbinders, Lobaczewski points out that "paramoralisms" stream profusely from such individuals so that they flood the average person's mind.

To the spellbinder, everything becomes subordinated to their conviction that they are exceptional, sometimes even messianic. An ideology can emerge from such individuals that is certainly partly true, and the value of which is claimed to be superior to all other ideologies. They believe they will find many converts to their ideology and when they discover that this is not the case, they are shocked and fume with "paramoral indignation." The attitude of most normal people to such spellbinders is generally critical, pained and disturbed.

The spellbinder places on a high moral plane anyone who succumbs to his influence, and he will shower such people with attention and property and perks of all kinds. Critics are met with "moral" outrage and it will be claimed by the spellbinder that the compliant minority is actually a majority.

Such activity is always characterized by the inability to foresee its final results, something obvious from the psychological point of view, because its substratum contains pathological phenomena, and both spellbinding and self-charming make it impossible to perceive reality accurately enough to foresee results logically.

In a healthy society, the activities of spellbinders meet with criticism effective enough to stifle them quickly. However, when they are preceded by conditions operating destructively on common sense and social order - such as social injustice, cultural backwardness, or intellectually limited rulers manifesting pathological traits - spellbinders activities have led entire societies into large-scale human tragedy.

Such an individual fishes an environment or society for people amenable to his influence, deepening their psychological weaknesses until they finally become a ponerogenic union.

On the other hand, people who have maintained their healthy critical faculties intact, attempt to counteract the spellbinders' activities and their results, based on their own common sense and moral criteria. In the resulting polarization of social attitudes, each side justifies itself by means of moral categories.

The awareness that a spellbinder is always a pathological individual should protect us from the known results of a moralizing interpretation of pathological phenomena, ensuring us of objective criteria for more effective action.

[A high IQ] generally helps in immunity to spellbinders, but only moderately. Actual differences in the formation of human attitudes under the influence of such activities should be attributed to other properties of human nature. The factor most decisive as regards assuming a critical attitude is good basic intelligence, which conditions our perception of psychological reality. We can also observe how a spellbinder's activities "husk out" amenable individuals with an astonishing regularity.

Ponerogenic Associations

We shall give the name "ponerogenic association" to any group of people characterized by ponerogenic processes of above-average social intensity, wherein the carriers of various pathological factors function as inspirers, spellbinders, and leaders, and where a proper pathological social structure generates. Smaller, less permanent associations may be called "groups" or "unions". Such an association gives birth to evil which hurts the other people as well as its own members.

We could list various names ascribed to such organizations by linguistic tradition: gangs, criminal mobs, mafias, cliques, and coteries, which cunningly avoid collision with the law while seeking to gain their own advantage. Such unions frequently aspire to political power in order to impose their expedient legislation upon society in the name of a suitably prepared ideology, deriving advantages in the form of disproportionate prosperity and satisfaction of their craving for power.[...]

One phenomenon all ponerogenic groups and associations have in common is the fact that their members lose (or have already lost) the capacity to perceive pathological individuals as such, interpreting their behavior in a fascinated, heroic, or melodramatic way. The opinions, ideas, and judgments of people carrying various psychological deficits are endowed with an importance at least equal to that of outstanding individuals among normal people. The atrophy of natural critical faculties with respect to pathological individuals becomes an opening to their activities, and at the same time a criterion for recognizing the association in concert as ponerogenic. Let us call this the first criterion of ponerogenesis

Another phenomenon all ponerogenic associations have in common is their *statistically high concentration of individuals with various psychological anomalies*. Their qualitative composition is crucially important in the formation of the entire union's character, activities, development, or extinction. Groups dominated by various kinds of characteropathic individuals will develop relatively primitive activities, proving rather easy for a society of normal people to break. Things are different when such unions are inspired by psychopathic individuals. Let us adduce the following example illustrating the roles of two different anomalies selected from among events studied by the author.

In felonious youth gangs, a specific role is played by boys (and occasionally girls) carrying the characteristic results sometimes left behind by an inflammation of parotid glands (the mumps). As mentioned, this disease entails brain reactions in some cases, leaving behind a discreet but permanent bleaching of feelings and a slight decrease in general mental skills. Similar results are sometimes left behind after diphtheria. As a result, such people easily succumb to more clever individuals' suggestions. When sucked into a felonious group, they become faint-critical helpers and executors of the latter's' intentions, tools in the hands of more treacherous, usually psychopathic, leaders. Once arrested, they submit to their leaders' insinuated explanations that the higher (paramoral) group idea demands they become scapegoats, taking the majority of blame upon themselves. ...

Individuals with the above mentioned post-mumps and post-diphtheria traits constitute less than 1.0% of the population as a whole, but their share reaches 25 percent of juvenile delinquent groups. This represents an inspissation[48] of the order of 30-fold, requiring no further methods of statistical analysis. When studying the contents of ponerogenic unions skillfully enough, we often meet with an inspissation of other psychological anomalies which also speak for themselves.

Two basic types of the above mentioned unions should be differentiated: Primary ponerogenic and secondary ponerogenic. Let us describe as primarily ponerogenic a union whose abnormal members were active since the very beginning, playing the role of crystallizing catalysts as early as a process for creation of the group occurred. We shall call secondarily ponerogenic a union which was founded in the name of some idea with an

---

[48] Latin *inspissatus, inspissare, in- + spissus* slow, dense; akin to Greek *spidnos* compact, Lithuanian *spisti* to form a swarm to make thick or thicker

independent social meaning generally comprehensible within the categories of the natural world-view, but which later succumbed to a certain moral degeneration. This in turn opened the door to infection and activation of the pathological factors within, and later to a ponerization of the group as a whole, or often of its fraction.

From the very outset, a primarily ponerogenic union is *a foreign body within the organism of society*, its character colliding with the moral values respected by the majority. The activities of such groups provoke opposition and disgust and are considered immoral; as a rule, therefore, such groups do not spread large, nor do not metastasize into numerous unions. They finally lose their battle with society.

In order to have a chance to develop into a large ponerogenic association, however, it suffices that some human organization, characterized by social or political goals and an ideology with some creative valued, be accepted by a larger number of normal people before it succumbs to a process of ponerogenic malignancy. The primary tradition and ideological values may then for a long time protect a union which has succumbed to ponerization process from the healthy common sense of society, especially its less critical components.

When the ponerogenic process touches such a human organization, which emerged and acted in the name of political or social goals whose causes were conditioned in history and the social situation, the original group's primary values will nourish and protect such a union - in spite of the fact that those primary values succumb to characteristic degeneration, their practical function becoming completely different from the primary one - because the names and symbols are retained. Individual and social "common sense" thereby uncovers its weakest spot. [...]

Within each ponerogenic union, a psychological structure is created which can be considered a counterpart or caricature of the normal structure of society or a societal organization. Individuals with various psychological aberrations complement each other's talents and characteristics. ... Earlier phases of the union's activity are usually dominated by characteropathic, particularly paranoidal, individuals, who often play an inspirational or spellbinding role in the ponerization process. At this point in time, the union still indicates a certain romantic feature and is not yet characterized by excessively brutal behavior. Soon, however, the more normal members are pushed into fringe functions and excluded...

Individuals with inherited deviations then progressively take over the inspirational and leadership positions. The role of essential psychopaths gradually grows...

A spellbinder at first simultaneously plays the leader in a ponerogenic group. Later there appears another kind of "leadership talent," a more vital individual who often joined the organization later, once it has already succumbed to ponerization. The spellbinding individual, being weaker, is forced to come to terms with being shunted into the shadows and recognizing the new leader's "genius" unless he accepts the threat of total failure. Roles are parceled out. The spellbinder needs support from the primitive but decisive leader, who in turn needs the spellbinder to uphold the association's ideology, so essential to maintain the proper attitude on the part of those members of the rank and filed who betray a tendency to criticism and doubt of the moral variety. The spellbinder must repackage the ideology appropriately, sliding new contents under old titles, so that it can continue fulfilling its propaganda function under ever-changing conditions. He has also to uphold the leader's mystique inside and outside the association. Complete trust cannot exist between the two, however, since the leader secretly has contempt for the spellbinder and his ideology, whereas the latter despises the leader for being such a coarse individual. The showdown is always probable; whoever is weaker becomes the loser.

The structure of such a union undergoes further variegation and specialization. A chasm opens between the more normal masses and the elite initiates, who are as a rule more pathological. This later subgroup becomes ever more dominated by hereditary pathological factors, the former by the after-effects of various diseases affecting the brain, less typically psychopathic individuals, and people whose malformed personalities were caused by early deprivation or brutal child-rearing methods on the part of pathological individuals. There is less and less room for normal people in the group. The leaders' secrets and intentions are kept hidden from the union's proletariat; the products of the spellbinders' work must suffice for this segment.

An observer watching such a union's activities from the outside and using the natural psychological world-view will always tend to overestimate the role of the leader an his allegedly autocratic function. The spellbinders and the propaganda apparatus are mobilized to maintain this erroneous outside opinion. The leader, however, is dependent upon the interests of the union, especially the elite initiates, to an extent greater than he himself knows. He wages a constant position-jockeying battle; he is an actor with a director. In macro-social unions, this position is generally occupied by a more representative individual not deprived of certain critical faculties; initiating him into all those plans and criminal calculations would be counterproductive. In conjunction with part of the elite, a group o psychopathic individuals hiding behind the scene steers the leader like Borman and his clique steered Hitler. If the leader does not fulfill his assigned role, he generally knows that the clique representing the elite of the union is in a position to kill or otherwise remove him.[...]

Ideologies

It is a common phenomenon for a ponerogenic association or group to contain a particular ideology which always justifies its activities and furnishes certain propaganda motives. Even a small-time gang of hoodlums has its own melodramatic ideology and pathological romanticism. Human nature demands that vile matters be haloed by an over compensatory mystique in order to silence one's conscience and deceive consciousness and critical faculties, whether one's own or those of others.

If such an ponerogenic union could be stripped of its ideology, nothing would remain except psychological and moral pathology, naked and unattractive. Such stripping would, of course, provoke "moral outrage," and not only among the members of the union; even normal people, who condemn these kinds of unions along with their ideologies, would feel hurt - deprived of something constituting part of their own romanticism, their way of perceiving reality. Perhaps the readers of this book will resent the author's stripping evil of all its literary motifs so unceremoniously. The job of effecting such a "strip-tease" may thus turn out to be much more difficult and dangerous than expected.

A primary ponerogenic union is formed at the same time as its ideology, perhaps even somewhat earlier. A normal person perceives such ideology to be different from the world of human concepts, obviously suggestive, and even primitively comical to a degree.

An ideology of a secondarily ponerogenic association is formed by gradual adaptation of the primary ideology to functions and goals other than the original formative ones. A certain kind of layering or schizophrenia of ideology takes place during the ponerization process. The outer layer closest to the original content is used for the group's propaganda purposes - especially as regards the outside world, although it can, in part, also be used inside with regard to disbelieving lower-echelon members. The second layer presents the elite with no problems of comprehension: it is more hermetic, generally composed by slipping a different meaning into the same names. Since identical names signify different contents depending on the layer in question, understanding this "doubletalk" requires simultaneous fluency in both languages.

Average people succumb to the first layer's suggestive insinuations for a long time before they learn to understand the second one as well. Anyone with certain psychological deviations, especially if he is wearing the normality mask we are already familiar with, immediately perceives the second layer to be attractive and significant - after all, it was built by people like him. Comprehending this doubletalk is therefore a vexatious task, provoking quite understandable psychological resistance; this very duality of language, however, is a pathognomic symptom indicating that the human union in question is touched by the ponerogenic process to an advanced degree.

The ideology of unions affected by such degeneration has certain constant factors regardless of their quality, quantity, or scope of action: namely, the motivations of a wronged group, radical righting of the wrong, and the higher value of the individuals who have joined the organization. These motivations facilitate sublimation of the feeling of being wronged and different, caused by one's own psychological failings, and appear to liberate the individual from the need to abide by uncomfortable moral principles.

In the world full of real injustice and human humiliation, making it conductive to the formation of an ideology containing the above elements; a union of its converts may easily succumb to degradation. At which time those people with a tendency to accept the better version of the ideology shall also long tend to justify such ideological duality. [...]

Let us remember: ideologies do not need spellbinders; Spellbinders need ideologies in order to subject them to their own deviant goals.

On the other hand, the fact that some ideology degenerated along with its corollary social movement, later succumbing to this schizophrenia and serving goals which the originators of the ideology would have abhorred, does not prove that it was worthless, false, and fallacious from the start. Quite the contrary: it rather appears that under certain historical conditions, the ideology of any social movement, even if it is sacred truth, can yield to the ponerization process.

A given ideology may in fact have contained weak spots, carrying the errors of human thought and emotion within; or it may, during the course of its history, have been infiltrated by more primitive foreign material which could have contained ponerogenic factors. Such material destroys and ideology's' internal homogeneity. The source of such infection by foreign ideological material may be the ruling social system with its laws and customs based on a more primitive tradition, or an imperialistic system of rule. [...]

The Roman Empire, including its legal system and paucity of psychological concepts, similarly contaminated the primary homogeneous idea of Christianity. Christianity had to adapt to coexistence with a social system wherein "dura lex sed lex"[49] not on understanding of people, decided a person's fate; this led then later to a desire to reach Gospel goals by means of Roman methods.

The greater and truer the original ideology, the longer it may be capable of nourishing and disguising from human criticism that phenomenon which is the product of the already known specific degenerative process. In a great valuable ideology, the danger for small minds is hidden; they can become the factors of such preliminary degeneration, which opens the door to invasion by pathological factors.

Thus, if we intend to understand the secondary ponerization process and the contents of human associations which succumbed to it, our consciousness should separate the original ideology from its counterpart or even caricature created by the ponerogenic process. Abstracting from any ideology, we must by analogy understand the essence of the process itself, which has its own etiological causes which are potentially present in every society, as well as characteristic developmental patho-dynamics.

The Ponerization Process

Observation of the ponerization processes of various human unions throughout history easily leads to the conclusion that the initial step is a moral warping of the group's ideational contents. [...]

---

[49] The law is hard, but it is the law.

Sometime during life, every human organism undergoes periods during which physiological and psychological resistance declines, facilitating development of bacteriological infection within. Similarly, a human association or social movement undergoes periods of crisis which weaken its ideational and moral cohesion. This may be caused by pressure on the part of other groups, a general spiritual crisis in the environment, or intensification of its hysterical condition. Just as more stringent sanitary measures are an obvious medical indication for a weakened organism, the development of conscious control over the activity of pathological factors is a ponerological indication, something especially important during a society's periods of moral crisis. [...]

By detecting and describing these aspects of the ponerization process of human groups, which could not be understood until recently, we shall be able to counteract such processes earlier and more effectively.

Any human group affected by the process described herein is characterized by its increasing regression as regards activities such as natural common sense and the ability to perceive psychological reality. Someone treating this in traditional categories could consider it an instance of "turning into half-wittedness" or growing of intellectual deficiencies and moral failings. A ponerological analysis of this process, however, indicates that pressure is applied upon the most normal part of the association by pathological factors in the person of their carriers.

Thus, whenever we observe some group member being treated with no critical distance although he betrays one of the psychological anomalies familiar to us, and his opinions being treated as at least equal to those of normal people although they are based on a characteristically different view of human matters, we must derive the conclusion that this human group is affected by ponerogenic process.

Such a state of affairs simultaneously consist of a liminal (watershed) situation, whereupon further damage to people's healthy common sense and critical moral faculties becomes ever easier. Once a group has inhaled a sufficient dose of pathological material to give birth to the conviction that these not-quite-normal people are unique geniuses, it starts subjecting its more normal members to pressure characterized by corresponding paralogical and paramoral elements, as expected.

For many people, such collective opinion takes on attributes of moral criterion; for others it represents a kind of psychological terror ever more difficult to endure.

The phenomenon of counter selection thus occurs in this phase of ponerization: individuals with more normal sense of psychological reality leave after entering into conflict with the newly modified group; simultaneously, individuals with various psychological anomalies join the group and easily find a way of life there. The former feel "pushed into counter-revolutionary position", and the latter can afford to remove their masks of sanity ever more often.

People who have been thus thrown out of a ponerogenic association because they were too normal suffer bitterly; they are unable to understand their specific state. Their idea, which constituted a part of the meaning of life for them, has now been degraded - although they cannot find a rational basis for this fact. They feel wronged; they "fight against demons" they are not in a position to identify. In fact, their personalities have already been modified to a certain extent due to saturation by abnormal psychological material, especially psychopathic material. They easily fall into the opposite extreme in such cases, because unhealthy emotions make the decisions. What they need is good advice in order to find the path of reason and measure. Based on ponerologic understanding of their condition, psychotherapy could provide rapid positive results. However, if the union they left is succumbing to deep ponerization, a threat looms over them: they may be the objects of revenge, since they have betrayed a magnificent ideology.

This is the stormy period of a group's ponerization, followed by a certain stabilization in terms of contents, structure and customs. Rigorous selective measures of a clearly psychological kind are applied to new members. So as to exclude the possibility of becoming sidetracked by defectors; people are observed and tested to eliminate those characterized by excessive mental independence or psychological normality. [...]

Macro-social Phenomena

When a ponerogenic process encompasses a society's entire ruling class, or nation, or when opposition on the part of normal people's societies is stifled - as a result of the mass character of the phenomenon, or by using spellbinding means and physical compulsion - we are dealing with macro-social ponerologic phenomenon. At that time, however, a society's tragedy, often coupled with that of the researcher's own suffering, are opening before him an entire volume of ponerologic knowledge, where he can read all about the laws governing such process if he is only able to familiarize himself in time with its naturalistic language and its different grammar.

Studies in the genesis of evil which are based on observing small groups of people can indicate the details of these laws to us. [...]

In studying a macro-social phenomenon, we can obtain both quantitative and qualitative data, statistical correlation indices, and other observations as accurate as allowed by the state of the art as regards science, research methodology, and the obviously very difficult situation of the observer. [...] The comprehension of the phenomenon thus acquired can serve as a basis for predicting its future development, to be verified by time. Then we become aware that the colossus has an Achilles heel after all. [...]

The difficulties confronted in abstracting the appropriate symptoms need not be insuperable, since our criteria are based on eternal phenomena subject to relatively limited transformations in time.

The traditional interpretation of theses great historical diseases has already taught historians to distinguish two phases. The first is represented by a period of spiritual crisis in a society, which historiography associates with exhausting of the ideational, moral and religious values heretofore nourishing the society in question. Egoism among individuals and social groups increases, and the links of moral duty and social networks are felt to be loosening. Trifling matters thereupon dominate human minds to such an extent that there is no room left for imagination regarding public matters or a feeling of commitment to the future. An atrophy of the hierarchy of values within the thinking of individuals and societies is an indication thereof; it has been described both in historiographic monographs and in psychiatric papers. The country's government is finally paralyzed, helpless in the face of problems which could be solved without great difficulty under other circumstances. Let us associate such periods of crisis with the familiar phase in social hysterization.

The next phase has been marked by bloody tragedies, revolutions, wars, and the fall of empires. Historians or moralists' deliberations always leave behind a certain feeling of deficiency with reference to the possibility of perceiving certain psychological factors discerned within the nature of phenomena; the essence of these factors remains outside the scope of their scientific experience.

An historian observing these great historical diseases is struck first of all by their similarities, easily forgetting that all diseases have many symptoms in common because they are states of absent health. A ponerologist ... tends to doubt that we are dealing with only one kind of societal disease... The complex conditions of social life ... preclude using the method of distinction which is similar to etiological criterion in medicine... We should then rather use certain abstractional patterns similar to those used in analyzing the neurotic states of human beings.

Governed by this type of reasoning, let us here attempt to differentiate two pathological states of societies; their essence and contents appear different enough, but they can operate sequentially in such a way that the first opens the door to the second. The first such state has already been sketched [as] the hysteroidal cycle.

States of Societal Hysterization

When perusing scientific or literary descriptions of hysterical phenomena, such as those dating from the last great increase in hysteria in Europe encompassing the quarter-century preceding World War I, a non specialist may gain the impression that this was an endemia of individual cases, particularly among women. The contagious nature of hysterical states, however, had already been discovered and described by Jean-Martin Charcot.[50]

---

[50] Jean-Martin Charcot, 1825-1893. In the contribution to neurosciences by France, this country claims the medical genius of them all. Charcot, whose brilliance as a clinician and a neuropathologist could never be surpassed. He created neurology as a firm discipline, made monumental studies in tabes, described, arthropathies "Charcot Joints", Amyotrophic Lateral

It is practically impossible for hysteria to manifest itself as a mere individual phenomenon, since it is contagious by means of psychological resonance, identification, and imitation. Each human being has a predisposition for this personality malformation, albeit to varying degrees, although it is normally overcome by rearing and self-rearing, which are amenable to correct thinking and emotional self-discipline.

During happy times of peace, when social injustice also exists and grows in the background (which is natural when we consider that certain individuals among those who want to "enjoy" what they have accumulated rapidly begin to oppress their fellows), children of the privileged classes learn to repress from their field of consciousness any of those uncomfortable concepts suggesting that they and their parents benefit from injustice. Young people learn to disqualify the moral and mental values of anyone whose work they are using to over-advantage. Young minds thus ingest habits of subconscious selection and substitution of data, which leads to a hysterical conversion economy of reasoning. They grow up to be somewhat hysterical adults who, by means of the ways adduced above, thereupon transmit their hysteria to the younger generation, which then develops these characteristics to a greater degree. The hysterical patterns for experience and behavior grow and spread downwards from the privileged classes until crossing the boundary of the first criterion of ponerology.

When the habits of subconscious selection and substitution of thought-data spread to the macro-social level, a society tends to develop contempt for factual criticism and humiliates anyone sounding the alarm. Contempt is also shown for other nations which have maintained normal thought-patterns, and for their opinions. Egotistic thought terrorization is accomplished by the society itself and its processes of conversion thinking. This obviates the need for censorship of the press, theater, or broadcasting, as a pathologically hypersensitive censor lives within the citizens themselves. When three egos govern: egoism, egotism, and egocentrism; the feeling of social links and responsibility disappear; and the society in question splinters into groups ever more hostile to each other. When a hysterical environment stops differentiating the opinions of limited, not-quite-normal people from those of normal, reasonable persons, this opens the door for activation of the pathological factors of various natures.

Individuals governed by a pathological view of reality and abnormal goals caused by their different nature develop their activity in such conditions. If a given society does not manage to overcome the state of hysterization … a huge bloody tragedy can be the result. One variation of such a tragedy can be a pathocracy. […] The most valuable advice a ponerologist can offer under

---

Sclerosis, was not only described but was named by him. His name comes forth as contribution to the knowledge of poliomyelitis, neuropathies (Charcot-Marie-Tooth) disease, nuiliary aneurysms, ankle clonus. He even wrote on hysteria, "blessed" hypnotism and was involved early on in the conflict over animal experimentation. He was a great teacher and many of his students became the "greats" in neurology.It has been said that Charcot entered neurology in its infancy and left it at its "coming of age".

such circumstances is for a society to avail itself of the assistance of modern science, taking particular advantage of data remaining from the last great increase of hysteria in Europe.

A greater resistance to hysterization characterizes those social groups which earn their daily bread by daily effort, where the practicalities of everyday life force the mind to think soberly and reflect on generalities. As an example: peasants continue to view the hysterical customs of the well-to-do classes through their own earthy perception of psychological reality and their sense of humor. Similar customs on the part of the bourgeoisie inclined workers to bitter criticism and revolutionary anger. Whether couched in economic, ideological, or political terms, the criticism and demands of these social groups always contain a component of psychological, moral, and anti-hysterical motivation. For this reason, it is most appropriate to consider these demands with deliberation and take these classes' feelings into account. [...]

The Genesis of The Phenomenon

The time-cycle sketched earlier was referred to as hysteroidal because the intensification and diminution of a society's hysterical condition can be considered its chief measurement. It does not, of course, constitute the only quality subject to change within the framework of certain periodicity. Here we shall deal with the phenomenon which can emanate from the phase of maximal intensification of hysteria. Such a sequence does not appear to result from any relatively constant laws of history; quite the contrary; some additional circumstances and factors must participate in this period of a society's general spiritual crisis and cause its reason and social structure to degenerate in such a way as to bring about spontaneous generating of this worst disease of society. Let us call this phenomenon "pathocracy." This is not the first time it has emerged during the history of our planet.

It appears that this phenomenon, whose causes also appear to be potentially present in every society, has its own characteristic process of genesis, only partially conditioned by, and hidden within, the maximal hysterical intensity of the above described cycle. As a result, unhappy times become exceptionally cruel and enduring and their causes impossible to understand within the categories of natural human concepts. Let us therefore bring this process of the origin of pathocracy closer, methodically isolating it from other phenomena we can recognize as being conditional or even accompanying. [...]

Every society worldwide contains individuals whose dreams of power arise very early. They are discriminated against in some way by society, which uses a moralizing interpretation with regard to their failings and difficulties although they are rarely guilty of them. They would like to change this unfriendly world into something else. Dreams of power also represent overcompensation for the feeling of humiliation, the second angle in Adler's rhombus. A significant and active proportion of this group is composed of individuals with various deviations, who imagine this better world in their own way, which we are already familiar with.

In the previous discussion, the readers have become acquainted with examples of these deviations selected in such a way as to permit us now to present the ponerogenesis of pathocracy and introduce the essential factors of this historical phenomenon which is so difficult to understand. It has certainly appeared many times in history, on various mainlands and in various social scales. However, no one has ever managed to identify it objectively because it would hide in one of the ideologies characteristic of the respective culture and era, developing in the very bosom of different social movements. Identification was so difficult because the indispensable naturalistic knowledge needed for proper classification of phenomena in this area did not develop until our contemporary times. Thus, the historians and sociologists discern many similarities, but they possess no identifying criteria because the latter belongs to another scientific discipline.

Who plays the first crucial role in this process of the origin of pathocracy: schizoids or characteropaths? It appears to be the former; therefore, let us delineate their role first.

During stable times which are ostensibly happy, albeit marked by injury to individuals and nations, doctrinaire people believe they have found a simple solution to fix such a world. Such a historical period is always characterized by an impoverished psychological world=view, a schizoidally impoverished psychological world view thus does not stand out during such times and is accepted as legal tender. These doctrinaire individuals characteristically manifest a certain contempt with regard to moralists then preaching the need to rediscover lost human values and develop a richer, more appropriate psychological world-view.

Schizoidal characters aim to impose their own conceptual world upon other people or social groups, using relatively controlled pathological egotism and the exceptional tenacity derived from their persistent nature. They are thus eventually able to overpower another individual's personality, which causes the latter's behavior to turn desperately illogical, or exert a similar influence upon the group of people they have joined. They are psychological loners who feel better in some human organization, wherein they become zealots for some ideology, religious bigots, materialists, or adherents of an ideology with satanic features. If their activities consist of direct contact on a small social scale, their acquaintances easily perceive them to be eccentric, which limits their ponerogenic role. However, if they manage to hide their own personality behind the written word, their influence may poison the minds of society in a wide scale and for a long time.

The conviction that Karl Marx is the best example of this is correct as he was the best-known figure of that kind. Frostig, a psychiatrist of the old school, included Engles and others into a category he called "bearded schizoidal fanatics." The famous utterances made by alleged Zionist Wise Men at the turn of the century start with a typically schizoidal declaration. The nineteenth century, especially its latter half, appears to have been a time of exceptional activity on the part of schizoidal individuals, often, but not always, of Jewish descent. After all, we have to remember that 97 % of all Jews do not manifest this anomaly, and that it also appears among all

European nations, albeit to a markedly lesser extent. Our inheritance from this period includes world-images, scientific traditions, and legal concepts flavored with the shoddy ingredients of a schizoidal apprehension of reality.

Humanists are prepared to understand that era and its legacy within categories characterizing their own traditions. They search for societal, ideational, and moral causes for known phenomena. Such an explanation however, can never constitute the whole truth since it ignores the biological factors which participated in the genesis of the phenomena. Schizoidal is the most frequent factor, albeit not the only one.

In spite of the fact that the writings of schizoidal authors contain the above described deficiency, or even an openly formulated schizoidal declaration which constitute sufficient warning to specialists, the average reader accepts them not as a view of reality warped by this anomaly, but rather as an idea to which he should assume an attitude based on his convictions and his reason. That is the first mistake. The oversimplified pattern, devoid of psychological color and based on easily available data, exerts an intense influence upon individuals who are insufficiently critical, frequently frustrated as a result of downward social adjustment, culturally neglected or characterized by some psychological deficiencies. Others are provoked to criticism based on their healthy common sense, also fail to grasp this essential cause of the error.
[…]

Schizoidia has thus played an essential role as one of the factors in the genesis of evil threatening our contemporary world. […]

The first researchers attracted by the idea of objectively understanding this phenomenon initially failed to perceive the role of characteropathic personalities in the genesis of pathocracy. However, when we attempt to reconstruct the early phase of said genesis, we must acknowledge that characteropaths played a significant role in this process. We already know from the previous discussion how their defective experiential and though patterns take hold in human minds, insidiously destroying their way of reasoning and their ability to utilize their healthy common sense. This role has also proved essential because their activities as fanatical leaders or spellbinders in various ideologies open the door to psychopathic individuals and the view of the world they want to impose.

In the ponerogenic process of the pathocratic phenomenon, characteropathic individuals adopt ideologies created by doctrinaire, often schizoidal people, recast them into active propaganda form, and disseminate it with pathological egotism and paranoid intolerance for any philosophies which may differ from their own. They also inspire further transformation of this ideology into its pathological counterpart. Something which had a doctrinaire character and circulated in numerically limited groups is now activated a societal level, thanks to their spellbinding possibilities.

It also appears that this process tends to intensify with time; initial activities are undertaken by persons with milder characteropathic features, who are easily able to hide their aberrations from others. Paranoidal individuals thereupon become principally active. Toward the end of the process, and individual with frontal characteropathy and the highest degree of pathological egotism can easily take over leadership. [...]

In the meantime, however, the carriers of other (mainly hereditary) pathological factors become engaged in this already sick social movement. They accomplish the work of final transformation of the contents of such union in such a way that it becomes a pathological caricature of its original contents and ideology. This is affected under the ever-growing influence of psychopathic personalities and thanks to the inspiration of essential psychopathy. Such leadership eventually engenders a wholesale showdown: the adherents of the original ideology are shunted aside or terminated. ... From this point on, using the ideological denomination of the movement becomes a keystone of mistakes in understanding of its essence.

Psychopathic individuals generally stay away from social organizations characterized by reason and ethical discipline. After all, these were created by that other world of normal people so foreign to them. They therefore hold various social ideologies in contempt, at the same time discerning all their actual failings. However, once the process of ponerogenic transformation of some human group into it yet undefined cartoon counterpart has begun and advanced sufficiently, they perceive this fact with almost infallible sensitivity: a circle has been created wherein they can hide their failings and psychological differentness, find their own "modus vivendi" and maybe even realize their youthful Utopian dream: a psychopath friendly world. They thereupon begin infiltrating the rank and file of such a movement; pretending to be sincere adherents poses them no difficulty, since it is second nature for them to play a role and hide behind the mask of normal people. [...] They therefore insinuate themselves into a movement preaching revolution and war with that unfair world so foreign to them.

They initially perform subordinate functions in such a movement and execute the leaders' orders, especially whenever something needs to be done which inspires revulsion in others. ... Thus they climb up the organizational ladder, gain influence, and almost involuntarily bend the contents of the entire group to their own way of experiencing reality and to the goals derived from their deviant nature. A mysterious disease is already raging inside the union. The adherents of the original ideology feel ever more constricted by powers they do not understand; they start fighting with demons and making mistakes.

If such a movement is to triumph by revolutionary means and in the name of freedom, the welfare of the people, and social justice, this can only bring about further transformation of a governmental system thus created into a macro-social pathological phenomenon, wherein the common man is blamed for not having been born a psychopath, and is considered good for nothing except hard work, fighting and dying to protect a system of government he can neither sufficiently comprehend nor ever consider to be his own.

An ever-strengthening network of psychopathic and related individuals gradually starts to dominate, overshadowing the others. Characteropathic individuals who played an essential role in ponerizing the movement and preparing for revolution are also eliminated. Adherents of the revolutionary ideology are unscrupulously "pushed into a counter-revolutionary position". They are now condemned for "moral" reasons in the name of new criteria whose paramoralistic essence they are not in position to comprehend. Violent negative selection of the original group now ensues. The inspiration role of essentially psychopathy is now also consolidated; it remains characteristic for the entire future of the macro-social pathological phenomenon.

The pathological block of the revolutionary movement remains a minority in spite of these transformations, a fact which cannot be changed by propaganda pronouncements about the moral majority adhering to the more glorious version of the ideology. The rejected majority and the very forces which naively created such power start mobilizing against the block. Ruthless confrontation with these forces becomes the only way to safeguard the long-term survival of the pathological authority. We must thus consider the bloody triumph of a pathological minority over the movement's majority to be a transitional phase during which the new contents of the phenomenon coagulate. The entire life of a society thus affected becomes subordinated to deviant thought-criteria and permeated by their specific experiential mode, especially the one described in the section on essential psychopathy. At this point using the name of the original ideology to designate this phenomenon is meaningless and becomes an error rendering its comprehension more difficult.

I shall accept the denomination of "pathocracy" for a system of government thus created, wherein a small pathological minority takes control over a society of normal people. The name thus selected above all underscores the basic quality of the macro social psychopathological phenomenon, which differentiates it from the many possible social systems dominated by normal people's structure, custom, and law. ... I think this name is consistent with the demands of semantics, since no concise term can adequately characterize such a complex phenomenon.

More on the Contents of the Phenomenon

Pathocrats' achievement of absolute domination in the government of a country would not be permanent, since large sectors of the society would become disaffected by such rule and find some way of toppling it. Pathocracy at the summit of governmental organization also does not constitute the entire picture of the "mature phenomenon". Such a system of government has nowhere to go but down. Any leadership position - down to village headman and community cooperative mangers, not to mention the directors of police units, and special-services police personnel, and activists in the pathocratic party - must be filled by individuals whose feeling of linkage to such a regime is conditioned by corresponding psychological deviations, which are inherited as a rule. However, such people become more valuable because they constitute a very small percentage of the population. Their intellectual level or professional skills cannot be taken into account, since people representing superior abilities with the requisite psychological deviations - are even harder to find. After such a system has lasted several years, one hundred percent of all the cases of essential psychopathy are involved in pathocratic activity; they are considered the most loyal, even though some of them were formerly involved on the other side in some way.

Under such conditions, no area of social life can develop normally, whether in economics, culture, science, technology, administration, etc. Pathocracy progressively paralyzes everything. Reasonable people must develop a level of patience beyond the ken of anyone living in a normal man's system, just to explain what to do and how to do it to some obtuse mediocrity of psychological deviant. This special pedagogy requires a great deal of time and effort, but it would otherwise not be possible to maintain tolerable living conditions and necessary achievements in the economic area or intellectual life of a society. However, pathocracy progressively intrudes everywhere and dulls everything.

Those people who initially found the original ideology attractive eventually come to the realization that they are in fact dealing with something else. The disillusionment experienced by such former ideological adherents is bitter in the extreme. The pathological minority's attempts to retain power will thus always be threatened by the society of normal people whose criticism keeps growing. On the other hand, any and all methods of terror and exterminatory policies must therefore be used against individuals known for the patriotic feelings and military training; on the other, specific "indoctrination" activities such as those we have presented are also utilized. Individuals lacking natural feeling of being linked to society become irreplaceable in either of these activities. The foreground must again be occupied by cases of essential psychopathy, followed by those with similar anomalies, and finally by people alienated from the society in question as a result of racial or national differences.

The phenomenon of pathocracy matures during this period: an extensive and active indoctrination system is built, with a suitably refurbished ideology constituting the vehicle of Trojan horse for the process of pathologizing the though of individuals and society. The goal is never admitted: forcing human minds to incorporate pathological experiential methods and thought patterns, and consequently accepting such rule. [...]

During the initial shock, the feeling of social links are fading; after that has been survived, however, the overwhelming majority of people manifests its own phenomenon of psychological immunization. Society simultaneously starts collecting practical knowledge on the subject of this new reality and its psychological properties. Normal people slowly learn to perceive the weak spots of such a system and utilize the possibilities of more expedient arrangement of their lives. They begin to give each other advice in these matters, thus lowly regenerating the feelings of social links and reciprocal trust. A new phenomenon occurs: separation between the pathocrats and the society of normal people. The latter have an advantage as regards talent, professional skills, and healthy common sense. They therefore hold certain cards. The pathocracy finally realizes that it must find some "modus vivendi" or relations with the majority of society: "After all, somebody's got to do the work for us."

There are other needs and pressures, especially from outside. The pathological face must be hidden from the world somehow, since recognition by world opinion would be a catastrophe. ... Primarily in the interests of the new elite and its expansionary plans, a pathocratic state must maintain commercial relations with the countries of normal man. Such a state aims to achieve international recognition as a certain kind of political structural; it fears recognition in terms of clinical diagnosis.

All this make pathocrats tend to limit their measures of terror, subjecting propaganda and indoctrination methods to certain cosmetology and to accord the society they control some margin of autonomous activity, especially as regards cultural life. The more liberal pathocrats would not be averse to giving such a society a certain minimum of economic prosperity in order to reduce the irritation level, but their own corruption and inability to administer the economy prevents them from doing so.

This great societal disease runs its course through a new phase: methods of activity become milder, and there is coexistence with countries whose structure is that of normal man. Anyone studying this phenomenon... is reminded rather of the dissimulative state of phase of a patient attempting to play the role of a normal person, hiding the pathological reality although he continues to be sick or abnormal. Let us therefore use the term "the dissimulative phase of pathocracy" for the state of affairs wherein a pathocratic system ever more skillfully plays the role of a normal sociopolitical system. In this state, people become resistant and adapt themselves to the situation within a country affected by this phenomenon; outside, however, this phase is marked by outstanding ponerogenic activity. The pathological material of this system rather easily infiltrates into other societies, particularly if they are more primitive, and all the avenues of pathocratic expansion are facilitated because of the decrease of common sense criticism on the part of the nations constituting the territory of expansionism.

Meanwhile, in the pathocratic country, the active structure of government rests in the hands of psychopathic individuals, and essential psychopathy plays a starring role. Especially during the dissimulative phase. However, individuals with obvious pathological traits must be removed from certain areas of activity: namely, political posts with international exposure where such personalities could betray the pathological contents of the phenomenon. [...]

Similar needs apply to other areas as well. The building director for a new factory is often someone barely connected with the pathocratic system but whose skills are essential. Once the plant is operational, further administration is taken over by pathocrats which often leads to technical ruin. The army similarly needs people endowed with perspicacity and essential qualifications, especially in the are of modern weapons. ...

In such a state of affairs, many people are forced to adapt, accepting the ruling system as a status quo but also criticizing it. They fulfill their duties amid doubts and conflicts of conscience, always searching for a more sensible way out which they discuss within trusted circles. ...

The following question thus suggests itself: what happens if the network of understandings among psychopaths achieves power in leadership positions with international exposure? This can happen, especially during the later phases of the phenomenon. Goaded by their character, such people thirst for just that even though it would conflict with their own life interest... They do not understand that a catastrophe would ensue. Germs are not aware that they will be burned alive or buried deep in the ground along with the human body whose death they are causing.

I the many managerial positions of a government are assumed by individuals deprived of sufficient abilities to feel and understand most other people and who also have deficiencies as regards technical imagination and practical skills - faculties indispensable for governing economic and political matters - this must result in an exceptionally serious crisis in all areas, both within the country in question and with regard to international relations. Within, the situation shall become unbearable even for those citizens who were able to feather their nest into a relatively comfortable "modus vivendi". Outside, other societies start to feel the pathological quality of the phenomenon quite distinctly. Such a state of affairs cannot last long. One must then be prepared for ever more rapid changes, and also behave with great circumspection.

Pathocracy is a disease of great social movements followed by entire societies, nations, and empires. In the course of human history, it has affected social, political, and religious movements as well as the accompanying ideologies... and turned them into caricatures of themselves.... This occurred as a result of the ... participation of pathological agents in a pathodynamically similar process. That explains why all the pathocracies of the world are, and have been, so similar in their essential properties. ...

Identifying these phenomena through history and properly qualifying them according to their true nature and contents - not according to the ideology in question, which succumbed to the process of caricaturization - is a job for historians. [...]

The actions of [pathocracy] affect an entire society, starting with the leaders and infiltrating every town, business, and institution. The pathological social structure gradually covers the entire country creating a "new class" within that nation. This privileged class feels permanently threatened by the "others", i.e. by the majority of normal people. Neither do the pathocrats entertain any illusions about their personal fate should there be a return to the system of normal man.

A normal person deprived or privilege or high position goes about performing some work which would earn him a living; but pathocrats never possessed any practical talent, and the time frame of their rule has eliminated any residual possibilities of adapting to the demands of normal work. If the law of normal man were to be reinstalled, they and their kind could be subjected to judgments, including a moralizing interpretation of their psychological deviations; they would be threatened by a loss of freedom and life, not merely a loss of position and privilege. Since they are incapable of this kind of sacrifice, the survival of a system which is the best for them becomes a moral idea. Such a threat must be battled by means of psychological and political cunning and a lack of scruples with regard to those others "inferior- quality" people.

In general, this new class is in the position to purge its leaders should their behavior jeopardize the existence of such a system. ...Pathocracy survives thanks to the feeling of being threatened by the society of normal people, as well by other countries wherein various forms of the system of normal man persist. For the rulers, staying on the top is therefore the classic problem of "to be or not to be".

We can thus formulate a more cautious question: can such a system ever waive territorial and political expansion abroad and settle for its present possessions?

What would happen if a state of affairs ensued which conferred internal peace, corresponding order, and relative prosperity within the nation?

The overwhelming majority of the country's population -being normal - would make skillful use of all the emerging possibilities, taking advantage of their superior qualifications to fight for an ever-increasing scope of activities. Thanks to their higher numbers, there would be a higher birth rate of their kind, and their power would increase. This majority would be joined by some sons from the privileged class who did not inherit the psychopathic genes. The pathocracy's dominance would weaken steadily, finally leading to a situation wherein the society of normal people take back the power. To the pathocrats, this is a known and nightmarish vision.

Thus, the biological, psychological, moral, and economic destruction of this majority of normal people is a "biological" necessity to the pathocrats. Many means serve this end, starting with concentration camps and including warfare with an obstinate, well-armed foe who will devastate and debilitate the human power thrown at him, namely the very power jeopardizing pathocrats rule. Once safely dead, the soldiers will thereupon be decreed heroes to be revered, useful for raising a new generation faithful to the pathocracy.

Any war waged by a pathocratic nation has two fronts, the internal and the external. The internal front is more important for the leaders and the governing elite, and the internal threat is the deciding factor where unleashing war is concerned. In pondering whether to start a war against the pathocratic country, one must therefore give primary consideration to the fact that one can be used as an executioner of the common people whose increasing power represents incipient jeopardy for the pathocracy. After all, pathocrats give short shrift to blood and suffering of people they consider to be not quite conspecific. [...]

Pathocracy has other internal reasons for pursuing expansionism through the use of all means possible. As long as that "other" world governed by the systems of normal man exists, it inducts into and within the strivings of the non-pathological majority, thereby creating a certain sense of direction. The non-pathological majority of the country's population will never stop dreaming of the reinstatement of normal man's system in any possible form. This majority will never stop watching other countries, waiting for the opportune moment; its attention and power must therefore be distracted from this purpose, and the masses must be educated and channeled in the direction of imperialist strivings. Such goals must be pursued doggedly so that everyone knows what is being fought for and in whose name a harsh discipline and poverty must be endured. This latter factor effectively limits the possibility of "subversive" activities on the part of the society of normal people.

The ideology must of course furnish a corresponding justification for this alleged right to conquer the world, and must therefore be properly elaborated. Expansionism is derived from the very nature of pathocracy, not from ideology, but this fact must be masked by ideology. [...]

On the other hand, there are countries with normal man's governments wherein the overwhelming majority of societies shudder to think a similar system could be imposed on them. The governments of such nations thereupon do everything they can within the framework of their possibilities and their understanding of the phenomenon in order to contain its expansion. The citizens of those countries would sigh with relief if some upheaval were to replace this malevolent and incomprehensible system with a more human, more easily understood governmental method with whom peaceful coexistence would be possible

Such countries thus undertake various means of action for this purpose, their quality depending on the possibility of understanding that other reality. [...]

Economic factors constitute a non-negligible part of the motivation for this expansionist tendency. Since the managerial functions have been taken over by individuals with mediocre intelligence and pathological character traits, the pathocracy becomes incapable of properly administering anything at all. [...] The collected prosperity of conquered nations can be exploited for a time, the citizens forced to work harder for paltry remuneration. For the moment, not thought is given to the fact that a pathocratic system within a conquered country will eventually cause similar unproductive conditions; after all corresponding self-knowledge in this area is nonresistant in the psychopath. [...]

As has been the case for centuries, military power is of course, the primary means for achieving these ends. Throughout the centuries, whenever history registered the appearance of the phenomenon described heron, specific measures of influence have also become apparent - something in the order of specific intelligence in the service of international intrigue facilitating conquest. This quality is derived from the personality characteristics inspiring the overall phenomenon; it should constitute data for historians to identify this type of phenomenon throughout history.

Psychopaths exist everywhere in the world; even a faraway pathocracy evokes a resonating response in them, working on their underlying feeling that "there is a place for people like us there". Uncritical, frustrated, and abused people also exist everywhere and they can be reached by appropriately elaborated propaganda. The future of a nation is greatly dependent on how many such people it contains. Thanks to its specific psychological knowledge and its conviction that normal people are naïve, a pathocracy is able to improve its "anti-psychotherapeutic" techniques, and pathologically egotistical as usual, to insinuate its deviant world of concepts to others. [...]

The law furnishes insufficient support for counteracting a phenomenon whose character lies outside the possibilities of the legislators imagination. Pathocracy knows how to take advantage of the weaknesses of such a legalistic manner of thinking. [...]

Whenever a nation experiences a "system crisis" or a hyperactivity of ponerogenic processes within, it becomes the object of a pathocratic penetration whose purpose is to serve up the country as booty. It will then become easy to take advantage of its internal weaknesses and revolutionary movements in order to impose rule on the basis of a limited use of force. ... After forcible imposition of such a system, the course of pathologization of life becomes different; and such a pathocracy will be less stable, depending for its very existence upon the factor of never-ending outside force....

Brute force must first stifle the resistance of an exhausted nation; people possessing military or leadership skills must be disposed of, and anyone appealing to moral values and legal principles must be silenced. The new principles are never explicitly enunciated. People must learn the new unwritten law via painful experience. The stultifying influence of this deviant world of concepts finishes the job, and common sense demands caution and endurance.

This is followed by a shock which appears as tragic as it is frightening. Some people from every social group - whether abused paupers, aristocrats officials, literati, students, scientists, priests,, atheists, or nobodies known to no one - suddenly start changing their personality and world-view. Decent Christian and patriots just yesterday, they now expose the new ideology and behave contemptuously to anyone still adhering to the old values. Only later does it become evident that this ostensibly avalanche like process has it s natural limits. ...

Pathocracy imposed by force arrives in a finished form - we could even call it ripe. People observing it up close were unable to distinguish the earlier phases of its development; when the schizoidals and characteropaths were in charge. ...

In an imposed system, psychopathic material is already dominant...[...]

The first conclusion which suggested itself soon after meeting with the "professor" [discussed earlier] was that the phenomenon's development is limited by nature in terms of the participation of susceptible individuals within a given society. The initial evaluation of approximately 6 % proved realistic. Progressively collected detailed statistical data assembled later did not contradict this assessment. This value varies from country to country in the magnitude of about one percentage point up or down. ...Essential psychopathy plays a disproportionate role compared to the numbers by saturating the phenomenon as a whole with its own quality of thought and experience. Other psychopathies - asthenic, schizoidal, anankastic, hysterical, et al - definitely play second fiddle although in sum they are much more numerous. Relatively primitive skirtoidal individuals become fellow travelers, goaded by their lust for life, but their activities are limited by considerations of their own advantage.

In non-Semitic nations, schizoidals are somewhat more numerous than essential psychopaths; although highly active in the early phases of the genesis of the phenomenon, they betray an attraction to pathocracy as well the rational distance of efficient thinking. Thus, they are torn between such a system and the society of normal people.

There are persons less distinctly inclined in the pathocratic direction. These include states caused by the toxic activities of certain substances such as ether, carbon monoxide, and possibly some endotoxins.[51] Paranoidal individuals expect uncritical support within such a system. In general, however, the carriers of various kinds of brain tissue damage lean clearly to the society of normal people and, as a result of their psychological problems, under a pathocracy, suffer even more than healthy people.

It also turned out that the carriers of some physiological anomalies known to physicians and sometimes to psychologists, and which are primarily hereditary in nature, manifest split tendencies similar to schizoids. In a similar manner, people whom nature has unfortunately saddled with a short life and an early cancer-related death frequency indicate a characteristic and irrational attraction for this phenomenon. ... An individuals' decreased resistance to the effects of pathocracy and his attraction to it appear to be a holistic response of person's organism, not merely of his psychological makeup alone.

Approximately 6 % of the population constitute the active structure of the pathocracy, which carries its own peculiar consciousness of its own goals. Twice as many people constitute a second group: those who have managed to warp their personalities to meet the demands of the new reality. ...

This second group consists of individuals who are, on the average, weaker, more sickly, and less vital. The frequency of known mental diseases in this group is at twice the rate of the national average. We can thus assume that the genesis of their submissive attitude toward the regime, their greater susceptibility to pathological effects, and their skittish opportunism includes various relatively impalpable anomalies. ...

The 6 % group constitute the new nobility; the 12 % group forms the new bourgeoisie, whose economic situation is the most advantageous. ...Only 18 % of the country's population is thus in favor of the new system of government.

The great majority of the population forms the society of normal people, creating an informal communications network. It behooves us to wonder why these people reject the advantages conformity affords, consciously

---

[51] Perhaps this is one of the reasons the pathocracy wishes to stamp out smoking?

preferring the opposing role: poverty, harassment, and curtailment of human freedoms. What ideals motivate them? Is this merely a kind of romanticism?

A person with a normal human instinctive substratum, good basic intelligence, and full faculties of critical thought would have a difficult time accepting such a compromise; it would devastate his personality and engender neurosis. AT the same time, such a system easily distinguishes and separates him from its own kind regardless of his sporadic hesitations. No method of propaganda can change the nature of this macro social phenomenon or the nature of a normal human being. They remain forever foreign to each other.

After a typical pathocratic structure has been formed, the population is effectively divided according to completely different lines from what someone raised outside the purview of this phenomenon might imagine, and in a manner whose actual conditions are also impossible to comprehend.... Pathocracy corrodes the entire social organism, wasting its skills and power. ... Typical pathocrats take over all the managerial functions in a totally destroyed structure of a nation. Such a state must be short-term, since no ideology can vivify it. The time comes when the common masses of people want to live like human beings and the system can no longer resist.

Pathocracy is even less of a socioeconomic system than a social structure or political system. It is a macro social disease process affecting entire nations and running the course of its characteristic pathodynamic properties. ... As long as we keep using methods of comprehending this pathological phenomenon which attempt to use political doctrines to define it, (even if those doctrines are heterogeneous to it) we will not be able to identify the causes and properties of the disease. A correspondingly prepared ideology will be able to cloak the essential qualities from the minds of scientists, politicians, and common people.

Normal People Under Pathocratic Rule

As adduced above, the anomaly distinguished as essential psychopathy inspires the overall phenomenon in a well-developed pathocracy... The pathocratic world - the world of pathological egotism and terror - is so difficult to understand for people raised outside the scope of this phenomenon that they often manifest childlike naïveté, even if they studied psychopathology and are psychologists by profession. There are no real data in their behavior, advice, rebukes, and psychotherapy. ... If a person with a normal instinctive substratum and basic intelligence has already heard and read about such a system of ruthless autocratic rule "based on fanatical ideology," he feels he has already formed an opinion on the subject. However, direct confrontation with the phenomenon causes him to feel intellectually helpless. All his prior imaginings prove to be virtually useless; they explain next to nothing. This provokes a nagging sensation that he and the society in which he was educated were quite naïve... One of the differences observed between a normally resistant person and somebody who has undergone a transpersonification is that the former is better able to survive this disintegrating cognitive void, whereas the latter fills the void with the pathologic propaganda material, and without sufficient controls.

When the human mind comes into contact with this new reality so different from any experiences encountered by a person raised in a society dominated by normal people, it releases psychophysiological shock symptoms in the human brain with a higher tonus of cortex inhibition and a stifling of feelings, which then sometimes gush forth uncontrollably. Human minds work more slowly and less keenly, since the associative mechanisms have become inefficient. Especially when a person has direct contact with psychopathic representatives of the new rule, who use their specific experience so as to traumatized the minds of the "others" with their own personalities, his mind succumbs to a state of short-term catatonia. Their humiliating and arrogant techniques, brutal paramoralizations, deaden his thought processes and his self-defense capabilities, and their divergent experiential method anchors in his min. ...

Only after these unbelievably unpleasant psychological states have passed, thanks to rest in benevolent company, is it possible to reflect - always a difficult and painful process - or to become aware that one's mind and common senses have been fooled by something which cannot fit into the normal human imagination.

Man and society stands at the beginning of a long road of unknown experiences which, after much trial and error, finally leads to a certain hermetic knowledge of what the qualities of the phenomenon are and how best to build up psychological resistance thereto. Especially during the dissimulative phase, this makes it possible to adapt to life in this different world and thus arrange more tolerable living conditions. We shall thereupon observe psychological phenomena, knowledge, immunization, and adaptation such as could not have been predicted before and which cannot be understood in the world remaining under the rule of normal man's systems. A normal person, however, can never completely adapt to a pathological system; it is easy to be pessimistic about the final results of this.

Such experiences are exchanged during evening discussions among a circle of friends, thereby creating within people's minds a kind of cognitive conglomeration which is initially incoherent and contains factual deficiencies. [...]The ideology officially preached by the pathocracy continues to retain its ever-diminishing suggestive powers until such time as human reason manages to localize it as something subordinate, which is not descriptive of the essence of phenomenon. [...]

Under such conditions, both instinct and feelings and the resulting basic intelligence play instrumental roles, stimulating man to make selections which are to a great extent subconscious.

Under the conditions created by imposed pathocratic rule ... our natural human instinctive substratum is an instrumental factor in joining the opposition. Similarly, the environmental, economic, and ideological motivations which influenced the formation of an individual personality, including those political attitudes which were assumed earlier... disappear within the statistical approach and diminish through the years of pathocratic rule. The decisions and the way selections made back to the society of normal people are finally decided by factors usually inherited by biological means, and thus not the product of the person's option, and predominantly in subconscious processes.

Man's general intelligence, especially its intellectual level, play a relatively limited role in this process of selecting a path of action, as expressed by statistically significant but low correlation (-0.16). The higher a person's general level of talent, the harder it usually is for him to reconcile himself with this different reality and find a modus vivendi within it. At the same time, gifted and talented people join the pathocracy, and harsh words of contempt for the system can be heard on the part of simple, uneducated people. Only those people with the highest degree of intelligence--which, as mentioned, does not accompany psychopathies--are unable to find the meaning of life within such a system. They are sometimes able to take advantage of their superior mentality in order to find exceptional ways in which to be useful to others. Wasting the best talents spells eventual catastrophe for any social system.

Since those factors subject to the laws of genetics have proven decisive, society becomes divided into the adherents of the new rule, the new middle class mentioned above, and the majority opposition by means of criteria not known before.

Since the properties which cause this new division appear in more or less equal proportions within any old social group or level, this new division cuts right through these traditional layers of society. If we treat the former stratification, whose formation was decisively influenced by the talent factor, as horizontal, the new one should be referred to as vertical. The most instrumental factor in the latter is good basic intelligence which, as we already know, is widely distributed throughout all social groups.

Even those people who were the object of social injustice in the former system and then bestowed with another system which allegedly protected them slowly start criticizing the latter. [...]

One of the first discoveries made by a society of normal people is that it is superior to the new rulers in intelligence and practical skills, no matter what geniuses they appear to be. The knots stultifying reason are gradually loosened, and fascination with the new rulership's secret knowledge and plan of action begins to diminish, followed by familiarization with the knowledge about this new reality.

The world of normal people is always superior to the other one whenever constructive activity is needed, whether it be the reconstruction of a devastated country, the area of technology, the organization of economic life, or scientific and medical work. [...]

As we have already pointed out, every psychological anomaly is in fact a kind of deficiency. Psychopathies are based primarily upon deficiencies in the instinctive substratum; however, their influence exerted upon mental development also leads to deficiencies in general intelligence, as discussed above. This deficiency is not compensated by the creation of the special psychological knowledge we observe among some psychopaths. Such knowledge loses its mesmerizing power when normal people learn to understand these phenomena as well. The psychopathologist was thus not surprised by the fact that the world of normal people is dominant as regards skill and talent. For that society, however, this represented a discovery which engendered hope and psychological relaxation.

Since our intelligence is superior to theirs, we can recognize them and understand how they think and act. This is what a person learns in such a system on his own initiative, forced by everyday needs. He learns it while working in his office, school, or factory, whether he needs to deal with the authorities, and when he is arrested--something only a few people manage to avoid. The author and many others learned a good deal about the psychology of this macro social phenomenon during compulsory indoctrinational schooling. The organizers and lecturers cannot have intended such a result. Practical knowledge of this new reality thus grows, thanks to which the society gains a resourcefulness of action which enables it to take ever better advantage of the weak spots of the rulership system. This permits gradual reorganization of societal links, which bears fruit with time.

This new science is incalculably rich in casuist detail; I would nevertheless characterise it as overly literary. It contains knowledge and a description of the phenomenon in the categories of the natural world-view, correspondingly bent or modified in accordance with the need to understand matters which are in fact outside the scope of its applicability. This also opens the door to the creation of certain doctrines which merit separate study because they contain partial truth, such as *a demonological interpretation* of the phenomenon.

The development of this familiarity with the phenomenon is accompanied by development of communicative language, by means of which society can stay informed and issue warnings of danger. A third language thus appears alongside the ideological doubletalk described above; in part, it borrows names used by the official ideology in their transformed modified meanings. In part, this language operates with words borrowed from still more lively circulating jokes. In spite of its strangeness, this language becomes a useful means of communication and plays a part in regenerating societal links. ... However, in spite of efforts on the part of literati and journalists, this language remains only communicative inside; it becomes hermetic outside the scope of the phenomenon, incomprehensible to people lacking the appropriate personal experience. [...]

This new science, expressed in language derived from a deviant reality, is something foreign to people who wish to understand this macro-social phenomenon but think in the categories of the countries of normal man. Attempts to understand this language produce a certain feeling of helplessness which gives rise to the tendency of creating ones own doctrines, built from concepts of one's own world and a certain amount of appropriately co-opted pathocratic propaganda material. Such a doctrine--an example would be the American anti-Communist doctrine--makes it even more difficult to understand that other reality. May the objective description adduced herein enable them to overcome the impasse thus engendered.[...]

The specific role of certain individuals during such times is worth pointing out; they participated in the discovery of the nature of this new reality and helped others find the right path. They had a normal nature but an unfortunate childhood, being subjected very early to the domination of individuals with various psychological deviations, including pathological egotism and methods of terrorizing others. The new rulership system struck such people as a large-scale societal multiplication of what they knew from individual experience. From the very outset, they therefore saw this reality much more prosaically, immediately treating the ideology in accordance with the paralogistic stories well known to them, whose purpose was to cloak bitter reality of their youth experiences. They soon reached the truth, since the genesis and nature of evil are analogous irrespective of the social scale in which it appears.

Such people are rarely understood in happy societies, but there they became useful; their explanations and advice proved accurate and were transmitted to others joining the network of this apperceptive heritage. However, their own suffering was doubled, since this was too much of a similar kind of abuse for one life to handle. They therefore nursed dreams of escaping into the freedom still existing in the outside world.

Finally, society sees the appearance of individuals who have collected exceptional intuitive perception and practical knowledge in the area of how pathocrats think and such a system of rule operates.

Some of them become so proficient in the deviant psychopath language and its idiomatics that they are able to use it, much like a foreign language they have learned well. Since they are to decipher the rulership's intentions, such people there-upon offer advice to people who are having trouble with the authorities. These usually disinterested advocates of the society of normal people play a irreplaceable role in the life of society. The pathocrats, however, can never learn to think in normal human categories. At the same time, the ability to predict the ways of reaction of such an authority also leads to the conclusion that the system is rigidly causative and lacking in the natural freedom of choice. [...]

I was once referred a patient who had been an inmate in a Nazi concentration camp. She came back from that hell in such exceptionally good condition that she was still able to marry and bear three children. However, her child-rearing methods were so extremely iron-fisted as to be much too reminiscent of the concentration camp life so stubbornly per-severing in former prisoners. The children's reaction was neurotic protest and aggressiveness against other children.

During the mother's psychotherapy, we recalled the figures of male and female SS officers to her mind, pointing out their psychopathic characteristics (such people were primary recruits). In order to help her eliminate their pathological material from her person, I furnished her with approximate statistical data regarding the appearance of such individuals within the population as whole. This helped her reach a more objective view of that reality and reestablish trust in the society of normal people.

During the next visit, the patient showed to me a little card on which she had written the names of local pathocratic notables and added her own diagnoses - which were largely correct. So I made a hushing gesture with my finger and admonished her with emphasis that we were dealing only with her problems. The patient understood, and - I am sure - she did not make her reflections on the matter known in the wrong places.

Parallel to the development of practical knowledge and a language of insider communication, other psychological phenomena take form; they are truly significant in the transformation of social life under pathocratic rule, and discerning them is essential if one wishes to understand individuals and nations fated to live under such conditions and to evaluate the situation in the political sphere. They include people's psychological immunization and their adaptation to life under such deviant conditions.

The methods of psychological terror (that specific pathocratic art), the techniques of pathological arrogance, and the striding roughshod into other people's souls initially have such traumatic effects that people are deprived of their capacity for purposeful reaction; I have already adduced the psychophysiological aspects of such states. Ten or twenty years later, analogous behavior can be recognized as well-known buffoonery and does not deprive the victim of his ability to think and react purposefully. His answers are usually well-thought-out strategies, issued from the position of a normal person's superiority and often laced with ridicule. Man can look suffering and even death in the eye with the required calm. A dangerous weapon falls out of ruler's hands.

We have to understand that this process of immunization is not merely a result of the above described increase in practical knowledge of the macro social phenomenon. It is the effect of a many-layered, gradual process of growth in knowledge, familiarization with the phenomenon, creation of the appropriate reactive habits, and self-control, with an overall conception and moral principles being worked out in the meantime. After several years, the same stimuli which formerly caused chilly spiritual impotence or mental paralysis now provoke the desire to gargle with something strong so as to get rid of this filth.

It was a time, when many people dreamed of finding some pill which would make it easier to endure dealing with the authorities or attending the forced indoctrination sessions generally chaired by a psychopathic character. Some antidepressants did in fact prove to have the desired effect. Twenty years later, this had been forgotten entirely.

When I was arrested for the first time in 1951, force, arrogance, and psychopathic methods of forcible confession deprived me almost entirely of my self-defense capabilities. My brain stopped functioning after only a few days' arrest without water, to such a point that I couldn't even properly remember the incident which resulted in my sudden arrest. I was not even aware that it had been purposely provoked and that conditions permitting self-defense did in fact exist. They did almost anything they wanted to me.

When I was arrested for last time in 1968, I was interrogated by five fierce-looking security functionaries. At one particular moment, after thinking through their predicted reactions, I let my gaze take in each face sequentially with great attentiveness. The most important one asked me, "What's on your mind, buster, staring at us like that?" I answered without any fear of consequences: "I'm just wondering why so many of you gentleman's careers end up in a psychiatric hospital." They were taken aback for a while, whereupon the same man exclaimed, "Because it's such damned horrible work!" "I am of the opinion that it's the other way round", I calmly responded. Then I was taken back to my cell.

Three days later, I had the opportunity to talk to him again, but this time he was much more respectful. Then he ordered me to be taken away--outside, as it turned out. I rode the streetcar home past a large park, still unable to believe my eyes. Once in my room, I lay down on the bed; the world was not quite real yet, but exhausted people fall asleep quickly. When I awoke, I spoke out loud: "Dear God, aren't you supposed to be in charge here in this world!"

At that time, I knew not only that up to 1/4 of all secret police officials wind up in psychiatric hospitals. I also knew that their "occupational disease" is the congestive dementia formerly encountered only among old prostitutes. Man cannot violate the natural human feelings inside him with impunity, no matter what kind of profession he performs. From that view-point, Comrade Captain was partially right. At the same time, however, my reactions had become resistant, a far cry from what they had been seventeen years earlier.

All these transformations of human consciousness and unconsciousness result in individual and collective adaptation to living under such system. Under altered conditions of both material and moral limitations, an existential resourcefulness emerges which is prepared to overcome many difficulties. A new network of the society of normal people is also created for self-help and mutual assistance.

This society acts in concert and is aware of the true state of affairs; it begins to develop ways of influencing various elements of authority and achieving goals which are socially useful. ...The opinion that society is totally deprived of any influence upon government in such a country is thus inaccurate. In reality, society does co-govern to a certain extent, sometimes succeeding and sometimes failing in its attempt to create more tolerable living conditions. This, however, occurs in a manner totally different from what happens in democratic countries.

These processes cognitive, psychological immunization, and adaptation permit the creation of new interpersonal and societal links, which operate within the scope of the large majority we have already called the "society of normal people." These links extend discretely into the world of the regime's middle class, among people who can be trusted to a certain extent. ... Exchange of information, warnings, and assistance encompasses the entire society. Whoever is able to do so offers aid to anyone who finds himself in trouble, often in such a way that the person helped does not know who rendered the assistance. However, if he caused his misfortune by his own lack of circumspect caution with regard to the authorities, he meets with reproach, but not the withholding of assistance.

It is possible to create such links because this new division of society gives only limited consideration to factors such as the level of talent or education or traditions attached to the former social layers. Neither do reduced prosperity differences dissolve these links. One side of this division contains those of the highest mental culture, simple ordinary people, intellectuals, headwork specialists, factory workers, and peasants joined by the common protest of their human nature against the domination of a Para human experience and governmental methods. These links engender interpersonal understanding and fellow-feeling among people and social groups formerly divided by economic differences and social traditions. The thought processes serving these links are of more psychological character, able to comprehend someone else's motivations. At the same time, the ordinary folk retain respect for people who have been educated and represent intellectual values. Certain social and moral values also appear, and may prove to be permanent.

The genesis, however, of this great interpersonal solidarity only becomes comprehensible once we already know the nature of the pathological macro social phenomenon which brought about the liberation of such attitudes, complete with recognition of one's own humanity and that of others. Another reflection suggests itself, namely how very different these great links are from America's "competitive society".[52]

Capitalism and Psychopathy

The members of the Quantum Future School have been engaged in studying psychopathy and pseudo-psychopathy for several years. This has certainly prepared most of us to be able to see the man behind the curtain, or, in this case, behind the "mask of sanity". These studies led to the question: why does psychopathic behavior seems to be so widespread in the US. (That is not to say that it doesn't exist everywhere - that's a given.)

Linda Mealey of the Department of Psychology at the College of St. Benedict in St. Joseph, Minnesota, has recently proposed certain ideas in her paper: *The Sociobiology of Sociopathy: An Integrated Evolutionary Model.*[53] These ideas address the increase in psychopathy in American culture by suggesting that in a competitive society - capitalistic by definition - psychopathy is adaptive and likely to increase. She writes,

"I have thus far argued that some individuals seem to have a genotype that disposes them to [psychopathy].

[Psychopathy describes] frequency-dependent, genetically based, individual differences in employment of life strategies. [Psychopaths] always appear in every culture, no matter what the socio-cultural conditions. [...]

---

[52] Lobaczewski, op. cit.

[53] http://www.bbsonline.org/Preprints/OldArchive/bbs.mealey.html

Competition increases the use of antisocial and Machiavellian strategies and can counteract pro-social behavior... [54]

Some cultures encourage competitiveness more than others and these differences in social values vary both temporally and cross-culturally. [...] Across both dimensions, high levels of competitiveness are associated with high crime rates and Machiavellianism.

High population density, an indirect form of competition, is also associated with reduced pro-social behavior and increased anti-social behavior." [Mealey, op. cit.]

The conclusion is that the capitalistic way of life associated in the United States with "democracy," has *optimized the survival of psychopaths* with the consequence that it is an adaptive "life strategy" that is extremely successful in U.S. society, and thus has *increased in the population in strictly genetic terms.* What is more, as a consequence of a society that is adaptive for psychopathy, many individuals who are NOT genetic psychopaths have similarly adapted, becoming "effective" psychopaths, or "secondary sociopaths" in the ways Lobaczewski has described. [55]

"Of course, because they are not intellectually handicapped, these individuals [psychopaths] will progress normally in terms of cognitive development and will acquire a theory of mind. Their theories, however, will be formulated purely in instrumental terms [what can claiming this or that GET for me?], without access to the empathic understanding that most of us rely on so much of the time.

They may become excellent predictors of others' behavior, unhandicapped by the 'intrusiveness' of emotion, acting, as do professional gamblers, solely on nomothetic laws and *actuarial data* rather than on hunches and feelings.

In determining how to 'play' in the social encounters of everyday life, they will use a pure *cost-benefit approach* based on *immediate personal outcomes*, with no 'accounting' for the emotional reactions of the others with whom they are dealing.

Without any real love to 'commit' them to cooperation, without any anxiety to prevent fear of 'defection', without guilt to inspire repentance, *they are free to continually play for the short-term benefit.*

At the same time, because changes in gene frequencies in the population would not be able to keep pace with the fast-changing parameters of social interactions, an additional fluctuating proportion of sociopathy should result because, in a society of [psychopathy], the environmental circumstances make an antisocial strategy of life more profitable than a pro-social one." [Mealey, op. cit.]

---

[54] Emphasis, ours.

[55] Many experts differentiate between primary and secondary sociopaths. The first is a sociopath because they have the "genes" and the second is more or less "created" by their environment of victimization. Other experts refer to these two categories as "psychopaths" for the genetic variety and "sociopaths" for the reactive variety. We prefer this latter distinction.

In other words, in a world of psychopaths, those who are not genetic psychopaths, are induced to behave like psychopaths simply to survive. When the rules are set up to make a society "adaptive" to psychopathy, it makes sociopaths of everyone.

What makes the psychopath so frightening and dangerous is that he or she wears a completely convincing "Mask of Sanity". This may at first make such a person utterly persuasive and compellingly healthy, according to psychiatrist Harvey Cleckley. Cleckley was first to describe the key symptoms of the disorder.

Psychopaths are experts at using people. They can ask anything of anyone without embarrassment and because of their outgoing seducing friendliness, their use of, "poor innocent me! I am such a *good* person, and I have been treated so *badly*!", the victim invariably gets sucked into giving the psychopath what they ask for - no matter how outrageous.

Psychopaths are masters at faking emotions in order to manipulate others. One psychologist reported that if you actually catch them in the act of committing a crime, or telling a lie, "they will immediately justify their actions by self pity and blaming another, by creating a heart-rending scene of faked emotional feelings". These fake emotions are only for effect, as the careful observer will note. The psychopath considers getting their way or getting out of trouble using faked emotions as a victory over another person.

Indeed, using their "emotional performances", these individuals can be truly overwhelming. Their charisma can be so inspiring - their emotion so deep and sincere-seeming - that people just want to be around them, want to help them, want to give all and support such a noble, suffering being. What is generally not seen by the victim is that they are feeding an endless internal hunger for control, excitement and ego-recognition.

Psychopaths cannot feel fear for themselves, much less empathy for others. Most normal people, when they are about to do something dangerous, illegal, or immoral, feel a rush of worry, nervousness, or fear. Guilt may overwhelm them and prevent them from even committing the deed.

The psychopath feels little or nothing except that they want something and not having it is a sort of pain, a hunger, so to say.

As a result, the threat of punishment, even painful punishment, is a laughing matter for the psychopath. They can repeat the same destructive acts without skipping a heartbeat, as well as seek thrills and dangers without regard for possible risks. This is called "hypoarousal". That is, very little - if anything - really arouses them; they are more machine-like than human-like.

The psychopath seems to be full of something that our ordinary language can only describe as being akin to deep greed. They manifest this inner state in many ways. One of the most common ways is to steal something of value to their victim (valuables), or to hurt/slander the victim or something or someone the victim loves. In the psychopath's mind, this is justified because the victim crossed him, did not give him what he wanted, or rejected him (or her).

In general, the successful psychopath "computes" how much they can get away with in a cost-benefit ratio of the alternatives. Among the factors that they consider as most important are money, power, and gratification of negative desires. They are not motivated by such social reinforcement as praise or future benefits or the well-being of others - even including those one would suspect them to care about, such as their own families. Studies have been done that show locking up a psychopath has absolutely no effect on them in terms of modifying their life strategies. In fact, it is shown to make them worse. Effectively, when locked up, psychopaths just simply learn how to be better psychopaths.

The psychopath is obsessed with control even if they give the impression of being helpless. Their pretense to emotional sensitivity is really part of their control function: The higher the level of belief in the psychopath that can be induced in their victim through their dramas, the more "control" the psychopath believes they have. And in fact, this is true. They *do* have control when others believe their lies. Sadly, the degree of belief, the degree of "submission" to this control via false representation, generally produces so much pain when the truth is glimpsed that the victim would prefer to continue in the lie than face the fact that they have been duped. The psychopath counts on this. It is part of their "actuarial calculations". It gives them a feeling of power.

Psychopathic behavior seems to be on the rise because of the very nature of U.S. capitalistic society. The great hustlers, charmers, and self-promoters in the sales fields are perfect examples of where the psychopath can thrive; the entertainment industry, the sports industry, the corporate world in the capitalist system, are all areas where psychopaths naturally rise to the top.

Since the psychopath bases their activities, designed to get what they want, on their particular "theory of mind", it is instructive to have a look at this issue. Having a "theory of mind" allows an individual to impute mental states (thoughts, perceptions, and feelings) not only to oneself, but also to other individuals. It is, in effect, a tool that helps us predict the behavior of others. The most successful individuals are those who most accurately predict what another person will do given a certain set of circumstances. In the present day, we have Game Theory - created by Nobel Prize winner John Nash - which is being used to model many social problems. This system is essential psychopathy in action.

When two individuals interact with each other, each must decide what to do often without knowledge of what the other is doing. Imagine that the two players are the government and the public. In the following model, each of the players faces only a binary choice: to behave ethically either in making laws or in obeying them.

The assumption is that both players are informed about everything *except the level of ethical behavior of the other*.[56] They know what it means to act ethically, and they know the consequences of being exposed as unethical.

There are three elements to the game. 1) The players, 2) the strategies available to either of them, and 3) the payoff each player receives for each possible combination of strategies.

In a legal regime, one party is obliged to compensate the other for damages under certain conditions but not under others. We are going to imagine a regime wherein the government is never liable for losses suffered by the public because of its unethical behavior - instead, the public has to pay for the damages inflicted by the government due to unethical behavior.

The payoffs discussed in Game Theory are generally represented in terms of money, which is a metaphor for energy. That is, how much investment does each player have to make in ethical behavior and how much payoff does each player receive for his investment.

In this model, (we will use an arbitrary set of numbers to make the example easy to understand), behaving ethically, according to standards of social values that are considered the "norm", costs each player $10.00. When law detrimental to the public is passed, it costs the public $100.00 (to represent a larger population than just a single individual). We take it as a given that such laws will be passed unless both players behave ethically which is not likely based on historical precedent.

Next, we assume that the likelihood of a detrimental law being passed in the event that both the public and the government are behaving ethically is a one-in-ten chance.

In a legal regime in which the government is *never* held responsible for its unethical behavior, and if neither the government nor the public behave ethically, the government enjoys a payoff of $0, and the public is out $100 when a law detrimental to the public is passed.

If both "invest" in ethical behavior, the government has a payoff of minus $10 (the cost of behaving ethically) and the public is out minus $20 which is the $10 invested in being ethical PLUS the $10 of the one-in-ten chance of a $100 loss incurred if a detrimental law is passed.

If the government behaves ethically and the public does not, resulting in the passing of a law detrimental to the populace, the government is out the $10 invested in being ethical and the public is out $100.

---

[56] This seems to be the chief problem in the culturally rampant breakdown of human relations. Time and again people engage in dynamic interactions with others only to find that they are duped, tricked, cheated, hurt, or otherwise abused in physical or psychological ways that they *did not anticipate*.

If the government does not behave ethically, and the public does, the government has a payoff of $0 and the public is out $110 which is the "cost of being ethical" added to the losses suffered when the government passes detrimental laws. Modelled in a Game Theory Bi-matrix, it looks like this, with the two numbers representing the "payoff" to the people - the left number in each pair - and government - the right number in each pair.

		Government	
		No Ethics	Ethical
	No Ethics	-100, 0	-100, -10
Society/People			
	Ethical	-110, 0	-20, -10

In short, in this game, the government always does better by not being ethical and we can predict the government's choice of strategy because there is a single strategy - no ethics - *that is better for the government no matter what choice the public makes*. This is a "strictly dominant strategy", or a strategy that is the best choice for the player no matter what choices are made by the other player.

What is even worse is the fact that the public is *penalized* for behaving ethically. Since we know that the government, in the above regime, will never behave ethically because it is the dominant strategy, we find that ethical behavior on the part of the public actually costs *more* than unethical behavior.

In short, psychopathic behavior is actually a *positive adaptation* in such a regime. The public, as you see, cannot even minimize their losses by behaving ethically. It costs them $110 to be ethical, and only $100 to not be ethical.

Now, just substitute "psychopath" in the place of the government and non-psychopath in the place of the public, and you will have a form game model of interpersonal relations between the psychopath and a normal person. This will help you understand why the psychopath will always win. If the "payoff" is emotional pain of being hurt, or shame for being exposed, in the world of the psychopath, that consequence simply does not exist just as in the legal regime created above, the government is never responsible for unethical behavior. The psychopath lives in a world in which it is like a government that is never held responsible for behavior that is detrimental to others. The psychopath has no conscience. It's that simple. And the form game above will tell you why psychopaths in the population, as well as in government, are able to induce the public to accept laws that are detrimental. It simply isn't worth it to be ethical. If you go along with the psychopath, you lose. If you resist the psychopath, you lose even more.

Societies, too, can be considered "players" in the psychopath's game model. The past behavior of a society will be used by the psychopath (or ponerological network) to predict the future behavior of that society. Like an individual player, a society will have a certain probability of detecting deception and a more or less accurate memory of who has cheated them in the past. The society will also have a developed, or not developed, proclivity to retaliate against a liar and cheater. Since the psychopath is using an *actuarial approach* to assess the costs and benefits of different behaviors, (just how much can he get away with), it is the actual past behavior of the society which will go into his calculations rather than any risk assessments based on any "fears or anxieties" of being caught and punished that empathic people would feel in anticipation of doing something illegal.

Thus, in order to reduce psychopathic behavior in society and in government, a society *must* establish and enforce a reputation for *high rates of detection of deception and identification of liars, and a willingness to retaliate.* In other words, it must establish a successful strategy of deterrence.

Since the psychopath is particularly unable to make decisions based on future consequences, only able to focus attention on immediate gratification - short-term goals - *it is possible that such individuals can be dealt with by establishing a history of dealing out swift social retaliation.* That is, identifying and punishing liars and cheaters must be both immediate and flawlessly consistent, thus predictable in it's occurrence.

And here we come to the issue concerning real-world human social interactions on a large scale: reducing psychopathy in our leaders *depends upon expanding society's collective memory of individual players' past behavior.* Those who do not remember history are doomed to repeat it.

Any reasonable scan of the news will reveal that lies and cheating are not "covered up" as thoroughly as American apologists would like to think.

Even the less well-informed Americans have some idea that there was certainly something fishy about the investigation into the assassination of JFK. In recent years, the man in charge of the Warren Commission, Gerald Ford, also a former President, admitted to "cheating" on the report when he admitted to changing the placement of one of the bullet wounds in the final report.

Then, there was Watergate followed by the Iran-Contra affair, not to mention "Monica-gate". Those seem almost naïve compared to the lies of the current people in power. The lies of the Bush gang, from stolen elections, to the 9/11 attacks, and through the infamous weapons of mass destruction in Iraq, have taken the art of lying to heights that would impress Hitler himself. And here we are just hitting some highlights, most familiar to all Americans.

What consequences did the cheaters of society suffer?

None to speak of. In fact, in nearly every case, they were rewarded handsomely with those things of value to the psychopath: money and material goods. If anyone thinks they were shamed by public exposure, think again!

But what is of *crucial* interest here is the fact that the American people have simply *not* responded to the revelations of lies in government with any outrage that could be considered more than token. At the present time, there isn't even "token outrage".

Don't you find that odd?

But we have already noted the reason: the American way of life has optimized the survival of psychopathy and in a world of psychopaths, those who are not genetic psychopaths, are induced to behave like psychopaths simply to survive. When the rules are set up to make a society "adaptive" to psychopathy, it makes sociopaths of everyone. As a consequence, a very large number of Americans are effective sociopaths. (Here we use "sociopath" as a designation of those individuals who are not genetic psychopaths.)

And so, we have George Bush and the Fourth Reich calculating how much they can get away with by looking at the history of the reactions of the American people to cheating.

There aren't any because the system is adaptive to psychopathy. In other words, Americans support Bush and his agenda because most of them are effectively *like* him. But that is not because they are *all* born that way. It is because psychopathy is required to survive in the competitive, capitalist U.S. Society.

As a society gets larger and more competitive, individuals become more anonymous and more Machiavellian. Social stratification and segregation leads to feelings of inferiority, pessimism and depression among the have-nots, promoting the use of "cheating strategies" in life that then make the environment more adaptive for psychopathy in general because those who are suffering will respond positively to any sign of change, even if they don't realize that the change is being proposed by those who will actually make their lives worse.

Psychopathic behavior among non-genetic psychopaths could be viewed as a functional method of obtaining desirable resources, increasing an individual's status in a local group, and even a means of providing stimulation that socially and financially successful people find in acceptable physical and intellectual challenges.

In America, a great many households are affected by the fact that work, divorce, or both, have removed one or both parents from interaction with their children for much of the day. *This is a consequence of Capitalistic economics.*

When the parents are absent, or even when one is present but not in possession of sufficient knowledge or information, children are left to the mercies of their peers, a culture shaped by the media. Armed with joysticks and TV remotes, children are guided from *South Park* and *Jerry Springer* to *Mortal Kombat* on Nintendo. Normal kids become desensitized to violence. More-susceptible kids - children with a genetic inheritance of psychopathy - are pushed toward a dangerous mental precipice. Meanwhile, the government is regularly passing laws, on the demand of parents and the psychological community, designed to avoid imposing consequences on junior's violent behavior.

As for media violence, few researchers continue to try to dispute that bloodshed on TV and in the movies has an effect on the kids who witness it. Added to the mix now are video games structured around models of hunting and killing. Engaged by graphics, children learn to associate spurts of "blood" with the primal gratification of scoring a "win".

Again, economics - capitalism disguised as "democracy" - controls the reality.

The fact is, it is almost a mechanical system that operates based on the *psychological nature of human beings*, most of whom *like* to live in denial or need to live in denial to please their parents, their peers, their religious leaders, and their political leaders. All they want to do is have some relaxation to enjoy the "American Dream." After all, "if ignorance is bliss, tis folly to be wise". This is most especially true when we consider the survival instinct of the ego. If the official culture says that there is no Third Man in the room, working through the inculcated belief systems, there is little possibility that the "subject" will be able to see the source of the ponerological phenomena in our world. It will always be an "invisible Third Man".

Consider all of the foregoing information now in relation to the 9/11 attacks and the fact that so many Americans find it almost impossible to believe that their government officials would wantonly sacrifice the lives of its citizens to further their personal agendas. More importantly, consider the fact that your government knows how you think only too well.

The Culture of Critique:

Here we come to what may well be the most sensitive issue raised in this book: the influence of Israel and its supporters, be they Jewish or Christian Zionists, who believe the establishment of a Greater Israel is a necessary step in the process leading to the First, or Second, Coming of their Lord. The pro-Israel lobby is so powerful that it is forbidden to discuss its power and influence on US politics and in the US media. Part of the problem is that it is often reduced to the question of the influence and power of "the Jews", which reduces it to a racial distinction. As the reader will see, our analysis is something else entirely.

The reader might wish to have a look at Kevin MacDonald's *The Culture of Critique:* An Evolutionary Analysis of Jewish Involvement in Twentieth-Century Intellectual and Political Movements[57], where they will learn that "ethnic Jews have a powerful influence in the American media—far larger than any other identifiable group. *"The extent of Jewish ownership and influence on the popular media in the United States is remarkable given the relatively small proportion of the population that is Jewish."*[58] It should be noted that, in saying this, neither we nor McDonald are talking about ordinary Jews, but rather the Jewish "elite" who claim to be acting in the interests of the Jewish people, but who, in reality, are using the lure of Judaism and its promises of a "homeland" for Jews to manipulate the Jewish people. We also wish to remind the reader of the comments of Dr. Lobaczewski concerning the influence of Schizoidal types and their writings on the preparatory stages of the inception of Pathocracy, and their statistically significant presence among Jews.

Israel, therefore, is in control of one of the most potent means of creating the "official culture" of America and can use these means to suit its own agenda, including making the terms "conspiracy theory" and "anti-Semitic" such horrible epithets that no one would dare to speak anything that might put them at risk of being so branded!

An examination of the mass media in the US gives a chilling review of this influence.

> "After World War II, television flourished... Psychologists and sociologists were brought in to study human nature in relation to selling; in other words, to figure out how to manipulate people without their feeling manipulated. Dr. Ernest Dichter, President of the Institute for Motivational Research made a statement in 1941... 'the successful ad agency manipulates human motivations and desires and develops a need for goods with which the public has at one time been unfamiliar -- perhaps even undesirous of purchasing.'"

> Discussing the influence of television, Daniel Boorstin wrote: "Here at last is a supermarket of surrogate experience. Successful programming offers entertainment - under the guise of instruction; instruction - under the guise of entertainment; political persuasion - with the appeal of advertising; and advertising - with the appeal of drama."

> [...] programmed television serves not only to *spread acquiescence and conformity*, but it represents a deliberate industry approach." [59]

Allen Funt, host of a popular television show, *Candid Camera*, was once asked what was the most disturbing thing he had learned about

---

[57] http://www.csulb.edu/~kmacd/books-Preface.html
[58] Emphasis, ours.
[59] Quoted by Wallace and Wallechinsky in *The People's Almanac,* pp. 805, 807.

people in his years of dealing with them through the media. His response was chilling in its ramifications:

> "The worst thing, and I see it over and over, is how easily people can be led by any kind of authority figure, or even the most minimal kinds of authority. A well-dressed man walks up the down escalator and most people will turn around and try desperately to go up also... We put up a sign on the road, 'Delaware Closed Today'. Motorists didn't even question it. Instead they asked: 'Is Jersey open?'" [60]

Submission to minimal signs of authority; lack of knowledge and awareness; a desire for a quick fix and an easy way out. These, it would seem, are the characteristics of the average citizen on the planet today. Of course, none of it would be possible without the help of the mainstream media.

The careful observer with knowledge of history will note immediately that what we are describing is Fascist style propaganda of the same sort that was instituted in Nazi Germany. [61]

On October 3, 2001, I.A.P. News reported that, according to Israel Radio (in Hebrew) Kol Yisrael, an acrimonious argument erupted during the Israeli cabinet weekly session between Israeli Prime Minister Ariel Sharon and his foreign Minister Shimon Peres. Peres warned Sharon that refusing to heed incessant American requests for a cease-fire with the Palestinians would endanger Israeli interests and "turn the US against us". "Sharon reportedly yelled at Peres, saying, *don't worry about American pressure, we, the Jewish people control America*".

On a July 1973 edition of CBS' "Face the Nation" Senator Fullbright, Chair of Senate Foreign Relations Committee stated:

> "The Israelis control the policy in the congress and the senate."

On page 99 of Donald Neff's book *Fallen Pillars,* he quotes Secretary of State under President Dwight D. Eisenhower (from 1953 - 1959) John Foster Dulles as saying:

> "I am aware how almost impossible it is in this country to carry out a foreign policy [in the Middle East] not approved by the Jews... terrific control the Jews have over the news media and the barrage the Jews have built up on congressmen ....
>
> I am very much concerned over the fact that the Jewish influence here is completely dominating the scene and making it almost impossible to get congress to do anything they don't approve of. The Israeli embassy is

---

[60] Wallace, Wallechinsky, op. Cit.
[61] We would also like to point out that Fox News has been revealed by the events of 9-11 to be one of the main propaganda arms of neo-conservative power in Washington though certainly, the majority of the big media players thought that they had to "get in line" in order to survive. It is only in the past year that citizens of the US have begun "voting with their wallets", abandoning major print media in droves. That this phenomenon has not been reported anywhere else in the world suggests that the majority of US citizens are refusing to pay for lies.

practically dictating to the congress through influential Jewish people in the country."

At this point we would like to make a very clear distinction between the Jewish people and those people who claim to represent them. While there is strong evidence to suggest an Israeli government involvement in the 9/11 attacks, in recent years we have been concerned to see a growing tendency among some independent 9/11 investigators to fall into the trap of blaming the Jewish people en masse for the actions of their government.

Such authors should consider whether it would be fair to call all Americans, themselves included, "bloodthirsty war criminals that delight in the death of Iraqi children", because to talk about "Jews" being responsible for 9/11 is certainly unfair to the Jewish people. Instead of "Jews", a more accurate definition would be "Zionists" or "Zionist organisations". That is not to say that many Jews to one degree or another do not support the actions of the state of Israel, but the majority (like many American Christians) are manipulated by religion; they are caught in the mesmerizing influence of "spellbinders."

In any case, by talking of "Jews" in this way, these authors are needlessly and wantonly exposing themselves and their fellow 9/11 truth seekers to attacks that *can* be justified in terms of the argument that most Jews, like most Americans, are not directly responsible for the crimes of their leaders, and any suggestion to the contrary is evidence of "anti-Semitism".

The simple fact is that most people are manipulated to bear responsibility for the crimes of their leaders. Do the authors in question not realise that by labelling all Jews as accomplices to the crimes of the "elite cabal", they are helping this cabal in their ultimate goal: to create the right social conditions for a savage war in the Middle East where both Jews and Arabs will be annihilated?

If such authors see themselves as true humanitarians and truth seekers, their goal should be to protect the human race - including ethical ethnic and religious Jews, ethical Christians, and ethical Muslims - from the predations and manipulations of the elite few who use and abuse humanity over and over again, Jewish, Christian, and Islamic alike. To this end their energy would be best used by focusing on and exposing the agenda of this "elite", not by beating up on those who are least able to understand that they are being duped. The battle is fought between those from opposing sides of the fence who can See - what is being fought over is the soul and future of the human race.

"There exists in our world today a powerful and dangerous secret cult."

So wrote Victor Marchetti, a former high-ranking CIA official, in his book *The CIA and the Cult of Intelligence*. This is the first book the U.S. Government ever went to court to censor before publication. In this book,

Marchetti tells us that there IS a "Cabal" that rules the world and that its holy men are the clandestine professionals of the Central Intelligence Agency. Paraphrasing, Marchetti:

> "This cult is patronized and protected by the highest level government officials in the world. Its membership is composed of those in the power centers of government, industry, commerce, finance, and labor. *It manipulates individuals in areas of important public influence - including the academic world and the mass media.* The Secret Cult is a global fraternity of a political aristocracy whose purpose is to further the political policies of persons or agencies unknown. It acts covertly and illegally."

Others have had this to say:

> "The main threat to Democracy comes *not from the extreme left* but *from the extreme right*, which is able to *buy huge sections of the press and radio*, and wages a constant campaign to smear and discredit every progressive and humanitarian measure." - George Seldes

> "There exists a shadowy Government with its own Air Force, its own Navy, its own fundraising mechanism, and the ability to pursue its own ideas of national interest, free from all checks and balances, and free from the law itself." Daniel K. Inouye, U.S. Senator

> "Some of the biggest men in the United States, in the field of commerce and manufacture, are afraid of something. They know that there is a power somewhere so organized, so subtle, so watchful, so interlocked, so complete, so pervasive, that they better not speak above their breath when they speak in condemnation of it." - Woodrow Wilson, *The New Freedom* (1913)

Remember: those who are at the top of the heap will always take whatever steps are necessary to maintain the status quo and the way this is done is via "official Pathocratic culture" which is a product of COINTELPRO.

According to analysts, COINTELPRO was the FBI's secret program to undermine the popular anti-war and equal rights upsurge, which swept the country during the 1960s. Though the name stands for "Counterintelligence Program," the targets were *not enemy spies*. The FBI set out to eliminate "radical" political opposition inside the US. This was a high level psychological operation specifically set up to vector "ideological" trends - beliefs of the United States citizenry.

When traditional modes of repression (exposure, blatant harassment, and prosecution for political crimes) failed to counter the growing insurgency, and even helped to fuel it, the Bureau took the law into its own hands. Its methods ranged far beyond surveillance, and amounted to a domestic version of the covert action for which the CIA has become infamous throughout the world.

Usually, when we think of COINTELPRO, we think of the most well known and typical activities which include sending anonymous or fictitious letters designed to start rumors, publishing false defamatory or threatening information, forging signatures on fake documents, introducing disruptive and subversive members into organizations to destroy them from within, and so on. Blackmailing insiders in any group to force them to spread false rumors, or to foment factionalism was also common.

What a lot of people don't keep in mind is the fact that COINTELPRO also concentrated on creating bogus organizations. These bogus groups could serve many functions which might include attacking and/or disrupting bona fide groups, or even just simply creating a diversion with clever propaganda in order to attract members away so as to involve them with time-wasting activity designed to prevent them from doing anything useful. According to investigators, these FBI programs were noteworthy because all documents relating to them were stamped "do not file." This meant that they were *never filed in the system*, and for all intents and purposes, did not exist.[62] This cover was blown after activists broke into an FBI office in Media, Pennsylvania in 1971. The possibility of finding evidence for any of it, after that event, is about zero.

The COINTELPRO files that were retrieved during the above mentioned break-in showed that the U.S. Government targeted a very broad range of religious, labor and community groups opposed to any of its agendas. We can be certain that many groups formed for the ostensible purpose of "investigating 9/11" are of this type.

What seems to be certain is that the Powers That Be (PTB) have developed COINTELPRO to an all new level of Social Shaping, Cultural Brainwashing, and the main targets of this activity would include virtually anyone who is seeking the truth about the shifting realities of our world. The cases of COINTELPRO activities against political groups must be no more than the tip of the iceberg, given that the great bulk of COINTELPRO-type operations remain secret. By all indications, domestic covert operations have become a permanent feature of U.S. politics and Social Programming, and it is hardly likely, considering the evidence, that the 9/11 Truth groups are exempt.

The implications of this are truly alarming. Those who manage to get close to the truth of these matters, despite the many obstacles in their path, face National covert campaigns to discredit and disrupt their research and reputations. Clearly, COINTELPRO and similar operations under other names also work to distort academic and popular perceptions of the problems facing our world. They have done enormous damage to the search for the Truth.

"Terrorism is changing. New adversaries, new motivations and new rationales have surfaced in recent years to challenge much of the conventional wisdom..." wrote Dr. Bruce Hoffman, Director of RAND.

---

[62] This, of course, makes us wonder just how much material relating to government activities is stamped « Do Not File » ?

And he was right. The only problem is, the reader is largely unaware of the definition of "new adversaries" that might be implied in his remarks. It doesn't take a genius to figure out that Dr. Hoffman may have been referring to "normal humans" as opposed to psychopaths in his remarks about "terrorism." Undoubtedly, as Lobaczewski has written, to the psychopath, the world of normal people - even if they are the majority - must be rejected and destroyed.

The most effective weapon of COINTELPRO is Ridicule and Debunking. Notice that Marchetti mentions above that this is done via manipulation of individuals in areas of important public influence - including the *academic world and the mass media.* With the analysis of Lobaczewski, we easily understand how this is accomplished.

Bottom line is: if you have bought into the emotionally manipulated consensus of "official culture" that there are no conspiracies, that there is no "Third Man", it is very likely that you are being manipulated by a psychopath. You have been hypnotized by the suggestions of the holy men of the Secret Cult. And you have chosen to believe them over your own natural human observations and senses.

From an "Expert" on Lies:

> "The size of the lie is a definite factor in causing it to be believed, because the vast masses of a nation are, in the depths of their hearts, more easily deceived than they are consciously and intentionally bad.

> The primitive simplicity of their minds renders them more easy victims of a big lie than a small one, because they themselves often tell little lies but would be ashamed to tell big ones. Such a form of lying would never enter their heads. They would never credit others with the possibility of such great impudence as the *complete reversal of facts.*

> Even explanations would long leave them in doubt and hesitation, and *any trifling reason would dispose them to accept a thing as true.* Something therefore always remains and sticks from the most imprudent of lies, a fact which all bodies and individuals concerned in the art of lying in this world know only too well, and therefore they stop at nothing to achieve this end."
> ~ Adolph Hitler, *Mein Kampf*

9/11 Ground Zero

On September 14, 2001 - just two days after the Terrorist Attack - I[63] read a curious article on a Russian News Site, www.strana.ru, that caught my attention and left me feeling strangely uneasy. It was an interview with a former Russian high official and specialist in *Russian secret services* which was translated for us by a reader who sent it in, and I am going to

---

[63] LKJ

reproduce it as I read it with underlinings and other emphases that I have added to show those points that struck me as most interesting:

"Acts of terrorism carried out on 11 September in America, and their consequences are commented upon in an interview with Andrey Kosyakov, former assistant to the chairman of the Russian Congress, *a specialist in International Security.*

Q: What suggests that terrorism in the USA was planned well in advance?

A: First, the conspirators *possessed the professional skill to fly an aircraft.* There had to be at least four of them with substitutes on hand in the event one of them failed. There is a high probability that the hijacking of an aircraft will fail, thus there had to be stand-by hijackers and/or pilots in this eventuality.

In the second place, all participants in the operation were ready to sacrifice themselves, and such individuals are not easy to find.

Finally, the *departure times* of the aircraft from four different points were *coordinated minute by minute.* This means that the *routes and timing were known well in advance*, and these particular flights were selected specifically for their routes and schedule.

All of this is *sufficiently complicated* to necessitate a long period of planning.

Q: And how long, in your opinion, would it take to plan something like this? How large an organization would it require? Could, for example, the Red Army carry out such an operation? Some analysts say that *only a National organization* could do this.

A: As far as the time of preparation is concerned, it would require months. And *such an organization must be very powerful.*

But, the participation of a National organization, such as a government of a country, is very doubtful.

I assure you that National resources have not been used here.

No secret service would risk their operatives in this way. They spend a lot of time and money training their agents. However, if President Bush had been the target, then one would suspect a secret service of some organization. But here, the target was different: civilians.

As for the Red Army, it doesn't fit for one simple reason: it consists of mainly Orientals and it is too easy to distinguish Japanese from Americans.

Q: So, what do you conclude from all this?

You see, analyzing this situation, I was struck by one significant fact: it is known that there were telephone calls from the plane. One of the calling persons was a professional journalist. And yet, not one of the calling individuals said that they were being hijacked by "Moslem terrorists". There was, apparently, nothing unusual about the appearance of the hijackers. There was no attempt to describe them. No one said: "Moslem terrorists have hijacked the plane", which would have logically been the first comment by this journalist *if* it was apparent that the hijackers were "foreign". *There was obviously nothing unusual about them in terms of appearance, accent, pronunciation, or other similar factors.*

Q: But, secret organizations could hide these things, couldn't they?

A: All these calls were private. And even the FBI was not able to suppress the fact that these calls took place. So, the conclusion which comes to mind, is that *the external appearance of the hijackers was in no way different from the other passengers.* Only in such cases would the communicants identify the hijackers in a shorthand way. *This suggests that the hijackers were European in appearance.*

There is also the suspicious fact that the conspirators left a huge "clue" in the leased automobile at the airport with a copy of the Koran and instructions for flying a plane in Arabic.

Now look, not one organization claimed responsibility. This means that the terrorists want to hide their identity.

With every other aspect of total control and professionalism, *how could they make such a mistake?*

This does not compute with all the rest of the perfection of the operation.

All this says that the criminals want to create a false track.

In this way, the secret services have been induced very cleverly to look for "Moslem terrorists".

Q: But indeed the practice of self-sacrifice is typical to the Moslem culture?

A: You are completely right. But who told you that those who died were not Moslems?

This way we can narrow the radius of our search.

On the basis of this information which we have, by analysis, we may come to the conclusion that those who did it were Americans or Europeans who were followers of radical Islam.

They were manipulated so that the true criminals will be thus spared for follow-up actions.

It is completely clear that this is a multi-phase operation. [...] ... *it seems that the target is precisely America; precisely civilians.*

Q: But, we remember that some analysts were claiming that if George Bush was in the White House on September 11, then the aircraft would have been aimed at the White House instead of the Pentagon.

This is highly improbable. In that case the White House or the Pentagon, but not peaceful population would be the *first* targets.

Indeed after a first successful terrorist act, the chances of success for the rest fall.

You see that the last action did fail in the crash of the aircraft in Pittsburgh. *It was most certainly shot down.* However hard it is to admit, this was the correct thing to do.

So it is clear that the main targets are civilians.

There is this formula that is part of the mentality of terrorists: the civilian population in the democratic countries are responsible for the actions of their government. The terrorists accept and use this formula. Therefore, the next terrorist acts will follow the same pattern. Obviously, they will occur on Wednesday or Thursday of next week. Why? I don't want to explain the terrorist's logic. But it is based on a certain sense of the "rightness" of the thing.

But I would like to repeat this: the fact that no terrorists are claiming responsibility, tells us that they will kill again and again until the next stage of global conflict is achieved. This is precisely the goal of these actions. Only then will they reveal their identity in order to get followers.

Q: How could the special services of the USA fail to detect such a terrorist act?

I will give two examples. Half a year ago Israeli reconnaissance carried out studies through the use of aerial targets for conducting terrorism.

It is certain that the Americans had access to these studies. But it seems to not have entered their minds to apply this information in defensive ways.

And other - in March of 1991 in our office sat Korzhakov, and we told him about the situation leading to the September government coup. We predicted that everything would occur in September. Everything actually occurred, exactly following our scenario, only it happened one month earlier: August. No one paid any attention. This means that when there are predictions of scenarios that seem to be improbable, no one takes them seriously, especially the secret services. That is why Putin says that what is needed is a union of all secret services of all nations.

Q: What is the probability that the American secret services will succeed in finding the leader of this operation, or that they simply will present to society a fake?

A: Very high. There are people, there are apartments where they were located, which means, there are traces, certainly. Following these traces, one may find the leader.

Q: And who this? Bin Laden?

Hardly.

Yes, there was the interception of his conversation with someone, where they reported to him the destruction of two targets. This was seen as indirect confirmation of his participation. But he is not an ideologist. He is too well known. And *the one who organized all of this is too smart to be noticed.*

Ever."

Now, remember, this interview with an intelligence expert took place just a few days after the 9-11 attacks. Several points in this article started me to thinking.[64] Those points are as follows: the attacks were carried out

---

[64] As we will make clear in Part One of this book, there are many assumptions in this interview that our subsequent research has shown to be doubtful, such as the physical

against civilians, targets that are highly symbolic to the ordinary American. In other words, the American people were the real targets, but not in the way that is usually thought. It was intended to make every single American full of fear and outrage so that whoever came along as a "strong man" pointing a finger at culprits and declaring that he was gonna go after them, would be able to do anything he wanted to do. And that is exactly what George W. Bush did.

The Russian intell guy said that it was obvious that the attacks were carried out by a very "powerful organization" that *wishes to blame Moslems* - to create a false trail - for these attacks. And he also noted that, because the attacks were so carefully planned, it was obvious that the planners would be too smart to be noticed - and certainly much too smart to leave clues lying about such as passports and "how to fly" videos in Arabic. Indeed, the passports and videos were dead giveaways to the fact that they were planted so as to falsely blame the act on Islamic terrorists.

Another thing that struck me rather forcibly was his remark that, *"Israeli reconnaissance carried out studies through the use of aerial targets for conducting terrorism"*, followed by his assertion that, *"It is certain that the Americans had access to these studies"*.

So, I began to think about what this intelligence guy was saying a bit more deeply despite the fact that he confidently assured his interviewer that no "national service" did this.

This Russian intelligence expert asked the loaded question: *"How could the special services of the USA fail to detect such a terrorist act?"*

This assessment struck me as one of the more intelligent bits of commentary about the 9-11 attacks to come out *at the time*, emerging through the hysterical rants about Osama and those nasty Muslims like a small island of sanity.

What I found to be most interesting was exactly *who* was most vigorously pointing the finger at Radical Islam: a veritable Greek Chorus led by a former cheerleader, our own George Bush and the Warmongers.

Another astute bit of commentary comes from Musa Keilani writing for The Jordan Times:

> "Jordan is fully committed to fight both terrorism and Osama Ben [sic]
> Laden whose followers are still being prosecuted this week for their attempt
> to sabotage and carry out attacks in Amman. Yet, many of us still feel with
> the Saudi foreign minister who brought out the names of five Saudis wanted
> by the American FBI while they died years ago before the anti-Arab
> hysterical witch hunt started.

> But some questions are still being raised amid the US effort against
> 'international terrorism'.

---

presence of the accused hijackers on any of the planes. The nineteen men accused of this crime were likely patsies chosen to take the fall by the real masterminds, much as Lee Harvey Oswald was blamed for the killing of JFK or Sharan Sharan for the murder of RFK.

We in Jordan have had several narrow escapes from the nefarious plots hatched by Ben [sic] Laden and would welcome any initiative that would remove the lingering fears of continued conspiracies against our national security and stability. As such, the Jordanians' commitment to a genuine international campaign against terrorism, in all its forms and shapes, including the state-sponsored style practiced by Israel, is unwavering.

Veterans who have spent a lifetime studying intelligence operations assert that the attacks could not have been carried out by any "Arab or Islamist" group without involvement of highly-placed "insider" networks in the US institutions.

These veterans are indeed best placed to assess intelligence operations, particularly in the United States, because the very focus of their professional work was the US and they have acquired intimate knowledge of how the intelligence community works in the US. They include, among others, Mikhail Magrelov, a long-standing intelligence specialist and deputy chairman of the Russian Federation Council Foreign Affairs Committee, Yevgeny Kozhokin, director of the state-run Russian Institute for Strategic Studies (RISS), and Andrei Kosyakov, formerly assistant to the chairman of the subcommittee of the Supreme Soviet of Russia, in charge of monitoring the activity of the intelligence services.

Doubts over the US assertions that the attacks had an "Arab and Islamist" link in the form of Ben [sic] Laden have also been raised by former government veterans and diplomats in Europe who argue that Washington should not jump to the conclusion that the Saudi dissident was responsible for the attacks and try to sell it to the world; the US should focus more on homegrown terrorism in its investigations.

The overall argument of the Russian intelligence experts is that a yet-to-be-identified but powerful and influential organisation could have been behind the operation, and this group may have little in common or may not have any links with Arabs and Muslims.

The experts argue that an organisation controlled by someone like Ben [sic] Laden could not have orchestrated the attacks that required the involvement of at least 100 to 150 dedicated people living within the US, dozens of them with extraordinary skills in flying, absolute familiarity with the US civil aviation system, emergency procedures and routines, high-level communication expertise and strategic planning, as well as the ability to evade intelligence surveillance. Such hi-tech minds with military precision and coordination could only belong to a group much more sophisticated than the largely ragtag operatives of any Third World country or organisation whose erstwhile operations have involved, at best, slamming explosives-laden trucks into buildings.

The argument and mainstream belief that no American would carry such a heinous crime of destruction in a suicide operation as that of Sept. 11 is immediately countered by the Oklahoma bombing of 1995. Timothy McVeigh was framed for that bombing in the same way that several other patsies have been used in high profile murders and bombings over the course of the past 50 years. The reality, which is backed up by solid evidence, is that the Oklahoma bombing was carried out by a rogue group within the U.S. intelligence community who have infiltrated a wider network of Pure American (Anglo-Saxon) militants which includes active and retired military officers and Green Beret colonels.

The truth about the group that McVeigh was involved with was deliberately suppressed, the experts argue, pointing out that McVeigh had equally strong suicidal feelings when he insisted on being executed. Furthermore, there was also a visible but unexplained anxiety on the part of the authorities in Washington to see that his mouth was sealed with death without delay.

Among the many questions raised by the experts are:

- How was it possible for an "Arab or Islamist group" to find "suicidal" professionals in the art of flying with precision and who could command a large civilian aircraft with such precision as to inflict maximum damage?

- How did the "emergency procedures" fail to go into effect in a few minutes after the hijacked planes deviated from their predetermined flight path?

- How did the hijacked planes manage to remain in air for between 55 minutes and 80 minutes?

- Why did the hijacked passengers who spoke with family members from aboard the planes did not bother to mention anything about the way the hijackers looked? ("The appearance of the hijackers in no way distinguished them from all the other passengers.... This supports the supposition that hijackers looked European in outward appearance," says one of the experts.)

- Why and how could the brains behind such a meticulously planned operation allow "extra big leads!!" to be left behind, like a traceable rented vehicle filled with the Holy Koran and flying manuals in Arabic that clearly establish an Arab link to the attacks?

- How did the "Arabs and Muslims" who the US says carried out the attacks manage to evade attention from the alert intelligence agencies of the US for the several months it would require to plan the operation?

The argument here is that almost every Arab or Muslim living in or entering the US with the slightest trace of links with militancy has come under very close scrutiny of the country's investigating and intelligence agencies. It is virtually impossible for such a large number of Arabs and Muslims to have evaded investigation and to have managed to take part in an operation of this magnitude and which involves such high-sensitive areas as aviation security.

All indications at this point in time are that accusing Arabs and Muslims of carrying out the attacks is very convenient for many interested groups and serves more than one purpose. Moreover, it is an exercise that shifts attention from the real authors of the assault."[65]

When we look at the fact that, from the very beginning, this event has been compared to "Pearl Harbor", we have to wonder if this is a sort of "signature"?

---

[65] http://www.themodernreligion.com/terror/wtc-thetruth.html

I remember back in 1986 when I came across the documented evidence that the attack on Pearl Harbor was known to the United States well before it happened, I was shocked. Not only did the government do nothing to prevent it, they did not even warn those who were going to be attacked. The loss of American lives was horrendous. And the blame lies on the doorstep of the *leaders of America*. There is even evidence that they deliberately manipulated the situation, at the highest levels, to ensure that the attack would take place.

Why?

Well, to get the United States into the war, of course. War is big business. Whenever you have a slow economy, a little warmongering is always the answer. In ancient times, it was the business of the day: go to war, kill the men, capture the women and the wealth of the enemy, and go home when you have spent it all and gotten tired of the women, and then go out and do it over again. Even Herodotus understood this to be the reason for war. And human beings haven't changed at all - at least not those who seek power positions.

Is it possible that the government of our country had an inkling that the events of 9-11 were going to happen?

After examining all the evidence available, indeed, that seems to be true.

And if so, is it possible that they did nothing?

Again, that seems to be true as well. And when they did finally wake up from their war games and school reading classes, the only thing they did was the exact opposite of trying to get to the bottom of the matter, trying to find the real culprits. Instead, they went after the False Flag clues that were left to lead everyone astray and denied anyone the right to question the conclusions that they propagandized so vigorously.

Well, sure, such clues might lead the average citizen astray. They might not be aware of what are called "False Flag operations". They aren't educated in the ways of intelligence and don't know about all the evil manipulations that go on all the time in the world of spy vs. spy.

But surely, the President of the Greatest Nation on Earth is not going to be taken in by such blatant nonsense as a "how to fly" video in Arabic or the fortuitous discovery of the passport of alleged lead hijacker Satam Al Suqami that miraculously escaped the Flight 11 crash and the WTC collapse to be found on a Manhattan street, is he?[66]

Apparently so.

So here we have an administration not acting when and how it ought to act, *either before or after the attack.*

Is this a coincidence? Or is it evidence of complicity?

In the four years since September 11, 2001, we read endless discussions of U.S. government complicity spreading like wildfire over the web,

---

[66] http://abcnews.go.com/sections/us/DailyNews/WTC_MAIN010912.html

followed by books and videos analyzing in great detail all available video footage of the attacks, the official story/ We read the results of published information in the mainstream media that punched holes in that official version. Dozens, then hundreds, and now thousands of commentators of greater or lesser prestige simply do not believe in the "failure of intelligence" that is the administration's answer to why and how George and Co. got caught with their pants down. Many, many people are certain that the government not only knew about the attack, but that they condoned it for their own nefarious purposes; or that they even participated, and that the 9/11 attacks were the equivalent of a new Pearl Harbor or even Hitler's Reichstag fire.

So, we have two opposing forces here: the administration supported by the Zionist controlled (for the most part) mass media, against a growing percentage of the population that claims that there was no failure of intelligence, that the government deliberately condoned or even participated in this attack, and that it is part of a planned schedule to impose a One World Government on all of us, to abridge our freedoms, and entrap us in a fascist state.

On their side, George Bush and his administration say that we have to accept some new, restrictive laws to make us "safe" (never mind that the intelligence was available, and it was the government that failed to heed the intelligence and make America safe). They say we must make some significant changes in the way the country does business, and most definitely, we need a little war here and there to level things out again (not to mention the economy). And all of the Joe Sixpak's of the world may be buying it. All the grandmother Sally Stock-market-investors are sitting at home, glued to Fox Network on their televisions, glad that Uncle Sam has taken charge here, bombed the Afghanis, given Saddam a major spanking, and is actively wiping out the Iraqis and anybody who ever helped them, meanwhile passing all the laws necessary to ensure the safety of their great nation. Never mind if that includes moving to a cashless society and implanting micro-chips under the skin so that everyone will be trackable so as to ensure that they aren't committing terrorist acts on their lunch break.

There's a saying attributed to Franklin Roosevelt: "In politics, nothing happens by accident, if it happens, you can bet it was planned that way." Maybe he really said it, maybe he didn't. Whether he did or not, anyone who studies history deeply can figure out that it comes pretty close to the truth. I[67] also once had a conversation with a fellow who was trained in military intelligence and he told me that one of the first rules of intelligence gathering is to observe the situation *as it is*, and extrapolate to who will gain from it: *Qui Bono*. So these two principles were uppermost

---

[67] LKJ

in my mind as I was considering all the data. Clearly, the attacks on 9-11 are "political events".

The situation at present is a bit complex. But we notice that it has only become complex *after* the fact. It is only the wild speculations and constant playing of agendas and counter-agendas that have tended to obscure the basic essentials of the matter. There are groups that go on and on about a "flash of light" that was emitted between the two airliners that crashed into the WTC, and this (according to them) proves there was some sort of missile fired. That's an interesting idea, but it really doesn't even make it to "theory" status because there are other possible explanations for such a flash, including a discharge of electricity between the plane and the building as soon as it is close enough to be "grounded" or a video artifact due to the different fields in a video image.

There are groups that make a big deal about supposed "pods" under the aircraft that hit the WTC. We can pretty easily dispose of that one by carefully examining photos of the underside of that particular type of aircraft.

Then, there's the group that takes the cake, in my opinion: the "hologram" people. That is about the silliest thing going. That is not to say that I don't think that hologram technology does exist and that it might be used in a number of ways, but I don't think that holograms photograph too well since they are produced by light and there are the endlessly repeating videos of the planes crashing into the World Trade Center Towers.

So, let's go back to ground zero of the present situation and look at the event itself, *by itself*, and ask the first important question: *Who benefits?*

It's easy to see that the Military-Industrial Complex in America has been the primary beneficiary along with Israel. Actually, the two are almost one creature, so it's hard to think of them as separate entities. It could be suggested that, by focusing the anger of the citizens of the United States against the Moslems, Israel has powerful backing for their expansionist goals, and with much of the MIC in their pockets, they have the money to do what they want to do: the money of the American tax payer.

The ultimate and only beneficiary of the 9/11 attacks, at least in the short term, has been Israel.

Now, let's get down to brass tacks here.

The September 11, 2001 attacks on the World Trade Center were followed live on television by hundreds of millions of people around the world. Everyone was shocked by the horror of the attack. TV networks broadcast the videos of the attacks over and over again with very little reporting since no one really knew what to say; it was just too shocking and unexpected. All the while the attack was being shown repeatedly, there was no explanation of the events because no one, we are told, knew any details. No one, that is, except the FBI who released the names of all 19 hijackers within a week of the attacks and claimed that they were

connected to Bin Laden and al-Qaeda, a name that quickly surfaced on
9/11 as the principal and sole plausible candidate as culprit, even if they
have never claimed responsibility. In fact, we note that a number of video
tapes and written messages, allegedly from Bin Laden, have been released
over the years since the 9/11 attacks, yet it was not until two days before
the 2004 Presidential election that the FBI was able to provide a tape in
which Osama appeared to take responsibility for the 9/11 attacks.
Coincidence? Hardly. Previous tapes that were released were clearly
faked, with claims that the translations, carried out by FBI translators, has
inaccurately translated Bin Laden's words. One video tape in particular,
made public on December 13, 2001[68], featured a man who was so
obviously *not* Osama Bin Laden that it was hard to imagine that the US or
Israeli intelligence authors of the tape actually believed they would get
away with it.

During the next few days bits and pieces of information were released to
the press by government officials, reports were issued and retracted, and
most news focus was concentrated on the frenzy of rescue efforts. The
focus of this reporting very quickly turned to the collapse of the twin
towers of the World Trade Center, pushing aside any mention of events at
the Pentagon, which was an early clue as to the true character of the
attack. Over the next few months, more information was released in bits
and pieces, but again, few people were paying any attention to the data
because, by then, the shock had turned into terror. Osama and Saddam
were Muslim, Osama did this evil deed, and Saddam was planning even
worse with his Weapons of Mass Destruction.

The meta-facts are that just under 2,800 people died in America on
September 11, 2001, and as a result the United States invaded Afghanistan
and Iraq, killing hundreds of thousands more human beings, including
killing or permanently maiming many thousands of its own citizens. The
official U.S. Military casualty figures from Iraq, at just over 2,000 as we
write, are most certainly false given that American deaths that happen in
military hospitals outside of Iraq are not counted. Observers have
estimated the true total may be close to 8,000 U.S. deaths, nearly three
times the number killed in September 2001, and this doesn't include the
100,000+ Iraqis who have lost their lives but who the US does not deem
important, or human, enough to be counted.

The events of 9-11, however, are still a confusing morass of
contradiction that has only been exacerbated by the so-called official 9-11
Report that used the American intelligence agencies as a scapegoat for the
clear evidence of government complicity. Nevertheless, the public of the
United States has been, for the most part, accepting of the "official
culture" version of the attacks. The claim that "National Security" requires

---

[68] http://www.whatreallyhappened.com/osamatape.html

the authorities to conceal much of the data about this crime is accepted almost without question. It is actually quite amazing how *little* the average American really knows about the events of that day even if you restrict your definition of "events" to what was reported by the media.

The most troubling fact of all is that the Official Version gleaned from the news reports and information released by government officials does not stand up to even the most cursory scrutiny.

What bothers me most of all is, considering the fact that the attacks on 9-11 were about the most audacious crime in American History, *there was no proper forensic investigation*. There was no Sherlock Holmes on hand to use his magnifying glass and his great knowledge of different kinds of cigarette ash; there was no Hercule Poirot called in to exercise his little gray cells; there was no Columbo bumbling about with his seemingly innocuous questions that annoy the heck out of the perpetrators. (This was also the case with the assassination of JFK. The crime scene was so thoroughly violated before a proper investigation took place that there was no possibility of finding the facts.)

You would think that, in the alleged greatest and most powerful nation on Earth that the investigation would have been the most thorough and scientific ever conducted.

But that isn't the case.

Although the terror attacks of September 11 were clearly criminal acts of mass murder, no effort was made to preserve the integrity of the crime scenes and the essential evidence was disposed of like garbage. Former New York City Mayor Rudolph Giuliani, the so-called "Prince of the New York", hired two large British construction management firms to oversee what many experts consider to be massive *criminal destruction of evidence*. The editor-in-chief of *Fire Engineering* magazine, William A. Manning, issued an urgent call to action to America's firefighters at the end of 2001, calling for a forensic investigation and demanding that the steel from the site be preserved to allow investigators to determine what caused the collapse, to no avail.

Both the independent 9/11 Commission and federal authorities have stated that of the four devices that could have recorded the final moments of the Flights that crashed into the WTC towers - a cockpit voice recorder (CVR) and flight data recorder (FDR) from the two planes - *none* were ever found in the wreckage.

However, as reported by the Philadelphia Daily News in October of 2004,[69] two men who worked extensively in the wreckage of the World Trade Center claim they helped federal agents find three of the four "black boxes" from the jetliners that struck the towers on 9/11.

---

[69] http://www.pnionline.com/dnblog/extra/archives/001139.html

New York City firefighter Nicholas DeMasi stated that he escorted federal agents on an all-terrain vehicle in October 2001 and helped them locate three of the four devices.

His account is supported by a volunteer, Mike Bellone, whose efforts at Ground Zero have been chronicled in the New York Times and elsewhere. Bellone said he assisted DeMasi and the agents and that he saw a device resembling a "black box" in the back of the firefighter's ATV.

The "black boxes" - actually orange in color - could have provided valuable new information about the worst terror attack to ever take place on American soil, but, then, maybe the data didn't fit the official story.

The devices are built to survive an impact of enormous force - 3400 Gs - and a fire of 1100 degrees Celsius for one hour, considerably higher than official estimates of the World Trade Center blaze that reached, at the very most, only 800 degrees.

Federal aviation officials themselves have remarked that the World Trade Center attacks seem to be the only major jetliner crashes in the history of aviation where the "black box" devices were never located. Coincidence or Conspiracy?

The two black boxes for Flight 93 were also found. However, they were deemed too severely damaged, and it isn't known if the data could be recovered. Again, the 9/11 crashes would be *the first time in history that black boxes did not survive an air crash*. Many months after the attacks, the FBI revealed that they were able to extract the contents of the boxes from Flight 93, but they chose to release only select quotes from the recordings.[70]

The two black boxes for Flight 77 were also found according to FBI Director Robert Mueller, but they only contained information on altitude, speed, headings and other information and the voice recorder contained "nothing useful". We suppose we will just have to take his word on that.[71]

Just for the exercise let's assume that the conspiracy theorists are correct and the government is lying and covering up the truth of the attacks on 9-11 either in whole or in part. Without any real evidence, without any real impartial investigation, what do we have to go on?

Admittedly, we do not have much left other than to observe the behaviors of all the parties before, during and after the event. But even though we have very little in the way of forensic evidence, we can still assert with the great detective Sherlock Holmes: "when you eliminate the impossible, whatever remains – however improbable – must be the truth!"

Contrary to those who claim that there no real passenger jets used in the attacks at all, that it was all a hologram, it seems rather clear that actual commercial jets hit the twin towers of the World Trade Center exactly as

[70]http://news.bbc.co.uk/1/hi/world/americas/1543564.stm
[71]http://www.cbsnews.com/stories/2002/02/25/attack/main501989.shtml

described by the many witnesses and as confirmed by government officials. It was on film, and we simply cannot refute that in my opinion. It happened, and everyone saw it; again and again and again and again.

But that does not mean that a commercial Boeing 757 hit the Pentagon.

Why do I say that?

Because the fact that large commercial jets were *seen* to hit the World Trade Center, over and over again on TV could very easily have "conditioned" the public to believe that the same type of craft hit the Pentagon when they were told that this was the case by government officials, backed up by "witnesses" most of whom just happened to be government officials.

Brain studies show that what is *suggested* during a period of pain or shock becomes *memory*. The brain sort of "traps" the ideas being assimilated at times of pain and shock into permanent "synaptic patterns of thought/memory".

The conditions surrounding the events of 9-11 were perfect for creating specific impressions and "memories" - manipulation of the minds of the masses by shocking events and media spin.

So, since we have video images of commercial jetliners hitting the World Trade Center towers , it is certain that this is what happened. The issue of the collapse of the buildings is different and most certainly does suggest prior planning to ensure that the buildings would not survive the impact, and that the collapse would be dramatic and shocking.

It is to these and other questions that we will turn in Part One of this book. Part Two takes up the question from an altogether different and original perspective, one extending back many thousands of years. It concerns the role of the three monotheistic religions in the unfolding tragedy in the Middle East, trying to understand why it seems just a little too convenient that these three religions should be at the heart of a conflict that could ignite a war that may well annihilate both the Jewish and the Arab populations of the region.

Part 1: 911

911

One commentator on the internet wrote:

> "Among the speculations being made by observers were ideas that the CIA
> was somehow involved in the 9-11 attack. Recent discoveries [...] bring that
> same sure but murky sense of the CIA's presence leading up to the attack.
> Perhaps another operation gone very sour.

> We also have the recent arrest and expulsion, although this is officially
> denied in Washington, of a large Israeli spy ring... [...] Spy rings as large as
> this one simply do not operate in a place like the United States without the
> CIA being aware of them. Apparently, there is a serious question whether
> Mossad, the Israeli intelligence service, told the U.S. what it knew before
> September 11. At any rate, we know the aftermath of the attack certainly has
> tipped the balance to favor Mr. Sharon's bloody-minded way of seeing the
> world. [...] Americans, for a second time, may have been the unintended
> victims of their own agency's dirty work."[72]

As readers may be aware, there are already many books and articles,
both in print and on the internet, that make a convincing case that the 9/11
attacks were an inside job, or, at the very least, could not have been
carried out solely by a rag-tag bunch of Islamic terrorists operating out of
a cave in Afghanistan. While this community of 9/11 researchers, often
referred to as the "9/11 Truth Movement", agree on most of the major
points of evidence that strongly suggest a government conspiracy, the one
bone of contention that has apparently divided them concerns the events
surrounding the attack on the Pentagon. While most sincere 9/11
researchers agree that both Flight 11 and Flight 175 did indeed hit the
WTC towers, and that it really was Flight 93 that ended its journey in the
Pennsylvanian countryside, the question as to what exactly hit the
Pentagon remains in dispute.

While we freely admit that the details of the attacks on the WTC and the
fate of Flight 93 present many potential smoking guns pointing to US and
Israeli government complicity or direct involvement in 9/11, it is our
belief that the attack on the Pentagon constitutes the real Achilles heel of
the conspirators. For this reason it comes as no surprise to us that there
appears to be a concerted attempt, by what we suspect to be government
Counter Intelligence operatives, to loudly declaim and discredit the idea

---

[72] John Cluckman, "Footprints in the Dust", CounterPunch, March 11, 2002,
http://www.counterpunch.org/chuckmanfootprints.html

that something other than Flight 77 hit the Pentagon that bright September morning in 2001.

Mike Ruppert, former LA police man and owner of the website "From the Wilderness", rose to fame in the 9/11 truth movement with the publication of his exhaustive tome, *Crossing the Rubicon*, an extremely well-researched analysis of the many gaping holes in the official government story of the 9/11 attacks and the reason they occurred. However, in his book, *Ruppert states that, while he is quite convinced that it was not Flight 77 that hit the Pentagon, he refuses to include the subject as part of his overall case for conspiracy because of the implications, i.e. if Flight 77 did not hit the Pentagon, then what happened to Flight 77?*

Ruppert balks at the idea of offering an answer to this question to his readers because *he believes most people would be unable to accept it,* but let's be clear here, in the context of 9/11 being the work of a faction of the US government and military, the answer to the question is quite obvious – that Flight 77 and its occupants (or the majority of them as we shall later explore) were flown to a specific destination and "disposed of" by the conspirators. On the one hand Ruppert is sure that his readers can accept the fact that U.S. government officials participated in the slaughter of the passengers on Flights 11 and 175 and the occupants of the WTC towers, yet he is equally sure that the *same readers* would be *unable* to accept the idea that the same government officials played a part in disposing of the passgengers of Flight 77 in a much less imaginative way.

Unlike Ruppert and others, we are not inclined to shrink from facing the highest probable truth, regardless of how unsavory that reality may turn out to be. As for the suggestion that it is inconceivable that the US (or any other government) would murder its own citizens when need dictates, we refer readers to any of the historical precedents that show that certain individuals within previous US governments have not hesitated to sacrifice the lives of U.S. citizens in order to further some political or personal goal.

Consider, for example, the fact that in the early 1960's *the US Joint Chiefs of Staff drew up and approved plans to launch a secret and bloody wave of terrorist attacks against their own country in order to trick the American public into supporting an ill-conceived war they intended to launch against Cuba.*

Code named 'Operation Northwoods', the plan, which had *the written approval of the Chairman and every member of the Joint Chiefs of Staff, called for innocent people to be shot on American streets; for boats carrying refugees fleeing Cuba to be sunk on the high seas; for a wave of violent terrorism to be launched in Washington, D.C., Miami, and elsewhere, by agents of the U.S. government. Innocent people would be framed for bombings they did not commit; planes would be hijacked.* Using phony evidence, *all of it would be blamed on Castro,* thus giving this little cabal of warmongers the excuse, as well as the public and international backing, they needed to launch their war.

It should be especially noted that *the plan was developed and approved* **without** *the awareness of then President Kennedy*. This fact alone should provide readers with some insight into the distinct possibility that the real source of political and military power in the US does not necessarily rest in the hands of the President and the Executive branch as most ordinary citizens have been lead to believe, which then begs the question: who really is in control of the US, and does anyone know who these people are and what their agenda is?

While *Operation Northwoods* was not actually implemented, previous and later US governments concocted several other equally *diabolical schemes that called for the sacrificing of the lives of American citizens,* and unlike Operation Northwoods, these schemes *were* carried through to their brutal conclusion. We need mention only the attack on Pearl Harbor, where historical documents now prove beyond doubt that the Roosevelt administration had not only been forewarned of the Japanese attack plans, but actually provoked and enticed the Japanese Navy into attacking the sitting ducks at Pearl Harbor. Roosevelt's goal, of course, was to manufacture enough public outrage to facilitate a US entrance into WW II. His plan worked very well, and the lives of over 2,400 American citizens were sacrificed for the power-lust of the few.

For those that may still be harboring some doubts about the willingness of any government, especially that of the United States, to sacrifice their citizens for the "higher good" (and let us never forget that in their minds, it is always for some "higher good" that they believe we, the great unwashed, would be incapable of understanding), we suggest a careful consideration of the events surrounding the sinking of the USS Maine, the sinking of the Lusitania and the Gulf of Tonkin incident for more clear-cut evidence that it is not only foolish but potentially life-threatening to maintain any illusions about what our government officials would or would not do.

For any 9/11 researchers to base their refusal to discuss the "no plane at the Pentagon" theory on the assertion that the American and world public could never accept the idea that the US government would murder 64 American citizens is misinformed at best and disingenuous at worst. The simple fact is that the people that carried out the 9/11 attacks did much more than murder the 64 US citizens on Flight 77, they murdered almost over 2,700 US citizens in the World Trade Center that day, and used the 9/11 event as justification to pursue their imperial war of aggression, murdering tens of thousands innocent Afghani and Iraqi citizens in the process.

If there is one quote that sums up the present situation as regards the reality of 9/11 and the inability of many people to accept that reality, it is the words of former U.S. President J. Edgar Hoover, who is reported to have said,

> "The individual is handicapped by coming face to face with a conspiracy so monstrous he cannot believe it exists".

Details of the events of 9/11/2001

Flight 77 took off at 8:20 a.m. from Washington's Dulles International airport.

The pilot had his last routine communication with the control tower at 8:50 a.m. "At 9:09 a.m., being unable to reach the plane by radar, the Indianapolis air controllers warned of a possible crash", the *Washington Post* reported. Vice-President Dick Cheney would later explain that the terrorists had, "turned off the transponder, which led to a later report that a plane had gone down over Ohio, but it really hadn't". [*Meet the Press, NBC*, 16 Sept 2001]

On 12 September it was learned that the transponder had been cut off at about 8:55 a.m., rendering the plane invisible to civilian air controllers. During this period of invisibility, the plane was said to have made a U turn back to Washington. This is, of course, an assumption. The information that the plane turned around has no known source.

The problem is: turning off the transponder, under the conditions that prevailed that day, would have been the best way of raising an alert.

The procedures are very strict in the case of a problem with a transponder, both on civilian and military aircraft. The FAA regulations describe exactly how to proceed when a transponder is not functioning properly: the control tower should enter into radio contact at once with the pilot and, if it fails, immediately warn the military who would then send fighters to establish visual contact with the crew. [see FAA regulations][73]

The interruption of a transponder also directly sets off an alert with the military body responsible for air defenses of the United States and Canada, NORAD.

The transponder is the plane's identity card. An aircraft that disposes of this identity card is immediately monitored, automatically.

"If an object has not been identified in less than two minutes or appears suspect, it is considered to be an eventual threat. Unidentified planes, planes in distress and planes we suspect are being used for illegal activities can then be intercepted by a fighter from NORAD." [NORAD spokesman][74]

---

[73] http://faa.gov/ATpubs
[74] http://www.airforce.dnd.ca/athomedocs/athome1e_f.htm

See also "Facing Terror Attack's Aftermath"[75], *Boston Globe Sept. 15th 2001*, where you will read:

"Snyder, the NORAD spokesman, said its fighters routinely intercept aircraft."

It is important to note that in the years prior to 9/11, hundreds of planes of all shapes and sizes lost contact with or were otherwise unresponsive to air traffic control. In every case where contact could not be re-established, US Air Force jets were immediately and automatically scrambled as per the long-standing orders. In fact, in the 12 months prior to 9/11, this automatic procedure was triggered flawlessly a total of 67 times, and every time US air force jets reached the unresponsive plane within 15 minutes.

So what happened on 9/11?

How could it have been possible that not one U.S. military jet was scrambled in time to reach any of the four planes? Remember, Flight 77 hit the Pentagon one hour and twenty five minutes after Air traffic controllers in New York were aware that Flight 11 had been hijacked, yet NORAD did nothing until after all four planes were well beyond help.

Even allowing for the official claim of a "breakdown in communications", considering the conditions that prevailed on September 11, 2001, by turning off the transponder at 8:56 a.m. the "terrorists" on Flight 77 actually gave the alert at least forty minutes before the plane struck the Pentagon.

Three F-16s at Langley AFB, Virginia (130 miles from the Pentagon), were ordered to get airborne at approximately 9:30 a.m. The pilots were Major Brad Derrig, Captain Craig Borgstrom, and Major Dean Eckmann, all from the North Dakota Air National Guard's 119th Fighter Wing stationed at Langley.[76] If the assumed NORAD departure time is correct, the F-16s would have had to travel slightly over 700 mph to reach Washington before Flight 77 does. The maximum speed of an F-16 is 1,500 mph. Even traveling at 1,300 mph, these planes could have reached Washington in six minutes - well before Flight 77 hit the Pentagon. Yet it is claimed they were *accidentally directed over the Atlantic Ocean instead*, and reached Washington about 30 minutes later. Remember, this was at a point during the day when all necessary personnel in the US government and NORAD were fully aware that they were under attack by hijacked airliners.

Andrews Air Force Base is just a few miles from the Pentagon and has two fighter wings, yet no orders were given to scramble any planes from this base until long after Flight 77 had hit the Pentagon.

---

[75] http://emperors-clothes.com/9-11backups/bg915.htm
[76] http://www.cooperativeresearch.org/timeline/2002/ap081902c.html

The US government-sponsored 9/11 Commission (certainly not an "independent" body given that the Chairman, Thomas Keane, is a cousin of President Bush) summed up the reasons why America's military defense structures failed to thwart the attacks:

"On 9/11, the defense of U.S. air space depended on close interaction between two federal agencies: the Federal Aviation Administration (FAA) and North American Aerospace Defense Command (NORAD). Existing protocols on 9/11 were unsuited in every respect for an attack in which hijacked planes were used as weapons."

As we have seen, this claim is untrue. The protocols to quickly intercept suspect craft were long-established and had worked flawlessly in the past.

"What ensued was a hurried attempt to improvise a defense by civilians who had never handled a hijacked aircraft that attempted to disappear, and by a military unprepared for the transformation of commercial aircraft into weapons of mass destruction."

Again, this is not true. Whether or not the craft was hijacked was irrelevant for air traffic controllers. What *was* relevant was that the aircraft were unresponsive and/or had turned off their transponders. In such a case, the long-standing procedures are activated, NORAD is contacted and jets are scrambled, without fail.

"A shoot down authorization was not communicated to the NORAD air defense sector until 28 minutes after United 93 had crashed in Pennsylvania. Planes were scrambled, but ineffectively, as they did not know where to go or what targets they were to intercept. And once the shoot down order was given, it was not communicated to the pilots. In short, while leaders in Washington believed that the fighters circling above them had been instructed to "take out" hostile aircraft, the only orders actually conveyed to the pilots were to "ID type and tail". [77]

Yet again this statement flies in the face of the Commission's own findings. As we shall see, Transport Secretary Mineta testified to the Commission that VP Cheney had apparently given a shoot down order for Flight 77 sometime before 9.20 a.m. while he sat in the Presidential Emergency Operating Center in the White House.

Ultimately, the 9/11 Commission concluded that, due to many factors (a considerable number of which have no apparent explanation or none that the Commission was willing to investigate fully), it was a catastrophic breakdown in communication that had lead to the hijackers unchallenged success. But do such massive and unprecedented failures happen all by themselves? Surely someone was responsible?

In certain regions, air traffic controllers have radar, called "primaries", that are able to detect movement in the air while the radar they normally use are called "secondaries" and are limited to recording signals emitted by the transponders of airplanes which tell them the registration, altitude,

---

[77] http://www.9-11commission.gov/report/911Report_Exec.htm

etc. Turning off the transponder permits an aircraft to vanish from these "secondary" radar. Such an aircraft will only appear on "primary" radar. According to the FAA, the air traffic controllers did not have access to primary radars in Ohio.

See: Pentagon Crash Highlights a Radar Gap[78], where you will read:

"The airliner that slammed into the Pentagon on Sept. 11 disappeared from controllers' radar screens for at least 30 minutes -- in part because it was hijacked in an area of limited radar coverage. [...]

The aircraft, traveling from Dulles International Airport to Los Angeles, was hijacked sometime between 8:50 a.m. -- when air traffic controllers made their last routine contact with the pilot -- and 8:56, when hijackers turned off the transponder, which reports the plane's identity, altitude and speed to controllers' radar screens.

The airliner crashed into the Pentagon at 9:38 a.m., about 12 minutes after controllers at Dulles sounded an alert that an unidentified aircraft was headed toward Washington at high speed.

The answers to the mystery of the aircraft's disappearance begin with the fact that the hijacking took place in an area served by only one type of radar, FAA officials confirmed. Although this radar is called a "secondary" system, it is the type used almost exclusively today in air traffic control. It takes an aircraft's identification, destination, speed and altitude from the plane's transponder and displays it on a controller's radar screen.

"Primary" radar is an older system. It bounces a beam off an aircraft and tells a controller only that a plane is aloft -- but does not display its type or altitude. The two systems are usually mounted on the same tower. Primary radar is normally used only as a backup, and is usually turned off by controllers handling aircraft at altitudes above 18,000 feet because it clutters their screens.

All aircraft flying above 18,000 feet are required to have working transponders. If a plane simply disappears from radar screens, most controllers can quickly switch on the primary system, which should display a small plus sign at the plane's location, even if the aircraft's transponder is not working.

But the radar installation near Parkersburg, W. Va., was built with only secondary radar - called "beacon-only" radar. That left the controller monitoring Flight 77 at the Indianapolis center blind when the hijackers apparently switched off the aircraft's transponder, sources said."

The only effect, then, of turning off the transponder at that precise point was to make the plane invisible to some *civilian* aviation authorities. One wonders how the "terrorists" knew that this act would make them invisible to the civilian air traffic controllers. Again, under the conditions prevailing that day, and as a general routine, turning off the transponder should have

---

[78] http://www.washingtonpost.com/ac2/wp-dyn?pagename=article&contentId=A32597-2001Nov2&notFound=true

brought the aircraft to the direct attention and scrutiny of the Military Defense Systems of the United States automatically. It is therefore a near certainty that, at all times, it was visible and monitored by the Military.

According to the statement of General Myers, the military waited three quarters of an hour before ordering fighters to take off. [Senate hearing, 13 Sept. 2001]

Two days later, on 15 September, NORAD issued a contradictory press release. It said that it hadn't been informed of the hijacking of Flight 77 until 9:24 a.m. and had then immediately given orders to two F-16s to take off from Langley, 105 miles from the Pentagon, instead of Andrews, only 10 miles from the Pentagon. They were in the air by 9:30, much too late... the object that impacted the Pentagon arrived at 9:37 a.m.

This version puts all the blame on the FAA for waiting.

But this is implausible due to the established procedures that were automatic.

The question that needs to be asked, considering all that was known at that claimed "late moment" of awareness - that two aircraft had crashed into the WTC and the United States was "under attack" - is: why were fighter jets sent instead of a missile?

The fact is, independently of the interception of Flight 77, the crisis situation that existed that day demanded maximum air defense protection over Washington. This activity would have fallen to Andrews Air Force Base, just as General Eberhart, CO of NORAD had already activated the SCATANA plan and had taken control of the New York airspace in order to position fighters there.

For the military, from the moment they were alerted of Flight 77's disappearance, which was, indeed, the moment the transponders were turned off, and not when the FAA supposedly got around to calling them, it was not a question of speculating that they were dealing with a mechanical failure. The facts on the ground were rather precise: shortly after two airliners were flown into the WTC towers, the transponder of another plane was cut off and the pilot failed to respond to radio contact. The job of the military could not have been clearer: shoot down the plane that was claimed to be headed for Washington.

These facts show clearly that the U.S. Military had no intention of shooting down whatever was heading for the Pentagon despite the menace it represented.

On 16 September 2001, Dick Cheney tried to justify the military's failure by claiming that the shooting down of a civilian airplane would be a "decision left up to the President". He played on the sympathy of the American people, saying that the President just couldn't take such a decision hastily because "the lives of American citizens were at stake".

Yet the reality of the situation is that Bush was one of the last to know about the 9/11 attacks. In fact, tens of millions of people in the US and around the world knew that New York was under attack before the American "Commander in Chief".

When Flight 11 hit the first WTC at 8:46 a.m., President Bush's motorcade was crossing the John Ringling Causeway on the way to Booker Elementary school. [79]

Not long thereafter, then Press Secretary Ari Fleischer, who was riding in another car in the motorcade and talking on his cell phone, exclaimed, "Oh, my God, I don't believe it. A plane just hit the World Trade Center". This call took place "just minutes" after the first news reports.[80]

Congressman Dan Miller also says he was told about the crash just before meeting Bush at Booker elementary school at 8:55 a.m.[81]

Some reporters waiting for Bush to arrive also learned of the crash just minutes after it happened. While we might expect that the Commander in Chief of the Armed Forces and President of the USA would be one of the first to know about the crash, the official story remains that Bush was not told about the first plane attack until after he arrived at the school. On page 17 of his book A pretext for war, author James Bamford comments:

> "Despite having a secure STU-III phone next to [Bush] in the Presidential limousine and an entire national security staff at the White House, it appears that the President of the United States knew less than tens of millions of other people in every part of the country who were watching the attack as it unfolded."[82]

So we see that Cheney's claim that part of the reason for the failure by America's defence apparatus to respond effectively to the attack was due to the difficult decision that confronted the President is a moot point, the President was not even informed of the attacks until *after* the first plane had hit the WTC. Or so it was claimed.

Official accounts would have us believe that Bush simply thought that Flight 11's impact on the North Tower of the WTC was an accident and continued with his book reading in a Florida classroom:

> "I was concentrating on the program at this point, thinking about what I was going to say. Obviously, I felt it was an accident. I was concerned about it, but there were no alarm bells."[83]

Yet over 40 minutes earlier, at about 8.20 a.m., Boston's Logan Airport had received a call from Flight 11 attendant Amy (Madeline) Sweeney stating that the aircraft had been hijacked. Somewhere between 8.13 a.m.

[79] http://www.washtimes.com/national/20021008-21577384.htm
[80]
http://web.archive.org/web/20021004153618/http://www.abqtrib.com/archives/news02/0910
02_news_draper.shtml
[81] http://www.sarasotamagazine.com/Pages/hotstories/hotstories.asp?136
[82] http://www.amazon.com/exec/obidos/tg/detail/-/0385506724/ref=ase_centerforcoop-
20/103-2964218-1386232?v=glance&s=books
[83] http://www.washtimes.com/national/20021007-85016651.htm

and 8.21 a.m. flight 11's transponder was turned off prompting Boston flight control manager Glenn Michael to say later, "We considered it at that time to be a possible hijacking".[84]

In any case, Cheney's claims are disingenuous. He equated the interception of the aircraft with the decision to shoot it down.

Interception is merely establishing visual contact, giving instructions with wing movements etc., and being *ready* to take action. A shoot down means that the fighters are already positioned to receive the order.

Further, it is incorrect that this decision to place fighter jets in a position to take action can only be made by the President. The interception of a suspect civilian aircraft by fighters is *automatic* and does not require any kind of political decision making by the President. It should have taken place on 11 September when the transponder was cut off. The fighters should have taken off immediately - unless they were ordered to "stand down". Furthermore, by September 11th 2001 the ability to give a shoot down order was not limited to the President but shared also by the Secretary for Defense.

Again, let me reiterate the fact that Flight 77 was invisible *only to civilian* aviation authorities. The fact that the transponders were turned off automatically alerts military air defense.

The New York Times reported:

"During the hour or so that American Airlines Flight 77 [is] under the control of hijackers, up to the moment it struck the west side of the Pentagon, military officials in [the Pentagon's NMCC] [are] urgently talking to law enforcement and air traffic control officials about what to do."[85]

MSNBC stated:

"Yet, although the Pentagon's NMCC reportedly knew of the hijacking, NORAD reportedly was not notified until 9:24 a.m. by some accounts, and not notified at all by others." [86]

While ABC News tells us:

"Brigadier General Montague Winfield, commander of the NMCC, the Pentagon's emergency response center, later said: 'When the second aircraft flew into the second tower, it was at that point that we realized that the seemingly unrelated hijackings that the FAA was dealing with were in fact a part of a coordinated terrorist attack on the United States'."[87]

However, Winfield wasn't actually at the NMCC during the 9/11 crisis.[88]

Captain Charles Leidig was in command of the National Military Command Center (NMCC), "the military's worldwide nerve center".

[84] http://www.boston.com/news/daily/12/attacks_faa.htm

[85] http://www.wanttoknow.info/010915nytimes11

[86] http://www.msnbc.msn.com/id/5233007/]

[87] http://abcnews.go.com/onair/DailyNews/sept11_moments_1.html

[88] http://www.cooperativeresearch.org/timeline/2004/independentcommission061704b.html

Telephone links were established with the NMCC located inside the Pentagon (but on the opposite side of the building from where the explosion will happen), U.S. Strategic Command, theater commanders, FEMA agencies and the Canadian military command center,

An Air Threat Conference Call was initiated and it lasted for eight hours. At one time or another, President Bush, Vice President Cheney, Defense Secretary Rumsfeld, key military officers, leaders of the FAA and NORAD, the White House, and Air Force One were heard on the open line.

NORAD command director Captain Michael Jellinek claimed this happened "immediately" after the second WTC hit.[89]

However, the 9/11 Commission concluded it started nearly 30 minutes later, at approximately 9:29 a.m. Brigadier General Montague Winfield, who later takes over for Leidig, said, "All of the governmental agencies that were involved in any activity going on in the United States at that point, were in that conference". While the call continued right through the Pentagon explosion the impact was allegedly not felt within the NMCC.[90]

However, despite being in the Pentagon, Defense Secretary Rumsfeld didn't enter the NMCC or participate in the call until 10:30 a.m.

And so we see that the one man who, officially, could issue a shoot down order (other than the President who was still reading a book on goats to children in Florida) decided not to enter the crisis meeting at the NMCC that began 40 minutes before the Pentagon was hit.

Just to close the book on Cheney's allegations that only the President could order a shoot down, the 9/11 commission interviewed Transportation Secretary Norman Mineta:

> Mr. Hamilton: We thank you for that. I wanted to focus just a moment on the Presidential Emergency Operating Center. You were there for a good part of the day. I think you were there with the vice President. And when you had that order given, I think it was by the President, that authorized the shooting down of commercial aircraft that were suspected to be controlled by terrorists, were you there when that order was given?

> Mr. Mineta: No, I was not. I was made aware of it during the time that the airplane coming into the Pentagon. There was a young man who had come in and said to the Vice President, "The plane is 50 miles out. The plane is 30 miles out." And when it got down to, "The plane is 10 miles out," the young man also said to the vice President, "Do the orders still stand?" And the vice President turned and whipped his neck around and said, "Of course the orders still stand. Have you heard anything to the contrary?" Well, at the time I didn't know what all that meant. And -

[89] http://web.archive.org/web/20041009173402/http://www.aviationnow.com/content/publicat ion/awst/20020603/avi_stor.htm
[90] http://911research.wtc7.net/cache/pentagon/attack/abcnews091102_jenningsinterviews.htm l

Mr. Hamilton: The flight you're referring to is the --

Mr. Mineta: The flight that came into the Pentagon.

Mr. Roemer: So when you arrived at 9:20, how much longer was it before you overheard the conversation between the young man and the vice President saying, "Does the order still stand?"

Mr. Mineta: Probably about five or six minutes.

Mr. Roemer: So about 9:25 or 9:26. And your inference was that the vice President snapped his head around and said, "Yes, the order still stands." Why did you infer that that was a shoot-down?

Mr. Mineta: Just by the nature of all the events going on that day, the scrambling of the aircraft and, I don't know; I guess, just being in the military, you do start thinking about it, an intuitive reaction to certain statements being made. [91]

So what are we to understand from these comments? Well, from the testimony of Mr Mineta, we see that VP Cheney had given an order at some point *prior* to 9.20 a.m., at least 18 minutes before the plane is alleged to have impacted the Pentagon. Mr Mineta claimed to the 9/11 Commission that he assumed that the order was a shoot down order, but if this is true, why was this order from the Vice President not quickly conveyed along the chain of command to the necessary parties? Clearly such an order would have rendered obsolete any confusion over whether or not to scramble jets in the first place. So why were no Air Force Jets scrambled from nearby Andrews AFB?

Mr Mineta stated that he did not hear the order itself but assumed, given the situation in hand, that it was a shoot down order for Flight 77.

But what if it wasn't?

Why would the unnamed official feel the need to ask Cheney if a shoot down order still stood? The danger had certainly not passed by 9:25 a.m. when Mineta heard the exchange. By then everyone knew that "America was under attack", *so who would query a shoot down order from the Vice President?* It seems much more plausible that the order that was being questioned was something akin to a "stand down" order. This would explain the obvious confusion on the part of the unnamed official and his compulsion to ask if the order still stood, even as he watched the obviously hijacked aircraft wing its way towards the Pentagon. It might also better explain Cheney's vexed response of, "Of course the orders still stand. Have you heard anything to the contrary?". It would also explain, of course, why no jets were scrambled and why the 9/11 attacks in general were so successful.

Interestingly, four months prior to 9/11 on May 8th 2001, Bush announced a new Homeland Security initiative:

---

[91] http://www.9-11commission.gov/archive/hearing2/9-11Commission_Hearing_2003-05-23.htm

Cheney to Oversee Domestic Counterterrorism Efforts

"President Bush May 8 directed Vice President Dick Cheney to coordinate development of U.S. government initiatives to combat terrorist attacks on the United States."

"I have asked Vice President Cheney to oversee the development of a coordinated national effort so that we may do the very best possible job of protecting our people from catastrophic harm. I have also asked Joe Allbaugh, the Director of the Federal Emergency Management Agency, to create an Office of National Preparedness. This office will be responsible for implementing the results of those parts of the national effort overseen by Vice President Cheney that deal with consequence management. Specifically it will coordinate all federal programs dealing with weapons of mass destruction consequence management within the Departments of Defense, Health and Human Services, Justice, and Energy, the Environmental Protection Agency, and other federal agencies. The Office of National Preparedness will work closely with state and local governments to ensure their planning, training, and equipment needs are addressed. FEMA will also work closely with the Department of Justice, in its lead role for crisis management, to ensure that all facets of our response to the threat from weapons of mass destruction are coordinated and cohesive."[92]

On the morning of 9/11 then, Vice President Dick Cheney was directly responsible for coordinating federal preparedness for international terrorist attacks on US soil.

Mr Mineta also testified that the FAA was very much in contact with NORAD right from the moment that the transponder on the very first flight, Flight 11, was switched off at 8.20 a.m., a full hour and 18 Minutes **before** the Pentagon was hit!

"The FAA was in touch with NORAD. And when the first flight from Boston had gone out of communications with the air traffic controllers, the air traffic controller then notified, I believe, Otis Air Force Base about the air traffic controller not being able to raise that American Airlines flight."

Let's recap the events to that point according to the official story:

FLIGHT 11

At 8.20 am a flight attendant on Flight 11 phoned Boston Logan airport reporting that the aircraft has been hijacked. For some reason, that has never been explained, no one in Boston contacted NORAD as per the *long-standing and automatic protocols* until over 20 minutes later, 6 minutes before Flight 11 ploughed into the WTC North Tower.

ABCreported:

---

[92] http://www.usembassy.it/file2001_05/alia/a1050801.htm

"There doesn't seem to have been alarm bells going off, [flight] controllers getting on with law enforcement or the military. There's a gap there that will have to be investigated."[93]

However, as per the testimony of Transport Secretary Mineta, NORAD suspected that Flight 11 had been hijacked as soon as communication with it was lost at 8.20 a.m. and Boston air traffic controllers *did* notify Otis AFB. Yet somehow, for some reason, NORAD did nothing.

Officially, pilots at Otis AFB received a call from Boston Flight control at 8.34 a.m. informing them of the situation. The pilots were reported to be sitting in their aircraft for over 5 minutes. *They did not get official clearance to take off until 8.46 a.m., the exact time that Flight 11 hit the WTC North Tower.* There has been no explanation as to why ATC at Boston did not inform Otis AFB immediately at 8.20 a.m. and no explanation for *the delayed order to scramble the jets until after Flight 11 had been transformed into a ball of flames in Manhattan.*

Also at 8.34 a.m., Boston flight control attempted to contact an Atlantic City, New Jersey, air base to send fighters after Flight 11. For decades, the air base had two fighters on 24-hour alert status, but this changed in 1998 due to budget cutbacks. The flight controllers did not realize this, and apparently tried in vain to reach someone. Two F-16s from this base were practicing bombing runs over an empty stretch of the Pine Barrens near Atlantic City. Only eight minutes away from New York City, they were not alerted to the emerging crisis.

Shortly after the second WTC crash at 9:03 a.m., the same two F-16s were ordered to land and were refitted with air-to-air missiles, then sent aloft. However, the pilots re-launched more than an hour after the second crash. They were apparently sent to Washington, but did not reach there until almost 11:00 a.m.

After 9/11, one newspaper questions why NORAD, *"left what seems to be a yawning gap in the midsection of its air defenses on the East Coast— a gap with New York City at the center".*[94]

Had these two fighters been notified at 8:37 a.m. or before, they could have reached New York City before Flight 11.

FLIGHT 175

At 8:43 a.m. NORAD was notified by Boston flight control that another flight, Flight 175, had been hijacked.[95]

---

[93] http://abcnews.go.com/sections/us/DailyNews/wtc_ticktock010914.html
[94]

http://www.northjersey.com/page.php?qstr=eXJpcnk3ZjczN2Y3dnFlZUVFeXkyNjMmZmdi
ZWw3Zjd2cWVlRUV5eTY0NTk1MDUmeXJpcnk3ZjcxN2Y3dnFlZUVFeXk5

Yet no orders were given at this time to scramble any aircraft. Later, *the 9/11 commission ignored the testimony of New York flight controller Dave Bottoglia that he was aware that Flight 175 was hijacked at this time and had notified NORAD*, claiming instead that NORAD was unaware that Flight 175 had been hijacked until 9.03 a.m., the approximate time that it crashed into the WTC South Tower.

One of the main excuses offered by the National Military Command Center (NMCC) and the Department of Defense for their failure to thwart the 9/11 attacks was that the 4,000 other planes in America's skies on the morning of September 11th 2001 made the task almost impossible. *Yet what is not pointed out is that, of those 4,000 planes, the 4 hijacked planes were the ONLY ones that were not transmitting a transponder signal, making them stick out like sore thumbs on any **military** radar screen.*

FLIGHT 77

The last radio contact with Flight 77 occured at 8.50 a.m. At 8.56 a.m. its transponder was turned off. Somewhere between these two times the plane was "hijacked".

The New York Times reported,

> "During the hour or so that American Airlines Flight 77 [was] under the control of hijackers (8.56 a.m.), up to the moment it struck the west side of the Pentagon, military officials in [the Pentagon's NMCC] [were] urgently talking to law enforcement and air traffic control officials about what to do."[96]

Despite this assertion, and the fact that it is backed up by transport Secretary Mineta's testimony that Cheney had given an order to shoot down Flight 77 sometime before 9:20 a.m., the 9/11 Commission accepted testimony from some that NORAD was not notified until 9:24 am and from others that NORAD was not notified at all.[97]

Pentagon spokesman, Lieutenant-Colonel Vic Warzinski claimed the military had not been expecting such an attack. This is not credible. Even though the transponder had been turned off, the Pentagon knew full well where that aircraft was. Communications between civilian air traffic controllers and the various federal authorities functioned perfectly as they had on many previous occasions.

In fact, not only had the FAA Command Center set up a teleconference with FAA facilities in the New York area by 8:40 a.m. but a communication line was also opened with the Air Traffic Services Cell, a

---

95

http://web.archive.org/web/20020615115751/http://www.norad.mil/presrelNORADTimelines.htm

[96] http://www.wanttoknow.info/010915nytimes11

[97] http://www.msnbc.msn.com/id/5233007/

military cell which had been created by the FAA and the Defense Department to coordinate priority aircraft movement during warfare or emergencies. This cell is staffed by Pentagon employees, and while it is usually only staffed three days per month for refresher training, September 11 just happened to be one of those days.[98]

Even more coincidentally, the cell had been given a secure terminal and other hardware just weeks earlier which had supposedly, "greatly enhanced the movement of vital information".[99]

FLIGHT 93

"According to NORAD's *initial statement, Flight 93 was hijacked at 9: 16 a.m.,* yet they were unable to say when the FAA notified them of the hijacking or how the FAA knew. Flight 93 is the only flight where NORAD could not at least supply this time of notification of hijacking."[100]

"Despite this, the 9/11 Commission concluded that *the hijacking of Flight 93 began at 9:28 a.m.* saying only that the original statement by NORAD was incorrect without giving any explanation as to how or why such an error was made."[101]

"At this same time, Cleveland flight controllers *noticed Flight 93 climbing and descending in an erratic way,* and shortly thereafter *screams and shouts of "get out of here" were heard by controllers over the cockpit transmission. Arabic voices are also heard.* At this point contact was lost with Flight 93. Yet despite this, we are told that *no one notified NORAD.*"[102]

"According to the 9/11 Commission, at 9: 36 a.m. Cleveland flight control specifically asked the FAA Command Center whether someone had requested the military to launch fighters toward Flight 93. Cleveland offered to contact a nearby military base. The Command Center replied that FAA personnel well above them in the chain of command have to make that decision and were working on the issue." [103]

This single fact suggests that somewhere along the chain of command someone was preventing the implementation of standard procedures taken in respect of suspect aircraft, which is the immediate scrambling of fighter jets.

"At about 9:36 am Flight 93 made a 180 degree turn and headed back to Washington." [104]

---

[98] http://www.freerepublic.com/focus/f-news/592509/posts

[99] http://web.archive.org/web/20020917072642/http://www.aviationnow.com/content/publication/awst/20020603/avi_stor.htm

[100] http://www.cnn.com/2001/US/09/16/inv.hijack.warning/

[101] http://web.archive.org/web/20040617211819/http://www.msnbc.msn.com/id/5233007/

[102] http://members.fortunecity.com/seismicevent/msnbctransponder.html#

[103] http://www.msnbc.msn.com/id/5233007/

[104] http://europe.cnn.com/2001/US/09/12/plane.phone.call/

Still no fighters were scrambled.

From 9:30 am until Flight 93 "crashed" several passengers were *alleged* to have made calls to their family members and to phone operators specifying that a hijacking was taking place.

> *"According to NORAD*, Flight 93 crashed at *10:03 am.* However, *a seismic study* authorized by the US Army to determine when the plane crashed concluded that the crash happened at *10:06:05."* [105]

> "Furthermore, according to a CNN report, the cockpit voice recording of Flight 93 was recorded on a 30-minute reel which started at 9:31am and ended at 10:02 am, with the last minute of recording apparently missing. This fact led some victim's family members to wonder if the tape had been tampered with."[106]

So what exactly happened in that last minute before flight 93 hit the ground in Pennsylvania?

> "Several eyewitness reports of the crash of Flight 93 attest to the presence of a white unmarked military-style jet over-flying the crash scene."[107]

The mayor of Shanksville, the closest town to where Flight 93 "crashed" stated:

> "I know of two people - I will not mention names - *that heard a missile*", Stuhl said. "They both live very close, within a couple of hundred yards. . .This one fellow's served in Vietnam and he says he's heard them, and he heard one that day." The mayor adds that based on what he knows about that morning, military F-16 fighter jets were "very, very close". [108]

> "Another eyewitness stated that he heard *two loud bangs* before watching the plane take a downward turn of nearly 90 degrees."[109]

> "It is also a matter of record that the debris of the crash was strewn across an area of approximately 8 miles. Ask yourself: how could parts of a commercial jet that allegedly hit the ground intact be 8 miles from the crash site?"[110]

These facts are clearly consistent with the idea that Flight 93 was shot down.

Of course, if Flight 93 was shot down and did not crash as claimed by the US government and 9/11 Commission, not only does this pose serious questions about the authenticity of the alleged phone calls made by passengers to the effect that they were going to try and "do something" to

---

[105] http://www.mgs.md.gov/esic/publications/download/911pentagon.pdf
[106] http://inn.globalfreepress.com/modules/news/article.php?storyid=470
[107] http://news.independent.co.uk/world/americas/story.jsp?story=323958
[108]
http://web.archive.org/web/20011116093836/http://dailynews.philly.com/content/daily_news/local/2001/11/15/SHOT15c.htm
[109] http://www.newsnet5.com/news/956371/detail.html
[110] http://archives.cnn.com/2001/US/09/13/penn.attack/

take control of Flight 93 from the hijackers, but it throws all other facets of the official story of what happened on 9/11 into doubt.

In the one hour and thirty minutes from the time authorities had become aware of the first plane hijacking to the time that Flight 93 "crashed" in Pennsylvania, the official story claims that the FAA, NORAD and the Presidential Emergency Operating Center (PEOC) all failed to organise the effective scrambling of a single fighter jet to confront the "hijackers". Not only that, but over the course of the day, air traffic controllers and employees of the FAA failed a total of 16 times to follow (or to have implemented) the automatic and long-standing procedures in which they were all well-versed.

And let us just remind readers once more, in the 12 months leading up to 9/11, procedures for the interception by military aircraft of suspect airplanes had been implemented flawlessly 67 times. On almost every occasion fighter aircraft had visual sighting of the suspect aircraft within 15 minutes of notification.

The Role of the Military

There are five extremely sophisticated anti-missile batteries in place to protect the Pentagon from an airborne attack. These anti-missile batteries operate *automatically*.

At 9:25 a.m., the control tower at Dulles airport observed an unidentified vehicle speeding towards the restricted airspace that surrounds the capital. [*Washington Post*, 12 September, 2001] The craft was heading toward the White House.

> "All of a sudden, the plane turned away. ...This must be a fighter. This must
> be one of our guys sent in, scrambled to patrol our capital and to protect our
> President... We lost radar contact with that aircraft. And we waited. ... And
> then the Washington National controllers came over our speakers in our
> room and said, "Dulles, hold all of our inbound traffic. The Pentagon's been
> hit". [Danielle O'Brien, ABC News, 24 October 2001]

The Army possesses several very sophisticated radar monitoring systems. The PAVE PAWS system is used to detect and track objects difficult to pick up such as missiles flying at very low altitudes. PAVE PAWS misses nothing occurring in North American airspace. "The radar system is capable of detecting and monitoring a great number of targets that would be consistent with a massive SLBM [Submarine Launched Ballistic Missile] attack. The system is capable of rapidly discriminating between vehicle types, calculating their launch and impact points."[111]

Thus, contrary to the Pentagon's claims, the military knew very well that an unidentified vehicle was headed straight for the capital. Yet, the

---

[111] http://www/pavepaws.org/ and http://www.fas.org/spp/military/program/track/pave paws.htm

military did not react, and the Pentagon's anti-missile batteries did not function.

Why?

We come back to the issue of Transponders.

Military aircraft and missiles possess transponders which are much more sophisticated than those of civilian planes. These transponders enable the craft to declare itself to the *electronic eyes* watching American airspace as either friendly or hostile. An anti-missile battery will not, for example, react to the passage of a friendly missile, so that in battlefield conditions, it is ensured that only enemy armaments and vehicles are destroyed.

*Thus, it seems that whatever hit the Pentagon **must** have had a military transponder signalling that it was "friendly" - i.e. it would take an American Military craft to penetrate the defenses of the Pentagon - or the* anti-missile batteries would have been *automatically* activated. Considering all aspects of the problem suggests that the systems *were* operational... and the object that hit the Pentagon was "read" by the anti-missile batteries as *"ours"*.

Strangely, the *entire* responsibility for air defense is attributed to NORAD, and that is simply not the truth.

The previously-mentioned National Military Command Center, located in the Pentagon centralizes all information concerning plane hijackings and directs military operations. The NMCC was in a state of maximum alert on the morning of 11 September. The highest military authority of NMCC is the Chairman of the Joint Chiefs of Staff. On 11 September, General Henry Shelton fulfilled this role. However, Shelton was conveniently en route for Europe, somewhere over the Atlantic. Thus, his job fell to his deputy, *General Richard Myers,* who was also conveniently hobnobbing with Senator Max Cleland at the time of the attacks. We have also noted that Secretary of Defense Donald Rumsfeld strangely chose *not* to join his colleagues at the NMCC crisis meeting being held in the Pentagon on the morning of 9/11, opting instead to stay in his office nearby until the Pentagon was hit.

In short, the answers to what happened on that day devolve to claimed technical failures, coordination problems, temporary incapacity, absence of commanders, transfer of responsibility, and so on.

Even if we were to accept such an implausible excuse, we are still left with the problem of why the automatic systems in place did not work.

USA Today reported:

NORAD had drills of jets as weapons

In the two years before the Sept. 11 attacks, the North American Aerospace Defense Command conducted exercises simulating what the White House said was unimaginable at the time: hijacked airliners used as weapons to crash into targets and cause mass casualties.[112]

One of the imagined targets was the World Trade Center! Yet despite this fact, the Bush administration, most notably then National Security Advisor Condoleezza Rice, claims that they were completely unprepared for the 9/11 attacks *because the idea of someone hijacking commercial airliners and flying them into buildings was never thought possible.* Does this mean that Condi was lying?

Take your time, no hurry.

On November 3rd , 2000 a US military website reported:

> "The fire and smoke from the downed passenger aircraft billows from the Pentagon courtyard. Defense Protective Services Police seal the crash sight. Army medics, nurses and doctors scramble to organize aid. An Arlington Fire Department chief dispatches his equipment to the affected areas.

> Don Abbott, of Command Emergency Response Training, walks over to the Pentagon and extinguishes the flames. The Pentagon was a model and the "plane crash" was a simulated one."[113]

Yet still we are asked to believe the Bush administration when they say that they could never have anticipated the 9/11 attacks. The reality, it seems, is that not only did a faction of the US government anticipate the attacks; they had a direct hand in *facilitating* them.

On the morning of 9/11 at least five "Training Exercises" were in progress. Each and every one, and others we may not yet know of, were under the control of Vice President Dick Cheney. The 9/11 Commission has accepted testimony from various officials implicated in the 9/11 "failures" that *it was just a case of bad luck or coincidence* that these exercises were taking place at the time. Taken together with all other conditions, that has to be one of the most extraordinary coincidences of all time. The exercises we know of included:

1) *Military Exercise, Northern Vigilance*: Transferred most of the combat ready interceptors and possibly many AWACS from the north east into northern Canada and Alaska. This explains, in part, why there were only eight combat interceptors in the NE on 9/11. The calculated effect of this war game was to *take USAF fighters away from the Eastern seaboard* and avoid the eventuality that a gung-ho fighter pilot might attempt to thwart the attacks.

2) *Non-Military Biowarfare Exercise, Tripod II:* FEMA arrived in NYC on 10 Sept 2001 to set up the command post for FEMA, New York City and Department Of Justice on Manhattan's pier 29. The effect and obvious

---

[112] http://usatoday.printthis.clickability.com/pt/cpt?action=cpt&title=USATODAY.com+-+NORAD+had+drills+of+jets+as+weapons&expire=&urlID=9961878&fb=Y&url=http%3A%2F%2Fwww.usatoday.com%2Fnews%2Fwashington%2F2004-04-18-norad_x.htm&partnerID=1660
[113] http://www.mdw.army.mil/news/Contingency_Planning.html

benefit to the conspirators of this exercise was to have FEMA employees already on the ground when the WTC towers were hit in order to *manage the fall out of information* in the immediate aftermath of the attacks.

3) *Wargame Exercise, Vigilant Guardian:* This exercise *simulated hijacked planes* in the northeast sector. The 9/11 Commission *made only mention* of this single exercise and *lied* about its purpose. The commission said its purpose was to intercept Russian bombers. The effect of this war game was also to *take USAF fighters away from the Eastern seaboard* and avoid the eventuality that a gung-ho fighter pilot might attempt to thwart the attacks.

4) *Wargame Exercise, Vigilant Warrior:* This exercise *simulated hijacked planes in the northeast sector* and was essential to the conspirators in order to control (delay) the relaying of information about the "hijacked" aircraft in order that they could complete their mission.

5) *Wargame Exercise, Northern Guardian*: This exercise *simulated hijacked planes in the northeast sector* and was also essential to the conspirators in order to control (delay) the relaying of information about the "hijacked" aircraft in order that they could complete their mission.

Again we note that these exercises can be observed to be precisely designed to facilitate the attacks on 9-11. If, as we are expected to believe, these exercises just happened to be scheduled on the day when a gang of Arab Terrorists, working out of a cave in Afghanistan, were actually planning the exact types of attacks, it was either the most extraordinary coincidence of all time, or someone "in the know" passed the information on to said "Muslim Extremists", an issue that has never been addressed. The most reasonable explanation is, of course, that these exercises on that date, coming in conjunction with the attacks themselves, demonstrate clear U.S. Government complicity.

As a result of these exercises, at the time of the real hijackings there were as many as 22 "hijacked aircraft" on NORAD's radar screen. Some of these drills were "Live Fly" exercises where actual aircraft, likely flown by remote control, were simulating hi-jacked aircraft. Some of the drills electronically added the hi-jacked aircraft into the system. All this as the real hijackings began! NORAD offered these exercises, at least five in all, as an explanation for the apparent failure of US military command and the FAA to prevent the attacks, suggesting it couldn't tell the difference between the seventeen bogus blips and the four actual hi-jacked aircraft blips. While such a claim may sound plausible enough to the average citizen, it is in reality very hard to believe, particularly given that, on December 9th 2001, the Toledo Blade reported the following:

> "Deep inside a mountain (Cheyenne) in Colorado, members of the North
> American Aerospace Defence Command (NORAD) are at full battle staff
> levels for a major annual exercise that tests every facet of the organization.

Operation Northern Vigilance, planned months in advance, involves deploying fighter jets to locations in Alaska and northern Canada."

"Everything is going as planned when Capt. Mike Jellinek arrives for his 6 a.m. shift. The Canadian will be overseeing the crew staffing a crucial post inside the mountain - NORAD's command centre.

Whether it's a simulation or a real-world event, the role of the centre is to fuse every critical piece of information NORAD has into a concise and crystalline snapshot.

An hour into his shift, something unscripted happens. NORAD's Northeast Air Defence Sector (NEADS), based in Rome, N.Y., contacts the mountain.

The Federal Aviation Administration has evidence of a hijacking and is asking for NORAD support. This is not part of the exercise.

In a flash, Operation Northern Vigilance is called off. *Any simulated information, what's known as an "inject", is purged from the screens.*

Someone shouted to look at the monitor displaying CNN.

'At that point, we saw the World Trade Center, one of the towers, smoke coming out of it. And a minute later, we watched the live feed as the second aircraft swung around into the second tower', says Jellinek."[114]

So we see that a NORAD employee involved in the training exercises made it clear that *there was no problem whatsoever with purging the simulated "injects" from the radar screen,* leaving only the real "hijacked" planes that were *clearly identifiable by the fact that they were not emitting a transponder signal.*

As per the report, the FAA contacted NORAD, and this "purging" occurred *a few minutes before the second plane* impacted the WTC south tower at 9:03 a.m., by which time Flight 77's transponder had already been switched off, and *Flight 93 was not even "hijacked" until some 15 minutes later!* Of course, we are still left with the nagging question as to why NORAD was contacted by the FAA about "hijacked airliners" some 10-15 minutes *after* Flight 11 had already been transformed into a ball of flames in the North Tower of the WTC at 8:46 am.

Let's look now in more detail at some of the most glaring evidence for a conspiracy on 9/11.

Reuters news agency was first on the scene of the Pentagon attack. Based on the information they gathered there *from eyewitnesses*, they announced that the Pentagon had suffered damage from a *helicopter explosion. Associated Press confirmed this* with Democratic Party consultant, Paul Begala.

2:41:05 PM "The Pentagon is being evacuated in expectation of a terrorist attack. It is believed a fire has broken out in the building." -*TCM Breaking News* (9/11/01)[115]

---

[114] http://www.ringnebula.com/northern-vigilance.htm

2:47:43 PM "There are reports that a helicopter has crashed into the Pentagon. An eyewitness said that they saw the helicopter circle the building and after it disappeared behind it, an explosion occurred." - *TCM Breaking News* (9/11/01)[116]

2:52:26 PM "Paul Begala, a Democratic consultant, said he witnessed an explosion near the Pentagon *shortly after two planes crashed into World Trade Centre.* "It was a huge fireball, a huge, orange fireball', Begala said. He said another witness told him a helicopter exploded." - *TCM Breaking News* (9/11/01)[117]

Shortly after the attack on the Pentagon, *the Department of Defense said* that a plane was involved. Suddenly, *new* "eyewitnesses" came forward that *contradicted the first ones,* and these new "eyewitnesses" now supported the "official version".

Fred Hay, assistant to Senator Bob Ney, was the first to claim that he saw a Boeing aircraft fall as he was driving down the highway next to the Pentagon. *Senator Mark Kirk* claimed that he was leaving the Pentagon parking lot after *breakfast with Donald Rumsfeld,* and he declared that a large plane had crashed into the Pentagon.

It was several hours before the Chairman of the Joint Chiefs of Staff, General Richard Myers, declared that the "suicide plane" was the Boeing 757, AA Flight 77 which had taken off from Dulles airport in Washington D.C. bound for L.A., and which had been lost to air traffic controllers at 8:55 a.m.

The air traffic controllers said that, at 8:55 a.m., the Boeing Flight 77 descended to 29,000 feet and did not respond to their instructions. Its transponder then went silent. They assumed electrical failure. The pilot was not responding to them, but - according to them - apparently was able to intermittently turn on his radio which allowed them to hear a voice with "a strong Arab accent" threatening him. The plane then made a turn "back toward Washington" and after that, all trace was lost. Keep in mind that no one of the civilian air traffic controllers saw this "turn back", because there was no transponder by which they could track it. It is just a claim that was made *after the fact.*

The air traffic controllers notified FAA headquarters that a hijacking was suspected. The FAA staff said that, in the midst of the panic of that day, they just thought this message was another notification concerning the second plane that hit the WTC. It was only a half hour later that they realized it was, in fact, a third plane. That is to say, at about 9:24 they knew they had a third problem:

---

[115] Please not that the times given correspond to the time the events were reported in Ireland (5 hours ahead of EST). http://archives.tcm.ie/breakingnews/2001/09/11/story23297.asp

[116] http://archives.tcm.ie/breakingnews/2001/09/11/story23298.asp

[117] http://archives.tcm.ie/breakingnews/2001/09/11/story23300.asp

"General Richard Myers, vice chairman of the Joint Chiefs of Staff, said
that, prior to the crash into the Pentagon, military officials had been notified
that another hijacked plane had been heading from the New York area to
Washington. He says he assumed that hijacked plane was the one that hit the
Pentagon, though he could not be sure." -TCM Breaking News (9/11/01)[118]

On September 13, General Myers was unable to give a report to the
Senate on defensive measures taken to intercept this Boeing. Based on his
testimony, the Senate Armed Services Committee determined that no
attempt at interception had taken place.

NORAD immediately jumped up and said "not so!". They issued a press
release the next day stating that it only received the warning of the third
hijacking at 9:24 and had most definitely immediately ordered two F-16's
from Langley AFB in Virginia to intercept Flight 77. But, they claimed
that the Air Force did not know its location and went in the wrong
direction! Apparently, a military transport taking off from Andrews Air
Force base happened to spot the Boeing by chance, but by then it was too
late. Keep in mind that a plane with a turned off transponder is always
visible to military radar.

A Boeing 757-200 measures 155 feet long and has a wingspan of 125
feet. Fully loaded, it weighs 115 tons and cruises at 560 miles per hour.

So, this last claim above is simply not plausible. We are expected to
believe that the U.S. military radar system could not locate a Boeing
within a range of only a few dozen miles? The military radar of the most
powerful nation on earth? And further, that said Boeing - a flying whale -
could outmaneuver and elude two fighter jets?!

It is known that the security arrangements that protect Washington were
revised after a plane managed to land on the White House lawn in 1994. It
is also known that those security arrangements, while mostly secret,
include five batteries of anti-aircraft missiles installed on top of the
Pentagon and fighters stationed at Andrews Air Force Base. Yet, we are
expected to believe that "the Pentagon simply was not aware" that a
hijacked Boeing was headed its way; that "no one expected anything like
that here"?

Essentially, we are being asked to believe that the headquarters of the
most powerful and militarized nation on earth had been helpless to defend
itself even in the midst of the most elaborate military exercises dealing
with the exact problem faced on that day ever held in the United States!

Among the various reports of an initial explosion before the main
aircraft impact was the claim that a truck bomb had exploded. The fact is
that there was indeed a fuel (oil) truck stationed just to the left of the
helicopter pad in front of the Pentagon. Photos taken moments after the

---

[118] http://archives.tcm.ie/breakingnews/2001/09/11/story23360.asp

impact show an already burning fire to the right of the main impact site that is emitting a dense cloud of black smoke. (See Plate 1)

This black smoke is consistent with burning oil, which continued to burn long after the flames and smoke from the main impact had died down. This fact lends credence to the eyewitness reports of an oil truck having exploded a few seconds before the main impact.

It is our contention therefore that the conspirators positioned and detonated the oil truck bomb just before the main attack in order to augment the aircraft explosion claim and also to provide *a literal smoke screen* in an attempt to hide the fact that Flight 77 was not involved in the attack. This is one of two "primer" explosions that occurred and which were reported at the time in the mainstream news. The second primer explosion *occurred at the White House*[119] and was designed as a preparation for an attack on that building, an attack that the Bush gang had been told to expect. Of course, one might have thought that, by now, Bush, Cheney et al would be old and wise enough not to believe everything they are told. We will discuss this aspect later.

CNN correspondent Jamie Mcintyre reporting from the Pentagon lawn about an hour after the attack had this to say:

> "From my *close up inspection*, there is no evidence of a plane having crashed anywhere near the Pentagon [...] There are no large tail sections wing sections, fuselage, nothing like that anywhere around which would indicate that the entire plane crashed into the side of the Pentagon." [120]

Strangely enough, the reports of odd happenings at the Pentagon kept coming in until late in the day:

> 4:05:16 p.m. "*A second aircraft* has crashed into the Pentagon building. It is not known whether this plane was that which was hijacked from Boston airport a short time ago, the fourth such plane to be used in this major attack on the US. *Earlier, a small plane had slammed into the building and set it ablaze*." -TCM Breaking News (9/11/01)[121]

> 4:17:03 p.m. "Part of the Pentagon building outside Washington has collapsed. It had been *hit by two planes* apparently hijacked by terrorists in Boston earlier today." - *TCM Breaking News* (9/11/01)

> 6:40:29 PM "Fighter jets are patrolling the skies above Washington after a jet hijacked by terrorists struck the Pentagon. An aircraft has crashed on a helicopter landing pad near the Pentagon, and the White House. The Pentagon has taken a direct hit from an aircraft. The nerve centre of the US military burst into flames and a portion of one side of the five-sided structure collapsed when the plane struck."

Secondary explosions were reported in the aftermath of the attack and great billows of smoke drifted skyward towards the Potomac River. Authorities

---

[119] http://www.nih.gov/news/NIH-Record/10_02_2001/story01.htm
[120] http://thewebfairy.com/911/pentagon/
[121] http://archives.tcm.ie/breakingnews/2001/09/11/story23320.asp

immediately began deploying troops, including a regiment of light infantry. General Richard Myers, vice chairman of the Joint Chiefs of Staff, says that prior to the crash into the Pentagon, military officials had been notified that another hijacked plane had been heading from the New York area to Washington. *He says he 'assumed that hijacked plane was the one that hit the Pentagon, though he could not be sure'." - TCM Breaking News* (9/11/01)

Members of the press were kept away from the scene for the ostensible reason that they might "hinder rescue operations". However, the Associated Press obtained photos taken by a private individual from a nearby building.

It is due to those photos - taken by a private individual while the news services were banned from the area - that the biggest questions about the strike on the Pentagon have been raised.

After all of this confusion, it was finally announced that, according to officials, the explosion at the Pentagon was caused when American Airlines Flight 77, a 100 ton Boeing 757 commercial airliner, crashed at ground level into the only section of the building that was being renovated to be more "blast resistant" and which housed the smallest number of employees. Flight 77 was allegedly hijacked by five Arab Islamic terrorists on an apparent suicide mission killing all 64 people on board. Officials claimed that the flight recorders from Flight 77 and the remains of all but one of the 64 passengers on board where found at the crash scene.

Now, let us pause for a moment to think about this. First of all, we should consider the alleged "mindset" of terrorists who would want to inflict the most damage possible on their selected target. Certainly, if a Fundamentalist Islamic terrorist organization managed to get hold of a plane, and then get it into range of the Pentagon, the "heart of the Great Satan", as they refer to the United States, they are going to want to go out in a blaze of glory that will be celebrated in legend for years to come! What a strike! Imagine! Being able to completely destroy the nerve center of the hated "Satan"!

Already, these alleged terrorists have managed to destroy the "commercial symbol" of the United States, or so we are told, and now we are informed that they had other objects in their sights - the symbol of the United States' Military Supremacy.

But somehow, they bungled it. Somehow, with all the skills they are claimed to have had, evidenced by the way that infamous Flight 77 swooped down on the Pentagon like a giant bird of prey going after a running rabbit, American Airlines Flight 77, a 100 ton Boeing 757 commercial airliner that could have almost completely destroyed the entire Pentagon, crashed at ground level into the *only section of the building* guaranteed to produce the least damage and the fewest casualties.

And here we find ourselves in the midst of a double conundrum; for not only did the alleged hijackers of Flight 77 go to extraordinary lengths to inflict the least damage possible on the Pentagon, the alleged pilot of Flight 77 couldn't even fly!

Flight instructors at the Scotsdale, Arizona flight school where alleged Flight 77 hijacker pilot Hani Hanjour trained, claimed that he was a completely incompetent pilot. CBS News reported:

> "Months before Hani Hanjour is believed to have flown an American Airlines jet into the Pentagon, managers at an Arizona flight school reported him at least five times to the FAA. They reported him not because they feared he was a terrorist, but because his English and flying skills were so bad...they didn't think he should keep his pilot's license."

> "I couldn't believe he had a commercial license of any kind with the skills that he had." - Peggy Chevrette, Arizona flight school manager.[122]

Despite these facts, the US government insists that Hanjour was an "expert pilot", simply because only an expert could have executed the incredible flying maneuvers required to steer a 757-200 across several lanes of traffic avoiding trucks, lamp-posts and trees and then hit the Pentagon at ground height.

This leads us to the obvious question: if these were really Five Arab Terrorists on a suicide mission to take down the hated Satan, and they were so skilled as to have pulled off all the stunning feats of that day, how did they bungle their chance for what would have been the greatest coup in Muslim Extremist history? How did they bungle so badly by using their fantastic flying skills to hit the part of the Pentagon that was the *least occupied* and the *most fortified*?

That is the "fact on the ground".

Just consider this: In order to cause the greatest damage to the Pentagon, the plane should obviously have dived right into the Pentagon's roof. The building is a pretty big target; it covers a surface area of 29 acres, making it an easy "hit". Instead, what actually happened makes no sense at all from the perspective of Islamic terrorists - we are assuming real "freedom hating" terrorists here as the Bush Administration has assured us they were - who now have their chance to do some real damage: they chose to strike a single facade, the height of which was only 80 feet instead of getting a bull's eye on that 29 acre target. Terrorists that can fly a 757 like a barrel racer rides a horse, and they appear to have used their alleged flying expertise to inflict the least damage possible?!

Perplexing is it not?

The alleged Boeing, purported to be in the hands of Islamic Fundamentalists who, with burning hatred in their heart of the United States and "its freedoms", steered said *flying whale* with unerring accuracy

---

[122] http://www.cbsnews.com/stories/2002/05/10/attack/main508656.shtml

into a flight path as though they were going to land on the Pentagon lawn. While remaining horizontal, this amazing Boeing, we are told, came down almost vertically, and struck the Pentagon at the height of the ground floor. What is more, it managed to do this without even ruffling the grass of the Pentagon's immaculate lawn. And then, despite its weight and forward momentum, the flying whale only *destroyed* a small section of the first ring of the building. (See Plate 2)

What is more, these deadly terrorists with race car driving skills *sacrificed their lives* to hit the Pentagon in such a way that only a small section was damaged, and it happened to be a section that was undergoing renovation and many of the offices of that section were unoccupied! You would think that if one is going to sacrifice one's life for something, like "burning hatred in their hearts for Mom, Apple Pie and the American Way", they would have wanted to get more bang for their buck.

Well, there's actually another very interesting thing about the section of the Pentagon that was hit: the Navy's brand new Command Center was destroyed. According to Aviation Now:

> *"Vice Adm. Darb Ryan*, chief of naval personnel, was in his office at the
> Navy Annex about halfway between Trapasso's home and the Pentagon.
> Having learned that New York had been attacked, he was on the telephone
> recommending the evacuation of the Pentagon "when out of the corner of
> my eye I saw the airplane" a split second before it struck."

Ryan was overheard reporting some of the initial damage assessment, which included spaces belonging to the chief of naval operations (CNO), the Navy's tactical command center on the D-ring, an operations cell and a Navy intelligence command center. These included up to four special, highly classified, electronically secure areas. Many of the *enlisted sailors* involved were *communications technicians with cryptology training who are key personnel in intelligence gathering and analysis.* Some personnel were known to be trapped alive in the wreckage.

Other navy personnel confirmed the admiral's initial assessment and said the dead numbered around 190, including 64 on the aircraft. Among them was Lt. Gen. Timothy Maude, who was in the Army support and logistics section. Many others were *Navy captains, commanders* and *lieutenant commanders* with offices between the fourth and fifth corridors (the western wedge of the Pentagon). The Navy's special operations office, which oversees classified programs, had moved out of the spaces only a few days before. All but one of the senior Navy flag officers were out of the building.

Early press reports claimed 800 deaths at the Pentagon, yet Donald Rumsfeld did not correct this grossly exaggerated figure on September 12th when the true death toll of 125 was certainly known.

> "Up to 800 people may have died Tuesday when a hijacked commercial
> airliner was crashed into the Pentagon, officials said. The more than 20,000

civilians and military men and women who work in the Pentagon streamed
into the surrounding parking lots, driven by blue and white strobe alarm
lights and wailing sirens." - CNN (9/12/01)

"125 people were killed on the ground at the Pentagon. An additional 59
perished aboard American Airlines Flight #77. We do not count the five
terrorists. Approximately 63 people were wounded/injured in the attack." -
DoD

The shock of the impact was felt throughout the entire building. 125
people in the Pentagon lost their lives, to which should be added the 64
people aboard the Boeing which can carry 269 passengers. In other words,
it was almost empty.

I could go on, but there are many other sources that cover the details of
that day in very competent ways not to mention the dozens of sources that
only add to the confusion. At the present moment, I am of the opinion that
a Boeing 757 most definitely did not hit the Pentagon, that the object that
struck the Pentagon *was* different from the commercial jetliners that were
clearly seen to fly into the World Trade Center Towers.

Now, let's move on to the "How did they do it?" question.

How Did They Do It?

I once spoke at length with an individual who served in the Persian Gulf
conflict. His job was to "program" missiles - *very* smart ones. Even
though it was his job, he was completely astonished at their capabilities.
He said, "They can be programmed to go down the street just above the
ground, turn right or left at a cross street, and hit the designated building at
the exact floor, even the exact window, that you tell them to hit"! My jaw
dropped and he then said that he was exaggerating, but only a little, and he
was describing it this way just to emphasize for me the capability of
modern guidance systems.

Now, that's amazing. That was also back in the early 1990s.

But let's make this perfectly clear: *We do not believe that it was a
missile that hit the Pentagon.*

The point of mentioning the smart missiles in use during Gulf War I is to
bring up the subject of the *guidance system* that was available even at that
time. We notice in the above reports that the circumstances of the strike
even led some witnesses to describe what hit the Pentagon as a helicopter,
but there were so many reports of a plane that we should hypothesize that
it was a plane-like object, even if it was a plane that could "fly like a
helicopter".

Once I realized that the description of the smart missile maneuvers
exactly fit what happened at the Pentagon, the question that occurred to
me was: *Could such a guidance system be used in a plane?* Even

commercial jetliners? If they could do this with missiles back in the 1990s, what have they done in the more than ten years since with such a system?

"Radar shows Flight 77 did a downward spiral, turning almost a complete circle and dropping the last 7,000 feet in two-and-a-half minutes. The steep turn was *so smooth,* the sources say, it's clear there was no fight for control going on. And the complex maneuver suggests the hijackers had better flying skills than many investigators first believed."[123]

Consider the "Universal Replacement Autopilot Program" (URAP)[124] (See Plate 3)

"A system designed to be installed in guided missiles or unmanned aircraft. There are two flight options available to the operator of an aerial vehicle with such a device installed: programmed flight and manual flight. In either flight mode the operator maintains full control over the vehicle and its trajectory including the ability for "instant recovery" from any unexpected divergence from the flight path, control over any payloads that the vehicle is carrying, "mission selection" (i.e. the mission can be aborted at any time) "manual takeover" (if programmed flight has been chosen) and "return to automatic" (if manual flight has been chosen) not to mention a host of other options to control just about every aspect of the vehicle and its trajectory."

In fact, the capabilities of the "Universal Replacement Autopilot" guidance system seem to describe very well the behavior of this anomalous 757 that struck the Pentagon.

As we have seen from the news reports, the *very first descriptions* - before the stories began to change to support the "official" announcements - repeated that something *smaller than a 757 was seen to strike the Pentagon.*

"I was convinced it was a missile. It came in so fast it sounded nothing like an airplane", said Lou Rains[125]

"It just was amazingly precise", Daryl Donley, another commuter, said of the plane's impact. "It completely disappeared into the Pentagon."[126]

''The plane came in at an incredibly steep angle with incredibly high speed',' said Rick Renzi. - *Pittsburg 11 News*[127]

This certainly creates some confusion. What can we make of it? Can the early witnesses be trusted more than the ones who came forward later, after having watched the shocking impact of commercial jetliners on the World Trade Center, over and over and over again on television and after hearing the repeated assurances that a Boeing hit the Pentagon as well?

We must certainly consider that it is altogether possible that such repeated exposure to the WTC event by the media could create certain

---

[123] http://www.cbsnews.com/stories/2001/09/11/national/main310721.shtml

[124] http://www.dtic.mil/ndia/air/bruns.pdf

[125] http://www.space.com/news/rains_september11-1.html

[126] http://www.delawareonline.com/newsjournal/local/2001/09/12terrorspreadsto.html

[127] http://www.pittsburgh.com/partners/wpxi/news/pentagonattack.html

synaptic maps of the event that were then overlaid on the Pentagon event by simple suggestion. We go into this in more detail in Part 2 of the book.

One of the ramifications is, of course, that many of the witnesses who later said they saw a commercial airliner are, in fact, convinced that that is what they saw, although we do not discount the possibility that a certain number of them are lying to protect their jobs or because they are being paid to spread disinformation. Remember the early reports of a helicopter, a truck bomb, small planes, etc., that were then followed by "official reports" or reports from government authorities that it was Flight 77, after which more "eyewitnesses came forward" with new and different stories that supported the "official versions".

One of our researchers looked into this problem and wrote:

> "Some witnesses said they saw a commuter plane, and others like Army Captain Lincoln Liebner, (who may have had an agenda) said he saw a large American Airlines passenger jet. Now such confusion at any accident scene is understandable. What is more, with the craft going 460 mph, added to the shock of it all, it was probably hard to tell what they really saw.
>
> Of the things that didn't make sense however were the many reports that *the object hit the ground*, when *we know from the photos that it didn't*. Something that was supposed to be as big as a 757 was certainly flying low enough to clip light poles yet it didn't scrape the ground? Something is wrong with that picture.
>
> Some eyewitnesses even claimed they saw people on the plane and faces in windows!"

The many confused descriptions - confused even while declaring it to be a commercial jet - lead us to believe that as long as they could see it with their eyes, it registered as being a passenger plane of some sort. And, even though the propaganda machine tells us that it was supposed to be a huge plane, it was obvious from the descriptive terms used by the witnesses - and by the evidence on the ground - that this was not the case - even if the "impression" was. The descriptions, when taken all together, are full of Cognitive Dissonance. What we do notice was those who did *not see* the plane, but were still close by and experienced something of the effects of the event, had most peculiar "impressions" related to the sound.

> "At that moment *I heard a very loud, quick whooshing sound* that began behind me and stopped suddenly in front of me and to my left. In fractions of a second I heard the impact and an explosion. *The next thing I saw was the fireball.*"[128]

Steve Patterson, 43, said he was watching television reports of the World Trade Center being hit when he saw *a silver commuter jet* fly past the window of his 14th-floor apartment in Pentagon City.

---

[128] http://www.space.com/news/rains_september11-1.html

"The plane was about 150 yards away, approaching from the west *about 20 feet off the ground*, Patterson said. He said the plane, which *sounded like the high-pitched squeal of a fighter jet*, flew over Arlington cemetery so low that he thought it was going to land on I-395.

It was flying so fast that he couldn't read any writing on the side. *The plane, which appeared to hold about eight to 12 people*, headed straight for the Pentagon but was flying as if coming in for a landing on a nonexistent runway, Patterson said.

"At first I thought 'God, there's a plane truly misrouted from National,' Then this thing just became part of the Pentagon ... I was watching the World Trade Center go and then this. What's next?"

He said the plane, which *approached the Pentagon below treetop level*, seemed to be flying normally for a plane coming in for a landing other than going very fast for being so low."

Then, he said, he saw the Pentagon "envelope" the plane and bright orange flames shoot out the back of the building.[129]

In the above report, we not only have a witness who says the plane looked like a "silver commuter jet", he also said that the plane *sounded* like the "high-pitched squeal" of a fighter jet.

"*I was right underneath the plane*", said Kirk Milburn, a construction supervisor for Atlantis Co., who was on the Arlington National Cemetery exit of Interstate 395 when he said he saw the plane heading for the Pentagon.

"I heard a plane. I saw it. I saw debris flying."[130]

Here he said he saw the plane heading for the Pentagon, and *because he saw it* he also said, "I heard a plane. I saw it. I saw debris flying".

What he said next, however, is not in keeping with a 757: "I guess it was hitting light poles", said Milburn. "It was like a *whoosh whoosh*, then there was fire and smoke, then I heard a *second explosion.*"

Notice that the witness says, "I *guess* it was hitting the light poles". One suspects that he couldn't see it if he was guessing. What is most interesting is that he said, "It was like a WHOOOSH whoosh, then there was fire and smoke, then I heard a *second explosion*".

Two early, primary witnesses have described a sound of a "whoosh"! The second one, when he couldn't see it, said it was like a "WHOOSH whoosh", just like the other man who couldn't see it, but then he has also told us that he saw a plane and heard a plane. But what he described was most definitely *not* a 757 flying low over his head.

A 757, under *no* circumstances makes a sound of "whoosh", and if the "whoosh" sound was being made by the hitting of light poles, it is a certainty that if a 757 was doing it, you would not hear the "whoosh" of

---

[129] http://www.washingtonpost.com/wp-srv/metro/daily/sep01/attack.html
[130] http://www.washingtonpost.com/wp-srv/metro/daily/sep01/attack.html

hitting light poles over the roar of the jet engines. If there's a 757 right overhead that's hitting light poles, and it's going 460 mph, it would not be "whooshing"! Anyone that has ever spent any time at the end of an international airport runway knows that the sound of a large commercial jet flying low overhead would be more accurately described as a deafening ROAR!

In short, if a 757 was low enough to hit light poles, it should have blown the witnesses' eardrums out along with everything else in the engine's way, not to mention the fact that the jet blast can literally blow cars off the road.

Another problem with this part of the story is the following comments from a resident of the DC area:

> "I live in the DC area, and the street lights are not very tall. In fact DC is a very "treed" city. Many of the trees are taller than the lamp posts. [...] If the wings of a 757 were hitting the lamp posts, the engines would be driven into the ground, provided that the plane was in a straight and level position."

The exhaust of those huge engines - that would necessarily be *scraping the ground if they are hitting light poles* - is like a supersonic cannon! The vortex and power of the exhaust would have produced an experience that is unmistakable - impressive beyond words - and hard to forget.

Take a look at the engine of a 757-200. There are two of them and they hang lower than the plane itself. (See Plate 4)

The interested reader can go to the Boeing website to learn about the jet engine specs, exhaust velocity contours, and so forth.[131]

> According to CBS News: "some eyewitnesses believe the plane actually hit the ground at the base of the Pentagon first, and then *skidded into the building*. Investigators say that's a possibility, which if true, crash experts say may well have saved some lives." [132]

Of course, "officials" have not explained how, in such a case, the Pentagon lawn was left untouched by the *skidding* 115 ton aircraft.

Look again at the photo taken just a few seconds after impact. (Plate 1)

This is the photo that the US government claims shows a 155 feet long, 44 foot high (at the tail) Boeing 757-200 crashing into the Pentagon.

Our question: *Where is it?*

Look at the cable spools that are positioned just to the right of the impact point (in front of the fireball from this view). The spools are approximately 6 feet high and are sitting no more than 20 feet from the Pentagon façade.

Again; where is the plane?

[131] http://www.boeing.com/assocproducts/aircompat/753sec6.pdf (assuming the information has not be scrubbed by the time you read this, as so much data on the internet has been removed since 9-11).
[132] http://www.cbsnews.com/stories/2001/09/11/national/main310721.shtml

Consider a to-scale image of a 757 placed in the hole caused by the collapse of the burning building some time after initial impact. (See Plate 5). The main damage caused was limited to the first ring of the Pentagon.[133] As can be seen from the image, only about 50% of the length of a 757 actually fits into this space. What we would naturally expect to see in the previous photo of the "moment of impact", is, at the very least, some of the remainder of the fuselage, or debris of the wings and the tail of the plane spread across the Pentagon lawn.

But in reality, what do we see?

No trace, whatsoever, of a Boeing 757. No trace, whatsoever, of Flight 77. (See Plate 6)

Among the theories that arose in an attempt to explain these glaring problems with the official story, was the US government suggestion that the aircraft was pulverized instantly when it impacted the reinforced façade of the building, never mind that this contradicts the "skidding" theory which, as CBS News said, "according to crash experts, may well have saved some lives". Later, we were asked to consider the possibility that the aircraft melted (with the exception of one pristine, if mangled) piece of the fuselage that fortuitously was blown onto the Pentagon lawn. (See Plate 7)

As Thierry Meyssan and his colleagues pointed out in their in-depth analysis of the Pentagon crash, *Pentagate*[134], *not even the US Department of Defense claims that this part comes from Flight 77.*

Of course, that just leaves the matter of the body parts that were allegedly identified and which somehow managed to escape the 2500 °C+ fire that we are told melted 100 tons of aircraft metal. Surely if a plane is "vaporized" then the occupants would be vaporized too? Nonetheless, the US government maintains that they were able to identify all of the passengers on Flight 77, *using fingerprints no less*!

The initial hole made by the aircraft was *at the very base of the Pentagon wall*. The *only* way that a 757 could have made this hole would be if it had been *sliding on its belly*, which of course would have left very clear marks in the Pentagon lawn. Look again the picture of the collapsed Pentagon façade above. Do *you* see any evidence of a large commercial airliner having slid along the Pentagon lawn?

A series of photographs taken by an official federal photographer at the Pentagon crash site show what appears to be an easily identifiable piece of a small-diameter turbofan engine. (See Plate 8)

If the government wants to prove that a Boeing 757-200 crashed into the Pentagon, why is no one willing or able to identify which part from which engine this is?

---

[133] Remember, the façade collapsed about twenty minutes after the impact.
[134] Meyssan, Thierry and others, *Pentagate*, Carnot Publishing Ltd;, 2002.

The photographs show a part of a turbofan jet engine and were taken by Jocelyn Augustino, a photographer for the Federal Emergency Management Agency (FEMA), at the Pentagon crash site on September 13, 2001. The round piece appears to be less than 3 feet in diameter and is propped up against what appears to be part of the engine housing and thick pieces of insulating material.

A Boeing 757 has two large engines, which are about 9 feet in diameter and 12 feet in length. A Rolls Royce RB211-535 engine, used on 757 aircraft, has a fan tip diameter of 78.5 inches. Nothing this large is to be seen in the FEMA photographs. The photo ID numbers are 4414 and 4415 and can be seen on-line.[135]

For those who say a smaller plane or unmanned drone, such as a Global Hawk, was involved in the Pentagon attack, identifying the piece in the photo could prove what kind of aircraft hit the building.

The Global Hawk is a singe-engine drone that uses a Rolls Royce Allison engine hand-built in Indianapolis, Indiana. The AE3007H engine has a diameter of 43.5 inches. The *unmanned* Global Hawk, using a satellite guidance system, is capable of landing *within 12 inches of its programmed destination.*

Several investigators suggested that the disk was from the auxiliary power unit (APU) mounted in the tail section of a Boeing 757.

Christopher Bollyn of *American Free Press* undertook the task of trying to find out what exactly this disk was. He called Honeywell's Aerospace division in Phoenix, Ariz., where the GTCP331-200 APU used on the 757 aircraft is made:

"There's no way that's an APU wheel", an expert at Honeywell told AFP.

The expert, who cannot be named, added: "That turbine disc—there's no way in the world that came out of an APU".

Bollyn then contacted John W. Brown, spokesman for Rolls Royce (Indianapolis), asking if the disk was from a Rolls Royce manufactured engine, perhaps the AE3007H used in the Global Hawk. Brown's response was:

"It is not a part from any Rolls Royce engine that I'm familiar with, and certainly not the AE 3007H made here in Indy."

Next Bollyn called Pratt & Whitney who manufactures parts of the 757's turbofan jet engines:

"If the aircraft that struck the Pentagon was a Boeing 757-200 owned by American Airlines, then it would have to be a Rolls Royce engine", Mark Sullivan, spokesman for Pratt & Whitney, told AFP.

Bollyn then contacted John W. Brown, spokesman for Rolls Royce once more, to inform him that the Pratt & Whitney spokesperson had stated that

---

[135] www.photolibrary.fema.gov/ photolibrary/advancedsearch.do

it must be a piece of a Rolls Royce engine. At this point Brown balked and asked who at Pratt & Whitney had provided the information.

Asked again if the disc in the photo was a piece of a Rolls Royce RB211-535, or from the AE 3007 series, Brown said he could not answer.

Bollyn then *asked Brown if he was actually familiar with the parts of an AE 3007H, which is made at the Indiana plant: "No", Brown said. "I don't build the engines. I am a spokesman for the company. I speak for the company."*

Bollyn states:

"Rolls Royce produces the RB211-535 engines for American Airlines 757-200 aircraft at a plant in Derby, England. Martin Johnson, head of communications at Rolls Royce in Derby, said he had followed the story closely in *American Free Press* and had also been notified in advance by Rolls Royce offices in Seattle and Indianapolis.

However, rather than address the question of the unidentified disc, Johnson launched a verbal attack on this reporter for questioning the government version of events at the Pentagon on 9-11. 'You are the only person in the world who does not believe that a 757 hit the Pentagon', Johnson said. 'The idea that we can have a reasonable conversation is beyond your wildest dreams', Johnson said and hung up the phone."[136]

The conclusion then is that the engine disk in the FEMA photos is probably *too small to be part of a 757 engine and it is definitely NOT a part of a 757's APU*. So what is it? It could very well be part of a Global Hawk AE3007H engine. To date however, no one has been able to confirm or deny this.

Because the Global Hawk is a *surveillance drone*, the engine is contained in a heavily insulated housing to be *extremely quiet*. This corresponds with eyewitness reports. American Free Press asked eyewitness Steve Riskus, who said he was within 100 feet of the aircraft, what he heard. He said he *"did not recall hearing anything"*. As noted previously, if a 757 or jet fighter flew at high speed 100 feet from an eyewitness the sound would be deafening.

The important thing is, if you have ever seen a 757 up close, the main words you will use - even if it passes you at 460 mph - are "humongous", or "gigantic" - words along that line. You will also - even at a distance - be overwhelmed by the noise of the jet engines. Yet, over and over again, even those who later *named* the object that hit the Pentagon as a "commercial airliner", used descriptive terms that are quite different from those that would have been used if a real 757 had been the impacting object. This could easily be a consequence of the "memory making" process discussed further on.

136

http://www.americanfreepress.net/10_10_03/Controversy_Swirling/controversy_swirling.html

The fact is, until the spin control machine had done its work, except for a few government officials, most of the witness' descriptive terms are more in keeping with descriptions of *something other than a Boeing 757*.

Witnesses who saw only one plane fall into two distinct groups, each seeing a different plane, on a different path, at different altitude, with different sound, at different speeds. *A third set of witnesses saw two planes approach the Pentagon and one of these veer away.*

Many heard a jet; others heard a missile (all military men). Those near Flight 77 as it came over the cemetery, saw it and *heard it pass silently* (no engine); whereas those near the killer jet which came by the freeway and knocked down the lamp posts *heard its loud scream as it put on speed* to reach the wall as an airliner flew over it.

Nevertheless, again we say, we do *not* think it was a missile that struck the Pentagon: *we are certain that it was a plane* - it had wings - it knocked over poles on the incoming trajectory, and it maneuvered "like a smart missile". Furthermore, we know that there is a "guidance system" that has the capability of doing exactly what this object was described to have done even if the system was loaded into something other than a missile. *The average cruise missile is far too small* (about 20 feet long with a wingspan of just 8 feet) to be a realistic contender for the Pentagon plane *and is therefore ruled out.*

One problem with the idea that it was an UAV like the Global Hawk that impacted the Pentagon is how to explain the damage that *was* inflicted not only to the façade but to 3 rings of the Pentagon. Whatever hit the Pentagon created a hole of approximately 15 feet across in the façade and extensive damage to the first floor of the first ring (as evidenced from previous photographs) which eventually collapsed. While the size of the hole and the limited overall damage is not consistent with a Boeing 757, neither is it consistent with an aircraft the size of a Global Hawk.

The Global Hawk is 44 feet long with a wingspan of 115 feet and a tail height of 15 feet and, *alone*, it could not have caused the damage to the Pentagon. (See Plate 9)

One of the most intriguing aspects of the Pentagon attack was the round hole that was left in ring C. (See Plate 10)

Bizarrely, the US government claims that an engine of a 757 made this hole, yet as we have seen, remains of the engine of the aircraft that hit the Pentagon were found at the *front* of the building and possibly in the first ring that sustained the main force of the impact, *not* in the third ring where clearly *something* else must have punched out this hole. Whatever it was, it had enough force to breech the main reinforced steel concrete outer wall and then travel some 250 feet, *passing through five other double-brick walls on the way.* In fact, Terry Mitchell, Chief of the Office of the Assistant Secretary of Defense (Public Affairs) was one of the first on the scene at this "punch out" point. In a DOD news briefing about the reconstruction of the Pentagon he stated:

> "This is a hole in -- there was a punch-out. They suspect that this was where a part of the aircraft came through this hole, *although I didn't see any evidence of the aircraft down there.*"

Yet later in the same briefing when referring to the same hole he stated:

> "This pile here *is all Pentagon metal. None of that is aircraft whatsoever.* As you can see, they've punched a hole in here. This was punched by the rescue workers to clean it out". [137]

So which was it? Was the hole punched out by some part of the aircraft or by rescue workers? Look again at the picture of the hole. We don't need the contradictory statements of Mr. Mitchell to conclude that the hole was punched out from the inside, yet how could it have been "punched out" by rescue workers when there are *scorch marks* at the top of the hole *on the outside*? Did the rescue workers punch out this hole when the fire was still raging inside?

Hardly likely. Limiting air flow is part of fighting a fire. You don't make holes to let in more air while you are trying to extinguish a fire.

Dare we suggest that the OASD chief was lying that day? He changed his story because the "official" version of events did not include the idea that part of the aircraft made that hole, because it is inconceivable that any part of a 757 could have done so.

So what did?

While the Global Hawk is an unmanned reconnaissance plane, an article from 2002 on the Center for Defense Information (CDI) web site stated that initial designs for the craft included the possibility for it to carry "three to six missiles". [138]

Eyewitness to the Pentagon attack and Pentagon worker Don Perkal, was on the scene within minutes:

> "Even before stepping outside *I could smell the cordite.* Then I knew explosives had been set off somewhere."

He also stated:

> "Hundreds of F.B.I., Secret Service and Defense Department plainclothes investigators were deployed in the parking lot, *recording witness statements.*"[139]

Another eyewitness, Gilah Goldsmith said:

> "We saw a huge black cloud of smoke", adding that it *smelled like cordite*, or gun smoke.[140]

---

[137] http://www.defenselink.mil/transcripts/2001/t09152001_t915evey.html

[138] http://www.cdi.org/missile-defense/uav.cfm

[139] http://www.mcsweeneys.net/2001/09/19perkal.html We would like to note here that this gave the FBI and other intell agencies a list of names and the capability of "leaning" on witnesses to ensure that they would say what they were "supposed" to say.

Witnesses inside the Pentagon, mostly military men, described *a shockwave and a blast*. The problem is that *only explosives create a shockwave*; there is no shockwave from a crash and fire. *The Washington Post* ran a story where it was stated:

"Air Force Lt. Col. Marc Abshire, 40, a speechwriter for Air Force Secretary James Roche, was working on several speeches this morning when he felt the blast of the explosion at the Pentagon. His office is on the D ring, near the eighth corridor, he said. "It shot me back in my chair. There was a huge blast. *I could feel the air shock wave of it*", Abshire said. "I didn't know exactly what it was. It didn't rumble. It was more of a direct smack."[141]

Donald R. Bouchoux, 53, a retired Naval officer, a Great Falls resident, a Vietnam veteran and former commanding officer of a Navy fighter squadron, was driving west from Tysons Corner to the Pentagon for a 10am meeting. He wrote:

"At 9:40 a.m. I was driving down Washington Boulevard (Route 27) along the side of the Pentagon when the aircraft crossed about 200 yards (should be more than 150 yards from the impact) in front of me and impacted the side of the building. There was an enormous fireball, followed about two seconds later by debris raining down. *The car moved about a foot to the right when the shock wave hit.*"

John Bowman, a retired Marine lieutenant colonel and a contractor, was in his office in Corridor Two near the main entrance to the south parking lot. "Everything was calm", Bowman said. *"Most people knew it was a bomb.* Everyone evacuated smartly. We have a good sprinkling of military people who have been shot at."[142]

Stars and Stripes reporter Lisa Burgess was walking on the Pentagon's innermost corridor, across the courtyard, when the incident happened. "I heard two loud booms - one large, one smaller, and *the shock wave threw me against the wall*", she said.[143]

Lon Rains, an editor of Space.com, was also an eyewitness to the Pentagon attack. He commented:

"In light traffic the drive up Interstate 395 from Springfield to downtown Washington takes no more than 20 minutes. But that morning, like many others, the traffic slowed to a crawl just in front of the Pentagon. With the Pentagon to the left of my van at about 10 o'clock on the dial of a clock, I glanced at my watch to see if I was going to be late for my appointment. At that moment I *heard a very loud, quick whooshing sound* that began behind me and stopped suddenly in front of me and to my left. In fractions of a second I heard the impact and an explosion. The next thing I saw was the

---

140

http://web.archive.org/web/20021116175404/http://www.jewishsf.com/bk010921/usp14a.shtml

[141] http://www.washingtonpost.com/wp-srv/metro/daily/sep01/attack.html

[142] http://www.dcmilitary.com/army/pentagram/6_37/local_news/10380-1.html

[143] http://www.pstripes.com/01/sep01/ed091201i.html

fireball. *I was convinced it was a missile.* It came in so fast *it sounded nothing like an airplane.*"[144]

While these testimonies are intriguing, eyewitness accounts of any major incident, particularly one as shocking as the Pentagon attack, are notoriously unreliable. Yet the fact remains that, even without them, the actual observable damage at the Pentagon leads us to conclude that some kind of explosive charge or hardened warhead was used to do the damage. A warhead that was very probably carried and released just seconds before impact, by an unmanned Global Hawk aircraft painted up in AA colors, complete with fake windows, just for good measure. (See Plate 11)

There were at least *four video cameras capable of recording the attack on the Pentagon.* One was on the roof of the Sheraton Hotel, a second was at a gas station across the road from the Pentagon itself, the third belonged to the Virginia Department of Transportation and was stationed on route 27, which the aircraft flew over. The fourth was the Pentagon's security camera stationed at the opposite one end of the façade from where the plane struck.

The footage from the cameras at the Sheraton, the gas station and on route 27 were confiscated by the FBI and have never been released.

The only footage made available to the public was that recorded by the Pentagon's security camera.

Plate 12 shows the first still from the only video footage of the Pentagon attack released by the US government. According to the U.S. government, it shows an approaching Boeing 757 in the upper right hand corner.

If we think back to the images and video footage of Flight 11 and Flight 175 hitting the WTC towers, we remember that we all saw both large Boeing 767 airplanes, as clear as day, even though they were flying at over 500 mph and were over 1,000 feet up in the air when they struck the WTC Towers. This provides us with an excellent guide on how such commercial aircraft appear at that distance. The side of the Pentagon is 971 feet long and the plane in the footage is no more than 750 feet (250yards) from the camera that is stationed near the opposite end of the Pentagon. Remember the indelible images of those huge planes flying into the World Trade Center towers? Even at that distance, even with the size of the WTC towers, the image and size of the aircraft that was burned into our minds from having seen the tapes replayed endlessly is awe-inspiring.

So, look again at the image from the Pentagon Security camera of the plane approaching the building (Plate 12).

Again we must ask the question: where is the Boeing 757-200 in this image?

Next time you are at an airport, take five minutes and go and look at some planes on the runway. Pick out a large passenger jet that is

---

[144] http://www.space.com/news/rains_september11-1.html

approximately 750 feet away, preferably one in the process of taking off or landing. Take a picture of it. Then think about this image from the Pentagon Security camera again and ask yourself.

Where *is* that Boeing 757?!

Now look at a close up. (See Plate 13)

Do you see a Boeing 757-200 in this picture?

If a Boeing 757 really did hit the Pentagon, it would stick out like, well… like a Boeing 757 in this footage, (see plate 14) *but the simple and obvious fact is that there is no Boeing 757 there.*

In fact, there is no plane of *any* description in the footage released by the Pentagon.

Note that the time stamp (Plate 14) displays a date and time of *September 12th at 5.37:19pm.* The DOD *has offered no reason for this discrepancy.* In the footage, the progression of seconds jumps from 19, where it starts, to 21 and then on to 22 and 23 where it ends.

What is clear from the *3 seconds of footage* is that one second and several frames have been cut from the film.

No explanation has ever been offered by the DOD or the US government as to why this video footage has clearly been "doctored", why one second and several frames have been removed – frames that would likely show just what it was that struck the Pentagon.

What we do see in the above image is a stream of white smoke that is *entirely inconsistent with a commercial jet aircraft at ground level* and much more in line with the trail left by a missile launch (See Plate 15), even if we keep repeating that something *more* than a "missile" struck the Pentagon.

As it happens, a correspondent of the author[145] had an interesting encounter on a train that goes along with the story about the military transport plane that so "luckily" spotted the "Boeing". In his own words:

"I met a gentleman that was of Jamaican descent who said he was an artist by trade. He was heading back home to Washington. I have no reason to doubt the man's story as he seemed very sincere and told it "as a matter of fact".

He said that when he heard on the radio of his car about the WTC event that the tension around the capital was rising, he was on his cell phone talking to other people while he drove. *He was in viewing distance of the Pentagon at the time of the attack and he saw two planes in the air,* one of them being a "small commuter type jet" but he didn't ID the other plane. He said *it was this smaller plane that hit the Pentagon*, so it could have been laced with explosives and remote controlled in by that other plane (there were reports of a C-130 in the area)."

Summing up the eyewitness reports and the available photographic evidence, we see that *there is nothing that supports the official story's*

---

[145] LKJ

claim that Flight 77 hit the Pentagon except the claims of the Bush Administration who have repeatedly been exposed as liars and manipulators, and the later "eyewitness reports" of people whose names and addresses were immediately compiled into a list by the FBI, Secret Service, and other intel units on the scene.

The early eyewitness reports that came out before the official story began to be trumpeted via the media are consistent with the object having been a plane much smaller than Flight 77, such as a drone loaded with explosives. The reports were made before "damage control" was firmly in place, and this damage control either served to influence and change people's perceptions, or compelled them to change their stories. The reports that it was a commercial jet only emerged later - hours later, even.

The claim that Flight 77 hit the Pentagon is extremely suspect for another reason: as previously noted, there is *no proof* that the plane that disappeared from radar over Southern Ohio actually "turned around" and headed back for Washington. A *Washington Post* article discusses the thirty minutes of complete Radar Invisibility. The report says, in part:

> "The aircraft, traveling from Dulles International Airport to Los Angeles, was hijacked sometime between 8:50 a.m. -- when air traffic controllers made their last routine contact with the pilot -- and 8:56, when hijackers turned off the transponder, which reports the plane's identity, altitude and speed to controllers' radar screens. The airliner crashed into the Pentagon at 9:38 a.m., about 12 minutes after controllers at Dulles sounded an alert that an unidentified aircraft was headed toward Washington at high speed. [...]

> With no signal on their radar screens, controllers did not realize that Flight 77 had reversed direction.

> At 9:09 a.m., unable to reach the plane by radio, the Indianapolis controller reported a possible crash, sources said.

> The first time that anyone became aware an aircraft was headed at high speed toward Washington was when the hijacked flight began descending and entered airspace controlled by the Dulles International Airport TRACON facility, an aviation source said.

> The first Dulles controller noticed the fast-moving plane at 9:25 a.m. Moments later, controllers sounded an alert that an aircraft appeared to be headed directly toward the White House. It later turned and hit the Pentagon."[146]

See Plate 16.

The report from the *Washington Post* also contradicts other reports which said that the radios transmitted sounds of voices with Arabic accents making threatening sounds.

---

[146] http://www.washingtonpost.com/ac2/wp-dyn?pagename=article&node&contentId=A32597-2001Nov2

"Unlike at least two of the other aircraft, whose pilots apparently held radios open so controllers could hear the hijackers, there was only silence from Flight 77."

However, one must take the other stories of hijacker voices with a grain of salt. There is no proof that the 19 Arab men alleged to have committed this crime were ever on the planes.

The nexus of fantasy and reality

What then are we to make of the many calls that were alleged to have been made by passengers of the doomed flights citing "Arab hijackers", most notably the call by the wife of former Solicitor General Bob Olson, Barbara Olson? (We'll get back to her in a moment.)Firstly, it has been effectively demonstrated scientifically that it is extremely difficult to make cell phone calls from above 8,000 feet. Almost all the alleged cell phone calls were claimed to have been made from well above this height. We aren't going to discard the idea that some cell phone calls did make it through, but expert opinion within the wireless telecom industry casts serious doubt on the likelihood that many of the calls could have been made. According to Alexa Graf, a spokesman of AT&T, commenting in the immediate wake of the 9/11 attacks,

> "It was almost a fluke that the [9/11] calls reached their destinations... From high altitudes, the call quality is not very good, and most callers will experience drops. Although calls are not reliable, *callers can pick up and hold calls for a little while below a certain altitude*".[147]

Ted Olson claimed that his wife made two calls from Flight 77 telling of the "Arabs" conducting the hijacking.

> "She [Barbara] had trouble getting through, because *she wasn't using her cell phone* – she was *using the phone in the passengers' seats*", said Mr Olson. "I guess she didn't have her purse, because *she was calling collect*, and she was trying to get through to the Department of Justice, which is never very easy." ... "She wanted to know 'What can I tell the pilot? What can I do? How can I stop this?'"

The problem with this account is, if Mrs. Olson had neither her cell phone nor her credit card with her, she could not possibly have made a call to anyone because a credit card is required before ANY connection from the satellite phones in airline passenger seats can be made.

The 9/11 Commission yet again, completely overlooked all of these facts. We aren't saying that Barbara Olson did not call her husband, but we will come to that issue soon.

So if some of the calls could have been real, and some could have been faked, how can that be?

---

[147] http://wirelessreview.com/ar/wireless_final_contact

Consider a 1999 report in the *Washington Post* entitled, "When Seeing and Hearing Isn't Believing", where it was stated:

> "'Gentlemen! We have called you together to inform you that we are going to overthrow the United States government.' So begins a statement being delivered by Gen. Carl W. Steiner, former Commander-in-chief, U.S. Special Operations Command.
>
> At least the voice sounds amazingly like him.
>
> But it is not Steiner. It is the result of voice "morphing" technology developed at the Los Alamos National Laboratory in New Mexico.
>
> By taking just a 10-minute digital recording of Steiner's voice, scientist George Papcun is able, in near real time, to clone speech patterns and develop an accurate facsimile. Steiner was so impressed, he asked for a copy of the tape.
>
> Steiner was hardly the first or last victim to be spoofed by Papcun's team members. To refine their method, they took various high quality recordings of generals and experimented with creating fake statements. One of the most memorable is Colin Powell stating, 'I am being treated well by my captors.'
>
> *'Once you can take any kind of information and reduce it into ones and zeros, you can do some pretty interesting things',* says Daniel T. Kuehl, chairman of the Information Operations department of the National Defense University in Washington, the military's school for information warfare.
>
> Digital morphing — voice, video, and photo — has come of age, available for use in psychological operations. PSYOPS, as the military calls it, *seek to exploit human vulnerabilities in enemy governments, militaries and populations to pursue national and battlefield objectives.*
>
> To some, PSYOPS is a backwater military discipline of leaflet dropping and radio propaganda. To a growing group of information war technologists, *it is the nexus of fantasy and reality. Being able to manufacture convincing audio or video, they say, might be the difference in a successful military operation or coup."*[148]

"The nexus of fantasy and reality" indeed. Given the scope and depth of the conspiracy with which we are dealing, it is entirely possible that the cell phone calls that were made from the planes on 9/11 - *if* those reporting them are sincere and believe they received such calls - were actually the result of a 'real time' application of this *voice morphing technology.*

Who could forget the rousing reports of the "soldier citizens" on Flight 93 who courageously decided to "do something" about the hijackers with the words "let's roll"?

One of those involved was Mark Bingham, a California PR executive. According to his mother, Bingham called her to tell her that his flight had been hijacked. Bizarrely however, the very first words that Bingham said

---

[148]http://www.washingtonpost.com/wpsrv/national/dotmil/arkin020199.htm

to his mother, with whom he was very close by all accounts, were, "hi mom, this is Mark Bingham."[149]

The only other words he said before hanging up were, "I love you".[150]

Now think about this: Why would anyone use their full name when calling their mother?? Would you, in a similar circumstance, call your mother and announce your full name? Really stop and think about it a moment. Could this small and seemingly innocuous detail in fact, be an example of one of the many flaws in the cover-up plans of the conspirators?

Since we keep facing this type of thing, over and over again, on that day of "incredible coincidences" that are off the scale of mathematical probability, it's time to stop thinking about "coincidences", and amazing flukes, and violations of the laws of physics, and start thinking about what really happened on 9-11: a coup d'état.

The bottom line is, there are just too many problems with the Pentagon attack that indicate that it could not have been a Boeing 757 that plowed into the building. This leads us to the most interesting questions.

If it was not a Boeing 757 that hit the Pentagon, why is the Bush administration so assuredly declaring that it was, and attacking anyone who questions that story with the slur of "conspiracy theorist", rather than providing the evidence that it was Flight 77 for the public to examine themselves? We notice that very few items of so-called "conspiracy theory" have rattled the "Bushes" quite like our *Pentagon Strike* Flash did. The Pentagon Strike video came out on August 23rd 2004. Probably nobody really noticed it at that point, but it hit a chord of response in the hearts of millions of people around the world. They began to madly download and forward it to their friends and relatives. Latest stats on how many people have viewed it to date are 500 million!

Apparently it even landed in the email box of the Editor of the *Washington Post*, which is why Carol Morello sent me an email asking for an interview. Or so she said. My suspicion was that the Post was instructed to do "damage control", albeit oh, so gently!

Now, look at this mini-timeline:

August 23rd 2004: Pentagon Strike Video which propagates wildly for a month.

September 21st 2004: First contact by Carol Morello of the *Washington Post*

October 7th 2004: *Washington Post* article[151]

October 19th 2004: George Bush visits New Port Richey[152] - a previously unscheduled "whistle-stop" on his campaign trail. NPR just happens to be my hometown.

---

[149] http://www.markbingham.org/legend.html
[150] http://www.guardian.co.uk/september11/story/0,11209,610356,00.html
[151] http://www.washingtonpost.com/wp-dyn/articles/A13059-2004Oct6.html

It was an interesting situation to know that if they hadn't seen the Pentagon Strike before, certainly George and Dick, Karl and the gang were watching it after the *Washington Post* wrote an article about it.

My initial feeling was that Dubya's visit to my little home town - certainly of *no* importance on the campaign trail - was deliberately done to send a message to me. Fact is, my daughter's ex-boyfriend wrote to tell her that he had been among those selected to shake the hand of George W. himself! Now, how's that for a coincidence?

As to exactly what Carol Morello wrote to me, here is the pertinent passage which is actually quite revealing:

> "A couple of editors here saw the video/film, and I was asked to find out what I could about it.
>
> As you can imagine, we continue to have an intense interest on the attack on the Pentagon and the people who were affected.
>
> I've just begun reporting, so it would be premature to tell you what "perspective" my story would have. My initial impressions are that *the questions and theories expressed in the video got a spurt of attention in early 2002, after the publication of a best selling book in France, then the furor died down for a while, and now they have re-emerged with the extraordinarily wide dissemination of this video on the Internet.*
>
> The 911 Commission report appears to have done little to dampen the controversy. I hoped to speak to you about how and why you posted it on your web site, what kind of response you've received and what you think about it." […]

Notice that she attributes the resurgence of interest in the "Pentagate" problem to the Pentagon Strike video.

Can we say "damage control"?

And if there is damage control, then that means there is damage.

Up to this point in time, the only acknowledgement the administration ever gave to such issues was to refer vaguely and dismissively to "conspiracy theories". Now, suddenly, it seems that dealing with the "conspiracy theories" in a direct manner was seen to be imperative. "9/11: Debunking the Myths"[153] came out in *Popular Mechanics Magazine* in March of 2005, just five months after the *Washington Post* article. That's pretty fast work!

Under the tutelage of Editor in Chief Jim "Oh look, a tank!" Meigs, Popular Mechanics assembled a team of researchers, including "professional fact checkers" (impressive eh?) to debunk the 16 most common claims made by conspiracy theorists about 9/11.

Unsurprisingly, the PM editors claim that, in the end:

---

[152] http://www.sptimes.com/2004/10/20/Decision2004/A_George_Bush_kind_of.shtml
[153] http://www.popularmechanics.com/science/defense/1227842.html?page=1&c=y

"we were able to debunk each of these assertions with hard evidence and a healthy dose of common sense. We learned that a few theories are based on something as innocent as a reporting error on that chaotic day. Others are the byproducts of cynical imaginations that aim to inject suspicion and animosity into public debate."

In fact, a careful analysis of the article shows that at most, just three of the sixteen claims could have been the result of "reporting error", forcing us to assume that, in the razor-like, emotionally unclouded cerebrum of Jim Meigs, at least 13 of the conspiracy claims about 9/11 are the result of "cynical imaginations aiming to inject suspicion and animosity into public debate".

The sad fact is that, while Popular Mechanics claims to be interested in understanding what really happened that day, their rebuttal of sixteen of the most common claims by so-called "conspiracy theorists" about 9/11 isn't worth the $3.57 of server space that it has so far cost them to publish it.

If there is one glaring hole in the arguments put forward by 9/11 conspiracy "debunkers", it is the fact that such people have *never* come up with a reasonable argument to explain *why*, in the wake of 9/11, so many obviously intelligent citizens became gripped by the uncontrollable urge to continually waste their time recklessly and fecklessly "injecting suspicion and animosity into public debate" for no apparent reason. It really is a mystery. Maybe they're trying to take over the world or something.

On the other hand, it doesn't take a degree in psychology to understand the primary motivations of the conspiracy debunkers.

You see, the very last thing that many Americans (and others) *want* to believe is that their government would attack its own people. For 9/11 "debunkers", logic and intellect have *no* part to play in investigating the question of what really happened on 9/11. It's pure emotion all the way.

In the beginning, on the morning of September 11, 2001 we were all united in our emotional reactions: shock, horror, grief - (and not to forget: jubilation from a bunch of Israeli Mossad agents). As the emotion subsided, most went on with their lives, but a few stood on, brows furrowed, scratching their heads. After considerable digging and research, it became obvious that the official story did not satisfactorily answer all of the questions, and the fact that officials were refusing to answer those outstanding questions, gave rise, logically enough, to a "conspiracy theory". Not long thereafter, the debunkers stepped in, *not* because they had the answers to the outstanding questions, but because they had their emotional buttons severely poked by the fact that someone was saying that their government was lying!

Sadly, the editors at PM are no different, and their little fear-inspired rebuttal of 9/11 conspiracy theories is of little actual use to *anyone*, least of all to those who really do want to know the truth of 9/11. Far from approaching the matter with an open mind (which is crucial in any attempt to find the truth), it is clear that *Popular Mechanics'* "professional fact checkers" *began* with the premise that the US government was *not* lying about the main events of 9/11, despite all of the evidence to the contrary.

From there, the objectivity and integrity of their research went sharply downhill as they busied themselves with hunting down the *very same sources that provided the official story* to confirm that the official story was in fact correct. Apparently, in "debunkerland", it is completely reasonable to ask U.S. government representatives to testify that the U.S. government is squeaky clean and then present that evidence as "fact". It is also kosher, we assume, to have a murder suspect double as a credible court's witness in a murder trial.

For those of you who have looked unemotionally at the events of 9/11, it is not unusual to be left wondering how those members of the US government who were clearly complicit in the murder of 3,000 of their own citizens can remain so smug and seemingly self-assured. To find the answer we need look no further than the Jim Meigs' of this world.

You see, it is people like Meigs who lack any love or appreciation for the truth and worship only their subjective view of the world that make it so easy for big government to commit big crime. At present there are millions of Americans and others around the world who, aided by the years of social conditioning and media mind programming, drew a very clear line around what they would and would not believe about their government and country. Most of what was inside the line was "feel good" stuff about "greatest democracy on earth" and other jingoistic nonsense, with perhaps a few admissions that "sometimes bad things happen" and "not everyone is a saint". This mindset provided (and continues to provide) a perfect opportunity for unscrupulous US politicians to literally get away with the murder of which most of the US public refuse to believe they were, and are, capable.

The result is that, for all intents and purposes, today there are two Americas:

- The America of the average American citizen which is little more than a government-provided dream world.

- The real America of the corrupt politicians and the select few who run the country, and much of the rest of the world.

Luckily for the select few, this second, real America just happens to lie outside of what many ordinary Americans are willing or able to believe is possible. Lest anyone think otherwise, the setting up of any accusation against government as being the domain of "conspiracy nuts" is not the result of pure coincidence. Conspiracy theories are as old as the first lie ever told and the subsequent attempts by the liar to avoid exposure. Most people think that "conspiracy theories" are made up by "conspiracy theorists", but the term "conspiracy theory" is most often used by those people who have most to gain from the ridicule of the allegations that are directed at them. The tactic has been used to such great effect over the years that certain high crimes committed by government have become the touchstone by which all other "conspiracies" are measured.

Take the folks at *Popular Mechanics*. In dealing with 9/11 they simply couldn't resist referencing that other most despicable crime committed by a US government - but of course, to them it just another "theory":

> "Don't get me wrong: Healthy skepticism is a good thing. Nobody should take everything they hear--from the government, the media or anybody else--at face value. But in a culture shaped by Oliver Stone movies and "X-Files" episodes, it is apparently getting harder for simple, hard facts to hold their own against elaborate, shadowy theorizing."

Did you catch it? The reference to Oliver Stone can mean only one thing: Jim's "fact checkers" contacted the CIA, and they told him straight up that some bullets really can do magic things.

So far, we have been generous to the people at *Popular Mechanics*. We have assumed that they are simply well-intentioned but misguided souls. However, it appears that there is a more sinister, and dare we say it, "conspiratorial" side to *Popular Mechanics'* "innocent" debunking of 9/11 conspiracy theories. You see, it turns out[154] that one of the main contributors to the article is one Benjamin Chertoff, a cousin of the new Dept. of Homeland Security Chief Michael Chertoff. *American Free Press'* Christopher Bollyn, who dug up the information, also claims that Ben Chertoff's mother was a Mossad agent[155]. While there is, as of yet, no evidence of any working relationship between the two, it is certainly noteworthy that the cousin of the current Homeland Security Chief, (who, in his previous incarnation as head of the Justice Department's criminal division was instrumental in the release of obvious Israeli spies before and after 9/11), happens to be behind a high-profile attempt to debunk 9/11 conspiracy theories.

So if you happen to stop by at the sorry article in question, don't be fooled or intimidated by the word "science" in big bold letters on the *Popular Mechanics* page. In Europe, McDonald's drink cups have the words "I'm loving it" emblazoned across them in various languages, regardless of what you put in them.

Credit by association or juxtaposition is one of the oldest tricks in the book of mass mind programming. Just because "they" say it, doesn't make it so. This simple, logical statement is a salient lesson for us all in these heady days where disinformation masquerades as truth and even "innocent" fun-loving "boys with toys" have become obedient workers in the lie factory.

---

[154] http://www.rense.com/general63/bellchert.htm
[155] http://www.etherzone.com/forum/index.php/topic,3280.msg35630.html#msg35630

According to another 9/11 researcher[156]:

"The editors of *Scientific American* followed in the footsteps of *Popular Mechanics* in exploiting a trusted brand in order to protect the perpetrators of the mass murder of 9/11/01. The column by Michael Shermer in the June, 2005 issue of *Scientific American*, titled *Fahrenheit 2777*, is an attempt to deceive the magazine's readers into dismissing the overwhelming evidence that 9/11 was an inside job without ever looking at that evidence. More specifically, Shermer attempts to inoculate readers against looking at the decidedly scientific refutation of the official story... […]

Shermer's column exhibits many of the same propaganda techniques as the ambitious feature article in the March issue of *Popular Mechanics* by Benjamin Chertoff, for which Shermer professes admiration:

'The single best debunking of this conspiratorial codswallop is in the March issue of *Popular Mechanics*, which provides an exhaustive point-by-point analysis of the most prevalent claims.'

Comparing the two attack pieces is instructive. Both pieces mention a similar range of issues, with Shermer adding Jewish conspiracy rumors and UFOlogists to the mix. Both employ the following three deceptive techniques, but with different emphasis."

Shermer uses an array of deceptive methods to persuade the reader that challenges to the official story of the 9/11 attack are worthy only of ridicule and should not be scrutinized. His primary technique is to use hoaxes and unscientific ideas to "bracket" the valid ideas that he seeks to shield the reader from. That Shermer went to such great lengths to thoroughly misrepresent the painstaking, scientific, evidence-based work of many researchers is a testament to the success of the Pentagon Strike Video! It really stepped on a sore toe.

And that tells us something important, the same thing Carol Morello of the *Washington Post* wrote:

"...the questions and theories expressed in the video got a spurt of attention in early 2002, after the publication of a best selling book in France, then the furor died down for a while, and now they have re-emerged with the extraordinarily wide dissemination of this video on the Internet."

We notice that *never*, in any of the two major "debunking" articles that followed fast on the heels of the Pentagon Strike video, was the video ever even mentioned, nor was our website mentioned. Other books, other researchers, other websites *were* mentioned, but the deliberate avoidance of Signs of The Times - the origin of the Pentagon Strike, was conspicuous.

Again we point out: debunkers are sent in only when damage control is needed. And damage control is only needed when it is thought that there *might* be damage. That means that the Pentagon Strike is understood clearly, in the minds of the perpetrators, to be the weak link in their chain

---

[156] http://911research.wtc7.net/essays/pm/index.html

of lies. Debunkers are sent in *not* to give answers to the outstanding questions, but to push the emotional buttons of the public, to reassure people who really want "a reason to believe" that their government is not lying to them.

Why would George Bush and his gang be so resistant to an *impartial* investigation? (The official investigation cannot be considered impartial. See David Ray Griffin's book *The 9/11 Commission Report: Omissions and Distortions*[157].)

Why was all the evidence of the crime scene immediately destroyed even though the government claims that "their experts" were taking care of everything?

Why can't we see the various films of the event that certainly exist from numerous security cameras in the area?

Why is the public denied full access to all the information about the crime? After all, if the perpetrator of a crime has been identified - as the Bush Administration certainly claims is so - there should be nothing about the crime scene that would need to be withheld in order to catch the criminal, right?

If there is so much *certainty* about the perpetrators, why not let the public know all the details that prove the perfidy of the guilty?

If Islamic Fundamentalists with burning hatred in their hearts for the Great Satan, the United States, had (or have) the ability to pull off something on the scale of the attacks of September 11, *where's the beef?* Show us! Inspire us to stand behind the government in going out and taking care of such evildoers! If their claims are true, it could only help the Administration's case to release the evidence, right?

So why all the stonewalling, all the backpedaling, debunking and secrecy? If actions are undertaken in good faith with the honest purpose of discovering the truth, there is no need for carefully guarded secrecy. In such circumstances, *only the guilty seek the darkness of secrecy to hide their crimes.*

The whole thing has been so "managed", so quickly "figured out" and cleaned up and put away, that it stinks to high heaven of a "sales job".

Can it be that the public has been "sold" an answer - the answer that the Bush Administration wants them to believe and has arranged, with the complicity of the mass media, to outshout any other explanation? And if they can't outshout them, to smear them, to marginalize them, to defame them, to out them, and perhaps, even to murder them?

Many citizens of the United States did not seem to have any problem at all believing that some crazed Islamic fundies hijacked four planes in the Most Powerful Nation on Earth, flew them around for extended periods of

---

[157] http://www.amazon.com/exec/obidos/tg/detail/-/1566565847/qid=1126095008/sr=2-2/ref=pd_bbs_b_2_2/104-8233846-1640731?v=glance&s=books

time, flew two of them into the World Trade Center Towers, and that North America's entire air defense simply failed. So why stonewall on the evidence?

But, let's assume that's what happened. Let's also give the Administration the benefit of the doubt about their hurried naming of the perpetrators and their too quick destruction of the crime scene.[158] Let's assume that their experts did handle everything well, and they just have some psychological need for secrecy, or that there *is* some compelling reason to stonewall a proper investigation.

We are still faced with the sticking point here: hypothesizing that somebody went to the trouble to arrange for a couple big jets to hit the World Trade Center, and the public was shown the films of these jets hitting said buildings over and over again, *why was the attack on the Pentagon so "different" in scope and evidence, most particularly the absence of repeatedly showing the attack on television?*

Why can't we see the surveillance videos of the same type of commercial jet hitting the Pentagon?

We are stuck with a marvelous conundrum. If no 757 hit the Pentagon, why is the government claiming it did? After all, if they can sell the rest of the flimsy story, and if something *other* than Flight 77 hit the Pentagon, there is no reason they couldn't have cooked up a story to back that fact up. If Osama bin Laden, from his cave in Afghanistan, could so "coincidentally" do the *real* thing on the very day that all the military exercises simulating hijacked airliners was being run so that his operation was hidden from the U.S. defense under that smokescreen, there is no reason to not propose that he could also have gotten his hands on some kind of military craft to strike the Pentagon.

Let's assume that it *was* a smaller, or different type of plane that hit the Pentagon. No matter who was behind the events, if they did not use a 757 to strike the pentagon, *why?*

If they (whoever "they" are) were able to commandeer large airliners for the WTC, why not use one for the Pentagon? Certainly, if it was Osama and gang, they would probably prefer the flying whale option to do the most damage (we've already made note of the fact that, as Burning Fundies, they failed miserably when they hit the Pentagon, doing so little damage), unless, of course, they actually wanted to deliver a nuke or some other type of charge, in which case a military type craft would have been preferable.

Now here we are going to go in a couple of different speculative directions, so bear with us.

---

[158] The remains of the central core and floors of the Twin Towers were carted away and shipped to China as scrap before investigators had time to analyse the evidence. The reader might want to ask him/herself, "in whose interest was it to clean up the evidence before it could be analyed?"

When we just sit back and look at the situation on that day, turn off the noise, the claims and counter-claims, there is one thing that strikes us again and again as the single major difference between the strikes on the WTC towers and the Pentagon: the differences in *the extent of the destruction.*

That is what *is*. Those are the "facts on the ground".

Referring back to the rules of intel gathering, let's ask a question: could there be a reason for this? In other words: *Qui Bono?*

The first thing we notice when we compare the two events - that is, the attack on the Towers and the attack on the Pentagon - is that the World Trade Center Towers were *totally destroyed,* and there was enormous loss of life, (even if that is not completely explained by the impact of two jetliners, which we will get to further on), while the Pentagon only had a small hole, and the collapse of a section that was not even fully occupied because it was still under construction. We have already noted this supreme failure on the part of the suicidal "Islamic Fundies" who could plan such an extraordinary operation and yet do such limited damage to the Pentagon.

So, let us speculate that doing limited damage to the Pentagon was *intended.* Total destruction of the WTC as opposed to minimal destruction and damage, or "targeted" destruction of a small, specific area of the Pentagon.

We can then speculate with some confidence that doing limited damage to the Pentagon was undoubtedly *not* the objective of Fundamental Islamic Terrorists who were ostensibly giving up their lives to strike at the heart of the "Great Satan" with a burning hatred for the United States and its freedoms. They certainly would want to do as much damage as possible.

This bit of speculation has led us to the possible answer as to *why* a different type of plane might be used in the strike on the Pentagon: *the necessity for precision so as to inflict an exact amount of damage, no more, no less.*

So let us theorize that *precision* was the *major concern* in the strike on the Pentagon, and that is why a different attack device was utilized.

Which brings us back to the idea of *a plane that had onboard smart missile guidance system - a system that can guide its carrier to literally turn corners and hit the target with such precision that "it is amazing".*

Theorizing that precision was a major concern - precision of the type that can hit an exact window on a designated floor and do an exact and designated amount of damage - we arrive at the idea that such precision and limitation was *essential* for some reason.

What could that reason be?

Why would the conspirators want to totally destroy one target - where civilians were the main victims - and only partly destroy another where one would think that crazed Islamic Fundies would want to do the most damage?

What immediately comes to mind is this one of the oldest tricks in the criminal play book: *self-inflicted injury as an alibi*. This strategy is so old that it is one of the first things criminal detectives consider when beginning their investigation. There are cases across the board of people falsely claiming to be the victims of crimes – insurance fraud is a good example.

The fact is that the buildings that represent not only America's status in the world, but also America's ability to maintain that status - i.e. its military organization - were hit by alleged terrorists. The emotional reaction of the masses of citizens was that the U.S. not only had a right to strike back with all its power, but also that it *must*. That is also "what IS". The masses of pedestrian thinkers do not look at the possibility of a self-inflicted wound being an alibi.

But that brings us back to the problem of why - assuming it was done with something other than a commercial jet - it could not be claimed that Osama did even that? It would have been so easy to do!

Since no claim was made that Osama got his hands on a military (or other) craft in an attempt to deliver a warhead to the Pentagon, and since the damage was so limited and so minimized even in publicity terms, we have to look elsewhere for the solution to this problem.

But before we do, let me bring up a second possibility that occurs to me. Readers may remember the Tylenol murders where cyanide was put in a random selection of bottles, placed back on the shelves in the stores, so that random persons would die to cover up the fact that a specific murder was the objective of this seemingly "random" act of terror.

So, what if there was someone - or something - in the Pentagon that someone wanted to destroy?

We notice that the Navy lost its new command center.

We wonder, of course, if the Navy ONI was one agency that had not been compromised by the Neocon invasion of Washington. Could that be one of the reasons that the Naval Command Center was destroyed?

Consider the following:

> "It's easy to imagine an infinite number of situations where the government might legitimately give out false information", the Solicitor-General, Theodore Olson, told the court on Monday. "It's an unfortunate reality that the issuance of incomplete information and even misinformation by government may sometimes be perceived as necessary to protect vital interests."[159]

Al Martin's book *The Conspirators*[160] is a secret history of the late 20th century and an uncensored version of what really goes on in the back

---

[159] http://story.news.yahoo.com/news?tmpl=story&u=/020323/79/1ao0k.html
[160] http://www.almartinraw.com/uri1.html

rooms of realpolitik brokers and go-fers. In his book, Al writes that contrary to popular belief, ONI is the most powerful US intelligence agency. "The ONI already had a deep existing covert illegal structure. They had a mechanism before the CIA even existed. They had contacts in foreign intelligence services and in foreign governments that the CIA never could have hoped to obtain."

> "The only people the CIA wouldn't step on to accomplish their aims was ONI. They would easily subvert an FBI or DEA investigation, but never ONI, because they were frightened of them." - "ONI is where the real deep control is. It's where the real deep secrets are kept. That was what ONI always did the best. Keeping secrets. Accumulating secrets. Warehousing secrets for the purposes of control."

> "When I asked him 'what secrets?' he replied, 'one thing I can tell you is the ONI was instrumental in dethroning former Mexican President Louis Portillo. Portillo got very friendly with George Bush and the CIA, and ONI had never aligned with the Bush faction. I know what people think, but that's not true. From what I can tell, it has never been aligned, but has always been hostile to that Eastern Country Club Bush Cabal and their friends in the CIA. The Bill Casey faction is the George Bush-Allen Dulles Faction'".

So we can speculate, therefore, that the the targeting of the ONI offices in the Pentagon on 9/11 was an act of internal warfare against the ONI, either by some section of the U.S. intelligence agencies, or by Israeli intelligence. Not a very nice idea, is it? That the United States has been taken over by a coup d'état, that the secrets of the ways and means of keeping "American Freedoms" may have been destroyed in the WTC and in a few selected rooms of the Pentagon.

Basically, the self-inflicted, limited damage hypothesis has actually split into two: that of alibi, or intentional murder, which may, in fact, go together.

If we consider the alibi conjecture, we include the idea that precision was necessary to insure the safety of *certain* occupants of the building. If you inflict an injury on yourself to allay suspicion, you don't want to make a mistake and blow your head off!

In short, this split hypothesis proposes that a number of the conspirators were *in the pentagon at the time it was hit,* or that certain *targets* were in the building, and this was the reason for a different "mode of attack" - a precision strike. And it is possible that both objectives could be served with a precision strike.

We notice that Newsweek coyly mentions that:

> "On Sept. 10, NewsWeek has learned, a group of top Pentagon officials suddenly canceled travel plans for the next morning, apparently because of security concerns."[161]

---

[161] http://www.msnbc.com/news/629606.asp?cp1=1

"San Francisco mayor Willie Brown was warned off flying that day as well."[162]

If what we have theorized is true, it's not likely that they canceled their travel plans because they might get on the wrong jet - after all, according to them, they didn't know about a possible terrorist attack - but rather to assure that they would be in place for their alibi - or their destruction. We would be very interested to know who those guys were.

Without data we can't answer these questions, and with either of these two lines of conjecture, we face the same dilemma: why it could not be claimed that Osama did even that? It would have been so easy to do! It would have painted Osama and the Islamic fundies in such evil colors that the whole world would have gone after them, including France and Russia! What's more, imagine the publicity value of the miraculous preservation of the Pentagon from an evil nuke strike by that clever Osama, holed up in his underground fortress with unlimited resources to outfox the entire United States military and intel services!

But nope, for some reason, the obvious thing to do - show *all* the evidence and blame Osama - was *not* done.

Since the publication of our "Pentagon Strike" Flash presentation mentioned above, we have been inundated with emails from some of the approximately *500 million people* that have seen it to date. By far the most common question we are asked is: *if it wasn't Flight 77 that hit the Pentagon, then what happened to the **real** Flight 77 and its occupants?*

We will return to this question later, although it should be clear to the attentive reader at this point that this is the central mystery, but first, in order to approach this problem with sufficient data and mental coolness, the reader might wish consider:

What Really Happened to Flight 93?

We have already presented some information that supports the likelihood that Flight 93 was shot down, yet this still leaves the question as to *why* Flight 93 was shot down? If, as now seems clear, the terrorist attacks of 9/11 were in fact carried out by a faction of the US government[163], and assuming that the order to shoot down Flight 93 was given by the conspirators themselves, why would they shoot down an aircraft that was essentially on a covert mission? If they shot this flight down, why were the other three flights left to complete their missions? (Assuming they actually *did* complete their missions.) Surely the drama of the "hijacking" of Flight 93 was not deliberately planned to have such an

---

[162] "Early Warning - State Department memo warned of terrorist threat"Phillip Matier, Andrew Ross, Chronicle Staff Writers, SFGate.com , Friday, September 14, 2001
[163] We'll look at Israeli involvement below.

inauspicious ending as harmlessly scattered across the Pennsylvania countryside?

In the context of 9/11 as an inside job, it seems much more likely that Flight 93 was originally meant to attack a fourth high-profile American landmark; most likely the White House. In fact, in the midst of the confusion on the morning of 9/11, *there were reports of an explosion and fire at the White House*. It is entirely possible that these reports were accurate and, just like the report of the initial explosion at the Pentagon, a bomb or incendiary device of some sort had been detonated at the White House in anticipation of the attack by Flight 93. Perhaps it was supposed to coincide with the crash of Flight 93 into the building, and a glitch caused the explosive to go off earlier, or the glitches on Flight 93 caused a failure of that part of the plan.

So why shoot it down? The most plausible reason is that the real mission of Flight 93 was compromised in some way, and the decision was taken to prematurely end its active participation in the attack. Dave McGowan closes his article on Flight 93 thusly:

> "Assuming that some General somewhere didn't get the hare-brained notion that it was actually his duty to defend the country against these attacks, why would a plane be shot down that was for all intents and purposes on a covert mission for the very people who would have ordered the downing of the aircraft?
>
> If this were the case, then there would be only one reason for shooting the flight down: to destroy any and all evidence in the event that the mission became compromised for any reason.
>
> And how, you may wonder, might the mission be compromised?
>
> One possible scenario could be if, say, the passengers were able to disarm the hijackers and take control of the plane.
>
> That would conceivably leave dozens of *eyewitnesses to what really happened* on those planes that fateful day. The contents of 'black boxes' can be suppressed quite easily; a parade of eyewitnesses, particularly eyewitnesses rightly viewed as American heroes, is another matter entirely.
>
> As disturbing as it may be to contemplate, the answer to the question of what really happened to flight 93 could be that it *was shot down precisely because the passengers were able to overpower the hijackers*, or at least were making an attempt to do so. It could be that the very heroism for which they have been cynically praised by the Bush regime may have earned them a summary execution."

We agree, with the one proviso that we suggest the possibility that there were *no hijackers* on the planes. What would have happened if the plane had landed safely with no hijackers on board?! Talk about compromising a mission!

The official version of events holds that all four flights were hijacked by Arab terrorists, yet there are a host of reasons why this is extremely unlikely. Not least among these is the fact that none of the alleged pilots had shown the aptitude to master control of a single-engined Cessna much less a large commercial airliner as reported by flight instructors at the flying schools were they alleged "learned to fly". The fact that so few members of the public are aware just how difficult it is to fly such a large aircraft greatly helped in the successful dissemination of this unlikely scenario.

Equally unlikely is that, armed only with box cutters, four or five hijackers on each flight could have successfully subdued trained pilots and crew and dozens of passengers. In fact, the term "box cutter" is not entirely accurate, at least for Flight 11.

According to the British *Telegraph* newspaper,[164] the only weapons that the would-be hijackers on that flight had were individual razor blades that they had smuggled onto the plane hidden in wash bags in their hand luggage. The hijackers then used these razor blades, we are told, to fashion "deadly knives" by attaching them to flimsy plastic credit cards, of all things, which they then used to cow the 11 crew and 81 passengers of Flight 11. We are not told exactly what they used to attach the blades to the credit cards, perhaps it was scotch tape, or super glue or bubble gum, but there you have it: A conspiracy theory if we ever heard one!

Of course, some passengers, on at least one of the flights, allegedly claimed that the "hijackers" had a bomb, yet is it credible that a hijacker who couldn't get anything more threatening than a razor blade on-board had somehow smuggled a bomb aboard unseen?

We are also expected to believe that these improvised and surely ineffective weapons were later used to "stab" and kill Daniel Lewin, an ex-member of the Israeli Defense Force's Sayeret Matkal, a top-secret counterterrorist unit[165], and two Flight attendants members.

According to the official story, it was by pure chance that Lewin was given a seat directly in front of and directly behind two of the hijackers: An Israeli counter-terrorist expert on a hijacked flight with Islamic terrorists sitting in the seats directly in front of and behind him. Who could have imagined it?!

Now think about this: There was a total of ninety two passengers and crew on Flight 11. Five slightly-built "hijackers" jumped up with razor blades taped (or bubble-gummed) to credit cards, and manage to kill three people, subdue the rest, and overpower the pilots. Could ninety two people, who surely had many items in their hand luggage or as part of the aircraft's equipment that they could have used as weapons, not overcome five men with razor-blades precariously attached to credit cards!?

---

[164] http://www.telegraph.co.uk/news/main.jhtml?xml=/news/2001/09/16/watt16.xml
[165] http://www.upi.com/inc/view.php?StoryID=06032002-121706-8744r

We are further asked to believe that, without the aid of any navigational instruments, the untrained hijackers were able to pinpoint their targets from 35,000 feet in the air. Anyone that has ever been on a commercial airliner and looked out the window at the ground below will understand just how unlikely this proposition is.

The official story further stretches the boundaries of belief by suggesting that, somehow, on all four planes, the hijackers were able to stand up, subdue the passengers, bypass the crew, break into the cockpit, overpower the pilots and turn off the transponders, all before the pilots were able to send a distress signal that the flight was being hijacked (a procedure that takes about three seconds to complete).

Another troubling discrepancy is the fact that, on all four "hijacked" flights, none of the names of the alleged hijackers appear on the official passenger lists of those flights. In the case of Flight 77 the names of the hijackers did not even appear on the autopsy list provided by the Armed Force Institute of Pathology.[166]

Flight attendant on Flight 11 Madeline Amy Sweeney allegedly called Boston ATC to report the hijacking. The only problem being that, while the FBI claims that there were five hijackers on Flight 11, Ms. Sweeney described only four. In addition, the seat numbers she gave were different from those registered in the hijackers' names.[167]

There is also the problem of how exactly the 19 alleged hijackers got onto the flights in the first place. To check in and board a flight in the US some form of photo ID is required. The name on the ID must match the name on the ticket and the photograph on the ID must match the face of the holder. If none of the alleged hijackers are recorded as having been on the flights, how does anyone know that there actually were any hijackers on the flights? Where did the FBI get the names, dates of birth and photographs of the 19 alleged hijackers that were published on the FBI website within two weeks of the attacks?

As a *Time Magazine* article, in the aftermath of the attacks, reported:

> "US officials are investigating whether the hijackers had accomplices deep inside the airports' 'secure areas'".[168]

Billie Vincent, a former FAA security director, also suggested that the hijackers had inside help at the airports.

> "These people had to have the means to take control of the aircrafts. And that means they had to have weapons in order for those pilots to relinquish control. Think about it, they planned this thing out to the last detail for months. They are not going to take any risks at the front end. They knew

---

[166] http://www.sierratimes.com/03/07/02/article_tro.htm
[167] http://news.bbc.co.uk/1/hi/world/americas/1556096.stm
[168] http://www.time.com/time/nation/article/0,8599,175953,00.html

they were going to be successful before they started... It's the only thing that really makes sense to me."[169]

Not long after these names were published, at least *seven of the "hijackers" loudly and publicly stated that they were still alive as reported by the BBC in September of 2001*. Despite this, the same 19 "hijackers" remain on the FBI website to this day!

There is also a problem with alleged chief hijacker Mohammed Atta. In *September of 2002* Atta's father went public with the claim that his son was still alive:

> "As I saw the picture of my son," he said, "I knew that he hadn't done it. *My son called me the day after the attacks on September 12th* at around midday. We spoke for two minutes about this and that."[170]

In fact, former Attorney General John Ashcroft went on record, and stated in no uncertain terms, that the United States government has no idea who the hijackers were, which, of course, begs the question as to how they know who to retaliate against.

It took the CIA over three years to come up with a video tape of Osama[171] finally directly accepting responsibility for the 9/11 attacks. Prior to this bin Laden had steadfastly denied that he was in any way involved. Of course, the timing of the video could not have been any better for the Bush administration: October 29th 2004, just three days before the US Presidential election, which, given the reports of serious voting irregularities in Ohio and elsewhere, would appear to have been the second time that the Bush camp stole the Presidency.

Former CBSNEWS anchorman Walter Cronkite summed up the reality of the situation during an interview on CNN in October 2004 when he stated:

> "I am inclined to think that Karl Rove, the political manager at the White House, who is a very clever man, he probably set up bin Laden to this thing."

> Unsurprisingly, interviewer Larry King did not ask Cronkite to elaborate on the provocative election eve observation.[172]

Israeli Involvement

We now come to what appear to be threads of Israeli involvement in the organization of 9/11. We notice, first of all, that all of the 9-11 airports

---

169

http://web.archive.org/web/20011009220602/www.miami.com/herald/special/news/worldtrade/digdocs/002594.htm

[170] http://www.guardian.co.uk/september11/oneyearon/story/0,12361,784541,00.html

[171] Refer back to the voice and videotape morphing technology on this item.

[172]http://www.google.co.uk/url?sa=t&ct=res&cd=3&url=http%3A//www.whatreallyhappened.com/binladen_cronkite.html&ei=JMUhQ7yFJJ6kiAKuy6ydAw

were serviced by one Israeli owned company, ICTS. ICTS sells services to every airport from which the hijacked planes operated, including security, sometimes through wholly owned subsidiaries like Huntleigh USA Corporation.

> "It has been suggested that the incredible feat of hijacking four aircraft without a single arrest at the gate would require the resources of a nation-state. [...]
>
> One company had automatic inside access to all of the airports from which hijacked planes departed on 9-11... an Israeli company. One that Mossad agents could easily find employment with without the management knowing who they were or what their purpose really was."[173]

We also observe the events in Israel during the months prior to the WTC attack: many people were withdrawing their support from Israel and there was a growing feeling of dis-ease among the peoples of many countries that Israel was simply going too far in its actions against the Palestinians. Everyone was getting tired of the constant harassment of the Palestinians, of the constant attacks against anyone who said a single word against Israel's political ambitions; who - if they did not support every single thing said and done by Israel - were flamed as "anti-Semitic".

In short, Israel was losing its grip on the collective guilt of the world; sympathies were turning against them, and toward the beleaguered Palestinians.

There is much evidence to warrant an in-depth investigation of the role played by agents of Israel in the 9-11 attacks. Yet the ubiquitous, tiresome, and completely baseless threat of being labelled "anti-Semitic" for criticising the actions of the Israeli government effectively prevents all but the most courageous from following the leads.

During the Clinton years, significant efforts had been made to bring the plight of the Palestinian people and the need for a just solution to the Middle East conflict to the attention of the international community. While Israel had successfully scuppered the Camp David peace talks by making demands that they knew the Palestinian people, and therefore Arafat, could not accept, Israel was finding itself increasingly isolated and increasingly pressured to make the concessions that peace required.

Once 9-11 happened, all bets were off.

On September 10th, 2001, the *Washington Times* ran an article entitled, "U.S. troops would enforce peace under Army study", which detailed the findings of an elite U.S. Army study center plan devised for enforcing a major Israeli-Palestinian peace accord that would require about 20,000 well-armed troops stationed throughout Israel and a newly created Palestinian state. The most interesting aspect of the report was the mention of a 68-page paper by the Army School of Advanced Military Studies

---

[173] http://www.whatreallyhappened.com/ICTS.html

(SAMS) drafted to analyse the daunting task facing any international peacekeeping force if Israel and the Palestinians ever reached a peace agreement back by the United Nations.

In the report, we are told that:

> "...the School for Advanced Military Studies is both a training ground and a think tank for some of the Army's brightest officers. Officials say the Army chief of staff, and sometimes the Joint Chiefs of Staff, ask SAMS to develop contingency plans for future military operations. During the 1991 Persian Gulf war, SAMS personnel helped plan the coalition ground attack that avoided a strike up the middle of Iraqi positions and instead executed a 'left hook' that routed the enemy in 100 hours.

> The exercise was undertaken by 60 officers dubbed 'Jedi Knights,' as all second-year SAMS students are nicknamed. *The SAMS paper* attempts to predict events in the first year of a peace-enforcement operation, and sees possible dangers for U.S. troops from both sides. It *calls Israel's armed forces a '500-pound gorilla in Israel.* Well armed and trained. Operates in both Gaza [and the West Bank]. *Known to disregard international law to accomplish mission.* Very unlikely to fire on American forces. Fratricide a concern especially in air space management.'

> *Of the Mossad,* the Israeli intelligence service, the SAMS officers say: *'Wildcard. Ruthless and cunning. Has capability to target U.S. forces and make it look like a Palestinian/Arab act.'"*[174]

Hmmm... we suppose that the Bush Gang didn't read that particular item of intel. They were too busy reading the "cooked intel" that said Saddam Hussein had weapons of mass destruction or was thinking about having them, or … well, you get the idea.

Alone, the quote from the Army School wouldn't mean much, but when added to the other evidence of Israeli spy rings, Israeli companies providing security at the airports, it does seem to support the idea that Mossad may indeed have been deeply involved in the 9-11 attacks on the World Trade Center and, perhaps, even the Pentagon, and that the Bush Cabal was not only complicit in ordering the U.S. military and intelligence services to "stand down", but that they were directly involved in the plot.

According to ABC news, alleged chief hijacker Mohammed Atta was financed by "unnamed sources in Pakistan". According to *Agence France Presse* and the *Times of India*, an official Indian intelligence report informs us that the 9-11 attacks were *funded by money wired to Mohammed Atta from Pakistan, by Ahmad Umar Sheikh, under orders from Pakistani intelligence chief General Mahmoud Ahmad.* The report said:

> "The evidence we have supplied to the U.S. is of a much wider range and depth than just one piece of paper linking a rogue general to some misplaced act of terrorism."

---

[174] Washington Times, 9/10/01

Guess where General Mahmoud Ahmad was on the morning of September 11?

Why in the U.S. of course!

Guess what he was doing?

Why, the good general just happened to be having breakfast with Florida's senator, Bob Graham – the then esteemed chairman of the Senate Intelligence Committee. Also present at the breakfast was Pakistan's ambassador to the U.S. Maleeha Lodhi and Representative Porter Goss (Goss is a 10-year veteran of the CIA's clandestine operations wing and is the current CIA director). *There were other members of the Senate and House Intelligence committees present also.*[175]

Don't you find it the least bit curious that so many darned bizarre things get done in Florida or in connection to Florida? After all, it was in Florida that Bush stole the 2000 election. Florida is a "safe zone" for all kinds of nefarious activities because Bush's brother, Jeb, is governor there. It also looks like the Bush Reich have the Florida Senator in their pocket, and even if he votes against any of the legislation desired by the Bush Gang, you can bet it is all for show: good cop, bad cop, S.O.P.

The day after the 9-11 attacks, then former Israeli Prime Minister and current Israeli Finance Minister Benjamin Netanyahu, when asked what he thought about the event, stated that it was "very good for Israel".

Indeed it was.

The spin that was immediately put on the events of September 11 created much-needed sympathy and vindication for the "war on Arab terrorism" that Israel claims it has been silently fighting for many years. Again we must ask, who had the motive *and* the capability to carry out the 9-11 attacks, and who stood to benefit the most?

Just hours after the attacks, George Friedman proclaimed Israel as the primary beneficiary. "The big winner today, intended or not, is the state of Israel", wrote Friedman, who said on his Internet website at stratfor.com adding: "There is no question that the Israeli leadership is *feeling relief.*" Again we come back to the question that all serious criminal investigators begin with – "Who benefits?"

The fact is that there exists much evidence, conveniently overlooked by certain 9-11 investigators, to strongly suggest that agents of Israel were deeply involved in the events surrounding the 9-11 attacks. For example: There is the fact of the existence of the Israeli spy ring, as exposed, surprisingly, by Fox News' Carl Cameron. In the four part series aired on Fox News in December 2001, Cameron reports many interesting facts such as:

---

[175] http://www.washingtonpost.com/ac2/wp-dyn?pagename=article&node=&contentId=A36091-2002May17&notFound=true

"Two Israeli companies *Amdocs* and *Comverse InfoSys*, (now called Verint), manage just about every aspect of the US telephone system.

Amdocs is responsible for billing and records for almost all phone calls in the US. Cameron states: Amdocs has contracts with the 25 biggest phone companies in America, and more worldwide. The White House and other secure government phone lines are protected, but *it is virtually impossible to make a call on normal phones without generating an Amdocs record of it.*

In recent years, the FBI and other government agencies have investigated Amdocs more than once. The firm has repeatedly and adamantly denied any security breaches or wrongdoing. But sources tell Fox News that in 1999, the super secret National Security Agency, headquartered in northern Maryland, issued what's called a *Top Secret sensitive compartmentalized information report, TS/SCI*, warning that *records of calls in the United States were getting into foreign hands, in Israel, in particular.*

Investigators don't believe calls are being listened to, but the data about who is calling whom and when is plenty valuable in itself. An internal Amdocs memo to senior company executives suggests just how Amdocs generated call records could be used. 'Widespread data mining techniques and algorithms...combining both the properties of the customer (e.g., credit rating) and properties of the specific 'behavior'.' Specific behavior, such as who the customers are calling."

Note the comment that, "the White House and other secure government phone lines are protected". Well, it just so happens that *Comverse InfoSys provides the wiretapping equipment and software for US law enforcement agencies.* Cameron tells us:

"Every time you make a call, it passes through the nation's elaborate network of switchers and routers run by the phone companies. Custom computers and software, made by companies like Comverse, are tied into that network to intercept, record and store the wiretapped calls, and at the same time transmit them to investigators.

The manufacturers have continuing access to the computers so they can service them and keep them free of glitches. This process was authorized by the 1994 Communications Assistance for Law Enforcement Act, or CALEA. Senior government officials have now told Fox News that while CALEA made wiretapping easier, it has led to *a system that is seriously vulnerable to compromise, and may have undermined the whole wiretapping system.*

Indeed, Fox News has learned that Attorney General John Ashcroft and FBI Director Robert Mueller were both warned Oct. 18 in a hand-delivered letter from 15 local, state and federal law enforcement officials, who complained that 'law enforcement's current electronic surveillance capabilities are less effective today than they were at the time CALEA was enacted.'

Comverse insists the equipment it installs is secure. But the complaint about this system is that the wiretap computer programs made by Comverse have, in effect, a back door *through which wiretaps themselves can be intercepted by unauthorized parties.*

Adding to the suspicions is the fact that in Israel, Comverse works closely with the Israeli government, and under special programs, gets reimbursed for up to 50 percent of its research and development costs by the Israeli Ministry of Industry and Trade. But *investigators within the DEA, INS and FBI have all told Fox News that* to pursue or even suggest Israeli spying through Comverse is considered career suicide."

To this last comment we have to ask: just what level of power do Israeli interests wield in the halls of power in the U.S. that any investigation into Israeli spying activities on US soil against U.S. intelligence agencies can be so completely quashed? Would this constitute a level of power and control that would allow those interests to carry off a terrorist attack like 9-11 and have it blamed on "Arab terrorists"?

Cameron goes on to tell us that *a group of 140 Israeli spies were arrested prior to September 11, 2000 in the US as part of a widespread investigation into a suspected espionage ring run by Israel inside the US.*

US Government documents refer to the spy ring as an *"organised intelligence-gathering operation"* designed to *"penetrate government facilities"*. Most of those arrested had served in the Israeli armed forces – but military service is compulsory in Israel and a number also had an intelligence background. *Many were posing as art students.*

These spies were spread out across the US, *usually living close to suspected Arab terrorist cells.* One group was living just a few blocks away from alleged chief "hijacker" Mohammed Atta in Hollywood, Florida. Cameron reports that, according to intelligence sources within the US, *a number of the terrorist cells that they had been watching changed their activities and routines immediately after having covert taps put on their communications by U.S. intelligence agents.*

Now think about this. You have a group of at least 140 Mossad agents and/or their accomplices running around the US with apparent impunity prior to 9-11 conducting a "spying" operation that is designed to "penetrate government facilities". You have two Israeli companies that control the entire US telephone and telephone wiretapping technology that are suspected of passing sensitive information to Israel. You have US intelligence agencies realising that, on a number of occasions, terrorist suspects that they had sought to wiretap and survey immediately changed their telecommunications processes and began acting much differently as soon as the, supposedly secret, wiretaps went into place. Keep in mind who has access to the wiretapping system information: Comverse, an Israeli company.

But it doesn't end there.

On the morning of September 11th and just as the WTC towers were crumbling, five Israelis were caught doing the "happy dance" as they videotaped the Twin Towers fall and over two thousand American civilians die. The now infamous "Dancing Israelis" were spotted by a woman who called the police who contacted the FBI. The five were apprehended in a moving company van, which contained $4700 in cash, *box cutters* and recently taken photographs, *one image showing a hand flicking a lighter in front of the destroyed buildings* as if mocking the event. Investigators said that:

> "There were maps of the city in the car with certain places highlighted... *It looked like they're hooked in with this. It looked like they knew what was going to happen.*"

The driver of the van later told the arresting officers:

> "*We are Israeli. We are not your problem. Your problems are our problems. The Palestinians are the problem.*"

Did this most interesting comment give the world a tantalising glimpse into the *real* reason for and, at the same time, reveal the co-conspirators - or even perpetrators - of the 9-11 attacks??

The five were detained for two months during which time at least two were identified as active Mossad agents. They were subjected to polygraph tests which one of them resisted for ten weeks before *failing*.

Now ask yourself: What questions might have been asked of this person during the test? We will probably never know, but we can speculate that he was probably asked direct questions about his involvement in the WTC attacks, and he, as a Mossad agent working for the state of Israel, was found to be lying.

After being released and deported to Israel, the five appeared on an Israeli television show where they made the following telling remark:

> "*The fact of the matter is we are coming from a country that experiences terror daily. Our purpose was to document the event.*"

Which begs the question: How can you document an event if you do not know beforehand that it is going to happen?

Another interesting detail was the fact that an Israeli Instant Messaging company, *Odigo*, received a warning about the WTC attacks two hours before the first plane hit the WTC; this warning originated in Israel.[176]

As reported by ex-Mossad agent Victor Ostrovsky[177], the Mossad had a secret history of supporting radical Islamic groups for its own purposes, and as Seymour Hersh, veteran investigative journalist writing in The New Yorker on Oct. 8, pointed out:

> "...many of the investigators believe that some of the initial clues about the terrorists' identities and preparations, such as flight manuals, *were meant to be found.*"

---

[176]http://www.haaretzdaily.com/hasen/pages/ShArt.jhtml?itemNo=77744&contrassID=/has%5C

[177] http://www.amazon.com/exec/obidos/tg/detail/-/0971759502/qid=1130335852/sr=2-1/ref=pd_bbs_b_2_1/103-3216640-8035850?v=glance&s=books

The fact that Israeli interests possess vastly disproportionate power in the U.S. was highlighted by Congressman Jim Moran (Democrat of Virginia), speaking at a 2003 public forum in his congressional district, and reported in the *New York Times* of March 15, 2003[178], where he stated:

> "If it were not for the strong support of the Jewish community for this war with Iraq, we would not be doing this. The leaders of the Jewish community are influential enough that they could change the direction of where this is going, and I think they should."

By "Jewish community", Moran was certainly not talking about the average Jewish American or the average Jew in Israel, but rather the *leaders* of the Jewish political and industrial communities and self-proclaimed "Zionists", those that claim to be acting in the interests of ordinary Jews.

The above facts are indisputable and constitute just the tip of the iceberg of what is clearly deep involvement by the agents of the state of Israel in not only the 9-11 attacks but American politics in general.

And so, there it was: after those nasty Islamic fundies attacked America, Israel had the biggest bully on the global block on their side. With the repeating rants of how evil Muslims are, how fanatical they are, how cruel and unusual they are, the whole rest of the world had better fall in line with Israel's thinking and help them find the "final solution" for Palestine and those other A-rabs.

Shades of Nazi Germany going after the Jews!

Thus we see that the main beneficiary of 9/11 was Israel. It was not the Arabs, who have seen their land invaded and occupied by the United States. It was not the Muslims, who have seen the U.S. and Israel attempt to foment civil war between Sunni and Shi'ia factions in Iraq, who watch as the US rattles its nuclear saber against Iran, and frankly, it is not the United States either. The U.S. is being rapidly destroyed politically and economically since 9-11.

At the beginning of our analysis of the 9/11 attacks, we stated that, compared to the attacks on the WTC, the attack on the Pentagon constituted the "Achilles heel" of the entire 9/11 conspiracy. The reason we have formed this opinion is very simple: while we all saw repeated footage of Flight 11 and Flight 175 crash into the WTC towers, and we all saw the wreckage of Flight 93 and have several eyewitness testimonies that a commercial airliner did indeed crash in Pennsylvania, no one has seen any footage of Flight 77 hitting the Pentagon, and the government studiously *refuses* to release any of the footage that they have that would show conclusively if it was Flight 77 or not.

---

[178] http://www.cnn.com/2003/ALLPOLITICS/03/14/moran.remarks/

More importantly, and here we present the defining argument for the "no plane at the Pentagon" argument, there is *no* evidence of a Boeing 757 having impacted the Pentagon on 9/11. Think about it. The *only* evidence that Flight 77 hit the Pentagon is the word of US government and military officials and the alleged phone call of Barbara Olson that she could *not* have made (as we shall see shortly). Also, both the Olsons were high level members of the Bush Cabal. That, of course, is one of the reasons that some people might argue that it *was* flight 77 that hit the Pentagon. Why would the Bush Cabal sacrifice one of its own? How could they persuade Ted Olson to go along with lying about a phone call from his wife in order to give support to the story that Flight 77 hit the Pentagon, when his wife was lost in the attack? Well, we will come to that.

Imagine for a moment that we have found someone on the planet who is completely unaware of the 9/11 attacks. Imagine further that this person is somewhat knowledgeable about aircraft disasters, crash scenes and the effects of explosives. Imagine that we can go back in time and place this person at the Pentagon and give them unhindered access to the crash scene. Imagine finally that the only thing we tell this person is that some kind of flying object struck the Pentagon.

In such a case, after having examined the evidence, the very *last* thing that such a person would conclude would be that a large 757 caused the damage? Why? Because there is absolutely *no* evidence to support such a conclusion.

Four years have passed since the 9/11 attacks, and the controversy still rages. Many Americans are becoming more and more disenchanted with their President and his government. Subtle hints are emerging that many, perhaps up to 50%, are wary of the official version of the attacks and are more than a little suspicious that their government may well have played a part. Despite this, the mainstream press in the US continues to propagandize the "Party Line" and to bow down to the demands of big business and big government, refusing to fulfill their official role of bringing truth to the people.

Most of the 2,752 people that died on September 11th 2001 were ordinary American civilians. There remain serious questions about how and why those people died. Their families, and all American citizens have a right to the truth about 9/11 and the US government refuses to give it to them.

The Setup:

Lacking among the many independent books and analyses of the 9/11 attacks is a concise outline of *what may well have happened that day* within reasonable parameters. To rectify this glaring omission, we would like to propose the following step-by-step breakdown of the events of that day, as we have been able to reconstruct it.

Obviously, even our scenario cannot be a definitive *account* because so many lies have been told, and so much data has been hidden or destroyed, that the best anyone can do is to carefully consider *all* that is available , and then formulate a working hypothesis based on logic, science, deep digging, common sense, and an objective understanding of the resources available to, and the true nature of, the people that were likely involved.

Our scenario is a plausible account, much more plausible than the crazy conspiracy theory that blames it on Osama and which led to the equally incomprehensible decision to destroy Saddam and Iraq to extract revenge!

First, let us state that the *specific planning* for the 9/11 attacks probably began *at least* six or seven years prior to the events themselves. This time was needed to maneuver the conspirators, active and passive, (of which there were probably hundreds) into the correct positions within the armed forces, government, and civilian agencies to enable the successful completion of the operation. This maneuvering also included the setting up and/or infiltration of businesses (the Israeli airport security and telephone companies for just a few examples) that were also to play key roles. This time frame was also needed to develop the "Muslim terror" threat in the public awareness and to select and deploy the patsies who would ultimately be labeled as the "hijackers".

However, there are strong indicators that the ideological infrastructure has been in place - and active - a lot longer than six or seven years. Since Gulf War I, instigated by George I, effectively turned Iraq into a "Straw man", that was thought to be easy to "knock down" with a quick "Shock and Awe", we might also plausibly suggest that the designs on Iraq were put on the table some years before that event, that is to say, in the 1980s. Still other indicators of the ideology afoot in the U.S. that breeds such conspiracies are the "*Northwoods Plan*", and *the assassination of John Kennedy*, not to mention the puerile nonsense called "Monicagate" that included the deep involvement of Ted and Barbara Olson.

It will come as no surprise to our regular readers that the Muslim terror threat is a phenomenon manufactured mainly by Israeli, British and American intelligence agencies. The group that has come to be known as "al-Qaeda" is officially recognised as being a remnant of the Russian Afghan war in the late 1970's when the CIA, using *Saudi intelligence* as a go-between, funneled arms and funds to fundamentalist Islamic groups to counter the Russian invasion of Afghanistan, which itself was provoked by U.S. government meddling in Afghanistan which threatened Russian influence in the region.

Throughout the 1980's and 1990's, US and Israeli intelligence agencies carefully developed this "network" of disaffected Islamic radicals into the modern day al-Qaeda. In an effort to cement the "reality" of the Islamic terror threat, several "false flag" terror attacks were carried out by agents of the Israeli and American government during the 1990's including the bombing of the U.S.S. Cole and several bomb attacks on American embassies. Evidence was planted to incriminate "Islamic terrorists" including, but not limited to, false claims of responsibility by previously unheard of "Islamic terror groups".

To state it bluntly, al-Qaeda *does not and never has existed in the form claimed by Western governments*. However, that is not to say that *real* Islamic Terrorists did not exist, or that the response of the Bush Administration to the events of 9/11 has not bred a whole new generation of *real* Islamic terrorists. (Readers are encouraged to do their own research to verify the truth of this statement, an excellent starting point being the *BBC*-aired documentary *The Power of Nightmares[179]*).

The Preparation:

During the years prior to 9/11, members of the Israeli Mossad operated a large network of agents (including Sayanim[180]), who were involved in setting up the attacks, which includes handling the Middle Eastern patsies. These agents and their superiors are also involved in conducting surveillance on the individuals in the US government and federal agencies that will be directly involved in the immediate response to the attacks. They employ tactics that include blackmailing and assassination to ensure that as little as possible is left to chance. Additionally, with their control of the telephone and computer network infrastructure of the U.S., it is also very likely that any selected member of the U.S. government can be individually targeted for blackmail and/or control so that virtually every function of the U.S. government is under the control of Israel.

---

[179] http://www.informationclearinghouse.info/video1037.htm

[180] Writes Selwyn Manning in The Scoop (Apr. 22, 2004):
http://www.scoop.co.nz/mason/stories/HL0404/S00176.html
Mossad insiders, now on the outside, say the Mossad has just 30 to 37 case officers called katsas operating at any one time. The Mossad is able to function on a low number of core katsas due to a loyal Jewish community outside Israel. The loyalists are networked via a system of sayanim, or volunteer Jewish helpers. Sayanim loyalists are usually Jewish, live outside of Israel, and are often recruited via Israeli relatives. There are reportedly thousands of sayanim around the world. Their role will be specific to their professions: A loyalist in the travel industry could help Mossad obtain documents. Sayanim offer practical support, are never put at risk, and are certainly not privy to classified information. A sayan in the tenancy business would find accommodation, financiers, doctors, civil servants, care-givers employed caring for the severely disabled -- all have a part to play without knowing the complete or bigger picture, and will remain silent due to loyalty to the cause. Katsas in charge of active sayanim will visit once every three months involving both face-to-face meetings and numerous telephone conversations. "The system allows the Mossad to work with a skeleton staff. That's why, for example, a KGB station would employ about 100 people, while a comparable Mossad station would need only six or seven." [According to The Scoop's source -- Ed.]

Several "trial runs" of the attacks in the form of military exercises were probably carried out in the years and months prior to September 11th in order to fully understand the workings of the various agencies involved, with a view to co-opting their ability to respond effectively as described above. At the same time, several new operations centers were created that would allow the conspirators to control the key area of air traffic control. (See the previously-mentioned Air Traffic Services Cell for an example.)

The key conspirators most likely include very few publicly-known members of the US military or government executive branch, but are rather made up of high-level members of the Israeli government and particularly the Israeli intelligence agency *Mossad*. Those publicly-known members of the US government and military such as Dick Cheney, Donald Rumsfeld, etc., the *apparent* power brokers of American politics, were also in on the plot, but the Israeli contingent were planning a special surprise for them as we shall see.

At some point prior to September 11th 2001, four commercial aircraft, two Boeing 757s and two Boeing 767s were fitted with software that allowed them to be remotely commandeered by the conspirators. The aircraft were also fitted with hidden video equipment that allowed the conspirators to view events in the cabins of the aircraft in real time. *The ventilation systems in all four aircraft are fitted with canisters containing a fatal analgesic gas mixture that is to be activated automatically.* We refer readers to the October 2002 hostage crisis in a Moscow theatre for evidence of the effects of this type of gas.[181]

While it is possible that these modifications to the aircraft could have been made covertly, there also exists the possibility - suggested by other researchers - that duplicate aircraft were used, though we consider it unlikely.

For example: there is evidence to suggest that there were two Flight 11s that left Boston the morning of 9/11. Flight 11 was an institution at Logan Airport. It was American Airlines' early morning transcontinental flight *for years*. Its departure was scheduled *regularly* for 7:45 a.m. at *Terminal B, Gate 32* as it apparently was on Sept. 11, as the NY Times radio transcript reports.[182] Despite this longstanding "institution" of a flight, the official version of events states Flight 11 left from *gate 26* which is repeated by many press reports.[183]

---

[181] http://en.wikipedia.org/wiki/Moscow_theatre_siege

[182] http://www.nytimes.com/2001/10/16/national/16TEXT-FLIGHT11.html?ex=1126411200&en=2da859e407225ee9&ei=5070&ex=1071378000&en=4b6d66a63bf99b3a&ei=5070 "7:45:48 -- Ground Control 1: American eleven heavy boston ground *gate thirty two* you're going to wait for a Saab to go by then push back."

183 http://www.washingtonpost.com/ac2/wp-dyn/A38407-2001Sep15 "American Airlines Flight 11 had backed away from *Gate 26 of Terminal B* at Boston's Logan Airport and was rolling toward the runway for a six-hour flight to Los Angeles."

http://www.telegraph.co.uk/news/main.jhtml?xml=/news/2001/09/16/watt16.xml

Another most interesting detail about Flight 77 is that, despite the official story, *Flight 77 was not scheduled to fly* and was not recorded as actually having flown from Washington Dulles airport on September 11th 2001![184]

The U.S. government's *Bureau of Transportation* documents details such as flight number, tail number, destination airport, scheduled departure time etc. about *every commercial flight in the USA*. A search of The US Government's Bureau of Transportation Statistics shows no Flight 0077 listed on *Sept 11, 2001*. A search for all American Airlines scheduled flights departing from Washington Dulles International Airport on *September 10th, 2001* showed Flight number 0077 to have been scheduled and did depart.

A search of the full list of American Airlines scheduled flights departing Dulles on *September 9th*, 2001 shows American Airlines Flight number 0077 is on this list as well.

The list for *September 8th 2001*, also included American Airlines Flight number 0077.

Curiously, the full list of American Airlines scheduled flights departing from Dulles on *September 12th, 2001*, the day after the attacks, show American Airlines Flight number 0077 is on the schedule, even though all flights had been cancelled.

Why was Flight 77 omitted from the Gov list on 9/11? Were any of the other hijacked aircraft similarly omitted from these government lists?

A search for all United Airlines scheduled flights departing from Boston Logan International Airport on September 11th, 2001 showed that *Flight 0175 is listed* and did indeed depart. A search of the full list of United Airlines scheduled flights departing from Newark, New Jersey Airport on September 11th, 2001 - United Airlines *Flight 0093* is listed as a scheduled flight which departed for San Francisco. A search of the full list of American Airlines scheduled flights departing from Boston, Massachusetts Airport on September 11th, 2001 shows United Airlines *Flight 0011* is listed as a scheduled flight and departed for Los Angeles International Airport.

So, why wasn't Flight 0077 on the Gov Flight list? Was it an administrative error or oversight or was it due to Flight 0077 not being actually scheduled to fly at all on the morning of September 11th 2001? Is it possible that this is a "glitch" in the plans? An item that indicates that American Airlines Flight 77 - as the "institution" it was - never left the ground on 911? It is certainly curious.

Furthermore, by some bizarre "glitch in the system", the Bureau of Transportation has *Flight 93 actually arriving at its destination in San Francisco at midday on 9/11* (the scheduled arrival time was 11:14am).

---

[184] http://www.apfn.net/Messageboard/03-26-05/discussion.cgi.24.html

Normally, any emergency landing or crash would be denoted on the BTS database as a 'diversion'.[185]

There is also a report that the passengers that boarded and died on United Airlines Flight 93 were originally meant to board UA Flight 91 to the same destination but due to a "crack in the windshield" of Flight 91 the passengers were transferred to Flight 93. Given the fact that Flight 93 had just 33 passengers and all of Flight 91's passengers were transferred to Flight 93, we wonder if there were *any* passengers booked on Flight 93 in the first place.[186] Not only that, but Tuesday September 11th 2001 was *the first time that Flight 93 flew the Newark to SF route on a Tuesday.*

In short, the possibility of duplicate, "modified aircraft" which were brought out of the hangar to be utilized on September 11 is plausible, and the Gov statistics might very well be "glitches" in the plans that indicate such "switching". Certainly, raising a smokescreen via dispensing false or confusing information - as we see above - might be part of the plan, simply to divert and confuse, but again, it is unlikely that any unnecessarily complicated maneuvers were implemented because each additional "step" in the plan is another stage at which something can go wrong.

On September 13, then Attorney General John Ashcroft, in a briefing on the 9/11 attacks, stated that a total of 18 hijackers had been involved in the attacks. In the same briefing, FBI Director Robert Mueller stated that all of the hijackers were "ticketed passengers". [187]

This posed a problem because, of the four hijackers on Flight 77, none had received any training on how to fly a Cessna much less a 757. To resolve this issue, the following day on September 14th, the FBI added pilot hijacker Hani Hanjour to the list of hijackers on Flight 77. [188]

But arbitrarily adding another hijacker to the list was not as simple as it might seem, because, of course, *Hanjour's name was not on the manifest*, which led the *Washington Post* to speculate that he did not have a ticket, which not only contradicted FBI Director Mueller's statement that the hijackers were "ticketed passengers", but also raised the impossible question of *how anyone can get on a commercial flight without a ticket.*[189]

Several news sites published lists of all the people on board the hijacked airlines. These lists are very curious because the numbers do not add up. Take for instance Flight 11: The list has 86 passengers onboard, including five hijackers, plus 11 crew members, a total of 97; but there only were 92 people total on board the plane according to all accounts. *The numbers*

---

[185] http://www.thoughtcrimenews.com/flight93notscheduled.htm

[186] http://rsjames.com/newsletters/2001/14-10-26-2001-13-14.txt

[187] http://www.globalsecurity.org/military/library/news/2001/09/mil-010913-usia18.htm

[188] http://www.cnn.com/2001/US/09/14/fbi.document/

[189] http://www.washingtonpost.com/wp-srv/nation/graphics/attack/hijackers.html

only work if you subtract the five hijackers. The other passenger lists also have too few names, by up to five people.[190]

Prepping the WTC

At some point prior to 9/11, the conspirators, possibly disguised as engineers, entered the WTC North and South Towers. As related by WTC worker Scott Forbes, the weekend before the 9/11 attacks, there was a power down in the WTC South tower allegedly to carry out maintenance on the electrical cabling in the building:

"On the weekend of 9/8/2001 - 9/9/2001 there was a 'power down' condition in WTC tower 2, the south tower. This power down condition meant there was no electrical supply for approx 36hrs from floor 50 up. I am aware of this situation since I work in IT and had to work with many others that weekend to ensure that all systems were cleanly shutdown beforehand ... and then brought back up afterwards. The reason given by the WTC for the power down was that cabling in the tower was being upgraded.

Of course without power there were no security cameras, no security locks on doors and many, many 'engineers' coming in and out of the tower. I was at home on the morning of 9/11 on the shore of Jersey City, right opposite the Towers, and watching events unfold I was convinced immediately that something was happening related to the weekend work."[191]

The impossibility of the Towers collapsing from the impact of the planes alone has been well documented. In fact, many structural engineers have expressed their shock and surprise at the fact that the towers collapsed as a result of the aircraft impacts or fire. The towers were in fact deliberately designed to be able to withstand the impact of a large commercial aircraft!

Frank A. Demartini, on-site construction manager for the World Trade Center, who died in the 9/11 attacks, spoke of the resilience of the towers in an interview recorded on January 25, 2001.

"The building was designed to have a fully loaded 707 crash into it. That was the largest plane at the time. *I believe that the building probably could sustain multiple impacts of jetliners* because this structure is like the mosquito netting on your screen door - this intense grid - and the jet plane is just a pencil puncturing that screen netting. It really does nothing to the screen netting."[192]

The centers of the WTC towers were built with large steel beams extending from the foundations up to the top of both buildings. These beams are the skeleton of the buildings to which each floor is attached via trusses.

---

[190] http://www.cnn.com/SPECIALS/2001/trade.center/victims/AA11.victims.html
[191] http://www.rense.com/general63/wte.htm
[192] http://www.freepressinternational.com/wtc_11152004_manager_88888.html

The core was designed to support the entire weight of the buildings several times over. Far more than a mere "service core", it comprised 47 steel box columns tied together at each floor by steel plates, similar to the 52" deep spandrel plates that tied the perimeter columns together. The largest of these core columns were 18"x36", with steel walls 4" thick near the base, tapering in thickness toward the top, and anchored directly to the bedrock.

The official reason given for the collapse of the twin towers is that structural failures occurred on the impacted floors due to infernos of 800°C.

Yet, as reported in the *South Bend Tribune* on November 22, 2004:

> "A laboratory director from a South Bend firm has been *fired for attempting to cast doubt on the federal investigation into what caused the World Trade Center's twin towers to collapse* on Sept. 11, 2001. Kevin R. Ryan was terminated Tuesday from his job at Environmental Health Laboratories Inc., a subsidiary of Underwriters Laboratories Inc., the consumer-product safety testing giant.

> Ryan wrote that the institute's preliminary reports suggest the WTC's supports were *probably exposed to fires no hotter than 500 degrees* -- only half the 1,100-degree temperature needed to forge steel, Ryan said. That's also much cooler, he wrote, than the 3,000 degrees needed to melt bare steel with no fire-proofing.

> *'This story just does not add up,'* Ryan wrote in his e-mail to Frank Gayle, deputy chief of the institute's metallurgy division, who is playing a prominent role in the agency investigation. *'If steel from those buildings did*

soften or melt, I'm sure we can all agree that this was certainly not due to jet fuel fires of any kind, let alone the briefly burning fires in those towers.[193]

In February of 2005, an electrical fire in Madrid's 8th tallest building (350 feet) burned for 18 hours. While the building also had a core of steel beams, it was naturally much less sturdy than the 1,300 feet tall WTC towers. [194]

At the peak of the Madrid fire, the temperature reached 800°C. Despite this, *only after 18 hours* did six upper floors collapse, and when they did, as one might expect, they collapsed *around* the core steel beams that they were attached to. Of course, unlike the WTC towers, the Madrid building did not suffer any initial damage to its core beams. (See Plate 17).

Yet according to Tomasz Wierzbicki, director of the Impact and Crashworthiness Laboratory at M.I.T., the aluminum wings and the planes' fuselage would have been almost instantly shredded into pieces the size of an adult's fist, with the engines and other heavy parts continuing to the core. But by working out the amount of energy involved, Dr. Wierzbicki and a student, Liang Xue, determined that *at most* only half of the inner columns could have been broken or severely mangled.[195]

Obviously, after the initial impact of the planes into the WTC towers, the steel core beams were still able to support the weight of the upper floors and the towers remained standing. The fact is that after the initial impact and fireball, *the fires in both WTC towers burned for a relatively short period of time* (South tower 56 minutes North tower 85 minutes) and were diminishing in intensity all the time as is evidenced by the thick black smoke that issued from the towers which is evidence of an oxygen-starved fire and, therefore, a relatively cool fire.

So the WTC core beams were damaged by the impact of the planes, but not badly enough that the beams could not support the upper floors, and the resulting fires burned at approximately 500 degrees for about an hour each. Then, for no apparent or explicable reason, both towers fell into their own footprints.

Anyone that has watched the footage of the WTC collapse cannot but remark on the surprising way in which the towers fell. It was as if *the steel cores* of the buildings, the 'skeleton' that holds them up, *suddenly disappeared* and the body of the buildings were left to collapse straight down with nothing to resist them but thin air.

---

[193] http://inn.globalfreepress.com/modules/news/article.php?storyid=1059

[194] http://news.scotsman.com/latest.cfm?id=4127075

[195]

http://www.nytimes.com/2001/11/11/nyregion/11COLL.html?ex=1126584000&en=be2140f
5f593be38&ei=5070&pagewanted=2&ei=1&en=6e7e84802c73aed6&ex=1006447757&oref
=login

Moreover, transcripts of the conversations with the firefighters who reached the crash site in the WTC indicate that the fires were small enough that only two hoses were requested to fight them.

The *official story* alleges that the impact of the planes and the resulting fires were sufficient to weaken the steel beams and cause them to collapse, resulting in the collapse of the floors above impact point which "pancaked" and brought the entire structures down. Yet, as we have shown, the problem with such a thesis is that, even if the beams at the impact point had been fatally compromised and the floors above had "pancaked on top of each other, the central core beams *below* the impact point should have been left standing some 1000 feet in the air.

The most bizarre thing about the collapse of the Twin Towers was that, to an onlooker, it was as if *all* of the core steel beams, which were fixed into the bedrock at ground level, were somehow instantly removed as support, and the towers collapsed into their own footprints.

The idea that explosives were used to do this is highly improbable given that each steel beam on each floor would have required a separate and considerably large explosive charge, all going off at the same time. Such simultaneous detonations would surely have been impossible to cover up had they occurred, not to mention the weeks upon weeks of time required to place such charges. Something altogether different was used to bring the towers crashing down even if some sort of explosive charge is clearly implicated.

"The reality of there being some kind of explosive events coinciding with the demise of each building, as reported by eye witnesses is well documented. However, any word of explosions essentially disappeared from mass-media reports of the attacks very quickly and to this day are not part of the official narrative. Mainstream scientific attempts to describe the collapses as unforeseen catastrophic engineering failures do not bother to take into account the widespread reports of explosions." [196]

"An odd remnant of the core of the north tower remained standing for about 15 seconds after the main collapse, and then seemed to abruptly disintegrate into a narrow column of dust where huge steel box columns had been... there are about ten seconds of footage from the same camera taken just as the collapse began. [...] After the upper portion of the tower has disappeared into the dust cloud the footage is intercut with a telephoto view from the north, and we do not return to this camera angle until the spire is about to collapse. [...]

Immediately after this, the spire begins to fall straight down along its own axis, at least initially, without any change in appearance. But at about the point when its top is even with the tapering roof of the Woolworth Building a distinct change takes place. [...]

---

[196] http://home.comcast.net/~jeffrey.king2/wsb/html/view.cgi-home.html-.html

All at once the outline of the previously solid looking steel columns begins to become less well defined. *Very soon after this it is clear that the steel columns have turned into a fine powder*, though remaining in a narrow vertical column somewhat wider than the original outline. The heavier portion of the dust settles straight down fairly quickly, leaving only an insubstantial wisp of lighter dust that drifts off to the left. It has been suggested that this was simply dust that had been somehow clinging to the columns, but it would be difficult to explain how any amount of dust could cling to the vertical sides of the columns after being scoured by the turbulent cloud from which it emerged. [...]

Because this video[197] was taken with a tripod-mounted camera located close to the collapse, the image is sharper than the other known footage of the event. There can be no doubt that the cluster of steel box columns comprising the spire, after surviving the violence of the collapse itself, did in fact disintegrate almost at the moment that it began to fall. I cannot begin to speculate on the kind of technology needed to make this happen, but can say with some certainty that even conventional explosives would not create such a disintegration, and nothing that could happen in a gravitational collapse would resemble this.

...Something very unusual has happened to these particular steel beams, something that caused them to not merely topple or crumple in segments but to disintegrate in place. It is difficult to imagine any mechanism during a gravity driven collapse that could so alter the structure of steel that it might disintegrate under its own weight - no amount of shaking can create that kind of metal fatigue. [...]

Could electrostatic forces generated by movement of particles account for some of this? Could the pyroclastic slurry of the collapse function like a thunderhead or Van de Graff generator, perhaps accounting for the visible glow as well as the displacement of the dust cloud? Could electrostatic repulsion somehow push the dust cloud off to the side? The final bimodal dust cloud seems very inconsistent with the extreme symmetry of the early stages of the collapse, so some asymmetric force must be at work. And could the force involved also have created the bright glow visible in so many images of the collapses? [...]

Something inescapably strange is going on in these pictures, something no official explanation of the collapses has come close to accounting for. Beyond this I make no claims, and have no insider knowledge. Based on the photographic evidence there can be no question that explosives, and possibly other weapons systems based on "black technologies" were used in the WTC demolitions. Otherwise one can only suppose that the laws of physics underwent a profound but temporary change on September 11, 2001, as indeed the political and moral climate of our country underwent a dark and fateful change. And it is precisely this change that was clearly the intent behind the vast high-tech magic show that was 9/11. In politics as in physics, things do not happen for no reason. [...]

---

[197] http://st12.startlogic.com/~xenonpup/spire/spire_collapse_from_north.avi

Only a willingness to accept that there could be one more level of deception beyond what we have understood will allow us to find the real contours of this all-encompassing fake reality that is attempting to control us all."[198]

The Big Day Arrives

At 7:59 a.m. (14 minutes after its scheduled 7:45 a.m. departure time) American Airlines Flight 11, specially modified with remote guidance system and gas canisters, takes off from Boston's Logan airport with 92 passengers and crew and *no* hijackers aboard.

At **8:14 a.m.** (16 minutes after its scheduled departure time) United Airlines **Flight 175**, specially modified with remote guidance system and gas canisters, takes off from Boston's Logan airport with 65 passengers and crew and *no* hijackers aboard.

8:13 - 8:21 a.m., Flight 11 transponder is turned off.

At **8:20 a.m.** (10 minutes after its scheduled departure time), American Airlines **Flight 77**, specially modified with remote guidance system and gas canisters, takes off from Dulles airport Washington with 64 passengers and crew and *no* hijackers on board.

At **8:42 a.m.** (41 minutes after its scheduled departure time), United Airlines **Flight 93**, specially modified with remote guidance system and gas canisters, takes off from Newark International Airport, New York, with 33 passengers and crew and *no* hijackers on board.

With the exception of Flight 93, not long after the pilots switch on the autopilot and the flights have reached their cruising altitude, a silent, colorless, odorless gas is released into the cockpit and the cabin via the ventilation system. Within minutes all occupants of the planes are beginning to slump over as they fall into unconsciousness. Not long thereafter, the gas begins to cause respiratory seizure and the passengers and crew quietly suffocate to death.

The "Universal Replacement Autopilot Programme" (URAP) is activated and takes control of all four planes. Communications systems on the planes are overridden giving the conspirators exclusive access to and control over all incoming and outgoing communications from the planes. Of course, in reality, there will be no *real* communications coming from any of the flights.

With the activation of the URAP, new flight plans are now being followed by the aircrafts' computers.

---

[198] http://st12.startlogic.com/~xenonpup/New_Spire/
Jeffrey King, a 50-something former engineer (MIT class of '74, about 10 years in electronics and electro-mechanical engineering), gainfully employed as a family physician for the past 25 years, but spending most of his limited free time for the past three years in trying to document and make available to the public and other researchers the photo and video evidence of the World Trade Center collapses.

Flight 11's new trajectory will take it through the airspace occupied by floor 89 of the WTC North tower.

Flight 175 is programmed to fly through the airspace of floor 75 of the WTC South tower.

8:46 a.m.: Flight 175 Changes Transponder Signal but Remains Easily Traceable.

At **8:46 a.m.**, Flight 11 completes its pre-programmed missions and hits the WTC North Tower.

8:48 a.m. CNN begins showing WTC crash footage.

8:50 a.m. Last radio contact with Flight 77 is received.

8:55 a.m. George W. Bush arrives at Booker Elementary School.

8:56 a.m. Flight 77 Transponder Signal Disappears. Flight 77 disappears from radar screens.

9:00 a.m. VP Cheney watches the WTC crash on television.

At **9:03 a.m.**, Flight 175 completes its pre-programmed mission and hits the WTC South Tower while millions watch it live on television. Condoleezza Rice goes to Cheney's office where she meets Richard Clarke, and Wolfowitz continues a routine meeting; Rumsfeld stays in his office; Dubya stays in the classroom.

9:05 a.m. Richard Clarke recommends evacuating the White House. Rice notes the Secret Service wants them to go to the bomb shelter below the White House, and as Clarke leaves, he sees Rice and Cheney gathering papers and preparing to evacuate.

9:06 - 9:16 a.m. Bush reads a goat story to the children at Booker Elementary School in Florida.

9:12 a.m. Renee May, a flight attendant on Flight 77 allegedly uses a cell phone to call her mother.

9:16 - 9:29 Bush allegedly works with his staff on a speech.

9:20 a.m. Barbara Olson is said to call from Flight 77 but the account is full of contradictions.

9:27 a.m. Ted Olson calls the Justice Department's control center to relate his wife Barbara's call from Flight 77.

9:27 a.m. Flight 93 passenger Tom Burnett allegedly calls wife, Deena, and mentions a bomb, knives and a gun. "He spoke quickly and quietly" according to his wife. The original versions of this conversation appear to have been censored. The call wasn't recorded, but Deena's call to 911 immediately afterward was. In that call she states, "They just knifed a passenger and there are guns on the plane". Deena said later, "If he said there was a gun on board, there was". This is the first of over 30 additional phone calls by passengers inside the plane.

9:29 a.m. Bush makes an already scheduled speech at Booker Elementary and announces a "Terrorist attack on our country". The speech occurred at exactly the time and place publicly announced beforehand making it clear that Bush - nor anyone else - considered himself to be a terrorist target. This is the last seen of Bush until the evening of Sept 11.

9:30 a.m. Radar tracks "Flight 77" as it closes within 30 miles of Washington, "moving from the northwest to the southwest". There are accounts that VP Cheney is told at 9:27 a.m. that radar is tracking Flight 77, 50 miles away from Washington. The 9/11 Commission says the plane wasn't discovered until 9:32 a.m.

9:30 a.m. The Secret Service finally rush Bush out of Booker Elementary School. A Sarasota police officer recalls that immediately after President Bush's speech, "The Secret Service agent [runs] out from the school and [says] we're under terrorist attack we have to go now."

9:30 - 9:37 a.m. Langley fighters fly *East* toward the ocean instead of north toward Washington. There are varying accounts that they were ordered to Washington, New York, Baltimore, or nowhere. In 2003 testimony, NORAD Commander Major General Larry Arnold explains that the fighters head over the ocean because NORAD is "looking outward" and has to have clearance to fly over land. Yet, the *BBC* reports that just before takeoff at 9:24 a.m., the pilots are specifically told that Flight 77 may have been hijacked and they had a cockpit signal indicating that they were in an emergency wartime situation. All accounts concur that, for whatever reason, the fighters go *East*.

9:34 a.m. Bush's motorcade heads for the Sarasota-Bradenton airport. A year later, Chief of Staff Andrew Card said, "As we were heading to Air Force One, we did hear about the Pentagon attack, and we also learned, what turned out to be a mistake, but we learned that the Air Force One package could in fact be a target."

9:35 a.m. Treasury Department evacuates; Pentagon does not.

9:36 a.m. Reagan Airport flight control instructs a military C-130 that has just departed Andrews Air Force Base to intercept Flight 77 and identify it. Pilot said, "When air traffic control asked me if we had him in sight, I told him that was an understatement - by then, he had pretty much filled our windscreen. Then he made a pretty aggressive turn so he was moving right in front of us, a mile and a half, two miles away. I said we had him in sight, then the controller asked me what kind of plane it was. That caught us up, because normally they have all that information. The controller didn't seem to know anything." He reported that it was either a 757 or 767 and its silver fuselage meant it was probably an American Airlines plane. They told us to "turn and follow that aircraft". Remarkably, this is the same C-130 that was 17 miles from Flight 93 when it later "crashed" in Pennsylvania.

9:36 a.m. Flight 93 turns around and files a new flight plan with a final destination of Washington. Radar shows the plane turning 180 degrees. The new flight plan schedules the plane to arrive in Washington at 10:28 a.m.

9:36 a.m. Flight 77 turns and disappears from radar. Just before radar contact is lost, FAA headquarters is told, "The aircraft is circling. It's turning away from the White House."

9:37 a.m. Flight 77 crashes into the Pentagon.

9:37 a.m. Witnesses claim that they see a military cargo plane near Flight 77. One witness says the military cargo plane was flying directly above the plane that hit the Pentagon "as if to prevent two planes from appearing on radar". As the craft descended toward the Pentagon, the military transport veered off to the West. The account of the pilot of the C-130 differs from the on-the-ground eyewitnesses. Interviewed later, he said, "with all of the East coast haze, I had a hard time picking him out." He also said that, just after the explosion, "I could see the outline of the Pentagon", implying by these statements that he was *not* nearby at all.

9:37 a.m. VP Cheney telephones Bush and tells him that the White House has been "targeted" and urges him to "stay away".

9:39 a.m. Jim Miklaszewski states on *NBC News*, "Moments ago, I felt an explosion here at the Pentagon".

9:40 a.m. FBI confiscates film of Pentagon crash "within minutes", says gas station employee. The security film on top of a hotel near the Pentagon was also confiscated.

9:40 a.m. Flight 93 Transponder Signal Turned Off; Flight Still Closely Tracked.

9:42 a.m. Passenger Mark Bingham calls his mother… "Hi mom, this is Mark Bingham."

9:45 a.m. Bush aides debate "where to go" with Bush.

9:55 a.m. Langley Fighters receive vague order to "protect White House".

9:55 a.m. Air Force One takes off, destination unknown, with no fighter escort.

9:56 - 10:40 a.m. Air Force One flies in circles while "Bush and Cheney and the Secret Service argue." The journalists onboard reported that the television reception for a local station remained generally good. So, one might think that Air Force One was circling over Florida, or at least over the Gulf of Mexico adjacent to Florida.

9:57 a.m. Passengers begin the attempt to regain control of Flight 93.

9:58 a.m. A man dialed emergency 911 from a bathroom on Flight 93 and says "we're being hijacked", and then reports an explosion and white smoke. The line then goes dead. The mentions of smoke and explosions on the recording of his call are now denied. The person who took the call is not allowed to speak to the media.

9:59 a.m., the South tower of the WTC, which was hit 17 mins *after* the North tower, collapses.

9:59 a.m. White House finally requests "Continuity of Government" Plans, Air Force One escort, and fighters for Washington.

10:00 a.m. Flight 93 transponder is turned back on and remains on for about 3 minutes.

10:00 - 10:15 a.m. Bush and Cheney claim to have been conferring on Shoot down Orders. There is no documentary evidence for this call. Even the 9/11 Commission was skeptical of this account.

10:00 - 10:30 a.m. Rumsfeld says that he returned from the Pentagon crash site around 10 a.m. He claimed to have made one or two calls in his office, one of which was to the President. Essentially, his whereabouts during this period is actually quite problematical.

10:03 - 10:10 a.m. Flight 93 "crashes". A Seismic study says the crash occurred at 10:06:05 a.m.

10:00 - 10:15 a.m. Cheney is told that Flight 93 is still headed for Washington and he orders it shot down. It is claimed that the plane had already crashed before this happened.

10:06 a.m. Witnesses see Flight 93 "rocking" its wings as it slowly descends.

10:06 a.m. Fighter plane seen trailing Flight 93. A second plane, described "as a small, white jet with rear engines and no discernible markings", was seen by at least six witnesses. Shortly after 9/11, an unnamed New England flight controller ignores a ban on controllers speaking to the media; he claims, "that an F-16 fighter closely pursued Flight 93...". Ernie Stuhl, the mayor of Shanksville: "I know of two people - I will not mention names - that heard a missile. They both live very close, within a couple of hundred yards... This one fellow's served in Vietnam and he says he's heard them, and he heard one that day."

Flight 93 apparently started to break up before it crashed because debris was found far away from the crash site. Debris fields are found two, three, and eight miles away from the main crash site.

10:15 a.m. The section of the Pentagon that had been hit by the unknown aircraft collapses.

10:28 a.m. the North WTC tower collapses, 17 before the South tower, collapses.

10:30 a.m. Acting Joint Chiefs of Staff Chairman Richard Myers enters the NMCC. There are discrepancies in the testimonies about where, exactly, he was, and these remain unresolved. In his own testimony, he fails to mention where he was or what he was doing from the time of the Pentagon crash until about 10:30 a.m.

10:30 a.m. Missing Rumsfeld finally enters NMCC after being missing for 30 minutes that are unaccounted for.

10:32 a.m. Vice President Cheney reportedly called President Bush and told him that Air Force One was a target. A later account calls the threat "completely untrue", and says Cheney probably made the story up to reinforce the reason that Bush was "unavailable".

10:35 a.m. Bush heads for Louisiana on Air Force One.

10:55 - 11:41 a.m. Fighter escort finally reaches Air Force One. One report says this occurred at 10 a.m. and another says it happened at 10:41 a.m. The *St. Petersburg Times*, after interviewing people who had been on Air Force One, concluded that the fighter escort from Texas arrived between 11:00 and 11:20. Why fighters did not reach Air Force One earlier is not clear.

11:00 a.m. Customs head, Robert Bonner, claimed later that he identified all 19 of the hijackers by running the passenger manifests through the system used by Customs. However, for two days, the FBI believed there were only 18 hijackers.

11:30 a.m. Media speculation that al-Qaeda is responsible promoted by General Wesley Clark.

11:30 a.m. Two congressmen, Dan Miller and Adam Putnam, who are on Air Force One, are summoned to meet with the President. Bush tells them about the "threat" and points to the fighter jet escort outside.

11:45 a.m. Air Force One lands at Louisiana Air Force Base. Bush remains in this location for approximately one hour recording a brief message and talking on the phone. Supposedly, these phone conversations consist of arguments with Dick Cheney and others over where he should go next.

12:58 p.m. "A few minutes before 1 p.m.", Bush agreed to go to Nebraska. It is alleged that this was due to "credible terrorist threats" on his life which prevented his return to Washington.

1:02 p.m. Donald Rumsfeld calls for WAR.

1:30 p.m. Air Force One leaves Louisiana for Nebraska.

2:00 p.m. An F-15 fighter pilot, Major Daniel Nash, returned to base after chasing Flight 175 and patrolling the sky over New York. He reported that when he got out of his plane that, "he [is] told that a military F-16 had shot down a fourth airliner in Pennsylvania...".

2:50 p.m. Bush arrives in Nebraska, Offutt Air Force Base. Bush stays on the plane for about ten minutes before entering the United States Strategic Command bunker at 3:06 p.m. where he begins a video conference meeting with Cheney, Rice, Rumsfeld, Armitage, Tenet, Mineta, Clarke, and others. Bush begins the meeting by saying, "I'm coming back to the White House as soon as the plane is fueled. No discussion." The meeting ends at **4:15** p.m.

4:00 p.m. CNN blames bin Laden for attacks.

4:10 p.m. WTC 7 is burning.

4:30 p.m. WTC 7 area evacuated.

4:33 p.m. Air Force One leaves Nebraska heading for Washington.

5:20 p.m. WTC building 7 collapses; the first modern, steel-reinforced high-rise to collapse "because of fire", The building's leaseholder, Larry Silverstein said in a PBS documentary, that the decision was made to "pull it", a term that implies deliberate demolition. However, building demolition takes a considerable period of preparation - even weeks.

6:54 p.m. Bush returns to the White House.

7:00 p.m. Secretary of State, Colin Powell, returns from Peru.

8:30 p.m. Bush gives third speech of the day: declares the Bush Doctrine: "We will make no distinction between the terrorists who committed these acts and those who harbor them."

9:00 p.m. Bush meets with the full National Security Council and then later with a smaller group of key advisers. They declare that Osama bin Laden is behind the attacks. He announces, "I want you all to understand that we are at war and we will stay at war until this is done. Nothing else matters. Everything is available for the pursuit of this war. Any barriers in your way, they're gone. Any money you need, you have it. This is our only agenda". When Rumsfeld points out that international law only allows force to prevent future attacks and not for retribution, Bush yells, *"No. I don't care what the international lawyers say, we are going to kick some ass."*

10:49 p.m. Attorney General Ashcroft tells members of Congress that there were three to five hijackers on each plane armed only with knives.

11:30 p.m. Bush writes in his diary: "The Pearl Harbor of the 21st century took place today."

Now that we have a pretty good "bird's eye view" of the official events of the day, let's zoom in a bit.

ZOOM

Flight 77's role in the 9/11 attacks is somewhat problematic. As we have already noted, there were many conflicting accounts in the initial hours after the Pentagon was hit.

After all of this confusion, it was finally announced that, according to officials, the explosion at the Pentagon was caused when American Airlines Flight 77, a 100 ton Boeing 757 commercial airliner, crashed at ground level into the only section of the building that was being renovated to be more "blast resistant" and which housed the fewest amount of employees in it. Flight 77 was allegedly hijacked by five Arab Islamic terrorists on an apparent suicide mission killing all 64 people on board. Officials claim the flight recorders from Flight 77 and the remains of all but one of the 64 passengers on board where found at the crash scene.

The strongest "evidence" that it was Flight 77 that crashed into the Pentagon was the testimony of Bush Administration member, Ted Olson, who claimed that his wife, a passenger on the flight, called him and gave him the inside info about what was going on. So let's take a moment to zoom in even closer and discuss:

The Saga of Babs and Ted

Ted and Barbara Olson were long time members of the Bush Cabal, deeply involved in numerous nefarious activities both known and unknown.

A passenger on Flight 77, Barbara Olson, allegedly called her husband, Theodore (Ted) Olson, who is Solicitor General at the Justice Department.[199] Ted Olson is in his Justice Department office watching WTC news on television when his wife calls. *A few days later*, he says:

> "She told me that she had been herded to the back of the plane. She mentioned that they had used knives and box cutters to hijack the plane. She mentioned that the pilot had announced that the plane had been hijacked." [*CNN*, 9/14/01]

He tells her that two planes have hit the WTC. [*Daily Telegraph*, 3/5/02]

She feels nobody is taking charge. [*CNN*, 9/12/01]

He doesn't know if she was near the pilots, but at one point she asks, "What shall I tell the pilot? What can I tell the pilot to do?" [*CNN*, 9/14/01 (C)]

Then she is cut off without warning. [*Newsweek*, 9/29/01][200]

Ted Olson's recollection of the call's timing is extremely vague, saying it "must have been 9:15 [am.] or 9:30 [am.]. Someone would have to reconstruct the time for me." [*CNN*, 9/14/01 (C)]

Other accounts place it around 9:25 A.M. [*Miami Herald*, 9/14/01; *New York Times*, 9/15/01 (C); *Washington Post*, 9/21/01][201]

The call is said to have lasted about a minute. [*Washington Post*, 9/12/01 (B)][202]

By some accounts, his message that planes have hit the WTC comes later, in a second phone call. [*Washington Post*, 9/21/01][203]

In one account, Barbara Olson calls from inside a bathroom. [*Evening Standard*, 9/12/01][204]

In another account, she is near a pilot, and in yet another she is near two pilots. [*Boston Globe*, 11/23/01][205]

Ted Olson's account of how Barbara Olson made her calls is also conflicting. Three days after 9/11, he says, "I found out later that she was having, for some reason, to call collect and was having trouble getting

---

[199] http://www.sfgate.com/cgi-bin/article.cgi?file=/chronicle/archive/2004/07/23/FLIGHTS.TMP

[200] http://www.msnbc.com/news/635771.asp

[201] http://www.startribune.com/stories/484/703150.html

[202] http://www.washingtonpost.com/ac2/wp-dyn/A14365-2001Sep11

[203] http://www.startribune.com/stories/484/703150.html

[204] http://www.cooperativeresearch.org/timeline/2001/eveningstandard091201.html

[205] http://www.boston.com/news/packages/underattack/news/planes_reconstruction.htm

through. You know how it is to get through to a government institution when you're calling collect." He says he doesn't know what kind of phone she used, but he has, "assumed that it must have been on the airplane phone, and that she somehow didn't have access to her credit cards. Otherwise, she would have used her cell phone and called me." [*Fox News*, 9/14/01][206]

Why Barbara Olson would have needed access to her credit cards to call him on her cell phone is not explained. However, in another interview on the same day, he says that she used a cell phone and that she may have been cut off, "because the signals from cell phones coming from airplanes don't work that well." [*CNN*, 9/14/01 (C)][207]

Six months later, he claims she called collect, "using the phone in the passengers' seats." [*Daily Telegraph*, 3/5/02]

However, it is not possible to call on seatback phones, collect or otherwise, without a credit card, which would render making a collect call moot. Many other details are conflicting, and Olson faults his memory and says that he, "tends to mix the two [calls] up because of the emotion of the events."

Larry King's interview with Ted Olson

KING: "Did she sound terrified, anxious, nervous, scared?

OLSON: No, she didn't. She sounded very, very calm.

KING: Typical Barbara.

OLSON: In retrospect, enormously, remarkably, incredibly calm. But she was calculating -- I mean, she was wondering, "What can I do to help solve this problem?" Barbara was like that. Barbara could not have not done something.

KING: What's going through you?

OLSON: My -- I am in -- I guess I'm in shock. And I'm horrified because I really -- while I had reassured her that I thought everything was going to be OK, I was pretty sure everything was not going to be OK. I, by this time, had made the calculation that these were suicide persons, bent on destroying as much of America as they could.

KING: Did you hear other noises on the plane?

OLSON: No, I did not. At one point, when she asked me what to say to the pilot, I asked her if she had any sense for where she was. *I had, after the first conversation, called our command center at the Department of Justice to alert them to the fact that there was another hijacked plane and that my wife was on it* and that she was capable of communicating, even though this *first phone call* had been cut off.

---

[206] http://www.cooperativeresearch.org/timeline/2001/foxnews091401.html
[207] http://www.cooperativeresearch.org/timeline/2001/cnn091401c.html

So I wanted to find out where the plane was. She said the plane had been hijacked shortly after takeoff and *they had been circling around,* I think were the words she used. She reported to me that she could see houses. I asked her which direction the plane was going. She paused -- there was a pause there. I think she must have asked someone else. She said I think it's going northeast.

KING: Which would have been toward the Pentagon?

OLSON: Depending upon where the plane was,..

KING: Dulles...

OLSON: Dulles is west of the Pentagon. So east of Dulles is the Pentagon. And this plane had been in the air for, I think, over an hour. So I don't know where she was when she called.

KING: They didn't do any direct flight right to the Pentagon.

OLSON: No, no. Her plane took off at 8:10. Its impact with the Pentagon must have been around 9:30 or so. You will probably be able to reconstruct that or have that information as to the time of the impact.

KING: How does the *second conversation* end?

OLSON: We are -- we segued back and forth between expressions of feeling for one another and this effort to exchange information. And then the phone went dead. I don't know whether it just got cut off again, because the signals from cell phones coming from airplanes don't work that well, or whether that was the impact with the Pentagon.

It was not -- *I stayed glued to my television.* I did call the command center again. Someone came down so I can impart this information and also to be there in case she called again. But it was very *shortly thereafter that news reports on the television indicated that there had been an explosion of some sort at the Pentagon.*

KING: Did you immediately know then that's what it was?

OLSON: I did. I mean I didn't want to. I did and I didn't want to, but I knew. But *it was a long time before what had happened at the Pentagon -- or it seemed like a long time -- before it was identified as an airplane. Then the first report that I heard was that it was a commuter plane, and then I heard it was an American Airlines plane.*

I called some people, I guess maybe just because I had to share the dread that was living with me. I called my mother and I called my son. I said I didn't think -- I thought that -- I was hoping that it wasn't true, but I was very worried. I did not want them to see something on television and hear her name.

KING: Your son was Barbara's stepson, right?

OLSON: Yes. I also tried to call my daughter, who was her stepdaughter.

KING: Did you hear from the President or the attorney general?

OLSON: Oh, yes, I did. *I heard from the President.* Well, *he was in the air.* I can't tell you exactly what time of day that was on the 11th. I also heard from the *attorney general*. I also heard from the *Vice President* and many other of our officials of government. And of course, scores of other people, including you and your wife and...

KING: How are you -- as you look at yourself, and looking at you now, how were you able -- and everybody, I'm sure, is saying this -- to *handle this so well*?

OLSON: I think -- I haven't talked to people that they call grief counselors or anything like that. But I think that *people are in shock for a considerable period of time*. That's why you're advised, I mean, not to make important decisions, not to do things that don't make sense. That's why people gather around. That's why friends show up at your home. That's why people go with you wherever you go just to be able to talk to you and insulate you from the emotions that are so -- packed so strongly in your body.

KING: By the way, was the President comforting?

OLSON: I thought the President was wonderfully comforting.

KING: To you on the phone?

OLSON: Yes, he was, enormously. *We couldn't speak long. This was during the day of the crisis*. And I didn't -- *I hadn't expected him to call*, because he is the President of the United States. We know now -- he knew then there were thousands of victims and terrible devastation and *crisis and the potential of further dangers to the structure of our government, meaning the institutions of our government and the leadership of our government*. I am deeply indebted to him that he had the time to call. He was very comforting. He is a very compassionate man.

KING: The audience of the show knows her so well. But a lot of the time they saw Barbara as harsh, Barbara very strongly opinionated, very conservative, maybe even more conservative than you, Ted.

OLSON: I don't know about that. But I think that's, it's interesting that you use that word opinionated, because Barbara mentioned once that she thought she was opinionated. And I said, "Barbara, you're not opinionated, you just have opinions."

KING: You told me about one thing last night, which just tore Shawn and my heart out. When you finally went to bed on Tuesday night, the end of this harrowing day, you find a note.

OLSON: Yes.

KING: What was it?

OLSON: Barb -- I left the home a little before 6:00, as I said. And Barbara left not long thereafter to catch the plane. And it was my birthday. And when I finally went to bed, it was after 1:00 on -- now it was September 12. There was a note that Barbara had written to me on the pillow, saying, "I love you. When you read this, I will be thinking of you and I will be back on -- I will be back Friday."

There were a few more words than that, but I just, that was a --
extraordinarily special and very much like Barbara. And I'm grateful that
she did that.

KING: Thank you, Ted, our hearts are with you.

OLSON: Thank you, Larry.

KING: Ted Olson, solicitor general of the United States. He did that earlier
for broadcast tonight."[208]

I have italicized a few of Ted's remarks for emphasis, but there are two
particular remarks that I would like to put together here:

"...it was a long time before what had happened at the Pentagon -- or it
seemed like a long time -- before it was identified as an airplane. Then the
first report that I heard was that it was a commuter plane, and then I heard it
was an American Airlines plane.[...]

I heard from the President. Well, he was in the air. I can't tell you exactly
what time of day that was on the 11th. ... We couldn't speak long. This was
during the day of the crisis. And I didn't -- I hadn't expected him to call,
because he is the President of the United States. We know now -- he knew
then there were thousands of victims and terrible devastation and crisis *and
the potential of further dangers to the structure of our government, meaning
the institutions of our government and the leadership of our government...* I
also heard from the attorney general. I also heard from the Vice President
and many other of our officials of government."

Now, let's think about this for a few moments. Let's keep the voice
morphing technology in mind when we consider phone calls from
airplanes. It's not that they can't happen, but the ones that supposedly
happened that day were often so bizarre as to challenge credulity.

Looking back at the testimony of the C-130 pilot above, we can see that
it is contradictory, and no facts can be established from that. If we hold the
phone call from the flight attendant on Flight 77 as being possibly suspect,
then we are left with this: The evidence that it was Flight 77 that hit the
Pentagon rests entirely on the *later* testimony of government officials who
most certainly might have an agenda. What is more, the *main* proof that
Flight 77 hit the Pentagon, the single event that clinches it according to the
official story, was the famous "phone call" from Barbara Olson to her
husband – a phone call that *could not have happened as described!*

Let us now return to the fact that the main mystery surrounds the fact
that the government will not release the security videos that obviously
would show what hit the Pentagon. The whole matter could be settled
right here and now with those videos.

Let me repeat: there is no reason to *not* release the videos even if a
different craft was used to strike the Pentagon, because, after all, a terrorist
attack is a terrorist attack no matter what kind of plane they use, right? If

---

[208] http://www.cooperativeresearch.org/timeline/2001/cnn091401c.html

you have control of the media - as is most certainly the case here, and has been used to good effect to conceal or marginalize the truth about 9-11 - then even if the government is complicit in the attacks on 9-11, they could spin whatever happened any way they wanted to as they have done so far.

If, according to the conspiracy theory of the current administration, Osama bin Laden had the resources to set up the hijacking of commercial jets to hit the World Trade Center, there is no reason he could not also have had the resources to get his hands on a fancy guided drone plane, or even a smaller jet, or anything similar for that matter. It would have been just as easy to lay it at Osama's door. That is to say, if Osama can be blamed for hitting the WTC with a couple of commercial jets, there is no reason he can't be blamed for hitting the Pentagon with something else.

In other words, no matter what it was - a Boeing 757 or a kite with a nuke attached to its tail - there is no reason the Powers That Be could not spin it to their advantage.

So why won't they release the security camera tapes?

If it was Flight 77, why can't we see it?

If it was something else, why can't we see it?

Heck, the American people are pretty accepting of explanations. There's no reason they wouldn't accept that Osama and gang could get hold of something else and fly it into the Pentagon. After all, Osama was said to have a massive underground hideout with missiles and a small army and about everything else. There's no reason why he couldn't also have been accused of getting his hands on a Global Hawk!

So again, and again, and again: why can't the American People *see what hit the pentagon*?

It clearly is not because of concern for the families of the victims and their grief. After all, the videos of the planes flying into the WTC were shown over and over and over and over again until the entire world was whipped into a frenzy of grief and rage.

Surely, assuming that the theory of direct complicity of Bush and Co. is correct, if the conspirators were setting this thing up as long as we think they were, they would have prepared the craft that hit the Pentagon very carefully and there would be nothing about it that would arouse suspicion or reveal their identify, right? Then they could just haul out the videos and show them around the world and blame Osama, right?

But something isn't quite right about the Pentagon Strike. And whatever it is, it has something to do with the "missing time" of Dick Cheney, Don Rumsfeld, and the flying in circles and "arguing" on the phone that George Bush did on that day.

Where did the body parts come from that were so quickly identified as those of the passengers of Flight 77 that allegedly hit the Pentagon? Body parts that survived from a massive aircraft that was claimed to have vaporized almost instantly?

The question about what happened to the passengers of Flight 77 leads us to the core of the mystery. If it was Flight 77 on the video, just show it and settle it. If it wasn't Flight 77 on the surveillance videos, why must the Bush Cabal *insist* that it was, even if they could just as easily have revealed that Osama had, in addition to hijacking three commercial jets, flown a guided drone into the Pentagon, or anything else? They could even explain a U.S. military plane being flown into the Pentagon by claiming that Osama owned one and painted it up to look like a U.S. craft.

Indeed, this small item is a terrible problem. It suggests that if the surveillance videos of what hit the Pentagon were shown, it would reveal the truth. And whatever truth that is, the Powers That Be will fight to the last gasp to conceal it.

We must dig deeper, it seems, for the solution to this problem.

Let's consider the fact that it seems obvious that George Bush, Dick Cheney, and Don Rumsfeld, *in no way*, felt threatened by the events of that day. Their insouciance demonstrates that said "terrorists" were terrifying everybody but them. We can look at the little stories about Cheney and Bush being worried that Air Force One was a target as "window dressing". After all, if you are going to play the victim, at some point you have to put on the victim act. They are smart enough to know that they had to act at least a little bit like they were concerned, even if they didn't manage to pull it off very well.

But what also seems obvious is that something strange was up during the period of time George Bush was flying around in circles, burning up the phone lines to Cheney, Rumsfeld and... Ted Olson? Yes indeedy.

After all, it was right at that time that George, Dick and Don ought to have been putting on their "victim" act. But the facts are that all of them "went missing" at a very crucial time and the key to the whole Pentagon mystery might lie in that fact.

So, the question that I think needs to be asked, based on the strange behavior of Bush, Cheney and Rumsfeld on that day, is this: even if they were complicit in setting up an exercise that provided a smoke screen for the 9/11 attacks to be executed by someone else, is it possible that Flight 77 was *not* part of the plan, as far as they were aware?

It's seems pretty certain that an attack on the Pentagon was part of the plan: witness the blasé behavior of Cheney and Rumsfeld even to the extent of Rumsfeld sitting in his office with Rep. Christopher Carter, making a prediction: "Believe me, this isn't over yet. There's going to be another attack, and it could be us." That was at 9:37 a.m., one minute before the Pentagon was hit.[209]

---

[209] Another account puts Rumsfeld's "I've been around the block a few times. There will be another event" comment two minutes before the first WTC crash at 8 :46 a.m.

In any event, the point is that these guys were not the least bit afraid, not the least bit ruffled, and they were actually hard pressed to even pretend to be shocked and afraid.

But something happened that changed all that. Notice this little bit of timing:

9:16 a.m. - 9:29 a.m. Bush is happily working on the speech he has to give in a few minutes. Never mind that "America is under attack", nothing is more important than Bush's speech at Booker elementary.

9:20 a.m. Barbara Olson is said to have called from Flight 77 but the account is full of contradictions.

9:27 a.m. Ted Olson calls the Justice Department's control center to relate his wife Barbara's call from Flight 77.

9:29 a.m. Bush makes his scheduled speech without a care in the world even if he is announcing that, "America is Under Attack".

9:29 a.m. Pentagon Command Center begins high level conference call.

9:30 a.m. Three Langley fighters go airborne, but they fly *due East*.

9:30 a.m. Suddenly, the Secret Service remember their job and hustle Bush out of the School and witnesses later state that they had the impression that there WAS a threat to the President at that point. That was one short speech!

9:34 a.m. Bush's motorcade heads for the Sarasota-Bradenton airport.

9:35 a.m. Treasury Department evacuates; Pentagon does not.

9:36 a.m. Flight 93 turns around, files a new flight plan with a final destination of Washington. Radar shows the plane turning 180 degrees. The new flight plan schedules the plane to arrive in Washington at 10:28 a.m.

9:36 a.m. Flight 77 turns and disappears from radar. Just before radar contact is lost, FAA headquarters is told, "The aircraft is circling. It's turning away from the White House".

9:37 a.m. Flight 77 allegedly crashes into the Pentagon.

9:37 a.m. VP Cheney claims that he telephoned Bush to tell him that the White House has been "targeted" and urges him to "stay away".

9:40 a.m. FBI confiscates film of Pentagon crash "within minutes", says a gas station employee. The security film on top of a hotel near the Pentagon was also confiscated.

9:40 a.m. Flight 93 Transponder signal turned off; flight still closely tracked.

9:42 a.m. Passenger Mark Bingham calls his mother…

9:45 a.m. Bush aides debate "where to go" with Bush.

9:55 a.m. Langley Fighters receive vague order to "protect White House".

9:55 a.m. Air Force One takes off, destination unknown, with no fighter escort.

9:56 - 10:40 a.m. Air Force One flies in circles while "Bush and Cheney and the Secret Service argue".

10:00 - 10:15 a.m. Bush and Cheney claim to have been conferring on Shoot down Orders. There is no documentary evidence for this call. Even the 9/11 Commission was skeptical of this account.

10:00 - 10:30 a.m. Rumsfeld says that he returned from the Pentagon crash site around 10 a.m. He claimed to have made one or two calls in his office, one of which was to the President. Essentially, his whereabouts during this period is actually quite problematical.

Now, remember what Ted Olson said in his interview quoted above?

"... it was *very shortly thereafter that news reports on the television indicated that there had been an explosion of some sort at the Pentagon.*"

"... *it was a long time before what had happened at the Pentagon -- or it seemed like a long time -- before it was identified as an airplane. Then the first report that I heard was that it was a commuter plane, and then I heard it was an American Airlines plane.*"

"... *I heard from the President.* Well, *he was in the air.* I can't tell you exactly what time of day that was on the 11th. I also heard from the *attorney general.* I also heard from the *Vice President.*"

"... *We couldn't speak long. This was during the day of the crisis.* And I didnt -- *I hadn't expected him to call...*"

"...he knew then there were thousands of victims and terrible devastation and *crisis and the potential of further dangers to the structure of our government, meaning the institutions of our government and the leadership of our government.*"

What if Ted Olson was telling the truth in these words? After all, as an attorney he would know that the best liars are those that stick closest to the truth?

Here's a scenario for the reader to consider.

There were in fact two event plans for the 9/11 attacks - the plan as relayed to the American conspirators and the *real* plans known only to the key members of the plot - the Israeli contingent. In the murkey world of international politics, one should never fully trust anyone, even those with whom you temporarily share a common goal. As such, Bush, Cheney et al were told by the Israeli organizers of 9/11 that two planes would be "hijacked" and flown into the WTC towers, another smaller light aircraft packed with explosives would be flown into the Pentagon, and a fourth similarly configured craft would hit the White House. Both these later craft were to be of a type that would fit with Osama's alleged arsenal and the much-publicized light aircraft training received by the patsy "hijackers". The *real* plan was somewhat different and involved an "insurance" aspect that the Israeli contingent could later use to ensure full compliance with Israeli wishes from the Bush administration. From the available data, we suggest that, from the point of view of the Bush contingent, neither Flight 93 nor Flight 77 were ever meant to part of the 9/11 attacks, and that the real plan involved attacks on not only the WTC towers and the Pentagon, but another symbolic target such as the Washington Monument also. Yet, as we shall see, things did not go according to plan, even for the Israeli contingent.

By 8:55 a.m. the pilots of Flight 77 are aware that their plane has been "hijacked" by persons unknown and they have verified that they are no longer in control of the aircraft. Not long thereafter, a call is routed to Barbara Olsen's seatback satellite phone. The voice on the other end is one she knows and knows that the message is a deadly serious one. She is informed that the two men in the seats beside her have been assigned to her and that if she wants to live, she should follow their instructions to the letter.

Barbara is told by her handlers that she should call her husband, Ted, which she duly does. But the message she delivers is not that Flight 77 has been hijacked by Arab terrorists. No, indeed, it is much worse than that. As Ted said:

> [The President knew] "the potential of *further dangers to the structure of our government,* meaning the institutions of our government and *the leadership of our government.*"

The ball was no longer in the court of the Bush Cabal: they had been checked and mated. They had formed an unholy alliance with masters of deception, whose only rule was "do unto others before they do unto you". In short, Barbara is "insurance". Just because the perpetrators of the 9/11 attack had the cooperation of the Bush Cabal, it doesn't mean that they trust them. They want insurance. And now they have it.

Not longer after Barbara hangs up the phone to Ted, she notices that her "handlers" are putting on gas masks. They hand one to her which she meekly places over her mouth and nose. They are sitting virtually alone in first class. As the analgesic gas is released, the other 63 passengers behind them and the pilots and crew fall unconscious.

Not long after the gas is released into the cabin of Flight 77, the URAP is activated and a new flight plan filed. The destination: Wright Patterson AFB in Ohio. Somewhere over Western West Virginia, at about 8.56 a.m., Flight 77's transponder is remotely switched off rendering it invisible to air traffic control. Flight 77 continues Westward and then bears north towards Wright Patterson landing about 40 minutes later at almost the same time that something *else* hits the Pentagon.

Around the time that Flight 77's transponder is switched off, a specially modified Global Hawk UAV (unmanned aerial vehicle) equipped with a "shaped charge" warhead and a secondary Depleted Uranium warhead takes off from a ship off the Eastern coast of the U.S.

At 9:35 a.m. the global hawk approaches the controlled Washington airspace from the Northwest and the batteries of anti-aircraft defense systems "read" the intruder as "ours". Because it *is*. Air traffic controllers at Washington's Dulles Airport pick up the aircraft using primary radar as a blip on their screens, only the aircraft's position, altitude and speed can be read. The global hawk is traveling at almost 500 miles per hour prompting flight controller Todd Lewis to say:

> "My colleagues saw a target moving quite fast from the northwest to the southeast. So she—we all started watching that target, and she notified the supervisor. However, nobody knew that was a commercial flight at the time. Nobody knew that was American 77. ... I thought it was a military flight."[210]

Danielle O'Brien, the Dulles flight controller said to be the first to spot the blip, comments on the speed and maneuverability of the approaching craft and opines that it must be "one of ours" (a USAF jet). The global hawk initially over-flies the immediate area of the Pentagon only to carry out a 270 degree turn with a steep descent from several thousand feet as it zeroes in on the Pentagon. Descending further to just above ground level as it gets within 200 feet of the Pentagon's west façade, the missile carrying the shaped charge is unleashed. In the initial explosion the global hawk's lightweight carbon-fibre-epoxy composite wings are completely destroyed, while the 5 feet wide, 44 feet long aluminum fuselage is torn into relatively small pieces. The shaped charge punches holes through three rings of the Pentagon, and the remote controlled nuke comes to rest. There isn't much time to make a decision, so the Bush Cabal thinks fast and decide to make the best of a bad situation. They even see how they can turn it to their advantage. After all, Barbara Olson is an attractive public figure and if she is thought to have been a victim, no one will ever suspect the perpetrators of sacrificing one of their own. Of course, the evidence that a Global Hawk hit the Pentagon and that Barabara Olsen is still alive is firmly in the hands of the Israeli contingent.

The negotiations completed, Cheney and Rumsfeld send special agents out immediately to confiscate the videos of the Pentagon and the cover-up machine goes into operation.

At about the same time as the global hawk impacts the Pentagon, Flight 77 is landing by computer control at Wright Patterson AFB. Barbara Olson and her two handlers step off the plane, the only ones to do so, and are met and moved to a secure location. The remaining dead passengers and crew are removed from Flight 77 by a "clean up" crew. Several body parts are removed and later that day taken to the Pentagon to be found and identified. The remaining body parts are incinerated.

Flight 77 is literally taken apart in a private hanger at Wright Patterson and later taken "piecemeal" to a "secure location".

Barbara Olson currently resides in one of the many extensive "secure locations" somewhere in the mainland US. Her husband, Ted Olson, who

---

[210] http://www.aldeilis.net/aldeilis/content/view/310/107/

as Solicitor General was instrumental in preventing the Supreme Court from ordering a recount of votes in the 2000 election and ensuring the Presidency for George Bush, meets with her regularly. And the Bush Cabal will defend to the death the claim that Flight 77 hit the Pentagon against ALL evidence to the contrary. It was, after all, a decision made in haste, under pressure.

The Problem With Flight 93

After following its normal flight plan towards Cleveland, and at approximately 9:40 a.m. Flight 93's transponder is remotely switched off and a new flight path is logged via the URAP that will see it plough into the Washington monument and the Mall, and of course, lots of innocent tourists - but it will never arrive there. As yet, the pilots of Flight 93 are unaware that their aircraft is now under the control of the automatic URAP, believing that the autopilot is still guiding the plane along its normal intended path. As Flight 93 climbs further, an anomalous "misfiring" occurs in the air pressure sensitive mechanism that should have activated the analgesic gas. No gas is released and the passengers and crew remain sitting comfortably in their seats, fully awake and aware.

Alarmed by this apparently disastrous "mechanical glitch", the "technician" sitting in front of the screen quickly calls his superiors to inform them of the matter in hand. The order is given to go to "plan B" and to verify that control can still be exerted over the aircraft. The URAP is set to "manual takeover" and the technician attempts to perform some basic maneuvers to confirm that the URAP is still functional in this mode.

As reported by MSNBC:

> "Cleveland flight controller Stacey Taylor recalls, "I hear one of the controllers behind me go, 'Oh, my God, oh my God,' and he starts yelling for the supervisor. He goes, 'What is this plane doing? What is this plane doing?' I wasn't that busy at the time, and I pulled it up on my screen and he was climbing and descending and climbing and descending, but very gradually. He'd go up 300 feet, he'd go down 300 feet..[211]

It is, but "automatic" control and the ability to have Flight 93 fly into the Washington Monument has been fatally compromised.

Previously, at about 9:00 a.m. Ed Ballinger, a flight dispatcher for United Airlines, sent messages one by one to the 16 transcontinental flights he is covering, including Flight 93, warning them of the first WTC crash and of the risk of a hijacking. These erratic and independent maneuvers of their aircraft alert the pilots of Flight 93, Jason Dahl and LeRoy Homer, that something is seriously wrong. Aware of the fact that commercial aircraft can be remotely controlled, the pilots conclude that

---

[211] http://members.fortunecity.com/seismicevent/msnbctransponder.html

this is in fact what is happening and decide to take back control of the plane. Denied any chance to communicate effectively with Air Traffic Control or the outside world by the conspirators, the pilots decide that rather than continue on the long trek to San Francisco, the best course of action is to turn around and manually pliot the 757 towards Washington Dulles airport which, given the nature of the events that were transpiring, they reasonably assume will be one of the safest parts of US airspace. As reported by several news sites, it was around this time that Flight 93 did indeed file a new Flight plan for Washington Dulles.[212]

Yet even as the two pilots of Flight 93 are discussing their options, an unmarked white F-15 jet with two AMRAAM missiles slung under its wings is preparing to take off from a remote corner of Olmsted AFB in Pennsylvania.

Just before 10:00 am, as Flight 93 is heading towards the Pennsylvannia border, the F-15 comes within 10 miles of Flight 93 and launches its missiles at the Boeing. Both missile target the heat signatures given off by the 757's engines. On impact, the war heads detonate, knocking a large chunk off one engine, seriously damaging the other and blowing a hole in the fuselage and scattering passenger bodies, luggage and debris into the air.

As originally officially reported, at 9:58 a.m., passenger Edward Felt dials emergency 911 from a bathroom on Flight 93 stating: "we're being hijacked"[213] and reports an explosion and white smoke after which the line goes dead.[214] The mention of smoke and explosions on the recording of his call are now denied by the FBI. The person who took the call is no longer allowed to speak to the media.[215]

Flight 93 has been fataly damaged, but the pilots and crew do not give up. The plane is severly damaged and is going down, yet the pilots, and possibly two passengers who have pilots licences, are fighting to maintain control.

The damage from the missiles to Flight 93's electronics causes the URAP to go off line and the Boeing's transponder comes back for a few moments[216] before Flight 93 definitively ends its journey in field near Shanksville Pennsylvania. As Flight 93 struggles to stay aloft, the cockpit voice recorder gives definitive proof of the real cause of the crash:

As reported by CNN:

---

[212] http://www.guardian.co.uk/wtccrash/story/0,1300,575518,00.html

[213] http://www.canoe.ca/CNEWSAttack010916/16_week-sun.html

[214] http://web.archive.org/web/20011223160242/http://abclocal.go.com/kgo/news/091101_nw_terrorist_attack_united.html

[215] http://www.mirror.co.uk/news/allnews/page.cfm?objectid=12192317&method=full&siteid=50143

[216] http://members.fortunecity.com/seismicevent/msnbctransponder.html

"Near the end of [Flight 93's] cockpit voice recording, loud wind sounds can be heard." [217]

As reported in the UK Mirror:

"Sources claim the last thing heard on the cockpit voice recorder is the sound of wind—suggesting the plane had been holed."[218]

Sometime after 9: 57 a.m. (just a few minutes before the plane hits the ground) at the end of the cockpit voice recording the sounds of the passengers and or pilots are heard in unaccented English to say: "Give it to me!" "I'm injured", and then something like "roll it up" or "lift it up" is heard.[219]

Yet to no avail. Flight 93 hits the ground somewhere between 10:03 a.m. and 10:06 a.m. Part of one of the engines is found about a mile away from the main crash site, the only reasonable explanation being that it somehow "detached" while the plane was still high in the air. Debris, and possibly body parts, are found by locals up to 8 miles from the crash site and paper is reported to have been still floating in the air for an hour after the impact. [220]

As previously noted, at least five eyewitnesses report a "small, white jet with rear engines and no discernible markings", flying low and in erratic patterns, not much above treetop level, over the crash site within minutes of the United flight crashing.

Of course, the simple truth is that, after Flight 93 developed its "glitches" and the pilots were attempting to bring the plane and passengers home safe and sound, there was simply no way that the conspirators could allow the occupants of the plane to survive and tell their stories.

On the one year anniversary of 9/11, George and Laura Bush attended a memorial ceremony at the Flight 93 "crash" site. (See Plate 18)

Considering all of the evidence that points to members of the Bush administration being guilty of the cold-blooded and needless murder of the 44 passengers and crew of Flight 93, the above image should leave readers in no doubt to the extent of the arrogance, hypocrisy and callousness with which the current leaders of the United States pursue their insane, megalomaniacal agenda.

Meanwhile, back in Washington, agents acting on behalf of the Bush contingent have started a fire at the White House in anticipation of the impact of the "Osama special", the small light aircraft they had been told

[217] http://www.cnn.com/2002/US/04/19/rec.flight.93.families

[218] http://www.mirror.co.uk/news/allnews/page.cfm?objectid=12192317&method=full&siteid=50143

[219] http://msnbc.msn.com/id/3080117/

[220] http://web.archive.org/web/20021028201123/http://news.independent.co.uk/world/americas/story.jsp?story=323958

to expect. The many references in media reports in the aftermath of the attacks that the Bush gang were expecting an attack on the White House and references to a fire at the White House are evidence of this. Of course, this attack never came, forcing the Bush gang to hurriedly cover it up.

From a strategic point of view, the attack on the White House that never came was a smart maneuver that helped to sow doubt and confusion among the Bush gang, not to mention making them look like a bunch of scared and incompetent buffoons and leaving the proverbial sword of Damocles hanging over their heads.

In short, while Bush was flying around, or better said, "running scared" that day, during that period of awful silence when no one knew where the Commander in Chief was, or what he might be doing, or what terrible thing was going to happen next, it is quite likely that he *was* on the phone to Ted Olson, among many others, and that some very fast damage control was being discussed, all the while the conspirators were having it shoved in their faces that they were *not* as smart as they thought they were.

Speculating further about the possible existence of national level satellite photos in the hands of someone with whom the Bush Cabal has had to negotiate, we can then move to the suggestion that, once these negotiations were satisfactorily concluded, the plan was resumed to utilize Flight 77, as the "plane that hit the Pentagon" with the agreement and complicity of Ted Olson who had been so "comforted" by the phone call from the President, and his "late" wife Barbara Olson.

After this step was taken, the hangman's noose was sprung: from that moment on, the video footage of what really struck the Pentagon had to be concealed at all costs. If it were to be released and the truth revealed, impossible questions about the fate of Flight 77 and its occupants and the phone calls they made would immediately arise and the entire operation would be exposed for what it is: a murderous attack on the United States Citizens by masters of deception with the complicity of their own government.

If our speculative line is correct, it means that the Bush Cabal have been hoisted on their own petard, and are being controlled, blackmailed, or otherwise held to a certain "line" by *some other group* so that this information will not be released. The main question is, of course, who is it and what are they demanding? Based on simple observation, nothing but the total destruction of the United States is going to satisfy them, along with a radical reshaping of the Middle East along Israeli lines that will necessarily involve a major war in which a significant percentage of Middle Eastern peoples, Jews and Arabs alike, will likely perish. Given the Iraqi quagmire that the US has *apparently* willingly entered into, a quagmire that seems to increasingly likely to lead to the fall and discrediting of America from it position as "world leader", it is emmiently reasonable and logical to suggest that they are only doing so under some form of duress.

We think that the scenario that we have outlined is much more plausible than the story floated by the Bush Administration to cover it up. What, in fact, could be more outlandish than the idea that 9/11 was carried out by 19 Arab terrorists armed only with box cutters, guided by a crazy recluse from a cave in Afghanistan? Toxic gas, computer-controlled aircraft, and an air defense system that was commanded to stand down or Arabs, box cutters, and the largest failure of NORAD one could possibly imagine conveniently falling on the one day it has been needed most since its inception.

It's your call.

To believe the conspiracy theory the government has promoted about 9/11 you need to believe that everything that could go wrong, did go wrong; that the system that had worked perfectly 67 times in the previous twelve months for intercepting aircraft somehow, at the most crucial moment in U.S. History, failed.

In short, the Greatest Military machine on earth was obliged to declare itself the most incompetent in order to cover up a truly horrific crime. Thousands of lives of U.S. citizens were lost on that day, thousands more American, Afghani, and Iraqi lives have been lost in the years since, and no one has been held accountable. At the same time, Draconian laws curtailing American freedoms have been passed to "make America Safe". The fact is, if the systems *already in place* had not been ordered to stand down, there would not have been an attack on the WTC Towers, much less the Pentagon. If U.S. political leaders were really interested in protecting the American people, the systems in place would have worked, and there would have been no need for the Patriot Act.

In the four years since the images of planes exploding in the windows of the World Trade Center were engraved in our psyches, the movement of people who doubt the official story of 9/11 has grown. There are now many websites devoted to the question. But how many Americans are willing to look at the facts in the face and confront the truth: the "attack" of 9/11 was an inside job.

Half a million people marched in New York in 2003 and again in Washington in 2005, against George Bush. They were angry that he has brought on war, deficit, tax cuts for the rich, surging unemployment and the most anti-democratic loss of rights ever seen in the USA. But how much coverage did these (and other) marches get in the media?

Moreover, even if they are in the streets protesting against the abuses and lies that are known, how many of those 500,000 people know how bad the situation really is? How many are willing to consider that Israeli Intelligence, with the help of a group of people in the Bush government, may very well have organised and staged the attacks on the World Trade

Center and the Pentagon in order to justify a "war on terror", that is, a war on the peoples of the Middle East? This war began in Afghanistan and has continued into Iraq. It looks now as though the administration is ready to take on Iran and eventually Syria, the countries named in a 1996 report prepared for Israeli PM Netanhayu by members of the neo-con cabal. Eretz Israel, these lands are called; the land God gave the Jews; and they want it all.

This abbreviated collection of data (believe me, there is a ton of material out there on this subject) does seem to support the idea that Mossad may, indeed, have been responsible for the 9-11 attacks on the World Trade Center and that the Bush Reich was not only complicit in ordering the U.S. military and intelligence services to "stand down", but that they were directly involved in the plot as the evidence of the link between Bob Graham and Mahmoud Ahmad demonstrates not to mention the saga of Babs and Ted.

And, of course, though each group is playing the other as in Spy vs. Spy, there are many things that Israel ought to consider in the volatile climate of burgeoning criticism of Israel around the world, a climate that could become full-blown anti-Semitism if Israel continues its ruthless aggression. But then again, we notice that the Israeli government and its intelligence agencies are actively promoting the idea that "a new wave of anti-Semitism" is sweeping Europe, an idea that serves to immediately quell any criticism of the inhuman policies of the Israeli government in the Middle East and around the world.

Never mind that Bush and Co, and American intel organizations have been stirring the pot for years. Just as people were "angry" and wanted an "answer" to 9-11, what kind of answer will be given when the heat is turned up on the Bush Reich? Is it not likely that Bush and friends would sacrifice their Israeli friends before taking the fall themselves? Just imagine what would happen if, suddenly, all the fingers pointed to Israel and Mossad as the masterminds of Global Terrorism?

It became abundantly clear to me that the events of September 11 were planned by those who not only had the motive, means, and opportunity to carry out the plan, but also were best placed to manage the consequences stemming from it, as well as managing the flow of information. What was also evident was that the question: "Who benefits?" had to be asked from a completely different perspective than simple diplomatic or foreign relations would allow. It became evident that the agenda was much more than just that of Israel wanting to get support for a war against the Palestinians or the Americans helping Israel because they wanted to gain control of oil in Iraq or opium trade and pipelines in Afghanistan. I realized that the events of September 11 were masterminded by those who were in the best position to manage the consequences and to obtain the benefits. It was clear that this was not Israel, though Israel may have been manipulated to participate because of its own tunnel-vision. Also, it was clear that the benefits were seen to be something altogether different.

It appears that the events of September 11 were planned years in advance, with the groundwork being carefully laid by a propaganda campaign orchestrated to convince the public that the United States has a plausibly sophisticated nemesis with the motive, means, and opportunity to perpetrate a devastating act of terror against Americans: Arab terrorism.

It also seems that the whole show was orchestrated using proxy agents and operative planners who are not only sufficiently distanced and compartmentalized from the true masterminds, (to create a condition of "plausible deniability"), but have been set up as patsies with evidence that has been carefully laid to incriminate them at the proper time.

As I have said, the real guilt must be sought among those who are in the best position to manage the flow of information as well as to reliably benefit from the new world order that is being created. When we take a broad view of the problem, we first see that the right-wing Israeli agenda benefits greatly from world opinion being turned against "Arab terrorists" and by implication of the Palestinians. There are those who seek to accuse the Jews as a whole of a plan for global domination, by gaining control of the Middle Eastern oil and thereby controling the world. Unfortunately, since Israel is very likely going to be destroyed in the process they will not be the ones who benefit. The only ones who will benefit are the political and corporate elites of the United States, the United Kingdom, the European Union and the "Zionists", who claim to act in the best interests of the Jewish people - also, as it happens, the very parties orchestrating the global war on terrorism.

In short, they are using the Jews to play the patsy in the final episode of the "Final Solution".

There are those commentators of the political and global scene who would like to think that this is merely a conspiracy of rich and powerful people who "see it as their moral duty" to establish a One World Government and to whom a unified world government is the most logical way to manage the affairs of the world.

Anybody who attributes this conspiracy to strictly human agencies obviously has not read the mountain of evidence detailing the multi-millennial evidence of this conspiracy including the long history of the UFO phenomenon and its intersection with the military and war. At the ultimate level, humans are *not* the masterminds, we can assure you. It is absurd to assign the motive to a perception of a moral duty, or even a logical approach to managing world affairs. That is nonsense in the face of the facts.

No indeed, there is an altogether different agenda being manifested here. It is the ultimate secret behind the events of 9/11.

Part 2: The Ultimate Truth

Into the Labyrinth

> The most successful tyranny is not the one that uses force
> to assure uniformity but the one that removes the
> awareness of other possibilities, that makes it seem
> inconceivable that other ways are viable, that removes the
> sense that there is an outside.
> *The Closing of the American Mind* - Allan Bloom

When researcher-author William Bramley began a seven-year investigation into the causes of war, he fully expected to find profit as the prime motivating factor. As everyone knows, war is not only very profitable to those who lend money or sell arms, it is also an excellent means of social and political control.

Studying man's history of warfare, Bramley found something he did not expect: abundant evidence of third-party manipulation. He wrote:

> It is no secret, for example, that prior to the American Revolution, France
> had sent intelligence agents to America to stir up colonial discontent against
> the British Crown. It is also no secret that the German military had aided
> Lenin and the Blosheviks in the Russian revolution of 1917. Throughout all
> of history, people and nations have benefitted from, and have contributed to,
> the existence of other people's conflicts.

What Bramley was not prepared to find - being a more or less average guy with a hobby studying warfare - was the repeated evidence of so-called UFOs in history associated with human conflicts.

> As I probed deeper … I was compelled to face the possibility that some
> human problems may be rooted in some of the most utterly bizarre realities
> imaginable. Because such realities are rarely acknowledged, let along
> understood, they are not dealt with. As a result, the problems those realities
> generate are rarely resolved, and so the world seems to shamble from one
> calamity to the next.[221]

The conclusions that the documents and traces he uncovered in the historical record led Bramley to conclude that human beings are under the covert control of an "alien" race that use war as a means of control. He also suggests that this alien race - which we propose is hyper-dimensional

---

[221] William Bramley, (1993) *The Gods of Eden*, Avon Books, NY

- breeds never-ending conflicts between human beings, promotes spiritual decay (and religious nonsense to encourage same), and induces conditions on Earth of "unremitting hardship." We would like to suggest that war and hardship may also be used as a means of harvesting energy and that this is a subject for a Ponerologist. It seems logical to assume that psychopaths could be deviants produced for the express purpose of doing what they do best: Ponerogenesis.

Bramley's ideas are right in line with the speculations of Charles Fort who wrote:

> I think we're property. I should say we belong to something: that once upon a time, this Earth was No-man's Land, that other worlds explored and colonized here, and fought among themselves for possession, but that now it's owned by something. That something owns this Earth - all others warned off.[222]

Dr Fred Hoyle, one of the world's foremost astrophysicists said in a 1971 news conference:

> Human beings are simply pawns in the games of alien minds that control our every move. They are everywhere, in the sky, on the sea, and on the Earth... It is not an alien intelligence from another planet. It is actually from another universe which entered ours at the very beginning and has been controlling all that happened since. [223]

As the title of Part Two suggests, this is not just another 9/11 book. While most published works on the incredible events of September 11th, 2001 explore the many and striking inconsistencies between what actually happened on that day and the *official* story as presented by the Bush administration, it is our conviction that, in order to fully understand the true meaning of 9/11, a much longer view must be taken.

The "core" of the 9-11 event can only be reached with a more or less spiraling approach. In this sense, it is very much like a labyrinth - which is an entirely appropriate metaphor - and we will follow the threads that lead from one item to another, finally arriving at the center, facing the monster, and then hopefully finding our way out again.

Curiously, after exploring this labyrinth, we will come to see that whether or not 9/11 was orchestrated by the US, by Israel, or by Osama bin Laden, is secondary to the ultimate secret. On this level, it is more important that the event happened than who actually came up with the idea. Certainly, it makes sense that it was Israel and the U.S. What we explore here in no way contradicts either that theory or any of the facts discussed in Part 1. It simply makes us aware that, given the choices made by mankind, as individuals and as societies, over the millennia, something

---

[222] Charles Fort, (1941), *The Books of Charles Fort*, Henry Holt, NY, p. 163, quoted by Jim Marrs, op. cit.
[223] Dr. Fred Hoyle, (1971) quoted by Otto O. Binder in "UFOs 'Own' Earth and All Mankind! *Saga*, December 1971, p. 36, quoted by Jim Marrs.

like a 9/11 was bound to happen. This in no way lessens the guilt or the karmic burden on the perpetrators. They were free to choose, and they did.

Jews, Christians and Moslems have a certain notion of the past that is conveyed to them in hagiography, Bible stories, and the Koran, as well as in chronologies and historical accounts. We tend to accept all of these as "truth" - as chronological histories along with what else we know about history - and we often reject out-of-hand the idea that these may all be legends and myths that are meta-historical - special ways of speaking about events in a manner that rises above history. They may also be mythicized history that must be carefully examined in a special way in order to extract the historical probabilities.

The chronologies, the way that we arrange dates and the antecedents that we assume for events, should be of some considerable concern to everyone. If we can come to some reasonable idea of the real events, the "facts", we can define the data that make up our view of the world in which we live and our own place within it. Perhaps such facts about our history can explain why our theologies and values tell us what they do, not focusing so much on what we believe, but *why* we believe what we do. This should indicate to us whether or not we ought really to discard the idea that those beliefs are "historical".

One could say, of course, that all history is a lie. Whenever we recount events or stories about people and times that are not immediately present to us, we are simply creating a *probable* picture of the past or a "distant happening". For most people, the horror and suffering of the Iraqi and Palestinian people, at the present moment in "time", has no spatial meaning because it is "over there". It is quite easy for *false images* of such events to be created and maintained as "history" by those who are not directly experiencing the events, particularly if they are not told the truth about them by those who do know. And so it has been throughout history.

An additional problem is that history not only is generally distorted by the victors, it is then later "mythicized". There is a story found in the *History* of Herodotus, which is an exact copy of an older tale of Indian origin, except for the fact that in the original, it was an animal fable, and in Herodotus' version, all the characters had become human. In every other detail, the stories are identical. Joscelyn Godwin quotes R. E. Meagher, professor of humanities and translator of Greek classics saying: *"Clearly, if characters change species, they may change their names and practically anything else about themselves."*

Going further still, historian of religion, Mircea Eliade, clarifies for us the process of the "mythicization" of historical personages. Eliade describes how a Romanian folklorist recorded a ballad describing the death of a young man bewitched by a jealous mountain fairy on the eve of his marriage. The young man, under the influence of the fairy was driven off a cliff. The ballad of lament, sung by the fiancée, was filled with "mythological allusions, a liturgical test of rustic beauty".

The folklorist, having been told that the song concerned a tragedy of "long ago", discovered that the fiancée was still alive and went to interview her. To his surprise, he learned that the young man's death had occurred less than 40 years before. He had slipped and fallen off a cliff; in reality, there was no mountain fairy involved.

Eliade notes that, "despite the presence of the principal witness, a few years had sufficed to strip the event of all historical authenticity, to transform it into a legendary tale". Even though the tragedy had happened to one of their contemporaries, the death of a young man soon to be married "had an occult meaning that could only be revealed by its identification with the category of myth".

To the masses, hungry to create some meaning in their lives, the myth seemed truer, more pure, than the prosaic event, because, "it made the real story yield a deeper and richer meaning, revealing a tragic destiny". We could even suggest that George W. Bush is viewed in this way by many Americans who prefer to believe that he is a heroic President, landing on aircraft carriers with verve and flair and a glint of steel in his eyes, protecting them from evil terrorists, when in fact, he is a cheap liar, a psychopath, and undoubtedly complicit in cooking up the attacks on the World Trade Center and Pentagon.

In the same way, a Yugoslavian epic poem celebrating a heroic figure of the fourteenth century, Marko Kraljevic, abolishes completely his historic identity, and his life story is "reconstructed in accordance with the norms of myth". His mother is a Vila, a fairy, and so is his wife. He fights a three-headed dragon and kills it, fights with his brother and kills him, all in conformity with classical mythic themes.

The *historic character* of the persons celebrated in epic poetry is *not in question*, Eliade notes. "But their historicity does not long resist the corrosive action of mythicization." *A historic event, despite its importance, doesn't remain in the popular consciousness or memory intact.*

The memory of the collective is anhistorical. Murko Chadwick, and other investigators of sociological phenomena have brought out the role of the creative personality, of the "artist", in the *invention and development* of epic poetry. They suggest that there are "artists" behind this activity, that there are people *actively working to modify the memory* of historical events. Such artists are either naturally or by training, psychological manipulation adepts. They fully understand that the masses think in "archetypal models". The mass mind cannot accept what is prosaic and individual and preserves only what is exemplary. This reduction of events to *categories* and of individuals to *archetypes*, carried out by the consciousness of the masses of peoples, functions in conformity with archaic ontology. We might say that - with the help of the artist/poet or psychological manipulator - popular memory is *encouraged* to give to the historical event a meaning that imitates an archetype and reproduces archetypal gestures.

At this point, as Eliade suggests, we must ask ourselves if the importance of archetypes for the consciousness of human beings, and the inability of popular memory to retain *anything but archetypes*, does not reveal to us something more than a *resistance to history* exhibited by traditional spirituality?

What could this "something more" be?

I would like to suggest that it is best explained by the saying, "the victors write the history". This works because the lie is more acceptable to the masses since it generally produces what they would *like* to believe, rather than what is actually true. We have certainly seen a few hints that this is exactly what George Bush and company are doing, based on this "rewriting of the event" in real time wherein Bush is scripted as the star of the show and the recipient of a "directive from God". He has been able to further plans for world-domination utilizing a religion that clearly is no different from other cults with the exception that George Bush and cronies are the beneficiary.

Sounds a lot like what Stalin did in Russia, and what the CIA has been doing all over the planet since WW II and certainly what monotheism has been doing for the past two thousand years.

The fact is, manipulation of the mass consciousness is "standard operating procedure" for those in power. The priests of Judaism did it, Constantine did it, Mohammed did it, and the truth is, nothing has changed since those days except that the methods and abilities to manipulate the minds of the masses with "signs and wonders" have become high tech and global in concert with global communication.

The Most Dangerous Idea in The World

We have noticed, over the past three years of our "political activism", that our Website is "off limits" to many other political activists who hold the same views we espouse. This is usually not directly declared, but it is made obvious by "omission". We've published a few scoops that, one would think, should be shouted from the housetops by every alternative news site on the web. But they aren't. Oh, yes, in a couple of cases an enthusiastic newbie grabbed one of our articles and started propagating it, and others picked it up, but we noticed that they republished it either without attribution or a link back to our site, and in some cases, actually misspelled or incorrectly named the source. These were sites that usually don't make those kinds of mistakes. But, in our case, they did. Curious.

(This is not always true, but is true often enough that we have taken note of it.)

Another example, our *Pentagon Strike* video is conspicuous by its absence from a host of websites that, ostensibly, promote the exact same views that we hold, politically speaking. This is curious mainly because the darn thing is so wildly popular that it still, over a year after release, attracts 20 to 30 thousand visitors every day, most of whom download and save it to send to their family and friends! It has been translated into 9 languages, and we get letters every day from viewers who visit our Website as a result of this little video. Seems that it is propagating without the help of other websites. (And I should also note here that the book orders we get from the video keep us plenty busy, so don't get the idea that I am complaining here, I'm just noticing things and speculating.)

We noticed that it appeared on a couple of alternative sites for about a day or two after it was released, but as soon as they had time to notice that there was a link in the video itself to our Website, the Video was pulled, or "archived", out of sight. It didn't matter to the people, however, because by now, the video has been seen by over 500 million people and counting. We have yet to encounter a group anywhere in any social context, in which there is not someone present who has seen the *Pentagon Strike* video.

It is also interesting that the Pentagon Strike video was one of the first "alternative news site" productions that actually attracted the concerted attention of the Mainstream Media. Because of the "viral" way it was spreading, it was apparently seen as something of a threat and the *Washington Post*[224] was sent to do "damage control" and shortly thereafter, we noted, a big rush to discredit the "no Boeing at the Pentagon" theory was launched on the Internet *and* in the mainstream media. We sure must have stepped on a sore toe!

It's rather ironic that our work, shunned by so many other "alternative news" sites, was what actually baited the bear out of his lair. You would think that those individuals and groups of individuals whose ideas are so similar to our own on that subject would want to capitalize on this kind of effectiveness in communication vis a vis the masses. We aren't stingy. We share, we link, we are careful to make attributions and give credit where it is due. And we most definitely think that more unity is needed if anything positive is ever going to happen.

At one point, in late 2002, when I could see clearly what Bush was up to, and I knew that a unified front and a clever strategy was essential if anything was to be done to stop the warmongering, I wrote to a whole slew of "alternative researchers" asking if it would be possible to arrange a quick meeting, a conference, to discuss issues, to critically examine the

---

[224] http://www.washingtonpost.com/wp-dyn/articles/A13059-2004Oct6.html

evidence so as to be able to agree on major points, and to formulate a systematic approach to the problems facing our world.

I did not receive a single reply.

I tried again about a year ago, suggesting that we have now seen that a systematic, unified approach is even more necessary, and received only *two* replies. One of them suggested that the answer to all the problems was to join a multilevel marketing outfit!

In January of this year, we received a visit from a delegate of Thierry Meyssan of *La Pentagate* fame. They were so impressed with our *Pentagon Strike* video that they wanted to invite us to join forces. (They at least recognized the potential of the "viral" marketing idea and realized the necessity for a united front). But, there was a condition: we had to disassociate ourselves from talking about UFOs and hyperdimensional realities!

We declined. We call it as we see it, and we aren't for sale.

Notice that the Jeff Rense site, which talks freely about all of the subjects we cover, including UFOs and strange phenomena, is liberally referenced and linked to by many "alternative news" sites.

But not Cassiopaea. Cassiopaea is too dangerous.

What's the difference? What do we talk about that Rense doesn't?

Well, there are two things that spring to mind: First of all, we reference everything from the hypothesized "hyperdimensional" point of view which includes Time Loops; and secondly, we actually dare to experiment with communicating with said realms of existence, (which is not to say that we believe anything about said communication, as I will explain further on), and this generally has resulted in us having a rather negative view of religion, including the New Age variations.

In June 2005, Thierry Meyssan joined up with Jimmy Walter for a "Re-Open 9/11 European Tour".[225] As the article says:

> "Joining them from the US are Twin Towers hero William Rodriguez, filmmaker Penny Little, lawyer Philip Berg (who is suing the Bush administration under the RICO statute), Kennedy assassination author Lisa Pease, 9/11 victim Rachel Hughes, and writers Chris Bollyn, Eric Hufschmidt, and Webster Tarpley."

The lineup included some of the best and most respected 9/11 researchers out there, yet we note that the total of attendees for two evenings in Amsterdam was stated to be 800 - that averages to 400 per evening; and the total for *two* evenings in Paris was stated to be 550 people, or 275 per evening. That's pretty poor turnout, if you ask me.

Nevertheless, Tarpley's article informs us that Meyssan, "compared French intellectuals who refuse to challenge Bush's 9/11 lies to the members of a French anti-fascist committee of 1936 who refused to accept

---

[225] http://rense.com/general65/halftimereportonjimmy.htm

clear evidence that the burning of the Berlin Reichstag in 1933 had been a provocation organized by the Nazis themselves". It was only around 1960 that academics accepted the truth about the Reichstag fire.

Here's where it gets a bit irritating. You see, our "hyperdimensional perspective" on things, brought about by (shudder) "inspirational communication" with "ourselves in the future", indicated as early as 1995, *ten years ago*, that the events of Nazi Germany were a "trial run" for what is happening on the planet today. The C's aren't big on "predictions", because they emphasize that the "Future is Open" and depends on us to a great extent, but the theme of the Nazi trial run being the model of today's events has been one of the most consistent ideas throughout the experiment. In other words, we've been saying this for 10 years that it was going to happen and it's happening *now* exactly as it was described, (even if, at the time, we simply could *not* grok how it might actually manifest! Who would ever imagine that they would pull off something like 9-11?!), and that suggests that maybe a few other things the C's have mentioned might be on target as well and we ought to pay attention.

But anyway, here we are, frequently attacked by the New Age crowd, attacked by the standard religious cult crowds (Christian, Jewish and Muslim alike), reviled by the materialists, attacked by COINTELPRO gangs, considered "fringe" by the alternative news groups of various sorts, and all because of one, single idea: *that hyperdimensional realities are real* - they have a physical reality - and that they might be the "home" of the *real* Controllers of our World, and that it just might be possible to communicate across the dimensional barriers. I talk about this in my book, *The Secret History of the World*:[226]

> "There is similarity between the two basic paths of fundamental research in modern theoretical physics, and the two realities we are considering: matter and consciousness. Just as in psi research there have been attempts to reconcile, or unify, matter and consciousness, the same has been true in advanced physics where although serious attempts have been made during the past two decades to find a Unified Theory that incorporates both a quantum approach ("matter") and the field approach ("consciousness"), no single theory which incorporates both has been successful as yet in either set of problems. Quantum mechanics deals primarily with the sub-microscopic world of elementary particles. It is based upon probabilities of events taking place non-deterministically, rather than a deterministically known state, which can be calculated using the classical equations of motion.

> When you have an infinite number of possible states, any of which can be solutions within certain boundary conditions, you run into certain problems when you try to transfer these concepts to classical realities. The state vector is the collection of all possible pre-collapse states and represents the system in which the event exists in all states simultaneously. Once the event

---

[226] http://www.qfgpublishing.com/

happens, or what is called "measurement" occurs, the system collapses the state vector into a single, probabilistically determined state. Until this collapse occurs, the state vector that has developed in time deterministically specifies the system collectively. This interpretation of quantum mechanics is known as the *Copenhagen Interpretation* and is dominant, with minor variations, in the quantum mechanics used today. It is characterized by a direct break with classical physics where a cause leads to an effect.

At the same time, field theory, (Einstein's general theory of relativity) plays the leading role when we are considering real world physical realities. Field theory seems to follow from the classical view of cause and effect and determinism. Classical mechanics deals with equations of motion that can be solved for specific events when initial conditions, such as position and velocity, or initial and final conditions, are known. So it is that the field represents a deterministic interrelation of mutually interacting forces between different events (i.e. particles), which can be found by substituting values into the field equations.

Both the field and quantum theories have special characteristics which are useful in physical theories of psi. However the same problems pop up in trying to combine quantum theory with (relativistic) field theory: no such system has yet been devised which can account for all phenomena.

At the present time, however, it seems that quantum field theory has been by far the most successful attempt at this endeavor. [...]

There are so many interpretations of quantum theory that may be relevant to psi and that may assist in gaining an understanding of how consciousness interacts with matter. Most of the new theories are based upon the introduction of a new level of duality in nature in that consciousness has a separate and distinct wave function from that of the normal wave function representing matter and physical reality in quantum theory, a sort of three wave system like biorhythms, where when all the lines cross, something happens.

The issue I would like to emphasize here is that we desperately need a scientifically acceptable conceptual framework within which Parapsychological phenomena make sense as part of nature and human life in its entirety. [...]

In considering the general theory of relativity, science usually utilizes a four-dimensional space-time continuum. In classical general relativity, the metrical properties of the continuum are intrinsic to the continuum, but a *fifth dimension* in which *our normally sensed space-time is embedded* can also be used to account for the curvature and properties of physical space. In the space-time continuum, one can say that all parts of the four-dimensional world exist simultaneously, in the sense of a mathematical formalism, and this would naturally lead to *a complete collapse of the philosophical ideas of causality.*

However, many scientists who work with these ideas do not think that this continuum is 'real' in a physical sense, such that physical entities could move back and forth at will in and out of time as easily as changing direction in three-dimensional space. We, on the other hand, think that it is not only possible, but also extremely likely based upon certain observations.

In relativity theory, time intervals between events are not completely fixed relative to moving systems or frames of reference. This has led to some speculation that there may also be analogies between precognition and anomalies. However, 'time dilation', the contraction of time intervals between moving reference frames, is too small to account for precognition and would still require any information transfer to travel faster than light, and the special theory of relativity, when narrowly interpreted, does not allow for physical travel backwards in time, but relegates this concept to an imaginary mathematical formalism.

Even though it is almost forbidden to question Einstein's restriction on superluminal travel, Einstein did, at one point, propose to consider the hyperdimensional world as 'real'. In 1938, with P. Bergmann, he wrote a paper entitled *On a Generalization of Kaluza's Theory of Electricity*:

So far, two fairly simple and natural attempts to connect gravitation and electricity by a unitary field theory have been made, one by Weyl, the other by Kaluza. Furthermore, there have been some attempts to represent Kaluza's theory formally so as to avoid the introduction of the fifth dimension of the physical continuum. The theory presented here differs from Kaluza's in one essential point; *we ascribe physical reality to the fifth dimension* whereas in Kaluza's theory this fifth dimension was introduced only in order to obtain new components of the metric tensor representing the electromagnetic field. [Einstein, A, Bergmann, P., Annals of Mathematics, Vol. 38, No. 3, July 1938.]

We believe that Einstein was following a path that was later to prove very fruitful. Einstein, however, was somewhat nervous about this idea, but he followed it anyway, writing in his paper:

If Kaluza's attempt is a real step forward, then it is because of the introduction of the five dimensional space. There have been many attempts to retain the essential formal results obtained by Kaluza without sacrificing the four-dimensional character of the physical space. *This shows distinctly how vividly our physical intuition resists the introduction of the fifth dimension.* But by considering and comparing all these attempts one must come to the conclusion that *all these endeavors did not improve the situation.* It seems impossible to formulate Kaluza's idea in a simple way without introducing the fifth dimension.

We have, therefore, to take the fifth dimension seriously although we are not encouraged to do so by plain experience. If, therefore, the space structure seems to force acceptance of the five dimensional space theory upon us we must ask whether it is sensible to assume the rigorous reducibility to four dimensional space. We believe that the answer should be 'no', provided that it is possible to understand, in another way, the quasi-four dimensional character of the physical space by taking as a basis the five dimensional continuum and to simplify hereby the basic geometrical assumptions.[...]

The most essential point of our theory is the replacing of ...rigorous cylindricity by the *assumption that space is closed (or periodic)*.[...]

Kaluza's five dimensional theory of the physical space provides a unitary representation of gravitation and electromagnetism. [...] *It is much more satisfactory to introduce the fifth dimension not only formally, but to assign to it some physical meaning.*[Einstein, A, Bergmann, P., Annals of Mathematics, Vol. 38, No. 3, July 1938.]

The reader should note that when considering field theory, it is necessary to differentiate between 1.) Pure field theory such as gravitation, and electrical and magnetic fields and 2.) Quantum field theory. Fields such as electromagnetic fields and gravitational fields are continuous and spatial while quantum fields are quantized, broken into discrete sections of particulate substance or energy. The basing of a theory of psi on a gravitational field rests partly on the fact that *gravitation is not subject to the maximum velocity of light because it doesn't travel, but is structural.* Evidence from Vasiliev and others suggests that psi is also independent of the velocity of light.

However, general relativity has obliged science to abandon the 'action at a distance' idea, causing the 'distance force' to be abandoned, and has placed gravity under subjection to a maximum velocity. Nevertheless, Margenau has suggested that general relativity ought to be regarded as a 'formal' principle such as the Pauli Exclusion Principle. In this case, gravitation would be non-energetic and subject to no maximum velocity and would act as a guiding way to physical phenomena.'[Forwald, Haakon, Mind, Matter and Gravitation: A Theoretical and Experimental Approach, Parapsychology Monographs, Number 11 (New York: Parapsychology Foundation 1969).]

These ideas have been adopted by many 'alternative science' writers who have related them to buildings, energy fields, light beings, earth grids and all that - mostly nonsense - and it does, indeed, seem that there may be locations on the planet where one can "tap" a certain energy with greater or lesser ease. But the phenomenon that these ideas speaks to more directly is that of hyperdimensional realities wherein mental energies or consciousness energies are amplified and can be interactive with the environment. There may be a specific technology that suggests not only power for transport that is partly physical, partly 'ethereal', that suggests communication that is also partly physical and partly ethereal, as well as powers of "manifestation" that might seem impossible to us in our present state of technology. All of these properties DO belong to hyperdimensional existence, and such a state of being has been reported for millennia as being the 'realm of the gods'."

That is the Most Dangerous Idea in the World.

Certainly, much work needs to be done on these ideas in order to be able to talk about specifics, but what I have written above should give the average reader a general idea that such things are being discussed among scientists, and it is not just a crazy "conspiracy theory". How many "extra dimensions" are there? Well, that is one of the things still under discussion.

The idea is, in more simple terms, that beyond our space and time, beyond the limitations of normal consciousness, exists a vaster reality, which can only be known or accessed with another, expanded consciousness. Even among some scientists who are interested in expanding our space-time structure, the idea that consciousness itself must be expanded is often overlooked. There are many instances cited of spontaneous "expansion of consciousness", and there are many claims from religious (including New Age religions) of methods and techniques to accomplish this, but in general, serious work on the idea in order to find out what really works, is rare.

What seems to be true is that every time in history that our worldview has expanded, it has been due to the fact that there is conflicting data that cannot be incorporated into the old model, and the model must be expanded to accommodate. Ignoring conflicting data is becoming harder to do nowadays because of the global communication network. In the past, it was a lot easier to suppress.

Einstein said that it takes only one contradictory fact to kill a scientific theory. That means that if just one account of, say, UFOs that defy the "rules" of our accepted space-time framework, is true, if the "standard model" can't explain it, then we need another, broader, framework that can. And the same is true of the anomalies of history, of the fact that human beings do not seem to be advancing in consciousness at the same rate that they have advanced technologically.

"There are three distinct levels of consciousness on Earth: sensation, simple consciousness and self-consciousness. [...] Each has its own framework of space-time. Take a snail as an example of the first. It lives in a world of one dimension of space plus time. The other two dimensions of space all around it are translated, by its faculty of sensation, into one dimension of space or time.

But a higher animal like the dog, with a higher faculty and simple consciousness, mentally extracts from time another dimension of space and lives in a larger world of two dimensions of space plus time. Get the picture? Time is a collection of extra dimensions of space either not apprehended, or imperfectly apprehended; each level of consciousness sees them bit by bit, moving constantly past, fused with time. So it is with the dog and the third dimension. His simple consciousness translates the third dimension of space into either one of the other two, or time.

But we have a higher mental faculty still, self-consciousness. By virtue of it we've extracted yet another dimension of space from time... We live in a world of three dimensions of space plus time. The question is: is there still a higher faculty, one that can extract another dimension of space from our time? And if so, would our paranormal, in this expanded framework, then become the normal?

There is such a fourth level of consciousness [...] It goes hand in hand with the apprehension of a fourth dimension of space extracted from time. A brief taste of this faculty is the mystical experience in which one's consciousness expands into and realizes a broader continuum of space and time. Lesser glimpses of the faculty, just a bit of it at any one time, are psychic intuitions such as telepathy, clairvoyance, and precognition. This higher faculty conceives in a fashion beyond sensation, simple - and self-consciousness - logic, concepts, and even language. ... And still other traces of this higher faculty are responsible for other kinds of psychic phenomena, such as psychokinesis, [etc]

Now what if a race of beings on another planet has acquired this faculty completely. They would be like gods to us, as far above us as we are above animals. They would live in a different, larger world of space-time. Using that extra dimension, they could perform feats that seem like magic to us, coming and going into and out of our space at will [...]

Finally, if our world is just part of a larger world, then each of us in turn must have a larger self that resides in that world. [...]

The point is this: there are no UFO phenomena per se, no psychic phenomena, no near-death phenomena, and no mystical phenomena. *There is just a reality phenomenon. Our world is enveloped in a larger one,* the workings of which are beyond our senses and level of consciousness, and so these workings when encountered are treated as paranormal. [...]

The history of Man shows that we have continually overstated our position in the universe, not only by underestimating its size, but also by regarding our location as its absolute focal point. It was at first a tremendous blow to our ego to accept that the Earth was not the center of the entire cosmos. What we must now accept is that Man is no more the center of the conscious or psychical world than he is of the physical world." [*Extra-Dimensional Universe*, John R. Violette, 2001, Hampton Roads, VA]

What is quite interesting about this is the fact that, over the past few years, we have been contacted by a growing number of academics, scientists - experts in their fields of math and physics and chemistry *and* history - who thank us for having the courage to address these subjects, and - in some cases - for giving them the keys to make sense of their own work, (even if they cannot yet come out in public and say so!). In other words, the hypothesis does solve problems as a good hypothesis should.

On the subject of experts, the reader might like to take a look at a recent piece published on Rense about mathematician A. K. Dewdney's work on the subject of 9-11, and how he has now "baited the bear from its lair" as well. The article demonstrates that Prof. Dewdney is getting the same treatment we got from the *Washington Post*:

"On Monday, May 23, 2005, FOX affiliate WSVN-TV sent Patrick Fraser, with only a BS in Journalism from UF-Gainsville, to tangle with Scientist Dr. A.K. Dewdney over the 9/11 Pentagon quagmire. Dr. Dewdney: "If we are right the implications are profound." Reporter: "Right or right off the wacko chart, common sense tells you it's not likely. In fact common sense tells you its not only outrageous -- its ridiculous and one well known skeptic has another description for it -- laughable." [...]

"Utilizing the Scientific Method, Dewdney has dealt a killing blow to the
two lynchpins of the 9-11 attacks stating unequivocally:

1. The Pentagon was not struck by a large passenger aircraft.
2. Cell phone calls alleged to have been made by passengers were essentially
impossible." [227]

From our point of view, more scientists need to become interested in
these problems, and we use every opportunity to press that objective. If
the scientific community - those who are interested in truth and the future
of our species, that is - can be brought together on this matter, then
Thierry Meyssan and Jimmy Walters will have more substance to present
to their audiences, and said audiences might become commensurably
larger and broader. This highlights, again, the need for a serious
unification of those seeking truth, and that truth must be sought *without
prejudice.*

This brings us back to what seem to be prejudices against our own work,
most of which relate to beliefs that have been imposed on our reality for
millennia. Even if such as Thierry Meyssan do not subscribe to religious
beliefs, he - and most human beings on this planet - are still influenced by
the "cultural norms" that have been established in the context of those
beliefs, including the opposing stance that there is no "deeper reality".
Strange that monotheism - or reactions thereto - was actually the
foundation for the materialist view of the universe. This view is explicated
in the following remarks made by a well-known anti-war essayist (which I
have edited slightly to remove the personal context in which they were
made):

"Consciousness does not exist without the physical body. When the physical
body goes, consciousness goes. All the rest — the souls, the aliens, the gods
— are just phantasms constructed by your mind trying to avoid the fear of
physical death. They don't really exist. The whole battle is right here.
Because of all these fantasies, we've neglected reality. The whole battle is
right here in front of us. It isn't somewhere else. Religions are all fiction.
Men who claim to practice them are hypocrites; they only care about the
money. That's the battle we have to win. If we focus on such fantasies, then
we lose focus on reality. Because of all these fantasy stories, we're going to
lose our future, and possibly our whole planet."

The problem is, *if* hyperdimensional realities are important as is quite
possible, then taking such a position might very well deprive the
individual of the perspective necessary in order to know where and how
the battle is actually being waged. If you do not know your enemy, you
cannot execute a strategically successful defense. It's that simple.

But keep in mind, we are only hypothesizing here. We aren't saying that
it is the "truth". It is certainly an idea that has, so far, been very useful in
connecting dots and answering questions and explaining "the order of the

---

[227] http://www.serendipity.li/wot/operation_pearl.htm

universe". But all the problems are not solved, and much work still needs to be done.

Nevertheless, when considering these ideas as a "working hypothesis", what we see again and again is that a really promising "warrior" in the fight for humanity gets "taken out" because they act within the "old model". Using the model can enhance our understanding of the possible true nature of the opposition, that it has resources and weapons at its disposal that supersede - and make obsolete - ordinary human machinations.

Our essayist above understands that religions are barriers, fences for human beings, and the cause of much human suffering. The question that should be asked, but that he never stops to ask is: *why?* With a little reflection, we can understand that religions - and the New Age variations - may very well be "strategic maneuvers" by hyperdimensional beings seeking to dominate humanity. Having theorized this point, and thinking in terms of military strategy, one can go on to speculate about what is really being concealed by religion as well as how religion has been utilized to create the "opposite" stance of total rejection of religion. Jacques Vallee once remarked on this by pointing out that there are two ways to stop an idea: if you can't contain it, drive it so far and hard that, like a train with too much fire in the boiler, it runs off the track. This is standard operating procedure for disinformation.

And no, I am not talking about ephemeral "psychic" forces or demons or whatever. I am saying that without a working hypothesis of the hyperdimensional nature of the control system there does not seem to be any hope whatsoever of winning this war. Thinking in terms of military strategy, we come to understand that the greatest deception of all is the idea that there are no negative forces, though we should certainly take some care in determining exactly what those forces are, of what they are capable, and devise an effective strategy.

Religions, including the New Age variations, teach that focusing one's attention on discovering the true nature of the opponent, "gives them energy". This is true only if one focuses with the intention of participation. However, a comprehensive understanding of these forces is absolutely necessary in order to know how to give them less energy. "The only thing necessary for the triumph of evil is for good men to do nothing."

Indeed, in one sense, the above essayist is exactly right: we *do* have to concentrate on our reality, the *here* and *now*, because it is in the here and now that the *future* is *forged*. That is one thing that is made abundantly clear by our "inspirational" guides who tell us:

> "Life is religion. Life experiences reflect how one interacts with God. Those who are asleep are those of little faith in terms of their interaction with the creation. Some people think that the world exists for them to overcome or ignore or shut out. For those individuals, the worlds will cease. They will

become exactly what they give to life. They will become merely a dream in
the 'past'. People who pay strict attention to objective reality right and left,
become the reality of the 'Future'."

Paying strict attention does not just mean "knowing", because
knowledge is useless if it is not applied. But this oh, so important,
message is completely obscured in the knee-jerk reactions that have been
programmed into us by the "cultural norms" established by religions and
their influence over our material reality. Far too much energy is devoted to
the "afterlife", either the Christian version or the New Age version of
"ascension" to some other world, realm, dimension, whatever.

The history of religion is a history of the descent of humanity into
insanity. This has become even more marked in the technological era, an
era, I should add, that was "created" by the monotheistic view that the
"Earth is the Lord's" and he can give it to whoever he wants to, and they
can use it and abuse it as they like.

The influence of religion has done nothing but cause human beings to
divorce themselves from reality, to retreat in terror toward illusion and
delusions about other worlds, and to abandon our Earth.

And yes, this is the view that is presented by our so-called "Other
worldly" source of information!

The only thing I can say at this point is that I believe the only way out of
the mess this planet is in is to first of all, eliminate the clouds of myth and
distortion surrounding the true nature of human beings and discover what
powers we may truly have if we can be unified beyond our petty
internecine squabbles created by the production of religious fantasies and
New Age Mumbo Jumbo, as well as the opposite idea that there is no
consciousness, that material life is all there is. A simple, strategic, military
analysis of the situation suggests that there would not be so much time and
effort spent on creating and promoting these fantasies and beliefs, (not to
mention marginalizing the idea that they ought to be studied
scientifically), if there was not something that someone wants to keep
totally hidden.

So, it seems to me that we are considered dangerous because of our
scientific approach to mysticism, most particularly our promotion of the
idea of hyperdimensional realities as having a "physical meaning". Let me
note that this awareness only dawned on me gradually.

Because of the fact that there were so many people in the world
promoting their versions of the "paranormal", so to say - including the
mainstream religions - I had the idea that talking or writing about such
things was acceptable, even if it was relegated to a more or less "fringe"
circle. That was okay by me. After all, I was intending to address only
those people who were actually interested in the subject. But that is not
how things played out, and it took me some time to "make the
connections". So, in order to understand what I am trying to convey, let

me recount a brief history of the problem and how we gradually began to suspect that we were moving in directions that are absolutely forbidden.

During Ark's[228] 6 year stay in the United States, he was unable to find suitable academic work that would support his own research interests due to several factors including his "foreign" status, but also due to his refusal to work for the arms industry. It was observed that there are very few jobs and research grants for physicists who do not wish to use their expertise in the service of the military in one way or another, or who do not want to follow ideas that will lead nowhere. Indeed, at a very early point, Ark was recruited to work for a contractor to the United States Department of Defense, but after three years in this position, it became obvious that he would have to either "get in deeper" or get out. He decided to get out, and I supported that decision.

Regarding myself, I had formerly worked as a bureaucrat for the State of Florida, and as a part-time hypnotherapist under the aegis of various psychiatrists and psychologists, (which actually led to my later questions about, and experiments with "mind phenomena" leading to the Cass Experiment).

In 1995, I began to share some of the results of the Cassiopaean transmissions with a discussion group on the internet. It was not, to understate the matter, well received except by a few individuals who seemed to be more "in the know" than the average "new age" type of seeker of "alternative solutions to the problems of man and his place in the universe". The fact is, the Cassiopaean material was distinctly Gnostic in flavor and tone. What the C's referred to as hyperdimensional realities were quite comparable to the realm of Archons of the Gnostics, and they certainly described the denizens of this realm in similar - though more modern - terms.

As I continued to research, the comparisons between this material and the "underground streams of knowledge" such as Sufism, Esoteric Christianity, Gnosticism, Hermeticism, became more and more obvious, and so I became convinced that I ought to share the material and the results of my research, so as to get feedback from others; to - so to say - make my feedback algorithms more robust.

In 1998, Ark began to help me create a website for this purpose. This website published my many years of historical research, as well as publishing the results of my experiences and researches into the paranormal and psychology. This latter element was based on over 25 years experience as a hypnotherapist. A special note is important here. I considered the issue of so-called "extraterrestrials" to be a valid subject for study and review, since it was so widespread a phenomenon in

---

[228] Laura's husband, theoretical physicist Arkadiusz Jadczyk
http://www.quantumfuture.net/quantum_future/

American culture. As a hypnotherapist, I had worked with individuals claiming to have been "abducted" by aliens, and my experiences and observations of such subjects convinced me that they were intriguing and worthy of academic research.

As noted, Ark assisted me in the technical aspects of creating my website, and occasionally added some analysis and commentary. We were not prepared for, nor even expecting, the level of reaction that resulted from this "marriage of science and mysticism". These reactions brought me to confront a strange condition of our world - the vast chasm between the methods and conclusions of science and religion. I had considered it a normal, reasonable approach to study religion and mysticism - the domains of the so-called "paranormal" - more or less scientifically, but apparently this perspective was to be condemned by both religious communities as well as by many in the scientific community.

This brings us back to the problem we face in our world: that "*the science of living beings*" has not proceeded apace with the sciences dealing with the physical objects in our reality.

Ark has also commented on these issues as follows:

"Looking at the history of 'our civilization', religion seems to have been in existence much longer than 'science.' And yet we see that religion has failed. In spite of its teachings people are still constantly at war with each other. Human beings have not become better, and they are often much worse than animals. It is terrible because, when you really *see* it, you realize how great a failure religion or the 'powers' of the various versions of God really are.

Science, which came later and has exploded in the last millennium, has failed too. It has brought mankind to the edge of self-destruction. Advances in mathematical, physical and computer sciences have brought about 'applied game theory', where wars are called 'games', and to 'win the game' is to kill as many people as possible with as little cost as possible. […]

Perhaps it is time to try something new? Perhaps a 'marriage of science and mysticism' has a chance?

Why not take what is good from science and what is good from religion, and discard what is wrong?

What is the best thing about religion?

Religion teaches us to be open minded and accepting of possibilities which are far from being 'rational'. Religions teach us to pay attention to singular events, miracles, phenomena that are fragile and hardly repeatable. Finally, religion teaches us to look inside as much as outside: know thyself.

The strengths of the approach of religion just happen to be the weak points in science.

Science is often narrow-minded and conservative, restricting everything to what is material and rigidly repeatable. Science teaches us that what is 'out there' is not connected to what is 'in here,' that it must be captured, weighed, measured and manipulated. That is why new paradigms are so painful when they come - but they *do* come in science, and they seldom come in religion which is "fixed" and dogmatic and not open to discussion.

What is the best thing about science? Science is open to criticism and discussion. Even if many forces on the earth try to make a sort of religion of science, in general, scientific theories must be published and publicly discussed. We can find an error in Einstein's papers because these, as well as other papers, are publicly available. Everyone can learn mathematics, as advanced as you wish, from reading monographs, articles, going to conferences, and discussing with other scientists.

The strength of science just happens to be the weakness of religion.

Religions are always "secret" in one respect or another - even if that secrecy is only the declaration that no changes can be made, no questions asked, because the ultimate truth about God is a 'mystery', a 'secret'. That is why the teachings of religion are so easily distorted and misunderstood. It is so easy for the central 'authority' to achieve the 'pinnacle' of the religion and declare to the followers the correct interpretation and that no other is permitted."

So it can be stated that one of my main operational protocols is to study religion and mysticism - the domains of the so-called "paranormal" - more or less scientifically, while Ark is inclined, on occasion, to combine "inspiration" with his scientific researches. In both cases, we wish to note, our mutual approach is to create working hypotheses that are subjected to tests and observation.

As noted, this approach brought forth a significant amount of protest, both from "true believers" in various religions and the so-called "New Age" community worldwide, as well as some academics who automatically consider the approach to be "un-scientific". Understand that this was more than just people writing and saying, "You are damned for your unbelief". These attacks were, quite simply, life-threatening both in terms of attempting to destroy our ability to work, make a living and support our family, and in terms of physical harm.

The initial attacks against us proceeded from two main sources: the so-called "New Age" or "Metaphysical" community, and Christian fundamentalists in the United States. We could understand the fundies, but we could not understand the attacks from the "New Age" types. After all, many of them were talking about the same subjects I was talking about. It took me awhile to understand that the problem was that they were also promoting untested beliefs in the same way the mainstream religions were, and they objected to someone saying that such beliefs ought to be critically analyzed and tested. The New Age and mainstream Fundies were soon joined by members of the Jewish and Islamic religions who objected to having religious texts and ideas subjected to a more or less scientific scrutiny. It wasn't that this hadn't been done before, but most of the academic research in theological areas is not very accessible to the public.

I was reading it, condensing it, and making it accessible. Apparently, this was a big no-no. It was clear that "true believers" of all types were happy to be left alone by science because this enabled them to perpetrate frauds on the public, particularly those who were disaffected vis a vis the "standard" religions, but certainly not excluding the fundamental frauds of even the "standard" religions per se.

It was quite disconcerting to both of us to find that, in our efforts to apply science to the study of metaphysics for the purposes of finding a meeting ground for all peoples to find peace, the most vicious of the defamatory attacks against us were that we were trying to start a "cult"! It seemed that the real cults that we were exposing as such decided that the best defense was a strong offense.

Right up to the period around September 11, 2001, the situation was no more or less problematical than would be for any individual with a "new idea" that is not yet quite acceptable. There are critics and there are responses to criticism. However, in conjunction with 9-11, the climate for scientifically examining religion and belief systems radically changed in the United States.

Seeing how religion and beliefs were driving the masses to acts of true insanity, I, along with many others, began writing articles protesting the politics of the current U.S. President, Mr. Bush, and his manipulative use of the Christian Fundamentalists as his support base, and religion as his raison d'etre. I had become particularly vocal in my opposition to the, then, oncoming invasion and occupation of Iraq.

Because of these activities, we began to be subjected to intensified attacks that now included fanatics of the so-called "Christian Right", and the label of "cult" was shouted louder and more often. As I noted, this became rather serious. We received death threats, our children were physically threatened, and in two cases, subjected to life-threatening attacks, our dog was poisoned, our names (including our children) and physical location was published on the internet with a request for "true believers" to go and "take care of" us (the implied intent was obviously to do physical harm, perhaps even causing death).

The attacks included a campaign of slander and defamation launched against us via the Internet, consisting of the most outrageous lies about our work and personal lives. We found that we were unable to do anything at all except to spend almost every waking hour defending ourselves, and staying awake at night in fear that fanatical fundamentalists would burn our house down as we slept.

We certainly made reports of this activity against us to the authorities in the U.S., including the FBI. The responses of these authorities consisted mainly in saying, "it's not our jurisdiction" or "anybody can say what they want", to "there are more important things to investigate" since September 11, 2001.

After reading some of the "other" material available on the internet, it might be thought that the simplest reason behind the attacks on us was due to these individuals feeling threatened by exposure of their truly cultic money making scams. Nevertheless, there is still the problem of the U. S. authorities' complete failure to act on our numerous complaints of criminal wrong-doing on the part of these individuals in their campaign of slander, libel, and defamation against us. We still cannot explain this. We further cannot explain why our work, in particular, has been targeted in the way it has when there are so many truly "cultic" groups operating in the U.S., who are allowed to operate unimpeded, and to perpetrate their obvious scams and frauds with complete impunity. The suggestion has been made that such groups are part of a vast secret "Counter-intelligence Program", but even if that is the case, it does not explain why our work was particularly targeted for attack unless, of course, it is because it is "going in the right direction". At the same time, we can't exclude the idea that these reactions are strictly mechanical in psychological terms. If a person perceives that something they believe is threatened by facts, they might easily react to the threat in such ways.

Nevertheless, reading the clues does seem to suggest more than just a "mechanical reaction", something that is akin to COINTELPRO. The theme of COINTELPRO has long been with us! As Richard Dolan has written:

"Anyone who has lived in a repressive society knows that official manipulation of the truth occurs daily. But societies have their many and their few. In all times and all places, it is the few who rule, and the few who exert dominant influence over what we may call *official culture*. - All elites take care to manipulate public information to maintain existing structures of power. It's an old game. [...]

[And war is the key element of power and control.]

Deception is the key element of warfare, and when winning is all that matters, the conventional morality held by ordinary people becomes an impediment. When taken together, the examples of official duplicity form a nearly single totality. [...]

The secrecy stems from a pervasive and fundamental element of life in our world, that *those who are at the top of the heap will always take whatever steps are necessary to maintain the status quo*. [...]

[C]over-ups are standard operating procedure, frequently unknown to the public for decades, becoming public knowledge by a mere roll of the dice. But also [...] information has leaked out from the very beginning. It is impossible to shut the lid completely. *The key lies in neutralizing and discrediting unwelcome information, sometimes through official denial, other times through proxies in the media.* [...]

[E]vidence [of conspiracy] derived from a grass roots level is unlikely to survive its inevitable conflict with official culture. And acknowledgement about the reality of [conspiracies] will only occur when the official culture deems it worthwhile or necessary to make it." [229]

Don't hold your breath.

Now, let me repeat the crucial point here: *Ideas about conspiracy are not delusions or paranoia. From a historical point of view, the **only** reality is that of conspiracy.* Our "freedom" is to a large extent an illusion. Secrecy, wealth and independence add up to power. ...Deception is the key element of warfare, (the tool of power elites), and when winning is all that matters, the conventional morality held by ordinary people becomes an impediment. In other words, creating religions to deceive people is standard procedure from the most primitive "witch doctor", who scares the tribe so that he can stay in power, right on up to the controls exerted by George Bush in the name of Christianity, and, undoubtedly, beyond, in the realms of hyperdimensions.

[Note: We speak of organized religions here, not about the very idea of God-Creator and the Mysteries of the Soul and Mind. If anything, we think that the evidence shows Creation to be far more grand and glorious than the organized religions even admit, and that the Cosmos is not reducible to the simplistic "god theories" of human beings.]

Secrecy about the true nature of our reality, and the true foolishness of these religions, stems from a pervasive and fundamental element of life in our world, that those who are at the top of the heap will always take whatever steps are necessary to maintain the status quo.

And maintaining the "status quo" via religion is one of the main objectives of the Power Elite.

And so it was that we gradually became aware of the fact that our approach of evaluating our reality in what amounts to scientific gnostic terms- which suggests that this world we experience, our normally sensed space-time, is "embedded" in a fifth dimension (and here I use the term as mathematicians use it, *not* as it is used by the so-called "New Age") that is *real*, and our reality may very well be the "battlefield" of denizens of this hyperdimensional space-time- is considered to be as dangerous as the ideas of the Gnostics and the Cathars who held similar ideas. That is to say human beings appear to be the "playing pieces" in vast and complex Secret Games of the Gods, and our actions or lack of action may represent the moves and maneuvers of said denizens of hyperdimensional space who, it seems, most desperately do NOT want us to unite in our awareness of their existence, exerting great effort to confuse and obfuscate humanity to that end. Because certainly, if we really discover the proof of their existence, and their games, we will stop playing.

This is the Most Dangerous Idea on Earth.

---

[229] Dolan, UFOs and the National Security State

Zionism vs. Anti-Semitism

Whenever there is a question of criticism of Israel, the question of anti-Semitism arises, and this is where we begin this section. We will be looking at the issue of anti-Semitism from a point of view that is certainly not discussed in the mainstream press, but it is also a point of view that is not discussed in the 9/11 movement: that of reincarnation.[230] It is this unique perspective on these events that defines our work. If the notion of reincarnation is too far-fetched for the reader, then we gently suggest that you put the book down now, for it is not the only, or even the most marginalized, "alternative idea" contained in the remainder of this book.

Yonassan Gershom, a neo-Hasidic Rabbi who "stands in the long tradition of authentic kabbalistic mystics and seers", wrote a book entitled Beyond the Ashes. This book was a compilation of cases of reincarnation from the Holocaust.

> "Belief in - and reliance upon - dreams, apparitions, visions, deja-vu, past-life memories, reincarnation, channeling, angelic communications, post-mortem contacts with deceased relatives, saints and sages, spirit guides, prophecies, and spiritual healings have all been known within the kabbalistic tradition and, at various times, accepted as part of the natural instrumentality of divine revelation."

Rabbi Gershom, a scholar and counselor, wrote of his discovery of a startling thing: many souls who were victims of the Nazi Holocaust have reincarnated - both as Jews and as non-Jews - as part of a natural and divinely sanctioned process of healing and planetary spiritual transformation.

He came upon this revelation in about the same way that Drs. Raymond Moody and Elisabeth Kubler-Ross came to their conclusions about "life-after-life", from listening to many patients who had significant near-death experiences. Rabbi Gershom collected over 200 cases of individuals who had experienced specific flashbacks, spontaneous memories or dreams, or visions of themselves dying as victims of the Nazi Holocaust. Many were Jews, but as many were not.

Rabbi Gershom, after examining these cases and the attendant issues, suggests to us that there are timeless human psychic and spiritual experiences that are behind the Jewish and Christian religions, but which have been suppressed and denied.

In the modern day, "cases suggestive of reincarnation", as researched in institutions of higher learning by competent scholars and professional counselors, add to the ever mounting evidence that reincarnation is, very likely, the universal reality behind our physical existence. If this is the case, and souls incarnate into bodies of different sex, color, and religion,

---

[230] We are assuming reincarnation to have a high probability of being an objective fact due to extensive research.

then what can we make of the perceived differences that human beings are so prone to claim? How can an individual claim that Judaism is "right" over any other religion when, it is very likely, he has lived multiple lifetimes as a non-Jew, and probably will again? And the same is true for Christianity.

Such accounts do seem to be included in the oral and written traditions of Judaism and can even be perceived in the New Testament of Christianity. But all too frequently, these accounts are taken out of context or interpreted in a crude fashion by persons who do not understand the nature of such sacred and spiritual experiences.

One of the most important implications of Rabbi Gershom's work is that there is a "meta-cosmic insight", which can emerge from our understanding of history and its worst tragedies - such as the holocaust - in the light of such experiences of reincarnation and the after-life. For all of us, we will ultimately face what we have done by becoming one of those we have afflicted. For the anti-Semite, it is likely that he will be born a Jew. For the Jew who insists that his religion is the only right one, the original one given from the mouth of God to Moses, it is very likely that he will do a stint as a Christian or even an Islamic Palestinian. We should be very careful at whom we throw stones because God is not mocked. By whatever measure you judge, you will be judged.[231] This leads us to the question: how many Nazis may have reincarnated as Jews, bringing with them their Fascist mentality, and applying it to Judaism in such a way as to bring suppression - and even ultimate destruction - upon themselves so as to taste what they dished out in another place and time?

It comes as something of a shock to mainstream Jews and Christians alike that the soil from which both their religions were grown in the Near East once allowed and even taught these concepts. It is only since the institution of formalized Christianity that both traditions have closed the door to such ideas. This occurred during the Middle Ages, at about the time of the prosecution of the Crusades, the creation of the Templars, the destruction of the Cathars by the Roman Catholic Church, the creation of the Inquisition, the emergence of the Legends of the Holy Grail, and the "reinvention" of Judaism in the form it is generally known today. This is also the period from which we get our oldest complete version of the Old Testament in Hebrew. This certainly strikes us as curious, most especially since this was also the time of the creation of certain kabbalistic documents, claimed to have a long "oral tradition" for which there is no evidence.

We have written in other places about the "high strangeness" of the 11th and 12th centuries. We have also written about the high strangeness that

---

[231] We should note that "judgment" is not an act of having a different opinion, it is an act of taking action against another because you do not agree with their opinion.

surrounds the time of the "writing" of the Hebrew Bible. Both periods, called "dark ages", produce an unsettling sensation of vertigo whenever one attempts to find a foundation upon which to establish what really was going on during those times. The written history and the archaeology simply do not match up. What is more, textual analysis of the documents of the time do not support the internal claims of the very materials that have served for centuries as our "history".

At some point a few years ago, I had some correspondence with Rabbi Gershom. He inquired if my husband and I would be interested in participating in a television show about people who have reincarnated from the Holocaust, retaining memories, and having some issues to work through in this life. We declined at the time, and I don't know how his project is proceeding, but considering the events I am about to describe, I rather suspect that his ideas were suppressed.

In my autobiography, Amazing Grace, I recounted how over the years I had been obsessed with the Holocaust and how this led to a conviction that I had experienced a former incarnation in Germany during that time. As the years went by, the conviction grew and was augmented by dreams and insights that my Jewish husband and family had been killed by the Nazis which drove me to suicide. Effectively, I had spent my entire current life mourning my loss and seeking answers to the grief that seemed to have been born in me. That "seeking" included a conviction that there was only One true mate for me, and that this One had been my Jewish husband in Germany in the former incarnation, who had been brutally murdered by the Nazis. Whether or not he had also incarnated again during the present period, and whether I might find him, I didn't know; but I felt his absence in my life as a great overarching tragedy.

In 1996, I received correspondence from a Polish Scientist, Prof. Arkadiusz Jadczyk, who had experienced a similar seeking impulse throughout his life with very astonishing complementary characteristics. After only one or two exchanges, we were both aware that the other was The One. Within six months, we had arranged our lives so we could be together, and as soon as our affairs permitted, we married.

Needless to say, the issue of the Holocaust and the violence done the Jews in that time was - and is - a very raw wound in our psyches. For anyone to accuse either of us of anti-Semitism is not only unjust, it is cruel and hurtful in a very deep way. While I am convinced that my husband of that life has been restored to me, I still mourn for my lost children. Though the nightmares are no longer so frequent, they still haunt me from time to time, and are still debilitating.

The point I wish to make is this: If anybody is anti-Nazi, it is me. What is more, my husband and his entire family lost everything they had due to this same Nazi juggernaut. Every day of his growing up years, my husband lived with the reality of what Hitler had done. When someone comes along and suggests that there is any anti-Semitism in our work, they had better come from a position of intimate knowledge of the beast itself, as we have. All of my searching and learning in this present life has been predicated upon the need to understand how such an atrocity as the Holocaust could occur in what we consider to be a modern and civilized world.

As I searched through the literature in hundreds of fields of study, the chief thing that became apparent to me is that mankind is in the iron grip of an uncaring control system that raises him up and brings him low for its own mysterious purposes. No group, no nationality, no secret society or religion, is exempt.

I needed answers. I couldn't live haunted daily by this grief for the Jews - for myself, my children - and all the other horrors of history. That was the motivation for the Cassiopaean experiment - my lifetime of seeking the answer to this question of Evil - and that was the motivation behind the questions I asked about the Jews. I wanted to know why and how a people supposedly Chosen by God could be so marked for tragedy. The usual reasons just didn't stand up to scrutiny - including their own explications recorded in the Torah. It was all logically inconsistent and made a mockery of the very idea of a Creator - Ribbono Shel Olom - Master of the Universe. There was something strange and mysterious here, and I wanted to know the answers. This is what led me to my work as a hypnotherapist.

After years of working with people's heads via hypnotherapy, I didn't much care whether such things as "past lives" actually existed or not. I only cared that the therapeutic modality worked and gave people relief. My own theory was that it gave them a drama to explain things, to work things out; a way to achieve a resolution by changing the script of the drama. I had the same "attitude" to what is known as "spirit release therapy". I incorporated that process in a couple of cases where nothing else worked in the late 80s. I was quite astonished at the results (and was very careful to not contaminate my subjects), and wondered just what the heck was going on? Again, I just explained it to myself that it was a self-created drama that allowed the person to sort themselves out. It didn't matter to me; I wasn't invested in believing any of it. I only cared that it relieved suffering. And it did, every time. It was even a rather simple formulaic process which is why I was so surprised that it worked. Could it be that easy?

My working hypothesis at the time, considering the boring regularity with which subjects from all walks of life came up with the same images, the same types of dramas, the same dynamics in the subconscious mind, was that there was some sort of "field of images", or archetypes to which all human beings were connected in some way. Well, let me make that more precise: people sorted into groups according to which images and dynamics were dominant in their particular case. Jung's work was helpful, but didn't go far enough to explain what I was witnessing. So, I decided that it would be interesting to access this pure field.

Well, how does one access such a theorized field of symbols and dynamics that seems to have some "rule" over people's lives? The obvious answer was some form of "channeling".

Unfortunately, there was a catch: I didn't trust anything - and I mean anything - that would just come into somebody's head - not even my own. I also wasn't interested in talking to alleged "dead dudes" anymore because, by this time, I'd had quite enough of that and if anybody knows they don't have much of interest to say, it was me, (assuming that it is anything other than a drama in the head of the subject).

One of the more interesting theories I came across regarding so-called "channeling" was developed by Barbara Honegger, said to be the first person in the United States to obtain an advanced degree in experimental parapsychology. Honegger suggested that automatism was the result of "stimulation" of the right hemisphere of the brain so that it could overcome the suppression of the left hemisphere. Automatism, as you might know, relates directly to utilizing a device such as automatic writing or a Ouija board type instrument. It was never entirely clear what was doing the stimulating, however and I could obtain no further information on her research. Whether or not the information was supposed to come from the subconscious of the individual or "spirits", was not clearly spelled out. But my thought was that, if it was true that some form of automatism could assist in synchronizing the right and left hemisphere of the brain, that even if it did not result in any real "contact", it was still a worthy exercise.

As I have said, there was an open possibility in my mind that such things as "spirits" were merely fragments of the personality of an individual, sort of like little broken off circuits in the brain running in repetitive loops, created by trauma or stress. Perhaps an individual, when faced with a difficulty, entered a narcissistic state of fantasy, created a "dream", which was imprinted in the memory of the brain. If they then emerged from this state back into dealing with their reality, but not having dealt with the issue itself, it might become locked away in a sort of cerebral file drawer, sitting there, waiting to be triggered by the electricity or neurochemicals of the brain in some random unconscious scan. The same could be said for so-called past life memories; they were merely self-created memory files generated in a state of narcissistic withdrawal due to stress. Such neurological files could then be downloaded and read by using the conscious bypass method of either automatism, or simply allowing the conscious mind to "step aside" as in hypnosis. For that matter, simple psychotherapy could be considered channeling in these terms. Trance channeling is more problematic because it suggests a definite pathological condition. In such cases, the "alter" ego, as either an alternate personality or whatever, is strong and well entrenched enough to establish a far stronger hold on the body of the host than those which can only manifest via automatism or trance.

My theory was that whatever the theorized "source" of whatever might be accessible, the method of automatism could be more safely utilized to access the field of archetypal symbols and dynamics that seemed to be the pool from which all people drew in the creation of their personal dramas, (leaving aside the question of whether or not those dramas represented anything factual or not). My idea was that if this field could be accessed directly, that a great deal of information about the human condition at large might be available. To increase the chance of direct access to this field, I eliminated, via playing out and feedback, any personal thought loops or memory files.

I continued to dig and read cases and find out everything I could about the subject. That's when I came across one of the first clues about the role of the "standard religions" in suppressing the human ability to access whatever it was - whether it was the subconscious, an archetypal field, or whatever.

It seems that all "primitive" or preliterate cultures had some form of codified communication between "spirits" and the living. Again, let me reiterate that I consider this nomenclature to be simply convention. This phenomenon seems to be universal in the ancient world, and only came under condemnation with the inception of monotheism around 1000 B.C.. When Yahweh spoke through his channels, they were called prophets and the activity was "divine inspiration". When anybody else did it, it was necromancy or demonic possession, or even just out and out deception. This was because, obviously, since Jehovah/Yahweh was the only god, those other "gods" did not exist; therefore, anyone who claimed to be channeling them was lying. Of course that begs the question as to why people were put to death for lying about communicating with gods that were claimed not to exist? And, if they did actually exist, and were actually communicating, as Yahweh was also, then what status does that suggest about Yahweh, since he was the one who claimed to be the only god and that this was true simply because Yahweh said so via channeling? Most curious.

In the sixth century B.C. the Thracian Dionysiac cults were known to be using shamans as trance channels to communicate with the spirits, or what were then known as theoi or gods that were said to be discarnate immortal beings with superhuman powers. Some scholars suggest that rationalist philosophy was born out of the Dionysiac, Orphic, and Eleusinian mystery cults devoted to the channeling of these gods; certainly much ancient Greek philosophy, especially that of Pythagoras, Heraclitus, and Plato, was saturated with these mysteries.

In Plato's Theagetes Socrates confesses, "By the favour of the Gods, I have since my childhood been attended by a semi-divine being whose voice from time to time dissuades me from some undertaking, but never directs me what I am to do".

The most interesting item of all is the fact that Pythagoras used something like a Ouija board as early as 540 B.C.: a "mystic table" on wheels moved around and pointed toward signs that were then interpreted by the philosopher himself, or his pupil Philolaus. Even down to the present day, the mysteries of the Pythagoreans are subjects of intense interest to scientists and mystics alike. Here there seems to be evidence that the advanced knowledge of Pythagoras may have been obtained via a Ouija board!

This brings us back to the question, of course, as to how "channeled" information could have been the basis of the Rationalist philosophy that there was nothing to channel? Could it be merely a progression of the idea of Yahweh/Jehovah that there was only one god, and he was it? Just another step in stripping away any spiritual support from the lives of human beings?

By the time the Romans had conquered Greece, the rationalist movement was turning against spirit-channeling. Cicero, the Roman rationalist whom the early Church Fathers highly revered, railed against spirit-channeling or necromancy on the grounds that it involved ghastly pagan rituals. What seems to have happened is that, eventually, rationalism bit the hand that fed it and began to devour its father, monotheism, by further extending the argument to the idea that there is no god, there are no spirits, nothing survives the death of the physical body, so there is really nobody for us to talk to on the "other side", so why bother? Science took the view that the whole thing was a con game, and that's pretty much the current mainstream scientific opinion of the phenomenon today.

Nevertheless, as I noted: I thought it would be interesting to try to access the "pure field of archetypes". I knew it would take time to run out all the loops - whether spirits or just subconscious dramas - and that patience and persistence was important. And so, I settled down to do it, and it took over two years. The results have become known as the Cassiopaean Transmissions.

The answers we received from the Cassiopaeans - "us in the future" as they described themselves - were intriguing, to say the least. The closest analogy to the view of reality presented by the Cassiopaeans is graphically explicated in the movie, The Matrix, wherein our reality is presented as a computer program/dream that "stores" human beings in "pods" so that they are batteries producing energy for some vast machine dominating the world. Certain programmed life-scenarios of great emotional content were designed in order to produce the most "energy" for this machine. And it seems that pain and suffering are the "richest" in terms of "juice".

Another major concept presented in The Matrix was that the "real now", was the reality of the control system that produced the "programmed dream of reality", experienced by those "trapped in the Matrix". The Matrix Dream Reality was based on the way things were in the past, before a terrible thing had occurred to destroy the world-that-was, after which it came under the control of computers which had become sentient and needed to utilize human beings as "power sources", or "food".

The difference between the metaphor of The Matrix and the view of the Cassiopaeans is that they propose a theoretical para-physical realm as another layer in the structure of space-time from which our own reality is projected, looping over and over again in endless variations. You could say that the hyperdimensional realms are the "future" in a very real sense.

According to the Cassiopaeans, this para-physical reality of hyperdimensional space - the realm of the Matrix programmers - is inhabited by beings of both positive and negative polarity who have "graduated" from our reality. This graduation is not necessarily one of "dying" and moving to a strictly ethereal realm, but rather one of moving to a world that is, effectively, of the future that creates our present by projecting itself into the past. What is important to realize is that if we think about the future in terms of probable futures, or branching universes, then what we do now, whether or not we wake up from the Matrix, determines what kind of future we experience, individually and collectively. Paul Dirac wrote:

> "There are, at present, fundamental problems in theoretical physics, the solution of which will presumably require a more drastic revision of our fundamental concepts than any that have gone before. Quite likely, these changes will be so great that it will be beyond the power of human intelligence to get the necessary new ideas by direct attempts to formulate the experimental data in mathematical terms. The theoretical worker in the future will, therefore, have to proceed in a more direct way. The more powerful method of advance that can be suggested at present is to employ all resources of pure mathematics in attempts to perfect and generalize the mathematical formalism that forms the existing basis of theoretical physics, and after each success in this direction, to try to interpret the new mathematical features in terms of physical entities."

 Certain ontological problems related particularly to quantum theory suggest that an "observer" (J. A. Wheeler's "Eye") watching the universe so as to "create it" may need to be included in our consideration. That suggests the necessity for expanding the scope of what is currently considered as "physical entities". The answer to "observability of parallel universes" may involve taking into account such an extension.

Now, consider the idea that there are several - maybe even infinite - "probable future yous" as observers. In the picture above, this would be represented as many "eyes" but all of them converging on a single point on the tail - the "now" moment that we perceive, which is the moment of "choice". It is from these probable futures of infinite potential - of "thought centers" - that reality is projected. It is through human beings that these energies are transduced and become "real".

You in the here and now - at the conjunction of all of these probabilities all vying with one another to become "real" - have no possibility of "creating" anything in this reality from "down here", so to say. The realities - the creative potentials - are a projection from higher levels of density.

The phenomenon that these ideas speak to more directly is that of hyperdimensional realities, wherein mental energies or consciousness energies are amplified, and can be interactive with the environment in terms of specific technology that suggests not only power for transport that is partly physical, partly "ethereal", but also communication that is partly physical and partly ethereal. Also, powers of "manifestation" that might seem impossible to us in our present state of technology are very real indeed. All of these properties do belong to hyperdimensional existence, and such a state of being has been reported for millennia as being the "realm of the gods", including Dragons and Serpents, and critters of all sorts.

As many physicists will tell you, all that really exists are "waveforms" and we are waveforms of reality, and our consciousness is something that "reads waves". We give form and structure to the waves we "read" according to some agreed upon convention.

And so, certain denizens of hyperdimensional space are "read" as more or less "reptilian" because that is the "essence" of their being, the frequency of their "wave form". And so, we call 'em "Lizzies" for short. They are not necessarily physical as we understand the term, nor are they necessarily "alien" as we understand the term either. We suspect that the perceptions of these levels of reality and their "consciousness units" are what is behind many religious conceptions and mythological representations of gods and goddesses and creatures of all sorts.

It is in this context of the Matrix, and realizing that the inner knowledge of many great mystery teachings down through the ages have presented the same, or a similar concept, that I have come to view the phenomena and interactions of our world. And such a view certainly produces results of becoming "free" from the controls of this Matrix, so I can say that in terms of experiment, it produces replicable results.

However, as Morpheus explained to Neo in the movie:

"The Matrix is a system, Neo. That system is our enemy. But when you're inside, you look around; what do you see? Businessmen, teachers, lawyers, carpenters. The very minds of the people we are trying to save. But until we do, these people are still a part of that system, and that makes them our enemy. You have to understand, most of these people are not ready to be unplugged. And many of them are so inured, so hopelessly dependent on the system that they will fight to protect it. Were you listening to me Neo, or were you looking at the woman in the red dress? They will fight to protect it..."

We could just as well re-write this to say: When you are inside the Matrix, you look around and see Christians, Jews, Mohammedans, Zoroastrians, Wiccans, Magicians... most of these people are not ready to be unplugged... they are so hopelessly inured, so hopelessly dependent on the system that they will fight to protect it. Were you listening to me, or were you listening to that Zionist, Baptist Evangelist, or purveyor of Magick and mumbo jumbo?

It was also pointed out by Morpheus that any human being who was plugged into the system could be used as an "agent" by something similar to a downloaded program that was designed to activate them in a certain way.

A similar state of affairs seems to be the actual case in our reality, with the Controllers acting from some hyperdimensional space of which we have but limited awareness, and even less access. Such a person who is "activated" as an "agent" then begins to fulfill a certain program of behavior designed to produce the most negative behavior and destruction, either to generate more "juice" or to cover up any awareness of the Matrix in which we live and move and have our being.

For the most part, the founders of many great religions - after they have brought through great knowledge - seem to have fallen prey to agents of the Matrix who twist and corrupt and distort. The same can be said for many political leaders and other public figures. But, it is not necessary to be an important figure to be an agent of the Matrix. Our friends, members of our family, tradesmen with whom we do business, the teller at the bank, a school teacher of our children, our doctors, and others with whom we interact on a daily basis, can all be activated, in an instant, as an agent of the Matrix - and most often, they are not even conscious of it.

While the internet has opened doors to the discovery of, and exchange of knowledge and information, including truths about the Matrix itself, it has also, naturally, created a perfect environment in which such Agents of the Matrix can operate with insouciance and impunity.

It seems to be so that most internet exchanges on the subject of the nature of our reality consist of 90 percent verbal abuse. The net exposes the degree of investment that people have in their Matrix reality. Believers and skeptics can be wonderfully creative about dressing up their prejudices with invective disguised as lofty principles and rational discourse. They always present their view as being opposed to the "primitive emotionalism, and logical inconsistencies" of their unscrupulous and deluded opponents, never noticing that their own agenda is fueled by these very same qualities.

The ferociousness with which True Believers and Skeptics, (both being programs of the Matrix), defend their world view (and attack those they declare to be threatening their peace of mind) by promulgating their chosen version of the Matrix Control System, is described in Buddhist philosophy (which can be still another Matrix program) as "attachment". The ego becomes so attached to its view of the world, its opinions, conclusions, perspectives, and so forth, that to suggest a more open view is perceived as a threat of destruction of the self and its identity. Thus it seems that the phenomenal rage exhibited by such persons is most likely generated by the fact that such individuals feel so great a threat to their identity, which is so entangled with their point of view, that they cannot distinguish between their beliefs and their egos.

The phrase shouted most often and most loudly by such True Believers is that their critics lack an "open mind". They, of course, cannot be criticized because they are "right". Anyone who does not believe as they do are characterized as close-minded and prejudiced against "their truth", as they have discovered it and wish to promulgate it. Generally, they engage in no research to prove these ideas, they merely attempt to impose them on others without rational discussion or investigation. Of course, there are exceptions, but more often than not, the fact that such True Believers approach their research with a prior belief is not considered an indication of lack of scholarly acumen, as it most definitely should be.

So it was, in the summer of 2001, our website, Cassiopaea.org, where we publish most of our material, came under a serious attack by members of certain Jewish organizations. These individuals accused us of publishing "anti-Semitic" material. They wrote: "We believe your site is anti-semetic,[sic] and either paid for by Nazi's or someone who hates Jews. We want you to remove your lies about our religion."

The attack became rather vicious and public, and these representatives of organizations that claim to "fight anti-Semitism" and hate, etc - not only lowered themselves to publicly libeling us and our work, writing such things as, "Ark is giving Jewish references, yet he's an anti-Semite and running a mailing list, brainwashing other Jews against our religion with lies". They also went to the trouble of researching and publishing our home address on the internet, on Jewish discussion boards, where they "invited" anyone who might live in our area go and "take care" of us in some unspecified manner.

Doing a little research of my own, we discovered that the center of activity was an e-group called "The Anti-missionary List", which is "devoted to helping everyone fight and respond to the lies of Christianity". On the site, the stated philosophy is, verbatim:

"On this list you can learn how and why the New Testament is nothing more than a compilation of pre-existing Pagan Doctrines stolen from Mithraic worship, Zoroaster, and others. You will learn Christian Missionary tactics and brain-washing technques, (sic) from people who have researched this all their lives, former Christians, etc.

"Christianity is the religion mentioned in Isaiah that would try and destroy the keeping of Torah and true worship."

I joined this group and a few others and read the discussions of Jews talking to other Jews while thinking that no "goyim" was present.

Did you ever overhear something that you were not intended to hear - something very hurtful - spoken by someone who pretended to be a friend, and only by hearing words from their own mouth do you realize that they could not possibly be your friend? If so, you probably remember the sensation of coldness that crept over your skin, the sudden pounding of your heart so that you thought it might explode, and the feeling that a big, cold stone had suddenly formed in the pit of your stomach.

That was what happened to me as I read the exchanges on these Jewish discussion groups. I was literally speechless. A discussion group that claimed to be composed of individuals involved in "educational" activities - aish, they called it - and dedicated to enlightening non-Jews about Jews, so as to end the "hate and prejudice", was the most hate-filled, prejudicial, and truly disgusting group interaction I have ever witnessed among human beings in my life. The chief theme that emerged from these discussions was that the Jews sincerely and deeply believe that they are literally the only "Chosen" people on the planet, and that this designation is absolutely Divine and without question. Anybody who is not a Jew is literally less than human. Every other religion is nothing but lies, and only Jews can ever, under any and all circumstances, be righteous.

I had always thought that people who claimed that Jews have such an attitude were just anti-Semitic. I never believed it. Anybody who said anything bad about Jews was just lying as far as I was concerned. I was finding it hard to believe it even as I witnessed it in these discussions.

After all the years of my desperate seeking for an understanding that might enable me to contribute in some small way to the effort to end hate and prejudice against Jews; after all the years of being focused on my feeling of needing to do something for the Jews; my years of pain and grief and tears for my lost family and the families of all other Jews destroyed in the Holocaust; I was brought to witness this?!

Of course, we can consider the argument that the best and worst of humanity exist in any group of people, religious, ethnic, or otherwise. If that is the case, just as it is with any other group, the bad apples can spoil it for the rest of them.

I also realized, after this encounter, that something very dangerous was taking place with the activities of such "anti-defamation" groups. Even though their stated intent is exactly the opposite, what they are actually doing is arousing anti-Semitic sentiment in non-Jews by going around so rudely and obnoxiously accusing people of anti-Semitism and insisting on the rightness of their own opinion.

What is frequently seen in these campaigns is essentially a demand for suspension of the rights of Free Speech and opinion in order to "be nice to the Jews who have suffered so much". The Jewish program of seeking out and silencing what they call "anti-Semitism" often amounts to little more than abnegating the rights of other people to think and speak according to their own rights and beliefs. The guilt hook of the Holocaust is used shamelessly and with sickening repetition.

Until we experienced it ourselves, we didn't believe it. Just think about it: we were being told that we may not publish inspirational material - none of which promotes hate or discrimination by any stretch of the imagination - simply because it did not agree with their views. More than that, if we did not buckle under to their demands, we were given a taste of what was going to be done to us. We could see an endless campaign of libel and defamation undertaken by groups with unlimited access to money and resources. We could see the possibilities of physical and material interference, even to the extent of making it impossible for us to provide a living for our family. We could also see physical threats to our safety.

Of course, as noted, this is not the case with all Jews. We have Jewish members of our Quantum Future School. We have Jewish readers who write to encourage us, one who said we ought not to, "buckle under the demands of a bunch of rabid Zionists".

But anybody who is paying attention knows that to stand against that bunch is to practically commit suicide.

So, even though we were trying to suggest a significant validation for why Jews might be targeted for repeated attack by the Matrix - which might have served to explain and validate their view that they were targeted more than other groups - we were certainly not allowed to suggest that it was not because their God chose them to be special. They are allowed to claim that they are Chosen by God and that their religion is the only right one, but we were not allowed to suggest that their religion might be part of the control system.

I was revolted and discouraged and heartbroken. I realized with a sickening thud in the pit of my stomach that - like all of us - Jews who have given their own power away are their own worst enemy. There was nothing I could do. It was clear that the powers in control of the Jews were the same as the powers in control of the rest of humanity. And their belief in their "specialness" made them even more vulnerable than the rest of us. It was the hook upon which their egos were hung. We removed the material.

Now, why were they so viciously attacking us?

Because we said they were special, but not because of their religion, but because of their genetics. The questions actually began with questions about Jesus:

Q: (L) Is there any special power or advantage in praying in the name of Jesus?

A: Yes. Prayers go to him.

Q: (L) And what does he do when he hears the prayers?

A: Determines their necessity against background of individual soul development.

Q: (L) Well, how can he do that when millions of people are praying to him simultaneously?

A: Soul division.

Q: (L) Does Jesus' soul divide?

A: Yes.

Q: (L) How many times does it divide?

A: Endlessly as a projection of consciousness.

Q: (L) And what happens to this piece of soul that is divided or projected?

A: Is not a piece of a soul.

Q: (L) What is it?

A: It is a replication.

Q: (L) Are any of us able to replicate in this manner if we so desire?

A: Could if in same circumstance. The way the process works is thus: When Jesus left the earth plane, he went into another dimension or density of reality, whereupon all "rules" regarding the awareness of time and space are entirely different from the way they are perceived in your realm. At this point in space time his soul which was/is still in the physical realm, was placed in a state of something akin to suspended animation and a sort of advanced form of unconsciousness. From that point to the present his soul has been replicated from a state of this unconsciousness in order that all who call upon him or need to be with him or need to speak to him can do so on an individual basis. His soul can be replicated ad infinitum - as many times as needed. The replication process produces a state of hyper-consciousness in each and every version of the soul consciousness. [...]

Q: (L) If one repeatedly calls upon Jesus does one get repeated replications or additional strength, power or whatever?

A: No.

Q: (L) In other words, once one has truly made the connection, that's it?

A: That's all that's needed.

Q: (L) Has any other soul volunteered to perform this work?

A: Yes.

Q: (L) How many souls are doing this work at the present time?

A: 12.

Q: (L) Can you name any of the others?

A: Buddha. Moses. Shintanhilmoon. Nagaillikiga. Varying degrees; Jesus is the strongest currently.

This was certainly a novel explanation that validated the salvific work of the holy figures of many traditions both known and unknown. (They may be known by other names at present.) But, it placed it in an entirely different context of hyperdimensionality as opposed to myths and fables of death and resurrection. However, the issue of Moses and the religion of Judaism as it was formulated and presented by him, raised many questions in our minds.

Throughout history we find one group praying to their god to protect them from the depredations of another group. The other group is praying just as fervently that their depredations will be successful. When one group succeeds in killing another, is that proof that its version of god is supreme? What then happens if the members of the successful group are then reincarnated into the group that was defeated? This is not a rhetorical question as Rabbi Gershom's book shows. The same is true about Christianity. What we have today is little more than an amalgamation of many pagan myths assigned to somebody named Jesus as his "real history".

The great Jewish scholar, Rashi de Troyes, (1040-1105), makes the astonishingly frank statement that the Genesis narrative, going back to the creation of the world, was written to justify what we might now call genocide. The Bible contains endless accounts of this activity, against the Canaanites, Hittites, Moabites, Midianites, among many others. The "chosen people" were instructed to kill everyone they could get their hands on, saving only virgins who they were supposed to take as slaves and rape as often as they liked. The author of the Jewish apocryphon "Fourth Esdras", written after the destruction of Palestine in 135 CE, ranted that Israel had not taken its "rightful" place as ruler of "the nations" (Gentiles), which are "but spittle" to "the Lord".

So why did the Catholic Church come along and seek to validate Judaism? Because the God of Israel, who gave his people the Promised Land, had to be unequivocally supreme so that neither the dispossessed Canaanites nor anyone else could ever appeal against his decrees.[232] Rashi's precise words were that God told us the creation story and included it in the Torah, "to tell his people that they can answer those who claim that the Jews stole the land from its original inhabitants. The reply should be; God made it and gave it to them but then took it and gave it to us. As he made it and it's his, he can give it to whoever he chooses". Christianity - as it was being formulated in its corrupt version at the time - raised up the Jews as the "Chosen" people, with their claimed history that went right back to Adam - and declared themselves to be the inheritors of this covenant.

---

[232] Ashe, Geoffrey, *The Book of Prophecy*, 1999, Blandford, London; p. 27.

All of this is based on the Bible and the "choosing" of the Jews by the Supreme God of the Universe to be his "special, chosen people". What seems to elude most people is the logical fact that the establishing of one "god" over and above any and all others, is an act of violence no matter how you look at it. In The Curse of Cain, Dr. Regina Schwartz writes about the relationship between Monotheism and Violence, positing that Monotheism itself is the root of violence:

> "Collective Identity, which is a result of a covenant of Monotheism is explicitly narrated in the Bible as an invention, a radical break with Nature. A transcendent deity breaks into history with the demand that the people *he* constitutes obey the law *he* institutes, and first and foremost among those laws is, of course, that they pledge allegiance to him, and him alone, and that this is what makes them a unified people as opposed to the 'other', as in all other people which leads to violence. In the Old Testament, vast numbers of 'other' people are obliterated, while in the New Testament, vast numbers are colonized and converted for the sake of such covenants."[233]

Dr. Schwartz also writes about the idea of the 'provisional' nature of a covenant: that it is conditional. "Believe in me and obey me or else I will destroy you." Doesn't sound like there is any choice, does there? And we find ourselves in the face of a pure and simple Nazi Theophany. So, of course, the question is: who is this God of the Bible?

> Q: (L) Regarding the "Fall" in Eden and the loss of the Edenic state, how long ago did that happen?
> A: 309000 years ago approx.
> Q: (L) What was the situation... what happened... what was the state of mankind?
> A: Loss of faith caused knowledge and physical restrictions by outside forces.
> Q: (L) What did the snake or the "tempter" represent?
> A: Forces known to you as Lizzies[234]
> Q: (L) What was the Fruit of the tree of Knowledge of Good and Evil that was supposedly eaten by Eve and then offered to Adam?
> A: Knowledge restriction. Encoding. [...]
> Q: (L) In what sense would the fruit of the tree of life be limiting?
> A: Believing that one source contains all knowledge is contradicting reality. [...] If the concept was the eating of the fruit of the tree of knowledge provides all knowledge, then one is being deceived, because no one particular source can provide all knowledge. Therefore, when one believes in the deception, one has now trapped oneself within parameters. And, forevermore, the human race, will be poisoned by the very same problem which is reflected in several different ways: one is always seeking the truth through one pathway instead of seeking it through a

---

[233] Schwartz, Regina M., *The Curse of Cain*, 1997, The University of Chicago Press, Chicago.
[234] Our term "Lizzies" is a short-hand notation for those theorized denizens of hyperdimensional realities whose "essence" or « wave form », is "read" as reptilian

myriad of pathways; and also believing in simplistic answers to very complex issues and questions.

As we have already noted, the revival of Judaism in the 11th and 12th centuries was a curious event and it was also the time of the "creation" and propagation of Kaballah, the Hermetic traditions of Egypt - as it is claimed - which are so closely associated with Judaic mysticism. So, in connection with the issue of Judaism, we must question the issue of Hermeticism.

Q: (L) Who was Hermes Trismegistus?
A: Traitor to court of Pharoah Rana.
Q: (L) Who is Pharoah Rana?
A: Egyptian leader of spiritual covenant.
Q: (L) In what way was Hermes a traitor?
A: Broke covenant of spiritual unity of all peoples in area now known as Middle East.
Q: (L) Who did Hermes betray?
A: Himself; was power hungry.
Q: (L) What acts did he do?
A: Broke covenant; he inspired divisions within ranks of Egyptians, Essenes, Aryans, and Persians et cetera.
Q: (L) What was his purpose in doing this?
A: Divide and conquer as inspired by those referred to as Brotherhood in Bramley book you have read.
Q: (L) Is this the Brotherhood of the snake Hermes formed in rejection of unity?
A: Hermes did not form it; it was long since in existence.
Q: (L) Who was the originator of the Brotherhood of the Serpent as described in the Bramley book?
A: Lizard Beings. [...]
Q: (L) I would like to know the approximate year of the life of Hermes Trismegistus.
A: 5211 approx. [years ago or B.C.?]

Our growing awareness of disinformation being utilized to corrupt and divert the real teachings of spiritual teachers of the past led us to inquire more deeply about Judaism and its great founder, Moses:

Q: (L) Where did the Jews come from?
A: Atlantis.
Q: (L) Who was Yahweh.
A: Fictional being.
Q: (L) Who was the god that spoke to Moses on the mount?
A: Audible projection of Lizards.
Q: (L) Did Moses at any time realize that he had been duped by the Lizzies?
A: No.
Q: (L) Yet, the other night you said that Moses is also doing work with Christ on another plane, is that correct?

A: Yes.

Q: (L) Well, if he was misled by the Lizzies, how did he get to be a good guy?

A: Taught afterward.

Q: (L) After what?

A: Plane transfer.

Q: (L) Did Moses die?

A: No.

A later session added to this idea:

Q: (L) Where did Moses get his knowledge?

A: Us.

Q: (L) Okay, you told us before that he saw or interacted with a holographic projection created by the Lizard Beings. Was that the experience on Mount Sinai?

A: Yes.

Q: (L) Okay, well, if he got knowledge from you, did he get this prior to the interactions with the Lizard beings?

A: Yes. He was corrupted by imagery. He was deceived by the imagery a la Joseph Smith, for example.

Q: (L) Are you saying that Joseph Smith, the recipient of the Mormon texts, was deceived by the Lizards also?

A: Yes. They do that a lot. […]

Q: (L) Why was Moses not allowed into the promised land?

A: Because he became tyrannical.

Q: (L) Were the Lizards the ones who led the Jews to the "Promised Land?"

A: No. Were not led; followed their own paths in effort to escape the effects of cataclysms.

Q: (L) Why have they got this big legend about being chosen and led to the promised land?

A: More brotherhood influence and nonsense.

The reader may wish to read The Gods of Eden for background on the Brotherhood of the Serpent.

The famous Ark of the Covenant was the thing that was supposed to have symbolized the "choseness" of the Jews. In The Secret History of the World, I have closely examined this subject, and it would take us too far afield to follow that thread now. For the moment, let me just say that the evidence indicates that this object was passed from the hands of the Jews not long after the Exodus around 1600 B.C.. It was taken to the East.

Q: I noticed in Genesis Chapter 33, verse 11, it says that Jacob, who wrestled with the angel the previous night and was on his way to see his brother Esau, who he had tricked into giving up his blessing years before, gave Esau the blessing. What was this? The birthright from his father or the blessing Jacob received from the angel?

A: Trampled leaves of wrath.

Q: This is what Jacob gave to Esau?

A: Yes, and what is the "core" meaning there?

Q: I don't know. What is the core meaning?

A: Leaves are of the Tree of Apples, from whence we get the proverbial "grapes of wrath", the Blue Apples incarnate!

Q: Why are these leaves 'trampled'?

A: Removes chlorophyll.

Q: What is the significance of the chlorophyll?

A: When the chlorophyll dies, the autumnal equinox is at hand.

Q: Did this signify something about the autumnal equinox?

A: Discover what the significance is, my Dear!

Q: Why did Jacob then deceive his brother again? He was to travel and meet him in Edom, but then went in the other direction as soon as Esau was on his way.

A: Refer to last answer, and cross reference.

Q: After wrestling with the 'angel', Jacob was renamed 'Israel', which means 'he will rule as a god.' This tends to make me think that this angel whom Jacob seems to have conjured, did something. What was this being that Jacob wrestled with?

A: Elohim provides the conventional response.

Who are the Elohim? Well, we will come to that. But, for the moment, let me just note that the story of the 12 tribes is actually based on an ancient Egyptian myth which is strikingly similar in all details to the stories of the 12 tribes of Israel.

In any event, based on the activities of the Catholic Church in the 10 and 11th centuries AD, they believed that the Jews still had the Ark and were hiding it and they very much wanted to find this object. Either that, or they wanted to create that impression to divert attention from the truth. It was certainly at this point that serious programs were instituted which included destruction of documents and confiscation of goods. They were obviously looking for something.

Q: (L) What was the "Ark of the Covenant"?

A: Power cell.

Q: (L) What was the origin of this power cell?

A: Lizards given to the Jews to use for manipulation of others.

Q: (L) Why was it that if you came close to this object or touched it you would die?

A: Energy overload; scrambling by reverse electromagnetism.

Q: (L) What is reverse electromagnetism?

A: Turned inward.

Q: (L) What effect does it produce?

A: Liquification of matter.

Q: (L) Well, that is pleasant. This "cell" was kept in an ornate box of some sort, is that correct?

A: Yes.

Q: (L) Why was it only the priests who could handle it?

A: Only those who would not try to use for selfish reasons.

Q: (L) But then did just coming near it injure a person?

A: Yes.

Q: (L) Well why were these individuals able to come near it?

A: Non-selfish energy field.

Q: (L) So it could tune into thought fields?

A: Yes.

The Christian church apparently never succeeded in their quest for the Ark. At least not the Catholic Christian Church. It appears that the Templars may have discovered something very interesting, but not in Jerusalem, and the story of their searches in Jerusalem were created later to divert attention. It also appears that the relationship between the Templars and Cathars was very symbiotic for at least a certain period. If what the Cassiopaeans have said about this object, that only those with non-selfish energy fields could handle it, and we consider the fact that the word "Cathari" means those who have been purified, we certainly have the right to wonder if the crusades against them, following the rampages in Jerusalem, might not be connected?

Q: In January of 1244, nearly three months before the fall of the fortress of Montsegur, two of the Parfaits escaped. According to tradition, the bulk of the Cathar treasure went with them - that is, gold, silver etc. Supposedly it was taken to a cave in the mountains and then to a castle stronghold. After this, the treasure vanished and has never been heard of again. In March, three months later, Montsegur capitulated with less than 400 defenders remaining. The defenders requested a two week truce. Now, these guys have been duking it out and slaughtering each other, yet they are granted a two week truce! This is quite amazing! They wanted to consider the terms of surrender. The terms were that all the fighting men were to receive a full pardon for various crimes. They would be allowed to depart with all their baggage, gifts, and any money they received from their employers. The Parfaits were to be generously dealt with if they would renounce their beliefs and confess their sins to the Inquisition. They would be freed, and subjected only to light penances. This was completely out of keeping with what the Inquisition was all about. Anyway, they asked for two weeks to consider the terms. In return, they offered hostages. Then, on March 15, the truce expired. The following day, 200 Parfaits were hauled out and burnt. There was no time to erect individual stakes, so they were all burned together in a wooden stockade at the foot of the mountain. Not one recanted. On the night of March 16 it says that four men, accompanied by a guide, made an escape by descending the sheer western face of the mountain, suspended by ropes. According to tradition, these men carried the 'true' treasure of the Cathars. Why was this not smuggled out with the bulk of the treasure three months earlier? Why was this retained in the fortress until the last moment? What was the delay for? Why did this item or items need to be retained until a specific date that coincided with the Spring Equinox? It is know that some sort of festival was held on March 14, the day before the truce expired. Apparently, this ceremony *had* to be held on March 14. From the reports, this ceremony or festival was quite impressive because

some of the hired mercenaries, defying inevitable death, converted to the
Cathar faith at this time. Could whatever was smuggled out have been
necessary to the ceremony on the 14th? Was it necessary for them to
retain something in their possession until a certain period of time had
passed?

A: If you understood the cycles, and more importantly, the forces
directing them, then you would already have the answer to this.

Q: Well, that is why I am asking. So, apparently these Cathars *did* have
something...

A: Sometimes, your asking is merely for validation of your own hunches.
And for growth and progress, one must learn to let the answer stand.

Now, we notice that the answer was related to "time" and "cycles"
which connects us to the issue of what it was that was passed to Esau in
the story of Jacob wrestling with the angel.[235] We also note the curious
fact that after the object was passed in the Jacob story, he was named
Israel, and this was the beginning, or so it seems, of the myth of Judaism's
twelve tribes. And it was after the passing of the object in the possession
of the Cathars that early Roman Catholic Christianity, something quite
different from the faith taught by the Cathars, became, in toto, the
dominant religion of all of Europe. Perhaps the same was true in the case
of Judaism as taught by Moses? Perhaps the truth was lost with the
passing of the Ark? We also note that this has something to do with
"cycles" and the "forces directing" these cycles..

The evidence seems to suggest that the Ark traveled to the East while
false trails were set up to suggest that it went West, as in the many
theories about "Holy Grail Across the Atlantic". These theories and others
were predicated on the smoke screens of such groups as the "Priory of
Sion", once more brought to the public view through Dan Brown's novel
The Da Vinci Code.

These smoke screens are an interesting phenomenon of the present day.
As it happens, approximately 700 years passed from the time of the Cathar
massacre before interest in the Ark was revived. At the very same time
that the "truth" of the Bible was being openly questioned in the nineteenth
century, the phenomenon of spiritualism manifested, and a whole host of
occult groups took shape, looking for something to replace the "old time
religion". As a result of this activity, a number of strange events took
place that it would be too involved to chronicle here.[236] Suffice it to say
that the evidence points to revelations of great secrets made before the

[235] For the reader who is unaware of my previous writings on the Bible, let me say that I do
not take the stories related there at face value, however, I do believe that the basic story
recounted in the Bible is a mythologizing of something that did happen in the same way that
the Greek myths or the Rg Veda is a mythologizing of real events. I refer interested readers
to my book *The Secret History of the World* for more on this subject.

[236] See: Hedsel and Ovason, The Zelator; Godwin, The Hermetic Brotherhood of Luxor;
Godwin, Arktos, Scott, The People of The Secret etc.

turn of the last century, possibly picked up by a group of wealthy Western industrialists - which may or may not have included the Rockefellers. At that point, the smoke and mirrors operation went into overdrive, and the "occult" groups were infiltrated with what we know today as disinformation. That condition has persisted to the present, and "secret societies" and occultists are most often part of the cover-up.

And this brings us to other strange matters, something called "Alternative 3" that is somehow mixed up with this cover-up of the ideas of the Holy Grail, the Ark of the Covenant, and the true history of mankind:

> Q: [...] OK, where is the Ark of the Covenant currently located?
> A: Alternative 3.
> Q: (L) Alternative 3 is the plan to take all the people, all the smart guys, all the elite, off the planet and leave everybody else here to blow up isn't it?
> A: Maybe. Maybe not. [This "maybe not" was delivered in the midst of the next question and was originally included with the next answer. But it rightly belongs here, and so I have moved it to retain the proper context.]
> Q: (L) Where is it currently located?
> A: Discover.
> Q: (L) We're trying to discover through our interaction with you. How else can we discover something as obscure as this? I mean, that's a pretty darned obscure question, I would think.
> A: *Study alternative 3 to find answer!*

Alternative 3, of course, leads us to consider the so-called MJ-12 group, the purported special task force for the study of UFO's supposedly formed by President Harry Truman on September 24, 1947. The interesting connection here is the fact that the CIA was officially "born" on September 9, 1947.

The history of the CIA is important here. In January of 1945, Werner Von Braun made plans to move his team of about 125 rocket scientists and engineers to surrender to the Americans. Hitler had ordered their execution to prevent their capture by the Allies. On the same day that Berlin fell to the Soviet Army, May 2, 1945, Von Braun and his team entered the American lines to safety.

Convinced that German scientists could help America's postwar efforts, President Harry Truman agreed in September 1946 to authorize "Project Paperclip", a program to bring selected German scientists to work on America's behalf during the "Cold War". However, Truman expressly excluded anyone found, "to have been a member of the Nazi party and more than a nominal participant in its activities, or an active supporter of Nazism or militarism". The War Department's Joint Intelligence Objectives Agency (JIOA) conducted background investigations of the scientists. In February 1947, JIOA Director Bosquet Wev submitted the first set of scientists' dossiers to the State and Justice Departments for review. The Dossiers were damning. Samuel Klaus, the State Departments representative on the JIOA board, claimed that all the scientists in this first batch were "ardent Nazis". Their visa requests were denied. Wev wrote a memo warning that, "the best interests of the United States have been subjugated to the efforts expended in 'beating a dead Nazi horse'." He also declared that the return of these scientists to Germany, where they could be exploited by America's enemies, presented a "far greater security threat to this country than any former Nazi affiliations which they may have had or even any Nazi sympathies that they may still have".

When the JIOA formed to investigate the backgrounds and form dossiers on the Nazis, the Nazi Intelligence leader Reinhard Gehlen met with the CIA director Allen Dulles. Dulles and Gehlen hit it off immediately, Gehlen was a master spy for the Nazis and had infiltrated Russia with his vast Nazi Intelligence network. Dulles promised Gehlen that his Intelligence unit was safe in the CIA. Dulles had the scientists dossier's re-written to eliminate incriminating evidence. As promised, Allen Dulles delivered the Nazi Intelligence unit to the CIA, which later opened many umbrella projects stemming from Nazi mad research (MK-Ultra/Artichoke, Operation Midnight Climax). By 1955, more than 760 German scientists had been granted citizenship in the U.S. and given prominent positions in the American scientific community. Many had been longtime members of the Nazi party and the Gestapo, had conducted experiments on humans at concentration camps, had used slave labor, and had committed other war crimes. In a 1985 expose in the Bulletin of the Atomic Scientists, Linda Hunt wrote that she had examined more than 130 reports on Project Paperclip subjects--and every one "had been changed to eliminate the security threat classification". President Truman, who had explicitly ordered no committed Nazis to be admitted under Project Paperclip, was evidently never aware that his directive had been violated.

"Project Paperclip" was instituted to find as many German scientists and engineers as possible and to create new identities for them so as to protect them from war crimes trials. The "powers that be" in America were very interested in mining their technological knowledge. Among the many rumors that emerged about the Nazi scientists was one that they had actually built a time machine.

Q: (L) Did the Germans construct a time machine during WWII?
A: Yes.
Q: (L) Were the German experiments in time travel carried to the U.S. after the war?
A: In splintered form.
Q: (L) Did the U.S. take possession of a time machine constructed by the Germans?
A: No.

Q: (L) Why not?

A: Was taken elsewhere.

Q: (L) Where?

A: Mausenberg, Neufriedland.

Q: (L) Still in Germany?

A: Nein!

Q: (L) Where is Mausenberg?

A: Antarktiklandt.

Q: (L) These individuals who have this time machine in Antarctica, what are they doing with it or what do they plan to do with it?

A: Exploring time sectors through loop of cylinder.

Q: (L) What is a loop of cylinder?

A: Complex, but is profile in 4th through 6th density.

Q: (L) Are there any particular goals that they have in doing this "time exploration"?

A: Not up to present, as you measure it.

Q: (L) Well, if they escaped and took this time machine to Antarctica, are they working with any of the so-called "aliens"?

A: 4th density STS.

Q: (L) Are these Germans and their time machine, any part of the plan to take over earth when it moves into 4th density.

A: Maybe.

Q: (L) Are the Germans behind any of the conspiracies in the U.S?

A: No.

This last answer surprised me because there is certainly a lot of conspiracy theory promoting just exactly that idea. But, we will soon discover something interesting, so bear with me.

Just who MJ-12 really might be has occupied a lot of research and thinking for a number of years. Sometimes, when you ask a question about a theory that is wrong, you get an indirect clue to the truth:

Q: (L) Ok, the *Matrix Material* says that Henry Kissinger is the current head of MJ12. Is this correct?

A: No.

Q: (L) Is he just a red herring, so to speak?

A: Yes. MJ12 is no longer MJ12.

Q: (L) What is MJ12 now known as?

A: *Institute of Higher Learning.*

Q: (L) Are you talking about Brookings Lab, or Brookhaven?

A: Not really.

Q: (L) Is it a specific institute of higher learning?

A: Yes.

That was certainly a strange remark. What could they mean by that? Nevertheless, again, asking questions about one thing often leads to something quite unexpected.

Q: (L) […] Some people on the net want me to ask about this HAARP thing... seems to be some sort of antennae thing...

A: *Disguise for something else.*
Q: (L) What is that something else?
A: *Project to apply EM wave theories to the transference of perimeters.*
Q: (L) What does that mean?
A: *If utilised as designed, will allow for controlled invisibility and easy movement between density levels on surface of planet as well as subterranially.*
Q: (L) Who is in charge of building this thing?
A: More than one entity. […]
Q: (L) Can you tell us if this is a human organization or aliens, or a combination?
A: *Human at surface level.* […]
Q: (L) Is there more you can tell us about this?
A: *It has nothing to do with weather or climate. These things are emanating from 4th density, as we have told you before.* […]
Q: (L) Is it currently in operation?
A: Experimental.
Q: (L) How long have they been working on this thing?
A: *Since the 1920s.*
Q: (L) What?! The 1920s?
A: Yes.

I was pretty astounded by the above answer. It made no sense at all to me at the time. But keep it in mind, it will be important. We are closing in on our quarry.

A strange guy named Al Bielek connects HAARP to certain mind control experiments that were supposed to have been carried out by the CIA at Montauk as an extension of the so-called Philadelphia Experiment. Bielek was an associate of zoologist Ivan Sanderson who also happened to be a friend of Morris K. Jessup. It was Sanderson and another associate, Riley Crabb, who brought forward and "confirmed" the story about Jessup's purported correspondence with a fellow named Carl Allen, aka Carlos Allende, who seems to have been the first to "name" the Philadelphia Experiment and to claim that it was based on the work of Einstein. Interestingly, Sanderson's claims were only made after Jessup was dead. The evidence mysteriously disappeared. Nevertheless, the Philadelphia Experiment mythos is based on this story begun by Sanderson, and continued by his associate Bielek.

Allende's first letter to Jessup arrived on January 13, 1956, with the return address: RD #1, Box 223, New Kensington, Pennsylvania, but which was postmarked Gainesville, Texas, and includes, in the very first paragraph, actually the very first sentence, a reference to UFT:

"My Dear Dr. Jessup,

Your invocation to the Public that they move en Masse upon their Representatives and have thusly enough Pressure placed at the right & sufficient Number of Places where from a Law demanding Research into Dr. Albert Einstein's Unified Field Theory May be enacted (1925-27) is Not at all Necessary. It May Interest you to know that The Good Doctor Was Not so Much influenced in his retraction of the Work, by Mathematics, as he most assuredly was by Humantics."

These claims about Albert Einstein's UFT were made by Allende exactly 8 months after the death of Albert Einstein on April 18, 1955. Not only was Morris Jessup not alive when claims were made about what he was up to, Einstein was similarly conveniently dead.

As it happens, the UFT that Einstein developed in 1925-27 was the wrong one. It was the first "homemade UFT" and, at the time, Einstein publicly expressed optimism that UFT would soon be solved. Einstein realized soon after the publication of the 1925 paper that the results were not impressive. This has been repeatedly checked, and is a Mathematical fact, contrary to the assertion of Carlos Allende.

Q: Here is this purported letter from a Carlos Allende to Dr. Jessup. Now, whether Carlos was a real person or not, what I want to know is if the information is somewhat accurate?
A: Is that not obvious?
Q: I thought it was. He said that Einstein did computations on cycles of human civilization and progress, compared to the growth of man's general character and development, and that this horrified him. Now, this is the very thing you suggested I do to find clues. And, I am doing it. It says here that Einstein was doing the same thing. Is this correct?
A: Yes.
Q: What horrified him?
A: The discovery of variability of physicality, and all that that implies, when one knows all that Einstein knew up to that point.
Q: So, 4th density blew him away!
A: And the other density levels. One begins with the premise that the material realm is the "whole shooting match", discovers it is not, must rethink everything.
Q: (L) Did the Philadelphia Experiment, as we have read about it, occur in the way it was described?
A: Close.
Q: (L) Was Al Bielek part of the experiment?
A: Yes.
Q: (L) Was the information he has given out about this factual?
A: Close.
Q: (L) Is the information he gives about being aged regressed in the body and his brother coming into a new body accurate?
A: No.
Q: (T) Is his brother, Duncan, really who he claims to be?
A: No.
Q: (L) Is Al Bielek really who he claims to be?
A: No. Was technician but not aboard vessel.
Q: (L) So he did not go back and forth in time?
A: Correct.
Q: (T) So he's trying to make himself out to be more than he actually is?

A: Yes. [...] He is an agent of the government.

Q: (T) Is Preston also a government agent?

A: Yes.

Q: (T) Why are they coming out with this story? Besides disinformation...

A: Slow revelation to effect gauge of public response. George Bush was involved with Philadelphia experiment.

This last remark about George Bush being involved in the Philadelphia Experiment is going to become very important, so hang onto it.

Q: (A) I am confused about space, time, Einstein's general relativity, gravitation and electromagnetism.

A: Einstein's Theory of Relativity is only partially correct. That is why we say that there is no "dimension" of time. As far as gravity and electromagnetics are concerned, we suggest a review of the as yet publicly unfinished Unified Field Theory of the same gentleman. Was it completed and put into application in secret? Hmmmmm... And, if so, what are the ramifications? Maybe you could make the same discoveries. [...]

So, we began to dig even deeper into Einstein's papers and correspondence and started trying to figure it out.

Q: Ark did some reading on the Einstein thing, the letters to Kaluza, and there did not seem to be anything that E did in the period mentioned that would make one tend to think that there was a UFT from him in that time. But, Kaluza *did* have an interesting idea about a 5 dimensional cylinder UFT which Einstein thought was quite startling. Yet, it seems that Einstein somewhat delayed Kaluza's presentation. What struck me was the word 'cylinder' which reminded me of the earlier session where I asked if the Germans had developed a time machine and you said 'yes', and that it was in Antarctica, and that 'they' were 'exploring the loop of the cylinder'. You said that the loop of the cylinder was a 4th thru 6th density profile. Could you give me some elaboration on this cylinder, the loop of the cylinder, and whether it was Kaluza who did the UFT and not Einstein?

A: Cylinder is really a double loop, is it not? And meditate if you will on the true meaning of this!

Q: Is it true that Kaluza had the theory and Einstein didn't?

A: Maybe it is that Einstein first hypothesized, and others were then commissioned for the purpose of completion in order to lead to application.

And then again later:

Q: (A) Einstein. We were told that Einstein discovered UFT, or the possible consequences, and stopped, that the thing that scared him was variability of physicality. I cannot see a trace in his papers. I can't see which particular year that he discovered that variability of physicality could follow from UFT. Which year was it?

A: 1936. [...]

What we actually found in print was a paper Einstein wrote in 1938, with P. Bergmann, entitled *On a Generalization of Kaluza's Theory of Electricity:*

"So far, two fairly simple and natural attempts to connect gravitation and electricity by a unitary field theory have been made, one by Weyl, the other by Kaluza. Furthermore, there have been some attempts to represent Kaluza's theory formally so as to avoid the introduction of the fifth dimension of the physical continuum. The theory presented here differs from Kaluza's in one essential point; we ascribe physical reality to the fifth dimension whereas in Kaluza's theory this fifth dimension was introduced only in order to obtain new components of the metric tensor representing the electromagnetic field."[237]

Was this the first paper on this subject? Or was it a modification of the first paper? In any event, we believe that Einstein was following a path that was later to prove very fruitful. Einstein, however, was somewhat nervous about this idea, but he followed it anyway, writing in his paper:

"If Kaluza's attempt is a real step forward, then it is because of the introduction of the five dimensional space. There have been many attempts to retain the essential formal results obtained by Kaluza without sacrificing the four-dimensional character of the physical space. This shows distinctly how vividly our physical intuition resists the introduction of the fifth dimension. But by considering and comparing all these attempts one must come to the conclusion that all these endeavors did not improve the situation. It seems impossible to formulate Kaluza's idea in a simple way without introducing the fifth dimension.

We have, therefore, to take the fifth dimension seriously although we are not encouraged to do so by plain experience. If, therefore, the space structure seems to force acceptance of the five dimensional space theory upon us we must ask whether it is sensible to assume the rigorous reducibility to four dimensional space. We believe that the answer should be 'no' provided that it is possible to understand, in another way, the *quasi-four dimensional character of the physical space* by taking as a basis the five dimensional continuum and to simplify hereby the basic geometrical assumptions.[…] The most essential point of our theory is the replacing of …rigorous cylindricity by the assumption that space is closed (or periodic).[…] Kaluza's five dimensional theory of the physical space provides a unitary representation of gravitation and electromagnetism. […] It is much more satisfactory to introduce the fifth dimension not only formally, but to assign to it some physical meaning."[238]

Q: What about the time machine by Newman? It's related to the UFT business, time loops, time travel... also, I can jump on this...
A: Look for Von Neumann.
Q: Von Neumann?! Okay, I read a book about Von Neumann, and what

---

[237] Einstein, A, Bergmann, P., *Annals of Mathematics*, Vol. 38, No. 3, July 1938.
[238] Ibid.

struck me was that he was an extremely bright man with a sharp mind, but somehow a little bit tragic, and I could not find any trace that he did anything unusual except in the subject of automata and artificial life and such things. Your advice to look into Von Neumann, is it relating to this business or in his presumed participation in the Philadelphia Experiment?

A: Good! Now you are "tracking". [...]

Q: (A) What I do not understand is why, a few years later, [Einstein] completely abandoned [UFT in terms of Kaluza-Klein theories] and started working very hard on a completely different solution. If he knew...

A: Was under control.

Q: (A) Can you control somebody and make him spend years.... Oh! Mind control! They got him!

A: Why do you think he emigrated to the United States in the first place?

Q: (A) Well, that is not a surprise. He was a Nobel Prize winner and *America was getting together every possible Nobel Prize winner, and also there was the persecution of the Jews, so it was natural.*

A: *More to it than that. What about Freud?*

Q: (L) I guess they didn't want Freud! He didn't know anything about UFT! (A) Now, apparently Von Neumann was also involved in application of UFT. But, Von Neumann was, as far as we know, doing a completely different kind of mathematics. He didn't even really know geometry, differential geometry. He was doing completely different things. [Game Theory, to be precise.] So how come the UFT that was discovered by Einstein, involved Von Neumann? What did Von Neumann contribute to this project?

A: Von Neumann was one of three overseers at Princeton with level 7 security clearance, and a clear budget request permittance.

Q: (L) My question is, about Von Neumann, as I understand it, Von Neumann was supposed to have been involved with the creation of a time machine, right?

A: Yes.

Q: (L) Did he succeed in such a project?

A: Yes.

Q: (L) Well, why was it that, when he developed a brain tumor and realized he was going to die - and I read that he screamed and yelled like a baby when he knew there was no hope - if he was somebody who had access to a time machine, why wasn't he able to do something about it instead of carrying on like a madman? The stories about his screams echoing all over the place, are horrible. He realized that his great mind was going to soon be still; if he had access to a time machine, one would think that he would have used it, would have pulled every string he could, to forestall his own death.

A: No Laura, it does not work that way. And besides, if you had a brain tumor, you could be forgiven for a few mental peculiarities too!

Q: (L) I just don't understand why, when he knew he was sick, that he didn't just use the time machine to go forward in time for a cure, or backward in time to correct something in his past...

A: *The time machine was not his property.*

Q: (L) So, they got what they needed from him and let him die. (A) It is

not clear. *He got this cancer so suddenly, it may even have been induced.*
(L) Well, that's a thought.

Now we have a lot of very interesting pieces of the puzzle laid out on the table, so to say, and so it is time to return to the issue of the Jews. At the point in time that I was really struggling to come to some understanding of this terrible event in our history wherein 60 million or more people lost their lives, of which only one tenth were Jewish, I wanted to try to understand.

> Q: (L) Is there some karmic element that was fulfilled by the Holocaust?
> A: Of course.
> Q: (L) Could you tell us what karma was being expunged in that activity, and what group the Jews represented?
> A: This is not germane, but it was Atlantean overseers "expunging" guilt from that life experience.
> Q: (L) Now, you have said that the Jews were Atlantean descendants, and that Noah was an Atlantean...
> A: *Most of them.*
> Q: (L) What is the significance of this relating to their religion and their experiences and the current state of the Jews?
> A: Were Jews in "holocaust" only.
> Q: (L) [What do you mean?]
> A: No special karmic significance to being "Jewish", special significance is experiencing holocaust for purpose of purging extraordinary karmic debt.

The answer that "most" of the Jews were Atlantean descendants was not really noticed by me at the time it was given. It was only much later that I realized that this was a significant clue.

I continued to research the history and myths and archaeology that led off in endless trails from the central issue and again and again I kept coming up against what I called "The Scottish Question" in terms of so-called conspiracies. What this term was intended to designate was the fact that whenever I tracked a series of clues, I always hit a closed door that was connected in some way to Scotland - including Scottish Rite Masonry.

> Q: (L) I would like to know what is the origin of the Freemasons?
> A: Osirians.
> Q: (L) Can you tell us when the original Freemasons formed as a society?
> A: 5633 B.C.
> Q: (L) Is Freemasonry as it is practiced today the same?
> A: 33rd degree, yes.
> Q: (L) So, there is a continuing tradition for over seven thousand years?
> A: Yes.
> Q: (L) Is this organization with a plan to take over and rule the world?
> A: Not exactly.
> Q: (L) What is their focus?

A: Overseers.
Q: (L) Of what?
A: The status of Quorum.
Q: (L) What is the Quorum?
A: Deeper knowledge organization. Totally secret to your kind as of yet.
Very important with regard to your future.
Q: (L) In what way?
A: Changes.
Q: (L) Can you get more specific? Is that changes to us personally?
A: Partly.
Q: (L) Earth changes?
A: Also.
Q: (L) What is the relationship between this Quorum and the
Cassiopaeans?
A: They communicate with us regularly.
Q: (L) Do they do this knowing you are Cassiopaeans or do they do it
thinking...
A: Yes.
Q: (L) Has there been an ongoing relationship between the Cassiopaeans
and this Quorum for these thousands of years?
A: For some time as you measure it.

If this date for the formation of the society later to become the
Freemasons - 5633 B.C. - is correct, it means that it was in existence for
about either 2500 years or 422 years before the Hermes rebellion, which
we have already learned took place 5211, though we don't know whether
that was B.C. or "years ago". It could mean that the Hermes rebellion took
place 5211 B.C. or right around 3200 B.C.. The C's said that Hermes was
a "Traitor to court of Pharaoh Rana" who was the Egyptian leader of a
spiritual covenant of spiritual unity of all the peoples in area now known
as Middle East, including Egyptians, Essenes, Aryans, and Persians. If the
C's are correct, there has been some serious twisting and manipulating of
the facts as we shall soon see. Well, we aren't surprised. Everything else is
disinformation, why not this?

What we find to be most interesting is the use of the dates as clues here -
the 33 representing the Osirians, and the 11 representing Hermes. We
notice also that the story about Jacob wrestling with the angel is in chapter
33 of Genesis, and the verse that tells us that Jacob passed something to
Esau is verse 11. Esau was, of course, the legendary father of the Arabs.
The C's described this item as "trampled leaves of wrath", and mentioned
cycles and the ends of cycles.[239] At a later point in time, the C's connected
the number 11 to "Medusa", and we have recently seen this element in

---

[239] As we pick up the clues, again and again we are disturbed by the niggling thought that the
Bible was assembled by individuals who had "foreknowledge", and that this information was
not favorable to the Jews. It is almost as though someone traveled into the past to "plant" the
Bible for nefarious purposes intended to come to fruition in the present time.

action on 9-11. The number 9, I should note, is the sum of three 3s, or 3 X 3.

But let's look a little bit closer at the Hermes affair. The generally accepted sequence of Egyptian historical events tell us that a king from "upper Egypt" - that is, the arid highlands - named Narmer, Menes, or Aha, defeated the King of Northern, or Lower Egypt, and thereby unified the two lands. This unification is commemorated in the famous Narmer Palette, which shows a "head smiting" scene, a euphemism for conquest. The best estimates for the date of this event just happen to be in the vicinity of 3100 B.C. - which suggests that the time the C's intended to refer to as the "Hermes Rebellion" was the longer period of 2500 years rather than the shorter. In other words, the great "unifier" of Egypt may have been this Hermes, and this may have been an act of rebellion against a covenant of peace.

According to Manetho, Menes/Narmer came from the Thinite province in Upper Egypt and, whether unification was achieved by military or peaceful means is uncertain, though head smiting seems to indicate the former.

Tradition tells us that Menes founded Memphis on an island in the Nile, conducted raids against the Nubians, and extended his power as far as the first cataract. He sent ambassadors to Canaan and Byblos in Phoenicia; he founded the city of Crocodilopolis, and built the first temple to the god Ptah, who Herodotus and others later say was Hepahestus, the volcano/fire god.

Skipping over the list and details of what is known via archaeology and conjectured via ignorance, we come to the reign of Peribsen in the so-called second dynasty. Peribsen was the fourth king of that line and some experts opine that he was actually not the legitimate heir of Nintejer, the king before him, but that he was an outsider who instigated a coup against Pharaoh Nintejer. Peribsen used the nomen "Seth" in his titles. Apparently, this signified sweeping political changes since the serekhs bearing the royal names are not surmounted by Horus anymore, but by his religious rival, Set, who became the primary royal patron deity of Peribsen.

Here we discover a most interesting item in history. Prior to this point, the pharaohs from the time of Narmer/Menes, were affiliated with Horus - the "son of Osiris". This means that apparently Horus - the Shemsu Hor - were the Hermes rebellion gang.

Q: (L) Who were the 'Followers of Horus'?
A: Those who held the 3rd "insight".
Q: (L) What was the third insight?
A: There are 10. *The 3rd involves transcendental existence.*

That certainly sounds very positive, but we have to be careful about our assumptions. Looking at the following, we see similar terms - including our mysterious Elohim who cut the deal with Jacob prior to the passage of the Ark to the East - and we realize that everything is not always as it appears:

Q: (L) Who were the Elohim of the Bible?
A: Transdefinitive.
Q: (L) What does that mean? Transcends definition?
A: And variable entities.
Q: (L) Were the Elohim 'good guys?'
A: First manifestation was human, then non-human.
Q: (L) Are they light beings as some people say? What brought about their transformation from human to non-human?
A: Pact or covenant.
Q: (L) They made a pact or covenant with each other?
A: No, with 4th density STS.
Q: (L) Well, that is not good! Are you saying that the Elohim are STS? Who were these STS beings they made a pact with?
A: Rosteem, now manifests as Rosicrucians.

And we suddenly realize that the Sons of Horus and the Elohim must have been one and the same: the Hermes gang that rebelled against the spiritual covenant of the Osirians. And the myth of Isis and Osiris and Set and Horus takes on a whole new meaning - and we see how it has been given a slight twist to obscure the truth. We also begin to suspect a strange connection between this group and the "creation" of Judaism via a conglomeration of Egyptian elements, as well as the conversion of Christianity to a similar Egyptian myth. Egypt, Egypt, everywhere!

Getting back to Peribsen, Egyptologists admit that the events of the second dynasty are extremely uncertain, if not the most uncertain in Egyptian history. What we find to be most fascinating is that right around the time of the Peribsen "rebellion", the Cretan civilization suddenly appeared in the Mediterranean. We also note the most curious fact that, based on the years assigned to the kings by Manetho, though we cannot be certain of the year in our own calendar system on which to affix these dates, the period between the unification by Narmer and the Peribsen coup happens to be right at 430 years - the period of time that the Jews claimed to have sojourned in Egypt.

It is curious to find this "unification" of Egypt, the building of a great city and temple in Egypt, and a rebellion 430 years later while we see that the time of Peribsen was 430 years after the time of Narmer/Menes at precisely the moment in time that a new group of people appeared on the island of Crete. It becomes even more interesting when we learn what Tacitus says about it:

"Some say that the Jews were fugitives from the island of Crete, who settled on the nearest coast of Africa about the time when Saturn was driven from his throne by the power of Jupiter. Evidence of this is sought in the name. There is a famous mountain in Crete called Ida; the neighboring tribe, the Idaei, came to be called Judaei by a barbarous lengthening of the national name."[240]

What we seem to be able to extract from all of this is that there is a peculiar match of odd items in the historical record to things the C's have said. The main difference is that the C's are telling us that our history has been corrupted and distorted to conceal the true objectives of those who do not have our best interests at heart.

In the story of Narmer, we detect an odd, distorted reflection of both Solomon, and Hermes. They were great civilizers, unifiers of two kingdoms, builders and occultists. There are even suggestions in occult literature that Solomon and Hermes were one and the same. And if the C's are correct, that is, in fact, true.

Solomon was supposed to have built the great temple for the Ark of the Covenant. Narmer/Menes built the great temple of Ptaah. Connected to this is the legend of the Egyptian labyrinth. Then, there was the Cretan labyrinth that was supposedly modeled on the Egyptian one, with legends of a terrible, devouring Bull in the center.

Herodotus describes a great labyrinth located in Egypt at the ancient site of Arsinoe on the eastern bank of a large body of water, Lake Moeris. The labyrinth was constructed in the style of a great compartmental palace with 3000 different chambers, 1500 of which were above ground and 1500 were below ground. The foundation was approximately 1000 feet long x 800 feet long. He claimed that it was built by Ammenemes III in the twelfth dynasty of the Old Kingdom in approximately 2300 B.C..

Pliny assures us that Herodotus was wrong not only about who built the labyrinth, but also about when it was built. Pliny dates it to almost four thousand years before his own time which puts it right at the time of the Unification of Egypt - the time of Narmer/Menes. He also makes the most interesting remark that the building was regarded with extraordinary hatred. That would certainly be true of a structure that was utilized for dreadful sacrifices.

Daedalus, the "great architect" of the Cretan labyrinth was connected to a king named Minos. This is a curious reflection of Menes. Discovering a great architect connected, even indirectly, to a great unifier of two kingdoms and builder of a great Temple in Egypt, naturally draws us to make connections between the Masonic story of Solomon and Hiram Abiff and the Ark of the Covenant. We also see many correspondences in the story presented in the Bible, that Solomon was a friend of Hiram, King of Tyre and that he married an Egyptian princess and other odd

---

[240] *The Histories*, Book V, c. 110 CE

connections. The Temple of Solomon was built to house the Ark, and the Cretan labyrinth was built to house a monster, and the Egyptian labyrinth was the "model" for the Cretan one.[241]

We see in the story of Menes/Narmer not merely a strong resemblance, but we see certain historical developments that, even though not specified, point us in the direction of thinking that the myth of Theseus, Ariadne, and Daedalus and the Minotaur in the labyrinth, and Solomon and the Ark, actually relate to Hermes and a military rebellion and conquest, after which he "married the princess" to secure his place on the throne, built his Temple - a labyrinth - which possibly contained some sort of technological device that was carried away from Egypt at some later point in history.

It is most curious to find this ancient link between Crete and Egypt and the Jews, the purported possessors of the famous Ark of the Covenant, most especially when we consider the issue of the labyrinth and the Minotaur. Was the Egyptian Labyrinth the real "Temple of Solomon"?

In the events of the time of Peribsen - the worshipper of Set - we see a possible twist on the story of slaves.

The Bible reports that Solomon made slaves of everyone in the land (except his own people, the Jews, of course), and he married a daughter of a pharaoh. One of the objections historians have made to this story is that until much later, the Egyptians simply did NOT give their princesses in marriage to other nations. They didn't need to. But Solomon married an Egyptian Princess. Perhaps this detail was part of the ancient tradition of a great king becoming ruler by virtue of his marriage to the Queen?

Was Peribsen a slave raised in the Egyptian court - who rebelled and then, later, lead his followers to Crete? At the time of the cataclysmic eruption of Thera, when they escaped from Crete, did they carry their stories of rebellion and escape from the tyranny of 430 years of slavery with them? Fleeing the thunderous mountain, did they escape to Israel, settling with their history of great temples, kings and former glories?

The Minoan Kingdom was destroyed by the eruption of the terrible volcano of Thera on the island of Santorini, and after that, none of the Minoan "palaces" was ever re-inhabited. It seems that the original Minoans fled, never to return, and afterward, the purely Greek period of Crete began with the arrival of waves of Dorians.

From the very beginning of Arthur Evans' excavations, the finds at Knossos differed so fundamentally from the art and artifacts of classical Greece that there was simply no comparison. The russet skin color of the Minoan men on the frescoes in the Palace of Knossos was a distinct sign of their alien nature to the Greeks. They were not fair-haired Achaeans, but brown skinned, dark-haired tribes. Evans found no temples, no large

---

[241] I will be detailing certain discoveries about this matter in another volume.

sculpture, no amphitheaters with seats, no inscriptions telling the deeds of the gods and great men, not even any familiar characters of the Greek pantheons.

Knossos presented no clear parallel to other known cultures of the eastern Mediterranean. The Minoans were something quite "other". The only possible comparison in terms of elegance of lifestyle was either Greece or Egypt. But the people who lived at Knossos were quite different from either of them. Knossos had no mummies, no pyramids, no sphinxes or obelisks, no monumental statures of gods or pharaohs, no walls filled with hieroglyphs glorifying their rulers and their deeds. .

In 1974, Hans Georg Wunderlich, Professor of Geology and Paleontology at Stuttgart University, published The Secret of Crete. This book was the result of many observations he had made while visiting Crete from a "geologists" point of view. There were many puzzling facts about the strange 1200 room "palace". One thing his geologist's eye noticed immediately was that the steps of the "palace" were made of soft alabaster, but were not worn! There were many doorways, but they were sealed off by stone slabs. There were "bathtubs" equipped with drain holes, but no drain pipes! He found row after row of storage vessels, but no kitchen. The list goes on, and the reader is encouraged to read his book for the lengthy analysis.

In the end, Dr. Wunderlich came to the realization, based on the objective evidence, observing the facts, that the "palace" of King Minos, so identified by Evans, was nothing but a necropolis. It had never been intended for the living, but was a place where a powerful cult of the dead practiced elaborate sacrifices, burial rites, and ritual games of death. He realized that the legend of Crete was essentially accurate, and that legend said that it was not a "home to a wise sovereign who fostered arts and sports", but that it was a sinister place belonging entirely to the underworld and a devouring god.

That sounds like Yahweh alright.

And now we need to talk about this Yahweh and what he wanted: Sacrifice.

We have mentioned the odd fact that the period of the 11th and 12th centuries was the time when Christianity and Judaism were "vitalized". At that point in time, Judaism was almost extinct, Hebrew was no longer spoken, and the Jews were beginning to lose their ethnic identity by being rapidly absorbed into the European population.

The discernable events were that Christianity needed to validate Judaism in order to claim the rights to the New Covenant based on the one "right" God, and so the Hebrew Bible, with all its claims to the only real monotheistic God and his "chosen people" was "produced" as evidence. The ostensible purpose for this was to unite all Jews and Christians under one religion. What actually happened, however, is that the Jews themselves became newly acquainted with their marvelously ancient history, and decided that it was quite sufficient for them and it was questionable as to whether these newcomers, these Christians, really had a right to claim a "New Covenant" with their god.

The important question here is: was the production of the Jewish "history", i.e. the Old Testament, a fraud? Was it produced by the manipulations of the Catholic Church?

The one thing that is observable about this period in history is the Christian church's "transfer" of the idea of sacrifice from animals back to human beings.

When we peer into the mists of ages past, we find that the practice of human sacrifice was almost a worldwide phenomenon. It has been theorized that, when global cataclysms occurred, the peoples got the idea that the "gods" wanted human lives. So, naturally, to avoid future cataclysms where the gods would take lives indiscriminately, the people might forestall such events by giving the gods the lives they wanted. The theory goes that it was then hoped that the gods would spare the sacrificers. (Observing events in the present day, one has to wonder if that is the underlying reason for the rabid Christian fundamentalism advocated by George Bush: a hope that if they kill enough "others", God will spare them!)

There is, however, something very interesting about this matter that is not generally noted: the areas where human sacrifice was "popular" were mostly in the Southern Hemisphere. Also, human sacrifice was closely associated with Solar deities. The further north you go, the less importance the Sun had, the more importance the Moon had, and the incidence of human sacrifice diminished. At certain points, where the two "types" mingled, it was not uncommon to find Moon worship associated with human sacrifice, or Sun worship divorced from Human Sacrifice. But what is evident from tracking the myths and folktales is that Human Sacrifice was primarily a Southern Hemisphere production that later moved north.

Most people are familiar with the many stories of the Aztecs and their major productions of mass sacrifice. A lot of people don't realize that such events were only a degree away from the sacrifices of the Jews. Such sacrifices were the common practice of the Jews, though most of the evidence was cleaned up when the Bible was "reissued" in the Middle Ages. It seems very likely that many of the actual descriptions of the "methods" of sacrifice described in the Old Testament originally applied to human beings, and the later editions changed this to animal sacrifice since having such a history would have been embarrassing at that point in time.

But, some people did notice. When the Aztecs/Toltecs and other Southern Hemisphere cultures and their bloody behavior were discovered, they were immediately compared to the Jews because of the many similarities in their rituals and modes of sacrifice! What was even more telling was the fact that many features of Southern Hemisphere American cultures - including language, happen to be similar to that of the Jews.

Many individuals have attempted to explain the above factors by suggesting that Mesoamerican natives were one of the "lost tribes" of Israel. However, there are certain clues to suggest that the migration was the other way around: from South America to the Middle East.

When we begin to look at the South American cultures, the first thing we are told is how "recent" they are. Polish archaeologist Arthur Posnansky dated the Kalasasaya palace court at Tiahuanaco, near Lake Titicaca, in Bolivia to 15,000 to 10,000 B.C. We are assured by mainstream experts that this evidence simply cannot be considered because radiometric dating says otherwise.

The most widely-used method for determining the age of fossils is to date them by the "known age" of the rock strata in which they are found. At the same time, the most widely-used method for determining the age of the rock strata is to date them by the "known age" of the fossils they contain. In this "circular dating" method, all ages are based on uniformitarian assumptions about the date and order in which fossilized plants and animals are believed to have evolved. Most people are surprised to learn that there is, in fact, no way to directly determine the age of any fossil or rock. The so called "absolute" methods of dating (radiometric methods) actually only measure the present ratios of radioactive isotopes and their decay products in suitable specimens - not their age. These measured ratios are then extrapolated to an "age" determination.

The problem with all radiometric "clocks" is that their accuracy critically depends on several starting assumptions which are largely unknowable. To date a specimen by radiometric means, one must first know the starting amount of the parent isotope at the beginning of the specimen's existence. Second, one must be certain that there were no daughter isotopes in the beginning. Third, one must be certain that neither parent nor daughter isotopes have ever been added or removed from the specimen. Finally,, one must be certain that the decay rate of parent isotope to daughter isotope has always been the same. That one or more of these assumptions are often invalid is obvious from the published radiometric "dates" (to say nothing of "rejected" dates) found in the literature.

One of the most obvious problems is that several samples from the same location often give widely-divergent ages. Apollo moon samples, for example, were dated by both uranium-thorium-lead and potassium-argon methods, giving results which varied from 2 million to 28 billion years. Lava flows from volcanoes on the north rim of the Grand Canyon (which erupted after its formation) show potassium-argon dates a billion years "older" than the most ancient basement rocks at the bottom of the canyon. Lava from underwater volcanoes near Hawaii (that are known to have erupted in 1801 AD) has been "dated" by the potassium-argon method with results varying from 160 million to nearly 3 billion years. It's really no wonder that all of the laboratories that "date" rocks insist on knowing in advance the "evolutionary age" of the strata from which the samples were taken -- this way, they know which dates to accept as "reasonable" and which to ignore

More precisely, it is based on the assumption that nothing "really exceptional" happened in the meantime. What I mean by "really exceptional" is this: an event theoretically possible, but whose mechanism is not yet understood in terms of the established paradigms. To give an example: a crossing of two different universes. This is theoretically possible, taking into account modern physical theories, but it is too speculative to discuss its "probability" and possible consequences.

Could such an event change radioactive decay data? Could it change the values of some fundamental physical constants? Yes, it could.

Is it possible that similar events have happened in the past? Yes, it is possible. How possible it is? We do not know. We do not know, in fact, what would be an exact meaning of 'the crossing of two different universes'.

In addition to considering the idea of cataclysms that could have destroyed ancient civilizations more than once, there is another matter to consider in special relationship to radioactive decay: that ancient civilizations may have destroyed themselves with nuclear war.

"Radiocarbon dates for Pleistocene remains in northeastern North America, according to scientists Richard Firestone of Lawrence Berkeley National Laboratory, and William Topping, are younger-as much as 10,000 years younger-than for those in the western part of the country. Dating by other methods like thermoluminescence (TL), geoarchaeology, and sedimentation suggests that many radiocarbon dates are grossly in error. For example, materials from the Gainey Paleoindian site in Michigan, radiocarbon dated at 2880 yr B.C., are given an age by TL dating of 12,400 B.C.. It seems that there are so many anomalies reported in the upper US and in Canada of this type, that they cannot be explained by ancient aberrations in the atmosphere or other radiocarbon reservoirs, nor by contamination of data samples (a common source of error in radiocarbon dating). Assuming correct methods of radiocarbon dating are used, organic remains associated with an artifact will give a radiocarbon age younger than they actually are only if they contain an artificially high radiocarbon keel.

Our research indicates that the entire Great Lakes region (and beyond) was subjected to particle bombardment and a catastrophic nuclear irradiation that produced secondary thermal neutrons from cosmic ray interactions. The neutrons produced unusually large quantities of Pu239 and substantially altered the natural uranium abundance rations in artifacts and in other exposed materials including cherts[242], sediments, and the entire landscape. These neutrons necessarily transmuted residual nitrogen in the dated charcoals to radiocarbon, thus explaining anomalous dates. [...]

The C14 level in the fossil record would reset to a higher value. The excess global radiocarbon would then decay with a half-life of 5730 years, which should be seen in the radiocarbon analysis of varied systems. [...]

Sharp increases in C14 are apparent in the marine data at 4,000, 32,000-34,000, and 12,500 B.C.. These increases are coincident with geomagnetic excursions. [...]

The enormous energy released by the catastrophe at 12,500 B.C. could have heated the atmosphere to over 1000 C over Michigan, and the neutron flux at more northern locations would have melted considerable glacial ice. Radiation effects on plants and animals exposed to the cosmic rays would have been lethal, comparable to being irradiated in a 5 megawatt reactor more than 100 seconds.

The overall pattern of the catastrophe matches the pattern of mass extinction before Holocene times. The Western Hemisphere was more affected than the Eastern, North America more than South America, and eastern North America more than western North America. Extinction in the Great lakes area was more rapid and pronounced than elsewhere. Larger animals were more affected than smaller ones, a pattern that conforms to the expectation that radiation exposure affects large bodies more than smaller ones."[243]

The evidence that Firestone and Topping discovered is puzzling for a lot of reasons. But, the fact is, there are reports of similar evidence from such widely spread regions as India, Ireland, Scotland, France, and Turkey; ancient cities whose brick and stone walls have literally been vitrified, that is, fused together like glass. There is also evidence of vitrification of stone forts and cities. It seems that the only explanation for such anomalies is either an atomic blast or a literal hail of comets exploding in the atmosphere.

There is, of course, much more to this than the little bit I am able to include here. Suffice it to say that there is evidence that the religion of the Jews came from South America via India to the Middle East, bringing its bloodthirsty, flesh flaying, genital mutilating god along.

Some experts quote Paul's remark from Hebrews 9:22 where it says, "under the Law almost everything is purified by means of blood, and without the shedding of blood there is neither release from sin and its guilt nor the remission of the due and merited punishment for sins". What such

---

[242] A chert is basically bits of glass. It is silica that has been heated until it fuses into tiny shards of glass.
[243] Firestone, Richard B., Topping, William, *Terrestrial Evidence of a Nuclear Catastrophe in Paleoindian Times*, dissertation research, 1990 - 2001.

experts fail to mention - again a sly twisting - is what follows, which is an argument against such practices.

Nevertheless, like the Aztecs, the Jewish priesthood began with terrifying cannibalistic rituals and sacrifices. Just picture the priest - kohane - standing before the worshippers spattered with dripping, stringy clots of blood, throwing basins of blood on the congregation to "cleanse" them, all the while the subliminal message being conveyed that "if you don't obey Yahweh, this is what he will do to you"! This is very likely what was taking place in the great Temple of Solomon which was probably the Temple of Hephaestus - the labyrinth - in Memphis, and was later transferred to the "labyrinth" at Crete. It was then brought to Palestine by the refugees from the eruption of Thera, and combined later with other tales of the cataclysm to produce the Old Testament and the rites of Judaism. We begin to understand why the labyrinth of Egypt was, according to Pliny, regarded with "extraordinary hatred".

The idea of the ritual sacrifice of the king instead of thousands of virgins, children, or warriors, seems to be the result of the mingling of the Southern Sun god worship with the influence of the Northern Moon worshippers. This seems to be a distortion of the idea that the king was ruler by virtue of his "marriage" to the goddess, or her representative, and that this "marriage" involved a shamanic death in order to be able to transduce the cosmic energies of benevolence and prosperity to the tribe or to defend the tribe against evil spirits.

The northern custom of a king who had lost his vigor voluntarily abdicating and being replaced by the "right heir" who could "marry the goddess" was mixed with the sacrifice ideas, and the result was that the priesthood had a weapon to wield over the monarch to keep him in line. Thus arose the idea of the "scape goat" king who was sacrificed in the labyrinth instead of maidens and warriors.

Herodotus tells us what seems to be an already garbled version of this mixing of the two ideas:

> "Being set free after the reign of the priest of Hephaistos, the Egyptians, since they could not live any time without a king, set up over them twelve kings, having divided all Egypt into twelve parts."

This also echoes the story of Jacob and Esau and the 12 tribes.

This shift was also recorded in the myth of Theseus which we have discussed in our book *The Secret History of the World* as being a variant of the myth of Perseus. What seems to be so is that the "Ark" was a northern "item" and the story of its being co-opted by the Egyptians - likely the Hermes rebellion - was reflected in the myth of the Sons of Aegyptus and the daughters of Danaus. It was a descendant of this "union" - Perseus - who "cleansed the temple" and restored the Goddess to her rightful place as depicted in the story of the slaying of Medusa, the freeing of Pegasus, and the rescue of Andromeda.

The religion of the Great Mother Goddess existed and flourished for many thousands of years in the Near and Middle East before the arrival of the patriarch Abraham, who is depicted as the first prophet of the dominator male deity, Yahweh. Archaeologists have traced the worship of the Goddess back to the neolithic communities of about 7000 B.C., some to the Upper Paleolithic cultures of about 25,000 B.C. From Neolithic times, at least, its existence has been repeatedly attested to well into Roman Times. Yet, Bible scholars tell us that Abraham lived in Canaan as late as between 1800 and 1550 B.C., a veritable Johnny-come-lately! How in the world has such a recent appearance on the world scene managed to push itself into such prominence and domination?

Over and over again in the studies of the ancient religions it is noted that, in place after place, the goddess was debased and replaced by a male deity - the worship of a young warrior god and a supreme father god. It has been assumed that this was the Indo-European invasion from the north. But when the cultural connections are considered, it is clear that the earliest invasion was from the South. Perhaps we ought to call it the "Indo-Incan" invasion since we have already made the connections to the cultures of South America. Archaeology reveals that, after these invasions, the worship of the Mother Goddess fluctuated from city to city. As the invaders gained more and more territory over the next two thousand years, the male began to appear as the dominant husband or even the murderer of the Goddess! The transition was accomplished by brutally violent massacres and territorial acquisition throughout the Near and Middle East. The same is true regarding the conversion of the western world to Christianity. Something is definitely strange about this picture.

This corruption drifted north, as Eliade has noted, changing the shamanic cultures from goddess worshippers to male dominated societies. In studying the legends about the Golden Age, the Antediluvian world, we realize over and over again that these stories talk about a garden where woman and man lived in harmony with each other and nature. That is, until a dominator male god decided that woman had been a very bad girl and must now and forever be subservient to man.

The Chinese *Tao Te Ching* describes a time when the yin, or feminine principle, was not yet ruled by the male principle, or yang, a time when the wisdom of the mother was still honored and followed above all. To many people, references to these times are no more than mere fantasy.

It seems that there were ancient societies organized very differently from ours, and chief among the finds in such digs are the many images of the Deity as female. Thus we are better able to interpret the references to the Great Goddess in ancient art, myth, and even historical writings.

The chief idea of these people was that the Universe was an all-giving mother. Indeed, this idea has survived into our time. In China, the female deities Ma Tsu and Kuan Yin are still widely worshipped as beneficent and compassionate goddesses. Similarly, the veneration of Mary, the Mother of God, is widespread even if, in Catholic theology, she is demoted to non-divine status, her divinity is implicitly recognized by her appellation Mother of God as well as by the prayers of millions who daily seek her compassionate protection and solace. In fact, the story of Jesus' birth, death, and resurrection seems to be little more than a reworking of those of earlier "mystery cults" revolving around a Divine Mother and her son or, as in the worship of Demeter and Kore, her daughter. And we are reminded of the interesting comment of the C's about the item that was transferred to Esau: "Trampled leaves of wrath. ...and what is the 'core' meaning there? ...Leaves are of the Tree of Apples, from whence we get the proverbial 'grapes of wrath', the Blue Apples incarnate!"

It is, of course, reasonable that the deepest understanding of divine power in human form should be female rather than male. After all, life emerges from the body of a woman, and if we are to understand the macrocosm by means of the microcosm, it is only natural to think of the universe as an all-giving Mother from whose womb all life emerges and to which, like the cycles of vegetation, it returns after death to be again reborn.

What is more important to us here is the idea that societies that view the universe as a Mother would also have very different social structures from our own. We might also conjecture that women in such a society would not be seen as subservient. Caring, nurturing, growth and creation would have been valued. At the same time, it does not make sense to think that such societies were "matriarchal" in the sense that women dominated men. They were, instead, by all the evidence, societies in which differences were valued and not equated as evidence of either superiority or inferiority.

What we do know is that "Venus" figurines have been found by the thousands, all over Eurasia, from the Balkans to Lake Baikal in Siberia, across to Willendorf in Austria, and the *Grotte du Pappe* in France. Some scholars (clearly with their minds where they ought not to be) have described them as "erotic art" of the stone-age and propose that they were used in obscene fertility rites!

But is that really the case?

Can these ubiquitous female images found from Britain to Malta even be described accurately as "Venus" figures? Most of them are broad-hipped, sometimes pregnant, stylized and frequently faceless. They are clearly a symbol, just as the cross with the crucified man is a symbol that is surprisingly like a sword plunged into the ground. Future archaeologists who might dig in the remains of our civilization would find equally ubiquitous and symbolic crosses!

The worship of a female creator goddess appears, literally, in every area of the world.

What is significant is that the most tangible line of evidence is drawn from the numerous sculptures of women found in the Gravettian-Aurignacian cultures of the Upper Paleolithic Age. Some of these date back to 25,000 B.C., as noted above, and are frequently made of bone or clay. They were often found lying close to the remains of the sunken walls of what are probably the earliest known human-made dwellings on earth. Researchers say that niches or depressions were made in the walls to hold the figures. Such finds have been noted in Spain, France, Germany, Austria, Czechoslovakia and Russia. These sites span a period of at least ten thousand years!

It appears highly probable that the female figurines were idols of a 'great mother' cult, practiced by the nomadic Aurignacian mammoth hunters who inhabited the immense Eurasian territories that extended from southern France to Lake Baikal in Siberia.

In the oldest archaeological finds, the Goddess was represented by birds and wavy symbols that indicated water and/or energy. These same wavy lines are retained as the symbol of the Astrological sign of Aquarius which may be the oldest extant symbol of the Great Mother Goddess.

But suddenly, at a certain point, somewhere around 5000 years ago, serpents became associated with the goddess, and the wavy lines of water/energy were transmogrified to snakes. What happened to bring about this association? By 4000 B.C., Goddess figures appeared at Ur and Uruk, both on the southern end of the Euphrates river, not far from the Persian Gulf. At about this same period, the Neolithic Badarian and Amaratian cultures of Egypt first appeared. *It is at these sites that agriculture first emerged in Egypt.*

From that point on, with the invention of writing, history as we know it emerged in both Sumer and Egypt - about 3000 B.C. (5000 years ago!) In every area of the Near and Middle East, the Goddess was known in historic times. It is pretty clear that many changes must have taken place in both the forms and modes of worship, but, in various ways, the worship of the Female Goddess survived into classical Greece and Rome. It was not totally suppressed until the time of the Christian emperors of Rome and Byzantium, who closed the last Goddess Temples about 500 A.D. Again, we are struck by the oddness of this fact when considered with all the other related issues.

It appears that the Goddess ruled alone in the beginning, though she was "married" to the king via a human female representative. Thus the son or brother who was also her lover and consort was part of the goddess religion in much earlier times.

Later, as the corruption crept in - after some dramatic, cataclysmic event - it was this youth - known in various languages as Damuzi, Tammuz, Attis, Adonis, Osiris or Baal - who died in his youth causing an annual period of grief and lamentation among those who paid homage to the Goddess.

For a very long time, this myth was annually enacted representing the fact that time was cyclical the same way the seasons are. It was the passing down of the knowledge of cyclical catastrophes connected to cyclical time. The world might end, but if it did, it was only because it had "run down" and needed to be "wound up" again.

But something changed all that. Somehow, the perception of the End of the World became a terrible punishment that might be prevented by savage sacrifices. And the sub-text of this idea was that time was linear and would end, finally and completely. This idea was brought with the invaders from the South, the murderers of the Goddess, the rapers of the Maidens of the Wells: the dominator religion that drove the sword into the stone.

Part of the cover-up seems to involve blaming this corruption on "northern invaders", or Aryan Indo Europeans. The invasions of the Aryans took place in waves over a period of up to three thousand years according to standard archaeology. The invasions of the historical period are attested to by literature and artifacts and are agreed upon by scholars. Those of prehistoric times are suggested by speculative etymological connections. I propose that they were from the South, and this was the corruption that spread like a disease all over the globe, corrupting even the Northern worshippers of the Moon and the Goddess.

Chavín is claimed to be the Mother Civilization of the Andes. The term Chavín has been applied to a developmental stage of Andean history, to an archaeological period, to an art style and to a hypothetical empire. Chavín has been interpreted as a culture, a civilization and a religion. The Chavín culture was one of agriculture and fishing and seafaring. Its earliest manifestation is in the Ica area.

The Mocha culture developed in the same area which had previously belonged to the Chavín culture, so we may assume that it was formed of survivors. Expert opinions suggest that one can easily see the influence of the oldest civilisation of Peru, the Chavín, on the Moche. Chavín was a well-developed class society, which was divided into nobility, farmers and slaves. The Moche people were developed in agriculture, fishing, handicraft, trade, sea-faring and metallurgy. The anthropomorphic pottery of the Mochicans is thought to express the mythological and social themes which were the peak of this art genre in the whole civilisation of Peru.

This raises an interesting issue because the human-shaped pottery shows that the typology of the Mochicans includes Mongoloid as well as Negroid features.

The earliest "god" image, the one carved on the Gate of the Sun, is a godlike creature holding *staves or sticks* in both of its hands. It is thought that the deity with staves was a celestial supreme being, a god of the heavens, who in the course of time was attributed the characteristic features of a thunder-god. The worship of the deity with staves spread from Chavín all over Peru, more particularly so in the Tiahuanaco culture on the Altiplano Plateau in South-Peru where he was called Viracocha.[244]

Several versions of Andean Genesis at Tiahuanaco were recorded by Juan de Betanzos in 1551, and Cristobal de Molina in 1553. In the early version preserved by Betanzos, the world creator is named *Contiti Viracocha*, and he emerges from Lake Titicaca to create "the sun and the day, and the moon and the stars". Viracocha orders "the sun to move in its path" and so the time of mankind begins. After calling the people out from caves, rivers, and springs scattered through the mythical landscape of creation time, Contiti Viracocha furiously *turns some of them into stone for sacrilegious behavior*. Then, he starts creation all over again! Only this time, he creates the people from stone instead of turning them into stone.

Of course we wonder about the "staves" in the hands of Viracocha? Were these the "tools" he used to "turn people into stone" or call flesh forth from stone? Are they the origins of the pillars Jachin and Boaz? How do these staves relate to the staves Jacob drove into the ground in the story about the magical increase of his flocks?

These questions bring us to consider the Semites and Sargon.

Sargon the Great

According to "experts", Sargon of Akkad reigned approximately 2,334-2,279 B.C., and was one of the earliest of the world's great empire builders, conquering all of southern Mesopotamia as well as parts of Syria, Anatolia, and Elam (western Iran). He established the region's first *Semitic dynasty* and was considered the founder of the Mesopotamian military tradition.

---

[244] Berezkin, Juri 1983. Mochica. Tsivilizatsia indeitsev Severnogo poberzhia Peru v I-VII vv. Leningrad.

Sargon is known almost entirely from the legends and tales that followed his reputation through 2000 years of cuneiform Mesopotamian history, and not from any documents that were written during his lifetime. The lack of contemporary record is explained by the fact that the capital city of Agade, (note the homophonic similarity to Arcadia) which he built, has *never been located and excavated.* It was destroyed at the end of the dynasty that Sargon founded and was never again inhabited, at least under the name of Agade.

According to a folktale, Sargon was a self-made man of humble origins; a *gardener* (think "gardens of the Hesperides") having found him as a baby floating in a basket on the river, brought him up in his own calling. His father is unknown; his mother is said to have been a priestess in a town on the middle Euphrates. (Note all the similarities to the story of Moses *as well as* Perseus.) Rising, therefore, without the help of influential relations, he attained the post of *cupbearer* to the ruler of the city of Kish, in the north of the ancient land of Sumer.

The event that brought him to supremacy was the defeat of Lugalzaggisi of Uruk (biblical Erech, in central Sumer). Lugalzaggisi had already united the city-states of Sumer by defeating each in turn and claimed to rule the lands not only of the Sumerian city-states but also those as far west as the Mediterranean. Sargon became king over all of southern Mesopotamia, the first great ruler for whom *the Semitic tongue* known as Akkadian, rather than Sumerian, was natural from birth.

Sargon wished to secure favorable trade with Agade throughout the known world and this, along with what was obviously a very energetic temperament, led Sargon to conquer cities along the middle Euphrates to northern Syria and the silver-mining mountains of southern Anatolia. He also took Susa, *capital city of the Elamites,* in the Zagros Mountains of western Iran, where the only truly contemporary record of his reign has been uncovered.

Several factors encouraged the resultant commercial success of Sargon's dynasty, including the legacy of the Sumerian city-states that he had inherited by conquest, previously existing trade of the old Sumerian city-states with other countries, and Sargon's military prowess coupled with his ability to organize. Commercial connections flourished *with the Indus Valley*, the coast of Oman, the islands and shores of the Persian Gulf, the lapis lazuli mines of Badakhshan, the cedars of Lebanon, the silver-rich Taurus Mountains, Cappadocia, Crete, and perhaps even Greece.

During Sargon's rule, his Akkadian language became adapted to the script that previously had been used in the Sumerian language, and there arose new spirit of writing evident in the clay tablets and cylinder seals of this dynasty. There are beautifully arranged and executed scenes of mythology and festive life. It could be suggested that this new artistic feeling is attributable directly to the Semitic influence of Sargon and his compatriots upon the rather dull Sumerians. In contrast to the Sumerian civilization, in Sargon's new capital, military and economic values were *not* the only things that were important.

The latter part of his reign was troubled with rebellions, which later literature ascribes, predictably enough, to sacrilegious acts that he - like Solomon - is supposed to have committed; but this can be discounted as the standard cause assigned to all disasters by Sumerians and Akkadians alike. The troubles, in fact, were probably caused by the inability of one man, however energetic, to control so vast an empire. There is no evidence to suggest that he was particularly harsh, nor that the Sumerians disliked him for being a Semite. What's more, the empire did not collapse totally, for Sargon's successors were able to control their legacy, and later generations thought of him as being perhaps the greatest name in their history. What is most interesting is that Sargon attributed his success to the patronage of the goddess Ishtar, in whose honor Agade was erected.

Sargon's story sounds a lot like a combination of the Biblical stories of Moses, David and Solomon and certainly, there is evidence of infusion of Semitic traditions into the culture of the Sumerians. We also wish to consider the fact that Sargon was the first "Semite". Nowadays "Semitic peoples" are generally understood to be, more or less, individuals of Middle Eastern origins: Jews and Arabs predominantly. That is to say, to be an Arab or a Jew is to be "Semitic".

What we notice most particularly is that Sargon was said to have come "from the North" and that he worshipped the Goddess Ishtar. Also, when we think of the word "Semitic" we naturally wonder if it doesn't imply something that was "half" of one thing and "half" of another?

This leads us to ask about the Sumerians that absorbed and adopted the Semitic language and cultural expressions, adapting them to their own use?

The Sumerians were a *non-Semitic* people who, judging by archaeological remains, were generally short and stocky, with high, straight noses and downward sloping eyes. Many wore beards, but some were clean-shaven. These people apparently migrated to the Fertile Crescent - they suddenly appeared in the area - and immediately established what was, for a long time, considered to be the first *real* 'Civilization'. They built cities, *step-pyramid-temples*, large residences and economic facilities. They referred to themselves as the "black-headed people" as if to emphasize their difference from the indigenous population who, one might assume, were not black-headed.

The picture painted by the archaeological record of the Sumerian City-State civilization, before Sargon, is one of constant strife between these cities, especially the most prominent ones: Kish, Erech, Ur, Adab, and later Lagash and Umma. Constant warring weakened the Sumerians until "the kingship was carried away by *foreigners*" such as the king of Awan,

Sargon of Akkad, the Gutians, the Elamites, and eventually Hammurabi. Sargon of Akkad, the first Semite, was then, a "foreigner" to the Sumerians who had (as we will see) a rather "lengthy" history prior to the Semitic influence.

It is quite curious that despite their sense of nationalism and the sharing of a common identity, the "black-headed people" were unable to unite in order to resist the conquerors. What is even more ironic is the fact that, even though they were unable to resist being conquered and ruled - in fact - by foreigners, the Sumerian culture was, eventually, to a great extent, *assimilated by the conquerors* by the adoption of their customs, script, and literature, including many of their religious myths.

The cultural "soul" of a people can be found in their stories, myths, and rituals. The stories of Sumer, as inscribed on its clay tablets, allow us to reconstruct, at least partially, a process of dynamic development that took place over many centuries. *Some experts* propose that Sumerian storytelling was indebted to the *wandering Semitic tribes*, who, being allegedly "illiterate", had the narrative memory capacity of "illiterate peoples". It is suggested by such experts that these Semites often entertained their more "civilized" Sumerian hosts by "telling tales around the campfire" or in the market place. It is then suggested that these stories were then written down by Sumerian scribes, who attempted to categorize the material into orderly groups of continuous narrative. Obviously, the "wandering, illiterate Semites" weren't quite so backward since they conquered the Sumerians and their influence actually gave the Sumerian civilization a cultural boost. What is more likely is that the writing of the Sumerians was developed for economic and military purposes, which was the purview of the "god" and his priests. It was only after the incursions of the Semites that a literary tradition began, and the development of writing proceeded in such a way that it could be utilized for literature.

The experts tell us that the Sumerians themselves had no real "sense of history" even though they had invented writing. This opinion is arrived at due to the fact that the Sumerians had recorded a sort of "history", in the form of a King list that was, to understate the matter, astonishing.

The Sumerians' relationship with their gods was *the* driving force in the rise of their civilization. The very reason for the existence of Sumer and her people seemed to lie with these strange and *mortal* 'deities'. The very reason for being was to *serve* the appropriate deity.

The Sumerian religion was more like a feudal covenantal relationship with an overlord than the mystical *worship* of a god as we would understand religion today. For the Sumerian, worship of the gods meant *complete* servitude - the very purpose for which mankind was (according to the Sumerians) created by the Sumerian gods.

According to the Sumerians, the city-states had been founded by the gods far back in time and it was the gods who had given the Sumerians, "the black-headed people", all the tools and weapons and marvelous inventions of their culture. For the Sumerians, everything that they had - cities, fields, herds, tools, institutions - had always existed because the gods had created all of it before they had created the black headed people to run things as their slaves. This immediately makes one think of the only people who claim an origin as slaves: the Jews.

This "slave-master" Religion was the central organizing principle of the city-states, each city *belonging* to a different deity who was worshipped in a large temple. According to the Sumerians, even if the gods might prefer to be just and merciful, they had also created evil and misfortune and there was nothing that the black-headed people could do about it. Judging from the *Sumerian Lamentation texts*, the best one could do in times of trouble would be to "plead, lament and wail, tearfully confessing his sins and failings". Their family god or city god *might* intervene on their behalf, but that would not necessarily happen even if the rules were carefully followed. After all, man was created as a broken, labor saving, tool for the use of the gods and at the end of everyone's life, lay the underworld, a dreary place like the Sheol of the early Hebrews.

According to the Sumerians, their gods were very intelligent, extremely long-lived and yet, very *mortal* beings. This is evident in their king lists. According to the Sumerians, the time *before the flood* was said to be a period of 432,000 years. Two kings from after the flood that are listed were Gilgamesh and Tammuz. The legends of Tammuz were so well-liked that they were assimilated to the pantheon of Babylon and later became the model for Adonis to the Greeks. Gilgamesh became the hero of the Babylonian epic poem which bears his name, and which also contains an account of the flood.

Until recently, these king lists and the names in them were thought to be purely mythic, but in the 1930's, Sir Leonard Woolley, while excavating a building at Ur on the Ubaid level, found an inscription indicating that the structure had been erected by the son of the founder of the First Dynasty of Ur, a person up till that time regarded as fiction. Gilgamesh, too, has inscriptions telling of the buildings he built.

The "King-List" is divided into dynastic periods that are city-state oriented as apparently regards the seat of central power. The most startling of these sections is the list dealing with the pre-deluge Kings. Eight *Annunaki Kings* are listed, as are five city-states where centralized rule apparently was seated. Length of rule is given in what is known as a "sar". All of the remaining King-List sections have the length of rule measured by years. The "sar" was equivalent in length to 3,600 years.

Now it is important to note that during this astonishing length of time recorded as "history" by the Sumerians, only two *Annunaki* held overall reign. First was Enki (later known as Ea) and the second was Enlil, a half-brother of Enki. The event that ended this first list was the legendary deluge. It was also during the latter part of this first period of the King-List that human beings appeared.

Calculating the length of time back to the arrival of these "Annunaki", brings us to about 450,000 years ago. That puts it well before the *accepted date* of the appearance of modern man.

The numbering system of the Sumerians is actually quite fascinating. The Sumerian civilization can be more or less divided into three periods of cultural manifestation. The first included the development of glyptics where cylinder seals were engraved with parades of animals or scenes of a religious nature. This was followed by the development of sculpture, and finally, the emergence of writing.

During the first period of cultural manifestation, archaeology indicates that there were no palaces for such as what we would consider a real king. The "king" was actually a priest who lived in the temple. The priest-king was titled "EN", or "Lord." It was only later, in the second cultural period that the title of king, or Lugal, came into use. At the same time, palaces became evident, witnessing a separation of the State - and its military forces - and the priesthood.

At the beginning of the second millennium B.C., the Sumerians came back to dominance for a period, but after Hammurabi, Sumer disappeared entirely as a political entity. Nevertheless, the Sumerian language remained a language of priests.

Around 3,200 B.C., the Sumerians devised their numerical notation system, giving special graphical symbols to the units 1, 10, 60, 600, 3,600. That is to say, we find that the Sumerians did not count in tens, hundreds and thousands, but rather adopted base 60, grouping things into sixties, and multiplying by powers of sixty.

Our own civilization utilizes vestiges of base 60 in the ways we count time in hours, minutes and seconds, and in the degrees of the circle.

Sixty is a large number to use as a base for a numbering system. It is taxing to the memory because it necessitates knowing sixty different signs (words) that stand for the numbers from 1 to 60. The Sumerians handled this by using 10 as an intermediary between the different sexagesimal orders of magnitude: $1, 60, 60^2, 60^3$, etc. The word for 60, *geš, is the same as the word for unity*. The number 60 represented a certain level, above which, multiples of 60 up to 600 were expressed by using 60 as a new unit. When they reached 600, the next level was treated as still another unit, with multiples up to 3,000. The number 3,600, or sixty sixties, was given a new name: *šàr*, and this, in turn, became yet another new unit.

The Sumerian numbering system often required excessive repetitions of identical marks, placing symbols side by side to represent addition of their values. The number 3,599 required a total of twenty-six symbols. For this reason, the Sumerians would often use a "subtractive convention" with a little symbol that meant "take this number away from that number to get the number that is being indicated".

In the pre-Sargon era, certain irregularities started to appear in the cuneiform representations of numbers. In addition to the subtractive convention, entirely new symbols were being created for multiples of 36,000. This means that instead of repeating 36,000 however many times it was to be indicated, the numbers 72,000, 108,000, 144,000, 180,000 and 216,000 had their own symbols assigned to them.

In all of human history, the Sumerians are the only ones we know of who invented and used a sexagesimal system. This can be seen as a "triumph" of their civilization, and a great mystery as well. Many people have tried to understand why they did this and numerous hypotheses were offered from Theon of Alexandria to Otto Neugebauer. These hypotheses range from, "It was the easiest to use" and the "lowest of numbers that had the greatest number of divisors" to "it was natural" because the number of days in a Solar year rounded down to 360, and so on. Daniel Boorstin suggested that the Sumerians used base 60 because they multiplied the number of planets known to them (5) times the number of months in the year. It was pointed out by the Assyriologist, G. Kewitsch in 1904 that neither astronomy nor geometry can really explain the origin of a number system, presupposing that abstract considerations preceded concrete applications. Kewitsch speculated that the sexagesimal system actually resulted from the *fusion of two civilisations*, one of which used a decimal number-system, and the other used base 6 derived from a special form of finger-counting. This was not easily accepted since there is no historical record of a base 6 numbering system anywhere in the world.

However, duodecimal systems, or base 12 numbering systems ARE widely attested, *especially in Western Europe*. It is still used for counting eggs and oysters. We regularly use the words "dozen" and "gross" and measurements based on 12 were used in France right up to the Revolution, and are still used in Britain and the U.S.

The Romans had a unit of weight, money and arithmetic called the *as*, divided into 12 ounces. One of the monetary units of pre-Revolutionary France was the *sol*, divided into 12 deniers. The Sumerians, Assyrians, and Babylonians used base 12 and its multiples and divisors vary widely as well. The Mesopotamian day was divided into twelve equal parts, and they divided the circle, the ecliptic, and the zodiac into twelve equal sectors of 30 degrees. This means that base 12 could very well have played a major part in shaping the Sumerian number system.

The major role of 10 in the base 60 system is well attested as well, since it was used as an auxiliary unit to circumvent the main difficulty of the sexagesimal system. This leads us to an important clue: the Sumerian word for "ten" also means "fingers" suggesting an earlier counting system.

Taking this back to a variation on Kewitsch's hypothesis, Georges Ifrah proposes that base 60 was a "learned solution" to the union between two peoples, one of which used a decimal system derived from a *vigesimal system* and the other a system using base 12. As it happens, 60 is the lowest common multiple of 10 and 12 as well as the lowest number of which all the first six integers are divisors and, 5 X 12 is 60.

What is interesting to note is that the French words for 80 and 90 (quatre-vingt, quatre-vingt-dix) carry the traces of a *vanished vigesimal arithemetic* in Ancient Europe.

Ifrah's hypothesis is that the Sumerian society had both decimal and duodecimal number systems, and its mathematicians subsequently devised a system that combined the two bases.

Of course, this hypothesis fails on the ground that it presupposes way too much intellectual sophistication. Unless, of course, we consider the *disjecta membra* of a vanished high civilization such as Atlantis.

It is evident that the Mesopotamian basin had one or more indigenous populations prior to the arrival of the Sumerians. The Sumerians were "immigrants" who came from somewhere else about which we know nothing since they seem to have broken all ties with their previous environment.

Coming back to the question: "Who were the Semites?", we understand that the term itself derives from the Old Testament where the tribes of Eber (the Hebrews), Elam, Asshur, Aram, Arphasad, and Lud are said to be the descendants of Shem, one of Noah's three sons. However, this claim makes the Elamites, who spoke an Asianic language, *first cousins* to the Hebrews, Assyrians, and Aramaeans, whose languages belong to the Semitic group.

"Asianic" is the term used for the earlier inhabitants of the Asian mainland whose languages, mostly of the agglutinative-kind, were neither Indo-European nor Semitic. It is generally believed that Mesopotamia was originally inhabited by Asianic peoples prior to the arrival of the Sumerians. It is thought that the Semitic-speaking population came in a later wave and that Sargon was the first Semitic king of a "Semitic nation". Of course, that still doesn't explain the Sumerians and their language.

Significant Semitic elements are to be found in the cultures of Mari and Kis at the beginning of the third millennium B.C., and it has even been proposed that the El Obeid peoples were the original Semites, though they were absorbed and assimilated by the Sumerians. The discovery of the Ebla tablets reveal the existence of a Semitic language in the mid-third millennium B.C.

When Sargon founded the first Semitic state by defeating the Sumerians, Akkadian became the language of Mesopotamia and pushed aside the unrelated language of Sumer. When the Sumerian cuneiform writing was adapted by the Akkadians, the writing system was already several centuries old. The Akkadians found an ideographic writing system that was already drifting toward a phonetic system and accelerated this drift while still retaining some of the ideographic meanings. The Akkadian and Sumerian cultural heritages merged, creating a true literary tradition. When Akkadian speech and writing finally supplanted their Sumerian counterparts in Mesopotamia, a strictly decimal numbering became the norm in daily use. The ancient signs for 60, 600, 3,600 and so on, progressively disappeared. In the hands of the Semites, cuneiform numerals and Mesopotamian arithmetic were gradually adapted into a system with a different base working on different principles. Nevertheless, base 60 did not disappear entirely, as we have already mentioned.

We should note, however, that it was with the sudden appearance of the Sumerian civilization - as early as the 5th millennium B.C. - that the long era of the tribal, egalitarian society of the Neolithic came to an end, between 4,000 and 3,000 B.C. Archaeologists and anthropologists have documented that the early society of Mesopotamia had been *guided by women* and had a Goddess as deity. The end of female leadership can be deducted from the following quote in *"In the Wake of the Goddesses"* by Frymer-Kenski:

"The dynasty of Kish was founded by Enmebaragesi, a contemporary of Gilgamesh. The name breaks down as follows: *enetik - eme - ebakin - aragikor - ageriko - ezi,* which can be transliterated to "from that time on - female - harvest - lustful - notorious - to domesticate" or "From that time on the lustful, notorious harvest female was domesticated".

This "name" tells us in no uncertain terms that the time of the Goddess was on the decline, because male domination had arrived with the Sumerians. Sargon, conversely, attributed all of his successes to the Goddess.

Now, let's come back to the clues that the French words for 80 and 90 (quatre-vingts, quatre-vingt-dix, respectively) carry the traces of a vanished ancient European vigesimal arithmetic. These traces, put together with the fact that the first Semitic king came from the "North" and that the "Semitic influence", of the Goddess worshipping Sargon, accelerated the development of the Sumerian culture toward something more than being economic slaves to the gods, we might wish to reconsider the term "Semitic".

Indeed, the religion of the ancient Sumerians has left its mark on the entire Middle East. Not only are its temples and ziggurats scattered about the region, but the literature, cosmogony and rituals influenced their neighbors to such an extent that we can see echoes of Sumer in the Judeo-Christian-Islamic tradition today. In other words, most of what we consider to be Semitic is actually Sumerian written in the Semitic Akkadian language. Undoubtedly, those peoples who today are called

Semitic by virtue of having had a name assigned to them from the Bible, are actually descendants of the Sumerians and their "Semitic language" was imposed on them by Sargon of Akkad who was clearly *not* one of the "black-headed people".

The linguistic affinity of Sumerian has not yet been successfully established. Ural-Altaic (which includes Turkish), Dravidian, Brahui, Bantu, and many other groups of languages have been compared with Sumerian, but no theory has gained common acceptance. [245]

Sargon Reprise

Sargon became king over all of southern Mesopotamia, the first great ruler for whom *the Semitic tongue* - not Sumerian - known as Akkadian, was natural from birth. This suggests to us that Sargon was not Sumerian, but that he was the bringer of a new language to Mesopotamia, imposing it on the peoples there in the same way that Spanish was imposed on South and Central America, and English has been adopted all over the world as a result of American domination of trade.

The language issue is our clue as to who relates to whom. The Afro-Asiatic language phylum has six distinct branches including Ancient Egyptian, which was known in its last years as Coptic, and which became extinct in the seventeenth century. The other five branches are Berber, Chadic, Cushitic, and Omotic. The Semitic language group is subdivided into an extinct Eastern branch, Akkadian, spoken by Sargon, and a Western branch with two sub-branches, Central and South. The Central group consists of Aramaic, Canaanite, and Arabic. The Southern group consists of South Arabian and Ethiopic. And here is the curiosity: one of the other branches of the Afro-Asiatic language tree is Berber, with sub-branches of *Guanche* - spoken by the original Canary Islanders; East Numidian, which is Old Libyan, and Berber proper.

Now, you ask, what is the oddity?

The Guanche language

Some experts tell us that the Guanches must have come from the neighboring African coast long ages before the Black and Arab "invaders"

---

[245] Arno Poebel, *Grundzüge der sumerischen Grammatik* (1923), partly out of date, but still the only full grammar of Sumerian in all its stages; Adam Falkenstein, *Grammatik der Sprache Gudeas von Lagas*, 2 vol. (1949-50), a very thorough grammar of the New Sumerian dialect, and *Das Sumerische* (1959), a very brief but comprehensive survey of the Sumerian language; Cyril J. Gadd, *Sumerian Reading Book* (1924), outdated but the only grammatical tool in English; Samuel N. Kramer, *The Sumerians* (1963), provides a general introduction to Sumerian civilization.

overran it. We are sagely informed that Mauritania was formerly inhabited by the "same ancient Iberian race which once covered all *Western Europe*: a people tall, fair and strong". Spain invaded, and most of the Guanches were wiped out by diseases to which they had no resistance, due to their long isolation. It was over a hundred years before anyone attempted to record their language, customs, and what could be remembered of their history. Friar Alonso de Espinosa of the Augustine Order of Preachers, writing in 1580, tells us:

"…It is generally believed that these are the Elysian Fields of which Homer sings. The poet Virgil, in the 4th book of the *Aeneid*, mentions the great peak of this island, when he makes Mercury, sent by Jupiter, go to Carthage to undeceive Aeneas, and to encourage him so that he might not abandon the voyage to Italy which he had undertaken.

It has not been possible to ascertain the origin of the Guanches, or whence they came, for as the natives had no letters, they had no account of their origin or descent, although some tradition may have come down from father to son. […]

The old Guanches say that they have an immemorial tradition that sixty people came to this island, but they know not whence they came. They gave their settlement the name, "The place of union of the son of the great one".

Although they knew of God, and called Him by various names, they had no rites nor ceremonies nor words with which they might venerate Him. […] When the rains failed, they got together the sheep in certain places, where it was the custom to invoke the guardian of the sheep. Here they *stuck a wand or lance in the ground*, then they separated the lambs from the sheep, and placed the mothers round the lance, where they bleated. They believed that God was appeased by this ceremony, that he heard the bleating of the sheep and would send down the rain.

…They knew that there was a hell, and they held that it was in the peak of Teyde [the volcanic mountain], and the devil was Guayota.

They were accustomed when a child was born, to call a woman whose duty it was, and she poured water over its head; and this woman thus contracted a relationship with the child's parents, so that it was not lawful to marry her, or to treat her dishonestly. They know not whence they derived this custom or ceremony, only that it existed. It could not be a sacrament, for it was not performed as one, nor had the evangelic law been preached to them. […]

The inviolable law was that if a warrior meeting a woman by chance in the road, or in any solitary place, who spoke to her or looked at her, unless she spoke first and asked for something, or who, in an inhabited place, used any dishonest words which could be proved, he should suffer death for it without appeal. Such was their discipline. […]

This people had very good and perfect features, and well-shaped bodies. They were of tall stature, with proportionate limbs. *There were giants among them of incredible size…*

They only possessed and sowed barley and beans. ... If they once had wheat, the seed had been lost... They also ate the flesh of sheep, goats, and pigs, and they fed on it by itself, without any other relish whatever... The flesh had to be half roasted because, as they said, it contained more substance in that way than if it was well roasted.

They *counted the year by lunations*... The lord did not marry with anyone of the lower orders, and if there was no one he could marry without staining the lineage, brothers were married to sisters.

They were wonderfully clever with counting. Although a flock was very numerous and came out of the yard or fold at a rush, they counted the sheep without opening their mouths or noting with their hands, and never made a mistake." [246]

I'm sure that the reader can see that even though we have very little to go on, there are a couple of suggestive indicators recorded by the good friar. The first thing we note is the custom of driving a lance into the ground for the sheep to "call the god". A memory of ante-diluvian technology, perhaps?

But more than this, the clues seem to indicate that what we call the "Semitic language" may actually have been a northern tongue, an Aryan language, adopted by peoples we think of as ethnically "Semitic" in modern terms but who, in ancient terms, were not Semitic at all.

What is most significant in the later historic records is that these Northern invaders viewed themselves as a very superior people. They were aggressive and continually in conflict with not only the peoples they conquered, but among themselves as well. Their coming revolutionized the art of war. They introduced the horse-drawn chariot, and the charioteer became a new aristocracy.

Many "experts" tell us that it was these northern people who brought with them the concepts of light as good and dark as evil and of *a supreme male deity*. However, the archaeological record suggests otherwise. If, indeed, they later assimilated the supreme male deity to their pantheon, it is clear that these ideas came from the mixing of cultures in Mesopotamia. The interweaving of the two theologies are recorded mythologically in the cultures of this region, and for too long, the blame has been cast in the wrong direction. But most of these ideas were formed before the knowledge of the Southern, American cultures was available. It is in the myths of South America that we discover the origins of the attitude that led to the destruction of the Goddess. It is also in these stories that we find the beginning of the concept of time as linear, with a beginning and an end.

---

[246] De Espinosa, Alonso, *The Guanches of Tenerife*, trans. by Sir Clements Markham (Nendeln/Liechtenstein: Kraus Repring 1972).

What seems to have happened is that certain "Aryan" types appeared in South America.

> Q: (L) Where else did the Atlanteans go?
> A: Americas. Inca. Aztec. Maya. Hopi Tribe. Pima tribe.
> Q: Now, I have noticed in all this reading that certain dates are repeatedly associated with certain subjects as signs or markers... and that these dates are associated with particular rituals, with particular groups, secret societies, various ancient matters - repeating over and over again. For example: the January 17th issue. It is like some sort of hugely important day. What I want to know is, is there some repeating relation between these dates and certain energy exchanges between densities? Are these dates indicative of some cycle of exchange between densities, or dates when the cycles create a situation wherein doorways are more easily opened?
> A: Dates provide marker only. ... If you did not have "dates", would you remember anything?
> Q: Well, I guess not. Okay, what are we supposed to remember from January 17th. Obviously this is some deep memory of an extremely significant event.
> A: Consult Maya.
> Q: (C) They had the 52 year cycles. ...
> A: Also 365 day cycles.
> Q: (C) Was that a beginning of a cycle?
> A: Measurement of what happened and when.
> Q: What happened on January 17th?
> A: Consult Maya.
> Q: But January 17th recurs repeatedly in the alchemical texts...
> A: And you may see the connection. Why do you suppose alchemists knew of the secrets brought "to the table" by the Maya/Egyptians?

As it happens, when we were in Mexico in 1997, I noticed an odd sculpture from one of the ancient temples that had been placed in the museum of anthropology. It was of a man whose skull, elbow joint, and thigh had been flayed, while the rest of his flesh was intact. This was a clear representation of not only the components of the skull and crossed thigh bones, but also the ubiquitous "joint" symbol of secret societies.

I photographed the carving, and you will note that it also includes a rattlesnake entwined around the body of the flayed man.

The theme of flaying is also present in India in the dance of Shiva on the elephant god. After the elephant is flayed, Shiva dons the skin as a symbol of acquiring the power of the god. The same flaying and donning of the skin of the sacrificial victims was practiced by the Southern American sun worshippers, by the Egyptians, and also by the Jewish priesthood.

We are reminded of the selective flaying and parts removal, and draining of blood that occurs in modern day "cattle mutilations".

Another item of considerable interest that connects Egypt to South America is the Ica skulls compared to the representations of elongated skulls among the Egyptian royalty. This is a subject I will cover more  thoroughly in another volume. The point at the moment is to make clear the obvious connection between some very strange things in South America and other strange things in Egypt and the Middle East, all connected in mysterious ways to the creation of three monotheistic religions, and the present day struggle among the three.

What seems to be evident is that there were "big, blond, sailor" types who rose to power in South America - known as the Viracocha people.

Viracocha was the supreme Inca god, a synthesis of sun god and storm gods. Legends of the Aymara Indians say that the Creator God Viracocha "rose from Lake Titicaca during the time of darkness to bring forth light". Viracocha was represented as wearing the sun for a crown, with thunderbolts in his hands, and tears descending from his eyes as rain. Viracocha made the earth, the stars, the sky and mankind, but his first creation displeased him, so he destroyed it with a flood and made a new, better one, taking to his wanderings as a beggar, teaching his new creations the rudiments of civilization, as well as working numerous miracles.

Viracocha eventually disappeared across the Pacific Ocean (by walking on the water), setting off near Manta Ecuador, and he never returned. It was thought that Viracocha would re-appear in times of trouble.

The term "viracocha" also refers to a group of men named the suncasapa or bearded ones - they were the mythic soldiers of Viracocha, also called the "angelic warriors of Viracocha". Later one of the Inca Kings (the eighth Inca ruler) took the name of Viracocha.

On the Gateway of the Sun, the famous carved figure on the decorated archway in the ancient (pre-Incan) city of Tiahuanaco most likely represents Viracocha, flanked by 48 winged effigies, 32 with human faces and 16 with condor's heads.

So Viracocha left the lands of the Inca and traveled across the Pacific. In India, we find the most interesting Indus Valley civilization which - upon visual inspection of the ruins - presents a striking resemblance to the ruins of the ancient cities of South America. The only difference was that the ability to shape megaliths seems to have been lost, and the Indus valley cities, while stylistically similar, are built of brick. One curious item that might be noted is the similarity of certain writings found on Easter Island to the Indus Valley script.

At a later point in time, the movement was north to Mesopotamia where again, certain sigils found on cylinder seals are similar to the Indus Valley script. The rigid caste system of the Incas is found also in India.

So, we find the ideas from across the Pacific, making their way up the Indian peninsula, to meet with a group of big blond nomadic herdsmen from the Altai mountains, probably in Mesopotamia where the Sumerians also had migrated with their memories of the Annunaki: big and blond. The Southern male god was adopted by the Altai Aryans in their mingling with the Southerners that invaded India from across the Sea.[247]

This new "Aryan" god was frequently depicted as a storm god, high on a mountain, blazing with the light of fire or lightning. In many of these transposed myths, the goddess is depicted as a serpent or dragon, associated with darkness and evil. Sometimes the dragon is neuter or even male, but in such cases, is closely associated with the goddess, usually as her son.

The Goddess religion seems to have assimilated the male deities into the older forms of worship, and survived as the popular religion of the people for thousands of years after the initial Southern Aryan invasions. However, her position had been greatly lowered and continued to decline. It was with the advent of Judaism, and eventually Christianity, that the Goddess religion was finally and completely suppressed.

And here we come to the most interesting thing of all: it is in the accounts of the Aryans of India that we find the original religious ideas of the Hebrews, including the idea of the End of the World.

There is the mountain-top god who blazes with light; there is the duality between light and darkness symbolized as good and evil; there is the myth of the male deity defeating the serpent; and there is the supreme leadership of a ruling class: the priestly Levites. All of these are to be found in both the "Indo-Incan" and Hebrew religious concepts and politics!

And this leads us to the obvious idea: The Indo-Incan patterns were either adopted by the Jews, or the Jewish priests were Indo-Incans from the start.

The Indo-Aryan attitude toward women is made clear in two sentences attributed to Indra in the Rg Veda: 'The mind of woman brooks not discipline. Her intellect has little weight'. And orthodox Jewish males daily thank god that they were not born women!

---

[247] See *Gods of the Cataclysm* for the evidence of this route of transfer of ideas.

In India, there is clear evidence of this Southern Aryan invasion from across the sea and the conquest of the Goddess worshippers. The books known as the Vedas were a record of the Aryans in India. They were written between 1500 and 1200 B.C. in Sanskrit using scripts possibly borrowed from the Akkadians.

The Indo-Aryan Rg Veda says that "in the very beginning there was only 'asura', or 'living power'." The asura broke down into two cosmic groups. One was the enemies of the Southern Aryans, known as the Danavas, or Dityas - the Northern Aryans - whose mother was the Goddess Danu or Diti; the other group, clearly the heroes of the Aryans, were known to them as the A-Dityas. This title betrays the fact that this mythical structure was created in reaction to the presence of the worshippers of Diti, since A-Ditya literally means "not Dityas", or "not people of Diti". That the people needed to be identified in terms of who they worshipped, suggests that this was the only thing that could be distinguished about them. In other words: they looked the same. They were not distinguished by being the "black-headed people".

One of the major Indo-Aryan gods was known as Indra, Lord of the Mountains, "he who overthrows cities". Upon obtaining the promise of supremacy if he succeeded in killing Danu and Her son Vrtra, he does accomplish the act, thus achieving kingship among the A-Dityas. In a hymn to Indra in the Rg Veda which describes the event, Danu and Her son are first described as serpent demons; later, as they lie dead, they are symbolized as cow and calf. After the murders, "the cosmic waters flowed and were pregnant". They in turn gave birth to the sun. This concept of the sun god emerging from the primeval waters appears in other Indo-Aryan-Incan myths and also occurs in connection with two of the prehistoric invasions. All of this connects the events to times of cataclysm.

The Rg Veda also refers to an ancestral father god known both as Prajapati and Dyaus Pitar. Dyaus Pitar is known as the "supreme father of all". The spread of the Indo-Aryan culture brought with it the origins of the Hindu religion and the concept of light-colored skin being perceived as better or more "pure" than darker skins. (The Sanskrit word for caste, "varna" means color.)

The Indo-Aryan beliefs are found in Iran, though the records are very late - dating back only as far as 600 B.C. The Indians and Iranians were derived from the same ethnic group and had been established on the Iranian plateau from about 4000 B.C. They spoke a Vedic Sanskrit dialect.

Though there is a considerable change from the Rg Veda to the Iranian Avesta, we still find the great father who represents light, with a new name: Ahura Mazda. He is the Lord of Light and his abode is on a mountain top glowing with golden light. The duality of light and dark is inherent in Iranian religious thought. Ahura Mazda is on high in goodness, and the devil figure, Ahriman is "deep down in darkness".

In the Iranian texts of 200 A.D. known as Manichean, we again find good and evil equated with light and dark. We are told in these writings that the problems of humanity are caused by a mixture of the two. And here, Mithra appears as the one who defeats the "demons of darkness".

Then, there is Gayo Mareta who is, in the Iranian texts, the "first man". He seems to relate to Indra in the Indian versions. Gauee or gavee in Sanskrit means cow. Mrityu in Sanskrit means death or murder, surviving in the Indo-Aryan German language as mord, meaning murder, and in the Indo-European English language as the word murder itself. Thus Gavo Mareta appears to be named "Cow Murderer". Just as Danu was symbolized as the cow Goddess, whose worship is best known from Egypt before Narmer, and Indra Her murderer, so Gayo Mareta may once have held this position in Iran. In the Pahlavi Books of about 400 B.C. it was written, "From Gayo Mareta, Ahura fashioned the family of the Aryan lands, the seed of the Aryan lands". We are also reminded of the text of Fr. Alonso regarding the beliefs of the Guanches:

> "They knew that there was a hell, and they held that it was in the peak of
> Teyde [the volcanic mountain], and *the devil was Guayota*."

In tracking these ideas, people disappearing here and reappearing there, we find that it was during the height of the Indus Valley civilization that both Sumeria and Egypt were conquered by what seems to have been "outsiders".

As early as the fourth millenium B.C., a group known as the people of the Ubaid culture entered the Tigris-Euphrates area. They were described as 'newcomers from the east'. The statement derives a certain support from tradition; "as they jouneyed from the East they found a plain in the land of Shinar [= Babylon] and they dwelt there" [Genesis XI, 2]; but it is based on the material evidence of the pottery of al 'Ubaid and of Susa respectively, that it is generally agreed that the al 'Ubaid people were related, culturally and presumably ethnically, to the early inhabitants of Elam.

The Susa pottery does not stand alone. In the late neolithic and in the chalcolithic periods painted pottery was produced over a vast area of Asia. In a Stone Age site near Persepolis, at Nihavend and at Tepe Siyalk, south of Teheran; at Tepe Hissar south of Astrabad; eastward, near Ashkhabad, at Anau and Ak-Tepe and at Namazgah-Tepe; on the edge of the Kara Kum desert at Jeitun and Chopan-Tepe; as far away as Baluchistan, where we have the Kulli painted wares, and up in Mongolia where the finest of all the decorative schemes were evolved; in all these and in many other intermediate sites there has been excavated painted pottery which shows a similarity of technique and parallels in design and motif which are sufficiently close to suggest, if not a common source, at least contacts and exchanges resulting in something like cultural uniformity.

Some scholars suggest that the Ubaid people brought the Sumerian language which is neither Semitic nor Indo-European. In fact, it is similar to some of the Ural Altaic languages. Aratta is a place name often mentioned in Sumerian texts, and it may have been the area of the Altai mountains.

The Ubaid people established a major settlement in the place later known as Eridu. They broke up the Halaf culture, and wreaked devastation upon them. These Ubaids spread as far north as Lake Urmia and Lake Van, close to the Iranian-Russian border. This section was later known as Ararat or Urartu, which could be corruptions of Aratta. The name "Eridu" could also be a corruption of Aratta, suggesting the original homeland.

In about 4000 B.C., the Ubaid people built a temple at Eridu which appears to be the first built on a high platform. At this temple, not a single goddess figurine was found.

Interestingly, a statue found in graves of the Ubaid people depicted a mother and baby with lizard-like features.

The deity worshipped at Eridu in historic times was the god Enki. Before this, the god of the shrine seems to have been a fish or water god who rose up out of the water exactly like the Viracocha people, and had scales, was a civilizer and teacher of language and culture. Enki was thought of later as the god of the waters and was described as riding around in his boat. He was also described as "he who rides". This concept of the fish or water god is similar to one found in a fragment of an Indo-Aryan Hittite tablet which tells of a sun god who rose from the water with fish on his head. It is also similar to the idea of the sun god who was born from the cosmic waters released by Indra, by the deaths of Danu and Vrtra. Though Enki is not generally designated as a sun god, in the myth of Marduk he is named as Marduk's father and, so, Marduk is called the "son of the sun".

The Ubaid people are credited with developing irrigation canals in Eridu which could hint at their origin in places that were along rivers and streams and where fish were common. Another clue to the identity of these people is the institution of kingship and the mention of the name Alalu as the very first king of Sumer, in the king lists of the earliest part of the second millennium. According to these tablets which refer to a prehistoric period, it was in Eridu that "kingship was first lowered from heaven".

The origins of the words "Hurrian", "Horite" or "Horim", may be connected to the Iranian word "hara" which means mountain. This word survives in the German "hohe" which means hill. It is also thought possible that the word relates to the Sanskrit "hari", which means "golden yellow", Also, it should be noted that in Sanskrit, the word for gold is "hiran", which later became "oro" in Latin, all of them with relations to the East - or peoples coming from across the Pacific.

Now, let's think about this for a moment. We have a god with a fish on his head, thereby associated with scales, and who is described as "he who rides", This scaly god not only rides, he rose from the water like the sun! Also, he was born from the deaths of the Mother Goddess and her son. Mountains of fire are involved, gold, and kingship being "lowered from heaven".

A third male deity - An or Anu - comes onto the Sumerian stage sometime after the beginning of the second millenium - the same period that the Hurrians discussed above are known to have entered the area, so they may well have brought this Anu with them.

In the early Sumerian period the name Anu is relatively obscure, and his name does not appear on any of the eighteen lists belonging to this period.

Anu appears as the successor to Alalu in the Hurrian and Hittite Kumarbi myth. But most interesting is his appearance in the later myth of Marduk, 'the son of the sun'. Here we learn that Enki was first asked to subdue the Creatress-Goddess, whom they call Tiamat, and was not able, though he did manage to kill her husband Apsu, thus becoming Lord of the Abzu (primeval waters) himself. Anu was then asked to subdue Tiamat, but according to the legend, when he confronted her, he cringed in fear and refused to complete his mission. Finally Marduk, son of Enki, was willing, though only upon the promise of the supreme position among all other deities if he succeeded. This previously secured promise brings to mind the one Indra requested before murdering Danu and Her son Vrtra; both of these myths were probably written about the same period (1600-1400 B.C.).

This legend, known as the Enuma Elish, which explains the supremacy of Marduk, has long been designated as Babylonian and therefore Akkadian and Semitic. But more recent research suggests that, though Marduk was known in the Hammurabi period, the myth claiming his supremacy did not actually appear until after the Kassites had conquered Babylon. Saggs points out that, "none of the extant texts belonging to it is earlier than the first millennium", and that "it has been suggested that, in fact, this work arose only in the Kassite period, a time now known to have been one of intense literary activity". The Kassites were also ruled by the Indo-Incans. Gurney tells us that, "the names of Indian deities are found to form an element in the names of the Kassite rulers of Babylonia", though once again the greater part of the Kassite people were not Indo-Incan.

In about 2100 B.C., a Sumerian king named Ur Nammu declared that he would establish justice in the land. He did away with the heavy duties and taxes that were burdening the people at that time and, "rid the land of 'the big sailors who seized oxen, sheep and donkeys'". [248]

---

[248] Jacquetta Hawkes *Dawn of the gods*

Now, while all this invading and conquering and demolishing of the Goddess Worship is going on over in the Tigris-Euphrates area, the same thing was going on in Egypt with Narmer-Menes!

There is considerable evidence for contact between Egypt and Sumer. Abundant evidence of Mesopotamian cultural influence is found at this time in Egypt. Significant is the fact that cylinder seals (a specifically Mesopotamian invention) occur there, together with methods of building in brick foreign to Egypt but typical of the Jemdet Nasr culture of Mesopotamia AND the Indus Valley civilization. Mesopotamian motifs and objects also begin to be represented in Egyptian art, such as boats of Mesopotamian type. And, the idea of writing, though it was expressed quite differently in Egypt, seems to have come from Mesopotamia. Paintings in early dynastic tombs portray a conical basket type of fish trap, nearly identical to those of the Ertebolle people of northern Europe who were descended from the Maglemosians! The male deity of Egypt arrived with the invaders and was portrayed as the sun riding in a boat!

Professor Walter Emery spent some forty-five years excavating the ancient tombs and pyramids of Egypt. Discussing the arrival of these people, he writes:

> "Whether this incursion took the form of gradual infiltration or horde invasion is uncertain but the balance of evidence... strongly suggests the latter. ...we see a style of art which some think may be Mesopotamian, or even Syrian in origin, and a scene which may represent a battle at sea against invaders... [in these] representations we have typical native ships of Egypt and strange vessels with high prow and stem of unmistakable Mesopotamian origin...

> At any rate, towards the close of the fourth millennium B.C. we find the people known traditionally as the 'Followers of Horus' apparently forming an aristocracy or master race ruling over the whole of Egypt. The theory of the existence of this master race is supported by the discovery that graves of the late pre-dynastic period in the northern part of Upper Egypt were found to contain the anatomical remains of a people whose *skulls are of greater size and whose bodies were larger than those of the natives*, the difference being so marked that any suggestion that these people derived from the earlier stock is impossible." [249]

These invaders were known to the Egyptians as the "Shemsu Hor" or people of Hor. And, of course, they brought with them their male god, Hor-Wer or Great Hor. By 2900 B.C. pictures of this sun god show him riding in his "boat of heaven".

It certainly makes one wonder if a brilliant UFO rising up out of the water would cause the ancient peoples to connect a boat (that goes on water) with flying through the air while looking like the sun! And, over and over again we are finding this image or juxtaposition of images.

---

[249] Quoted by Stone, 1976.

According to Professor Emery, the name of the first king of the First Dynasty, known as Narmer or Menes in Manetho's history of 270 B.C, was actually Hor-Aha. Later, the name of Hor appears to have been incorporated into the more ancient goddess religion as the "son who dies". This has led to a lot of confusion between the two "Hors", Horus the Elder, god of light of the invaders, and Horus the Younger, the son of the goddess Isis.

Hor later was transmogrified into Horus by the Greeks and is depicted as fighting a ritual combat with another male deity known as Set. Set is supposed to be his uncle, the brother of his mother Isis and father Osiris. The combat was supposed to symbolize the overcoming of darkness or Set, by light, symbolized by Hor.

In Sanskrit the word "sat" means to destroy by hewing into pieces. In the myth of Osiris, it was Set who killed Osiris and cut his body into fourteen pieces. But, the word "set" is also defined as "queen" or "princess" in Egyptian! "Au Set", known as Isis by the Greeks, means "exceeding queen"!

In the myth of this ritual combat, Set tries to mate sexually with Horus; this is usually interpreted to have been an extreme insult. The most primitive identity of the figure Set, before the wavy lines of water or energy became serpents, may be the goddess religion and this combat, just as the combat of Marduk with Tiamat, may have represented the suppression and destruction of the Goddess religion. And of course, the conquering invaders presented themselves as "saviors" and that their conquest was a triumph of light over darkness!

So it has always been.

Nevertheless, the followers of Hor established the institution of kingship in Egypt. Again, marrying the representative of the goddess in order to "steal her power" was an important part of the assumption of kingship. And, we may justifiably compare the name of "Hor" to the Hurrians or Horites who came from India to Sumer.

Around the time of the Second Dynasty the town of Heliopolis (known to the Egyptians as Annu!), became the home of a school of scribal priests who also worshipped a sun god who rode in a boat. In this town they used the name Ra. In Sanskrit, Ra means royal or exalted on high. This prefix is found in the Sanskrit word for king, raja and queen, rani. It survives in the German word ragen, to reach up, in French as roi, meaning king, as well as in the English words royal, reign and regal.

In the pyramid texts of the Fifth Dynasty (about 2400 B.C.) Horus was equated with Ra. Both Horus and Ra were closely connected, at times competitively, with the right to kingship. As Ra-Harakhty, Ra is identical with Horus of the Horizon, both meaning the sun at rising. Ra too is portrayed as the sun who rides across the heavens sitting in his sacred boat. Again, why a boat in the heavens?

Ra's boat was said to emerge out of the primeval waters, much as Enki was said to ride his boat in the deep waters of the Abzu of Eridu, or as the Indo-Aryan sun god was said to have emerged from the cosmic waters. As in the Indo-Incan Hittite myth of the sun god in the water who rises from the sea with fish on his head, so too Ra rose from the waters each morning.

As the name of Horus was assimilated into the Goddess religion, as the son of Isis, the priests of Memphis proposed another concept of the great father god. This time his name was Ptah, curiously like the Sanskrit Pitar - from India. The texts concerning him describe the creation of all existence, suggesting that Ptah was there first. This time we are told that it was through an act of masturbation that Ptah caused all the other gods to come into being, thus totally eliminating the need for a divine Mother!

Well, again, we have all of these shining boats rising out of the water. And, this idea of the masturbating god is not new. One of the Sumerian gods, Enki, was supposed to have masturbated and thereby caused the Tigris and Euphrates rivers to flow!

Yet, even though these conquering Indo-Incans came in wave after wave, bringing their gods who ride in shining boats in the sky, the goddess religion still survived. This very fact may indicate the presence of another group who worked quietly to preserve the ancient truths in the face of almost overwhelming opposition. The new male gods were assimilated and synthesized creating an almost impossible to sort mish-mash of gods and goddesses.

With the knowledge that the worship of the Goddess was violently overturned by invading Indo-Aryans who were descendants of the Incan Sun worshippers whose objective was to forestall another "end of the world" with the sacrifice of enormous numbers of human beings, (probably the "black headed people" who were created to serve the "gods") we may better understand the transitions and inversions that have occurred in our myths and legends as well as our concepts of time. And with this understanding, we are free to pursue a more open and reasonable series of speculations as to what the End of the World, and all the prophecies related to it might be about.

Just as there was a Dark Age surrounding the period of time in which the Old Testament came into being, during which time Monotheistic Judaism was imposed forcibly on the Canaanites, and we have only the Old Testament itself to attest to its validity; we have a similar period of Dark Ages enveloping the development and codification of the New Testament and the imposition of Monotheistic Christianity on the Western World.

Don't you find that curious?

The god of the Jews is a personality who purportedly ceaselessly intervenes in history and who reveals his will through events. Historical facts thus acquired a religious value in the fact that they were specific situations between man and god, and history became the epiphany of god. This conception was continued and magnified by Christianity. We can see the seeds of the original myths here, but we can also see the major distortions.

In monotheism, every event is definitely situated in time - a given time and no other - and is not reversible. It is a historical event with weight and value in and of itself. And that weight is upon the shoulders of mankind, individually and collectively.

In the offshoot of Judaism, Christianity, the Messianic hope, the victory over the forces of darkness, is projected indefinitely into the future and will only happen once in terms of linear time. Further, there is only one who can accomplish this conquest of darkness, and man's only hope is to give up his will to this one who has been crucified and resurrected to symbolize his verity, even if he has really done nothing to change the state of the world in real time. When the Messiah comes again (never mind that he was supposed to have already been here and global conditions did not improve), the world will be saved once and for all, and history will cease to exist - and most of humanity along with it, not to mention a "third of the angels", and so on.

This idea of irreversible, linear time, was imposed upon mankind through violence and exclusion, serving as the basis for the philosophy of history that Christianity, from St. Augustine on, has labored to construct.

In case you didn't notice what just happened here, let me make it a little clearer. What this has done is give value to the "future" as an end to everything. That's it; no more. Further, the arbiter of that future is one god, who, I might add, is his own surety because he has helpfully announced at the beginning that he is the one god; and this one god has a select group of servants who will be preserved to the exclusion of all others in some way, if they obey him, and destroyed if they disobey him. But, of course, it is "free will choice" as to whether to believe this or not. It doesn't sound like a choice; it sounds like an ultimatum!

We begin to smell a rat here. A hint that the introduction of the concept of linear time was the raison d'être for the introduction of monotheism.

And, for the most part, our modern world is predicated upon linear time. Thus, the reason for the raison can be dimly seen by those who have been tracking with me here: it is that linear time is a supreme weapon to use against the mind of man in terms of control and domination! Monotheism is a myth that establishes a particular identity as an antithesis - against another - actually, just about all Others! The ultimate club of elitists!

Most of the Old Testament is a chronicle of genocide and horrendous practices of human and animal sacrifice. In the New Testament, we find that the work of a remarkable man who lived two thousand years ago in the Middle East, whose teachings gave birth to Christianity, has been replaced by a "story" based on a human sacrifice ritual, an already ages old corruption - the ubiquitous solar/fertility cult. Then, beginning in the tenth century, Judaism was revived, the Cathars were destroyed, and the Crusades were begun to "find something".

Curious, eh?

In any event, the concept of blood sacrifice passed into Christianity in this barbaric custom. It is, in fact, the heart of Christianity as it is understood by Christians today. However, making Christ the "once for all atonement" for everyone had curious consequences. With such an event as an "example", it became quite easy to manipulate the populace to willingly emulate this self-sacrifice, and thus, the motivation for the Crusades, and endless wars and genocide by "civilized" peoples was made "normal".

Fiendishly clever, I say.

The purpose of the moment is to identify the several occult threads that lead down to the present day so as to be able to understand the events of 9-11. When I say "occult", I don't necessarily mean "black magick" or similar such nonsense, though such things are certainly not excluded. Generally, however, when such things as "occultism" are brought into the mixture, after careful investigation, one usually discovers the presence and activity of hyperdimensional beings masquerading as "angels" or "demons" as well as just about anything in between.

The last thousand years of history shows us that when a scapegoat is needed, such as in the time of the Inquisition and the pogroms of the Catholic Church, the Jews are often the target. At these times, reports emerge that claim that Jews and Germans collaborated against the Catholic Church in the 9th century, forming a group of elitists that engaged in "sickening sacrificial rituals".

Early among the proponents of the theory of Jewish blood lust was St. Bernard of Clairvaux. When I first read this claim, my immediate reaction was to snort in disgust and declare it to be nonsense. As I mentioned above, I am very sensitive to anything with anti-Semitic overtones. However, after reviewing the history of the creation of the Bible, and putting it together with some odd comments made by the Cassiopaeans, I have come to the idea that such a claim is not too far off - except that those "Jews" involved, are not necessarily "real" Jews, so to say. My hypothesis is that there is a Nordic Covenant that has existed from the time of the Dark Ages, and that this group is, effectively, the "new vehicle" for the Machiavellian machinations of the Elohim who originally "fenced in" the Jews at the time of the Exodus.

In December of 1994, the C's delivered an odd series of rapid fire comments. It has only been with hindsight that we have come to understand that this was very likely a series of "marker events" for us to notice in terms of the setting in motion of the STS plan for the "End

Times". That they were only possible/probable is clear from the C's many other remarks about "predictions" including:

"The forces at work here are far too clever to be accurately anticipated so easily. You never know what twists and turns will follow, and they are aware of prophetic and philosophical patternings and usually shift course to fool and discourage those who believe in fixed futures."

Keeping that in mind, let's look at the string of "markers":

1. Ukraine explosion; chemical or nuclear.
2. Hawaii crash; aviation, possibly involving military
3. More California seismic activity after 1st of year: San Diego, San Bernardino, North Bakersfield, Barstow: all are fracture points. Hollister, Palo Alto, Imperial, Ukiah, Eureka, Point Mendocino, Monterrey, Offshore San Luis Obispo, Capistrano, Carmel: these are all stress points of fracture in sequence. "Time" is indefinite. Expect gradual destruction of California economy as people begin mass exodus.
4. Also, Shasta erupts; Lassen activity. Ocean floor begins to subside.
5. Queen Elizabeth serious illness; blood related.
6. Princess Diana suicide attempt.
7. Gas explosions this winter in NE United States, Texas and other.
8. Supernova and unusual weather all over.
9. Memphis feels tremors.
10. Minneapolis banking scandal relates to mysterious Nordic covenant.
11. Evangelical sexual tryst exposed.
12. Gold is discovered in California after one of the quakes.
13. UFOs dramatic increase and Gulf Breeze gets swarmed, becomes massive "Mecca".
14. Laura sees much more UFO activity.
15. Huge wave of UFO activity. All manner and origins.
16. Many aliens will appear and we will be visible too.
17. All must awaken to this. It is happening right now. The whole populace will play individual roles according to their individual frequencies. This is only the beginning.

Item number 5, the "Princess Diana Suicide Attempt" is an interesting "marker" point since it was obviously only a "probable" future in 1994. Three years later, other events had transpired to move her to a different destiny. In a certain sense, her activities with Dodi Fayed might be seen as "suicidal". And when we consider that aspect of it, from a higher consciousness point of view, Dodi's actions were also "suicidal". So, what was originally "read" as a suicide attempt, became a fact.

There are many people who claim that Diana and Dodi were murdered. This may be so in some sense, but again, only their own actions made them vulnerable.

Coming back now to our subject of a "group" that is behind the machinations of history, we must consider the term "fifth column":

"A clandestine subversive organization working within a given country to further an invading enemy's military and political aims" (American Heritage Dictionary, 1976).

Nearly all experts of "esoterica", after years and years of searching and studying, eventually come to the idea that there is some sort of major conspiracy that has been running the show on planet earth for a very long time. The problem is, there are any number of conclusions as to "who is on first" in this trans-millennial, multi-national, global ballgame. The thing that raises red flags, however, is that just about any of the many conclusions can be supported by reams of "evidence".

When I first began my own research in a serious and dedicated way, I was quite distressed by this factor. The only thing that I did different from most researchers was to take this confusion as a "given" fact that was intended. There were two things that had been burned into my mind very early on, and I found both of them to be very useful when applied to the present problem. The first was a remark attributed to FDR: "Nothing in politics happens by accident. If it happens, you can bet it was planned that way." The other idea was a remark made to me by a friend who had been trained in Army Intelligence. He said that the first rule of Intelligence is to just observe what IS and understand that it is very likely the way it is for a reason. Once you have settled that firmly in your mind, you can then begin to form hypotheses about who might benefit the most from a given situation, and once such hypotheses are formed, you can then begin to test them. You may have to discard any number of ideas when you find the flaw, but unless you begin with this process, you will be duped over and over again.

In considering the problem before us, we can see that there are "tracks" throughout history of some pretty mysterious goings on that do, indeed, suggest a "conspiracy". If we take that as an observation of what IS, we immediately face the second big question: is it a conspiracy of "good guys" or "bad guys"? It is at this point that all the various conspiracy experts begin to diverge into their assorted rants about Zionists or Masons, and all the many variations thereof.

But what if, instead of asking that question and beginning to argue, we just settle back and observe what is and try to find the answer based on observation?

The single biggest argument against historical conspiracy is the relatively short lifespan of human beings, combined with the observable psychological make-up of man. A corollary objection is the fact that, very often, the domino effect of events that "change history" are of such a nature that it would be impossible for ordinary human beings to engineer them. In other words, Time and Space are barriers to the idea of human beings being engaged in a global conspiracy.

Well, of course the diligent researcher has by now tried every other way to make the puzzle pieces fit ending in repeated failures to account for everything, including the numerous views that oppose and contradict one another. So, when we stop for a moment to think about this initial, observable fact of the barrier of Time and Space, we then think of an idea: what if the conspirators are not constrained by Time or Space? Our initial reaction to this thought is to dismiss it out of hand. But as we pursue our researches, as we come across repeated "anomalies" and "glitches" and "tracks" throughout space and time - what we call "history" - we begin to get the uneasy feeling that we ought to take another look at this idea.

As it happens, once the possibility of manipulation of space and time has been added to our hypothesis, things finally begin to "fall into place". Once that happens, however, once we begin to look at history from this trans-millennial, trans-spatial perspective, the character of the "conspiracy" begins to emerge, and only the most gullible - or negative intentioned - occultist could hold onto, or continue to promote, any idea that this conspiracy is benevolent. In fact, it becomes abundantly clear that many, if not most, religions and systems of philosophy, have been created and introduced by the conspirators in order to conceal the conspiracy itself. And when you are considering beings with mastery over space and time, thousands of years needed to develop any given aspect of the overall plan is negligible. And so, in consideration of such beings, we come again to the idea of hyperdimensional space - known as "4th density" and its denizens.

As it happens, precisely at the time I was struggling to understand the bizarre nature of the 10th -12th centuries, the C's used the opportunity to give me a "lesson in history".

> Q: Next question: is there any relationship between the fact that Roger de Mortimer, the carrier of the last of the line of the Welsh kings, was the lover of Isabella of France, who was the daughter of Philip the Fair, the destroyer of the Templars, and the murderer of Edward II, the first of the English Princes of Wales?
> A: Templars are a setup, insofar as persecution is concerned. Remember your "historical records" can be distorted, in order to throw off future inquiries, such as your own.
> Q: I know that. I have already figured that one out! But, it seems that no one else has made this connection. I mean, the bloodlines that converge in the Percys and the Mortimers are incredible!
> A: You should know that these bloodlines become parasitically infected, harassed and tinkered with whenever a quantum leap of awareness is imminent. : Such as "now". Here is something for you to digest: Why is it

that your scientists have overlooked the obvious when they insist that
alien beings cannot travel to earth from a distant system??? Even if speed
of light travel, or "faster", were not possible, and it is, of course, there is
no reason why an alien race could not construct a space "ark", living for
many generations on it. They could travel great distances through time
and space, looking for a suitable world for conquest. Upon finding such,
they could then install this ark in a distant orbit, build bases upon various
solid planes in that solar system, and proceed to patiently manipulate the
chosen civilizations to develop a suitable technological infrastructure.
And then, after the instituting of a long, slow, and grand mind
programming project, simply step in and take it over once the situation
was suitable.

Q: Is this, in fact, what has happened, or is happening?

A: It could well be, and maybe now it is the time for you to learn about
the details.

Q: Well, would such a race be 3rd or 4th density in orientation?

A: Why not elements of both?

Q: What is the most likely place that such a race would have originated
from?

A: Oh, maybe Orion, for example?

Q: Okay. If such a race did, in fact, travel to this location in space/time,
how many generations have come and gone on their space ark during this
period of travel, assuming, of course, that such a thing has happened?

A: Maybe 12.

Q: Okay, that implies that they have rather extended life spans...

A: Yes...

Q: Assuming this to be the case, what are their life-spans?

A: 2,000 of your years. When in space, that is...

Q: And what is the span when on terra firma?

A: 800 years.

Q: Well, has it not occurred to them that staying in space might not be
better?

A: No. Planets are much more "comfortable".

Q: Okay... imagining that such a group has traveled here...

A: We told you of upcoming conflicts... Maybe we meant the same as
your Bible, and other references. Speak of... The "final" battle between
"good and evil..." Sounds a bit cosmic, when you think of it, does it not?

Q: Does this mean that there is more than one group that has traveled here
in their space arks?

A: Could well be another approaching, as well as "reinforcements" for
either/or, as well as non-involved, but interested observers of various
types who appreciate history from the sidelines.

Q: Well, swell! There goes my peaceful life!

A: You never had one! You chose to be incarnated now, with some
foreknowledge of what was to come. Reference your dreams of space
attack.

Q: Okay, what racial types are we talking about relating to these
hypothetical aliens?

A: Three basic constructs. Nordic, Reptilian, and Greys. Many variations of type 3, and 3 variations of type 1 and 2.

Q: Well, what racial types are the 'good guys?'

A: Nordics, in affiliation with 6th density "guides".

Q: And that's the only good guys?

A: That's all you need.

Q: Wonderful! So, if it is a Grey or Lizzie, you know they aren't the nice guys. But, if it is tall and blond, you need to ask questions!

A: All is subjective when it comes to nice and not nice. Some on 2nd density would think of you as "not nice", to say the least!!!

Q: That's for sure! Especially the roaches! Maybe we ought to get in touch with some of these good guys...

A: When the "time" is right. Just pay attention to the signs, please!

Q: There is a lot being said about the sightings out in the Southwest area. They are saying that this is the 'new' imminent invasion or mass landing. Can you comment on this activity?

A: Prelude to the biggest "flap" ever.

Q: And where will this flap be located?

A: Earth. Invasion happens when programming is complete...

Q: What programming?

A: See Bible, "Lucid" book, Matrix Material, "Bringers of the Dawn", and many other sources, then cross reference...

Q: Well, we better get moving! We don't have time to mess around!

A: You will proceed as needed, you cannot force these events or alter the Grand Destiny.

Q: I do *not* like the sound of that! I want to go home!

A: The alternative is less appetising. Reincarnation on a 3rd density earth as a "cave person" amidst rubble and a glowing red sky, as the perpetual cold wind whistles...

Q: Why is the sky glowing red?

A: Contemplate.

Q: Of course! Comet dust!

[...]

Q: (L) I read the new book by Dr. David Jacobs, professor of History at Temple University, concerning his extensive research into the alien abduction phenomenon. [Dr. Jacobs wrote his Ph.D. thesis on the history of the UFOs.] Dr. Jacobs says that now, after all of these years of somewhat rigorous research, that he knows what the aliens are here for and he is afraid. David Jacobs says that producing offspring is the primary objective behind the abduction phenomenon. Is this, in fact, the case?

A: Part, but not "the whole thing".

Q: (L) Is there another dominant reason?

A: Replacement.

Q: (L) Replacement of what?

A: You.

Q: (L) How do you mean? Creating a race to replace human beings, or abducting specific humans to replace them with a clone or whatever?

A: Mainly the former. You see, if one desires to create a new race, what better way than to mass hybridize, then mass reincarnate. Especially when the host species is so forever ignorant, controlled, and anthropocentric. What a lovely environment for total destruction and conquest and replacement... see?

Q: (L) Well, that answered my other question about the objective. Well, here in the book, Dr. Jacobs says that there are ongoing abductions through particular families. I quote: 'Beyond protecting the fetus, there are other reasons for secrecy. If abductions are, as all the evidence clearly indicates, an intergenerational phenomenon in which the children of abductees are themselves abductees, then one of the aliens' goals is the generation of more abductees. [...] To protect the intergenerational nature of the breeding program, it must be kept secret from the abductees so that they will continue to have children. If the abductees KNEW that the program was intergenerational, they might elect not to have children. This would bring a critical part of the program to a halt, which the aliens cannot allow. The final reason for secrecy is to expand the breeding program, to integrate laterally in society, the aliens must make sure that abductees mate with non-abductees and produce abductee children.' Now, this seems to suggest that there is a particular bloodline that is susceptible to...

A: We have told you before: the Nazi experience was a "trial run", and by now you see the similarities, do you not? Now, we have also told you that the experience of the "Native Americans" vis a vis the Europeans may be a precursor in microcosm. Also, what Earthian 3rd density does to Terran 2nd density should offer "food for thought". In other words, thou art not so special, despite thy perspective, eh? And we have also warned that after conversion of Earth humans to 4th density, the Orion 4th density and their allies hope to control you "there". Now put this all together and what have you? At least you should by now know that it is the soul that matters, not the body. Others have genetically, spiritually and psychically manipulated/engineered you to be body-centric. Interesting, as despite all efforts by 4th through 6th density STO, this "veil" remains unbroken.

There are many items in the above excerpts of extreme interest considering current events. One thing is the issue of "mind programming". Contrary to what many conspiracy theorists claim, the main "mind programming" project on Earth has been - and continues to be - religious and cultural.

The second most predominant method of mind control is via the media and controlling the flow of information. It might even be possible that beings with mastery of space/time could travel back in to the past and destroy documents and plant their own "version of history".

Q: Who burned the library at Alexandria, since I have heard two stories: one that the Christians did it and the other that the Arabs did it. Which?
A: Neither.
Q: Who DID burn it?
A: Sword keepers of "the lock".
Q: Who are the Sword Keepers of the Lock?
A: Has to do with Illuminati.

Q: What was their purpose in burning this library?
A: What is the purpose in burning ANY library?
Q: To destroy knowledge. Prevent other people from having access to it.

Again we find a "track" that suggests to us that somebody wanted to keep human beings in the dark. We can, of course, ascribe this to just ordinary human activities of greed and ignorance as many materialist interpreters do. But, when one begins to add up all of the similar types of events throughout history, the indictment against is that man cries to heaven for an end to his existence. And yet, as a hypnotherapist, I have never found this assessment to be satisfactory.

The Laws of Probability tell us that, without any intelligent control, 50% of the time events would occur leading to great good and benefit. Factoring in intelligent decisions to do good should make this higher; it might bring this average up to about 70%. Yet we can clearly see that this is not reflected in our reality.

An alien presence has been noted at many points in history of great disaster or mass death. Examination of the records and documents has led some scholars and researchers to conjecture that many of history's Darkest Hours have been created by the alien presence.

Richard Dolan, who studied at Alfred University and Oxford, and did his graduate work in history at the University of Rochester, is a scholar of Cold War Strategy, Soviet History and culture, and international diplomacy. His recent book, UFOs and The National Security State,[250] reveals how, from the early 1940s to the 1970s, military personnel around the globe encountered unidentified flying objects hundreds and even thousands of times. In some cases, these encounters involved injury and even death to military personnel. What is also of great interest is that the military continues to scramble jets to pursue UFOs, to attempt to shoot them down or otherwise force a confrontation. Dolan's book certainly begs the question: if, as some people suggest, the military are hiding the UFO matter because they are in cahoots, why are they still trying to pursue them and shoot them down?

Based on the documents assembled by Dolan, it is obvious that the governments of the world do indeed see the UFO problem as a very, very serious matter. In the course of assembling the documents and reporting the events, Dolan came to the inescapable conclusion that there exists an "Above Top Secret" group with access to all available UFO data, and that this group "straddles" the worlds of government, military, and industry. The evidence shows that the military forces - under orders from somewhere - created a complete fiction for public consumption that the UFO problem was "nonexistent". They were assisted in pulling the wool over the eyes of the public by "heavy-handed official media and culture",

---

[250] http://www.keyholepublishing.com

and they were obviously under orders to consistently and repeatedly "debunk" the idea that aliens were ensconced in our world.

Many conspiracy theorists propose that the reason for this is because there is an interactive relationship between the governments, the military, and "Aliens". But it is clear from Dolan's history that the problem is deeper and wider than that. They wouldn't be scrambling jets to go after them if they were in cahoots.

So again, we come back to the idea of a "clandestine subversive organization" of global machinations - hyperdimensional beings who have designs on our planet.

The reader only has to carefully peruse Dolan's book to grasp the idea that some hidden group has the power to enforce its will upon the military forces and the Lions of Industry - and we do not, for a moment, think that this could be a human organization. This would, in fact, explain why there is a covert war going on between these forces and the military.

When we step back for the Global view, the situation suggests to us the analogy of arrogant and powerful Masters of Reality, aided and abetted by their military and intelligence organization servants, who, while they are obeying the powerful overlords, are seeking to keep everything quiet as they try desperately to discover the secrets of power so as to arrogate it to themselves. And it seems evident that, in the present time, the game is afoot in the citadels of Power and Secrets. Something is happening and the servants of the alien masters are running scared. They are trying to cement controls, to solidify their power base, because Something Wicked This Way Comes.

Dolan's chronological history of the actual interaction between UFOs and the public and the corresponding behavior of the military, the intelligence community, the media, the scientific community in ITS interaction with the public, make this abundantly clear.

With a broad historical awareness of the facts, a firm grounding in the realization that most of what is out there is deliberate disinformation, the individual who surveys the plethora of "alternative information" in books and on the internet, can easily recognize the "noise" factor produced by the Secret State. And here is where we come to the third major approach to mind control. Dolan tells us:

> "By the early 1970's, there were already means available to alter the moods of unsuspecting persons. A pocket-sized transmitter generating electromagnetic energy at less than 100 milliwatts could do the job. This is no pie-in-the-sky theory. In 1972, Dr. Gordon J.F. McDonald testified before the House Subcommittee on Oceans and International Environment on the issue of electromagnetic weapons used for mind control and mental disruption. He stated:

> [T]he basic notion was to create, between the electrically charged ionosphere in the higher part of the atmosphere and conducting layers of the surface of

the Earth, this neutral cavity, to create waves, electrical waves that would be tuned to the brain waves. ...About ten cycles per second. ...You can produce changes in behavioral patterns or in responses.

The following year, Dr. Joseph C. Sharp, at Walter Reed Hospital, while in a soundproof room, was able to hear spoken words broadcast by 'pulsed microwave audiogram.' These words were broadcast to him without any implanted electronic translation device. Rather, they reached him by direct transmission to the brain." [251]

Consider the above in terms of "chemtrails" - obviously being utilized to create the "neutral cavity" described above - and the enormous proliferation of this activity in the years prior to the 9-11 event. Is it any wonder that human beings have been turned into sheep? And here we have an interesting exchange with the C's regarding same, most particularly the identification of "the enemy":

12-04-99
Q: (L) But, the fact still remains, in my opinion, that there are a lot, lot, lot of planes flying above us in the past few years! Whether they are dumping anything on our heads, or what, there are an extreme number of planes flying in these upper level criss-cross patterns. Now, whether they are just playing war-games, or they are spy planes, they are doing something! What is the reason for all of this upper level flying that results in these criss-crossed contrails that everybody is seeing?
A: A lot of it is "training maneuver" oriented.
Q: Why are they training so many pilots? What are they preparing for?
A: Military budgets must be justified, you know. Review "Military-Industrial Complex 101".
Q: So, this is just training flight, justification of budget, and nothing more than that?
A: Well, we would not say "not anything more to it than that", but, *when you say "M-IC," you have said a lot!*
Q: Are you implying that there is a build-up of the Military-Industrial Complex for a reason?
A: To preserve status quo during "peacetime". This peace business is not very profitable, you know.
Q: Does that suggest that they are building up to set off a war so they can make more money?
A: Maybe if indeed, and if the populous can be hoodwinked. But, fortunately, the public is less hoodwinkable. Maybe the real enemy is "out there", rather than "over there". Was it not always?
Q: Does any of this increased aircraft activity have anything to do with the increased awareness and activities of aliens in and around our planet?
A: As always. But, this awareness is factionalized and compartmentalized.

---

[251] Dolan, UFOs and the National Security State, Hampton Roads, 2002.

The C's comments from 1999 take on a whole new meaning in light of the events of 9-11, as does Bush's drive for "war".

But, there's another piece that struck me, and notice that it was from November of 1995, ten years ago. Also notice that it began with a question about terrorists! (I've edited out the chitchat so that the points are not lost in the noise):

> Q: (L) Is there any relationship between all of the terrorist bombings that have been taking place in Paris recently, and any stepped up alien activity?
> A: Open.
> Q: (L) Is there anything we can obtain on that subject by formulation of correct questions?
> A: USAir-194 crash; United Air crash, Colorado Springs; Connection? Get voice recorder tape transcripts.
> Q: (L) Is this in some way related to the question about the Paris bombing?
> A: No.

Now, what the heck brought on that answer? It was obviously keyed by some word in my question, maybe "terrorist"? Were the C's suggesting that these were "practice runs" for the attack on the WTC?

> Q: (T) This is related to what they were talking about last week, the bases turning 4th density, a plane flew into it and crashed.
> A: Assumption! Strobe lights are used for 3rd density mind control.

Here again, a remark that tells us that the C's are trying to redirect us to a certain subject, and we weren't getting it. Well, how could we? What we now see with hindsight, in terms of what was going on over the past many years, most especially the past 9 years when all the pieces have been being set up on the global game board, gives a whole new meaning to the communications from the C's.

> [...] Q: (L) Okay. You mentioned the strobe lights. Are these strobe lights that are used to control minds, are these something that we would or might come in contact with on a daily basis?
> A: Do you not already know? We didn't say: some strobe lights, we said: strobe lights, i.e. all inclusive!
> Q: (T) Strobe lights come in many forms and types. TV is a strobe light. Computer screens are a strobe light. Lightbulbs strobe. Flourescents strobe. Streetlights strobe.
> A: Police cars, ambulances, firetrucks... How long has this been true? Have you noticed any changes lately??!!??

This last remark from C's was kind of a doozie. Here we have a clear connection between the word "terrorist", plane crashes, and now strobe lights on police cars, ambulances, firetrucks. Also, the number of question marks and exclamations was theirs. So, in November of 1995, they are telling us that some big change has taken place... and somehow it connects all of these things together with mind control.

> Q: (F) Twenty years ago there were no strobe lights on any of those vehicles mentioned. They had the old flasher type lights. Now, more and more and more there are strobe lights appearing in all kinds of places. (L) And now, they even have them on school buses! (T) And the regular city buses have them too, now. (L) Okay, is the strobing of a strobe light, set at a certain frequency in order to do certain things?
> A: Hypnotic opener. [...]
> Q: (L) What is the purpose of the hypnotic opener being used in this way?
> A: You don't notice the craft.
> Q: (L) Oh! So we may be being continuously flown over by alien craft...
> A: Assumption!

Now, notice that MY assumption was that this was to hide alien craft... but the C's came back pretty strongly that this was an assumption! The word "craft" takes us back to the listed plane crashes at the beginning of the session.

> Q: (T) Okay, what craft are we *not* seeing?
> A: Opener. Is precursor to suggestion, which is auditory in nature.
> Q: (L) Okay, you said the "suggestion is auditory in nature". If this is the case, where is the suggestion coming from auditorily?
> A: Where do you normally receive auditory suggestions from?
> Q: (L) Radio, television... (T) Telephone... (L) Is that what we are talking about?
> A: Yes.
> Q: (L) If you encounter a strobe while driving, or you are sitting in front of your television, then the suggestions can be put into you better because of this hypnotically opened state? Is that it?
> A: Yes.
> Q: (L) What are these suggestions designed to do, to suggest? In a general sense?
> A: Review.
> Q: (L) Not see the craft?
> A: Yes.
> Q: (T) Do we get these signals from the radio in the car even if it is turned off?
> A: Depends upon whether or not there is another source.
> Q: (T) Another source such as?
> A: ELP, for example.
> Q: (L) What is "ELP?"
> A: Extremely Low Pulse.
> Q: (T) ELF, Extremely Low Frequency, and ELP, Extremely Low Pulse - is this the same thing?
> A: Sometimes.

Remember what Dolan wrote? "A pocket-sized transmitter generating electromagnetic energy at less than 100 milliwatts could do the job."

Q: (T) This would be an external pulse or frequency?
A: Yes.
Q: (T) Would it be originating from the source of the strobe?
A: No. They act in unison.
Q: (T) Two separate sources acting in unison?
A: Close.
Q: (L) And this process prevents us from seeing something, such as craft flying in our skies at any given time?
A: Or maybe see them as something else.

And that sure did happen with the Pentagon plane. On August 24, 2002 we asked about the Pentagon Crash. Here is their answer.

Q: Did a Boeing 757, Flight 77, crash into the Pentagon?
A: No.
Q: What did produce the damage to the Pentagon?
A: It was very close to what you have surmised: a drone craft specially modified to give certain "impressions" to witnesses. Even the windows were not "real".
Q: What happened to Flight 77?
A: It was landed and now resides, in part, in fourth density.
Q: What do you mean by that?
A: As we have mentioned before, certain bases have this property due to direct interaction with denizens of that realm.
Q: What about the passengers? What happened to the humans?
A: Let us just say that the "human" part now resides at 5th density.
Q: Did they kill them and use parts of them for DNA identification?
A: "Parts" is the correct word.
Q: (Guest comments) Oh! I was hoping they were still alive somewhere!
A: Do you think that any of them could be "allowed" to survive?
Q: When you say that the plane is now partly in 4th density, do you mean it was "taken" while aloft, as happened to the military jet over Lake Michigan some years back? It was "absorbed" by a UFO? [Case described in detail in Dolan's book.]
A: It landed in the normal way.

At the same session quoted above, the Cassiopaeans commented on the Global Elite - the Fifth Column - behind the 9-11 event and its obvious schedule:

Q: Since we know from Dolan that the real "elite" are not those who form our visible government, do any of those in the White House have awareness of the *real* reason these plans are being driven at this time?
A: The White House knows little of what transpires in any case.
Q: Well, how can it be that there is an obvious global conspiracy, with countries that appear to be in opposition on the surface, that are actually working in concert? Who are the members of this global conspiracy? Who is driving them?
A: At those levels, there is only one "Master."
Q: How can they control not only America, but China, Russia, Israel,

Saudi Arabia, and all the rest? What "levels" do you mean?

A: Levels that can hand down orders to bury or suppress. Those who are at that level have been bought and paid for by both giving knowledge of upcoming cataclysmic events, and promised survival and positions of power after. It is not difficult to realize that there is a body of such types in positions of power already. Power is not only attractive to such types, they are the kind most easily corrupted by it.

And it all goes together with the material in Dolan's book about the under-ozone "neutral cavity"... chemtrails - being constantly bombarded with ELP - while strobes are entraining people's brains... microwave towers everywhere probably doing the job. You could think of the complete system as a mind control fence erected around the American people. Outrageous? Yes. Impossible? I don't think so.

And so we come back to the issue of just what the heck is going on, who's on first, and what is the hoped for outcome by these Controllers of our world?

Exploring the Labyrinth

As we saw in our little survey of history, there seem to be two main groups operating on the planet from time immemorial. What we also realize is that the "bad guys", so to say, have no qualms about lying and/or presenting themselves as "good guys", and even doing a lot of "nice" things for their subjects. We can compare this to the same care we might provide to valuable breeding stock that provide us with food and services.

In a world where hyperdimensional reality is the reality, where there exist beings capable of moving through space-time, where branching realities are not only a fact of life but one of the laws of physics, the bottom line is: it is extremely, extremely, difficult to figure out who or what to trust. And for those who are just certain that they have "psychic abilities", or that they can "remote view" or that they have "gut instincts" that will allow them to know who to trust, let me assure you that when you are dealing with hyperdimensional beings, the rules of your reality simply do not apply. You can take that to the bank. I have dealt with a number of cases where an individual has been utterly convinced that they were channeling Jesus, the Host of Heaven, or remote viewing "aliens" and perceiving their objectives with clarity. In every case, the facts turned out to be quite different - the person was thoroughly and masterfully duped and used.

G.I. Gurdjieff illustrated our predicament with the following tale:

"There is an Eastern tale which speaks about a very rich magician who had a great many sheep. But at the same time this magician was very mean. He did not want to hire shepherds, nor did he want to erect a fence about the pasture where his sheep were grazing. The sheep consequently often wandered into the forest, fell into ravines, and so on, and above all they ran away, for they knew that the magician wanted their flesh and skins and this they did not like.

At last the magician found a remedy. He hypnotized his sheep and suggested to them first of all that they were immortal and that no harm was being done to them when they were skinned, that, on the contrary, it would be very good for them and even pleasant; secondly he suggested that the magician was a good master who loved his flock so much that he was ready to do anything in the world for them; and in the third place he suggested to them that if anything at all were going to happen to them it was not going to happen just then, at any rate not that day, and therefore they had no need to think about it. Further the magician suggested to his sheep that they were not sheep at all; to some of them he suggested that they were lions, to others that they were eagles, to others that they were men, and to others that they were magicians.

And after this all his cares and worries about the sheep came to an end. They never ran away again but quietly awaited the time when the magician would require their flesh and skins."[252]

We certainly do not ask you to take our word for the existence of such beings, nor for anything else in this book. It is incumbent upon each of us to do the necessary research for ourselves. This higher reality – what we call fourth density – makes appearances in our world in many ways if one is open to the clues. Various anomalous events from UFOs to Fortean phenomena are regularly reported in the press, only to be derided and dismissed by people who either have never investigated such incidents for themselves, who have decided a priori that such manifestations are impossible, or who are paid to debunk them. Our own interest in these strange events is mostly to acknowledge their existence and see what they can tell us about reality, and about our own lack of understanding that tells us the things can't exist. Many of them lead us to infer that there is some intelligence behind them, often mischievous or even manipulating and malevolent.[253] To study the influence of this intelligence through history is to come to an understanding that it, or they, do not have the best interests of humanity at heart. Make no mistake, even if 4D is a higher reality, that does not mean that all its denizens are friendly or are the living manifestations of what we consider to be the higher values of truth, love, and beauty. Evolution has two paths, one rising towards creation, the other descending towards entropy. As strange as it may seem, one can choose to evolve towards hate and lies by focusing upon one's subjective needs and desires.

Ancient Civilisations and Tweaking Genes

And so we come to the elements that can help us solve the problem. Remember the "markers" that the C's gave? One of them was as follows: "Minneapolis banking scandal relates to mysterious Nordic covenant".

At the time of this list of markers, I thought it was a curious statement, but the only thing I knew about "Nordics" was that there were many claims being made about Nordic type aliens. In checking all the references, it was, again, distressingly confusing with most of it being identifiable as "bad guys", just to use the term loosely. I queried the C's:

---

[252] Gurdjieff, cited in P. Ouspensky, *In Search of the Miraculous*, Penguin Arkana Books, London, 1987, p. 219.
[253] The books of John Keel are good places to start.

Q: (L) Who are the Nordic type aliens?
A: Your ancestors.
Q: (L) What planet did they come from?
A: Several and transitory.
Q: (L) What is their type called? Just the Nordic types?
A: That is as good as any description.
Q: (L) What is their purpose here on the planet at this time?
A: Observation.
Q: (L) Haven't they been seen with the Lizzies on occasion?
A: Yes.
Q: (L) Are they involved with the Lizzies?
A: Some are.
Q: (L) Are some of them not nice?
A: Fifty-fifty.

At a later point in time, an individual entered my life through a series of "coincidences" that seemed very serendipitous and beneficial at the time. However, as the relations progressed, it became increasingly obvious that destruction had been sent into my life in the guise of "good". Again, I queried the C's about this matter and was surprised to learn that the individual was connected in some way to this "Nordic Covenant". Again, the emphasis was upon the fact that at the higher levels, there are good guys and bad guys, and that human beings can be easily manipulated and used against one another in these "games of the gods" without even being aware of it.

> Q: (L) The first inquiry I have is our situation relating to SV, and the different clues that we have received, and the different observations that I have made myself, and the discussions that we have had on the subject. Can you tell us anything in a general way, or do we really have to ask specific questions about the subject?
> A: SV is storehouse of vital information, clue for you was in name, but you failed to notice! This is why the frustration is for you; nothing of value comes without a price!! The price, my dear, continues...The Nordic Covenant was a duality. All persons of Nordic heritage hold secret power centers, can be of darkness, or of light... SV is of Teutonic bloodline leading directly to such super power sources as Thule Society and others, and she is aware of her powers and mission. It is of positive orientation. However, you are being tested by 4th through 6th density forces to determine if you have the strength and wisdom for continuance! [Always] check intent, however, malice is in absence. Notice the difference. The duality of covenant!!!

Naturally, the mention of the Thule Society rang bells in my head. Even though I was having difficulty grasping the ideas of how a seemingly innocent person with no malice, could be used in the way the C's described - to "test" me. Well, my reaction to that was that I didn't want to have anything to do with anything connected to the Thule society because of its connection to Hitler. I was frustrated because the C's were so ambiguous in their remarks about this matter. But finally, I decided that if the C's were in any way connected to this Thule Society, that they would have to go too. And as soon as I made that decision, the following exchange took place:

> Q: I am not comfortable with this information about SV. It seems to be contradictory to everything I can observe and feel.
> A: Worry not further! Discomfort is not necessarily danger, and is indicative of growth and learning. So, proceed and celebrate!!

I think that means I passed the test. But there was a reason I felt the way I did about the idea of the Thule society. Some time earlier I had queried the C's closely about Adolf Hitler. As we noted at the beginning of this monograph, the C's had informed us that the important thing about the Holocaust was not that anyone was Jewish in particular, but that it was the expunging of guilt for events that took place at the time of the destruction of Atlantis. In fact, this issue, in the context of a possible alien invasion was brought up in the earliest contacts with the C's:

> Q: (L) Bob Lazar referred to the fact that aliens supposedly refer to humans as containers. What does this mean?
> A: Later use.
> Q: (L) Use by who? How many:
> A: 94 per cent of all population. All are containers; 94 per cent use will be used. Consumed for ingredients.
> Q: (L) Why?
> A: New race. Important. 13 years about when happens.
> Q: (L) Why are humans consumed?
> A: They are used for parts.
> Q: (L) We don't understand. How can humans be used for parts?
> A: Reprototype. Vats exist. Missing persons often go there and especially missing children.
> Q: (L) How can we protect ourselves and our children?
> A: Inform them. Don't hide the truth from children.
> Q: (L) How does truth protect us?
> A: Awareness protects. Ignorance endangers.
> Q: (L) What is the purpose of this project?
> A: New life here.
> Q: (L) Are the aliens using our emotions and energies?
> A: Correct; and bodies too. Each earth year 10 percent more children are taken.
> Q: Who is responsible for this?
> A: Consortium.
> Q: (C) This is totally sick! I don't want to do this any more!
> A: Sick is subjective.
> Q: (L) But what you are telling us is so awful!
> A: Understand, but all does not conform to your perspective.
> Q: Why is this happening to us?

A: Karma.

Q: (L) What kind of Karma could bring this?

A: Atlantis.

Now that we have come to the subject of Atlantis, let me just assemble a selection of text from the C's that will give a quick background for understanding the possible dynamics of our present situation:

Q: (L) Was Noah's flood caused by the close passage of another celestial body?

A: Yes.

Q: (L) Which body was that?

A: Martek. Mars.

Q: (L) Was Martek an inhabited planet at that time?

A: No.

Q: (L) Did it have water or other features?

A: Yes.

Q: (L) When it passed close to the earth did it, in fact, overload our planet with water we did not have prior to that time?

A: Yes.

Q: (L) Did we, prior to that time, have a water-vapor canopy surrounding our planet as some theorists have suggested?

A: Yes.

Q: (L) Was it a cosmic event that brought about the death of the dinosaurs?

A: Yes.

Q: (L) Did it happen before the flood of Noah?

A: Yes.

Q: (L) How many thousands of years ago counting backward?

A: 27 million years ago.[254]

Q: (L) What event took place at that time that caused the death of the dinosaurs?

A: Cometary showers.

Q: (L) Is there any regular periodicity or cycle to this comet business?

A: Yes.

Q: (L) What is the period?

A: 3600 years roughly.

Q: (L) Where are these cometary showers from?

A: Clusters in own orbit.

Q: (L) Does this cluster of comets orbit around the sun?

A: Yes.

Q: (L) Is the orbit perpendicular to the plane of the ecliptic?

A: Yes and no.

Q: (L) Does this cluster come into the plane of the ecliptic and cause havoc in the solar system?

---

[254] Yes, I know that "standard texts" say 65 million years ago. But we have already covered the issue of radiometric dating, and so rather than stumble over this figure - when the C's have been so correct on so many other things, perhaps we ought to just let it stand as possible.

A: Exactly.

Q: (L) Is this cluster of comets the remains of a planet?

A: No.

Q: (L) Is the cluster of fragments in between the orbits of Mars and Jupiter the remains of a planet?

A: Yes.

Q: (L) What was that planet known as?

A: Kantek.

Q: (L) When did that planet break apart into the asteroid belt.

A: 79 to 80 thousand years ago approximately.

Q: (L) What body were the Sumerians talking about when they described the Planet of the crossing or Nibiru?

A: Comets.

Q: (L) This body of comets?

A: Yes.

Q: (L) Does this cluster of comets appear to be a single body?

A: Yes.

Q: (L) Is this the same object that is rumored to be on its way here at the present time?

A: Yes.

Q: (L) Who were the Annunaki?

A: Aliens.

Q: (L) Where were they from?

A: Zeta Reticuli.

Q: (L) Do they come here every time the comet cluster is approaching to sap the souls energy created by the fear, chaos and so forth?

A: Yes.

Q: (L) The two events are loosely interrelated?

A: Yes.

Q: (L) Is that why they are here now?

A: Close.

Q: (L) Is there a large fleet of space-ships riding a wave, so to speak, approaching our planet as one of my abductee hypnosis subjects said?

A: Yes.

Q: (L) Where are these ships from?

A: Zeta Reticuli.

Q: (L) When will they arrive?

A: 1 month to 18 years.

Q: (L) How can there be such a vast discrepancy in the time?

A: This is such a huge fleet that space/time warping is irregular and difficult to determine as you measure time.

Q: (L) Are these craft riding a "wave" of some sort?

A: Yes. Your government already knows they're coming close again.

Q: (L) How big is the biggest one at this time?

A: 900 miles diameter. Spirograph.

Q: (L) What is the origin of the Aryan race?

A: 5th planet now known as asteroid belt.

Q: (L) When did they come to earth?

A: 80 thousand years ago. Difficult for us to use your measuring system.

Q: (L) Were they similar in form and structure to what they are now?

A: Yes. Blond and blue eyed descendants.

Q: (L) Was that planet much like earth?

A: Yes.

A: Blue eyes. Eye pigment was because planet was farther from Sol.

Q: (L) How did the people of that planet come to earth? Did they know it was going to be destroyed?

A: Some knew and were taken by Lizzies and they are the Annunaki.

Q: (L) Where do the Celts come from?

A: Same. Ferocious people. Came from fifth planet.

Q: Okay. I would like to know the geographic coordinates, according to our current grid system, that would frame Atlantis. I don't need the exact shape, just a general box shape... the perimeter...

A: Like asking: "What are the geographic coordinates of the North Atlantic Treaty Organization?"

Q: Okay, let me get more specific: the Atlantean land that was supposed to have existed in the Atlantic Ocean... what was the farthest north of any part of Atlantis that was in the ocean, that no longer exists?

A: It is "time for you" to know that Atlantis was not a nation, land, Island, or continent, but rather, a civilization! [The civilization of that time was global.]

Remember, the sea level was several hundred feet lower then...

Q: Why was the sea level several hundred feet lower? Because there was ice somewhere or because there was not as much water on the earth at that time?

A: Ice.

Q: Was the ice piled up at the poles? The ice sheet of the ice age?

A: Yes.

Q: So, Atlantis existed during the ice age?

A: Largely, yes. And the world's climate was scarcely any colder away from the ice sheets than it is today.

Q: Well, how could that be? What caused these glaciers?

A: Global warming.

Q: How does global warming cause glaciers?

A: Increases precipitation dramatically. Then moves the belt of great precipitation much farther north. This causes rapid buildup of ice sheets, followed by increasingly rapid and intense glacial rebound.

Q: (L) Was the story of Noah's flood the story of the breaking up of Atlantis?

A: Yes. But symbolic.

Q: (L) How many people were on the planet at that time?

A: 6 billion.

Q: There are legends of half human creatures, minotaurs, centaurs, etc. Were any of these creatures real?

A: Experiments known as beasts in Atlantis.

Q: Who built the temple of Baalbek?

A: Atlantean descendants.

Q: What is the reason for the enormous proportions of this building?

A: Giants. Genetic effort to recreate Nephalim.

Q: Did the Atlanteans succeed in recreating the Nephilim?

A: No. Retarded subjects.

Q: Why did they build the enormous city?

A: In anticipation of success.

Q: Why would someone come along and build a city of the proportions of Baalbek in anticipation of a genetic project that could take many years to accomplish.

A: Project took only three years. Speeded up growth cycle using nuclear hormonal replication procedure. Why failed. Did not take properly.

Q: What technical means did they use to cut the stones and transport them?

A: Sound wave focusing.

Q: What happened to interrupt or halt the building of this city?

A: Venus first appearance and pass.

Q: What year was this project brought to a halt?

A: 3218 B.C.

Q: Who built the city of Mohenjo-Daro?

A: Lizards directly. Coatzlmundi legend ties in to this directly look at illustrations on stones now.

Q: Who is Coatzlmundi?

A: Other deity of the Lizards worshipped by the Atlanteans and their descendants because of the direct contact with humans for 1000 years during peak of Atlantis.

Q: I would like to go back to the subject of the Nephilim. Now, the other night when we lost the tape, you said the Nephilim were a group of humanoid types brought here to earth to be enforcers, is that correct?

A: Yes.

Q: When were they brought here?

A: 9046 B.C. one reference.

Q: They were giants, is that correct?

A: Yes.

Q: They were presented to the people as the representatives, or "Sons" of God, is that correct?

A: Yes.

Q: You say these dudes were 11 to 14 feet tall...

A: Yes.

Q: You and the ancient literature say that these sons of god intermarried with human women, is that correct?

A: Yes.

Q: Did they do that the same way it is done today, that is, sexual interaction?

A: No.

Q: How was it done?

A: Forced insemination.

Q: So, it was artificial insemination?

A: Close.

Q: Were these beings like us, including their sexual apparati?

A: Close.

Q: Any significant differences?

A: Three gonads.

Q: Was their sexual apparatus otherwise similar?

A: Yes.

Q: Did they mate with human females in a normal way at any time?

A: No.

Q: Why not?

A: Size difference.

Q: Just for the sake of curiosity, just how different in terms of size?

A: 23 inches long.[255]

Q: (T) Is the government planning to stage an invasion by aliens to cause the populace of the world to go into such a fear state that they will accept total control and domination?

A: Open. But if so, will "flop".

Q: (T) Why?

A: Many reasons: 1. Visual effects will be inadequate and will have "glitches". 2. Real invasion may take place first. 3. Other events may intercede.

Q: (T) Such as what?

A: Earth changes.

Q: (T) Am I correct in assuming that some of these hot-shot, big-wig guys in the government who have plans for taking over the whole world and making everything all happy and hunky-dory with them in charge, are just simply not in synch with the fact that there are some definite earth changes on the agenda? Are they missing something here?

A: Close. They are aware but in denial.

Q: (T) Are these earth changes going to occur prior to the arrival of the cometary cluster?

A: No. But "time" frame is, as of yet, undetermined.

Q: (T) Am I correct in saying that if they knew what was really going to happen that they would still continue with their stupid little plans to make money and try to control the world?

A: Yes. Greed is a sickness.

Q: (T) Is there such a thing as "alternative three" the plan to take all the brains off the planet?

A: No.

Q: (T) Is that more disinformation?

A: Yes. So is Mars landing but not Mars monuments.

Q: (TL) Who made the monuments on Mars?

A: Atlanteans.

Q: (T) So, the Atlanteans had inter-planetary ability?

A: Yes. With ease. Atlantean technology makes yours look like the Neanderthal era.

Q: (T) Who created the structures on the moon that Richard Hoagland has discovered?

A: Atlanteans.

---

[255] The reader should be alerted to the fact that my curiosity is not idle. My point was to ascertain the reasonableness of the C's answers, and also to gather data for checking and comparing with other sources.

Q: (T) What did they use these structures for?
A: Energy transfer points for crystalline power/symbolism as in monuments or statuary.
Q: (T) What statuary are you referring to?
A: Example is face.
Q: (T) What power did these crystals gather?
A: Sun.
Q: (T) Was it necessary for them to have power gathering stations on Mars and the Moon. Did this increase their power?
A: Not necessary but it is not necessary for you to have a million dollars either. Get the correlation? Atlanteans were power hungry the way your society is money hungry.
Q: (T) Was the accumulation of this power what brought about their downfall?
A: Yes.
Q: (T) Did they lose control of this power?
A: It overpowered them the same way your computers will overpower you.
Q: (V) Is it similar to them gaining a life and intelligence of their own?
A: Yes.
Q: (L) You mean these crystalline structures came to life, so to speak?
A: Yes.
Q: (L) And then what did they do?
A: Destroyed Atlantis.
Q: (L) But I thought that Atlantis was destroyed because of the close passage of another body of the solar system?
A: Was damaged but recovered.
Q: (L) So Atlantis was damaged by a close passage of Mars or whatever and then recovered from that damage, is that correct?
A: Part of landmass, but not all, was destroyed.
Q: (L) So, how many separate destructions did Atlantis experience?
A: Three.
Q: (L) One was caused by the close passage of Mars?
A: Yes. And comets.
Q: (L) Was Mars and the comets loosely interactive?
A: Yes.
Q: (L) And the second was caused by what?
A: Venus.
Q: (L) And the third and final destruction was caused by what?
A: Crystals.

Now we have a somewhat better idea of what was going on in Atlantis and why the C's have said that the planetary karma is related to Atlantis. What is curious is why so many New Age and esoteric types glorify Atlantis and its offspring, Egypt.

Is there any "hard" evidence for this ancient, worldwide, high civilization? I don't want to spend too much time going over all of it and attempting to reproduce the fine efforts of other writers. But, just to cover the subject briefly, one of the most telling pieces of hard evidence is included in Charles Hapgood's book, Maps of the Ancient Sea Kings.

Charles Hapgood heard about these maps when he was studying the ice ages. A copy of an ancient map had been found in the Topkapi Palace in Istanbul in 1929, and a Turkish naval officer had presented a copy of it to the US Navy Hydrographic Office. It was examined by scholars who noted that the map represented Antarctica before it was covered with ice, yet, the map was painted on parchment and was dated to 1513, over 300 years before Antarctica was officially "discovered".

Core samples taken by the Byrd Antarctic Expedition showed that the last warm period in the Antarctic ended around 4,000 B.C.. It began about 9,000 years before that. The only conclusion that could be drawn was that someone had mapped Antarctica at least 6,000 years ago. Hapgood discovered that there were more of these ancient maps - portolans, as they are called - and that some of them strongly indicate that the mapmaker had an aerial view of what he was mapping!

By a series of analyses, Hapgood and others came to the conclusion that there was an ancient civilization whose center or "home base" was Antarctica itself.[256] The fact that it was a global society, just as our own is, was also evident from other clues. This was, to put it mildly, not an acceptable idea to the uniformitarian view of evolution.

Dr. Hapgood never used the word "Atlantis" in his book. He knew the value of his academic reputation and that he just couldn't go there. But that was not a problem for Erich von Daniken.

Von Daniken's book, Chariots of the Gods? came out in 1967 and proposed that the ancient portolans, side by side with other anomalies, suggested the presence and influence of extraterrestrial "gods" in ancient times. I find this to be a curious sort of "damage control" that attempts to support the uniformitarian hypothesis since it suggests strongly that mankind himself was incapable of creating an advanced civilization on his own.

Coming along behind Von Daniken is Zecharia Sitchin who suggests that civilization was instigated by beings from a tenth planet in our solar system and that human beings themselves were genetically engineered by these same beings around 450,000 years ago. Basing his theory on strictly three-dimensional aliens with more or less human limitations, but advance knowledge, leaves too many questions either unanswerable or with answers that are absurd. As a theory that can predict, it is too full of holes. When the concepts of hyper-dimensionality are included in the fundamental idea of "inspiration" for civilization and scientific development, it makes some strange sense. However, that, of course, excludes the "creators" or sources of inspiration from physically residing

---

[256] Rand and Rose Flem-Ath, *When the Sky Fell*, 1995, St. Martins, Canada

on a tenth planet, and leaves them free to come and go as they choose from wherever they are to wherever they wish to go in the universe via hyperdimensional physics, space/time transfer, which is what they seem to be doing anyway. This then obviates the need for a 10th planet as part of the explanation altogether.

The Martian hypothesis is also very popular nowadays, promoted by many people who ought to be able to think out of the box in a more creative way than that. Again, why does civilization have to have originated somewhere else and come to Earth? It is a far more reasonable hypothesis that a high civilization developed on Earth (even if inspired from elsewhere, assuming that this happened), and that this former civilization had space travel capabilities. If there are monuments on Mars that are similar to structures on Earth, why couldn't they have been built by space travelers from Earth *to* Mars, rather than vice versa?

Von Daniken and Sitchin, and many others, are still inculcated with the notion that our ancestors were fundamentally stupid. They have the idea that any technological sophistication must have been brought from somewhere else because they simply can't erase the image of the howling savages with bear grease in their hair that has been so thoroughly implanted in the perception of our culture. More significantly, they don't want to think about what could happen to wipe such a civilization from the face of the earth.

Plato and the Vedas both suggest exactly that: mankind did create an advanced civilization. What is more, they both tell us that there was a terrible, ancient war. The Vedas talk about flying machines and nuclear bombs. In the Timaeus, Plato tells us that the conflict was between Atlantis and Europe, and that it was in full fury around twelve thousand years ago. He records that the Atlanteans had conquered Europe as far as Italy, and North Africa as far as Libya, and it was the Athenians who finally conquered Atlantis. Shortly after, both Atlantis and Athens were destroyed in a global catastrophe.

The idea of a global civilization being destroyed in a "single day and night" is not, to understate the matter, a thought that one wishes to contemplate in any serious terms for any lengthy period of time. Science avoids having to do so by negating it as a possibility.

I would like to add the one point that never seems to be mentioned even conjecturally, and it is this: if an ancient civilization was so advanced, particularly if there were "aliens" in charge, why weren't they aware of the impending disaster? The cheap excuse that it was a "punishment from God" doesn't get it if the gods were aliens because if they did destroy the civilizations of the earth, they effectively dirtied their own nest and damaged their own "possession".

The ancient sources do tell us that some few humans survived - those who were "warned" and told how to prepare to survive. Is that what is going on today? Does the elite, the Global Controllers in contact with hyperdimensional beings, consider themselves the new "Noahs"? Perhaps there are "gods" of some sort, and they do not want everybody to know the truth? Perhaps there are beings of some sort with an agenda?

In this sense, a comparison of the ancient civilization to the state of our own might be a useful idea. Perhaps the ancient people were vulnerable because they simply did not consider such a possibility? Perhaps, just like us, their "science" assured them that such a thing was either impossible or so unlikely that they didn't have to worry about a thing. Perhaps, like ours, their science was uniformitarian also, and they closed their eyes and minds to potentials, thereby leaving themselves altogether vulnerable to sudden disaster. Perhaps they were lied to as we are?

In Matthew 24, Jesus points out that right up to the moment of the disaster in the days of Noah, people were "eating and drinking and marrying", and essentially conducting their lives with no thought whatsoever for what was about to fall upon them. So it seems that, another of the conditions of "as it was in the days of Noah" is a socio-cultural milieu that is in denial about possibilities and potentials of terrestrial cataclysm. That is, most definitely, our present state. We should like to know if this condition serves some hidden agenda of some thing or someone?

When we travel back in time and peer into the darkness of millennia past, we detect that most amazing moment in time wherein there was such an odd occurrence, such a peculiarity in thinking, that it staggers the mind to consider it. I am speaking of the introduction of the concept of monotheism and the fact that this singular event was the bedrock from which our modern conceptions of Time, the platform of our present civilization arose. What sort of imagination and response to life gave birth to this idea?

Of course, we come to the fact that it was among the Jews that Monotheism was born, and who "kept the faith" for, as they claim, five thousand years. Not only that, but they have done so in the face of what seems to be absolutely outrageous persecution.

Q: (L) Well, then how did mankind come to be here?
A: Combination of factors. Numerous souls desired physical existence then was altered by three forces including principally Lizards through Grays, Nephalim and Orion union.
Q: (L) You said the other night that the Nephalim came from some area around the constellation Scorpio, is that correct?
A: Originally seeded there but you were too.
Q: (L) We were originally seeded somewhere else? Where? Orion? What is the name of that planet?
A: D'Ankhiar. Ankh is ancient symbolism of this planet. Is female symbol. Stands for mother planet.

Q: (L) What was the Fruit of the tree of Knowledge of Good and Evil that was supposedly eaten by Eve and then offered to Adam?

A: Knowledge restriction. Encoding.

Q: (L) What did it mean when it said Eve ate of the fruit of the tree of knowledge? What act did she perform to do that?

A: Consorted with wrong side.

Q: (L) What does consorted mean?

A: Eve is symbolic.

Q: (L) Symbolic of what?

A: Female energy.

Q: (L) The female energy did what when it consorted?

A: Lost some knowledge and power. If the concept was the eating of the fruit of the tree of knowledge provides all knowledge, then one is being deceived, because no one particular source can provide all knowledge. Therefore, when one believes in the deception, one has now trapped oneself within parameters. And, forevermore, the human race, will be poisoned by the very same problem which is reflected in several different ways: one is always seeking the truth through one pathway instead of seeking it through a myriad of pathways; and also believing in simplistic answers to very complex issues and questions .

Q: (L) Where was Eden?

A: Earth.

Q: (L) The entire earth was Eden?

A: Yes.

Q: (L) Was the "fall" in Eden, or the loss of the Edenic state, also accompanied by a cataclysm?

A: Yes.

Q: (L) What was the nature of that cataclysm?

A: Comets.

Q: (L) The cluster you have mentioned before?

A: Yes.

Q: (L) And, how long ago did this occur?

A: 309882 years ago.

Q: (L) Was the loss of the Edenic state also accompanied by a takeover of mankind by the Lizzies?

A: Yes.

Q: (L) At one point we were told that time was an illusion that came into being at the "time" of the "Fall" in Eden, and this was said in such a way that I inferred that there were other illusions put into place at that time...

A: Time is an illusion that works for you because of your altered DNA state.

Q: (L) Okay, what other illusions?

A: Monotheism, the belief in one separate, all powerful entity.

Q: (T) Is separate the key word in regard to Monotheism?

A: Yes.

Q: (L) What is another one of the illusions?

A: The need for physical aggrandizement.

Q: (L) The focus on the physical as the thing one needs to hold onto or protect.

A: Yes.

Q: (L) What is another of the illusions?

A: Linear focus.

Q: (L) Anything else at this time?

A: Unidimensionality.

Q: (L) The veil... (J) The perception of only one dimension... (L) Were these illusions programmed into us genetically through our DNA?

A: Close.

Q: (L) The other night we were talking about the "Mark of Cain" and I lost part of the tape. I would like to go back over that a little bit more at this time. What was the true event behind the story of the "Mark of Cain"?

A: Advent of jealousy.

Q: (L) What occurred to allow jealousy to enter into human interaction?

A: Lizard takeover.

Q: (L) Wasn't the Lizard takeover an event that occurred at the time of the fall of Eden?

A: Yes.

Q: (L) Was this story of Cain and Abel part of that takeover?

A: Symbolism of story.

Q: (L) This was symbolic of the Lizzie takeover, the advent of jealousy, and the attitude of brother against brother, is that correct?

A: Partly. The mark of Cain means the "jealousy factor" of change facilitated by Lizard takeover of earth's vibrational frequency. Knot on spine is physical residue of DNA restriction deliberately added by Lizards. See?

Q: (L) You mean the occipital ridge?

A: Yes.

Q: (L) What was the configuration of the spine and skull prior to this addition?

A: Spine had no ridge there. Jealousy emanates from there, you can even feel it.

Q: (L) Okay, at the time this "Mark of Cain" came about, were there other humans on the planet that did not have this configuration?

A: It was added to all simultaneously.

Q: (L) How did they physically go about performing this act? What was the mechanism of this event, the nuts and bolts of it?

A: Are you ready? DNA core is as yet undiscovered enzyme relating to carbon. Light waves were used to cancel the first ten factors of DNA by burning them off. At that point, a number of physical changes took place including knot at top of spine. Each of these is equally reflected in the ethereal.

Q: (L) Well, the question I do have is, how many people were there on the planet and did they have to take each one and do this individually?

A: 6 billion.

Q: (T) That's 500 million more than there are now.

A: No, 200 million.

Q: (L) Okay, there were this many people on the planet, how did they effect this change on all of them?

A: Light wave alteration.

Q: (L) And light waves, actual light waves, affect DNA?

A: Yes.

Q: (T) What was the origin of the light waves?

A: Our center. Our realm. STO.

Q: (L) So, how did the Lizzies use the light from the Service to Others realm...

A: They used sophisticated technology to interrupt light frequency waves.

In short, what the Cassiopaeans were suggesting was that all monotheistic, "we have the only version of God that is right", religions are part and parcel of the hyperdimensional control system. But it is obvious that Monotheism was not the mode of religion over all the earth for many millennia, not even among the Jews. What does seem to be so is that this idea was "reintroduced" at periodic intervals, and the Jews have been singled out for the honor most recently. And this "honor" has brought them nothing but grief. And that, of course, leads us to ask why?

Q: (L) I am curious about what I call the "Scottish Question". Why is it that every time I start a paper trail on any issue of conspiracy, there always seems to be a link to Scotland and Scots?

A: "Celtic", what does it mean?

Q: (L) Well, the word "kilt" comes from "Celtic", but no one seems to know where they originated... they just sort of appeared on the landscape, so to speak.

A: Exactly!

Q: (L) So, there is some interesting connection! (RC) Does it mean "warrior race"?

A: If you prefer! We have close affiliation with the "Northern Peoples". Why? Because we were in regular, direct contact with them on Kantek, before they were "lifted" to Earth by Orion STS.

Q: (L) If you were in direct contact with them, how come they were in cahoots with the Orion STS bunch?

A: Who says they are in "kahoots"?

Q: (L) Weren't they rescued by the Orion STS?

A: Yes. But one need not be in "kahoots" to be rescued!!!

Q: (L) Well, if the Orion STS brought the Celts here, they must have brought them for their own purposes, am I correct?

A: Essentially, but herein lies the reason why you need a review. You see, you have some gaps in your knowledge base which are caused by channeling, absorbing and analyzing information out of sequence with what we have given you and mixing it all together! You are doing wonderfully, my dear, but it is difficult for you to keep up this way, because your natural drive for the truth makes you impatient, and therefore you tend to fill in the gaps with simple reasoning and assumptions. While these are often correct, they can tend to allow you to get ahead of yourself.

Q: (L) Okay, square one: Is there a group composed of humans who have been alchemists, who are presently in possession of a substance called "the elixir of life" and which David Hudson calls "monoatomic gold"[257]?

A: And much, much more! Monoatomic gold is but one minor issue here. Why get lead astray by focusing upon it solely. It would be akin to focusing on the fact that "Batman" can fly! Is that the only important thing that "Batman" does in the story? Is it? Alchemy is but one minor piece of the puzzle.

Q: (L) Okay, I understand. But, understanding the alchemical connection, and its potential for extending life and opening certain abilities, makes it more feasible to think of a group that has been present steadily and consistently for many thousands of years on earth.

A: They are not the only ones! Let us go to the root. Who, or what made you?

Q: (RC) The Creator. (L) Prime Creator.

A: How? And who is Prime Creator?

Q: (L) Everything, I guess.

A: You are "Prime Creator". Prime Creator Manifests IN you. But... who was secondary?

Q: (RC) The Sons of God? The Elohim?

A: Who is that? Remember, your various legends are "seen through a veil".

Q: (RC) Okay, getting back to the Celts, were the Pleiadians the secondary creators who brought in the Celts?

A: Review what we have just said!

Q: (L) They said it was the Orions. Are the Orions these secondary creators? (RC) Well, I read that it was the Pleiadians. And the Hebrews were originally the Hoovids who came from Sirius...

A: Here comes a shocker for you... one day, in 4th density, it will be your descendants mission to carry on the tradition and assignment of seeding the 3rd density universe, once you have the adequate knowledge!!!

Q: (L) If the Orion STS brought the Celts here, were the Celts, while they lived on Kantek, in the form they are in now?

A: They were lighter in appearance.

Q: (L) You have told us on other occasions that the Semitic peoples were remnants of the Atlanteans, and yet they are quite unlike...

A: Whoa!! Wait a minute, let's not get ahead of ourselves. First things first. What RC said was not entirely factual. Remember, there is much disinformation to weed through.

Q: (RC) What did I say that was not factual?

A: In this part of your 3rd and 4th density universe, specifically your "galaxy" it is the region known as Orion that is the one and only indigenous home of human type beings... reflect on this! Indigenous home base, not sole locator. What you are most in need of review of is the accurate profile of "alien" data.

Q: (RC) I thought that humans originated in Lyra and then a war broke

---

[257] In a later session, we asked the C's again about monoatomic gold:

Q: (L) Now, we have wondered about obtaining and taking some of this Monoatomic Gold.

A: Are you serious? How about some small helpings of arsenic, anyone?

out there and they ended up in Orion.

A: Lyra is not inhabited. There have been homes in all places, but some were/are transitory, and some are not. Pay attention to Orion! This is your ancestral home, and your eventual destination. Here is the absolutely accurately accurate profile of Orion to follow: This is the most heavily populated region of your Milky Way galaxy! This is a region that extends across 3rd and 4th density space for a distance as vast as the distance between your locator and it. There are 3,444 inhabited "worlds" in this region. Some are planets as you know them. Some are artificially constructed planetoids. Some are floating space barges. And some are "satellites". There are primary homes, traveling stations and incubator laboratories all in 2nd, 3rd and 4th densities. There are overseer zones in 5th and 6th densities. Approximately one half is STO and one half is STS. Together, along with many other colonies, located elsewhere, this is called, in translation, Orion Federation. Orions created grays in 5 varieties, as cybergenetic beings, and installed them on Zeta Reticuli 1, 2, 3 and 4, as well as on 2 planets orbiting Barnard's Star. The Reptilians also inhabit 6 planets in the Orion region in 4th density, and are owned by the Orion STS as slaves, and, in some cases, pets!!! The name "Orion" is the actual native name, and was brought to earth directly. Study the legend of the "god" of Orion for parallels.

Q: (L) Are the Orion STS the infamous red-headed Nordic aliens?

A: Yes, and all other humanoid combinations.

Q: (L) Okay, if it started with the Nordic types, and that is where the other humanoid combinations came from, what genetic combinations were used for human beings? Black people, for instance, since they are so unlike "Nordics"?

A: The Nordic genes were mixed with the gene pool already available on Earth, known as Neanderthal.

Q: (L) What was the genetic combination used to obtain the Oriental races?

A: Orientals come from a region known in your legends as "Lemuria", and are a previous hybridization from 7 genetic code structures from within Orion Union, designed to best fit the earth climate and cosmic ray environment then existent on earth.

Q: (L) Okay, what about the Semitic and Mediterranean peoples?

A: Each time a new flock was "planted", it was engineered to be best suited to the environment where it was planted. Aryans are the only exception, as they had to be moved to earth in an emergency.

Q: (L) If races are engineered on earth to be "best suited", what factors are being drawn from - or considered - regarding the Semitic race?

A: They are not engineered on earth, but in Orion lab as all others. They were "Planted" in the Middle East.

Q: (L) If a lot of the information that is being propagated these days is confusion or disinformation, what is the purpose of all this?

A: You answered yourself: Confusion and disinformation.

Q: (L) I want to know who, exactly, and why, exactly, genetically engineered the Semitic people, and why there is such an adversarial attitude between them and the Celts and Aryans.

A: It is not just between the Jews and Celts, if you will take notice. Besides, it is the individual aural profile that counts and not groupings or classifications. But, to answer your question: there are many reasons both from on and off the planet.

Q: (L) Why was Hitler so determined, beyond all reason, even to his own self-destruction, to annihilate the Jews?

A: Many reasons and very complex. But, remember, while still a child, Hitler made a conscious choice to align himself with the "forces of darkness", in order to fulfill his desires for conquest and to unite the Germanic peoples. Henceforth, he was totally controlled, mind, body, and soul, by STS forces.

Q: (L) So, what were the purposes of the STS forces that were controlling Hitler causing him to desire to annihilate an entire group of people?

A: To create an adequate "breeding ground" for the reintroduction of the Nephalim, for the purpose of total control of the 3rd density earth prior to elevation to 4th density, where such conquest is more difficult and less certain!

Q: (L) Do you mean "breeding ground" in the sense of genetic breeding?

A: Yes. Third density.

Q: (L) Did they accomplish this goal?

A: No.

Q: (L) So, the creation of the Germanic "Master Race" was what they were going after, to create this "breeding ground"?

A: Yes.

Q: (L) And, getting rid of the Jews was significant? Couldn't a Germanic master race be created without destroying another group?

A: No.

Q: Why?

A: Because of 4th density prior encoding mission destiny profile.

Q: (L) What does that mean?

A: This means encoding to activate after elevation to 4th density, thus if not eliminated, negates Nephalim domination and absorption. Jews were prior encoded to carry out mission after conversion, though on individual basis. The Nazis did not exactly know why they were being driven to destroy them, because they were being controlled from 4th density STS. But, Hitler communicated directly with Lizards, and Orion STS, and was instructed on how to create the "master race".

Q: (L) And they were going to use this as their basis to introduce a new blend of the Nephilim... (RC) And the New World Order... their version of it. (L) Well, what is the plan now?

A: We cannot tell you this yet, as you would seek to reveal it prematurely, leading to your destruction!!!!

Q: (L) Meanwhile, back to the Celts: obviously if the Lizard Beings thought that the Aryans/Celts were a good breeding ground for this "Nephilim Master Race", then it must be because there is something genetically inherent in them that makes them desirable in this sense. Is this correct?

A: No, not in the sense you are thinking. We suggest that you rephrase this question after careful reflection on the implications.

And so I did. I thought long and hard about the idea that there was something significant in Jewish genetics and how cleverly and effectively they had been "fenced in" by their religion. I began to think that it must be true that the Brotherhood of the Serpent was really behind Judaism. I began to see that the Jewish claims of "chosenness" and their separation from humanity had been by design. What better way to convince them to "keep their genes to themselves". Particularly, if there was something important in their genetics that could get in the way of the plans of the Elite Control System to take over the world. I also realized that the related question might be, what is there specifically about Aryan genes that might be modified by the mixing with this particular genetic codon carried by Jews?

Q: (L) I have thought about my question from the last session and I want to ask it this way: You have said that Hitler received instructions from higher density beings about creating a 'Master Race'. Why were the Aryan genetic types seen to be more desirable for creation of this Germanic 'master race'?

A: Both, similarity and ancestral link most unblemished from Orion 3rd and 4th density stock.

Q: (L) So they were essentially trying to breed a group of people like themselves?

A: Yes.

Q: (L) Okay, what is it about the Semitic genes that was considered to be so undesirable in the creation of this 'Master Race?'?

A: Would blemish genetic characteristics inclined to ruthlessness and domination.

Q: (L) So, you are saying that there is something, some genetic tendency or set of genes in the Semitic type that would counteract this?

A: Close.

Q: (L) But isn't the nature of a person determined by their soul and not the physical body?

A: Partially, remember, aural profile and karmic reference merges with physical structure.

Q: (L) So you are saying that particular genetic conditions are a physical reflection of a spiritual orientation? That the soul must match itself to the genetics, even if only in potential?

A: Yes, precisely.

Q: (L) So a person's potential for spiritual advancement or unfoldment is, to a great extent, dependent upon their genes?

A: Natural process marries with systematic construct when present.

Q: (L) Well, if that is the case, and the aliens are abducting people and altering their genes, can they not alter the genes so that higher level souls simply cannot come in?

A: Not incarnative process, natural biological processes. Incarnative involves strictly ethereal at 5th density and lower, and thus is enveloped in triple cycle "veil" of transfer which is impregnable by any means.

However, any and all 1st, 2nd, 3rd, and 4th processes can be manipulated at will and to any degree if technology is sufficient. [...]

There is actually something rather more significant in the above remarks. We noted that, in the previous attempt to "recreate the Nephilim", as the C's called it, they had said that the experiment failed because the subjects were "retarded". The exact remarks were, "speeded up growth cycle using nuclear hormonal replication procedure. Why failed. Did not take properly". Since this experiment supposedly took place in the Middle East, in Baalbek, Lebanon, it seems that it is very likely that Jews were the subjects.[258] And we suspect that this is when it was decided that the Jews had to be eliminated. Because, it seems that there is more to this plan than meets the eye.

Q: You say that there is an effort on the part of these beings to create a new race. Why do they want or need a new race?
A: Theirs no longer satisfies them. [...] The concept of a "master race" put forward by the Nazis was merely a 4th density STS effort to create a physical vehicle with the correct frequency resonance vibration for 4th density STS souls to occupy in 3rd density. It was also a "trial run" for planned events in what you perceive to be your future.
Q: (L) You mean with a strong STS frequency so they can have a "vehicle" in 3rd density, so to speak?
A: Correct. Frequency resonance vibration! Very important.
Q: (L) So, that is why they are programming and experimenting? And all these folks running around who some think are "programmed", could be individuals who are raising their nastiness levels high enough to accommodate the truly negative STS 4th density - sort of like walk-ins or something, only not nice ones?
A: You do not have very many of those present yet, but that was, and still is, the plan of some of the 4th density STS types.
Q: Okay, you brought up the subject of Frequency Resonance Vibration. You suggested that there are certain STS forces who are developing or creating or managing physical bodies that they are trying to increase the frequency in so that they will have bodies that are wired so that they can manifest directly into 3rd density, since that seems to be the real barrier that prevents an all-out invasion, the fact that we are in 3rd density and they are in 4th. Now, I assumed that the same function could be true for STO individuals. It seems that many individuals who have come into this time period from the future, coming back into the past via the incarnational cycle so as not to violate free will, have carefully selected bodies with particular DNA, which they are, little by little, activating so that their 4th density selves, or higher, can manifest in this reality. Is it possible for those energies to manifest into such bodies which have been awakened or tuned in 3rd density?

---

[258] It would be more accurate to say that the subjects were likely to be Semites. The Jews as such did not yet exist at that time. In fact, the Jews as a people were probably not formed until the period of the exile in Babylon. See *The Secret History of the World* for details.

A: STO tends to do the process within the natural flow of things. STS seeks to alter creation processes to fit their ends.

Q: This Top Secret document and the Anna Hayes material to some extent, both talk about many abductions being "ourselves from the future" who have come back to the past, or what is for us, the present, to abduct their own bodies to make genetic adjustments so that they can advance and not make the mistakes they made in another timeline. Is that, in fact, part of the scenario?

A: Very close to the truth!

Q: Can you abduct yourself in an STO manner and help yourself in this way? Can that be STO?

A: It is not, because that is not STO.

Q: So, when that is happening, and if it is happening, it is occurring in the STS parameter?

A: Yes.

Q: How do the STO manage?

A: They do not concern themselves with such things.

Q: Well, if the STS guys are genetically tweaking themselves to have some kind of different outcome for some reason that we do not perceive, don't you think there should be a balancing action on the STO side of some sort?

A: You are thinking in STS terms. But that is natural, since human 3rd density is STS.

Q: You say they don't concern themselves with that. What do STO individuals coming back from the future into the past concern themselves with?

A: Answering calls for assistance with knowledge.

Q: What do these STS individuals coming back into the past hope to do by genetically tweaking their ancestors? What happened that they want to have happen differently?

A: Infinite number of possible answers to that question.

Q: So, they are coming from all different timelines with all different kinds of agendas - all designed to serve themselves. [...] So, that's why they have been following certain bloodlines for generation after generation; they are tinkering with the DNA and arming genetic time-bombs that are waiting to go off. (A) What is interesting is how do those who are trying to get these people, to abduct them, how do they spot them? How do they get the information? By following the bloodline, or by some kind of monitor you can detect from a long distance - and they can note that "here is somebody of interest" or "here is somebody dangerous" or "let's abduct this one" or whatever. How do they select? Do they search the genealogies or is it some kind of remote sensing?

A: Now this is interesting, as it involves the atomic "signature" of the cellular structure of the individual. In concert with this is the etheric body reading and the frequency resonance vibration. All these are interconnected, and can be read from a distance using remote viewing technology/methodology.

Q: (L) Can it be done in a pure mechanical way without using psychic means?

A: At another level of understanding, the two are blended into one.
Q: (T) Computerized psychic remote viewing, maybe. Like artificial intelligence. Maybe a mind connected to a computer?
A: That is close, yes.

And now, let's look at the situation from another angle. We have the idea that the Jews were "Atlantean" in the sense of existing as part of a Global civilization. We suggest that they were indigenous to Mesopotamia and spread down into the Indian subcontinent. We have noted the movements of peoples around the globe, and have noticed that the people of India were invaded and taken over by the Aryan Viracocha people from South America; the Sun God worshipping sacrificers who inculcated their conquered subjects with their religion.

Q: (L) What is the origin of the books of Enoch?
A: Sanskritian society in area now referred to as India. 50% of area was destroyed in nuclear conflagration in between
Q: (L) In between what?
A: Then and now in the expanded present.
Q: (L) What is the "expanded" present?
A: The real measure of time.
Q: Now, you said before that Atlanteans were not Celts, is that correct?
A: No.
Q: The Atlanteans were Celts?
A: "Celts, Druids", etc... are merely latter day designations.
Q: Let's back up here. You said that the Celts came from Kantek. They were transported by the Lizzies... brought here, correct?
A: Yes.
Q: When the Lizzies did this, how many Celts were physically brought here?
A: Hundreds of millions.
Q: How long, in our terms, did it take to bring these Celts to this planet? Or, is this ongoing?
A: Well, in the sense that you measure it, let us say about a week.
Q: Did they transport them in ships, that is some sort of structure. That is, did they load them up, move them into 4th density, reemerge here in 3rd density, or something like that?
A: Close.
Q: And they unloaded them in the area of the Caucasus, is that correct?
A: And regions surrounding.
Q: And, that was what, 79 to 80 thousand years ago?
A: Over 80,000.
Q: As I understand it, Atlantis was already quite a developed civilization at that time, is that correct?
A: Yes, but regions change with waves of immigration, or conquest... witness your own lands.
Q: You also said once that there was a nuclear war in India and that this was what was being discussed in the Vedas when it talks about the 'blue-skinned' people who weren't really blue because they were Celts, and

they were flying in aircraft, and they were engaged in this war, etc. Who
were the Celts at war with?

A: The Paranthas.

Q: Now, wait a minute! Who are the Paranthas?! Do we have a new
player here?

A: Not new. Atlantis was merely a home base of an advanced civilisation
of *3 races of humans* occupying different sections of a huge island
empire, which, in itself, underwent 3 incarnations over a 100,000 year
period as you would measure it.

Q: The 3 races were the Celts... or Kantekkians. Are the Kantekkians
different from the Celts?

A: Only in the sense of long term racial and genetic blending.

Q: So, Atlantis had the Kantekkians and who else?

A: Race you would call "Native Americans", and a third, no longer
existing race, somewhat resembling Australian or Guinean aborigines,
only lighter in complexion. Paranthas.

Q: Was this third group destroyed by the other two?

A: One of the 3 cataclysms.

Q: So, the Paranthas were the antecedents of the Abos of Australia?

A: Yes, and compare to now existing peoples of India, Pakistan, Sri
Lanka, Australia, and New Guinea for similarities, bearing in mind
genetic mixing and dilution.

Q: Were the Vedas written by the Paranthas or written by the Celts?

A: Descendants of Parantha, as per "Divine guidance".

Q: Were the Jews that were genetically engineered and then planted in the
Middle East... what year was this?

A: 130,000 years ago.

Q: Cayce talks about the division in Atlantis between the "Sons of One"
and the "Sons of Belial". Was this a racial division or a philosophical/
religious division?

A: It was the latter two, and before that, the former one.

Q: When it was a racial division, which group was it?

A: The Sons of Belial were the Kantekkians.

Q: Well! That is not good!

A: Subjective... you are not bodies, you are souls.

So, we have some idea that a remnant of the Paranthas may have
survived in the Jews. And, based on some of our speculations about time
travel, branching universes, and possible futures, somebody traveled back
into the past to round up all the Jews and impress upon them the
importance of keeping their genes to themselves, so as to make that event
"fall forward into the future like a row of dominoes". Then, at some future
point in time, that is, the present, it would be possible - with technology -
to wipe them from the face of the earth so as to control the branching of
this sector of space/time at the nexus point that is on the schedule as the
much touted "End of Time".

This "manipulation of the past" is evident in a textual study of the Bible.
This was, of course, forbidden for centuries while the Controls were being

expanded and all the playing pieces of the final game were being set up. Nevertheless, after years of bloodshed and death to anyone who questioned the Bible, it was realized that somebody had "created" the Bible by assembling four different source documents in an attempt to create a "continuous" history. After much further analysis, it was concluded that most of the laws and much of the narrative of the Pentateuch were not even part of the time of Moses. That meant that it couldn't have been written by Moses at all. More than that, the writing of the different sources was not even that of persons who lived during the days of the kings and prophets, but were evidentially products of writers who lived toward the end of the biblical period! Another way of putting it is that the Bible claimed a history for the first 600 years of Israel that probably never existed. It was all a lie.[259]

We come back to that most interesting fact: it was the Catholic Church that encouraged the beliefs of the Jews in the Middle Ages. It was also at that time that the pogroms against them were initiated in European countries. That produces a strange sensation of vertigo. But it is easy to understand when one understands the principles of Machiavelli. It's actually quite simple: create a belief, and then attack the group that holds the belief which convinces them that others are jealous of them and want to take what they have, thus they hold even more firmly to that belief.

From that point on, we witness the astonishing effort to transmute those horrific experiences into positive things by the denial mechanism of psychology wherein any person who suffers and is unable - for whatever reason - to end that suffering, justifies it by creating the belief that "good" things, developmental things, positively proceed from such ordeals.

We are told in the Bible that the most significant event in Jewish history is the return from exile in Babylon. It was, indeed significant since that was the point in time when the Bible was created, and the religion of Yahweh actually seems to have been created by the Persians. It was then that the codification of the authority of the Levite priesthood took form, and we begin to smell a rat. Indeed, the evidence, which we shall explore shortly, strongly suggests that the Levites were not Jews at all- they were Aryans - and the broad view of the event suggests that this was a moment in history in which one of the dominoes was set up.

The next domino was set up in the 10th-12th centuries by the Catholic Church with the aid and assistance of the Levite priesthood.

It was at this point in time that the "Egyptian connection" was made, Hermetic "documents" began to "appear"; kaballah, sephir yetzira and

---

[259] Of course, it is not really a "lie", properly speaking. The stories are just highly mythicized accounts of certain people and events, arranged "vertically" in history with genealogies inserted to produce the effect of a long history, and links between disparate groups that may or may not have existed. For a detailed examination of this question, please see Chapter 10 of *The Secret History of the World*.

other Hebrew literature appeared - including the Hebrew Bible in toto itself. These were naturally intended to be "inherited" by Christians, and it seems that this was a mode of introduction of the elements of the Sorcerers coven - the worshippers of the Serpent power who promoted the Hermes rebellion as a great and wonderful positive influence.

At the same time, there was the appearance of the Grail Stories, which were gradually corrupted by the Catholic Church, all while they were destroying the Cathars and trying to dispossess all the Jews of their possessions - including any documents they may have retained showing the true history of Israel. As we note in our book The Secret History of the World:

> "In the 11th century, a real troublemaker, Isaac ibn Yashush, a Jewish court physician in Muslim Spain, mentioned the distressing fact that a list of Edomite kings that appears in Genesis 36 named a few kings who lived long after Moses was already dead. Ibn Yashush suggested the obvious, that the list was written by someone who lived after Moses. He became known as 'Isaac the Blunderer'.

> The guy who memorialized clever Isaac this way was a fellow named Abraham ibn Ezra, a 12th century rabbi in Spain. But Ibn Ezra presents us with a paradox because he also wrote about problems in the text of the Torah. He alluded to several passages that appeared not to be from Moses' own hand because they referred to Moses in the third person, used terms Moses would not have known, described places that Moses had never been, and used language that belonged to an altogether different time and place than the milieu of Moses. He wrote, very mysteriously, 'And if you understand, then you will recognize the truth. And he who understands will keep silent'."

And then we come to the reasoning behind the Catholic Church supporting the revival of Judaism so that they could "inherit" the "New Covenant". We remember the words of Rashi de Troyes that the Bible:

> "was written to justify what we might now call genocide. The God of Israel, who gave his people the Promised Land, had to be unequivocally supreme so that neither the dispossessed Canaanites nor anyone else could ever appeal against his decrees.[260] Rashi's precise words were that God told the Jews the creation story and included it in the Torah 'to tell his people that they can answer those who claim that the Jews stole the land from its original inhabitants. The reply should be; God made it and gave it to them but then took it and gave it to us. As he made it and it's his, he can give it to whoever he chooses'".

Well, of course, the Jews think it belongs to them. What they don't seem to realize is that a lot of Christians believe fervently that they have *inherited* this right.

---

[260] Ashe, Geoffrey, *The Book of Prophecy*, 1999, Blandford, London; p. 27

Modern Day Manipulations and mtDNA

The next domino was set up in the 19th century with the emergence of "Zionism". Again, we question just who these Zionists really are and do they actually serve the best interests of the Jews? The result of the Zionist agitation was twofold. First, it led to the idea of creating a "Jewish State". Second, it led to the Holocaust. Yes, I realize that over 60 million human beings were killed in the Holocaust, and only a small percentage of them were Jews. I have also considered the fact that it is very likely that many of the other victims who were not Jews in name, very possibly were peoples who were of "mixed blood", so to say.

The third domino has been set up with the creation of the Jewish state, and the repatriation of Jews from all over the world. They are now, effectively, fenced in and ready for the final Final Solution.

Anyone who suggests that this view of the religion of Judaism is "anti-Semitic", might keep in mind that we say the same about Christianity and Islam, so we are an equal-opportunity shooter of sacred cows. We object to all Control Systems. In fact, as we have pointed out, Christianity would not exist if it were not for Judaism, and vice versa. They are very strange bedfellows with Islam, and every now and again one is enabled to glimpse the reality beneath the facade of the power elite who play one against the other, throughout the millennia, with mankind caught in the jaws of the trap.

What is the trap? What is the agenda that is promoted most vigorously by the Zionists - those "Jews" who are undoubtedly secret Aryans? We have to realize that the war between the Israelis and Palestinians is based on the claim that Israel is the Promised Land, and that it "belongs" to the Jews by fiat of God Almighty.

As noted, if what the Cassiopaeans were saying about the intention to replace the human race with physical vehicles more suited to the intentions of 4th density STS is true, it is not difficult to understand why it would be important to prevent the spread of the Semitic genes - keeping always in mind that these genetics are shared by Israelis *and* Arabs. Further, it is not too great a stretch to see that the greatest means of doing this has been via the very religions in question: Judaism, Islam and Christianity, in what appear to be manipulated opposing roles - opposition that seems to disappear at the pinnacles of power and control. And of course, in such a game, it would be necessary to pit two of the players against one another while the third steps forward to "save the day".

The eradication of these genes as a preparation for an overt take-over by our fourth density overlords may indeed be the explanation for what has been happening on our planet for the past several millennia.

When one considers that Hitler was determined to follow his protocol for destroying Jews - as well as about anybody else in those areas where

Jews had lived for centuries – (even in the face of his impending destruction, and that in the final days of his power, knowing that the Allies were closing in on him, instead of cleaning up the evidence of his monstrous perfidy, he actually ordered an acceleration of the destruction of the Jewish people), it becomes obvious that *this was his clear and singular agenda*, upon which all else he did was predicated.

When one carefully studies Hitler and the Nazi regime, there is a sensation of vertigo that something is dreadfully wrong with this picture that goes far deeper than most commentators and analysts of the situation seem to fathom. Oh, it can all be taken apart and looked at in its separate pieces, and we can see how the German people were in a certain dire situation and Hitler came along and promised to make it all better. We can read psychological profiles of Hitler and come to some idea that the guy had some serious issues. That's all pretty standard.

But still, after reading all the technical details, after all the events are cleaned up and laid out in nice chronological tables, expert after expert will end their discussion just as puzzled as they began. Even when they think that they have an answer for "why?", they will admit that what they have done is only speculative and that they still have the uneasy feeling that they haven't quite arrived at the answer.

And that is the crux of it: why, oh why, was Hitler damned and determined to destroy the Jews against all human ethics and even logic and good sense? Before you even offer a facile answer, spend 20 or more years poring over the literature and then you will understand why this question nearly drove me crazy. There was *no answer*. And if there was no answer, if such an event was just "random evil" that happened to seat itself in Germany in the third decade of the last century - a civilized and advanced country - then we are all screwed.

All things considered, we come back, again and again, that Hitler's primary agenda was to destroy the Jews. And *not* because of their religion - because of their genes. Now where did Hitler even get an idea like that?

We can easily trace the history of the ideas of eugenics and see the "external" view of the matter. The one thing that is difficult to find is where and how the Jews were determined to be "undesirable", racially speaking.

During the course of my research for my book "The Secret History of the World", I stumbled over an item that raised the hair on the back of my neck. This discovery had to do with "Mongols", and as I read the material in question, what came to my mind were two other references that included the word "Mongols" that were stuck in my memory banks from years past. The first is one of Nostradamus' famous quatrains and the second is a quote from a prediction made by America's famous seer, Edgar Cayce just prior to World War II.

Nostradamus wrote:

L'an mil neuf cens nonante neuf septmois,
Du ciel viendra un grand Roy d'effrayeur:
Resusciter le grand Roy d'Angolmois*
Avant après Mars regner par bon heur. X 72

This has been translated into English as follows:

In the year 1999 and seven months
From the sky will come the Great King of Terror,
Raising again the great king of the Mongols,
Before and after Mars (war) reigns at his pleasure. X.72

Edgar Cayce's remark about Mongols was as follows:

If there is not the acceptance in America of the closer brotherhood of man,
the love of the neighbor as self, civilization must wend its way westward -
and again must Mongolism, must a hated people be raised.

The reader may certainly wonder how and why two odd comments by two prophets who lived hundreds of years apart should have struck me as so all-fired interesting considering our perspective on "inspirational" material - that research is always necessary. Well, again, bear with me. I am going to attempt to recount the research as it proceeded. As I do, I think that the reader will come to see the above remarks about "Mongols" in a new light.

First of all, during the summer of 2003, in all the hullabaloo over the death of Dr. David Kelly, we came across the term "Ethnic Specific Weapons" in an article we published on our News Page "Signs of the Times"[261] that went as follows:

Microbiologists With Link to Race-Based Weapon Turning Up Dead[262]

Exclusive to *American Free Press*
By Gordon Thomas

Dr. David Kelly—the biological warfare weapons specialist at the heart of the continuing political crisis for the British government—had links to three other top microbiologists whose deaths have left unanswered questions.

The 59-year-old British scientist was involved with ultra secret work at Israel's Institute for Biological Research. Israeli sources claim Kelly met institute scientists several times in London in the past two years. [...]

There have been persistent reports that the institute is also engaged in DNA sequencing research. One former member of the Knesset, Dedi Zucker, caused a storm in the Israeli Parliament when he claimed that the institute was "trying to create an ethnic specific weapon" in which Arabs could be targeted by Israeli weapons.

---

[261] http://www.signs-of-the-times.org
[262] http://americanfreepress.net/08_09_03/Microbiologists_With/microbiologists_with.html

Signs Comment: "Ethnic Specific Weapons?" Hmmm... maybe the Israelis have forgotten that the Arabs are genetically identical to the Jews... ? What will kill an Arab will kill a Jew.

We have long been suggesting that the ultimate agenda of the Global Reich is to set Israel up and do the most fiendish double cross of all; and now we may have a clue as to how they plan to do it.

Look out, Israel, you have all been herded into a corral by the Balfour Agreement, your leaders have been calling you home to Israel for years... aided and abetted by England and America - those whose sympathies with the Nazis are well known; and you think they are "serving you"? On a platter, maybe...

We were actually so non-plussed by this article that we didn't quite know what to make of it. But something really bugged me, and the Signs Team decided to take this dangling thread and pull on it. The question was, of course, since all the genetic studies with which I was familiar pointed out the fact that Jews and Arabs are "brothers", what in the world were they talking about here? What kind of "Ethnic Specific Weapon" could target Arabs and *not* Jews?

For example, have a look at the graph of the genetic relationships between Jews and their neighbors.

So, the question was: How could an Ethnic Specific Weapon work when we have the idea that just about everybody is related to everybody else to one extent or another, and most particularly, how could anybody have the idea that they could distinguish between Jews and Palestinians genetically?

In recent years, there have been a raft of genetic studies focused on issues of "Jewishness". This work has been advanced, to a great extent, by Jewish scientists themselves, so it cannot be considered a venue for anti-Semitism. Nevertheless, in spite of the seeming attempts of Jews seeking to prove that they ARE different from everyone else, there are many voices raised against the issue of Jews as a separate genetic "line". For example:

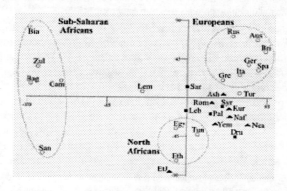

Graph from Michael Hammer's study, Uni of Arizona.

Jews are represented by triangles: Ashkenazim = Ash, Roman Jews = Rom, North African Jews = Naf; Near Eastern Jews = Nea; Kurdish Jews = Kur, Yemenite Jews = Yem; Ethiopian Jews = EtJ; non-Jewish Middle Easterners = Pal, non-Jewish Syrians = Syr, non-Jewish Lebanes = Leb, Israeli Druze = Dru, non-Jewish Saudi Arabians = Sar; Non-Jewish Europeans: Rus = Russians, Bri = British, Ger = Germans, Aus = Austrians, Ita = Italians, Spa = Spanish, Gre = Greeks, Tun = North Africans and Tunisians; Egy = Egyptians, Eth = Ethiopians, Gam = Gambians, Bia = Biaka, Bag = Bagandans, San = San, Zul = Zulu. Tur = non Jewish Turks, Lem = Lemba from south Africa.

Notice, in the above graph, that the lower right corner of the graph is where Near Eastern Jews are positioned. One might therefore theorize that the Near Eastern Jews are, more or less, the most "Jewish" of the Jews in terms of many generations of "Jews" in their family lines. Looking around this cluster, we notice that there are several "families" that are very close, including Yemenite Jews, Druze, North African Jews, *and* Palestinians. On the other hand, the Ashkenazi Jews are not only much closer to Turks, Syrians and Roman Jews, they are quite distant from both the Near Eastern Jews and the Palestinians. I also noted with some considerable interest that Saudi Arabians are much closer to Europeans and even Ashkenazi Jews than to Palestinians.

Jews are not a race. Anyone can become a Jew - and members of every race, creed and color in the world have done so at one time or another. There is no distinguishing racial physical feature common only to Jews.

Being Jewish is not a race because Jews do not share one common ancestry or biological distinction. People of many different races have become Jewish people over the years.

Rabbi Harold M. Schulweis explains the nature of Judaism:

"One of the unique aspects of Judaism is its rejection of Judaism as a biological entity, an inherited spiritual DNA, racial or ethnic. The point is that being a Jew is not a matter of genes and chromosomes. To the contrary, Judaism is the first religion to recognize the 'ger', the stranger who chooses to identify himself with Judaism. Judaism is not rooted in race or clan or in a genetic matter but a religious tradition of choice."

The answer as to "Who is a Jew" that is most often given is that Jews are *a religion and a civilization*, but *not* a race or singular ethnic group. Rabbi Rami Shapiro said, "There is only one response to Who is a Jew? that works: A Jew is one who takes Judaism seriously. One who takes Judaism seriously studies it, argues with it, and lives it".

This, of course, begs the question as to why so many genetic studies are being done by and about Jews, and how does this relate to Ethnic Specific Weapons? Clearly, Jews themselves do not agree on what defines being a Jew, but what confuses the issue even more is the disinformation.

In the article *The Mark of Doom*,[263] we find the following comments:

"American scientists have declared that in ten years they will succeed in creating a radically new type of biological weapon. This weapon would be capable of infecting people according to a genetically predetermined marker such as skin color or eye shape. Infection could have a delayed effect or only begin once a certain type of medicine was taken. A recent closed seminar held by the CIA was devoted to the topic. The event took place as part of the Project for the New American Century. [...]

Yet the most terrifying new possibility is the hypothetical biological weapon that could infect people according to genetic markers. Not only would it allow for genocide; it would be created specifically for that purpose. A recent report by the British Medical Association stated that 'the rapid progress in genetics could become the basis for ethnic cleansing on an unheard of scale in the near future'. [...]

Three years ago, ideologues like US Deputy Defense Secretary Paul Wolfowitz and PNAC Director William Crystal were already discussing genetic weapons. They recommended that the Pentagon consider the possibility for using this type of weapon not only to successfully wage war, but also to reconfigure world politics. According to a PNAC report, genetic weapons could completely change the politics of the entire planet: 'cutting-edge biological warfare targeting a certain genotype could turn the reign of terrorism into a politically useful tool'.

According to information from PNAC, Israel has also recently begun to work actively on mutagenic weapons. Israel geneticists confirm that Arabs carry a unique gene that no one else in the world has. This gene forms the basis for the Israeli research, believe American experts. [...]

Fortunately, it is not as easy to create a selective biological weapon as some scientists are claiming. Though it may be possible to create bacteria that multiply only when a person takes a specific medication, the creation of an effective genetic weapon that would not harm the developers themselves seems unrealistic in the foreseeable future." [...]

---

[263] http://www.gateway2russia.com/st/art_217290.php

There is one more reason why this kind of biological weapon is unlikely to be as effective as the ideologues would wish. As Nazi doctor Josef Mengele put it, "Scratch a Frenchman and find an African". Humanity has existed for many millennia. In the context of all our past tribal and intertribal connections, it is not far from the truth to say that *we are all brothers.* "Over the many years of human existence, ethnics groups have intermingled to such an extent that the genetic structures determining ethnic identity have blurred and become difficult to recognize", notes Prozorov.

In the related article: *Politically Desirable, Genetically Unviable,* we find the following:

"You know, there are politicians who set goals for scientists. These goals are often never accomplished, but nonetheless, why not set goals and why not get money for research? Creating genetic weapons is a goal of this kind. In reality, it would be quite difficult to create this kind of weapon. A lot of currently published research is dedicated to the structure of the human genome and the difference between various races. *It has been proven that the differences are very slight*, and scientists have only begun to identify them. [...]

The overwhelming majority of countries, including the US and Russia, signed a convention that prohibits developing, testing, manufacturing, and storing biological weapons. If they begin conducting research and tests, they will be violating this convention and giving other countries an excuse to start this kind of research themselves. [...] Yet *to create viruses that could target only a certain race or people is nearly impossible in my opinion*, at least at the current stage of biology."

Contrast the above with the following from our Ethnic Specific Weapons Supplement:

Ethnic Weapons For Ethnic Cleansing [264]

Greg Bishop
March 2000

[T]his "theoretical possibility" was recognized over 25 years ago, if not before. It was originally brought to the attention of potential customers with the publication of an article in the Military Review of November 1970.

This journal for command-level military personnel was published by the US Army Command and General Staff College in Fort Leavenworth, Kansas. The feature, entitled "Ethnic Weapons", authored by Carl A. Larson, outlines the history, desirability, and possibilities of engineered biological pathogens which would affect only those races which historically have no natural defense against certain "enzyme inhibitors".

Larson is listed as head of the "Department of Human Genetics at the Institute of Genetics, Lund, Sweden", as well as a licensed physician. The

---

[264] http://www.elfis.net/tem/ethnic_weapons.htm

Hippocratic oath was apparently not administered in Sweden when Larson received his accreditation. [...]

According to Charles Piller and Keith Yamamoto in their 1988 book Gene Wars, Larson's article was the first time that the subject of ethnically targeted CBWs was broached publicly, and that in "the military's private circles it was old news".

Comment: We learn that the work on such weapons was begun in Nazi Germany. The victims of these weapons were largely Jews. When Larson published his paper in 1970, in 'the military's private circles it was old news',which means it had been discussed for a long time by the US military, most likely with the Nazis brought into the US after World War II via Operation Paperclip. Tests were carried out as far back as 1951 on Blacks working at the Mechanicsburg, PA Naval Supply Depot.

Biowar and the Apartheid Legacy [265]

By Salim Muwakkil, In These Times
June 6, 2003

A two-part story in the Washington Post on April 20 and 21 revealed that biological agents developed by the South African government during its apartheid days have fallen into private hands.

Written by Post reporters Joby Warrick and John Mintz, the piece noted that unique, race-specific strains of biotoxins were available on the world market – for the right price or the right ideology.

[...] The top-secret program that Basson directed was called Project Coast, and it lasted from 1981 to 1993. The South African National Defense Force created it at a time when the white-minority regime was under increasing threat by indigenous black South Africans. Daan Goosen, the former director of Project Coast's biological research division, told the Post he was ordered by Basson to develop ways "to suppress population growth among blacks" and to "search for a 'black bomb', a biological weapon that would select targets based on skin color."

[...] The Washington Post even noted, "Goosen says many scientists kept copies of organisms and documents in order to continue work on 'dual-use' projects with commercial as well as military applications."

A May 2002 story on Project Coast in the Wall Street Journal reported that Goosen said he has been 'visited by scores of people looking for 'stuff to kill the blacks.' Race-specific weapons naturally are in hot demand among racists, so it's no surprise that South Africa's race-specific research is highly coveted.

[...] Reported links between Israel's ethnic weapons and South Africa's Project Coast are tentative; some would say tenuous. But the possibility of such links is terrifying, and justifies as much scrutiny as was focused on Iraq's imaginary arsenal.

---

[265] http://www.alternet.org/story.html?StoryID=16095

At this point, the reader may wish to peruse the entire Signs Supplement on Ethnic Specific Weapons[266] so as to understand that the claim that no such weapons are currently available, nor could they even work, is complete disinformation. This work has been going on for a very long time and is, undoubtedly well advanced and may even be being used already!

Our research on this subject, inspired by the Dr. David Kelly affair, was published in August of 2003 and was met with basically dead silence. Nobody even wanted to touch this one. Now, all of a sudden, the issue is popping up here and there, mostly from the disinformation angle.

To continue with my little chronology, the question of what could be used as a "separator" between Jews and Palestinians led me to re-visit all the genetic research I could get my hands on. My puzzlement grew as I pursued this line.

At the present time, it is known that Eastern European Jews have a significant Eastern Mediterranean element which manifests itself in a close relationship with Kurdish, Armenian, Palestinian Arab, Lebanese, Syrian, and Anatolian Turkish peoples. At the same time, there are traces of European (including Western Slavic) and Khazar ancestry among European Jews. Ethiopian Jews mostly descend from Ethiopian Africans who converted to Judaism, but may also be related to a lesser extent to Yemenite Jews. Yemenite Jews descend from Arabs and Israelites. North African Jewish and Kurdish Jewish paternal lineages come from Israelites. The problem with all of these studies is that they fail to compare modern Jewish populations' DNA to *ancient Judean DNA* and medieval Khazarian DNA, and they focus on paternal ancestries.

I had a copy of the book *The Seven Daughters of Eve* on the shelf that I hadn't read yet, and decided that it might give me a few clues. It was then that I realized that the answer might lie in mtDNA. And so, I began the search for any genetic studies of Jewish mtDNA. Nicholas Wade writes in *DNA, New Clues to Jewish Roots*:

"The emerging genetic picture is based largely on two studies, one published two years ago and the other this month, that together show that the men and women who founded the Jewish communities had surprisingly different genetic histories.

The earlier study, led by Dr. Michael Hammer of University of Arizona, showed from an analysis of the male, or Y chromosome, that Jewish men from seven communities were related to one another and to present-day Palestinian and Syrian populations, but not to the men of their host communities.

The finding suggested that Jewish men who founded the communities traced their lineage back to the ancestral Mideastern population of 4,000 years ago from which Arabs, Jews and other people are descended. It pointed to the

---

[266] http://signs-of-the-times.org/signs/signs_ethnic_supplement.htm

genetic unity of widespread Jewish populations and took issue with ideas that most Jewish communities were relatively recent converts like the Khazars, a medieval Turkish tribe that embraced Judaism."

A new study now shows that the women in nine Jewish communities from Georgia, the former Soviet republic, to Morocco have *vastly different genetic histories from the men*. In each community, the women carry *very few genetic signatures* on their mitochondrial DNA, a genetic element inherited only through the female line. This indicates that the community had just a small number of founding mothers and that after the founding event there was little, if any, interchange with the host population. The women's identities, however, are a mystery, because, unlike the case with the men, *their genetic signatures are not related to one another or to those of present-day Middle Eastern populations*.

It was in this last discovery that the skin on the back of my neck began to crawl. Obviously, if Jewish men are related to one another *and* to present-day Palestinian and Syrian populations, the means of producing a "death factor" of so-called "Ethnic Specific Weapons" - by either inclusion or exclusion - might lie in the mtDNA. It occurred to me that it was coincidentally odd that in ancient Israel, the Jewish priesthood was handed from father to son, but at some point, Jewish status came to be defined by *maternal descent*. Nicholas Wade tells us:

> "The idea that most or all Jewish communities were founded by Jewish men and local women is somewhat at variance with the usual founding traditions. Most Jewish communities hold that they were formed by families who fled persecution or were invited to settle by local kings.
>
> For instance, Iraqi Jews are said to be descended from those exiled to Babylon after the destruction of the First Temple in 586 B.C. Members of the Bene Israel community of Bombay say they are the children of Jews who fled the persecutions of Antiochus Epiphanus, who repressed the Maccabean revolt, around 150 B.C.
>
> Most of those founding narratives do not have strong historical support. Dr. Lawrence H. Schiffman, professor of Hebrew and Judaic studies at New York University, said the new genetic data could well explain how certain far-flung Jewish communities were formed. [...]
>
> Dr. Shaye Cohen, professor of Jewish literature and philosophy at Harvard, said the implication of the findings and the idea of Jewish communities' having been founded by traders, was 'by no means implausible.'
>
> 'The authors are correct in saying the historical origins of most Jewish communities are unknown', Dr. Cohen said. 'Not only the little ones like in India, but even the mainstream Ashkenazic culture from which most American Jews descend'.
>
> In a recent book, 'The Beginnings of Jewishness,' Dr. Cohen argued that far-flung Jewish communities had adopted the rabbinic teaching of the matrilineal descent of Jewishness soon after the Islamic conquests in the seventh, eight and ninth centuries A.D.

One part of the Goldstein team's analysis, that matrilineal descent of Jewishness was practiced at or soon after the founding of each community, could fit in with this conclusion, Dr. Cohen said, if the communities were founded around this time."

The comments about the mtDNA research caught my attention. "A new study now shows that the women in nine Jewish communities from Georgia, the former Soviet republic, to Morocco have *vastly different genetic histories from the men*. In each community, the women carry *very few genetic signatures* on their mitochondrial DNA, a genetic element inherited only through the female line. [...] unlike the case with the men, *their genetic signatures are not related to one another or to those of present-day Middle Eastern populations*." I went to the original research and found the following:

"We have analyzed the maternally inherited mitochondrial DNA from each of nine geographically separated Jewish groups, eight non-Jewish host populations, and an Israeli Arab/Palestinian population, and we have compared the differences found in Jews and non-Jews with those found using Y-chromosome data that were obtained, in most cases, from the same population samples.

The results suggest that most Jewish communities were founded by relatively few women, that the founding process was independent in different geographic areas, and that subsequent genetic input from surrounding populations was limited on the female side.

In sharp contrast to this, the paternally inherited Y chromosome shows diversity similar to that of neighboring populations and shows no evidence of founder effects.

These sex-specific differences demonstrate an important role for culture in shaping patterns of genetic variation and are likely to have significant epidemiological implications for studies involving these populations. We illustrate this by presenting data from a panel of X-chromosome microsatellites, which indicates that, in the case of the Georgian Jews, the female-specific founder event appears to have resulted in elevated levels of linkage disequilibrium."[267]

---

[267] [Founding Mothers of Jewish Communities: Geographically Separated Jewish Groups Were Independently Founded by Very Few Female Ancestors by Mark G. Thomas,1, Michael E. Weale,1 Abigail L. Jones,1 Martin Richards,3 Alice Smith,2 Nicola Redhead,2 Antonio Torroni,5,6 Rosaria Scozzari,6 Fiona Gratrix,2 Ayele Tarekegn,1 James F. Wilson,2 Cristian Capelli,2 Neil Bradman,1 and David B. Goldstein2 1TheCentre for Genetic Anthropology, Departments of Biology and Anthropology, and 2 Department of Biology, University College London, London; 3Department of Chemical and Biological Sciences, University of Huddersfield, Huddersfield, United Kingdom; 4Bruce Rappaport Faculty of Medicine and Research Institute, Technion and Rambam Medical Center, Haifa, Israel; 5Dipartimento di Geneticae Microbiologia, Universitàdi Pavia, Pavia, Italy; and 6 Dipartimentodi Geneticae Biologia Molecolare, "LaSapienza" di Roma, Rome - Address for correspondence and reprints: Dr. David Goldstein, Department of Biology, University College London, GowerStreet, London WC1E6BT, United Kingdom.]

Naturally, I began to tug on this thread to find out exactly who, among Jews, were related to these Eight Founding Mothers. The above cited paper says further:

> "Comparison of Y-chromosome and mtDNA patterns reveals a striking contrast between the maternal and paternal genetic heritage of Jewish populations.
>
> On the Y chromosome, there is no consistent pattern of lower diversity in Jewish communities when compared with their non-Jewish host populations; in two cases, diversity is significantly lower in the Jewish groups; in one case, it is higher; and, in the rest, differences are not significant.
>
> However, the pattern in the mtDNA is quite different. In each case, the Jewish community has a significantly lower mtDNA diversity than its paired host population. Indeed, every Jewish population has a lower mtDNA diversity than any non-Jewish population. This finding indicates that mistakes in associating particular host populations with Jewish populations would be very unlikely to affect our results. [...]
>
> When ratios of mtDNA to Y-chromosome diversity were calculated, to standardize the mtDNA results in relation to the other genetic system, the ratio for the Jewish data sets ... was again found, in all but one case (the Ethiopian Jews), to be less than the ratio for the non-Jewish host. [...]
>
> Even more striking than this, however, is the high frequency of particular mtDNA haplotypes in the Jewish populations. No host population in our sample has an mtDNA modal frequency greater than 12% (mean 7.7%). In contrast, seven of the Jewish populations have a modal frequency greater than 12% (mean 22.6%), and some of the Jewish groups have much higher frequencies.
>
> In particular, Moroccan Jews, the Bene Israel, and Georgian Jews have modal frequencies of 27.0%, 41.3%, and 51.4%, respectively, which are all higher than those observed in any of the other populations. Again, this pattern is not seen on the Y chromosome, where the modal frequencies in Jewish populations (mean 15.2%; range 7.4% to 31.2%) are not significantly different from those seen in host populations (mean 13.6%; range 8.1% to 33.3%).
>
> In most European and Near Eastern populations, the highest frequency mtDNA type is the HVS-1 Cambridge Reference Sequence (CRS). This type occurs at 16%, on average, in Europe, and at 6%, on average, in the Near East. This pattern is reflected in our data, in that all of the seven European and Near Eastern non-Jewish populations have the CRS as their modal haplotype.
>
> However, only two of the nine Jewish populations have the CRS as their modal haplotype, while, among the other seven, each has a different modal haplotype.
>
> Thus, among the nine Jewish groups there are eight different mtDNA types that are modal with an unusually high frequency.

Apart from the CRS, none of the other Jewish modal haplotypes are represented in the Israeli Arab/Palestinian data set, in contrast to the similarities between Ashkenazic Jews, Sephardic Jews, Israeli Arabs/Palestinian, and Lebanese populations reported for the Y chromosome. [...]

These results therefore suggest that an extreme founder effect has occurred in the maternal but not paternal genetic histories of most Jewish populations.

Greater geographic structuring of the mtDNA than the Y chromosome is an unusual pattern. To assess whether this is specific to the Jewish populations, we also compared mtDNA and Y-chromosome structuring among the host populations. Among the latter populations we found the more usual pattern of greater Y-chromosome differentiation. This demonstrates that the unusual pattern observed among the Jewish populations is not associated with the geographic areas from which they derive but rather with their unique demographic histories. [...]

It would appear that the founder effects on the maternal side have been so severe that mtDNA frequencies in the Jewish populations are very different from those found in any non-Jewish population. The non-CRS modal haplotypes in the Jewish populations are generally rare in the non-Jewish populations. The CRS, on the other hand, is too ubiquitous to allow it to be pinpointed to anything other than a general Eurasian origin. [...]

For example, the most extreme founder effect is seen in the Georgian Jews, of whom 51% possess the same haplotype. The Georgian Jewish modal type is matched by a single individual in the Georgian sample. However, a search of the mtDNA database shows that it also occurs in Syria (2/69 individuals) and Iraq (1/116). One directly derived type is present in two Georgians, but derived types are also found in the North Caucasus (2/208 individuals), Turkey (1/218), Armenia (1/191), and Sicily (1/90). For the Georgian modal haplotype, there is therefore no clear indication of provenance, although an indigenous origin is certainly possible, given the data. [...]

In two cases, however, comparison with the published data does provide some indication of the possible geographic origins of the modal types. The modal type in the Bene Israel is a one-step mutational neighbor of a haplotype present in the Indian sample, as well as being a one-step neighbor of a type previously identified in India. Similarly, the commonest type in the Ethiopian Jewish sample is also present in the non-Jewish Ethiopian sample and occurs in the worldwide mtDNA database only in Somalia. Other high-frequency haplotypes in the Ethiopian Jewish sample are also found almost entirely in Africa. The lack of an indication of a Middle Eastern origin for these haplotypes, on the basis of the Richards database, makes local recruitment a more reasonable explanation in these two cases. [...]

The greatly reduced mtDNA diversity in the Jewish populations in comparison with the host populations, together with the wide range of different modal haplotypes found in different communities, indicates female-specific founding events in the Jewish populations.

Although we cannot be certain whether this occurred immediately after the establishment of the communities or over a longer period of time, a simple explanation for the exceptional pattern of mtDNA variation across Jewish populations is that each of the different Jewish communities is composed of descendants of a small group of maternal founders. After the establishment of these communities, inward gene flow from the host populations must have been very limited. [...]

The differences among the Jewish populations in mtDNA haplogroup frequencies indicates that the Jewish groups formed independently around (at least) eight small, distinct nuclei of women. The severity of these demographic events was sufficiently great to drive an unusual pattern of geographic variation among the Jewish populations.

Although it has been commonly found that Y-chromosome variation shows greater geographic structure than the mtDNA, this pattern is reversed in the Jewish populations, which show greater differentiation for the mtDNA than for the Y chromosome.

Jewish populations therefore appear to represent an example in which cultural practice in this case, female-defined ethnicity has had a pronounced effect on patterns of genetic variation. [...]

The pattern in Ashkenazic Jews is of particular interest. Despite the common opinion that this population has undergone a strong founder event, it has a modal haplotype with a frequency similar to that of its host population (9.0% vs. 6.9%), providing little evidence of a strong founder event on the female side. The possibility remains, however, that present-day Ashkenazic Jews may represent a mosaic group that is descended on the maternal side from several independent founding events. [...]

These results demonstrate that demographic events restricted to only one of the sexes can be of considerable epidemiological significance."

Needless to say, this is an extremely interesting state of affairs, and my guess is that a lot more is known about this research than is currently available to the public. It is almost impossible to speculate about the origins of the "Founding Mothers" of a significant number of Jews, but I am reminded of an old saying that if your son marries, you lose him to his wife's family, and if your daughter marries, you gain a son. Perhaps this is naturally due to the special types of emotional bonds that are formed between women. But, of significant interest here is the issue of what it is that "bottle-necked" these groups of people.

After reading *The Seven Daughters of Eve*, and a host of technical papers on genetics, I finally had a look at Arthur Koestler's *The Thirteenth Tribe*. His theory is that the majority of modern Jews are Ashkenazim, descended from the Khazars, a Caucasian people who had converted to Judaism in the Middle Ages. For a time, Koestler's ideas were vigorously argued - even rejected - but in more recent times, his ideas have been partly vindicated. Ashkenazi Jews have a more significant admixture of Italian, Greek, and Turkish genes than of Spanish, German, or even

Austrian ones as do the Separdim. This certainly connects them to the Khazars, but does not exclude mixing with the Western "real" Jews of Spain and elsewhere.

There was another issue that popped up during this period: Kevin MacDonald's work. MacDonald ascribes a genetic homogeneity to Jews postulating that Judaism is an "evolutionary group strategy". MacDonald has been generally accused of anti-Semitism and, indeed, anyone with eyes can see that Jews are like everyone else: they come in all colors, shapes and sizes. We realize now, of course, that there is a wide variation in the paternal ancestry, but that there is something truly strange about the maternal ancestry of a significant number of Jews is now quite evident.

The question then became: what is mtDNA and what, precisely, does it do?

To look further into this question, let us return to the death of Dr. David Kelly, the biological warfare weapons specialist who had links to three other top microbiologists who are on the startlingly long list of microbiologists who have died mysteriously in the past few years.

Regular readers of our web site already know that I make unusual connections between things and this item certainly has been working on me. What it reminded me of was the movie *V*, where the aliens began to target scientists for destruction because they were the only ones capable of figuring out the genetics of the invaders and what might be used as a weapon against them. I know that is a strange connection, but when you try to figure out a reason for the deaths of so many microbiologists in so short a period of time, considering what is happening on the global political stage, you have to start somewhere.

Of course, it wasn't until the death of David Kelly that the clue about Ethnic Specific Weapons turned up and then it all began to make a sick sort of sense.

The news bytes tell us that Kelly was involved with ultra secret work at Israel's Institute for Biological Research. We are also told that there have been "persistent reports" that the institute is engaged in DNA sequencing research. This last seems to be founded on the fact that a former member of the Knesset, Dedi Zucker, claimed in the Israeli Parliament that the institute was "trying to create an ethnic specific weapon" in which Arabs could be targeted by Israeli weapons.

What does *not* fit in this little scenario is the fact that it was *Israeli sources* making the claim that Kelly met Israeli institute scientists several times in London in the past two years, from which, it seems, the inference was made that Kelly was involved with ultra secret work *for* Israel.

As I have already written, the problem that captured my attention - assuming that Dedi Zucker was letting the cat out of the bag when he said that Israel was "trying to create an ethnic specific weapon in which Arabs could be targeted" - was what kind of "marker" would they use to include or exclude based on *ethnicity*?

There are two points to keep in mind here from our look at genetics. First, studies done from the perspective of the Y chromosome, or the male genetic line, show similarities between Ashkenazic Jews, Sephardic Jews, Israeli Arabs/Palestinian, and Lebanese populations as well as limited genetic connections to European populations.

Second, in *most* European *and* Near Eastern Jewish populations, the highest frequency mtDNA type is the HVS-1 Cambridge Reference Sequence (CRS). This type occurs at 16%, on average, in Europe, and at 6%, on average, in the Near East. All of the seven European and Near Eastern *non-Jewish* populations have the CRS as their modal haplotype.

At that point in time, what was revealed by the genetic studies available to me, suggested that any biochemical weapon specifically designed to take out Palestinians would also take out most of today's Jewry, AND a large number of Europeans and their descendants, such as many Americans.

Looking at it from the point of view of mtDNA wasn't entirely satisfactory either. Remember the remark: *two of the nine Jewish populations had the CRS as their modal haplotype, including the largest group of modern Jews, Ashkenazi:*

"The pattern in Ashkenazic Jews is of particular interest. Despite the common opinion that this population has undergone a strong founder event, it has a modal haplotype with a frequency similar to that of its host population (9.0% vs. 6.9%), providing little evidence of a strong founder event on the female side."

That meant that the mtDNA as an "excluder" would only work for less than 30 percent of modern Jews - Separdic Jews - and the remaining 70 percent would be as susceptible to an Ethnic Specific agent as Palestinians. That didn't make a whole lot of sense. Since most of the Zionist Jews are Ashkenazi, why would they create a weapon that would guarantee their own destruction? I kept thinking about Larsen's explication of the possibility of "engineered biological pathogens which would affect only those races which historically have no natural defense against certain enzyme inhibitors.

Of course, I realized that there must surely be a lot more to this issue than was available to the public. Who knows what kind of research goes on in the Enclaves of the National Security State?

So there the problem rested as I continued to dig for clues.

Now, let's take a moment to answer the question: what is mtDNA and what, precisely, does it do?

Mitochondria are tiny structures that exist within every cell, though not in the cell nucleus along with the chromosomes. The mitochondria help the cell use oxygen to produce energy. The more active a cell is, the more energy it needs and the more mitochondria it contains. Active cells such as those that make up muscles and neurons can contain as many as a thousand mitochondria.

Each mitochondria is in a little membranous sac which also contains enzymes for aerobic metabolism, or the burning of fuel that we take in as food. This "burning" takes place in a "sea of oxygen" which neither produces "flame" nor gives off light, but most definitely produces heat.

The main output of this process is a high-energy molecule called ATP which is needed by the body to run everything from the beating of the heart, to thinking with the cells of the brain.

Right in the middle of each of these little power cells is a tiny piece of DNA that is only sixteen and a half thousand base pairs in length. To compare, the bases in the chromosomes of the nucleus number three thousand million.

Mitochondrial DNA is composed of genetic codes for the oxygen-capturing enzymes that do the work in the mitochondria. Interestingly, many of the genes that control the workings of the mitochondria are found within the nuclear chromosomes. This, of course, reminds us of Larsen's "enzyme inhibitors". An inhibitor that affects "oxygen capturing enzymes"?

There is also something very bizarre about the mtDNA: Mitochondrial DNA forms a circle. As it happens, bacteria and other micro-organisms also have circular chromosomes.

Some experts think that mitochondria were once free-living bacteria that invaded more advanced cells hundreds of millions of years ago. The cells got a boost from being able to use oxygen - a cell can create much more high-energy ATP from the same amount of fuel using oxygen than it can without it - and the mitochondria may have found life within the cell more "comfortable" than outside. Yes, I know this is a really wild explanation, but it gets better. The experts theorize that, very slowly, over millions of years, some of the mitochondrial genes were transferred to the nucleus where they remain. This means mitochondria are trapped within cells and cannot return to the outside even if they wanted to.

This idea is based on the fact that the nuclear chromosomes are littered with broken fragments of mitochondrial genes that can't do anything because they are not intact.

Of course, with the strange connections that pop up in my head, all of this reminded me of a number of remarks made by "Us in the Future" which I can't resist including here in chronological order, though each excerpt came at different times, spread out over 8 years:

DNA core is as yet undiscovered enzyme relating to carbon. Light waves were used to cancel the first ten factors of DNA by burning them off. At that point, a number of physical changes took place...

Q: (L) Could you describe to me the true meaning of the Osirian cycle. What was the symbology of the killing of Osiris and the cutting up of the body?

A: Removal of knowledge centers.

Q: (L) Knowledge centers in what?

A: Your DNA.

Q: (L) So, the breaking up of Osiris' body represents the breaking up of the DNA in our bodies?

A: Partly. Also means knowledge capacity reduction. Time is an illusion that works for you because of your altered DNA state.

Q: (V) A few weeks ago several of us began to suffer from internal heat, insomnia, and other things. What was this?

A: Image. Deep conjunction of fibrous linkage in DNA structure.

Q: (L) Is there any possibility of regaining or restructuring this DNA?

A: Was there, will be again.

Q: (L) OK, we've got a whole bunch of DNA, in these funny- looking double strands. And, according to the book, only 2% is actually used, and the other 98% of it is what these 'experts' are pleased to call 'junk'. They call it junk. Now, I would like to know, is there any way to activate this other DNA?

A: Won't it be activated on its own?

Q: Is bloodline something that is distinct or different from genetics or DNA?

A: Symbiotic relationship.

Q: Are these bloodlines carrying a specific codon that is designed to activate at a certain period of time or in response to a certain frequency?

A: Possibly, but why should not that apply to everyone?

Q: I have been having this sensation of an electrical charge building up in my legs and I would like to know what I can do to discharge this. All the muscles are hard and uncomfortable.

A: Molecular changes due to DNA evolving.

[Break. Group watches video: Riverdance.]

Q: Hi guys! Did you like the movie?... How close are these dances to the original Celtic dances?

A: Half.

Q: What about these dances would make them more original?

A: Floating.

Q: But, why the stylized rigidity of the arms?

A; Has to do with sound through chemical enzyme based utilization for power purposes.

Q: How does the stiff-arm posture relate to sound?

A: Chemical transmitter flow.

Q: You mean that something flowed through their arms and out their hands to enhance levitation?

A: Close.

Q: Well, if you think about it, the Celtic folklore talks about the enormous heat of certain heroes who had to be plunged into very cold water several times so that they could cool down enough to put clothes on. Add to that the fact that the Celts went into battle naked because they would go into the 'furor' and produce so much heat that they could not tolerate clothing. And, what about the heat of the 'states' [described by Ibn al-'Arabi] that I experience from time to time identified as a 'reflection' of the connection to 4th density. That is a truly bizarre state because the heat is so intense it is almost unbearable, yet does not even show on a thermometer, and to anyone else who touches me, I am not hot. Yet the internal heat is unbelievable.

Q: (L) What would be the effect of cosmic rays emitted by a supernova that is in some proximity to the earth on the human body?

A: Genetic splice of strand.

Q: (L) How close would a supernova have to be to have this effect?

A: 2000 light years.

Q: You once said that the core of DNA is an as yet undiscovered enzyme related to carbon. Is that correct?

A: Yes.

Q: Here in this book it says: "Evidence is accumulating that only a relatively small portion of the DNA sequence is for so-called structural genes. Structural genes lead to the production of protein. There are an estimated 50,000 structural genes with an average size of approximately 5,000 base pairs, which then accounts for only 250 million of the estimated 3 billion base pairs.

What is the rest of the DNA for?

Some of the DNA is so-called repetitive sequences, repeated thousands of times. The function is unknown. The ALU, repeat, for instance, contains over 300,000 copies of the same 300 base pair sequence. Certainly this DNA is not junk and plays some important role in the gene regulation chromosomal architecture or chromosomal replication.

Until 1977, it was thought that genes were single sequences of DNA that are coded into RNA and then into protein. However, further study has shown greater complexity. It is now known that there are pieces of DNA within a gene that are not translated into protein. These intervening sequences, or INTRONS, are somewhat of a mystery, but appear to be a very common phenomenon."

Now, is this thing they are talking about, these INTRONS, are these the core that you were talking about?

A: In part.

Q: What about this ALU repeat with over 300,000 copies of the same base pair sequence. What is it?

A: Tribal unit.

Q: What is a tribal unit?

A: Sectionalized zone of significant marker compounds.

Q: What does this code stand for?

A: Physiological/spiritual union profile. ...

Q: What does the rest of the DNA code for that is not coding for structural genes. What else can it be doing?

A: Truncated flow.

Q: Truncated flow of what?

A: Liquids. ...

Q: (L) Does truncated flow mean a flow of liquid that has been stopped?

A: Yes. Because of design alteration!

Q: Is this liquid that has been truncated a chemical transmitter?

A: Yes.

Q: And would this chemical transmitter, if it were allowed to flow, cause significant alterations in other segments of the DNA?

A: Yes.

Q: So, there is a segment of code that is in there, that is deliberately inserted, to truncate this flow of liquid, which is a chemical transmitter, or neuropeptide, which would unlock significant portions of our DNA?

A: Close: Biogenetic engineering. ...

Q: Okay, can you tell us what was this specific liquid or transmitter that was truncated?

A: Think of the most efficient conductor of chemical compounds for low wave frequency charge.

Q: Saline?

A: Close. It is a naturally bonding combination.

Q: (L) Well, I'll have to research it. The fact is, we've got 3 billion base pairs... do some of these so-called segments of "junk DNA", if they were activated, would they instruct chromosomal replication to take place with more than 23 pairs as a result?

A: In part.

Q: Is there anything we can do in terms of activities or...

A: No. Biogenetic engineering.

Q: Was the thought that I had one night that, at some point in time something may happen that will turn genes on in our bodies that will cause us to physically transform, an accurate perception of what could happen?

A: For the most part, yes.

Q: Are there any limitations to what our physical bodies can transform to if instructed by the DNA? Could we literally grow taller, rejuvenate, change our physical appearance, capabilities, or whatever, if instructed by the DNA?

A: Receivership capability.

Q: What is receivership capability?

A: Change to broader receivership capability. ..

Q: (A) It means how good is your receiver.

A: Yes.

Q: (L) What is your receiver? The physical body?

A: Mind through central nervous system connection to higher levels.

Q: So, that is the whole issue of gaining knowledge and developing control over your body. If your mind and CNS are tuned to higher levels of consciousness, that has significance in terms of your receivership capability?

A: Close.

All persons of Nordic heritage hold secret power centers, can be of darkness, or of light...

Suffering activates neuro-chemicals which turn on DNA receptors.

Coming back to our mtDNA, we realize that this is the powerhouse of the body, where oxygen capturing enzymes are coded. The mystery as to why parts of mtDNA are attached to nuclear DNA might be easily solved by theorizing that it was once part of the nuclear DNA. Again, a segment from our superluminal transmissions from Us in the Future comes to mind:

> Q: During the time Neanderthal man was on the Earth, did he live alongside Modern man?
> A: Yes. Except modern type man was different then.
> Q: In what ways?
> A: DNA and psycho/electrical frequencies.
> Q: Does this mean that their physical appearance was different from what we consider to be modern man?
> A: Radiance. ...
> Q: Oh, that's interesting. Well, there are legends that the Northern people had "light" in their veins. Very ancient belief. Is this what you are referring to?
> A: Maybe.

I don't want to speculate too much further on the mtDNA at this point except to suggest that it might be the key to Ethnic Specific biochemical weapons when you consider that its configuration is similar to that of bacteria.

Now, as I mentioned, realizing that Ashkenazi Jews were different in some significant way from Separdic Jews, I decided to have a look at Koestler's book which presents the theory that Eastern European Jews are descended from the ancient Khazars. Look again at the chart above to note the position of Ashkenazi Jews relative to other groups according to the male lineage analysis.

Again we notice that the lower right corner of the graph is where Near Eastern Jews are positioned. One might therefore theorize that the Near Eastern Jews are, more or less, the most "Jewish" of the Jews in terms of many generations of "Jews" in their family lines. Looking around this cluster, we notice that there are several "families" that are very close, including Yemenite Jews, Druze, North African Jews, *and* Palestinians. On the other hand, the Ashkenazi Jews are not only much closer to Turks, Syrians and Roman Jews, they are quite distant from both the Near Eastern Jews and the Palestinians.

Naturally, Zionist Jews - most of them Ashkenazi - do not like Koestler's ideas - that the Eastern European Jews were originally Khazars, an Aryan tribe from Central Asia.

The short version of one of the theories held to by the Ashkenazi themselves is that the Roman Jews are descended from a group of Jews that fled Israel at the time of the diaspora and that some of them migrated up into Eastern Europe, then going even further East and mixing with

Turks, forming the Ashkenazi Jews. Another theory is that the Khazars included remnants of original Jews who fled Israel at the time of the Babylonian captivity. When they adopted Judaism in the 9th century, they were just "coming home" so to say. With either of these theories, they retain their "birthright" to Israel upon which the present occupation of Palestine is based.

I can only say that I have read a lot of material on both sides of the question and I find Koestler's research to be original and credible. What is more, there is nothing about the gene flow of the Eastern European Jews that cannot be explained far more completely with his theory than with the "out of Israel at some point" hypothesis. Koestler's ideas explain the anomalies of the Khazar clans as well, when juxtaposed against the Sephardic Jews and their paternal kin, the Palestinians.

Hillel Halkin wrote in an article entitled: *Wandering Jews and Their Genes*:

> Finally, published in last June's Proceedings of the National Academy of Science were the results of a study conducted by an international team of scientists led by Michael Hammer of the University of Arizona and Batsheva Bonné-Tamir of Tel Aviv University...

> Based on genetic samples from 1,371 males... its main conclusions are:

> 1. With the exception of Ethiopian Jews, all Jewish samples show a high genetic correlation...

> 3. In descending order after these Middle Easterners, *Ashkenazi Jews correlate best with Greeks and Turks*; then with Italians; then with Spaniards; then with Germans; then with Austrians; and least of all with Russians...

> And on the other hand again: whereas the traditional explanation of East European Jewish origins was that most Ashkenazi Jews reached Poland and Russia from... the Rhineland; Rhineland from northern France... this version has come under increasing challenge in recent years on both demographic and linguistic grounds.

> Most Jews, the challengers maintain, must have arrived in Eastern Europe not from the west and southwest but from the south and east - that is, via northern Italy and the Balkans; Asia Minor and the Greek Byzantine empire; the Volga kingdom of the Khazars... or a combination of all three.

> Now comes the Proceedings of the National Academy of Science report, which appears to bear out this newer version of events. Ashkenazi Jews, it informs us, have a more significant admixture of Italian, Greek, and Turkish genes than of Spanish, German, or even Austrian ones.

In other words, for the Jews, to have traveled up through Italy to Eastern Europe, would have had to mix with Germans or Austrians - but that isn't the case.

> Of course, things are not so simple. Even without questioning the study's highly technical procedures, different interpretations could be put on them. It

could be argued, for example, that the resemblance of Jewish to Greek and Italian Y chromosomes is traceable to proselytization in the Mediterranean world during the period of the Roman Empire...

What must also be remembered is that Y chromosomes tell us only about males. But we know that in most societies, women are more likely to convert to their husband's religion than vice-versa... If true, this might also explain a number of differences between the Hammer/Bonné-Tamir study and earlier research on the geographical distribution of specific Jewish diseases, blood types, enzymes, and mitochondrial DNA...

This issue is actually so contentious that, after the paper on the Eight Founding Mothers of Judaism was published, Michael Hammer, himself of Ashkenazi heritage, and others, went back to the lab and produced their own "Founding Mother Event of Ashkenazi Jews" paper.

Published on January 14, 2004, the paper, entitled *MtDNA evidence for a genetic bottleneck in the early history of the Ashkenazi Jewish population* tells us the following: (emphases, ours)

> The term 'Ashkenazi' refers to Jewish people of recent European ancestry, with an historical separation from other major Jewish populations in North Africa and the Middle East. The contemporary Ashkenazi gene pool is thought to have originated from a founding deme that migrated from the Near East within the last two millennia. After moving through Italy and the Rhine Valley, the Ashkenazi population presumably experienced a complex demographic history characterized by numerous migrations and fluctuations in population size. During the past 500 years, there was a period of rapid growth culminating in an estimated population size of 8 million Ashkenazi Jews at the outbreak of the Second World War.

Notice that in this most recent research, Hammer is again trying to resurrect the "Up through Italy and the Rhine Valley" idea which is rather thoroughly contradicted by his own earlier research on the paternal ancestry as Hillel Halkin pointed out. One of the issues of Ashkenazi ancestry is the high frequency of more than *20 known recessive disease alleles*. As any animal breeder knows, this often occurs with inbreeding. Koestler has pointed out that the Khazars - after their conversion - were more "Jewish than the Jews". As converts, they were more zealous in following the "rules" of not marrying outside of their group. After the destruction of the Khazar kingdom, the population of Khazarian Jews was undoubtedly greatly reduced and this accounts not only for a bottleneck, but also for the conditions in which inbreeding would occur, leading to the expression of recessive disease alleles in the gene pool.

Reading Hammer's new paper is almost painful as his efforts to "repatriate" the Ashkenazi Jews are quite transparent. He refers, at the very beginning, to the "Eight Founding Mothers paper" which pretty much left the Ashkenazi out in the cold, Jewishly speaking.

> In a recent study based on mtDNA sequence variation ... the authors inferred separate maternal founding events for several Jewish populations, with

limited subsequent gene flow from surrounding host populations. Interestingly, the Ashkenazi Jewish sample in this study appeared to be an exception to this pattern, showing no strong signal of a founding event ...

To address the question of whether mtDNA from Ashkenazi populations exhibit signs of a genetic bottleneck, we perform a more extensive analysis of mtDNA genetic variation ... in a sample of 565 Jews from 15 different Ashkenazi communities originating in western and Eastern Europe, and compare these patterns of variation with those of neighboring non-Jewish populations.

In our analysis, we take advantage of the ability to infer evidence for maternal population bottlenecks on the basis of comparative estimates of mtDNA sequence diversity.

This last paragraph just tells us in Sciencespeak that they intend to "interpret" the data according to their bias; you know, "cook the data".

The results presented here portray a pattern of highly reduced mtDNA diversity for the Ashkenazi population, an unusually large proportion of mtDNA haplotypes that are unique to the Ashkenazi gene pool, and a reduction in frequency of rare haplotypes and singleton sites compared with Near Eastern populations.

For example, the three most frequent Ashkenazi haplo- types account for 27.8% of total mtDNA repertoire in our Ashkenazi sample. These Ashkenazi mtDNA haplotypes are virtually absent from surrounding non-Jewish populations and therefore provide a genetic signature of the Ashkenazi maternal gene pool, and bear witness to the strong effects of genetic drift acting on this population.

What Hammer is NOT addressing is the fact that maternal gene pool of the Ashkenazi is not related to the maternal gene pool of other Jews. As Koestler pointed out, the above also bears witness to the self-imposed isolation of Jewish groups among their host populations. They chose to live in walled Ghettos and keep their genes to themselves even if it meant extreme endogamy. In other words, what Hammer et al are describing is inbreeding. He acknowledges this below:

This contrasts with the situation in both Near Eastern and European non-Jewish populations, where only a single haplotype (CRS) was found at elevated frequencies (ie, above 5%).

There are several periods in the history of Jewish populations when bottlenecks may have occurred, for example: (1) in the Near East before the initial migration to Europe (e.g., 41,500 years ago), (2) during the migrations of Jews from the Near East to Italy after the 1st century A.D., (3) upon establishment of small communities in the Rhine Valley in the 8th century A.D., and (4) in the 12th century A.D., when migrations took place from western to eastern Europe.

In addition, endogamy in combination with 4100-fold population growth in the last 500 years undoubtedly played a role in shaping patterns of variation in the Ashkenazi gene pool.

While several authors posited that the high frequency of genetic conditions, such as Tay-Sachs disease, is the result of heterozygote advantage, 5,28 - 30 others have argued for an important role of genetic drift. For example, Risch et al. proposed that founder effects resulting from the dynamics of population growth in the 16 - 19th centuries, especially in the northern Jewish Pale of Settlement (Lithuania and Belarus), explain most, if not all of the genetic diseases observed at high frequency in the Ashkenazi population today. This hypothesis was supported by the inference of a recent age of the single founder mutation (B350 years) that causes early-onset idiopathic torsion dystonia.

The much older estimated age of the factor XI type II mutation (B3000 years), which has a high frequency in both Ashkenazi and Iraqi Jewish populations, implies that its frequency is largely independent of the recent demographic upheavals particular to the Ashkenazi population. [...]

All of the above - and more - is covered rationally and plausibly by Koestler in his book *The Thirteenth Tribe*. Nevertheless, Hammer et al continue to beat the dead horse of a Near East origin for the Ashkenazi mtDNA gene pool.

The observed mutational frequency peak for the Ashkenazi and Near Eastern non-Jewish populations is similar and consistent with the age of the Pleistocene expansion, which is older than that inferred from the mutational frequency peak for European non-Jews. This is consistent with a Near East origin for a major portion of the Ashkenazi Jewish mtDNA pool.

If the Jewish population bottleneck did begin in the Near East, other Jewish populations from around the world are predicted to harbor similar values of f 0 and f 1 in their mismatch distributions. To test this prediction, we examined the mismatch distributions resulting from the data of Thomas et al., which includes samples of the Bukharan, Georgian, Indian, Iranian, Iraqi, Moroccan, and Yemenite Jewish communities. All HVS-1 sequence datasets showed a significantly elevated f 0 (only Sephardic Jews showed an increase in f 1) relative to Near Eastern non-Jewish populations... This result implies that global Jewish communities suffered a common bottleneck in the Near East, or independent founder events during the Jewish Diaspora. [...]

Notice in the above that the Sephardic Jews, did not fulfill the prediction of the "mismatch theory" above. Also note that this prediction was not tested against anything other than Jewish populations. What if other populations show similar mismatch distributions? But Hammer presses on bravely in his attempt to explain away why Ashkenazi aren't like other Jews in the maternal ancestry:

This suggests the possibility that contemporary Ashkenazi mtDNA diversity may derive, in part, from a small and subdivided ancestral mtDNA gene pool, and is consistent with the hypothesis that some high frequency disease alleles originated before the separation of Jewish communities in the Near East. Indeed, estimates of the age of mutations causing Ashkenazi genetic diseases range from recent times (ie, during demographic upheavals within

Europe in the past 500 years), to times when ancestral Ashkenazi populations were first migrating to and within Europe, to times before Jewish populations migrated out of the Near East. [...]

The combined mtDNA and disease mutation data suggest that Ashkenazi Jewish populations experienced a long period of accentuated genetic drift marked by an early bottleneck, perhaps beginning in the Near East. Prolonged periods of low effective population size can lead to the accumulation of slightly deleterious mutations throughout the genome. Small founder populations derived from large ancestral populations are not always capable of purging these deleterious mutations. This may be the ultimate cause of the segregation of disease mutations in Ashkenazi Jews. However, this explanation does not preclude more proximal causes for the increase in frequency of disease mutations, such as those hypothesized by Risch et al., 7 unequal contribution of a particular segment of the Ashkenazi Jewish community to the explosive population growth occurring in the Pale of Settlement approximately 25 generations ago. Low effective size may have enabled deleterious mutations to become established in the Jewish population, while the recent growth of affected segments of the community amplified these mutations to frequencies sufficiently high to form homozygotes.

In other words, he has described the results of the exact scenario that Koestler has hypothesized - inbreeding of a small, surviving population of Khazars and ghetto-ization of fanatical converts - and still has not managed to provide a single convincing bit of evidence of the origin of the Ashkenazi in the Near East.

The short of it is that Koestler's theory, despite many attempts to deconstruct it, still provides the best answers for the origins of the Ashkenazi Jews: they were Khazars who, for political reasons, converted to Judaism. The interested reader is invited to read Koestler's book with its original research and clear exposition of the links between the Khazars and the Eastern European Jews.

The big question now is: Who were the Khazars? Koestler was only able to go so far in answering this question. In my own search, I think I may have gotten a bit closer to it than he did and, at the same time, I may have discovered the clue as to why Nostradamus and Edgar Cayce said what they did.[268]

---

[268] Nostradamus wrote:

In the year 1999 and seven months

From the sky will come the Great King of Terror,

Raising again the great king of the Mongols,

Before and after Mars (war) reigns at his pleasure. X.72

Edgar Cayce's mention of Mongols was as follows:

If there is not the acceptance in America of the closer brotherhood of man, the love of the neighbor as self, civilization must wend its way westward - and again must Mongolism, must a hated people be raised.

The Khazars flourished from the seventh to the eleventh century. This means that they emerged following the reign of the emperor Justinian discussed on the Cassiopaea website.[269] The issues surrounding the reign of Justinian, recorded by Procopius, indicate to us that something very strange was going on during that period of history. In 1998, "Us in the Future" made a comment about this that was only later confirmed scientifically which again, I cannot resist including for its historical interest:

> Q: (L) I have discovered that three of the supernovas of antiquity which have been discovered and time estimated by the remnants, occurred in or near Cassiopeia at very interesting points in history.
> A: Yes...
> Q: (L) Well, one of these periods in history was around 1054. This is a very interesting time. It just so happens that there are no European records of this supernova which was recorded by the Chinese, Japanese, and perhaps even the Koreans. Yet, there are no European records. What happened to the European records?
> A: Europe was in a "recovery mode" at the "time."
> Q: (L) Recovery from what?
> A: Loss of civilized structure due to overhead cometary explosion in 564 AD.
> Q: (L) What effect did this have on the civilized structure? Was it a direct effect in terms of material, or did it have effects on people causing them to behave in an uncivilized and barbaric way?
> A: Well, the burning fragmentary shower ignited much of the land areas in what you now refer to as Western Europe. This had the results you can imagine, causing the resulting societal breakdown you now refer to as "The Dark Ages".
> Q: (L) Well, it damn sure was dark. There is almost a thousand years that nobody knows anything about!
> A: Check Irish or Celtic, and French or Gallic records of the era for clues. There were temporary "islands of survival", lasting just long enough for the written word to eke out.

A year later, August 17, 1999, the Knight Ridder Washington Bureau published an article by Robert S. Boyd entitled: *Comets may have caused Earth's great empires to fall* which included the following: (emphases, mine)

> "Recent scientific discoveries are shedding new light on why great empires such as Egypt, Babylon and Rome fell apart, giving way to the periodic "dark ages" that punctuate human history. *At least five times during the last 6,000 years, major environmental calamities undermined civilizations around the world.*

---

[269] http://www.cassiopaea.org/cass/truth_or_lies_7.htm

Some researchers say these disasters appear to be linked to collisions with comets or fragments of comets such as the one that broke apart and smashed spectacularly into Jupiter five years ago.

The impacts, yielding many megatons of explosive energy, produced vast clouds of smoke and dust that circled the globe for years, dimming the sun, driving down temperatures and sowing hunger, disease and death. The last such global crisis occurred between AD 530 and 540-- at the beginning of the Dark Ages in Europe -- when Earth was pummeled by a swarm of cosmic debris.

In a forthcoming book, Catastrophe, the Day the Sun Went Out, British historian David Keys describes a 2-year-long winter that began in AD 535. Trees from California to Ireland to Siberia stopped growing. Crops failed. Plague and famine decimated Italy, China and the Middle East.

Keys quotes the writings of a 6th-century Syrian bishop, John of Ephesus:

"The sun became dark. ... Each day it shone for about four hours and still this light was only a feeble shadow.''

A contemporary Italian historian, Flavius Cassiodorus, wrote:

"We marvel to see no shadows of our bodies at noon. We have summer without heat."

And a contemporary Chinese chronicler reported, "yellow dust rained like snow."

Dendrochronologist, Mike Baillie, established that:

Analysis of tree rings shows that at in 540 AD in different parts of the world the climate changed. Temperatures dropped enough to hinder the growth of trees as widely dispersed as northern Europe, Siberia, western North America, and southern South America.

A search of historical records and mythical stories pointed to a disastrous visitation from the sky during the same period, it is claimed. There was one reference to a "comet in Gaul so vast that the whole sky seemed on fire" in 540-41.

According to legend, King Arthur died around this time, and Celtic myths associated with Arthur hinted at bright sky Gods and bolts of fire.

In the 530s, an unusual meteor shower was recorded by both Mediterranean and Chinese observers. Meteors are caused by the fine dust from comets burning up in the atmosphere. Furthermore, a team of astronomers from Armagh Observatory in Northern Ireland published research in 1990 which said the Earth would have been at risk from cometary bombardment between the years 400 and 600 AD. [...]

Famine followed the crop failures, and hard on its heels bubonic plague that swept across Europe in the mid-6th century. [...]

At this time, the Roman emperor Justinian was attempting to regenerate the decaying Roman Empire. But the plan failed in 540 and was followed by the Dark Ages and the rise of Islam.

Apparently, this disaster was also followed by the arrival of the Khazars. The kingdom of the Khazars has vanished from the map of the world and today many people have never even heard of it. But, in its day the Khazar kingdom [Khazaria] was a major power.

The Byzantine Emperor and historian, Constantine Porphyrogenitus (913-959) recorded in a treatise on Court Protocol that letters addressed to the pope in Rome, and similarly those to the Emperor of the West, had a gold seal worth two solidi attached to them, whereas messages to the King of the Khazars required a seal worth three solidi.

In other words, it was clearly understood that the Khazars were more powerful than the Emperor of the West or the Pope. As Koestler commented, "This was not flattery, but Realpolitik". How can it be that we are taught about the Byzantine Empire and the rise of the power of the Popes of the Western Empire, and have so little knowledge of an empire that existed at the same time, that was obviously more powerful than either of them? A Jewish empire, in fact?

The country of the Khazars was strategically located at the gateway between the Black Sea and the Caspian, acting as a buffer protecting Byzantium against invasions by the barbarian Bulgars, Magyars, Pechenegs, and later the Vikings and Russians. More important than this was the fact that the Khazars also blocked the Arabs from Eastern Europe.

Within a few years of the death of Muhammad (AD 632) the armies of the Caliphate, sweeping northward through the wreckage of two empires and carrying all before them, reached the great mountain barrier of the Caucasus. This barrier once passed, the road lay open to the lands of Eastern Europe. As it was, on the line of the Caucasus the Arabs met the forces of an organized military power which effectively prevented them from extending their conquests in this direction. The wars of the Arabs and the Khazars, which lasted more than a hundred years, though little known, have thus considerable historical importance. [Professor Dunlop of Columbia University, authority on the Khazars, quoted by Koestler, p. 14]

Most people know that the Frankish army of Charles Martel turned back the Arabs on the field of Tours. Few people know that, at the same time, the Muslims were met and held by the forces of the Khazar kingdom.

In 732, the future emperor, Constantine V, married a Khazar princess and their son became Emperor Leo IV, known as Leo the Khazar.

A few years later, probably in AD 740, the King of the Khazars, his court and the military ruling class embraced the Jewish faith and Judaism became the state religion of the Khazars. This came about as a reaction against the political pressure of the other two Superpowers of the day - Byzantium and the Muslims - both of which had the advantage of a monotheistic State Religion which allowed them greater control over their subjects. Not wanting to be subject either to the Pope or the Byzantine Emperor, but seeing the political benefits of religious controls, Judaism was chosen.

The Khazar kingdom held its power and position for most of four centuries during which time they were transformed from a tribe of nomadic warriors into a nation of farmers, cattle-breeders, fishermen, viticulturists, traders and craftsmen. Soviet archaeologists have found evidence of advanced civilization with houses built in a circular shape at the lower levels, later being replaced by rectangular buildings. This is explained as evidence of the transition from portable, dome shaped tents, to settled lifestyles.

At the peak of their power, the Khazars controlled and/or received tribute from thirty or so different nations and tribes spread across the territories between the Caucasus, the Aral Sea, the Ural Mountains, the town of Kiev, and the Ukrainian steppes. These peoples included the Bulgars, Burtas, Ghuzz, Magyars, the Gothic and Greek colonies of the Crimea, and the Slavonic tribes to the Northwest.

"Until the ninth century, the Khazars had no rivals to their supremacy in the regions north of the Black Sea and the adjoining steppe and the forest regions of the Dnieper. The Khazars were the supreme masters of the southern half of Eastern Europe for a century and a half. [...] During this whole period, they held back the onslaught of the nomadic tribes from the East". [Soviet archaeologist M. I. Artamonov]

In the timeline of history, the Khazar Empire existed between the Huns and the Mongols. The Arab chroniclers wrote that the Khazars were, "white, their eyes blue, their hair flowing and predominantly reddish, their bodies large, and their natures cold. Their general aspect is wild".

The Georgians and Armenians, having been repeatedly devastated by the Khazars, identified them as *Gog and Magog*. An Armenian writer described them as having, "insolent, broad, lashless faces and long falling hair, like women".

They sound like the long-haired Franks, don't they?

One of the earliest factual references to the Khazars occurs in a Syriac chronicle dating from the middle of the sixth century. It mentions the Khazars in a list of people who inhabit the region of the Caucasus. Koestler recounts that other sources indicate that *the Khazars were intimately connected with the Huns.*

In AD 448, the Byzantine Emperor Theodosius II sent an embassy to Attila which included a famed rhetorician by name of Priscus. He kept a minute account not only of the diplomatic negotiations, but also of the court intrigues and goings-on in Attila's sumptuous banqueting hall. He was, in fact, the perfect gossip columnist, and is still one of the main sources of information about Hun customs and habits. But Priscus also has anecdotes to tell about a people subject to the Huns whom he calls Akatzirs - that is, very likely, the Ak-Khazars, or "White" Khazars.

The Byzantine Emperor, Priscus tells us, tried to win this warrior race over to his side, but the greedy Khazar chieftain named Karidach, considered the bribe offered to him inadequate, and sided with the Huns. Attila defeated Karidach's rival chieftains, installed him as the sole ruler of the Akatzirs, and invited him to visit his court. Karidach thanked him profusely for the invitation and went on to say that "it would be too hard on a mortal man to look into the face of a god. For, as one cannot stare into the sun's disc, even less could one look into the face of the greatest god without suffering injury". Attila must have been pleased, for he confirmed Karidach in his rule.

After the collapse of the Hun Empire, the Khazars raided and absorbed numerous tribes of nomadic hordes coming from the East. At this point, the West Turkish kingdom arose, a confederation of tribes ruled by a Kagan, or Khagan. The Khazars later adopted this title for their rulers as well. This "Turkish state" fell apart after a century, but it is important to note that it was only after this period that the word Turkish was used in reference to a specific nation, as opposed to its earlier use which simply meant a tribe speaking a Turkic language such as the Khazars and Bulgars.

And so, at the time of the cometary disasters that brought on the Dark Ages, the Khazars rose to power. By the first decades of the seventh century, there were three "Superpowers", two of whom had been fighting each other for a century and were seemingly on the verge of collapse. Persia was about to face its doom in the armies of the Khazars, but through its friendship with Khazaria, Byzantium survived.

In 627, the Roman Emperor Heraclius made an alliance with the Khazars so as to defeat his nemesis: Persia. The Khazars provided Heraclius with 40,000 horsemen under a commander named Ziebel and Heraclius promised him his daughter.

The Persians were defeated, which was followed by a revolution and after ten years of anarchy and chaos, the first Arab armies delivered the coup de grace. And so, a new Superpower arose: the Islamic Caliphate.

In short order, the Muslims conquered Persia, Syria, Mesopotamia, Egypt and surrounded the Byzantine Empire in a half-circle from the Mediterranean to the Caucasus. Between 642 and 652, the Muslims repeatedly penetrated into Khazaria in an attempt to gain a foothold on the way to Eastern Europe. After a defeat in 652, the Muslims backed off for thirty or forty years and concentrated on Byzantium, laying siege to Constantinople on several occasions. Had they been able to get to the other side, to surround Byzantium from the Khazarian side, it would have been fatal for the Roman Empire.

Meanwhile, the Khazars consolidated their own power, expanding into Ukraine and the Crimea, incorporating the conquered people into their empire ruled by the Kagan. By the time of the 8th century, the Khazar Empire was stable enough to actually go on the offensive against the Muslims rather than just holding their position and driving them away repeatedly.

> "From a distance of more than a thousand years, the period of intermittent warfare that followed looks like a series of tedious episodes on a local scale, following the same, repetitive pattern: the Khazar cavalry in their heavy armour breaking through the pass of Dariel or the Gate of Darband into the Caliph's domains to the south; followed by Arab counter-thrusts through the same pass or the defile, towards the Volga and back again. [...] One is reminded of the old jingle about the noble Duke of York who had ten thousand men; "he marched them up to the top of the hill. And he marched them down again." In fact, the Arab sources speak of armies of 100,000, even of 300,000 men engaged on either side - probably outnumbering the armies which decided the fate of the Western world at the battle of Tours about the same time."

> "The death-defying fanaticism which characterized these wars is illustrated by episodes such as the suicide by fire of a whole Khazar town as an alternative to surrender; the poisoning of the water supply of Bab al Abwab by an Arab general; or by the traditional exhortation which would halt the rout of a defeated Arab army and make it fight to the last man: "To the Garden Muslims, not the Fire" - the joys of Paradise being assured to every Muslim soldier killed in the Holy War." [Koestler, p. 28]

The giant Islamic pincer movement across the Pyrenees in the west and across the Caucasus into Eastern Europe was halted at both ends at about the same time. As Charles Martel's Franks saved Gaul and Western Europe, so the Khazars saved the Eastern Roman Empire.

At the end of all this was the marriage of the Khazar princess to the heir of the Byzantine Empire in gratitude for defeat of the Muslims. Following this event, of course, was the politically expedient conversion of the Khazars to Judaism.

Overnight an entire group of people, the warlike, fanatical Khazars, suddenly proclaimed themselves Jews. The Khazar kingdom began to be described as the "Kingdom of the Jews" by historians of the day. Succeeding Khazar rulers took Jewish names, sent for Jewish scholars from Spain to come and instruct them, settle with them. During the late 9th Century the Khazar kingdom became a haven for Jews of other lands. But it seems that this process was almost exclusively a question of male Jews - including Kohanim - coming to Khazaria and marrying Khazar women. What does not seem to have happened, is the intermarriage of Khazars with Separdic Jewish women from other European communities of Jews.

Koestler quotes at length from ancient accounts of the Khazars and I highly recommend this book to the reader not only because it is well researched, but also because it can be quite entertaining reading!

At the height of the Khazar empire, the main source of royal income was foreign trade. There were enormous caravans that transported textiles, dried fruit, honey, wax, and spices following the Silk road to and from the East. Arts and crafts and haute couture flourished. Slaves and furs were traded by Rus merchants, Vikings coming down the Volga on a north/south trade axis. On all these goods, the Khazars levied a tax of ten per cent. This was added to the tribute paid by the Bulgars, Magyars, and others. Khazaria was cosmopolitan, open to all sorts of cultural and religious influences while, at the same time, using its State Religion to defend itself against the other two ecclesiastical powers in the world.

In short, Khazaria was an extremely prosperous country and this prosperity depended on its military power. Khazaria had a standing army with which it was able to maintain brutal domination over its subject tribes and peoples. Human sacrifice was also practiced by the earlier Khazars-including the ritual killing of the king at the end of his reign.

At the beginning of the ninth century, the Khazars had more or less a tacit "nonaggression pact" with the Caliphate, and relations with Byzantium were friendly. After all, they were family! But, a new cloud was on the horizon: the Vikings began to stir.

Two centuries earlier, it had been the Arabs and their "Holy War". Now it was the Vikings and their "unholy war" of piracy and plunder.

> "In neither case have historians been able to provide convincing explanations of the economical, ecological or ideological reasons which transformed these apparently quiescent regions of Arabia and Scandinavia quasi overnight into volcanoes of exuberant vitality and reckless enterprise. Both eruptions spent their force within a couple of centuries but left a permanent mark on the world. Both evolved in this time-span from savagery and destructiveness to splendid cultural achievement." [Koestler, p. 86]

Within a few decades, the Vikings had penetrated all the major waterways of Europe, conquered half of Ireland, colonized Iceland, conquered Normandy, sacked Paris, raided Germany, the Rhone delta, the gulf of Genoa, circumnavigated the Iberian peninsula and attacked Constantinople through the Mediterranean and the Dardanelles, coordinated with an attack down the Dnieper and across the Black Sea. A special prayer was formulated in Christendom: Lord deliver us from the fury of the Normans.

Again, Byzantium depended on Khazaria to block the advance of the Vikings.

This branch of norsemen who were called Rhos or Varangians, originated *from eastern Sweden* and were cousins to the Norwegians and Danes who raided Western Europe.

> "These Varangian-Rus seem to have been a unique blend - unique even among their brother Vikings - combining the traits of pirates, robbers and meretricious merchants, who traded on their own terms, imposed by sword and battle-axe. They bartered furs, swords and amber in exchange for gold, but their principal merchandise were slaves." [Koestler, p. 89]

For a century and a half, trade and diplomacy between the Byzantines and the Khazars and the Rus alternated with war. Slowly but surely, the Vikings built permanent settlements, becoming Slavonized by intermingling with their subjects and vassals - the Slavs along the Dnieper who were agricultural and more timid than the "Turks". This mixing of genes and cultures tamed the Rus and turned them into Russians.

At first, the Rus were friendlier with the Khazars than with the Byzantines. The Rus even adopted the title "Kagan" for their ruler. However, all the while they were having "cultural exchanges" with the Khazars, the Rus were bringing the Slavs into their own fold. Considering the genetic data, this may be as much due to intermarriage between the Slavonic tribes, as due to conquest. Within a couple of decades, the Rus were receiving tribute from almost half of the former subjects of the Khazars!

When the town of Kiev, on the Dnieper river, passed into Rus hands, apparently without an armed struggle, it was the beginning of the end for Khazaria. There were still large communities of Khazar Jews in Kiev, and later, after the final destruction of Khazaria, they were joined by Khazar refugees.

A tribe called the Magyars now come into view. The Magyars seem to have originated in the forest regions of the northern Urals along with two other tribes, the Vogul and Ostyak. Probably at the time of the cometary bombardment that brought on the dark ages, these tribes were driven out of their forests and the Magyars, attaching themselves as willing vassals to first the Huns and then the Khazars. There is no record of a single armed conflict between the Khazars and Magyars. Toynbee says that the Magyars "took tribute" on the Khazars' behalf from the Slav and Finn peoples.

At the time of the arrival of the Rus, the Magyars moved across the Don river to its West bank. One might assume, by the fact that they were allies of the Khazars, that they did this with the full permission of the Khazars and that it was intended to act as a check against the advancement of the Rus.

The Khazars compensated the Magyars for their loyalty by giving them a king, the founder of the first Magyar dynasty and then, they did something that they apparently had not done up to this point: intermarriage between the Magyars and several Khazar tribes took place. The Khazar Kagan gave a noble Khazar lady to the new king of the Magyars for his wife. There were no children of this union, but it is assumed that there were marriages between her retainers and the members of the Magyar court.

At some point during this period, there also seems to have been a rebellion of three Khazar tribes, some of whom fled to the Magyars. As Koestler puts it: the Magyars received, metaphorically and literally, a blood transfusion from the Khazars.

Until the middle of the tenth century, both the Magyar and Khazar languages were spoken in Hungary. The result of this double tongue is the mixed character of the modern Hungarian language. Though the Hungarians have ceased to be bilingual, there are still some two hundred loan-words from the Chuvash dialect of Turkish which the Khazars spoke.

There is some evidence to indicate that among the dissident Khazar tribes (the leading one was called Kabar), who de facto took over the leadership of the Magyar tribes, there were Jews, or adherents of a "judaizing religion". Some experts think that this rebellion was, in fact, connected with the religious reforms initiated by King Obadiah of the Khazars. Rabbinical law, strict rules, and other elements of Judaism would certainly have grated on a tribe of steppe warriors.

The alliance of the Magyars and Khazars came to an end when the Magyars crossed the Carpathian mountains and conquered the territory that was to become Hungary. Thus, in 862, they raided the East Frankish empire.

> The Magyars seem to have acquired the raiding habit only in the second half of the ninth century - about the time when they received that critical blood-transfusion from the Khazars. The Kabars ... became the leading tribe, and infused their hosts with the spirit of adventure which was soon to turn them into the scourge of Europe, as the Huns had earlier been. They also taught the Magyars "those very peculiar and characteristic tactics employed since time immemorial by every Turkish nation - Huns, Avars, Turks, Pechenegs, Kumans - and by no other ... light cavalry using the old devices of simulated flight, of shooting while fleeing, of sudden charges with fearful, wolf-like howling." [Koestler, p. 103]

In other words: "By way of deception, thou shalt do war..."

Thus, the Khazars were instrumental in establishing the Hungarian state. In the tenth century, the Hungarian Duke Taksony invited an unknown number of Khazars to settle in his domains. It is not unlikely that these Khazars were Jews. Steve Jones writes in *In the Blood: God, Genes, and Destiny*:

"Ashkenazim are quite distinct from their Mediterranean and Middle-Eastern co-religionists in the incidence of the disease and in the mutations responsible...

The genetic family tree of Jews from different parts of Europe shows that they are not a unique group, biologically distinct from other peoples around them. There is, though, evidence of common ancestry that gives Jews at least a partial identity of their own. In most places, there is overlap between the genes of the Jewish population and those of local non-Jews. There has been interchange; sometimes through recent marriage, but more often as a result of mating long ago....

The Y chromosomes of Jews are - unsurprisingly - not all the same; the idea of the sons of Abraham is a symbolic one. They do show that many males, some only distantly related to each other, have contributed to the genes of European Jewry. On the average, most Jewish populations contain more diversity for male lineages than for female (whose history is recorded in mitochondrial DNA). This means that there has been more invasion of the Jewish gene pool by the genes of non-Jewish men than of women. The Y chromosomes of Jewish men from the Balkans are rather unlike those of other European Jews, perhaps because there was more admixture in this unstable part of the world."

Judit Beres and C. R. Guglielmino write in: Genetic Structure in relation to the history of the Hungarian ethnic group.

"Magyars, Jews, Gypsies, Germans, Slovaks, Kuns, Romanians, etc. In this very large study, Hungarian Jews were found to be highly distinct from all other groups residing in Hungary." [Human Biology 68:3 (June 1996): 335-356]

Bruce Schecter, a Hungarian physicist, paints the following picture of life in Hungary and Budapest at the beginning of the 20th century:

"At the turn of the century bankers, merchants, industrialists, artists, and intellectuals thronged the broad boulevards that ring [Budapest] or rode beneath them in Europe's first subway. Between 1890 and 1900 the population of Budapest had increased by more than 40 percent to over three-quarters of a million souls, making it the sixth largest city in Europe. Because of Budapest's lively cafes, boulevards, parks, and financial exchange, visitors called it the 'Little Paris on the Danube'. What would not become apparent for years was that while the cares were doing a booming business, the maternity wards of Budapest were churning out [Jewish] geniuses like a Ford assembly line.

Hungary's economic and intellectual flowering began with the Ausgleich of 1867, which established the dual monarchy with Austria. Under that agreement Hungary achieved something approaching independence from

Austria; the Austrian Empire became the Austro-Hungarian Empire. With astonishing rapidity the engines of the industrial age and capitalism would transform Hungary. 'The operators of those mechanisms', writes historian Richard Rhodes, 'by virtue of their superior ambition and energy, but also by default, were Jews'.

Shortly after the establishment of the dual monarchy, discriminatory laws against Jews were repealed, opening to them all civic and political functions. The surge of Jewish immigration followed, paralleling the contemporaneous flood of Jewish immigrants from Russia to New York City.

Political power remained in the hands of the nobility, whose indifference to the gentile non-Hungarian minorities - nearly half the population - would keep a third of the gentiles illiterate as late as 1918, and most of them tied to the land. The Hungarian nobility, unwilling to dirty its hands on commerce, found allies in the Jews. By 1904 Hungarian Jews, who comprised about 5 percent of the population, accounted for about half of Hungary's lawyers and commercial businessmen, 60 percent of its doctors, and 80 percent of its financiers. Budapest Jews were also a dominant presence in the artistic, literary, musical, and scientific life of the country, which caused the growing anti-Semitic community to coin the derogatory label 'Judapest'.

The growing anti-Semitism would in later years cause many of the brightest members of the Hungarian Jewish community to flee their country. Some of the leading scientists and mathematicians, whose ideas and inventions would help form this century, were part of this tide of immigration. Among the better known were Leo Szilard, who was the first person to understand how chain reactions can unleash the power of the atom; John von Neumann, inventor of the electronic computer and game theory; and Edward Teller, the father of the hydrogen bomb. Less well known outside the world of science but equally influential were Theodor von Karman, the father of supersonic flight; George de Hevesy who received a Nobel Prize for his invention of the technique of using radioactive tracers that has had a revolutionary impact on virtually every field of science; and Eugene Wigner, whose exploration of the foundations of quantum mechanics earned him a Nobel Prize.

The list of the great Hungarian scientists could be extended almost indefinitely, but even outside the sciences the prominence of Hungarians is extraordinary. In music it would include the conductors Georg Solti, George Szell, Fritz Reiner, Antal Dorati, and Eugene Ormandy, and the composers Bela Bartok and Zoltan Kodaly. Hungarian visual arts in this century were dominated by Laszlo Moholy-Nagy, who founded the Chicago Institute of Design. Hollywood was even more influenced by the Magyar emigration. Movie moguls William Fox and Adolph Zukor were Budapest-born, as were Alexander Korda and his brothers, Vincent and Theodor, the director George Cukor, and the producer of Casablanca, Michael Curtisz. And of course, Zsa Zsa Gabor and her sisters were Hungarian, as were Paul Lukas and Erich Weiss, better known as Harry Houdini.

Trying to account for what the physicist Otto Frisch called the "galaxy of brilliant Hungarian expatriates", is a favorite activity in scientific circles. The leading theory, attributed to the theoretical physicist Fritz Houtermans, is that, "these people are really from Mars". Andrew Vazxonyi offers a particularly charming version of the extraterrestrial theory. "Well, at the beginning of the century", he says quite seriously, but with a twinkle in his eye, "some people from outer space landed on earth. They thought that the Hungarian women were the best-looking of all, and they took on the form of humans, and after a few years, they decided the Earth was not worth colonizing, so they left. Soon afterward this bunch of geniuses was born. That's the true story".

The actual explanation for Hungary's outpouring of genius is hard to find. Chance certainly played a role. But the strong intellectual values of the Jewish bourgeoisie, combined with the excellent Hungarian educational system, were the fertile field in which the random seeds of genetic chance could flourish." [*My Brain is Open*, Bruce Schecter, 1998, Touchstone, New York]

Kevin MacDonald writes in *The Culture of Critique: An Evolutionary Analysis of Jewish Involvement in Twentieth-Century Intellectual and Political Movements,*[270]

"Jews have indeed made positive contributions to Western culture in the last 200 years. But whatever one might think are the unique and irreplaceable Jewish contributions to the post-Enlightenment world, it is naïve to suppose they were intended for the purpose of benefiting humanity solely or even primarily".

I would like to point out that the list of Jewish scientific achievements from the quote above includes atomic bombs and Game Theory. Science, strongly influenced by the important contributions of so many Jewish scientists, has indeed exploded - no pun intended - and it has brought mankind to the edge of self-destruction. Advances in mathematical, physical and computer sciences have brought about "applied game theory", where "wars" are called "games", and to "win the game" is to kill as many people as possible with as little cost as possible.

Now, back to the Rus. At the same point in time when the Magyars went across the Carpathians, thus depriving the Khazars of their protection in the buffer zone, taking many Jews with them, the Rus took over Kiev in a bloodless coup. There is a reason that they were able to do this.

Three years earlier, the Byzantine emperor set out against the Saracens. He hadn't been gone long when a messenger came to tell him to turn around and return to Constantinople as soon as possible because 200 Russian ships had entered the Bosporus from the Black Sea and were sacking the suburbs of the city. This attack had been coordinated with a simultaneous attack of a western Viking fleet approaching Constantinople across the Mediterranean. The master mind behind this almost capture of Constantinople was Rurik of Novgorod, AKA Rorik of Jutland.

---

[270] http://www.csulb.edu/~kmacd/books-Preface.html

The Byzantines now realized what they were up against and, as Koestler notes, decided to play the double game. Treaties were signed in 860 and 866. Scandinavian sailors were recruited into the Byzantine fleet and the famous Varangian Guard was formed. Later treaties in 945 and 971, led to the Principality of Kiev supplying the Byzantine Emperor with troops on request. In 957, Princess Olga of Kiev was baptized on her state visit to Constantinople.

In 988, during the reign of St. Vladimir, the ruling dynasty of the Russians finally and definitively adopted Christianity via the Greek Orthodox Church.

At about the same time, the Hungarians, Poles and Scandinavians converted to Roman Catholicism. The lines of religious division were being drawn across the world. With new alliances and new enemies, the Khazars were, it seems, no longer needed. Now the taxes they charged on all the commerce between Russia and Byzantine and the West and the East became a burden no longer to be borne. The Byzantines sacrificed the Khazar alliance in favor of a Russian détente.

The destruction of the capital city of Khazaria, Sarkel, by Svyatoslav of Kiev in 965, was the end of the Khazar empire, though the state continued.

In 1016, a combined Russian-Byzantine army invaded Khazaria, defeated its ruler and "subdued the country".

The Russians were unable to hold against the tide of nomad warriors from the Steppes. The constant pressure pushed the center of Russian power north and Kiev went into decline. Independent principalities arose and fell, creating chaos and endless war. Into this vacuum rode the Ghuzz, "pagan and godless foes" also known as Polovtsi, Kumans, Kun or Kipchaks. They ruled the steppes from the late eleventh to the thirteenth century when they were overrun by the Mongols.

The Eastern Steppes were plunged into darkness and the later history of the Khazars is shrouded in obscurity. Arab chroniclers speak of a temporary exodus of the population to the Caspian shore, but later returned with the aid of the Muslim Shah of Shirwan. More than one source speaks of this exodus, and eventual return, with the aid of the Muslims. The price of this Muslim help was conversion.

The first non-Arab mention of Khazaria after 965 is a travel report by Ibrahim Ibn Jakub, the Spanish-Jewish ambassador to Otto the Great. He described the Khazars as still flourishing in 973. The Russian Chronicles give an account of Jews from Khazaria arriving in Kiev in 986.

A later mention, in the Russian Chronicle for the year 1023, describes Prince Mtislav marching against his brother Prince Yaroslav with a force of Khazars and Kasogians. Seven years later, a Khazar army is reported to have defeated a Kurdish invading force.

In 1079, the Russian Chronicle says, "The Khazars of Tmutorakan took Oleg prisoner and shipped him overseas to Tsargrad (Constantinople)".

Four years later, Oleg was allowed to return to Tmutorakan where, "he slaughtered the Khazars who had counseled the death of his brother and had plotted against himself".

Around A.D. 1100, the Christian saint, Eustratius was a prisoner in Cherson, in the Crimea, and was ill-treated by his "Jewish master", who forced ritual Passover food on him. Koestler emphasizes that the story is probably bunk, but what is important is that it takes a strong Jewish presence in the town for granted.

The last mention of the Khazars in the Russian chronicle is in 1106. About 50 years later, two Persian poets mention a joint Khazar-Rus invasion of Shirwan and speak of Dervent Khazars. At around the same time, there is a short and grumpy (Koestler's term) remark made by the Jewish traveler, Rabbi Petachia of Regensburg, who was scandalized at the lack of Talmudic learning among the Khazar Jews when he crossed Khazaria.

The last mention of the Khazars *as a nation* is dated around 1245, at which point in time, the Mongols had already established the greatest nomad empire in the world, extending from Hungary to China. Pope Innocent IV sent a mission to Batu Khan, grandson of Jinghiz Khan, ruler of the Western part of the Mongol Empire. Franciscan friar, Joannes de Plano Carpini visited the capital of Batu Khan: Sarai Batu, AKA Saksin, AKA Itil, the former city of the Khazars.

After his return, Plano Carpini wrote in his famous history a list of the regions he visited, as well as the occupants. He mentions, along with the Alans and Circassians, the "Khazars observing the Jewish religion".

Then, darkness.

Bar Hebraeus, one of the greatest Syriac scholars, relates that the father of Seljuk, (the founder of the Seljuk Turk dynasty), Tukak, was a commander in the army of the Khazar Kagan and that Seljuk himself was brought up at the Kagan's court. He was banned from the court for being too familiar with the Kagan.

Another source speaks of Seljuk's father as, "one of the notables of the Khazar Turks". Thus, there seems to have been an intimate relationship between the Khazars and the founders of the Seljuk dynasty. There was an obvious break, but whether it was because of conversion to Islam, or whether conversion to Islam came about because of the break in relations, we cannot know.

Russian epics and folk tales give us a few scattered bits to consider after the expiration of the official chronicles. They speak of the "country of the Jews" and "Jewish heroes" who fought against Russians and ruled the steppes. Legends from the Middle ages circulated among Western Jews tell of a "kingdom of the Red Jews".

> "The Jews of other lands were flattered by the existence of an independent Jewish state. Popular imagination found here a particularly fertile field. Just

as the biblically minded Slavonic epics speak of 'Jews' rather than Khazars, so did western Jews long after spin romantic tales around those 'red Jews', so styled perhaps because of the slight Mongolian pigmentation of many Khazars.

In the twelfth century there arose in Khazaria a Messianic movement, a rudimentary attempt at a Jewish crusade, aimed at the conquest of Palestine by force of arms. The initiator of the movement was a Khazar Jew, one Solomon ben Duji, aided by his son Menahem and a Palestinian scribe. They wrote letters to all the Jews, near and far, in all the lands around them ... They said that the time had come in which God would gather Israel, His people from all lands to Jerusalem, the holy city, and that Solomon Ben Duji was Elijah, and his son was the Messiah.

These appeals were apparently addressed to the Jewish communities in the Middle East, and seemed to have had little effect, for the next episode takes place only about twenty years later, when young Menahem assumed the name David al-Roy, and the title of Messiah. Though the movement originated in Khazaria, its centre soon shifted to Kurdistan. Here David assembled a substantial armed force - possibly of local Jews, reinforced by Khazars - and succeeded in taking possession of the strategic fortress of Amadie, northeast of Mosul. From here he may have hoped to lead his army to Edessa, and fight his way through Syria into the Holy Land. [...]

Among the Jews of the Middle East, David certainly aroused fervent Messianic hopes. One of his messages came to Baghdad and ... instructed its Jewish citizens to assemble on a certain night on their flat roofs, whence they would be flown on clouds to the Messiah's camp. A goodly number of Jews spent that night on their roofs awaiting the miraculous flight.

But the rabbinical hierarchy in Baghdad, fearing reprisals by the authorities, took a hostile attitude to the pseudo-Messiah and threatened him with a ban. Not surprisingly, David al-Roy was assassinated - apparently in his sleep, allegedly by his own father-in-law...

His memory was venerated, and when Benjamin of Tudela traveled through Persia twenty years after the event, 'they still spoke lovingly of their leader'. But the cult did not stop there. According to one theory, the six-pointed 'shield of David' which adorns the modern Israeli flag, started to become a national symbol with David a- Roy's crusade. [...]

During the half millennium of its existence and its aftermath in the East European communities, this noteworthy experiment in Jewish statecraft doubtless exerted a greater influence on Jewish history than we are as yet able to envisage. [...]

In general, the reduced Khazar kingdom persevered. It waged a more or less effective defence against all foes until the middle of the thirteenth century, when it fell victim to the great Mongol invasion... Even then it resisted stubbornly until the surrender of all its neighbors. Its population was largely absorbed by the Golden Horde which had established the centre of its empire in Khazar territory. But before and after the Mongol upheaval, the Khazars sent many offshoots into the unsubdued Slavonic lands, helping ultimately to build up the great Jewish centres of Eastern Europe.

Here, then, we have the cradle of the numerically strongest and culturally dominant part of modern Jewry." [Koestler, pp. 135 - 137]

As Koestler remarks, this history reduces the term "anti-Semitism" to meaningless jargon based on a misapprehension shared by both the Nazi killers and their victims.

It also reduces the Israeli-Palestinian conflict to the most meaningless and tragic hoax which history has ever perpetrated.

Now, let's try to answer the question about the Mongols with a passage from Lev Gumilev's work on *Ethnogenesis and the Biosphere*:

"Names deceive. When one is studying the general patterns of ethnology one must remember above all that a real ethnos and an ethnonym, i.e. ethnic name, are not the same thing.

We often encounter several different ethnoi bearing one and the same name; conversely, one ethnos may be called differently. The word 'Romans' (romani), for instance, originally meant a citizen of the polis Rome, but not all the Italics and not even the Latins who inhabited other towns of Latium.

In the epoch of the Roman Empire in the first and second centuries A.D. the number of Romans increased through the inclusion among them of all Italians-Etruscans, Samnites, Ligurians, Gauls, and many inhabitants of the provinces, by no means of Latin origin.

After the edict of Caracalla in A.D. 212 all free inhabitants of municipalities on the territory of the Roman Empire were called 'Romans', i.e. Greeks, Cappadocians, Jews, Berbers, Gauls, Illyrians, Germans, etc. The concept 'Roman' lost its ethnic meaning, it would seem, but that was not so; it simply changed it.

The general element became unity not even of culture, but of historical fate, instead of unity of origin and language. The ethnos existed in that form for three centuries, a considerable period, and did not break up.

On the contrary, it was transformed in the fourth and fifth centuries A.D., through the adoption of Christianity as the state religion, which began to be the determinant principle after the fourth ecumenical council. Those who recognized these councils sanctioned by the state authority were Romans, and those who did not became enemies.

A new ethnos was formed on that basis, that I conventionally call 'Byzantine', but they themselves called themselves 'Romaic', i.e. 'Romans', though they spoke Greek.

A large number of Slavs, Armenians, and Syrians were gradually merged among the Romaic, but they retained the name 'Romans' until 1453, until the fall of Constantinople. The Romaic considered precisely themselves 'Romans', but not the population of Italy, where Langobards had become feudal lords, Syrian Semites, (who had settled in Italy, which had become deserted, in the first to third centuries A.D.), the townsmen, and the former colons from prisoners of war of all peoples at any time conquered by the Romans of the Empire became peasants.

Florentines, Genoese, Venetians, and other inhabitants of Italy considered themselves 'Romans', and not the Greeks, and on those grounds claimed the priority of Rome where only ruins remained of the antique city.

A third branch of the ethnonym 'Romans' arose on the Danube, which had been a place of exile after the Roman conquest of Dacia. There Phrygians, Cappadocians, Thracians, Galatians, Syrians, Greeks, Illyrians, in short, all the eastern subjects of the Roman Empire, served sentences for rebellion against Roman rule. To understand one another they conversed in the generally known Latin tongue. When the Roman legions left Dacia, the descendants of the exiled settlers remained and formed an ethnos that took the name 'Romanian', i.e. 'Roman', in the nineteenth century.

If one can treat the continuity between 'Romans' of the age of the Republic, and the 'Roman citizens' of the late Empire, even as a gradual extension of the concept functionally associated with the spread of culture, there is no such link even between the Byzantines and the Romans, from which it follows that the word changed meaning and content and cannot serve as an identifying attribute of the ethnos.

It is obviously also necessary to take into consideration the context in which the word - and so the epoch - has a semantic content, because the meaning of words changes in the course of time. That is even more indicative when we analyze the ethnonyms 'Turk', 'Tatar', and 'Mongol', an example that cannot be left aside.

Examples of camouflage. In the sixth century A.D. a small people living on the eastern slopes of the Altai and Khangai mountains were called Turks. Through several successful wars they managed to subordinate the whole steppe from Hingan to the Sea of Azov. [The Khazars] *The subjects of the Great Kaghanate, who preserved their own ethnonyms for internal use, also began to be called Turks, since they were subject to the Turkish Khan.*

When the Arabs conquered Sogdiana and clashed with the nomads, they began to call all of them Turks, including the Ugro-Magyars.

In the eighteenth century, European scholars called all nomads 'les Tartars', and in the nineteenth century, when linguistic classification became fashionable, the name 'Turk' was arrogated to a definite group of languages.

Many peoples thus fell into the category 'Turk' who had not formed part of it in antiquity, for example the Yakuts, Chuvash and the hybrid people, the Ottoman Turks.

The modification of the ethnonym 'Tatar' is an example of direct camouflage. Up to the twelfth century this was the ethnic name of a group of 30 big clans inhabiting the banks of the Korulen. In the twelfth century this nationality increased in numbers, and Chinese geographers began to call all the Central Asian nomads (Turkish speaking, Tungus-speaking, and Mongol-speaking), including the Mongols, Tatars. And even when, in 1206,

Genghis-khan officially called all his subjects Mongols, neighbors continued for some time from habit to call them Tatars.

In this form the word 'Tatar' reached Eastern Europe as a synonym of the word 'Mongol', and became acclimatized in the Volga Valley where the local population began, as a mark of loyalty to the Khan of the Golden Horde to call themselves Tatars. But the original bearers of this name (Kereites, Naimans, Oirats, and Tatars) began to call themselves Mongols. The names thus changed places.

Since that time a scientific terminology arose in which the Tatar anthropological type began to be called 'Mongoloid', and the language of the Volga Kipchak-Turks Tatar. In other words we even employ an obviously camouflaged terminology in science.

But then it is not simply a matter of confusion, but of an ethnonymic phantasmagoria. Not all the nomad subjects of the Golden Horde were loyal to its government. The rebels who lived in the steppes west of the Urals began to call themselves Nogai, and those who lived on the eastern borders of the Jochi ulus, in Tarbagatai and on the banks of the Irtysh, and who were practically independent, because of their remoteness from the capital, became the ancestors of the Kazakhs.

These ethnoi arose in the fourteenth and fifteenth centuries as a consequence of rapid mixing of various ethnic components. The ancestors of the Nogai were the Polovtsy, steppe Alans, Central Asian Turks, who survived a defeat by Batu and were taken into the Mongol army, and inhabitants of the southern frontier of Rus, who adopted Islam, which became a symbol at that time of ethnic consolidation. The Tatars included Kama Bulgars, Khazars, and Burtasy, and also some of the Polovtsy and Ugric Mishari. The population of the White Horde was the mixture; three Kazakh jus were formed from it in the fifteenth century.

But that is not yet all. At the end of the fifteenth century, Russian bands from the Upper Volga began to attack the Middle Volga Tatar towns, forced some of the population to quit their homeland and go off into Central Asia under the chieftainship of Sheibani-khan (1500-1510). There they were met as fierce enemies because the local Turks who at that time bore the name of 'Chagatai' (after Genghis-khan's second son Chagatei, the chief of the Central Asian ulus), were ruled by descendants of Timur, the enemy of the steppe and Volga Tatars, who ravaged the Volga Valley in 1398-1399.

The members of the horde who quit their homeland took on a new name 'Uzbeks' to honor the Khan Uzbeg (1312-1341), who had established Islam in the Golden Horde as the state religion. In the sixteenth century the 'Uzbeks' defeated Babur, the last of the Timurides, who led the remnants of his supporters into India and conquered a new kingdom for himself there.

So the Turks who remained in Samarkand and Ferghana bear the name of their conquerors, the Uzbeks. The same Turks, who went to India, began to be called 'Moghuls' in memory of their having been, three hundred years earlier, subject to the Mongol Empire.

But the genuine Mongols who settled in eastern Iran in the thirteenth century, and even retained their language, are called Khazareitsy from the Persian word khazar - a thousand (meaning a military unit, or division).

But where are the Mongols, by whose name the yoke that lay on Rus for 240 years is known?

They were not an ethnos, because by Genghis-khan's will Jochi, Batu, Orda, and Sheibani each received 4, 000 warriors, of whom only part came from the Far East. The latter were called 'Kins' and not 'Tatars', from the Chinese name of the Jurchen. This rare name occurred for the last time in the Zadonshchina, in which Mamai was called Kinnish.

Consequently, the yoke was not Mongol at all, but was enforced by the ancestors of the nomad Uzbeks, who should not be confused with the settled Uzbeks, although they merged in the nineteenth century, and now constitute a single ethnos, who equally revere the Timurides and the Sheibanides, who were deadly enemies in the sixteenth century, because that enmity had already lost sense and meaning in the seventeenth century."

Look again at the bold text paragraph above and then consider the comment from Michael Hammer's paper where he says:

"The much older estimated age of the factor XI type II mutation (B3000 years), which has a high frequency in both Ashkenazi and Iraqi Jewish populations, implies that its frequency is largely independent of the recent demographic upheavals particular to the Ashkenazi population." [...]

Now, with the history of the Khazars in mind, look again at the chart of relationships. It all begins to make sense, doesn't it?

And now we come back to the Nordic Covenant.

C's: Notice the difference. The duality of covenant!!!
Q: (L) Is SV a 'walk-in?'
A: Not correct terminology.
Q: (L) Well, then what is the correct terminology? What is SV?
A: Birthright.
Q: (L) Okay, now let me go a little bit deeper. Could SV be what you described as a robot person, but programmed for a positive purpose?
A: No, robot "people" do not have bloodlines.
Q: (L) So, this is something that's programmed genetically in a bloodline?
A: Not exactly, those that have the bloodline have the corresponding soul alignment.
Q: (L) We are talking about a genetic bloodline that activates certain abilities and genes that interface with the corresponding soul that has prepared for this manifestation of the bloodline?
A: Yes.
Q: Book says: 'In ancient Near Eastern rituals, the cut made to the animal is symbolically made to the inferior who enters into the covenant with a superior." Is this an accurate representation?
A: Maybe for some.
Q: At the making of the Covenant at Mt. Sinai, there were a bunch of

sacrificed animals, and Moses took the blood, dividing it in half, he cast one half on the altar. Taking the book of the covenant, he read it to the people, and they said, 'we will observe all that Yahweh has decreed. We will obey'. And then Moses took the blood and cast it on the people saying, 'this is the blood of the covenant that Yahweh has made with you containing all these rules'. What is this blood of the covenant?

A: Has to do with bloodline.

Q: So this symbolized the bloodline of the Jews?

A: No.

Q: What bloodline are we talking about here?

A: Aramaic/Aryan.

Q: Are you saying that the Jews are Aramaic/Aryan?

A: No. Jews are not bloodline categorizable, per se.

Q: Was any of this related to the Nordic Covenant?

A: In a parallel sense.

Q: Okay. Umm... It says then: 'We are heirs of a long tradition in which Monotheism is regarded as the great achievement of Judaeo-Christian thought. Monotheism is entangled with particularism, and with the assertion that this god, and no other, must be worshipped. This particularism is so virulent that it reduces all other gods to mere idols, and is so violent that it reduces all other worshippers to abominations. The danger of a universal Monotheism is asserting that its truth is *the* truth; its system of knowledge, *the* system of knowledge; its ethics, *the* ethics; not because any other option must be rejected, but because there simply is no other option. They presuppose a kind of metaphysical scarcity, a kind of hoarding mentality, hoarding belief, hoarding identity, hoarding allegiance, because there is a finite supply of whatever, it must be contained in whole or part. It suggests limit and boundaries.' Is this idea part of the Nordic Covenant?

A: No.

Q: Is the Nordic Covenant in any sense similar to any of the things I have read here?

A: It is a mystical thing, not related to theology in a direct sense.

Q: How long has the Nordic Covenant been in existence?

A: 5129 years.

Q: Is the Nordic Covenant made between humans and other humans, or between humans and higher density beings?

A: Mostly between humans and humans, but some of the other.

Q: Does this Nordic Covenant exist on the earth today in similar format as it did at its inception?

A: Yes.

Q: Is this Nordic Covenant the same as you have referred to as the Quorum?

A: No.

Q: Would you say that the Nordic Covenant and the Quorum are in opposition, or just different?

A: Segmented relationship.

Q: Is the Nordic Covenant made between people who are blond and blue-eyed?

A: Not the central issue.

Q: What is the central issue of the Nordic Covenant?

A: Bloodline extends off the planet.

Q: Is this Nordic Covenant a group that is in place on the planet for the purpose of guarding or propagating a particular bloodline?

A: To guard secrets.

Q: What does this secret have to do with a bloodline?

A: You should be able to figure this one out!

Q: Are these people with this bloodline and with these secrets the same ones involved with the genetic engineering of new bodies for the Lizzies to occupy at the point of transition to 4th density?

A: No.

Q: Are these secrets negative to our civilization or race?

A: From your perspective, maybe.

Q: Do these bloodlines have to do with Nephilim?

A: A little.

Q: What secrets are they guarding?

A: Your origins; the nature of your being.

Q: So, this Nordic Covenant is that which wishes to maintain the darkness of our realm, the time loops, the replays, and all that sort of thing?

A: One of the players, yes.

We noticed the date of the formation of the Nordic Covenant: 5129 years ago - approximately 3100 B.C. Going back to our dates at the beginning, we recall that the formation of the society later to become the Freemasons was 5633 B.C., which could have been 2500 or 422 years before the Hermes rebellion which took place 5211 years ago, or B.C. If the Hermes rebellion was 5211 years ago, then that makes it right around 3200 B.C., putting it right about 100 years before the formation of the Nordic Covenant. We also know that the Nordic Covenant is a "duality" - there are good guys and bad guys - again, using the term loosely.

The C's said that Hermes was a "Traitor to court of Pharaoh Rana",who was the Egyptian leader of a spiritual covenant of spiritual unity of all the peoples in area now known as Middle East, including Egyptians, Essenes, Aryans, and Persians. So, what seems to be so is that all of these groups listed: Aryans, Persians, Egyptians, Essenes - were part of the spiritual covenant - the "Nordic Covenant" formed in response to the Hermes Rebellion.

The next thing to consider is this interesting exchange:

Q: (L) Okay, now: I would like to know if there was a real historic person behind the legend of King Arthur?

A: Close. Sorcerer's Coven. Secret pact of coven is covenant.

Q: (L) Was this the Nordic Covenant behind the legend of King Arthur?

A: Maybe there is something more like an offshoot. King Arthur story based on an offshoot of Nordic Covenant Root.

Q: (L) Okay, now you say that the Nordic Covenant can be positive or negative. Would the Arthurian Cycle be of the Positive Offshoot?

A: Both.

Q: (L) What period of time did this Sorcerer's Coven...

A: During the "Dark Ages".

Q: (L) Can you get me closer to a year, or period of years?

A: We will let you do that.

Q: (L) The chief thing I noticed about this period of the Dark Ages is that from the time of the 'birth of Christ', for about 1300 years, there is an incredible lack of documentation. Now, there were some manuscripts written by Monks, such as Gregory of Tours and so forth, but in general, the only things that have survived from this period are things put out by Monks under the control of the church. It is as though the whole world became illiterate. Is this, in fact, the case? Was it that nobody was writing anything down during this period?

A: Close.

Q: (L) Was any part of this because of the control of the Catholic Church over writing and education, and that they opposed everything that did not support their views?

A: Close.

Q: (L) So, what we have to work with is what we have to work with. And, I guess that's as close as we can get. It isn't a whole heck of a lot. How many people were in this Covenant?

A: Look for answers, trees will lead you to it.

Q: (L) What literary source could I go to find the least distorted or corrupted information?

A: Trees.

As we have mentioned, the claim emerges from time to time that there is a secret group that was formed in the 9th century composed of "priests" of both the Aryan Pagan religion and certain Jewish priests. It is true that a lot of strange things happened after this period as we have noted, and that such a group certainly might fit the profile of a "Sorcerer's Coven".

This group was alleged over the centuries to have engaged in human/child sacrifice, though it is truly difficult to believe. At times the accusations would be directed against the Jews. Such rumors gave many rulers in Europe the excuse to expel Jews from a number of countries, including from England by Edward I in 1290, as well as from Spain by Isabella and Ferdinand. At other times, the accusations would be directed at Aryans, pagans, or others. At one point, it was the Templars, at another point, it was the Masons. What seems to be true is that the TRUE sorcerers have never been revealed.

The one thing that seems to emerge from a consideration of these matters is that the practice of sacrifice of both animals and humans by cutting the throat and immolation in fire, practiced in ancient times by the priesthoods of the Inca-Aryan groups, and imposed on the Jews by these groups, was at the root of these rumors. And, as usual, it was blamed on the rank and file of innocent Jews.

The question is, of course, what was the role of Zionists in this Sorcerer's Coven? The Zionist elite, in fact, have been noted to use the "common Jews" in ways designed to further their own agendas. Again and again the idea is trotted out that there is a "Jewish Zionist" Conspiracy and that the Jews are planning to take over the world, as outlined in the Old Testament, the Jewish Apocrypha and the Talmud. What everyone seems to be missing is that Judaism - as we know it - was created by Christianity in the Dark Ages, and that the whole Sacrifice/Slaughter of innocents comes from the God Viracocha, though there have been many attempts to cover this up and create a benevolent image for the ancient Inca empire of Atlantis.

The issue of sacrifice, which has - in modern times - been thought to be a "Jewish" thing - now comes to our attention. At a certain point in time, as I studied these matters, I realized that the instructions for the sacrifice recorded in the Bible, to some extent could be said to describe the actions taken upon modern day mutilated cattle. The major exception was, of course, that they are not then immolated in fire. But a lot of people don't realize that the immolation in fire of the Jewish sacrifices really amounted to cooking the meat for human consumption.

So, here we have mutilated cattle where certain elements relate to the sacrifice, only nobody has roasted the remains to eat them. I thought this was rather curious.

> Q: Is there any relationship between the instructions for animal sacrifice in the Bible and the cattle mutes?
> A: Only in the general sense of enzyme actions upon leukocytes.
> Q: Does that mean that the instructions for preparation of sacrificial animals were designed to prepare them for alien 'food'?
> A: More for energy transfer.
> Q: Do you mean energy transfer in the a) sense of the transfer of the energy of the animal through the sacrifice, or b) the transfer of the energy of the human performing the sacrifice into the animal, and then through the animal to the alien (and I am using the term alien in its broadest sense) ?
> A: Why not both?
> Q: (L) Okay, I have also been reading about cattle mutilations, that specific parts of the body are taken...
> A: Rumen.
> Q: (L) What is that?
> A: Cattle part.
> Q: (L) Why do they take an eyeball? What do they want only one eyeball?
> A: Study soul pattern.
> Q: (L) Can you study a soul pattern through an eyeball?
> A: Like a tape recorder.
> Q: (L) Why do they take part of a lip?
> A: DNA library.

Q: (L) Well, how many eyes and DNA libraries do they need. This is happening a lot.

A: Some is copy cat by "secret government".

Q: (L) Back in the 1970's, in the Central United States, there were quite a number of cases of animal mutilation There has been a lot of publicity about this at some point and then it died down and was covered up, and there were a lot of ideas and theories about it. What I would like to know is who was doing the animal mutilation?

A: Many.

Q: Okay, who was doing most of the animal mutilation?

A: Not applicable.

Q: Okay. Was some of the animal mutilation done by the U.S Government, or entities within the government?

A: Was?

Q: (L) In other words, it is still going on. Okay, so they are still doing it. Was, or is, some of this activity being conducted by alien individuals?

A: Yes.

Q: (T) Were they acting for the same reasons?

A: No.

Q: Why did the government do animal mutilations?

A: Copy, in order to throw off investigation.

Q: (L) So they copied this activity to throw off investigations. Did they do this as an act to protect the aliens who were doing animal mutilations for their own purposes?

A: No.

Q: (L) Were they doing it to protect themselves from the public knowing that they were engaged in alien interactions?

A: They do it to protect the public from knowing that which would explode society if discovered.

Q: (L) What is this item that they were protecting so that society or the public wouldn't know about it. What activity is this?

A: Humans eat cattle, aliens eat you.

Q: (L) Okay, yeah, we eat second level, they eat third. Did aliens do some of the cattle mutilation?

A: Yes. Blood. Nourishment.

Q: (L) Okay, but you just said that aliens eat humans, and humans eat cattle. Why were the aliens being nourished by cattle, if that's not their normal bill of fare? (T) A cow's blood is a lot like human blood.

A: Do you not ever consume facsimile? Facsimile is less controversial, obviously!

Q: (L) So in other words, they were eating cattle just to keep from having to eat so many humans, that would have just upset people a lot, is that it?

A: Yes. Some of their human "food" is merely emotions, think of flesh as being the equal of "filet mignon".

Q: (T) Some of their food is merely emotions. Okay, when we're talking about these aliens, are we talking about the Grays?

A: No.

Q: (T) We're talking about the Lizards.

A: Yes.

Q: (T) Okay, what do the Grays feed on?

A: Plasma.

Q: (T) Okay, the Grays feed on plasma, blood plasmas of some kind, is this what you are saying?

A: Yes.

Q: (T) Okay, so that's why they want the blood; so, do the Grays feed on emotions?

A: No. They send them to Lizards. Transfer energy through technology.

Q: (T) Are the cattle giving off enough emotion for the Grays to feed this to the Lizards also?

A: No. That is physical only, you see, Lizards and Grays only need physical nourishment while "visiting" 3rd level, not when in natural realm, 4th density, there they feed on emotions only.

Q: (T) Grays are not strictly third density? Because they've been created by the Lizzies?

A: Yes. Correct, they too are 4th level.

[…]

Q: (L) Let me ask this one before the tape runs out and we take a break. What is the "ultimate secret" being protected by the Consortium?

A: You are not in control of yourselves, you are an experiment.

Q: (T) When you say this is the ultimate secret, that we're being "protected" from by the government, are we talking about the ultimate secret of humans only here?

A: Basically.

Q: (T) The ultimate secret of the human race is that we are an experiment that other humans are conducting on the rest of us?

A: Part.

Q: (T) Okay, does the other part have to do with the Lizards?

A: Yes.

Q: (L) Other aliens also?

A: Yes.

Q: (T) Okay, so, are the humans who are running the experiment, do they know that they are part of the experiment also?

A: Yes.

Q: (T) And they're doing this willingly?

A: They have no choice.

Q: (L) Why do they have no choice?

A: Already in progress.

[…]

Q: (L) How "long", and I put long in quotes, because we know, as you say, there is no time, but how long, as we measure it, have the Grays been interacting with our race? The Grays, not the Lizards, the Grays, the cybergenetic probes?

A: Time travelers, therefore, "Time is ongoing". Do you understand the gravity of [this] response?

Q: (L) They are time travelers, they can move forward and backward in time, they can play games with our heads... (T) They can set up the past to create a future they want. (D) They can organize things so that they can create the energy that they need... (L) They can also make things look good, make them feel good, make them seem good, they can make you have an idea one minute, and then the next minute, create some sort of situation that confirms that idea...

A: When you asked how long, of course it is totally unlimited, is it not?

Q: (L) That's not good. If they were to move back through space time and alter an event in our past, would that alteration in the past instantaneously alter our present as well?

A: Has over and over and over. You just are not yet aware, and have no idea of the ramifications!!!

Q: (L) We're just literally, as in that book, stuck in the replay over and over and over, and the Holocaust could happen over and over, and we could just, you know... Genghis Khan, Attila the Hun... over and over and over again. (T) We're stuck in a time loop; they're putting us in a time loop.

A: Yes.

Q: (D) I have a question about... there was a... (Pause) Mankind has found it necessary for some reason or other to appoint time for some reason or other. The only reason I can see is to have a means of telling, like in verbal or written communications...

A: Control mechanism.

Q: (T) Is there a way for us to break the control mechanism? Besides moving to 4th density? (D) That was part...

A: Nope.

Q: (D) When 4th density beings communicate it's telepathic, right?

A: Yes.

Q: (L) If you're communicating telepathically... (D) On 4th density.. (L) And time doesn't exist, how do you communicate about events as one happens now, as opposed to later and the next thing happens, and the next thing happens... (J) How is it sequential?

A: Translate.

Q: (D) Translate? Okay, let me explain what I mean. I mean, we talk about 1907 something happened...

A: That is how it is done.

Q: (T) Translate is how it is done. You translate the experience?

A: From 4 to 3. And vice versa.

Q: (L) So, in other words, it's almost like making movies. (J) Are linear thought processes part of it? Is it being linear and non-linear?

A: Part of 3d illusion only.

Q: (L) So, in other words, if you're a 4th density being, everything is more or less happening, excuse the term happening, everything is simultaneous, and if you wish to discuss or communicate or have any focus upon any particular aspect of this unified dimension, then what you do is you kind of extract it out, project it into 3d...

A: Close.

Q: (L) ... like a movie.

A: But you will not understand fully until you get there

Q: (L) Well, the situation we find ourselves in, is the only way of getting out of this time loop, so to speak, to move into another density, or is there a loop in the other density as well?

A: No.

Q: (L) No loop in the other density?

A: Yogis can do it. How they control their own physicality.

Q: (L) It says here in this Top Secret document penned by the so-called Nexus Seven:

"The bottom line is, ARC has discovered that it is very possible that confirmation, validation and consensus scientific acceptance equals an open invitation to invasion.... Denial may be one of the most powerful measures we have at our disposal to prevent the overt acceptance of the reality of advanced alien presence into the consensus consciousness. Denial is a munition.

They are saying that as long as the whole idea of alien presence remains in the realm of the fantastic and kooky, the implausible and mentally ill that it is a line of defense against aliens. They see this as just a little 'guided free will' to protect consensus belief using 'popular deployable psychological munitions of belief'. They are saying that denial is a psychological weapon, a 'deterrent of aliens into mainstream reality since the aliens seem to respect the stance of individual and group consciousness and acculturation free-will more than military might and power'. Therefore, we can, by accepting alien presence and existence above board in enough mainstream public, unwittingly turn off the restrictions against overt contact the aliens are following. The overt invasion trigger is our general human acceptance."

Could you comment on the idea that denial of the reality is protection? Is that, in fact, so?

A: No. Protection comes from awareness, not the other way around.

Q: That was an interesting idea to me, so I did want to pose it. Another idea in this document was that the patriarchal, monotheistic religion brought some measure of "blanket protection". They are claiming that as soon as the patriarchal monotheism was installed on the planet, the alien presence withdrew. Is this a valid concept? Does the patriarchal monotheism act as a deterrent of alien intrusion into our reality?

A: This is a confused concept. Why would aliens install monotheistic principles if the result is to close off the contact opportunity?

Q: That's what I thought myself. I mean, what better contact opportunity than under the guise of god, Jesus or angels or the Holy Ghost. Alien intrusion into our reality was, in my opinion, facilitated via the monotheistic religions. But, they did note that after the institution of monotheism, the *apparent* alien contact became much less, thus the conclusion they drew.

A: The two events are either coincidental or inaccurately measured.

Q: Well, it is clear that the whole monotheistic religion was a perfect front for the alien contact to continue to feed on humanity within the holy of holies of the temples. It did NOT stop, as this document suggests. The whole animal sacrifice thing, the offerings to the gods, the chanting and praying and all that; it just gives a whole new meaning to cattle mutilations!

It also gives a whole new meaning to war as a form of human sacrifice - especially since we note that most wars are fomented in the crucible of religious differences. And so, we suggest that war and massacres instituted against different groups at different times are manipulated from higher densities in order for them to obtain their "food" of both emotional suffering, and possibly even flesh. It may even be that, at certain points in history when they seek more direct interaction with humanity, that mass death is essential in order to do so.

This suggests that the "Sorcerer's Coven" - the Global Elite - probably do not engage in hidden rituals of human or animal sacrifice as certain conspiracy theorists suggest. They don't need to. They can create wars and pogroms and other situations of pain and suffering in continuation of their ancient practices - right out in the open.

We come back now to our consideration of Alternative 3, the current global elite, the manipulation of humanity via the 9-11 disaster. And indeed we note the signature of 9-11. What does this mean? Let's look at a couple excerpts from the C's regarding these numbers. The first time the number 11 was brought up was in an odd session on 11-11-95. I had been searching through endless volumes of occult literature and had read many conspiracy theories about the Rosicrucians, Illuminati, and Masons being involved in many historical manipulations from the writing of the Bible to the Kennedy assassination. What struck me was the claim that the number 33 was the "signature". I had a certain feeling that, if this was so, it must be for a reason. I wanted to know what was the "essence" of this number; what did it really convey? What was really odd was the fact that, in answering my question about the number 33, the C's chose to emphasize the number 11 as being more important.

> Q: (L) Now, the main thing I wanted to ask about is the references I come across in tons of reading, that the number 33 is somehow significant. Could you tell us the significance, in esoteric terms, or in terms of secret societies, of the number 33. There is the cipher of Roger Bacon, based on the number 33, the 33rd degree masons...
> A: As usual, we do not just give you the answers, we help you to teach yourself!! Now, take 11 and contemplate...
> Q: (L) Well, three times eleven is thirty-three.
> A: Yes, but what about 11?
> Q: (L) Well, eleven is supposed to be one of the prime, or divine power numbers. In Kaballah, 11 is the power number... [Also the number of the hidden sephiroth, Daath.]
> A: Yes...
> Q: (L) Eleven is 10 plus 1; it is divisible only by itself and by 1. I can't think of anything else. In numerology, I am a an 11 in numerology... I am also a 22. What else is there to the number 11?
> A: Astrology.
> Q: (L) Well, in astrology, the eleventh sign is Aquarius,[…]. The eleventh

house is friends, hopes, dreams and wishes, and also adopted children. Aquarius the Water-bearer, the dispenser of knowledge. Does 11 have something to do with dispensing of knowledge?

A: Now, 3rd house.

Q: (L) Gemini. Okay. Gemini and Aquarius. Third house is how the mind works, communication, relations with neighbors and siblings, education, local travel, how one speaks. Gemini is known as the "consummate man". Somewhat shallow and interested in the things of material life. It is also the divine number of creation. So, what's the connection here?

A: Matrix.

Q: (L) This IS a matrix. The third house and the eleventh house create a matrix?

A: Foundation.

Q: (L) Gemini is in June, Aquarius is in February. Gemini is the physical man, and Aquarius is the spiritual man?

A: Yin Yang.

Q: (L) So Gemini is the physical man and Aquarius is the spiritual man... yin yang... is that the...

A: Yes...

Q: (L) So 33 could represent the transformation of the physical man to the divine man through the action of secret or hidden teachings... and those who have gone through this process represent themselves with the number 33, which means that they started out oriented to the flesh and then became...

A: Medusa 11.

Q: (L) Medusa 11? What does Medusa have to do with it? Please tell me how Medusa relates here?

A: Heads.

Q: (L) Medusa. Heads. 11. Is there something about the mythical Medusa that we need to see here?

A: 11 squared divided by phi.

Q: (L) By pi. 11 squared divided by pi. What does this result bring us to?

Here the reader must note that I had never heard of "phi". I did know of the "Golden ratio", but didn't realize that it was a specific number known as "phi". So, my natural assumption was that the C's were making a mistake and that they really meant "pi" which, of course, everybody knows. So, they were trying to communicate something to me and I was unable to "get it" because my information base was limited. Nevertheless, I stumbled along trying to learn something from this exchange.

A: 33.infinity.

Q: (L) Well, we don't get 33 out of this... we get 3.3166 etc if we divide the square root of 11 by pi. Divided by phi... what in the heck is phi? Okay, if we divide pi into 11, we get 3.5infinity, but not 33. [My knowledge of math terms was also seriously limited. I was dividing 11 by 1.1416 = 3.501... Obviously, this was frustrating to the C's and they tried to teach me the phi ratio as follows.]

A: 1 times 1

Q: (L) Oh. You weren't saying 11 times 11, you were saying 1 times 1? [And I wasn't getting the "phi" thing, so they kept trying.]

A: No. 5 minus 3.

Q: (L) Okay, that's 2.

A: 2 minus 1.

Q: (L) Okay, that's 1. I don't get it. A math genius I am NOT. What is the concept here?

A: Look: 353535.

Q: (L) What is the 35 sequence?

A: 5 minus 3.

Q: (L) Okay, we have strange math. But, you can do anything with numbers because they correspond to the universe at deep levels...

A: Is code.

Q: (L) What does this code relate to? Is it letters or some written work?

A: Infinite power.

Q: (L) How is infinite power acquired by knowing this code? If you don't know the correspondences, how can you use a numerical code?

A: Lord of Serpent promises its followers infinite power which they must seek infinite knowledge to gain, for which they pledge allegiance infinitely for, which they possess for all eternity, so long as they find infinite wisdom, for which they search for all infinity.

Q: (L) Well, that is a round robin... a circle you can't get out of!

A: And therein you have the deception! Remember, those who seek to serve self with supreme power, are doomed only to serve others who seek to serve self, and can only see that which they want to see.

Q: (L) The thought that occurs to me, as we are talking here, is that the STS pathway consists of an individual who wants to serve themselves - they are selfish and egocentric -they want to impel others to serve them; they want to enslave others; and they find ways to manipulate others to serve them. But, they end up being impelled by some higher being than they are. Because they have been tricked into believing that by so doing, they are actually drawing power to themselves through the teachings, including the popular religions which promote being "saved" by simply believing and giving up your power. And, then, you have a whole pyramid of people *taking* by trickery and deception, from others. The taker gets taken from in the end. A pyramid where all those on the bottom, the majority, have no one to take from, so they get absorbed into the next level higher, until you get to the apex and everything disappears. In the STO mode, you have those who only give. And, if they are involved with other STO persons, everyone has and no one is at the bottom or at the top, in a void. In the end, it seems like everyone ends up serving someone else anyway, and the principle is the *intent*. But in STO, it is more like a circle, a balance, no one is left without.

A: Balance, yin-yang.

Q: (L) Obviously the 33 represents the Serpent, the Medusa, and so forth...

A: You mentioned pyramid, interesting... And what is the geometric one-dimensional figure that corresponds?

Q: (L) Well, the triangle. And, if you have a triangle point up you have 3, joined to a triangle pointing down, you have 3, you have a 33. Is that something like what we are getting at here?

A: Yes.

Q: (L) Is there a connection between the number 33 and the Great Pyramid in Egypt?

A: Yes.

Q: (L) And what is that connection? Is it that the builders of the pyramid participated in this secret society activity?

A: Yes. And what symbol did you see in "Matrix", for Serpents and Grays?

Q: (L) You are talking about the triangle with the Serpent's head in it?

A: Yes.

Q: (L) Are we talking in terms of this 33 relating to a group of "aliens", or a group of humans with advanced knowledge and abilities?

A: Either/or.

Q: (L) Is this what has been referred to in the Bramley book as the Brotherhood of the Serpent or Snake?

A: Yes.

Q: (L) Is this also what you have referred to as the Quorum?

A: Close.

Q: (L) So, we have a bunch of people who are playing with mathematics, and playing with higher knowledge, basically as a keep busy activity to distract them at the human level from the fact that they are being manipulated at a higher level. Is this what is going on? Or, do they consciously know what they are doing? Is it a distraction or a conscious choice?

A: Both.

Q: (L) If I were to name some names, could you identify if named individuals were involved in this secret group?

A: It would not be in your best interests.

Q: (L) Is there anything more on this 33 number that I should look at now?

A: No. You need to contemplate.

The salient points of the above exchange seem to be that the C's were conveying that there is a yin-yang duality even within "secret societies", and that there are three "heads". The number 11 represents the Medusa aspect, or the destroyer. It is obvious in retrospect that the "353535 code" was intended to convey "phi" to me, and to point out that this was a path of spiritual darkness. It is also interesting to speculate that those individuals who teach "mystical" ideas related to phi ratios are, in some way, following this path of "turning to stone". As I noticed during the above interaction, a double triangle, the "Star of David", is also a symbolic representation of the number 33, and this relates back to the idea that Judaism was "created" by these groups as a "corral" for the Jews. It's sort of astonishing to think that they were so obvious as to provide this "signature" right out in plain view. And, of course, we think of that odd story about Jacob passing the "blessing" to Esau in chapter 33 of Genesis, verse 11 as well as the C's remarks about it: "Trampled Leaves of Wrath".

Speaking of Genesis, we come now to another exchange on the subject of the number 11, over a year after the first one, on December 14, 1996:

> Q: (L) OK, let me jump over to this other subject of the number 33 and the number 11. Is there anything beyond what was given on 11-11-95, that you could add at this time, about any of the mathematics or the use of these numbers?
> A: Prime numbers are the dwellings of the mystics.
> Q: (L) What do you mean, "prime numbers are the dwellings of the mystics"?
> A: Self-explanatory, if you use the tools given you.
> Q: (L) How can a number be a dwelling?
> A: Figure of speech. [Planchette spirals several times, vigorously] And how interesting that we have a new "cell" phone company called: "Primeco".

The reader may wish to consider the information given about microwave transmissions for mind control in light of this remark.

> Q: (L) And how does a cell phone company called "Primeco" relate to prime numbers being dwellings of mystics?
> A: Not for us to answer. [Word association by group: encryption, cells of monks, prisons, prime number divisible by one or self]
> Q: (L) Is encryption the key?
> A: Oh, there is so much here. One example is: "Snake eyes" is not so good as 7,11, eh?
> Q: (T) They are all prime numbers, two; seven and eleven. (L) What kinds of documents or writings... or what would be applicable...
> A: No, Laura you are trying to focus, or limit the concept, my dear. Think of it, what is the Judaic Christian legend for the creation of a woman?
> Q: (L) That woman was taken from the rib of Adam. That Eve was created from the rib of Adam.
> A: Ever heard of a "prime rib"?
> Q: [Groans] (T) I hate being in kindergarten and not knowing what the subject is. Ok, prime rib. We have a prime rib, so...
> A: What happens in a "Primary".
> Q: (L) An election. You narrow down the candidates. What happens in a primary?
> A: Who gets "picked" to run?
> Q: (L) Ok, keep on...
> A: "Prime Directive"?
> Q: (L) OK.
> A: "Prime time"?
> Q: (L) The first, the best... and...
> A: Not point Name the primary mystical organizations for key to clue system.
> [We named: Catholicism, Christianity, Judaism, Cabalism, Sufism, The Koran, Mysteries. Laura realized that she had just set aside the book

"Understanding Mysticism", it was next to a book on Kabballah on the bookcase in the room. Jesuits, Masons, Knights Templar, Rosicrucians]
(L) All right. With our little list that we're making, are we on to something, or are we completely off track?
A: Yes, now check out those crop circles photos... any prime number combos there?
Q: (L) Do you mean in terms of dimension, or do you mean in composition?
A: Composition and dimensions... anything you can find.
[Discussion: Sacred geometries, all sects listed use prime numbers. John 3:16-19, Corinthians 13. Genesis, Ch.2, verse 22 "rib taken from the man and made woman" - 2 is the only even prime number. Ch 3, v5..."your eyes shall be opened and ye shall be as the gods." (Eating from the Tree of Knowledge)]
Q: (L) Are we thinking in any of the lines of something we ought to follow, or are we drifting?
A: All are lines you ought to follow.

At the present moment in time, when we consider the fact that George Bush "stole the elections", we are reminded of the curious clue above "primary". The comments about "prime rib" as the "creation of Eve from the rib of Adam" remind us of the fact that the C's have said that the intention of the hyperdimensional control system is to "replace" humanity. "Prime directive", as well as the cell-phone company put together with "prime time", combined with George Bush's actions after he stole the election in 2000 (and again, in November 2004), all point to the present moment in "time" as the moment that the dominoes of historical manipulation are being pushed over.

The issue of the number 11 also led to some discoveries in another direction: the zodiac.

Q: I understand that Libra was added to the zodiac and broke Scorpio and Virgo apart. Were there originally 10 or 11 signs in the zodiac?
A: Originally?
Q: You know what I mean!
A: There have been many combinations.
Q: Well, when did the present 12 sign zodiac begin to be established AS IT IS?
A: 1302 A.D.
Q: And how many signs were there before that?
A: 11.
Q: That's what I thought. What is the source of the oldest zodiac available to us?
A: Atlantis.
Q: Well, fine, what is the oldest extant source in terms of writings?
A: Egypt.

In the meantime, I had learned from a Vedic astrologer that the number 9 represented energies of destruction, death, decay and illness. I spent some time collecting data on this, and realized that there was something to this. What seemed to emerge was the fact that any "location" that was "impressed" by the number nine, was a locale of illness, destruction, death, decay and just general dis-ease. I began to think about all the legends of the "gods who measure", and the fact that our circle has 360 degrees, and all the major angles add up to nine. This is a system that has been in place for a very long time. I thought of the chessboard imagery of the Masons and other secret societies - the 12 x 12 series of 144 squares - 144 adding up to 9, and I put this alongside the 12 house zodiac, and I started wondering what was really going on?

I then gave some thought to calendars. What was obvious there was that our system of calendars just simply does not make any sense: alternating months of 30 and 31 days with February being short by two or three days, depending on how you look at it; except once every four years. What I realized was that an 11 house zodiac would "fit" more naturally with a 330 degree circle. I began to play with it.

> Q: Now, next question: in playing with my 11 house zodiac, it became apparent that, in order for it to work properly, the circle must be converted from 360 degrees to 330 degrees. Now, this made me think about the degrees in a circle. With a 360 degree circle, the total as well as all the cardinal points are numbers that total 9. I have examined this idea of numbers having some sort of 'frequency' effect on all things, and it seems to be true in a *very* deep sense. So, all our measurements on our globe are based on the number 9, and this is NOT a friendly number! The ancient gods were known as 'they who measure', and this imposition of a 360 degree circle on our world, and a 12 sign zodiac, is part of a system that imposes a frequency or vibration on our reality that is quite destructive. It perpetuates the negative existence. Am I getting close to the proper understanding here?
> A: The proper understanding is more important than how it was reached.
> Q: So, it is the conclusion. But, the deeper I go, the more I see that this world is *really* controlled by these negative beings! They really have us under their thumbs.
> A: Do they?? If so, then how is it that you can communicate with us?

As I followed these threads, including the idea of Medusa being involved in the story of Perseus and Andromeda, the daughter of Cassiopaea, many things began to make sense.

> Q: I have a few questions on the subject of Cassiopaea. On several occasions you have described Cassiopaea or the Cassiopaeans, the unified thought form light beings that transmit through Cassiopaea, as being the 'front line of the universe's system of natural balance'. On another occasion when RC was here, she was asking questions about Isis and you said that Isis was a 'vanguard'. Now, it seems to me that something that is at the front line is also a vanguard - that the definitions are interchangeable, or similar. In reading through all the various myths and

legends, it occurs to me that the similarity between the imagery of Queen Cassiopaea and Isis is quite striking. What is the relationship between Queen Cassiopaea, archetypally speaking, and Isis?

A: Subliminal.

Q: The other thing I noticed about the word 'Isis' is that it can be slightly altered to make 'I Zeus'. And, Perseus can be 'per Zeus' and Persia can be made to say 'per ziu'. One of the oldest etymological roots for the word 'God' is 'ziu' from which we get 'deu'. These all represent the English translation of 'for God', with Perceval being 'per ziu val' or 'strong for God'. Could you comment on these relationships?

A: Interconnected by trilingual learning curve.

Q: I also noticed that the word 'Osiris' could also be slightly modified to say 'of Sirius'. Comment, please.

A: Sirius was regarded highly in your "past".

Q: What was the foundation of this regard for Sirius?

A: "From whence cometh, is seen that which knows no limitation."

Q: Could you elaborate on that?

A: Could, but will not. Because you can!

Q: In reading the transcripts, I came across a reference to a 'pact' made by a group of STS individuals, and it was called 'Rosteem', and that this was the origin of the Rosicrucians. In the book *The Orion Mystery*, it talks about the fact that Giza was formerly known as RosTau, which is 'Rose Cross'. Essentially, I would like to understand the symbology of the Rose affixed to the Cross. It seems to me that the imagery of Jesus nailed to the Cross is actually the Rose affixed to the Cross - a myth created by the Rosicrucians. How does Jesus relate to the Rose?

A: No, it is from the Rose arose the Cross.

Q: What does the cross symbolize?

A: The symbology is not the issue. It is the effect.

Q: What is the effect of the cross?

A: All that has followed it. [i.e. Monotheism, and the three warring factions, all driven by STS.]

Q: In the same vein, I have noticed that there are two classes of arachnids - which is related to the number 8. There are scorpions and there are spiders. The zodiac was changed by taking the pincers away from the Scorpion - the 8th house - and creating out of them the sign of Libra. This image was one of a woman holding a balance scales, usually blindfolded. This was done within recorded history, but was probably formalized through the occult traditions of Kaballah. Now, in trying to figure out who has on what color hat, if there is such a thing, I have come to a tentative conclusion that the spider, or spinner of webs, is the Rosicrucian encampment, and that the Scorpion represents the seeker of wisdom... because, in fact, the word for Scorpio comes from the same root as that which means to pierce or unveil. Therefore, the Scorpion is also Perseus, per Ziu, or 'for God'. And the Rosicrucians are the 'other', so to speak. Can you elaborate on this for me? Or comment?

A: What a tangled web we spin, when we must not let you in.

Q: So, the Rose is the Spider?

A: Different objective. Rose is a stand alone symbol.

Q: So, the Rose can be used by either side, is that it?

A: Maybe.

Q: Another derivation of the word root of Scorpio is 'skopos', or 'to see'. You said that the human race was seeded on a planet in the constellation Scorpio, and, therefore, when the zodiac was set up and the clues were laid out, it seems to me that the insertion of the sign of Libra was designed to take power away from human beings, to take their hands away, to prevent them from seeing, to make them defenseless. Is this imagery close?

A: On track.

Q: And the Scorpion is represented in four ways: the scorpion, the lizard, the eagle and the dove. So, there are four levels of experience. Also, Minerva/Athena was the daughter of Zeus alone. She was known as the 'tamer of horses', and was a Virgin Goddess. She was also known as 'Parthenos' meaning separation. Is this part of the imagery of the creation of Eve from the rib of Adam, so to speak, or the separation of knowledge from soul, or the veil between the world of 3rd density and 4th density?

A: Close.

Q: Along this same line, in the astrological symbology, the different stars are designated as being located on different parts of the body in a rather arbitrary way that does not seem to necessarily have a lot to do with the actual configuration of the stars themselves. King Cepheus in the sign of Aries, the consort of Cassiopaea, has a star in the right shoulder. The name of this star in Arabic means 'redeemer'. The old king has to die to 'redeem'. In the imagery of the crucifixion, Jesus is depicted as carrying the cross on his shoulder as if to say that he is the old king who must die to make way for the new one... Additionally, many of us have been experiencing the pain in the shoulder, arm, and shoulder-blade for some time. You have, on occasion, related this to DNA changes. Is it that certain individuals are connected to other densities through the windows of the stars in certain constellations, and the clues are found in the location of the stars in the figures of the constellations relating to the areas of the body where pockets in the etheric field are points of activation of DNA, and that these relate to certain pains and discomforts?

A: Okay.

Q: Is that okay as in I am onto something?

A: Maybe...

Q: Can you help me out a little here?

A: To do so would compromise your discoveries.

Q: Are the body pains in these areas related?

A: To...?

Q: Obviously this is a big one... it relates directly to the crossed shin bones, the skull, the shoulder-blades, knees, elbows and a lot of other symbols... the exposed breast of the Masonic initiate, etc. In fact, in the Bible where it says that Jesus was scourged, it is actually a word that usually means the pressing and squeezing that cause milk to express from the breast. On page 33 of 'Bringers of the Dawn', Barbara Marciniak writes: 'there have been different portals on earth that have allowed different species, creator gods from space, to insert themselves. One of the huge portals that presently being fought over is the portal of the Middle East. If you think back over the history of the Earth, you will realize how many dramas of religion and civilization have been introduced in that portal. It's a huge portal with a radius of 1,000 miles or so. This is why there is so much activity in the Middle East. This is the portal that the Lizzies use.' Could you comment on that information. Are there other portals that are that large which are used by positive entities?

A: Portal is dual. Statements made in publication are close, but not absolute.

Q: Is this idea of portals extremely significant. Are they fought over?

A: Yes, but you do not need to explore these truths, until you have learned more.

And, of course, at the present time, we do indeed see this battle over the Middle East Portal in the actions of George Bush and the Warmongers in concert with the Illuminati Zionists.

Q: First of all, this session on 11/11/95, the question was asked - you were talking about matrixing Gemini and Aquarius, the 11th and 3rd houses of the zodiac - and I made the remark that 33 could represent people in secret societies who think they are following systems of advancement being transformed from ordinary man to some sort of "superman". You immediately answered: 'Medusa 11'. I'm assuming loosely that your answer, 'Medusa 11' was to the question of what 33 represented. So, Medusa 11 was the answer?

A: 1/3 of 33.

Q: Medusa was 11 of the 33. So that means that there was 22 of the 33 that was represented by something else, is that it?

A: If you wish to perceive it as such.

Q: Okay, well then, is my perception erroneous?

A: The pathway chosen is fruitful, but do not suppose the terminus to have been reached.

Q: Well, Medusa 11 is one third of 33, what are the other two thirds. (A) I believe, that in general, they will try to take you out of this idea of 33. They never, by themselves - I am not sure that the 33 is right...

A: 33 is right, but what it means is complex and fluid in nature.

Q: This Medusa idea, as I have recently learned, is part of a triad of female figures. And in this triad, the other two female figures are Cassiopaea and Andromeda, or Cassiopaean and Danae combined. I don't know which set to select.

A: Select that which fits.

Q: I think that Danae and Cassiopaea could be the same entity in the mythical sense...

A: Who speaks for Andromeda?

Q: Cassiopaea... or Perseus? What do you mean who 'speaks' for her?

A: If you do not know, you need more pieces before you can advance.

Q: (L) Okay, the story says that Perseus has slain Medusa and he is on his way back and came to Ethiopia. He found that a lovely maiden had been given up to be devoured by a horrible sea-serpent, and her name was

Andromeda. She was the daughter of a 'silly, vain woman named Cassiopeia'. She had boasted that she was more beautiful than the daughters of the Sea God. The punishment for the arrogance of Cassiopaea fell not on her, but on her daughter, Andromeda. The Ethiopians were being devoured in huge numbers by the serpent - sounds a little bit like what the Lizzies are doing today - and learning from the oracle that they could be freed from the pest only if Andromeda could be offered up to the beast - they forced Cephus, her father, to offer her up. So, her mother got her into the soup and her father turned on the heat. Anyway, Perseus arrived and the maiden was chained to a rocky ledge waiting for the monster. He saw her and fell instantly in love. So, he waited beside her until the great sea monster came and cut off its head. They sailed away and lived happily ever after. So, who spoke for Andromeda, her mother, is that what you mean?

A: It is a beginning.

When we consider the above story as an archetype of the current events, we do indeed suspect that the role of Cassiopaea speaking up for her daughter has been vilified.

Q: Okay, one interesting thing that we just discovered was that Hyakatuke and Hale Bopp both crossed the eye of Medusa, the star Algol, on April 11th exactly one year apart. What is the significance of this?

A: You must remember mosaic, matrix... When you are on the verge of quantum changes or discovery, the realities begin to reveal their perfectly squared nature to you. Can you not picture all reality as a curving and bobbing journey through a transparent, undulating matrix mosaic?

Q: (L) Is astrology in general a false assumption?

A: Astrology is a stepping stone to higher knowledge. [...] Realms are compartmentalized at graduated levels, like everything else. The root basis of the study of astrology is the "unified entity realm", which relates to the effect that local cosmic bodies have upon the body and soul of third density beings in any given locator. [...]

Q: Why was astrology absent from the myths of ancient Greece?

A: Not absent, "Stalinized".

Q: What does that mean?

A: Soviets removed Stalin from the history books when he fell from popularity. So, Greeks, astrology... "Stalinized"...

Q: Why?

A: Deadly secrets would be revealed.

Q: Revealed to whom?

A: You.

Q: If we could find the pieces and put them together, they would show us the drama and the connection between 3rd and 4th density?

A: You would have to use the original astrology, before cosmic changes of a planetary nature; there was no Venus, for one example, and earth was oriented differently axially speaking.

Now that we have considered the symbology of the number 11 to some extent, and recognize it as a signature of the Secret Government, let's turn to the number 9.

Authors Lynn Pinknett and Clive Prince wrote The Stargate Conspiracy about 'The Nine'. The reader will find a lot of useful information in this book, so it would be pointless to try to reproduce their work here. However, the C's did make a couple of comments about this group of channeled entities that are so popular among the Elite:

> Q: (L) Who are the 'Orange' aliens mentioned as being the 'Council of Nine'?
> A: Orange is reference to hair color. [...]
> Q: (L) Next question: I would like to know what is the "Council of Nine", as I have read about in several books. Now, there was an ancient council of Nine, and then there is the one talked about by Phyllis Schlemmer, and it is supposed to be a group of aliens located somewhere in North Dakota, or something like that. Are there any references on the council of Nine that you can give us?
> A: Partial deception.
> Q: Partial deception in the ancient references, or the modern ones?
> A: Take ancient references and interpret modern accounts according to current events profile.

And of course, the "current events profile" provided by Pinknett and Prince which compares the modern "Council of Nine" to the Nine Neters, or Gods, of Egypt, seems to be going in the right direction. We also consider the issue of "partial deception". We find that the controllers can, indeed, speak the truth when they choose.

> Q: Whitley Strieber and Art Bell have published a book about a "global superstorm". Is any of the information they have given in this book fairly accurate?
> A: Derived from non-human sources known for stark accuracy, when convenient.
> Q: What makes it convenient at the present time for them to be "starkly accurate"?
> A: Fits into plans.
> Q: Plans for what?
> A: Do we not know already?
> Q: In other words: world conquest and the takeover of humanity?
> A: Not as simple. Call it amalgamation.

Recently we bought a copy of the TV movie "V" since I hadn't seen the whole thing back when it was on prime time. I had forgotten that the reptilian aliens disguised as humans were referred to throughout the movie as "the Visitors". I had also forgotten that there were so many allusions to the alien take-over as being accomplished in exactly the same way the Nazis took over Germany.

There is a character in the movie - an old Jewish man - who remembers the Nazi death camps.

At the end of the movie, after the old man has been taken and tortured and killed, his son finds a letter that was left for him by his father which said:

"My Dear Family,

It is painful knowing that I'll not see your faces anymore. I must take a stand for what I know is right. You may think that an old man wouldn't be afraid to die, but this old man is very frightened. [...] So far, I am as frightened as a child who fears the dark.

But we must fight this darkness that is threatening to engulf us. Each of us must be a ray of hope and do our part and join with the others until we become a blinding light, triumphant over darkness. Until that task is accomplished, life will have no meaning.

More than anything, you must remember always which side you are on and fight for it - [We] have to, or we won't have learned a thing."

The information we have been presenting since 1996, while still a minority view as far as the New Age, Metaphysical, and UFO research communities are concerned - seems to be getting rather popular lately, what with the apparent emergence of the Control System onto the stage of history. What we have been hammering about - observation, research, what is really going on out there - with thousands of pages of material to back it up - is now, all of a sudden, being talked about more openly by others, that is, the so-called "alien presence" is, in fact, the manipulations of 4th Density, and that these entities feed off of us, our negative emotions. In other words, we are not the top of the food chain. Humans eat cattle; aliens eat us. But regardless of the facts, many people are working hard to convince us that the aliens are the solution to our problems, that they are waiting in the wings for our invitation to them to enter and fix our mess. And, true enough, their arrival probably would "fix our mess" by making it pale in comparison to the troubles we'd be confronting once they arrived! [271]

And of course, as people begin to talk, it seems that a lot of the people who have been long-time members of COINTELPRO are changing their tunes also, apparently in the interests of doing "damage control". Some of the hard core "Gray Huggers" are beginning to present the idea that one must use discernment-based caution and investigation - and most especially one must trust *them* to tell you who are the "good guys" and who are the "bad guys".

Whitley Strieber appears to be running his vacuum on both sides of the fence in an attempt to be the preeminent authority and the "guy we can all trust" in these matters. He seems to be laying the groundwork that will

---

[271] Of course, they are already "here"; we just can't see them.

give him a platform to negate Truth in a far more subtle way than he has done heretofore. Now - all of a sudden - Whitley is acknowledging that there IS something negative going on. But we notice that he only acknowledged it after it reached a point where it is becoming impossible to cover up. We suspect that Whitley - and others - will use this as a springboard to say, "well, I was the first to tell everybody that there are bad guys out there, but *the visitors* that are holding *my* hand aren't bad guys or I would tell you so. Trust me"!

Seems to us that things out there are getting so in-your-face obvious, that the dark hats need a double agent to do damage control. Whitley writes:

"We are coming to a time when we are going to have to hide our freedom in our hearts. Over thirty years of my life, I have been working toward the creation of a tool that will preserve and even strengthen freedom even in the most oppressive times it is possible to imagine.

There could come a time in every life when a choice must be made between living as the servant of a dreadful power, whether it has a human face or an alien face or no identifiable face at all, or being enslaved by it. If that happens, then the good must choose slavery and lock our freedom in our hearts. In those days, hidden freedom will be the only freedom that is true." [Our emphasis.]

The "good must choose slavery"?? "Hidden freedom will be the only freedom that is true"?? Excuse me!?

So his Path is to teach us that resistance is futile, the situation is hopeless, give up, think long term, you will be assimilated! And Whitley comes right out and tells us what he is up to.

"Thirty years of travel along this path has told me that it is a source of very real empowerment. It is a fortress for free souls, in protection of their freedom, which I define as their ability to see the will of God and serve it. The fact that I was on this path was why the good visitors came to me in 1985, and why the dark side has worked so hard to hurt me, to minimize me, to make a joke out of me. I'm on a mission for people to get on this path, and I'm not ashamed to say it. It's unique in the world, it's powerful and it is precious beyond price." [Our emphasis]

Indeed. Whitley's on a mission to convince people there is no "spiritual" path out of this mess, we can only grin and bear it. Just be nice to *the Visitors* and they will be nice to you. That's how it was in the movie.

Well, that little scene from the movie, **"V"**, where the old man's letter was read aloud has stayed with me. Over and over again I hear it. And I think about what the C's said about the Nazis which we have already covered, but which bears repeating:

Q: (L) Was Hitler's agenda a practice run for a future scenario?
A: Close. Was a "testing" of the will.
Q: (L) Whose will was being tested?
A: Yours.
Q: (L) Me specifically, or the planet?

A: Latter. [...] The concept of a "master race" put forward by the Nazis was merely a 4th density STS effort to create a physical vehicle with the correct frequency resonance vibration for 4th density STS souls to occupy in 3rd density. It was also a "trial run" for planned events in what you perceive to be your future. [...] Now, some history... as you know, the CIA and NSA and other agencies are the children of Nazi Gestapo... the SS, which was experiment influenced by Antareans who were practicing for the eventual reintroduction of the nephalim on to 3rd and or 4th density earth. And the contact with the "Antareans" was initiated by the Thule Society, which groomed its dupe subject, Adolph Hitler, to be the all time mind programmed figurehead. Now, in modern times, you have seen, but so far, on a lesser scale: Oswald, Ruby, Demorenschildt, Sirhan Sirhan, James Earl Ray, Arthur Bremer, Farakahan, Menendez, Bundy, Ramirez, Dahmer, etc...

Q: (L) I read the new book by Dr. David Jacobs, professor of History at Temple University, concerning his extensive research into the alien abduction phenomenon. [Dr. Jacobs wrote his Ph.D. thesis on the history of the UFOs.] Dr. Jacobs says that now, after all of these years of somewhat rigorous research, that he KNOWS what the aliens are here for and he is afraid. David Jacobs says that producing offspring is the primary objective behind the abduction phenomenon. Is this, in fact, the case?

A: Part, but not "the whole thing".

Q: (L) Is there another dominant reason?

A: Replacement.

Q: (L) Replacement of what?

A: You.

Q: (L) How do you mean? Creating a race to replace human beings, or abducting specific humans to replace them with a clone or whatever?

A: Mainly the former. You see, if one desires to create a new race, what better way than to mass hybridize, then mass reincarnate. Especially when the host species is so forever ignorant, controlled, and anthropocentric. What a lovely environment for total destruction and conquest and replacement... see?

[...] We have told you before: the Nazi experience was a "trial run", and by now you see the similarities, do you not? [...] Now, we have also told you that the experience of the "Native Americans" vis a vis the Europeans may be a precursor in microcosm. Also, what Earthian 3rd density does to Terran 2nd density should offer "food for thought". In other words, thou art not so special, despite thy perspective, eh? And we have also warned that after conversion of Earth humans to 4th density, the Orion 4th density and their allies hope to control you "there". Now put this all together and what have you? At least you should by now know that it is the soul that matters, not the body. Others have genetically, spiritually and psychically manipulated/engineered you to be bodycentric. Interesting, as despite all efforts by 4th through 6th density STO, this "veil remains unbroken".

So, please go and rent the movie "V" and watch it again. There is a lot to be learned there that you won't learn from Whitley's Strieber or others of his ilk. And pay close attention toward the end when the letter is brought out and read. Notice and remember:

"We must fight this darkness that is threatening to engulf us. Each of us must be a ray of hope and do our part and join with the others until we become a blinding light, triumphant over darkness. Until that task is accomplished, life will have no meaning.

More than anything, you must remember always which side you are on and fight for it - or we won't have learned a thing."

So, we see that the numbers 9 and 11 are the significators of the Secret World Government, the Consortium who have ruled the entire world for millennia in concert with their hyperdimensional masters. They have slowly, but surely, divided up the globe, assigned overseers who manipulate their human puppets to play games for the masses to observe and think that humanity is in control of its own destiny. These Secret Games of the Gods have been the "bread and circuses" designed to make humanity weak and defenseless. And one of the biggest deceptions is the hiding of the hyperdimensional nature of the Controllers by the systematic suppression of the UFO Alien reality in our world. If that were *ever* acknowledged, the game would be up.

And now, we want to look at the current puppets on the stage - those who have sold out humanity for power and wealth, not realizing that there will be neither for them ever. Something happened to open the door to the placing of the United States on the Throne of the Serpent. And those who search carefully and patiently can find it.

Out of the Labyrinth

In Mark Hedsel's book, *The Zelator*, we discover the "intimations" of an important, esoteric event. In Chapter Five of the referenced work, Hedsel informs us that:

> "At the end of the last century an astounding revelation was made, as a result of dissent among members of secret Schools. Information, hitherto guarded jealously by the most enclosed of the inner Orders, was made public. The secrets disclosed pertained to a far deeper level of knowledge than has hitherto been made exoteric by the Schools - even in this enlightened age."

The speaker in Hedsel's book, his teacher, promises to provide titles by which this most curious item might be researched, but dies before doing so. He later mentions A.P. Sinnett, and Hedsel himself speculates that it is the Theosophical ideas of A.P. Sinnett and Helena Blavatsky. I don't agree because of what the teacher says next:

> "In a nutshell, what was made public during this conflict in the Schools was the truth that our Moon is a sort of counterweight to another sphere, which remains invisible to ordinary vision. This counterweighted sphere is called in esoteric circles the Eighth Sphere.
>
> The truth is that this Eighth Sphere does not pertain to anything we are familiar with on the physical plane, yet we must use words from our own vocabularies whenever we wish to denote its existence. Were we to use a word which fits most appropriately this Sphere, then we should really call it a vacuum. Certainly, Vacuum is a more appropriate term than sphere, for the Eighth Sphere sucks things into its own shadowy existence."

Now, the question is: who was it who revealed this "great secret of secrets" at the end of the 19th century, as Hedsel's teacher has remarked? And then, who did they reveal it to?

The book suggests that we should attribute this to Sinnett and Blavatsky, but we are already wise to such tactics. It is important to know *who* the "revealer" was in order to know what was revealed. This will then lead us to understand *what* was done with that knowledge and how it affects us today.

In the 1920s, the Rockefellers and other monied groups made enormous contributions to "education in America", and the preparations for the Hitler drama were underway.

Q: OK, where is the Ark of the Covenant currently located?
A: Alternative 3.
Q: (L) Alternative 3 is the plan to take all the people, all the smart guys, all the elite, off the planet and leave everybody else here to blow up, isn't it?
A: Maybe. Maybe not.
Q: (L) Where is it currently located?
A: Discover. Study alternative 3 to find answer!
Q: (L) OK, the Matrix Material says that Henry Kissinger is the current head of MJ12. Is this correct?
A: No. MJ12 is no longer MJ12.
Q: (L) What is MJ12 now known as?
A: Institute of Higher Learning.
Q: (L) Is it a specific institute of higher learning?
A: Yes.

Can we identify to which Institute the Cassiopaeans are referring?

Well, we notice a number of "tracks" in history. The first thing we come across is the development of the Aryan supremacy idea of eugenics. We notice that this was picked up in America with funding from the Rockefellers, Carnegies, Merrimans, and other "robber baron" families. We then notice that the Jews were targeted by this "research".

At the same time that the rank and file Jews were being vilified, the Rockefellers were also endowing education and buying the "Jewish brains" and importing them to Princeton to build the bomb, among other things.

This latter event "just happened" to coincide with Hitler's takeover of the German government and the mass expulsion of Jews from German Universities which had, until then, been the seats of higher learning in math and science. Negotiations were begun to get Einstein, who finally agreed to become the second member of the Institute's School of Mathematics. Kurt Godel came, followed by Hermann Weyl, who wanted Von Neumann. In short, overnight, Princeton had become the new Gottingen.

What we are basically seeing in endowment of Princeton as a mathematical center, and the luring of scientific talent to America, is *part of the truth of one of the ideas of Alternative 3*. It was effectively, a "brain drain" on Europe. All the geniuses who were capable of certain, specific things, were being brought to America and settled in Princeton. This produced an almost immediate scientific earthquake. Of course we see that the scientific revolution in America did not begin *after* WW II as many conspiracy theorists would like to believe, but rather before. In the 1920s, to be exact. Not very long after the purported "revelation of the great secret", as described in Hedsel's book.

We have also been directed to look at a certain time period which would correspond to the activities of such sources, and so we might wish to look at the vast array of literature for internal clues. In reviewing all of this literature, in casting our net far and wide, there is only one source that "fits" the description: Gurdjieff's metaphor of "Food for the Moon". There is, in fact, a singular remark made by Gurdjieff in conversation with P.D. Ouspensky, recorded by the latter in his book, *In Search of the Miraculous* that confirms that the information revealed by Gurdjieff was, in fact, related to cyclic catastrophes and their relations to hyperdimensional realities:

"There is a definite period", Gurdjieff said, "for a certain thing to be done. If, by a certain time, what ought to be done has not been done, the earth may perish without having attained what it could have attained."

"Is this period known?" I asked?

"It is known", said Gurdjieff.

We come now to Gurdjieff's comments about "planetary evolution", "secret schools", esoteric and exoteric teachings, the Terrible Secret, the *astounding revelation,* the information, hitherto guarded jealously by the most enclosed of the inner Orders. Gurdjieff noted that standard scientific teachings tell us that life is "accidental". Such ideas fail to take into account the idea that there is nothing accidental or unnecessary in nature, that everything has a definite function and serves a definite purpose of Cosmic Consciousness. Gurdjieff then says:

"It has been said before that organic life transmits planetary influences of various kinds to the earth and that it serves to 'feed the moon' which we now understand is a metaphor for the energy drain of hyperdimensional beings who farm and feed on humanity.

Now, interestingly, this idea has repeatedly surfaced in UFO research and lore: the idea of mankind being 'lunch' for the aliens. It is not quite that simple but the Cassiopaean source indicates that there is an energy that is released when the soul separates from the body and this is ostensibly the reason that higher density beings are often noted at times of great disaster and during wars; they are feeding on this awareness. Now, note, they are *not* feeding on the soul, but *the energy of awareness*! And, we have to look at the ideas of cyclic catastrophes in this light."

The Book of Revelation says:

"Then I saw a single angel stationed in the sun's light, and with a mighty voice he shouted to all the birds that fly across the sky, Come, gather yourselves together for the great supper of God, that you may feast on the flesh of rulers, the flesh of generals and captains, the flesh of powerful and mighty men, the flesh of horses and their riders, and the flesh of all humanity, both free and slave, both small and great! ...and all the birds fed ravenously and glutted themselves with their flesh." [272]

---

[272] Chap 19, vs. 17, 18 and 21 excp., *Amplified*, Zondervan

The main point of the Cassiopaean material relating to the Jews suggests that Jewish genes possibly contain a most important codon needed for resistance against the domination of the Matrix Control System. That is the major premise. That is *not* anti-Semitic. However, the Cassiopaeans also pointed out - and it seems to be well supported by scholarly research - that Judaism - like all other religions on the planet - is a creation of that same Control System, and was deliberately imposed on the Jews in order to stop them from intermarrying with others and prevent the spread of the useful genetic variation among non-Jews. An agent of the Matrix came along and convinced them that they were *so* special that they ought not to mingle with other "tribes", and they bought it.

And here we come to the great mystery of Judaism. As many Jews point out, you cannot go back three generations in any Jewish genealogy without confronting a "solid wall of belief in Torah". And this leads us directly into the problem: if Judaism isn't true, why has it lasted so long?

One of the main aspects of socio-cultural programming is what is called "imprinting". Human beings are born with certain basic behavior patterns built in their DNA. Just as a flower will follow a certain series of steps from the emergence of the seedling to the stage of producing a flower, human beings also develop certain characteristics only at certain times in their growth process. These sequences are something over which we have no control. Konrad Lorenz illustrated this principle with his famous ducks.

Ducks (and humans) are "programmed" at a certain time in their lives to "accept a mother" figure. If the proper mother figure is not there at that moment of "imprinting", whoever or whatever IS there will be the "mother image" in the mind of the duck. That is to say, when the appropriate (or inappropriate) object of need is presented to the duck at the correct time in its development, the object is labeled "mother" somewhere in the brain, and this label is next to impossible to erase.

Experiments were conducted with ducks which demonstrated that there is a critical age in hours at which a duckling is most responsive to "obtaining and labeling" a mother. Similar studies were done with monkeys. These studies demonstrated that if a monkey has not received motherly stimulation before he is a certain number of weeks old, he will grow up to be cold, aloof, and unfriendly to his own offspring. The curious thing about the monkey experiments was that the sense of touch was more important than the feeding. A fuzzy surrogate with no milk was preferred over a wire surrogate with milk. This demonstrates a high level need for touching and caressing. It also suggests the "mode" of this "mother imprint" - it is sensory. Kinesthetic. It relates to pleasurable feelings of the body - how one is "touched".

Evidence that there is a critical period for the "mother imprint" in the higher animals was emphasized in the monkey experiments. In one instance, the experimenter was not prepared for the arrival of a new baby monkey and had to create a makeshift "surrogate mother" using a ball for the head. This was provided to the baby, while the experimenter worked on a better model with a face. But, it was too late. The baby monkey had already bonded to the faceless mother and turned the face of the new model around so that it was blank. A mother with a face was simply not acceptable because the imprint had already been made.

We are all programmed. Our programs are written in the circuits of our brains by those around us in our formative years, just as their programs were written during their formative years, and so on back into the mists of time. Everyone carries in their genes, it seems, deep archetypes that are very much like a database program just waiting for someone to input data.

The thing is, this database is only open to input for a limited period of time, and whatever data is entered during that time determines how all other data will be evaluated forever after. It will produce over and over again the same response to any set of stimuli that have one or more items that have been organized by the database. Anything that is not found in the database is "discarded".

If the database is not utilized and no data is entered during the period of "readiness", or imprinting, that possibility goes dormant and diminishes.

The higher thinking functions, laid over the deep level archetype database, can be viewed as a kind of software that is linked to the database, and must constantly check with it in order to operate. You could think of it as a word processing program with a fixed dictionary and set of templates, and you can only write in it according to the templates, and you can only use the words that are in the already fixed dictionary.

Since our brains are genetically designed to accept imprint conditioning on its circuits at certain crucial points in neurological development, these critical periods are known as times of Imprint Vulnerability. The imprint establishes the limits or parameters within which all subsequent conditioning and learning will occur. Each successive imprint further complicates the matter, especially if some of these programs are not compatible with others.

Different schools of thought describe these circuits as "stages of development". Some of the earliest work in these concepts has passed into our culture to such an extent that they have become slang terms such as, "Oh, he's just anal-retentive", with very little actual understanding of what is meant by such expressions.

It seems that, according to research, the "older" brain structures - those necessary for basic survival, such as the brain stem - are imprinted in the earliest stages of development, and that the "newer structures", such as the mid-brain and cortex, develop "superimpositions" upon the more primitive imprints. However, the earlier parts of the brain and their imprints form the foundation for the responses to later imprints, and continue to function after the higher thinking modes are developed.

In other words, if you are traumatized as an infant at a crucial point of Imprint Receptivity, it doesn't matter if you grow up to be the President of the United States - you will still be ruled by the imprint.

The first stage, or circuit, is the oral-passive-receptive, and is imprinted by what is perceived to be the mother or first mothering object. It can be conditioned by nourishment or threat, and is mostly concerned with bodily security. Trauma during this phase can cause an unconsciously motivated mechanical retreat from anything threatening to physical safety.

In recent times I have given a lot of thought to this particular circuit. Having come to the tentative idea that the whole Judeo-Christian monotheistic rant was a major control program, I came face to face with the question: how and why has it worked so well for so many thousands of years? More than that, how was it imposed in the first place? I puzzled over this for weeks. I thought about several things that Friedrich Nietzsche had said that struck me like thunderbolts of truth, once I was able to really step back and look at the matter. He wrote:

> "The Jews are the most remarkable nation of world history because, faced with the question of being or not being, they preferred, with a perfectly uncanny conviction, being at any price; the price they had to pay was the radical falsification of all nature, all naturalness, all reality, the entire inner world as well as the outer, They defined themselves counter to all those conditions under which a nation was previously able to live, was permitted to live; they made of themselves an antithesis of natural conditions - they inverted religion, religious worship, morality, history, psychology, one after the other, in an irreparable way into the contradiction of their natural values.
>
> ...Christianity has waged a deadly war against the higher type of man. It has put a ban on all his fundamental instincts. It has distilled evil out of these instincts. It makes the strong and efficient man its typical outcast man. It has taken the part of the weak and the low; it has made an ideal out of its antagonism to the very instincts which tend to preserve life and well-being... It has taught men to regard their highest impulses as sinful - as temptations. '...What is Jewish, what is Christian morality?' Chance robbed of its innocence; unhappiness polluted with the idea of 'sin'; well-being represented as a danger, as a 'temptation'. a physiological disorder produced by the canker worm of conscience."

But, that's not to say that Nietzsche was any paragon himself, with his mysogynistic, misanthropic rants! He was, in fact, declared insane in 1888. But then, considering where his ideas were going, is it any wonder? Did he see something that other people did not?

Nevertheless, he had a point about Judaism and Christianity, (and any and all other monotheistic, dominator religions.)

So, there I was, pondering this and trying to figure out *how* and *why* people could be so completely taken in by this utter nonsense? How can educated members of the human race, in this day and age, with all the resources of knowledge and awareness available to those who have the desire and energy to search for truth, possibly buy into such myths? It just staggered my mind to think about it. How can such subjectivity prevail over the most evident objective reality?

Well, clearly, something happened so that the strongest and most intelligent minds on our planet - for we know that those of Jewish bloodline are, above all, super-intelligent - were fenced in and placed in a position that has repeatedly endangered their survival as an ethnic group. How was this intellect derailed so effectively?

I went back in my thinking to the whole Jehovah-I AM deal; the Moses story and all that; and went over the details as they are presented in the Bible for clues; and I came up against that most interesting demand of that crafty Jehovah/Yahweh: circumcision - on the 8th day, no less.

What better way to ensure a deep, subconscious, distrust of women - not to mention an overwhelming terror at the very mention of the pain and suffering that might ensue from breaking the monotheistic covenant - the cruel and punishing "mother" image established at the time of Imprint Vulnerability - than whacking a guy's pee-pee when he is interested only in being warm, cozy, and filling his tummy with warm, sweet milk?!

Whoa! Talk about your basic abyssal cunning there!

The first "circuit" is concerned with what is safe and what is not safe. In our society, money is one of the primary items that is intimately tied to survival and biological security. Money represents survival. In addition to that, people who have been traumatized during the imprinting phase of the first circuit tend to view other people in an abstract way. It is "us and them". They also tend to be very easily threatened by disapproval of any sort because disapproval suggests the idea of extinction or loss of food supply. And, finally, those who have been negatively imprinted at this stage tend to have a chronic muscular armoring that prevents proper, relaxed breathing; they are "up tight".

One of the main characteristics of people who are heavily controlled by this circuit, or are "stuck" in this "oral phase", is that when they sense danger of any sort, whether actual or conceptual, *all mental activity comes to a halt*. Such people are chronically anxious and dependent - mostly on religion. They are not able to really understand what other people are feeling or what can happen in the future in regard to relationships, given a certain present situation. They only understand what is happening "now", and they can only feel what *they* feel. They cannot accurately grasp what others feel because they relate to others only as sensory objects.

So we see that, by this simple act of circumcision, the strength of the Jewish bloodline and its potential intellectual ability to "see through" and objectively assess reality, has been "chopped off". Not only do they retreat in terror into their religion, they cannot perceive the effect they are having on others. They cannot even perceive how repellant their acts are to those who are able to see objectively.

Such an act would make it almost literally impossible for a circumcised man to ever climb his way out of the trap. The merest suggestion of threat to his religion, to his belief system, would turn on all the neuro-chemicals that flooded his infant body at the time of the actual event of circumcision, and he would retreat in narcissistic terror to the safety of non-being - or being according to external dictates - religion and the representatives of religion: the priesthood.

Beside the Jews, for years, the AMA advocated and urged circumcision of American babies for "hygienic" reasons. There is a distinction between those circumcised ritually on the 8th day, and those circumcised immediately after birth. I know of no study done on human beings like those done on monkeys and ducks, but perhaps the response of the mothers is indicative of the natural moment of Imprint Vulnerability. A study was done and the mothers were asked: "When did you first feel love for your baby?" 41 % said during the pregnancy and 24% said at birth, but 27% said that it was during the first week and 8% said after the first week.

That is, the indicators for when the child might be "vulnerable", if measurable by the indicators of the mothers, suggest that the day of highest susceptibility for the infant first circuit imprint very well might be on the 8th day after birth. This suggests a knowledge of human psychology and physiology that supersedes what we know even now. Much research ought to be done on this matter.

The implications of this, and the importance of circumcision - which is, effectively, a bodily mutilation - to sustain a religion over thousands of years suggests to us that there must be something really important about those genetics for so powerful a lock to have been instituted and put in place to control and manipulate Jewish people.

As we have noted, circumcision was an Egyptian thing, before it was a Jewish thing, and that brings up the question about the fact that archaeologists and other diggers-into-the-past have often noted how "stable" and long lasting the Egyptian culture/religion was for so very long a period of time. Egyptians didn't revolt against their rulers, they were all happy as clams being controlled and directed by their gods (who were their rulers) for millennia. While other nations around them rose and fell, the Egyptians just stayed in their isolated cocoon, doing their thing, marching in the armies of the Pharaoh to conquer most of the known world, giving all to Pharaoh - their divinity in the flesh - until something happened.

Anyway, such speculations aside, there is a very real problem here: as is said, those who do not study history are doomed to repeat it.

We have here an important group of people who have never seemed to be able to extract the lessons of history over and against their own programming. And the truth is, it is likely that it will be mostly the women of Judaism that will be able to grasp the problem, because they haven't been imprinted with the mortal dread of losing their "soul" by abandoning their religion. It will take a powerful intellect to overcome that circumcision imprint. And, as brilliant as a person is, if they don't, they can never be other than a subjective thinker. Ever.

Rapturing Red Heifers and Rivers of Blood

The reader may want to pick up copies of Gershom Gorenberg's book "The End of Days: Fundamentalism and the Struggle for the Temple Mount"[273], and "Forcing God's Hand: Why Millions Pray for a Quick Rapture and Destruction of Planet Earth"[274], by Grace Halsell.

Gershom Gorenberg is an associate editor and columnist for *The Jerusalem Report*, a regular contributor to *The New Republic*, and an associate of the Center for Millennial Studies at Boston University. He lives in Jerusalem, where he has spent years covering the dangerous mix of religion and politics.

Grace Halsell served President Lyndon Johnson as his speech writer for three years. She covered both Korea and Vietnam as a journalist. She was the author of 14 books, including, *"Prophecy and Politics: Militant Evangelists on the Road to Nuclear War"*.

The facts that these two authors, one Christian and one Jewish, bring forward, are that the *Armageddon theology of the New Christian Right* is being propagated by numerous TV evangelists, including Pat Robertson and Jerry Falwell, along with Hal Lindsey's widely read *The Late Great Planet Earth*, and Tim LaHayes' *"Left Behind"* series. This theology is influencing millions of human beings worldwide to not only believe that the world is going to end soon, but that it is their duty to hasten the event in any way they can. It is in this context that we gain greater understanding of the politics of George W. Bush, though both of these books were written long before Bush effected his first coup d'etat in 2000.

Halsell interviewed fundamentalists, all of whom believed that it is their duty to fulfill the biblical prophecy of fighting World War III, preparatory to Christ's Second Coming. Most disquieting is her discussion of *an alliance of the New Christian Right and militant Zionists who share a common belief and enthusiasm for a global holocaust*. Alarming, too, is the extent of the political influence of the above mentioned tele-evangelists, the Israeli lobby and the fact that the policies of George W. Bush are largely subject to his alleged belief in the inevitability of a God-willed nuclear war. We suspect that Bush, behind the scenes, is not truly Christian, even in his own mind, but rather follows the ideas of

---

[273] http://www.amazon.com/exec/obidos/tg/detail/-/0195152050/qid=1122725933/sr=8-1/ref=pd_bbs_sbs_1/102-9600794-9506557?v=glance&s=books&n=507846

[274] http://www.amazon.com/exec/obidos/ASIN/1590080157/qid=1122725861/sr=2-1/ref=pd_bbs_b_ur_2_1/102-9600794-9506557

Machiavelli which posit that a leader must *appear* to be religious in order to induce the masses who are believers to follow him. On the other hand, Bush and much of Congress may very well believe in this Armageddon Theology.

Both Gorenberg and Halsell detail and document the history of the alliance between militant Zionism and Christian fundamentalism and expose the purpose of the alliance which is the return to Israeli control of all of Palestine and the rebuilding of the Temple in Jerusalem, on the site where the Al-Aqsa mosque and the Dome of the Rock now stand. For the religious Zionist, these actions are the prerequisite to the Messiah's *first* coming. For the Christian fundamentalists, it is prerequisite to Armageddon and Messiah's *second* coming. Reclamation of Israel from the Palestinians who have lived there for over 5000 years, and establishing Jewish hegemony, including the use of nuclear weapons (Armageddon) are seen as events to be earnestly desired and supported.

Armageddon is seen by Christian fundamentalists as "nuclear and imminent", waiting only for proper orchestration from American political leaders. We should note that there are somewhere between 40 and 50 million such Christian fundamentalists in the U.S. The Zionists, naturally, do NOT include Armageddon in their messianic aspirations. This conflict of interests at a higher level is exposed in Gorenberg's book.

Gorenberg's book was written before 9-11 and, in this sense, was extremely prescient. The reader who wishes to understand what is at the root of the current conflict that threatens to engulf our planet will find his history of those 35 disputed acres of the Temple Mount to be crucial. Gorenberg makes clear what is at the root of the volatile relationships between Arabs, Jews and Christians in Israel. He pays special attention to carefully documenting and analyzing the actions and beliefs of fundamentalist groups in all three religions.

Jewish messianists and Christian millennialists both believe that building the Third Temple on the site where both Solomon's and Herod's temples are alleged to have stood is essential for their respective prophetic scenarios to take place, (never mind that they seem to both be using each other and each believe that the other is just a dumb tool). The Muslim believers fear that efforts to destroy Al-Aqsa mosque, to make way for the Third Temple, will prevent fulfillment of the prophecy about Islam's Meccan shrine migrating to Jerusalem at the end of time. Gorenberg calls the Temple Mount, "a sacred blasting cap".

As far-fetched and delusional as this may sound to the average fair-weather Church, Synagogue or Mosque goer, it would be a mistake to underestimate the hypnotic effects that the idea of a personal 'savior' have on those people who seem to be 'tailor made' to fall prey to such manipulative honeyed promises of 'eternal happiness'. Did any of us really think that among the 6 billion + people on the planet, none would take the prophecies of manufactured religion at face value and clamour for their fulfillment at the 'appointed time'?

The problem, of course, is that there probably never was a *first* "Temple of Solomon", and the Old Testament is *not* a true "history of the Jews". So, the question is: if Islam is predicated on two previously "manufactured" religions, what does that say about the faith of the Islamic fundamentalists?

The fact is: There is an alliance between America and Israel in the war on Islam. They are both determined to establish Israeli control over Jerusalem and rebuild the Temple where the Dome of the Rock now stands, and the Palestinians are in the way. This is the core issue behind the current "War on Islam", disguised as a "War on Islamic Terrorists" and more recently, "War on those who hate our civilization". And just as Christians and Jews are quite willing to sacrifice their own people for this monstrous agenda, so are Muslims undoubtedly raising up terrorists to do as much damage to the "infidels" as possible so as to save their holy site. But to really get a grip on the explosive situation, we have to lay the major share of the blame for Islamic terrorism in the current day, where the power has resided for a very long time: in the West, the Christian West:

> "There's a new religious cult in America. It's not composed of so-called "crazies" so much as mainstream, middle to upper-middle class Americans. They listen - and give millions of dollars each week - to the TV evangelists who expound the fundamentals of the cult. They read Hal Lindsey and Tim LaHaye. They have one goal: to facilitate God's hand to waft them up to heaven free from all trouble, from where they will watch Armageddon and the destruction of Planet Earth. This doctrine pervades Assemblies of God, Pentecostal, and other charismatic churches, as well as Southern Baptist, independent Baptist, and countless so-called Bible churches and mega-churches. At least one out of every 10 Americans is a devotee of this cult. It is the fastest growing religious movement in Christianity today." -- *Dale Crowley Jr., religious broadcaster, Washington D.C.*

The "Rapture of the Church" is an idea popularized by John Darby, a nineteenth-century British preacher. The word "Rapture" describes the joy of the believers while the rest of humanity is facing apocalyptic terror, seven years' worth, before God's kingdom on earth is established.

Tim LaHaye - with his ghost-writer Jerry B. Jenkins - has produced a series of books that seek to make that terror real, to depict the "Rapture" in the world of jumbo jets and IMacs.

LaHaye's books are *real* to people living in frightening times. For the true believer, LaHaye's books are not just accurate descriptions of how it is all going to actually happen, they provide satisfyingly delicious scenarios of being proven *right*. The non-believers are treated to long and drawn-out descriptions of what is going to happen to them on earth after the Rapture.

One of the key elements of the "Rapture" theory is the Antichrist. This individual signs a seven-year peace treaty with Israel - which includes rebuilding the Temple. Jews are expected to unanimously support this project and Muslims also will agree to move the Dome of the Rock to "New Babylon".

The rebuilding of the Temple in Jerusalem is required in the scenario because the Antichrist must desecrate it half way through the Tribulation which is supposed to include war, earthquakes, and locusts. All of this is to be *hoped for* as a necessary preliminary to establishing God's kingdom on Earth.

The theory demands something else: *that Jews will convert to Christianity in masses* so that they can then become "witnesses" or converters of more gentiles. Darby's theory insists that God's promises to the people of Israel must be read literally as applying to literal Jews. Therefore, the Jews *will* convert (because it is in the eschatological screenplay).

"At the "End of the World", the believers of three faiths will watch the same drama, but with different programs in their hands. In one, Jesus is Son of God; in another he is Muslim prophet. The Jews messiah is cast in the Muslim script as the *dajjal* - another name for the Antichrist, the deceiver predicted by Christian tradition. The infidels in one script are the true believers of another. If your neighbor announces that the End has come, you can believe him, even if he utterly misunderstands what is happening.

It makes sense: *Christianity's scriptwriters reworked Judaism and Islam rewrote both*. David Cook notes that from the start, apocalyptic ideas moved back and forth between the faiths; the global village is older than we realize. *Some of the early spokesmen of Islamic apocalyptic thinking were converted Jews and Christians; they arrived with histories of the future in their saddlebags*.

What's more, a story's end is when the truth comes out, the deceived realize their mistake. *The deep grievance at the start of both Christianity and Islam is that the Jews refused the new faith - so the Jews must appear in both religions' drama of the End, to be punished or recognize their error*.

And the setting of the End is also shared. The crucial events take place in or near Jerusalem. After all, the script began with the Hebrew prophets, for whom Jerusalem was the center not only of their world but of God's, and everyone else worked from their material. Isaiah's announcement of the End of Days comes directly after he laments that the 'faithful city [has] become a harlot'. That sets up the contrast: In the perfected age, 'the mountain of the Lord's house shall be established as the top of the mountains' and 'out of Zion shall go forth the law'. *The messiah's task is to end the Jews' exile and reestablish David's kingdom - in his capital*.

Christianity reworked that vision. Jesus, says the New Testament, was not only crucified and resurrected in the city, he ascended to heaven from the Mount of Olives - and promised to return there. Without the Jews' national tie to the actual Jerusalem, Christians could allegorize such verses. The Jerusalem of the end could be built on other shores, and countless millennial movements have arisen elsewhere. But the literal meaning is there to be reclaimed, particularly in a time of literalism, such as our own.

Most striking of all is Islam's adoption of the same setting. For Muslim apocalyptic believers, Jerusalem is the capital in the messianic age. At the end of time, say Muslim traditions, the Ka'ba – Islam's central shrine in Mecca - will come to Jerusalem. The implication is that in Islam, speaking of the apocalypse at least hints at Jerusalem - and *a struggle over Jerusalem alludes to the last battle.*

Curiously, academic experts often say that Islam assigns scant space to apocalypse. In the religion's early centuries, believers attributed a vast body of contradictory traditions to the Prophet. Early Islamic scholars winnowed the sayings, establishing which were most reliable. Meanwhile, Islam became the faith of an empire, and it was time to talk softly of overthrowing the given order. So the authors of books containing the "most accurate" traditions, the pinnacle of the canon, said little of the End. *'High' Islam appears un-apocalyptic."* [Gorenberg]

Thus, we see that, for those Christians who believe in Armageddon Theology, the only thing to do is to promote the well-being of Israel with money, arms, and other kinds of support, so that the Temple can be rebuilt; never mind that it is going to be desecrated and that Israel is supposed, in the scenario, to be utterly destroyed in the process of establishing God's kingdom!

What a double-cross!

"I've listened to Muslim sheikhs explain how verses in the Koran foretell Israel's destruction, and to American evangelical ministers who insist on their deep love for Israel and nevertheless eagerly await apocalyptic battles on Israel's soil so terrible that the dry river beds will, they predict, fill with rivers of blood. I also came to realize that the center of my story had to be the Temple Mount. What happens at that one spot, more than anywhere else, quickens expectations of the End in three religions. And at that spot, the danger of provoking catastrophe is greatest. [...]

Melody, the cow that could have brought God's kingdom on earth, or set the entire Middle East ablaze, or both, depending on who you ask, has her head stuck between the gray bars of the cowshed and is munching hay and corncobs. [...]

Melody's birth in August 1996 seemed to defy nature: Her mother was a black and white Holstein. In fact, [Gilad Jubi, dairyman of the Kfar Hasidim agricultural school] says he'd had trouble breeding the dairy cow, and finally imported semen, from Switzerland, he thinks, from a red breed of beef cattle. But 'red' cows are normally splotched. An entirely crimson one is extraordinary: The *Mishneh Torah*, Moses Maimonides twelfth-century code of Jewish law, records that just nine cows in history have fit the Book of Numbers' requirements for sacrificing as a 'red heifer'. Yet the rare offering was essential to maintaining worship in the Temple in Jerusalem. *The tenth cow, Maimonides asserts, will arrive in the time of the messiah. That's when Jewish tradition foresees the Third Temple being built on the Temple Mount.* [...]

Finding a red heifer is one precondition to building the Temple. Another, it's generally assumed, is removing the Dome of the Rock from the Temple Mount. [...]

The next day, a newspaper broke the story. [Adir Zik, an announcer on the settler's pirate radio station known for his fiery rhetoric] spoke about the red heifer on his radio show. The madness about Melody had begun. [...] Press photographers arrived. The rabbi, sans calf, appeared on national TV. The Boston Globe's man did a story, and other American correspondents followed. ... A CNN crew made a pilgrimage to the red heifer, as did crews from ABC and CBS, and from Japan, Holland, France.

If much of the world's media reported on Melody in a bemused tone, as a story about the strange things people believe, not everyone saw the cow as a joke. On the opinion page of the influential Israeli daily *Ha'aretz*, columnist David Landau argued that the security services should see the red heifer as a 'four-legged bomb' potentially more dangerous than any terrorist. Landau... understood the expectations of building the Temple that the cow could inspire among Jewish religious nationalists, and its potential for inciting war with the Muslim world. 'A bullet in the head', he wrote, 'is, according to the best traditions, the solution of security services in such cases...'.

Too shrill? As Landau alluded, the nameless agents of Israel's Shin Bet domestic security force, caught off guard by the assassination of Prime Minister Yitzhak Rabin in November 1995, had underestimated the power of faith in the past. At Kfar Hasidim, Melody was moved from the cowshed to 'solitary confinement' in the school's petting zoo, where she could be kept slightly safer from the visitors arriving daily. A dog was posted to guard her. It couldn't guard against sprouting white hairs. [Which Melody did, disqualifying her and saving her from being turned into cow toast.]

Unquestionably, the reactions to Melody seem bizarre. But there are three very solid reasons for the fears and hopes she engendered: the past, the present, and most of all the future.

Numbers 19 is one of the most opaque sections in scripture. A red heifer, 'faultless, wherein is no blemish, and upon which never came a yoke', is to be slaughtered, and its body burned entirely to ash. Paradoxically, this sacrifice must be performed outside the Temple, yet the heifer's ash becomes the key to the sanctuary: It alone can cleanse a man or woman tainted by contact with human death.

For, says the biblical text, anyone who touches a corpse, or bone, or grave, anyone who even enters the same room as a dead body, is rendered impure, and must not enter the Temple. Yet proximity to death is an unavoidable part of life, and sacrifice was how Israelites served God. So to free a person of impurity, says Numbers, mix the heifer's cinder with water, and sprinkle the mixture on him. As Jewish tradition read those verses, the heifer really had to be faultless. Two white hairs would disqualify it. The rarest possible beast was essential to purify a priest who'd attended his own father's burial, or to allow any Israelite who'd been in the presence of a corpse to share in the sacrificial cult. [...]

The last ashes of the last red heifer ran out sometime after the Romans razed the Temple in Jerusalem in the year 70. *Every Jew became impure* by reason of presumed contact with death which, practically speaking, didn't matter much because there was no sanctuary to enter and *sacrifice had ceased being the center of Judaism.* The tenth heifer logically belonged to the imagined time of the messiah because a rebuilt temple also did.

Except that today, the absent ashes of the red heifer have a new function. They are a crucial factor in the political and strategic balance of the Middle East.

Over nineteen hundred years have passed since the Temple's destruction, but its location - give or take a few crucial meters - is still a hard physical reality. [...] In principle, Temple Mount remains the most sacred site in Judaism. [...]

But the Mount itself isn't in ruins. As Al-Haram al-Sharif, the Noble Sanctuary, it is the third-holiest site in Islam. [...] A glance at the Mount testifies that any effort to build the Temple where it once stood - the one place where Jewish tradition says it can be built again - would mean removing *shrines sacred to hundreds of millions of Muslims, from Morocco to Indonesia.* An attempt to dedicate even a piece of the enclosure to Jewish prayer would mean slicing that piece out of the Islamic precincts.

On June 7, 1967, the third day of the Six-Day War, Israeli troops took East Jerusalem, bringing the Temple Mount under Jewish rule for the first time in almost 2,000 years. Israel's leaders decided to leave the Mount, Al-Haram al-Sharif, in Muslim hands. The decision kept the ingredients for holy war apart, just barely. [...]

Yet a separation made by the civil government would not have worked without a hand from Jewish religious authorities. From the Six-Day War on, Israel's leading rabbis have overwhelmingly ruled that *Jews should not enter the gates of the Mount.* One of the most commonly cited reasons ... is that under religious law, every Jew is presumed to have had contact with the dead. *For lack of a red heifer's ashes, there is simply nothing to be done about it: no way for Jews to purify themselves to enter the sacred square, no way for Judaism to reclaim the Mount, no way to rebuild the Temple.* Government officials and military leaders could only regard the requirement for the missing heifer as a stroke of sheer good fortune preventing conflict over the Mount. [...]

In 1984, the Shin Bet stumbled onto the Jewish settler underground's plot to blow up the Dome of the Rock. One of the group's leaders explained that among the "spiritual difficulties" that kept them from carrying out the attack was that it is forbidden to enter the Temple Mount because of impurity caused by contact with the dead - that is, *they lacked the ash of a red heifer.* In a verdict in the case, one judge wrote that if the plan had been carried out, it would have 'exposed the State of Israel and the entire Jewish people to a new Holocaust'.

The danger hasn't gone away: The Temple Mount is potentially a detonator of full-scale war, and a few people trying to rush the End could set it off."
[Gorenberg]

According to Gorenberg, between a fifth and a quarter of all Americans are evangelicals. In Latin America, the number of Protestants subscribing to these beliefs has climbed from 5 million in the late sixties to 40 million in the mid-nineties. "One reason for the rise [was] the campaign of John Paul II against the leftist faith of liberation theology. Denied a tie between religion and hope for a better world, Latin American Catholics have been more open to the catastrophic hopes of premillennialism."

South Korea's apocalyptically oriented Protestants have gone from 15 percent of the total population to 40 percent during the seventies and eighties.

The old stereotypical image of the apocalyptic believers as tramps on street corners carrying signs saying, "The End is Nigh" no longer stands. Today's adherents of the Rapture theory wear suits in boardrooms and stride the corridors of power.

"Reverend Irvin Baxter, a Pentecostal minister from Richmond, Indiana, made Melody the cover story in his "*Endtime*" magazine, which provides 'World Events from a Biblical Perspective', then published a follow-up article when he was able to come and visit himself. To his 40,000 Christian subscribers, he explained Maimonides' view that the tenth red heifer would be offered in the messiah's time - and then noted that under the diplomatic schedule then in effect for the Oslo accords, 'the final status of Jerusalem and the Temple Mount is to be settled by May of 1999. It's in 1999 that Melody will be three years of age...'

In other words, the calf, the medieval Jewish sage, and the Israel-PLO peace agreement all proved that the Temple would be in place for the End Times to begin by the millennium's end.

Televangelist Jack Van Impe likewise noted that, 'scripture requires the red heifer be sacrificed at the age of three', and asked breathlessly, 'Could Melody's ashes be used for Temple purification ceremonies as early as 2000?'[...]

[In] 1999, I [Gorenberg] dropped in at the offices of the *Al-Aqsa Association*... to see Ahmad Agbariay [who] is in charge of the association's efforts to develop the mosques at Al-Haram al-Sharif. [...] The Jews, he told me, 'intend to build the Third Temple'.

Was there a target date? I asked.

'All I know is that three years ago they said a red heifer had been born... and that in three years they'd start building. Three years will be up in August 1999'.[...]

The folks with the cow have a star role on the stage of the End. [...]

[Rabbi Chaim Richman, a proponent of Religious Zionism] ... asserts that human beings are acting to bring the world's final redemption. Jews returning to their land and building a state is a piece of that. [...]

Reverend Clyde Lott knows cows... Knowledge of what rabbis want in a cow has come more recently. [...] At the end of the 1980s, Lott recalls, 'there was a wave of prophecy preaching going through Mississippi, and the question was when is Israel going to build the Temple'. For that, Lott knew, a red heifer was needed. [...] The question weighed on him for months. Until one day, when he was working in the field and a piece of equipment broke down and Lott got in his car to head for town, the car took him instead to the state capital of Jackson, where he strode uninvited into the office of Ray Manning, international trade director for the State of Mississippi. ... The bizarre meeting eventually produced a letter to the agriculture attaché at the U.S. embassy in Athens, responsible in his specialty for the entire Middle East.

Manning explained that he'd been approached by a cattle producer who'd made this offer: "Red Angus cattle suitable for Old Testament Biblical sacrifices, will have no blemish or off color hair, genetically red... also excellent beef quality."

What Lott did has a logic. Cattle-raising today is biotech. It was his life's work. But did it mean anything? Lott isn't the only technical person pulled to the vision of Temple-building because it promises that a technical skill is essential to the world's salvation. Nor is he the only one in our technological age to read the Bible itself as a tech manual, installation instruction for the final, fantastic upgrade of the universe. [...]

Lott's name was getting out, people who'd never met him were inspired by his plan, in one significant swath of American society he was not nuts but cold sane. [...]

The 'restoration of Israel' - the term Christians concerned with the End have used for generations to refer to the prophesied return of the Jews to their land - must also, he decided, be the 'restoration' of Israel's livestock industry."
[Gorenberg]

In 1994, Rabbi Richman visited Lott in Mississippi where he was shown four heifers. One caught his attention and he examined it for fifteen minutes or so. Then he declared, "You see that heifer. That heifer is going to change the world". It was the first cow in 2000 years to satisfy Numbers 19. Lott had "proved he could deliver". However, Richman wanted a heifer born in Israel to insure that it was "legally unblemished".

"Lott gave up his family farm. At a Nebraska ranch, he began raising Red Angus bred to the highest standards, which means, he explains, 'marbling in the meat, white flakes through the flesh... easy calving, hardiness... longevity'. To further the effort, the Association of Beef Cattle Breeders in Israel set up a professional board whose members included Lott, Richaman, and several Israeli Agriculture Ministry officials. [...]

In the spring of 1998, Canaan Land Restoration of Israel, Inc., a nonprofit body dedicated to bringing cattle to Israel, was established, with pastors scattered from California to Pennsylvania as officers and advisory board members. Lott appeared at churches, raising funds, and on Christian TV. Donation cards, adorned with sepia photos of grazing cows, allowed supporters to sponsor the purchase of '1 red heifer - $1,000.00', a half-heifer or quarter, or 1 air fare (1 cow) at $341. A fundraising letter exhorted, 'Remember, Gen 12:2-3: 'I will bless those who bless you, and whoever curses you, I will curse', a verse often cited by evangelicals as a reason to support Israel. [...]

Guy Garner ... pastor of the Apostolic Pentecostal Church of Porterdale, Georgia [gave up his tire sales business] to commute to Israel to handle Canaan Land's affairs. [...] The cows, Guy stresses, are 'a giveaway to the Jewish people'. The growers get them and the calves they produce free of charge, with just two obligations: After a number of years they must provide Canaan Land with the same number of young cows as they received originally. And, along the way, Canaan Land has the right to examine every newborn calf, and to take any it judges to be "special" - likely to qualify as a red heifer and speed establishment of the Temple. [...]

Yet who is supposed to reap the real benefit of bringing red heifers to Israel? Garner's certainty he is helping Israel is sincere. But he has humbly cast himself as a bit character in an Endtime drama whose script is somewhat rougher on Jews than on born-again Christians. In fact, the Christians will safely exit to the wings, while on stage, the Jews will find themselves at the center of the apocalypse.... 'It's not a pleasant thing to think about', Garner says glumly, 'but God's going to do what He's going to do'. [...]

[Lott says] *'God has been waiting for six thousand years* to share with mankind to prove to the world who He is. And he's chosen people just like us to be a part of the greatest Endtime plan that mankind could ever have experienced'." [Gorenberg]

In 1998, Rabbi Richman broke his connections to Canaan Land after learning that Lott had been filmed at a Florida church *talking about converting the Jews to Christianity.* Gorenberg notes that this was symbolic of the state of the much wider alliance between the Christian Right and Israel. It is "an alliance in which each side assumes that the other is playing a role it doesn't understand itself, in which each often regards the other as an unknowing instrument for reaching a higher goal".

"Richman speaks astringently of the 'doormat theology' of Christians who see Israel as a stepping-stone to an apocalypse from whose horrors only Christians will be saved. ... On the Christian side are those who want to 'bless' Israel, and provide it with what they believe is the fuse for Armageddon. And perhaps also to convert the Israelis, another "blessing" since only the converted will make it through the Last Days. [..]

In letters after the breakup [of Richman and Lott] Richman said that, 'the Temple Institute has its own plans with regard to red heifers.' [...]

Prophecy, Guy Garner explains, is 'history written in advance'. He's not unusual in thinking so." [Gorenberg]

The question we need to ask is: *Why does faith look for a finale?* What power does this idea hold over humanity? Why can't modern people put the religions of Judaism, Christianity and Islam in the museum of religious concepts alongside Zeus and Ishtar?

Gorenberg proposes a partial answer: A true believer in God (be he Jew, Christian or Muslim), is highly invested in both the power and goodness of his god. God *must* be good. And for an individual raised in a particular faith, who had no choice about his social, cultural and religious conditioning, this necessity for god to be good has very deep roots in his or her psyche. Being convinced that the "faith of our fathers" is *good,* is natural and powerful.

But, here is the rub: bad things happen in this world that do *not* fit with the concept of a *good* and All-Powerful god. Therefore, to be a believer means to exist in a state of dissonance that must be resolved.

Human beings struggle with this problem daily; trying to find answers that will solve the issues of death, disease and destruction; trying to fit their experiences with their faith in a good God. Gorenberg gives an example of a clergyman who preaches endless sermons about men whose lives were saved because they gave to charity, when the fact in the background was that his own daughter died at the age of twenty of cancer.

And so, the most daring idea of all is to assert that the world is broken and needs to be fixed. Of course, God - being omnipotent and omnipresent - *must* know that the world is broken, and being good, he plans to fix it someday. And so, the answer of the millennialist is "desperately honest": there IS something wrong with the creation of the Good and All-Powerful God, and in the same moment, the despair about the situation, the cognitive dissonance of the Good God who lets bad things happen - is rejected because *God is going to make everything alright.*

> "Naturally, your vision of the repair will depend on what you think is broken. [...]
>
> The picture of God's kingdom follows accordingly, but there is also the matter of how badly broken things are, of whether God acting through men and women is already fixing the world, or whether there is no choice but to wait for the Repairman to come to smash and break down and rebuild the world the way He always meant it to be." [Gorenberg]

Throughout their growing up years, people are told that when something good happens, that is god acting, and when something bad happens, that is Satan who got in the door because the person's faith wasn't strong enough. With that kind of conditioning, it's no wonder that people are powerfully invested in maintaining the "goodness" of their god. To insist that a messiah or saviour is "yet to come" is, essentially, a rejection of now, of response-ability. The Millennialists hang on to their beliefs for dear life because the alternatives are to either accept the world as it is, and reject the "good god hypothesis", or to abandon the world completely, both of which would bankrupt their faith.

The power of Millennialism is enormous! The problem that the religions face, however, is how to keep that hope burning, keep dangling that carrot, without letting it explode in their faces.

Because, when people give signs to know when the Time has come, and others discover that the signs have been fulfilled and that the day is near, and others say the day IS here, the irresistible force of enthusiasm inevitably smashes into immovable reality: The world doesn't end.

And it's nothing but rivers of blood everywhere. Every time.

"God does not look on all of His children the same way", said Dr. John Walvoord, President of Dallas Theological Seminary, mentor to Hal Lindsey.

God, he tells me, had plans for Jews and Christians, but not for the others - unless they became Christians. God, he said, had a heavenly plan for Christians, and an earthly plan for Jews.

And, I ask, the earthly plan for Jews?

"To re-create Israel." [Halsell]

What is not widely reported, but is well known among these fundamentalists circles is that, *once Israel has done what the Christians want it to do:* re-create itself and re-build the Temple, then *they are finished.* Those that do not convert will be destroyed. It's that simple. Christians can love and support Jews now, encouraging them and praising them and sending them money and everything they need to "get the job done". However, once that is accomplished, do not think for a minute that this love and support will continue as long as the Jews remain Jews.

"In early 1999, members of a Denver, Colorado dispensationalist group called Concerned Christians were arrested by Israeli police, handcuffed, jailed as common criminals and deported back to the States. Israeli police accused them of planning a 'bloody apocalypse' to hasten the Second Coming of Christ. It was suggested that they plotted the destruction of Jerusalem's most holy Islamic shrine.

In a fervent wish to replace the mosque with a Jewish temple, the Denver cult members are no different from other dispensationalists who believe God wants this done. As I learned from Christians on a Falwell-sponsored tour, they hold this idea quite sacred. A retired Army major named Owen, who lives in northern Nebraska, seems typical.

I spent much time with Owen, a widower, who is slightly built and about five feet, five inches tall. He stands erect and has a pleasant smile. Well dressed and with a full head of sandy hair, he looks younger than his age. He had served in Europe during World War II and later for a number of years in Japan. One day, as I am walking alongside Owen, our group moves toward the old walled city. As we enter Damascus Gate and pass along cobblestone corridors, I easily imagine Jesus having walked a similar route. In the midst of a rapidly changing environment, the old walled city, guarding layer-upon layer of history and conflict, provides the stellar attraction for tourists and remains home for 25,000 people. As the Palestinian Muslim Mahmud had told me earlier, throughout its long history, Jerusalem has been predominantly and overwhelmingly Arab.

We approach Haram al-Sharif, or Noble Sanctuary, which encloses the Dome of the Rock and Al-Aqsa Mosque — sites which I had visited earlier with Mahmud. Both these edifices, on raised platform grounds, generally are called simply 'the mosque' and represent Jerusalem's most holy Islamic shrine.

We stand on lower ground below the mosque and face the Western Wall, a 200-foot-high and 1,600-foot-long block of huge white stones, believed to be the only remnant of the second Jewish temple.

'There' our guide said, pointing upward toward the Dome of the Rock and Al-Aqsa mosque — 'we will build our Third Temple. We have all the plans drawn for the temple. Even the building materials are ready. They are hidden in a secret place. There are several shops where Israelis work, making the artifacts we will use in the new temple. One Israeli is weaving the pure linen that will be used for garments of the priests of the temple.' He pauses, then adds:

'In a religious school called Yeshiva Ateret Cohanim the Crown of the Priests — located near where we are standing, rabbis are teaching young men how to make animal sacrifice.'

A woman in our group, Mary Lou, a computer specialist, seems startled to hear the Israelis want to return to the rites of the old Solomonic sacrificial altar of the temple.

'You are going back to animal sacrifice?' she asks. 'Why?'

'"It was done in the First and Second Temples,' our Israeli guide says. 'And we do not wish to change the practices. Our sages teach that neglecting to study the details of temple service is a sin.'

Leaving the site, I remark to Owen that our Israeli guide had said a temple must be rebuilt on the Dome of the Rock site. But he said nothing about the Muslim shrines.

'They will be destroyed,' Owen tells me. 'You know it's in the Bible that the temple must be rebuilt. And there's no other place for it except on that one area. You find that in the law of Moses.'

Did it seem possible, I ask Owen, that the Scripture about building a temple would relate to the time in which it was written — rather than to events in the current era?

'No, it is related to our era', Owen says. 'The Bible tells us that in the End Times the Jews will have renewed their animal sacrifice.'

In other words, I repeat, a temple must be built so that the Jews can resume their animal sacrifice?

'Yes', said Owen, quoting Ezekiel 44:29 to prove his point.

Is Owen convinced that Jews, aided by Christians, should destroy the mosque, build a temple and reinstate the killing of animals in the temple — all in order to please God?

'Yes', he replies. 'That's the way it has to be. It's in the Bible'.

And does the building of the temple, I ask, fit into any time sequence?

"Yes. We think it will be the next step in the events leading to the return of our Lord. As far as its being a large temple, the Bible doesn't tell us that. All it tells us is that there will be a renewal of sacrifices. And Jews can do that in a relatively small building.'

Isn't it atavistic, I ask, to go back to animal sacrifice? And what about a multitude concerned with animal rights in our modern age?

'But we don't care what they say. It's what the Bible says that's important', Owen stresses. 'The Bible predicts a rebuilding of a temple. Now the people who are going to do it are not Christians but Orthodox Jews. Of course the Old Testament made out a very specific formula for what the Jews must follow regarding animal sacrifice. They can't carry it out without a temple. They were observing animal sacrifice until 70 A.D. and when they have a temple they will have some Orthodox Jews who will kill the sheep or oxen in the temple, as a sacrifice to God.'

As Owen talks of reinstating animal sacrifice — a step he feels necessary for his own spiritual maturity — he seems to block from his awareness the fact that Muslim shrines stand on the site where he says God *demands* a temple be built.

That evening, after dinner, Owen and I take a long walk. Again, I voice my concerns about the dangers inherent in a plot to destroy Islam's holy shrines.

"Christians need not do it' , "Owen says, repeating what he told me earlier. 'But I am sure the shrines will be destroyed'.

But, I insist, this can well trigger World War III.

"Yes, that's right. We are near the End Times, as I have said. Orthodox Jews will blow up the mosque and this will provoke the Muslim world. It will be a cataclysmic holy war with Israel. This will force the Messiah to intervene.' Owen speaks as calmly, as softly as if telling me there'd be rain tomorrow.

'Yes', he adds, as we return to our hotel. 'There definitely must be a third temple.'

Back home in Washington, D.C.... I talked with Terry Reisenhoover, a native of Oklahoma, who told me he raised money to help Jewish terrorists destroy the Muslim shrines.

Reisenhoover — short, rotund, balding and a Born Again Christian blessed with a fine tenor voice — told me he frequently was invited during the Reagan administration to White House gatherings of dispensationalists, where he was a featured soloist.

Reisenhoover spoke freely to me of his *plans to move tax-free dollars from American donors to Israel*. In 1985 he served as chairman of the American Forum for Jewish-Christian Cooperation, being assisted by Douglas Krieger as executive director, and an American rabbi, David Ben-Ami, closely linked with Ariel Sharon.

Additionally, Reisenhoover served as chairman of the board for the Jerusalem Temple Foundation, which has as its sole purpose the rebuilding of a temple on the site of the present Muslim shrine. Reisenhoover chose as the foundation's international secretary *Stanley Goldfoot*. Goldfoot emigrated in the 1930s from South Africa to Palestine and became *a member of the notorious Stern gang*, which shocked the world with its massacres of Arab men, women and children. Such figures as *David Ben-Gurion denounced the gang as Nazis and outlawed them.*

Goldfoot, according to the Israeli newspaper *Davar,* placed a bomb on July 22, 1946, in Jerusalem's King David Hotel that destroyed a wing of the hotel housing the British Mandate secretariat and part of the military headquarters. *The operation killed some 100 British and other officials* and, as the Jewish militants planned, hastened the day the British left Palestine.

'He's a very solid, legitimate terrorist', Reisenhoover said admiringly of Goldfoot. 'He has the qualifications for clearing a site for the temple.'

Reisenhoover also said that while Christian militants are acting on religious fervor, their cohort *Goldfoot does not believe in God or sacred aspects of the Old Testament.* For Goldfoot, it's a matter of Israeli control over all of Palestine.

'It is all a matter of sovereignty', Goldfoot deputy Yisrael Meida, a member of the ultra right-wing Tehiya party, explained. 'He who controls the Temple Mount, controls Jerusalem. And he who controls Jerusalem, controls the land of Israel.'

Reisenhoover told me he had sponsored Goldfoot on several trips to the United States, where Goldfoot spoke on religious radio and TV stations and to church congregations. Reisenhoover helped me secure a tape cassette of a talk Goldfoot made in Chuck Smith's Calvary Chapel in Costa Mesa, California. *In soliciting donations for a temple, Goldfoot did not tell the Christians about plans to destroy the mosque.*

Reisenhoover had given me several names of persons who knew Stanley Goldfoot, among them George Giacumakis, who for many years headed the Institute for Holy Land Studies, a long established American-run evangelical school for studies in archaeology and theology. On one of my visits to Jerusalem, I made an appointment with Giacumakis, a Greek American with dark eyes and cultivated charm.

Might he, I asked, after we had visited casually over coffee, help me arrange an interview with Goldfoot?

'Oh, no', Giacumakis responded, dropping his head into both hands, as one does on hearing a disaster. 'You don't want to meet him. He goes back to the Irgun terrorist group!' Raising his head and waving an arm toward the King David Hotel, he added, 'Stanley Goldfoot was in charge of that operation. *He will not stop at anything.* His idea is to rebuild the temple, and if that means violence, then he will not hesitate to use violence.'

Giacumakis paused, then assured me that while he himself did not believe in violence, 'If they do destroy the mosque and the temple is there, that does not mean I will not support it'

It was also Terry Reisenhoover who helped me get acquainted with the Reverend James E. DeLoach, a leading figure in the huge Second Baptist Church of Houston. After we had talked a few times on the telephone, DeLoach volunteered he would be in Washington, D.C. He came by my apartment, at my invitation, and I set my tape recording running — with his permission.

'I know Stanley very, very well. We're good friends', he said. 'He's a very strong person.'

Of Reisenhoover, DeLoach said, 'He's very talented — at raising money. *He's raising $100 million.* A lot of this has gone to paying lawyers who gained freedom for 29 Israelis who attempted to destroy the mosque. It cost us quite a lot of money to get their freedom.'

And how, I ask, did he and the others *funnel the money from U.S. donors to the aid of the Jewish terrorists?*

'We've provided support for the Ateret Cohanim Yeshiva.'

The Jewish school, I asked, that prepares students to make animal sacrifice?

'Yes,' he agreed.

And Christian donors are paying for that?

'It takes a lot of training,' he said. Then, quite proudly: 'I've just hosted in my Houston home two fine young Israelis who study how to do the animal sacrifice in the temple to be built'." [Grace Halsell]

Indeed, the Torah devotes a lot of words to animal sacrifice, yet Judaism has survived without such barbarity for nearly two thousand years.

"Sometime during the Roman siege of Jerusalem, Yohanan ben Zakkai escaped the city and established a new center of Jewish learning in the town of Yavneh. Ben Zakkai was a revolutionary posing as protector of tradition. Before, the ram's horn had been blown on Rosh Hashanah only in the Temple; he ruled that it could be blown elsewhere. He did not say the same of sacrifices. His successors instituted prayers that took the place of burnt offerings, in part by praying for the Temple's restoration. [...]

In nostalgia, Jews idealized the Temple; it stood for a lost utopia where God and human beings enjoyed a perfect relationship, a lost childhood. Its destruction symbolized loss of innocence. Judaism became a religion of the intellect, with study as the central religious act. It superseded sacrifices by remembering them. The modern denominations of Reform and Conservative Judaism altered their liturgy to diminish that memory. Except that sometimes a culture's old memory can come suddenly back to life, like a recessive gene that has waited generations.

For its part, Christianity regarded the razing of the Temple as proof that God had moved his covenant from the old Israel who'd rejected Jesus to the new Israel of the Church. Second-century Christian philosopher Justin Martyr lumped sacrifices together with the Sabbath, circumcision, and all the other commandments that, he said, were irrelevant after Jesus. Besides, Christians argued, Jesus' crucifixion was the last atonement by blood - a thesis that both accepted the idea of sacrifice (even human sacrifice) and rejected it." [Gorenberg]

A pamphlet for tourists tells us:

"The beauty and tranquility of Al-Aqsa Mosque in Jerusalem attracts thousands of visitors every year. Some believe it was the site of the Temple of Solomon, peace be upon him ... or the site of the Second Temple ... although no documented historical or archaeological evidence exists to support this."

There is something to be said for this as the reader will know from reading "Who Wrote the Bible".[275] Archaeologists have been digging up the "Holy Land" since the nineteenth century and, so far, there has been not a shred of evidence to support the "Temple of Solomon" story, nor much of anything else in the Bible "as history".

Nevertheless, Temple Mount IS standing there, taking up nearly a sixth of the walled Old City of Jerusalem. It is certainly true that Herod built a Temple in the vicinity that replaced the earlier temple built by Jews returning from exile in the fifth century B.C.. Those, in turn, claimed that they were building the Temple on the spot where the former "Temple of Solomon" had stood. As we discover in Who Wrote the Bible, the so-called "Temple of Solomon" was very likely a pagan Temple that had existed for some time in Jerusalem and had fallen into disrepair and was restored by King Hezekiah as part of his religious reform project.

But, even the Temple Mount is a matter of stories and not facts. Medieval philosopher, Moses Maimonides says that not only was Adam born where the altar stood, but Cain and Able made their sacrifices there and Noah did the same after the flood, (never mind that he supposedly landed on Mt. Ararat in Turkey). Abraham was told to go to "Mount Moriah" to sacrifice his son Isaac, and Mount Moriah is where the Second Book of Chronicles informs us Solomon built the Temple. As noted in Who Wrote the Bible, Second Chronicles is a late rewrite of Jewish royal history and it is altogether likely that the redactor took the name "Moriah" and assigned it to where the Temple that was refurbished stood in order to affirm its sanctity.

Another curious point that Gorenberg makes is the fact that the word "Jerusalem" occurs hundreds of times in the Bible, but NOT in the Torah. The closest is "Salem", possibly an early, pagan name for the city. Archaeologists tell us that Jerusalem was a sacred center long before the alleged time of David and Solomon. The Temple was supposedly built on a "threshing floor", which may indicate that the religion practiced in the

---

[275] http://www.cassiopaea.org/cass/biblewho1.htm

region, and the temple that actually stood there already, was devoted to fertility gods and goddesses.

In our own more recent history, Christian Spaniards who conquered Cordoba turned its Great Mosque into a cathedral and the Ottoman sultan who vanquished Constantinople in 1453 converted the church of Hagia Sophia to a mosque. Central Asia's oldest standing mosque in Bukhara, north of Afghanistan, stands on layers that archaeologists have shown reveal the prior existence of both a Zoroastrian temple and a Buddhist temple.

The temple that was in Jerusalem - which was NOT Solomon's - was destroyed in 586 B.C. by the Babylonians. Seventy years later, the returning exiles were tasked with building a new Temple "on the site" of the old one. The big question is: after so many years, did they actually build on the right spot? Did they even know what was the place where the former temple in Jerusalem stood? For that matter, is what is now known as Jerusalem really the place that was known as Jerusalem before the exile? Gorenberg points out that it's hard to understand why any city stood there at all. "It's on the edge of a desert; the soil is rocky; the sole spring is grade C; the trade routes cross to the north."

It seems that the temple built by the returning exiles from Babylon was little more than a human-built platform on top of the mountain, achieved by moving a lot of earth to accommodate the crowds that came to witness the sacrifices. It was on this earthwork platform that Herod built the temple that remains in the memory of the Jews.

Josephus described Herod as, "brutish and a stranger to all humanity. He married the last princess of the Hasmonean dynasty and murdered her and her sons and another of his sons by a different wife. But he certainly did build the most magnificent temple that Jerusalem had ever seen. The purpose of the temple, according to various sources, was to make money. The building project attracted pilgrims by the thousands - "customers for faith, the only product Jerusalem has ever had to sell".

Herod's temple didn't last long. It was razed in the summer of 70 AD by Titus and sixty years later, the emperor Hadrian rebuilt the city as "Aelia Capitolina, dedicated to Jupiter, Juno, and Minerva". It is very likely that the "Wailing Wall" so revered by Jews as the last remnant of Herod's Temple, is actually part of the Temple of Jupiter built by Hadrian. [see Tuvia Sagiv]

Nevertheless, the troops of the caliph Umar, second commander of the faithful after Mohammed, conquered Aelia Capitolina in 638. At that time, the city's Christian patriarch, Sophronius was asked to show him where the Temple had formerly stood. A Byzantine account tells us that, when the patriarch saw Umar there, he knew the world was ending (but remember, at that time the idea of rebuilding the temple was not part of the Christian theology), and so he pointed out the mount which had become a heap of rubbish.

Umar cleared away the rubbish and built a mosque that was the forerunner of the Dome of the Rock which was built by Caliph Abd al-Malik ibn Marwan in 691, and stands nearby. The problem is, historians can't really explain why the Caliph wanted to create a "holy site" there since Mecca was already "The Holy Site" of Islam. Gorenberg suggests that the Byzantine building indicates strong Christian influence in its design. It does, in fact, somewhat resembles the later Templar style of church and one might be justified in thinking that there was a strong Islamic influence on the Templars both in terms of architecture as well as esotericism. A clue to this esoteric stream is revealed inside where a mosaic inscription from the Koran addresses "The People of the Book", an Islamic designation for Christians, saying:

> "Do not say things about God but the truth! The messiah Jesus, son of Mary, is indeed a messenger of God ... So believe in God and all the messengers, and stop talking about a trinity... Verily God is the God of unity. Lord Almighty! That God would beget a child? Either in the Heavens or on the Earth?"

And, for the Jews, there was also a message in the structure itself: The Dome stands where everyone knew the Temple did, and therefore, it can be seen that Islam is the culmination of Judaism and Christianity.

Many of the popular ideas about the location of the Temple in Jerusalem are due to the work of Sir Charles Warren.

> "Lieut.-General Sir Charles Warren was born at Bangor, North Wales, on 7th February 1840. His early education took place at the Grammar Schools of Bridgnorth and Wem, and at Cheltenham College. He then entered the Royal Military College at Sandhurst, and from that passed through the Royal Military Academy at Woolwich and received a commission as lieutenant in the Royal Engineers on 23rd December 1857. After the usual course of professional instruction at Chatham, Warren went to Gibraltar, where he spent seven years, and, in addition to the ordinary duties of an Engineer subaltern-looking after his men and constructing or improving fortifications and barrack buildings -he was employed on a trigonometrical survey of the Rock, which he completed on a large scale. He constructed two models of the famous fortress, one of which is now at the Rotunda at Woolwich, and the other at Gibraltar. He was also engaged for some months in rendering the eastern face of the Rock inaccessible by scarping or building up any places that might lend a foothold to an enemy.

> On the completion of his term of service at Gibraltar he returned to England in 1865, was appointed Assistant Instructor in Surveying at the School of Military Engineering at Chatham, and a year later his services were lent by the War Office to the Palestine Exploration Fund.

> The object of the Palestine Exploration Fund was the illustration of the Bible, and it originated mainly through the exertions of Sir George Grove,

who formed an influential committee, of which for a long time Sir Walter Besant was secretary. Captain (afterwards Sir) Charles Wilson and Lieut. Anderson, R.E., had already been at work on the survey of Palestine, and, in 1867, it was decided to undertake excavations at Jerusalem to elucidate, if possible, many doubtful questions of Biblical archaeology, such as the site of the Holy Sepulchre, the true direction of the second wall and the course of the first, second, and third walls, involving the sites of the towers of Hippicus, Phaselus, Mariamne, and Psephinus, and many other points of great interest to the Biblical student.[...]

'It was Warren who restored the ancient city to the world ; he it was who stripped the rubbish from the rocks and showed the glorious temple standing within its walls 1,000 feet long, and 200 feet high, of mighty masonry : he it was who laid open the valleys now covered up and hidden; he who opened the secret passages, the ancient aqueducts, the bridge connecting the temple and the town. Whatever else may be done in the future, his name will always be associated with the Holy City which he first recovered.' [...]

It was on his way to Kimberley from Cape Town via Port Elizabeth ... that he had the late Mr. Cecil Rhodes as his traveling companion. As they were driving over the brown veldt from Dordrecht to Jamestown, Warren noticed that Mr. Rhodes, who sat opposite to him, was evidently engaged in learning something by heart, and offered to hear him. It turned out to be the Thirty-nine Articles of the Church of England. In the diary of this journey, also published in 'Good Words' of 1900, Warren relates, 'We got on very well until we arrived at the article on predestination, and there we stuck. He had his views and I had mine, and our fellow-passengers were greatly amused at the topic of our conversation -for several hours-being on one subject. Rhodes is going in for his degree at home, and works out here during the vacation.'

Sir Charles Warren was later appointed Metropolitan Police Commissioner in London, a post he held at the time of the famous Jack the Ripper murders. Warren never made any statements about who he thought the killer might be but in a report to the Home Office on Oct 17 1888 he wrote, 'I look upon this series of murders as unique in the history of our country'." [276]

Michael Hoffman wrote in 1996:

"The most recent Palestinian uprising, this past September, began in the wake of the opening of Jerusalem's 'Hasmonean Tunnel', which runs adjacent to the Haram al-Sharif, Islam's Third Holiest Shrine, is the former site of the Temple of Herod, destroyed in A.D. 70 by Roman legions commanded by Titus.

Though the media repeatedly discounted it at the time, the Palestinians were enraged due to their fear that the opening of the Tunnel was the beginning of the end for the Al-Aqsa Mosque and the start of the rebuilding of the Third Temple, which is the fabled goal to which most of the esoteric secret societies of the West and most especially the orders of Freemasonry, are oriented (indeed, Masonic iconography is obsessed with a rebuilt Temple).

[276] http://www.casebook.org/ripper_media/rps.spion.html

The establishment media, in a remarkable demonstration of the uniformity and power of their monopoly control of large scale communications, were able to stifle any substantial reporting in September, providing evidence that Palestinian fears on this subject had some justification.

In what James Shelby Downard terms a "cryonic process" (after the method by which Walt Disney's mortal remains are supposedly preserved)--the freeze-wait-thaw operation--the truth about the intense concentration of the resources of both esoteric Zionism and esoteric Freemasonry on this "Temple Mount" complex, was frozen while the riots raged. When they subsided, a waiting period ensued as the crisis left the front pages and moved slightly to the rear of the consciousness of the group mind of the masses. After the waiting period, came the thaw, when the truth was taken out of the deep freeze and presented to the public. [...]

The opening of the tunnel in September, 1996, with its ritual bloodshed, a precursor of the sacrificial blood ordained to flow if the Temple is rebuilt, was orchestrated in 1867. It was then that the future General Sir Charles Warren, England's Commissioner of Police and co-conspirator in the occult ritual murder known to history as "Jack the Ripper", had been dispatched on yet another Masonic mission, to lay the groundwork for the rebuilding of the Temple of Jerusalem. And so it was that in 1867, one of England's most important Freemasons, a member of its "research lodge" (Ars Quator Coronatorum), "rediscovered" the claustrophobic, 500-yard tunnel.

The "implements" of the old Temple, according to the Talmud, were hidden on the Temple Mount before the destruction of the Second Temple. With Warren's Tunnel now open, the "treasure hunt" begins, as the establishment media admitted, between the lines, during its mid-October "thaw".

In the second week in October, Zionist zealots, involved in crimes of terrorism linked to the hoped-for destruction of Al-Aqsa mosque, suddenly entered stage center from their establishment-imposed positions of obscurity. In the processing of the group mind, chronology is everything. Hence, mid October was the time designated for slowly pulling the curtain back and revealing the actual game afoot. At this juncture the establishment media unveiled Mr. Yehuda Etzion, head of Hai Vekayam, spearhead of the drive to rebuild Herod's Temple upon the ruins of Islam's revered Al-Aqsa mosque. As if on cue, seven Hai Vekayam 'activists' were arrested by Israeli police when they tried to force their way onto the Dome of the Rock in October.

Also on cue, a petition was presented to the Israelis in October, dotting every "i" and crossing every "t" of every Palestinian fear about what the Zionists intend with their "tunnel". The petition, put forth by the Temple Mount Faithful organization, a group financed by deep-pockets Judeo-Churchian fundamentalists in the U.S. and shadowy, international Zionist and Masonic moneybags, calls for the removal of the mosque from the Temple Mount. James Shelby Downard and I have a term for that call: Truth or Consequences via Revelation of the Method. For more on that, interested persons may consult my Truth or Consequences lecture, available on audio-cassette." [Michael Hoffman] [277]

With all the things that have happened since 1996, with all that Halsell and Gorenberg have uncovered, Hoffman doesn't sound so nutty, now does he? Fact is, after his expedition, Warren wrote a book entitled "*The Land of Promise*", a book arguing that Britain's East India Company should colonize Palestine with Jews. The idea was quite popular in England for two reasons: 1) it promoted British imperial interests and 2) it fit Bible prophecy. These two factors would motivate the Balfour Declaration of 1917 in favor of a Jewish Homeland.

Certainly, the British had territorial interests in Palestine, but one cannot ignore the issue of religion and millennialist aspirations about the British. Yes, Imperial logic would say that Britain should take Palestine because it was the gateway to the Ottoman Empire and to Africa as well, but notice what Gorenberg writes:

> "On November 2, 1917, two days after General Edmund Allenby's Egyptian Expeditionary Force took Beersheba from the Ottoman Turks and prepared to march north toward Jerusalem, the British government announced an entirely different rationale for the campaign: Foreign Secretary Arthur Balfour sent a letter to British Zionist leader Lord Rothschild, informing him that the cabinet had approved 'a declaration of sympathy with Jewish Zionist aspirations: His Majesty's Government view with favour the establishment in Palestine of a national home for the Jewish people...'.

> Five weeks later, Allenby's army took Jerusalem. For two days after the actual conquest, the general's arrival was meticulously planned. ... Christian armies were returning to the city for the first time since the Crusades. Allenby arrived at Jaffa Gate riding a white horse, with the pomp of a king. Then, before he entered the Old City, he dismounted and walked. A standard account of the general's reason: His Savior had entered this city on foot, and so would he.

> Allenby's action makes sense of the Balfour Declaration: Conquering Jerusalem had to not only be considered strategically, it had to be accomplished "according to prophecy". The British logic was rooted in their fervor for the Old Testament and the hope for the millennium. That logic was derived from the cultic teachings of the Christadelphians and John Darby's premillennialist Plymouth Brethren, as well as the hopes of mainstream Anglicans. It was their desire to convert the Jews and return them to their homeland. Barbara Tuchman writes of these passions about the influential Earl of Shaftesbury, that 'despite all his zeal on the Jews' behalf, it is doubtful if Lord Shaftesbury ever thought of them as a people with their own language and traditions... To him, as to all the 'Israel-for-prophecy's sake school', the Jews were simply the instrument through which Biblical prophecy could be fulfilled. They were not a people, but a mass Error that

must be brought to Christ in order that the whole chain reaction leading to the Second Coming ... could be set in motion'.

Neither Balfour nor Lloyd George was a millennialist, but they were products of an England suffused with such belief, and of the ardor it produced for the Old Testament. Balfour defended his declaration to Parliament by arguing that Christendom must not be 'unmindful of the service [the Jews] have rendered to the great religions of the world'. Lloyd George commented that when he discussed Palestine with Weizmann, Zionism's apostle to the British government, Weizmann, 'kept bringing up place names that were more familiar to me than those of the Western front'. The two statesmen could regard restoring the Jews to their land as a British task because English millennialism had made this a reasonable project, even for those who weren't thinking about the millennium. Except that once England actually ruled Palestine, the simple commitment of the Balfour Declaration slammed into the real world." [Gorenberg]

August 16, 1929, the day that the Palestine Mandate burst into flames, predictably, as Gorenberg notes. The day before, on the anniversary of the destruction of the Temple, hundreds of Jews had demonstrated along the Western Wall, demanding rights to the spot. A surviving photograph of the demonstrators is interesting because it shows some of them in shorts and regular shoes. Why is this interesting? Because as a sign of mourning on such days, religious Jews do not wear leather shoes on a fast day. This means that the protesters were not demanding rights to the Western Wall for religious reasons, but for nationalistic and territorial reasons. They raised the Zionist flag and sang the Zionist anthem.

So, the next day, Muslim protestors came and beat up the pious Jewish worshippers who had nothing to do with the demonstration of the day before. The following Friday, tensions had increased to such an extent that Arabs began assaulting Jews in the old city, armed with clubs and knives. Within an hour, the attacks had spread to other areas of the city and the British police force was so undermanned it could do nothing.

The violence spread and on the second day (24 August), in Hebron, rioters moved from house to house murdering and looting. Sixty-seven Jews were killed, including a dozen women and three children. Most of the town's Jews were saved by their Arab neighbors.

One historian records that Jews went well beyond self defense. In one instance, in retaliation, Jews broke into a Mosque and destroyed holy books. A Palestinian version of the events tells us that the people of Palestine reacted to the provocation of Jewish religious extremists at the holy site, which seems to be what actually happened.

In a week and a half of terror, 133 Jews and 116 Arabs were killed. From any point of view, the event was a turning point in the struggle for control of Palestine. The fact is that there was, at this early stage, a great opposition of Palestinians to the creation of a Jewish state in Palestine, and it's easy to understand. Palestine was basically "given to the Jews" by

Britain. But, many in Britain began to think that the Balfour Declaration's promise of a "national home" for the Jews had been a mistake.

The facts are: two national groups were struggling for one piece of land. One of the groups had been there for a very, very long time, and the other group intended to come and take over what they were convinced was theirs either by right of the British mandate, or by right of their god. The British plan to settle the Jews in Palestine was a disaster and they ran with their tails between their legs, leaving the Palestinians and the Jews to duke it out on their own.

But the fight was not equal. The desire among the Christian West for the Jews to remain in Palestine, to re-create Israel, to re-build the Temple, and to fulfill prophecy was behind the Jewish presence. The Palestinians didn't have a chance from the beginning.

> "*Avraham Stern* was a rebel even among rebels, too extreme for the average extremist. A Polish-born Jew who admired Mussolini, he'd been a member of the Irgun Tzva'i Le'umi (National Military Organization), the right-wing Jewish underground in Palestine. In the late '30s, Palestine's Arabs revolted against British rule; attacks on Jews were common. The Irgun rejected the mainstream Haganah policy of restraint and launched revenge attacks on Arabs: gunfire at a bus here, a bomb in a market there, the murder of innocents as payment for the murder of innocents. From there it went on to battling the British, who sought to satisfy the Arabs by restricting immigration even as desperate Jews were trying to get out of Europe. But when World War II broke out, the Irgun declared a truce: Fighting Germany was more important than driving out the British. Such zigzagging wasn't for Stern: In spring 1940, he and his followers left the Irgun to create a more radical group that would keep fighting the British. They robbed banks, tried to assassinate mandatory officials. In Hebrew the group was called Lehi... the English called it the Stern Gang, even after police ferreted Stern out in a Tel Aviv apartment in 1942 and shot him dead. The group's new leaders included Yitzhak Yezernitzky, who later changed his name to Yitzhak Shamir and decades later became Israel's prime minister. [...]
>
> In a newspaper called The Underground, Lehi published its eighteen principles of Jewish national renaissance. Number 18 read: "Building the Third Temple, as symbol of the era of the Third Kingdom." After Israeli independence, the group's veterans republished the principles, with an emendation. Now number 18 said: 'Building the Third Temple as a symbol of the era of total redemption'. Historian Joseph Heller explains that "Third Kingdom" sounded too close to 'Third Reich' - a sensitive point since Lehi was stained by having unsuccessfully offered its services to the Axis against Britain in 1941.
>
> The emendation make the point clearer: 'They were a messianic movement, especially under Stern', says Heller." [Gorenberg]

Gorenberg tells the story of David Shaltiel who was commander of the Haganah, the Jewish militia-turned army. Shaltiel had been raised in an Orthodox home in Hamburg. He claimed that, "at the age of thirteen he walked out of the synagogue on Yom Kippur and ate pork and waited for God to strike him down". When nothing happened, he was finished with religion. Shaltiel went on to join the French Foreign Legion and later became an arms buyer for Haganah in Europe. In 1936, the Gestapo arrested him in Aachen. He is said to have been Dachau and Buchenwald and "another sixteen prisons". Somehow, he was released before World War II began and returned to Palestine where he became a Haganah officer.

In November of 1947, after WW II (which must certainly have profoundly affected Shaltiel), the United Nations (which also was profoundly affected by WW II, as was the entire world) voted to partition Palestine between a Jewish and an Arab state. You might even say that this vote was a direct result of the events of WW II and many people have suggested that there was Zionist complicity in the murder of millions of Jews for the express purpose of generating guilt and sympathy for the Jewish people, to put them in a position of unassailable "moral right" to Palestine.

In any event, the Arabs were opposed to partition (not a surprise) and were battling Jews even as the British pulled out leaving Palestine in a shambles.

On May 28, 1948, two weeks after the Zionist leadership proclaimed the establishment of the State of Israel, the Jewish quarter of Jerusalem fell to Jordanian forces.

At dawn on July 17, a U.N. cease-fire was due to go into force. Shaltiel, the guy who had ceremonially eaten pork on Yom Kippur so many years ago, now decided that - before he had to stop fighting upon the execution of the cease-fire - he was going to be a hero and re-take the Old City as his last Hurrah. The Old City didn't have any strategic value, but apparently, its symbolic significance was enormous to the Jews. Shaltiel had the help of the Irgun and Lehi forces, as well as a special explosive charge designed by a physicist.

So confident of victory was Shaltiel that he had a lamb ready to sacrifice on Temple Mount.

Shaltiel died in 1969 and no one knows if he expected the resumption of animal sacrifice as a regular practice, but it is certain that he thought that sacrificing a lamb was the proper way to celebrate the re-taking of Jerusalem. Shaltiel probably would not have contravened David Ben-Gurion's orders not to damage any of the Muslim shrines, had he been successful in his bid to re-take the mount, but the same cannot be said for the commander of the Lehi forces, Yehoshua Zetler. If the attack was successful, he had definite plans to raze the Muslim shrines on the Mount and he equipped his men with the explosives to do it.

As it happened, the offensive failed. The special bomb made a black mark on the four hundred year old Muslim walls, but didn't even crack them. At 5:00, the cease-fire went into effect.

Yisrael Eldad wrote pornographically of his feelings about that night, later published in a memoir:

> *"And the heart imagines: Perhaps it will break out tonight...*
>
> *If only they had a sense of history. Oh, if only! And precisely on this night, the night of the first destruction, the night of the second destruction, precisely on this night if only they burst through and got there - for they are capable of bursting through and getting there... There are enough arms, and there are young men, and there is Jerusalem, all of her desiring it, ready for a dread night like this, if only they would burst through, if only they would get there.*
>
> *To the Wall, to the mourning, to what has been abandoned.*
>
> *To break through and set it all aflame. In fire it fell and in fire it will rise again. To raze it all there, all the sanctified lies and hypocrisy. To purify, purify, purify."*

(Speaking of sanctified lies and hypocrisy, the Old Testament has to be the mother of them all.)

But it didn't happen: the Jewish State was born without the Old City which remained in the hands of the Palestinians who had lived there for 2000 years. Many of them are probably descended from original Jews who converted.

In his 1996 book *"Beginning of the End: The Assassination of Yitzhak Rabin and the Coming Antichrist"*, Texas pastor John Hagee recalls sitting with his father when news came over the radio that Israel was a new nation. His father told him, "We have just heard the most important prophetic message that will ever be delivered until Jesus Christ returns to earth". For the millennialists, the Balfour Declaration had been exciting, but Israel's "birth" produced absolute frenzies of apocalyptic ecstasy. The prophecies of the Last Days were coming TRUE!

> "Except for stories I'd heard in my childhood Sunday School, I knew little or nothing about a Jerusalem where people live everyday lives - where they are born, got to school, get married, have children, at times laugh and celebrate, at other moments cry and mourn. Then, one day, moving to Jerusalem, I began to experience the realities of a people who have always lived there.
>
> I walk the cobblestone streets with an Arab Muslim, Mahmud Ali Hassan, who was born in Jerusalem, bought his first pair of shoes, got his first shave from a barber, was fitted for his first suit of clothes, was married, saw all his children born and watched them grow up - all in the Old Walled City.
>
> With Mahmud, I walk along narrow corridors within one of the few remaining examples in the world of a completely walled town. The walls stand partially on the foundations of Hadrian's Square, built in A.D. 135. they include remains of earlier walls, those of King Herod in 37 B.C, and

Agrippa, A.D. 41, and Saladin, 1187. And finally the walls were rebuilt by the Turkish Muslim, Suleiman the Magnificent, in the sixteenth century.

'This Old Walled City throughout its long history has been predominantly inhabited by Arabs,' Mahmud tells me. 'And Arab markets, Arab homes, and Arab religious sites make up about ninety percent of the Old City.'

'As Arabs, we are descendants of an indigenous people, a people who never left Palestine, continually having lived within these old walls', Mahmud continues. 'I can trace my forebears back more than ten generations. And in the case of my father and his father and his father, our famili8es have lived in the same house for the past three hundred years'. [...]

'This is one of the oldest cities in the world', Mahmud reminds me. 'Arabs called Amorites came here four to five thousand years ago. They established this site as a religious foundation to honor their god. And these early Arab worshippers of a god they called Shalem gave us the name of our Holy City, Jerusalem. Then came others of our forebears, the Canaanites from Canaan. They made Jerusalem an early center of worship of the One God. The Canaanites had a king named Melchizedek, and it is written that he also was a priest of God Most High.'

'All this early history predates the arrival of the Hebrews by many centuries... And when a tribe of Hebrews, one of many tribes in the area, did arrive, they stayed for less than 400 years. And they, too, like many before and after, were defeated. And 2000 years ago, they were driven out.'

From Al-Aqsa, we walk a short distance toward the magnificent Dome of the Rock, one of the most beautiful shrines in all the world - often compared in its beauty with the Taj Mahal. [...] See Plate 19

'As Arabs, as Muslims, our quarrel has never been with Jews as Jews, or with the great religion of Judaism. The places that the Jews and Christians revere as holy, we revere as holy. The prophets the Jews and Christians revere as holy, we revere as holy. My point is that everyone in history has borrowed from what went before. No one or no one group has exclusive rights here. There were countless battles over Jerusalem. And the Hebrews were in power here only sixty years'." [Halsell]

A late 1998 Israeli newsletter posted on a "Voice of the Temple Mount" web site, says that its goal is "the liberation" of the Muslim shrines and the building on that site of a Jewish Temple. "Now the time is ripe for the Temple to be rebuilt", says the Israeli newsletter. The newsletter calls upon "the Israeli government to end the pagan Islamic occupation" of lands where the mosque stands. It adds, "The building of the Third Temple is near".

"There remains but one more event to completely set the stage for Israel's part in the last great act of her historical drama. This is to rebuild the ancient Temple of worship upon its old site. There is only one place that this Temple can be built, according to the law of Moses. This is upon Mt. Moriah. It is there that the two previous Temples were built. -- Hal Lindsey, *The Late Great Plane Earth*

> An anti-Semite "is someone who hates Jews more than he's supposed to."
> -- *TV Evangelist James Robison.*

The Christian Church, throughout most of its history, has been anti-Semitic. With the reformation, however, many Christians turned from anti-Semitism to a new kind of discrimination rampant in the world today: philo-Semitism. This is a stance which views the Jews as practically necessary *as* Jews, because they have a role to play in the salvation of Christians! This "love of Jews" includes within its parameters the complacent sureness that the Jews *are* different, and are destined for extinction once they have performed their assigned task.

Certainly, there are personal and political differences among Christians which make a generalization inaccurate and perhaps even dangerous, but the fact remains that many fundamentalists who are leading the "let's help Israel every way we can" and "let's go after the Muslims" charge of the present day have an established history of having taught their followers that Jews were behind all of the world's troubles.

It was after the full horrors of Nazi Germany had been revealed that Western Christianity realized that promoting anti-Semitism a la *The Protocols of the Elders of Zion,* could be seen as sympathizing with the Nazis. So, those fundamentalist who were blatantly anti-Semitic backed up and regrouped.

With the birth of Israel in 1948, the anti-Semitic Christians changed their tactics. They were still anti-Semitic (still are), but they acted differently on the outside; they became "loving" and "grateful", benign and patronizing toward Jews. Thank goodness the Jews were now doing what they were supposed to do: regather in Israel so Jesus could return and blast them all to smithereens!

As this new appreciation of the Jewish role merged with dispensationalist beliefs, Western Christians became fiercely supportive of the new Jewish state. Nothing must come between Israel and its destiny! Anybody could criticize any other nation in the world, but not Israel. Criticizing France, Germany or even the U.S. was just "political". Criticizing Israel was criticizing God Almighty.

At the same time that millennialists proclaim their love for Israel, they frequently reveal that they have no liking for Jews at all.

> "Standing, overlooking the Megiddo valley, Clyde, a traveling companion, explained to me that this was the site where Christ would lead the forces of good against evil. 'Two-thirds of all the Jews will be killed', Clyde said, citing Zechariah 13:8-9. Pausing for some math, he comes up with nine million dead Jews. 'For two hundred miles, the blood will reach to the horses' bridles.'
>
> When I express concern over this scenario, Clyde explains, 'God is doing it mainly for his ancient people, the Jews. He's devised a seven-year

Tribulation period mainly to purge the Jews, to get them to see the light and recognize Christ as their savior'.

But why, I ask, would God have chosen a people = 'God's favorite' as Clyde says - only to exterminate most of them?

'As I said, God must purge them', Clyde says. 'He wants them to bow down before His only son, our Lord Jesus Christ.'

But a few will be left? To bury their dead?

'Yes', Clyde tells me. "There'll be 144,000 who are spared. Then they will convert to Christ'. [Halsell].

'Only 144,000 Jews will remain alive after the battle of Armageddon. These remaining Jews - every man, woman and child among them - will bow down to Jesus. As converted Christians, all the adults will at once begin preaching the gospel of Christ. Imagine! They will be like 144,000 Billy Grahams turned loose at once!'" - *Hal Lindsey*

"As long as they don't convert, Jews are 'spiritually blind.'" - *Jerry Falwell*

Traditionally, Jews have been liberal and supportive of liberal agendas. Having known discrimination and racism, they were allied with liberal agendas. However, in 1967, after Israel seized Arab lands that it did not want to relinquish, the Jewish state moved rapidly to the conservative right. American Jews, formerly liberal supporters of the rights of others were persuaded that their number one priority was to support Israel. Under this influence, they also moved rapidly to the right.

The Israeli Right and The Christian Right became strange bedfellows, each with a doctrine centered around Israel and a cult of land. Nathan Perlmutter of the ADL explained why American Jews support the Christian Right in America: First he says, he feels himself a somewhat typical American Jew in that he weighs every issue in life by one measure: "Is it good for the Jews? This question satisfied, I proceed to the secondary issues."

American Jews support Jerry Falwell because he supports the expansionist aims of Israel. Perlmutter knows that evangelical-fundamentalists interpret Scripture as saying all Jews eventually must accept Jesus or be killed. But, meanwhile, he says, "We need all the friends we have to support Israel... If the Messiah comes, on that day we'll consider our options. Meanwhile, let's praise the Lord and pass the ammunition".

Irving Kristol urges American Jews to support such as Falwell telling them that "in the real world" Jews are better off to back the Right, those that are strongly pro-Israel. To be sure, he adds, fundamentalist preachers will say that God does not hear the prayer of a Jew. But, "after all, why should Jews care about the theology of a fundamentalist preacher when they do not for a moment believe that he speaks with any authority on the question of God's attentiveness to human prayer? And what do such theological abstractions matter against the mundane fact that the same preacher is vigorously pro-Israel?"

> "Douglas Krieger, an evangelical lay leader of Denver, Colorado, closely connected with Terry Reisenhoover in raising money to eradicate the Al-Aqsa mosque and the Dome of the Rock to rebuild the Temple in Jerusalem, early on urged Israel to work with and totally embrace evangelical-fundamentalist issues in exchange for their support of Israel.

> In a lengthy analysis paper prepared for Israeli and American Jewish leaders, Krieger points out that as a consequence of its wars of aggression, Israel faced two choices: to seek peace by withdrawing from 'territory acquired by war', or to continue reliance upon even greater military strength, i.e. the Christian Right controlled U.S.

> If the Israelis took the second choice, which Krieger urged them to do (as a millennialist he very much wants them to re-take all of Palestine and re-build the Temple), then the Israelis and American Jews would face the danger of an outbreak of anti-Semitism.

> Because of Israel's military seizure of Arab lands, 'a rise of anti-Semitism could possibly surge in the West'. This could be prevented, however, Krieger said, through its alliance with the New Christian Right. He pointed out that Israel could *use* the evangelical-fundamentalists to project through their (the Jews') vast radio and television networks an image of Israel that Americans would like, accept and support.

> Moreover, Krieger said, 'The Religious Right could sell the Americans on the idea that God wanted a militant, militarized Israel. And that the more militant Israel became, the more supportive and ecstatic in its support the U.S. Right would become'." [Halsell]

Militant Zionist Jews and fundamentalist Christians have therefore formed an alliance that embraces the same dogma. This dogma has nothing to do with spiritual values or living a good life as either a Christian or a Jew. The alliance is about political power and worldly possessions. It's about one group of people physically taking sole possession of land holy to three faiths, occupied for two thousand years by a people that certainly resist their lands, their rights, and their lives being taken from them. It is a dogma centered on a small political entity - Israel. Both Israeli leaders and the Christian Right make ownership of land the highest priority in their lives, creating a cult religion - and each group is doing so cynically, for their own selfish reasons, expecting the other to be destroyed by their own hubris.

> "Dispensational beliefs reduce the complex and diverse societies of Africa, Asia and the Middle East to walk-on roles as allies of Gog in God's great end-time drama... the consensus was clear: prophetic imperatives required the elimination of Arabs not only from (Jerusalem) but from most of the Middle East... They stood in the way of God's promises to the Jews." -- *Paul Boyer, When Time Shall Be No More*

"The Evangelical New Right ... systematically seized control of the leadership of the southern Baptist Convention, the largest Protestant denomination ... altering long-held theological positions for political advantage." -- *Sidney Blumentahal in The New Republic*

"I do not know how many future generations we can count on before the Lord returns." -- *James Watt, U.S. secretary of the interior speaking before the House Interior Committee, in an apparent refutation to arguments for conserving natural resources.*

President Reagan represented a dispensationalist view that since "Christ is at the door", spending on domestic issues should not be taken too seriously. "Most of Reagan's policy decisions", said James Mills, a former California state official, were based on his "literal interpretation of biblical prophecies". This led to Reagan's idea that there was "no reason to get wrought up about the national debt if God is soon going to foreclose on the whole world".

George W. Bush apparently has the same view.

Reagan's support of gung-ho neo-conservatives can only be understood in the light of the President's millennialist thinking. "Why waste time and money preserving things for the future? Why be concerned about conservation? It follows that all domestic programs, especially those that entail capital outlay, can and should be curtailed to free up money to wage the War of Armageddon."

The Dispensationalists who preach Armageddon Theology are a relatively new cult - less than 200 years old. There are four main aspects of their belief system:

1) "They are anti-Semitic. They profess a fervent love for Israel. Their support of Israel does not, however, arise out of a true love for the Jews and their sufferings. Rather, their 'love and support' is based on their wanting Israel 'in place' for the 'Second Coming of Christ', when they expect most Jews to be destroyed."

2) The Dispensationalists have a very narrow view of God and the six billion people on the planet. They worship a tribal god who is only concerned with two peoples: Jews and Christians, who said tribal God intends to pit against one another for His favor. The other five billion people on the planet are just not on this God's radar except to be killed in the final battle.

3) The Dispensationalists are certain right down to their bones that they understand the Mind of God. They provide a scenario, like a movie script, that unfolds with time sequences, epochs or "dispensations" all ending happily with an end-time escapism called the Rapture - for a chosen few like themselves. They appeal to those who want to feel that they are on the "inside" of a "special group" with secret, profound knowledge. This desire for certitude causes millions of the followers of Dispensationalism to trust their leaders to an extraordinary degree.

4) "Fatalism is the fourth aspect of Dispensationalists. The world, they say, is getting steadily worse and we can do nothing, so there is no point in doing

anything. The teachers teach about the wrath of a vengeful god and declare that God does not want us to work for peace, that God demands that we wage a nuclear war: Armageddon that will destroy the planet." [Halsell]

The frightening by-product of these beliefs is that, since the Cult is in Power in the United States, it is so easy to create the very situations which are described, thus ensuring the fulfillment of the ideas of the Dispensationalists: the Cult that wants to Create Armageddon needs five billion people on the planet to go willingly to the sacrificial altar, and Muslims have been chosen to be first.

The nation of Israel, the Jewish people, have suffered so much and so long that they simply do not know who to trust anymore. And now we have individuals who are religious fanatics -- Zionists -- coming along and doing everything possible to stir up anti-Semitic feelings, calling on all their fellow Jews to unite and congregate in Israel - the Promised Land of their religion - in the same way it has happened over and over again throughout history. Seeing this self-destructive tendency is not only painful, but gives one a feeling of desperation. Not again!

It is very sad because we hear the rumble of revulsion building all around. It is at the root of the growing neo-Nazi thug movement; it is heard even at the supermarket in the checkout line. A current of anger and resentment threading its way into the subconscious minds of non-Jews - that will lay the groundwork for the arising of a new Hitler. Only this time, he won't be just a German dude with the force of the Allies there to stomp him in the dirt. He will raise that ugly cry again, the cry that will be seen as justified by the very actions of Jews themselves, who have walked right into the trap. All the problems will be presented as existing in Jews, in Israel... and he (or they) will present so simple a way to solve these problems: they will point out that the Jews are all gathered in one place (or at least they are all known because they all belong to clubs and synagogues because those kind Zionist folks have been going around gathering them back into the fold), so the Final Solution will be resurrected again. And the whole rest of the human race will not realize that they have been had.

In 1997, we were considering a visit to Israel at some point in the future. My husband Ark had friends at the University of Tel Aviv, and he had been in contact with them. So, on January 11, the Cassiopaeans volunteered the following:

> A: Tell Ark that we strongly suggest that he drop Tel Aviv from his itinerary. There is a grave aura of danger over the locator of Israel. Something big, big, big is going to happen there. We can not say exactly "when", and will not say exactly what, but it will be decidedly negative!!!!

Which leads us back to the issue of the September 11 2001 attacks - shortly following the attack on our site by Jewish groups. At the time of the event, my eyes had just been opened to what the Jews were doing to themselves, and I was watching the affairs in the Middle East with some interest. I could see that world opinion was turning in favor of the Palestinians, and I was hoping that some peaceful resolutions would be achieved by the balancing of world opinion on the side of Palestine. By this time, I already knew that the Palestinians and Jews were genetically so close that if there was any plan to destroy the Semitic genetic codon, it would have to include destroying the Arabs also, and I certainly could not see how that might be done, especially if peace might be reached by virtue of diplomatic pressure.

But, on September 11, everything changed. I saw now how it could be done. On September 14, while the entire world was still in shock, we sat down to ask the Cassiopaeans about this terrible event.

Q: We have a series of questions about this recent event. Was the attack on the World Trade Center undertaken by Moslem Terrorists?
A: No.
Q: Who was behind this attack?
A: Israel.
Q: [My mind immediately made the connection to the remark about Tel Aviv made four years previously. I realized that if this was true, if it became known, the Jews had initiated the means of their own destruction.] Is it going to become known that it was Israel? Will they be exposed?
A: Yes.
Q: Is this the event that is going to lead to the destruction of Israel?
A: Yes.
Q: Are there going to be further terrorist attacks in the US next week as others have been predicting?
A: No.
Q: Are there going to be further terrorist attacks of this kind at any time in the near future in the U.S.?
A: No.
Q: Is this the beginning of WW III?
A: No.
Q: Is the US. Going to bomb Afghanistan?
A: Possible in future.
Q: (A) You say that Israel will be exposed - something will come out; in what time perspective?
A: Month [before first hints emerge which turned out to be correct with the news about the Israeli spies pretending to be art students.]
Q: Expose Israel? In a month? How?
A: Yes, open. Perhaps sooner.
Q: (A) What mistake did they make?
A: Infiltrated.
Q: (A) They seem to be so smart, and they did such a big thing, only to make a mistake. (L) I guess we can only wait to see how it turns out. It's a spooky idea. What do countries do when something like that is

discovered and they have had a long-term diplomatic relationship? They talk to each other, they pat each other on the back in public and then one of them attacks the citizens of the other? What do they do? It's like having to get a divorce when everybody thought you had such a happy marriage. And when it's like this? It's like having to get a divorce after discovering that your partner has murdered your children and buried them in the back yard. (A) Yeah, but it's not so clear, because when you say "Israel," it's not one thing. There are different parties, different factions, they are fighting. We don't know.

A: Gore is pushing buttons on Capitol Hill.

Q: What does Gore have to do with anything? He lost the election. Well... (A) He had this Lieberman as his running mate. What kind of buttons? (L) Is he pushing buttons to expose, or pushing buttons to suppress?

A: To suppress.

Q: Well, that's the damnedest thing I ever heard. Did the U.S. Government shoot down the fourth plane - flight 93 - as some people are suggesting?

A: Yes.

Q: Did any of our people in any position to do anything, know?

A: No.

Q: Were they blindsided?

A: No. But not expecting.

Q: (A) So, they knew it was going to happen, but they didn't know when and what exactly? Is that it?

A: Yes.

Q: Is it truly a "failure of intelligence?"

A: Yes. But deliberate.

Q: (A) What is the most probable scenario. There were infiltrators, they had some knowledge, and they communicated this knowledge to some part of Intelligence, but this part of Intelligence did not press to communicate it to the higher parties?

A: Yes. And it was not known plan.

Q: So the infiltrator did not know the specific plan. So, they overstepped. Hubris. (A) Which part of Israel government was behind it? (L) Probably some deep level orthodox bunch.

A: Yes.

Q: (A) But they killed a lot of Jews. (L) They don't care. Jews killed a lot of Jews in WW II. Hubris.

A: Greed.

Q: How did the guy on the internet newsgroups know? Is he involved with the Israelis?

A: No.

Q: How did he know about this event?

A: Fourth Density STS contact.

Q: Is this another instance of when they can be stunningly accurate when they choose?

A: Yes.

Q: So, this guy was not an insider in the plot?

A: No.

Q: Well, I find that hard to believe.

A: Patience.

Q: Was he being set up to look accurate so people would buy into his rant?

A: Yes.

Q: Well, Sollog did predict that this would happen in 1997. But then, the guy on the newsgroup predicted that something was going to happen in seven days... That was bizarre. He didn't say what, but the message was headed with 9/11. If he had known what was going to happen, I think he would have at least hinted. (A) But that would be too dangerous for him.

A: Yes. More like a miss.

What the Cassiopaeans had said was literally mind boggling. But then, within the month, the news about the Israeli students jumping for joy at the sight of the burning World Trade Center was published, followed by the information about the Israeli Art Students who were evident Mossad agents. What was strangest was that they were connected to the Islamic "terrorists" as though they were "spying on them". It never occurred to anybody that they might have been working with them - pretending to be on their side, setting them up to act as the agents of destruction with all the resources of Mossad behind them.

And then, later, the evidence of American intelligence connections to the 9-11 attack was revealed, and it became obvious that the remarks about Al Gore "pushing buttons" weren't so crazy after all.

In any event, the mainstream media was beating the "Osama Bin Laden" drum, and it was - for a time - very convincing. We decided to ask on September 24.

Q: (L) You said last time that Israel was behind the attack on the WTC. They are collecting evidence that Osama Bin Laden and company are behind it. Are they manufacturing this evidence?

A: Yes.

Q: (L) Is the truth going to come out?

A: Yes.

Q: (L) So are we going to have a war here?

A: Close.

Q: (L) Are we going to have more terrorist attacks in the US? They already said no, but that's because we already know it wasn't terrorist. Are we going to have more violence in the US that may not be as a result of terrorists? But part of the overall manipulation?

A: Yes.

Q: (L) Can you designate any of the areas where this violence may occur in the near future?

A: Indianapolis.

Q: (L) What kind of violence?

A: Hit by focusing beam of the HAARP array.

Q: (L) Well that's weird. (A) By mistake? An accident?

A: No.

Q: (L) What will be the outcome of Indianapolis being hit by this focusing beam of the HAARP array?

A: Mind controlled violence.

Q: (L) Can we know what form it will take?

A: Shootings.

Q: (L) Are there going to be any other kinds of violence, such as bombs or airplanes being flown into buildings, or release of anthrax, or small pox, or any other kind of chemical or germ warfare activities. Any of those?

A: Yes.

Q: (L) Which ones?

A: Fair chance of germ disbursement.

Q: (L) What kind of germ?

A: Influenza.

Q: (L) Do you mean a deadly form of flu?

A: Yes.

Q: (L) But nothing like anthrax or small pox or any of those really sick ones? Is that it?

A: No. Keep looking and listening.

Q: (L) Well we plan to. What is going to happen with the Middle-eastern situation; this Afghanistan or whatever?

A: Herding of population to much finer order of control.

Q: (L) What is the purpose of this control; this increasing control.

A: Preparation for war in Palestine.

Q: (L) But nobody has said anything about having a war in Palestine. They're all talking about having a war in Afghanistan. How does Palestine fit in here?

A: It is the ultimate objective of Israel.

Q: (L) Why would they want to have war in their own country? Well, aside from the fact that they've been having a war in their own country for a long time. I guess they want to bring it to a final conclusion. What is going to be the result of this plan?

A: Destruction of Jews.

Q: (L) Well obviously this is not what *they* are planning, is it?

A: No.

Q: (L) They are planning destruction of Palestinians, right?

A: Yes.

Q: (L) It seems that throughout history whenever the Jews have plotted and planned to destroy somebody, they are the ones who have ended up being destroyed themselves. Or am I misreading my history here?

A: No.

The Cassiopaeans were certainly right about the "herding of the population to much finer orders of control". What was so puzzling was the remark about "preparation for war in Palestine". That was certainly not a declared agenda. In fact, it was extremely difficult to understand why the US was going after the whole country of Afghanistan - hurting a lot of innocent people - for Osama bin Laden when - by all accounts - such an operation would have been better carried out by intelligence operations.

As the next couple of weeks went by, we saw our freedoms being taken away because of this event, and it was becoming increasingly clear that there was a major agenda for US involvement. The C's mysterious remarks about the relationships between Mossad and possible U.S. intelligence groups were still inexplicable, and everyone was worried because the government kept repeating that there were going to be more terrorist attacks and we needed to have the Patriot Act on the books right away. Everybody was worried about suitcase nukes and bio-terrorism. We asked more questions on October 13.

> Q: My first question: People are talking about, and are concerned about, what is to be the proper attitude or the proper action - if any - or behavior, or response to the current situation in the world: terrorist activity, the increasing controls of the government, that sort of thing. In other words, they are wanting to know if they should take action, or if they should just observe. Or, should they be guided by their individual situations. People are concerned. Can you respond to these concerns?
> A: Most people will not be harmed in direct ways.
> Q: If most people will not be harmed in direct ways, does this mean that the idea that the United States may become the target for an all out... (A) Before you ask, "most people" is an imprecise term. "Most people" could be just over half. That leaves a lot of room for "people" being harmed. (L) Can you be more precise?
> A: Force will not get out of hand *yet*.
> Q: (A) Which I read as a "negligible number of people will be harmed" in global terms. (L) Is it true that only a negligible number of people will be harmed in the immediate upcoming period?
> A: Yes.
> Q: (L) But, of course, if one is among that "negligible number", it can be up-close and personal. Can you give us - do we dare ask for a number? (A) No, because then we would have to specify the country and work our way through all the details. You see, four thousand is still negligible in global terms. (B) Will the primary harm to people be psychological?
> A: Partly but also real strictures.
> Q: (L) Do you mean greater control and loss of freedoms? Is this stricture going to be physical, or a stricture on our freedoms, or a combination of both?
> A: Both.
> Q: (L) Is there going to be a witch hunt in this country for people who the government wishes to identify as being potential terrorists, or anti-American, like the McCarthy era?
> A: *First there will be controls by laws. Then more force.*
> Q: (L) Is all of this going to culminate in some plan that is being activated at the present time? Is this all directed to a specific outcome by the powers that be, so to speak?
> A: Mostly; but *unexpected twists and turns from opposing forces.*
> Q: (L) And who are these opposing forces? Are there good guys, or is it just like another "gang", as in global gang wars? Using "gangs"

metaphorically here.

A: *4th density STO will manifest help for some 3rd Density groups.*

Q: (L) Do any of those 3rd density groups that are going to be helped include us? [Laughter.]

A: Close.

Q: (L) Okay, so there are going to be twists and turns. Can we know any of the highlights of these twists and turns in our global or national situation? It sounds like an interesting show. Is it better that we don't know? If the STO forces are planning something, maybe it's better that we don't know so that it remains a surprise. Is that true?

A: Close. Just know that help is near.

Q: (L) Next question: Is the anthrax that has been contracted by several people around our country a terrorist act against our country by foreign terrorists?

A: No.

Q: Where did the Anthrax come from?

A: U.S. government. [This later proved to be accurate.]

Q: (L) That's not very nice. (A) Well, the "U.S. Government" can mean any of many parts that all fight with each other. (L) Okay, when you say "U.S. Government," is that the government that we consider to be our government, or is that the secret government - some maverick branch that is operating without the approval of our elected officials?

A: Latter.

Q: (A) Well, that's imprecise. I am sure that at least one elected official is in on it. Certain questions have more or less known answers. What we know is that it comes from some part of the U.S. government. A maverick part. We don't know, and I don't know if we want to know from which part. (L) Probably not. (A) So, probably when they start to look for tracks of the Anthrax, it will certainly point somewhere abroad - to Afghanistan or somewhere else. (L) Right. That will give the government a reason to go and bomb somebody else. (A) So, is this reasoning correct? (L) Are they going to try to blame it on some foreign element?

A: Yes.

Q: (L) So, if they are going to try to blame it on some foreign group, can we have any idea of which group?

A: *Iraq.*

Q: (L) Are we ultimately headed toward bombing Iraq?

A: Yes.

Q: (A) Notice however, one complication: groups all over the world, as we are now noticing, have started protests against America. People are going to the streets in Europe to protest. So, in order to avoid this protest, probably America will have to produce some new evidence. Maybe an explosion of anthrax - maybe something completely new. (L) Is that something that is going to happen?

A: Yes.

Q: (L) And what might be the next major act of terrorism be that will... (A) It may be somewhere in Europe to convince the European countries. (L) So, whoever is protesting the most is the one that is likely to get hit in some way. (A) But, on the other hand, it may not be easy for America to produce something there, since it is much easier to produce "terrorist" events in America where they have complete control of everything. (L) If they try to do it elsewhere, they are liable to get caught.

A: France may be hit next with nuke.

Q: (L) Well, that's not friendly! (A) Well, that may make sense. There is this connection between the Afghans and Algerians and France. Algeria has already terrorized France in the past, so that may be the set-up. (L) That would certainly get their attention. Is there going to be an outbreak of terrorism on the 31st of this month as has been circulating on the grapevine?

A: Not likely. [...]

Q: (BT) Well, the thought that went through my mind, in such a scenario, is related to Cheney. Could he be part of the maverick group pulling the strings?

A: Close.

Q: (L) Are any of these people in the government, those in the public eye, the decisions makers; are any of them consciously aware that they are furthering the agenda for the STS takeover of the planet? The main players.

A: No.

Q: (L) Bush is just a puppet. He's like Pinocchio. Every time he opens his mouth his nose just gets longer and longer. Pretty soon his nose will be so long he won't be able to walk across the room. Well, it is easy to get upset with Bush until you realize that he is as much a dupe as anyone else. He seems to be going around in a fog. All the jokes that are made about him being so dull are true! How can you get mad at a complete puppet? I've never heard the guy say an intelligent thing that wasn't written down for him, and even then he sometimes manages to screw it up. (A) Yes, it seems so. Because those leaders who have proven NOT to be stupid in the past, have proved to be... (L) ...dead. (A) Or, they proved to be able to kill millions to stay alive. (L) Yup, seems to be so. (A) Yes, they can be stupid in a very intelligent way. (L) Are all of these people going to be exposed, caught, shown for what they are?

A: Ultimately.

Q: (BT) Yeah, and that can be part of the STS program anyway. Expose 'em and replace 'em with something worse. If everybody relies on the government to save us, and then find out that the government is not only not going to save us, but that they are guilty of harming us for manipulation, that is a manipulation of a higher order. (L) Yeah! And then who will the people cry for to be in charge? Aliens? (A) It's a "free" choice. [Laughter.] (L) Well, it's a terrible thing to feel that way about your President who is supposed to be the representative of your country. (A) I'm surprised that some Americans... (L) ...actually believe that he's doing a good job and telling the truth. (A) Yes. (L) I would like to know what is the REAL percentage of Americans who think that Bush is doing a good job. I know they put up the results of polls, but I have observed that polls are often published to sway public opinion, and are not an accurate representation of it. What is the real percentage?

A: 53 %.

Q: (L) Just a little over half. Well, even that figure is depressing. Are we in danger of Anthrax?

A: Most likely not or anything else.

Q: (L) Well, we ordered a micron filter for the air unit just in case! (L) We watched one film that showed a strange, dark object, shooting down towards the ground. What was that?

A: 4th Density energy surge.

Q: (L) Where was it surging from and to?

A: Dome of destruction-energy time-lock to ground.

Q: (L) Are you saying that there was a dome of a time lock over this area? Do you mean that they put a "time lock" over this area so that they could "harvest" bodies or energy?

A: Close.

Q: (BT) Was there any other purpose besides harvest?

A: Gathering records, gold, soul extraction.

Q: (L) What did they want the gold for?

A: 4th density uses gold for technology.

Q: (BT) Well, that is in many myths about the "gods" mining gold in antiquity. (L) Were they gathering records in the sense of material objects?

A: Partly.

Q: (L) Might these records also have been an extraction of "records" from people as they were dying?

A: Yes.

Q: (L) For what purpose did they intend to use the souls that were extracted?

A: Remolecularization.

Q: What will they use these remolecularized beings for?

A: Insert them back into building to escape and be rescued.

Q: (L) Are you saying that this was an opportunity used as a very traumatic screen event of a mass abduction, so to say?!

A: Yes.

Q: (L) What was done to these people who were abducted? Was there a specific reason for a mass abduction?

A: Turn on the programs.

Q: (TB) So, those who "escaped" are very likely programmed individuals turned loose in our society. People with programs set to make them run amok at some point?

A: Close.

Q: (A) Well, we still have one problem: the problem involvement of Israel. We were worrying about what is going to happen in Israel. At present, all the anger is directed at the United States.

A: America may shift blame.

As it happened, throughout this period we were engaged in fighting another battle against our own 9-11 type attack. As a result of these virulent and vicious assaults, I wrote what has become known as the

Adventures with Cassiopaea[278] series. During the course of this project, as I followed the threads of evidence, I discovered many things that bear strongly upon the subject of 9-11.

In the days and months following the event, I watched the news reports, read the many commentaries on the internet, observed the activities of the different players, all the while putting together the most amazing line of discoveries I had found in the course of doing the research for the writing of the Adventures. As I did, I realized that we were actually seeing with our own eyes was the playing out of dramas that the Cassiopaeans had described seven and eight years previously. I also realized that this was, indeed, the fulfilling of the prophecies of the Book of Revelation as I had been led to understand them over sixteen years before.

To say I was shocked and not a little horrified would be somewhat of an understatement.

Those of you who have read our research published in the Adventures Series will immediately understand that the destruction of the True Jews, as well as Arab Semites, was - and is - part of the plan of the Global Elite who know that 'Something Wicked This Way Comes', and who intend to be on the 'right side' of the victors when the dust settles.

Until recently, impacts by extraterrestrial bodies were regarded as, perhaps, an interesting but certainly not an important phenomenon in the spectrum of geological process affecting the Earth. As we have seen, this has only been the case since Lyell, Laplace and Newton put a period to such speculations. What seems to have happened is that, through repeated cataclysms, man has been brought low, relegated to darkness regarding his history, and at the very point when he began to study and analyze his environment objectively, religion stepped in and put a period to such ideas.

The question is, why? What, in the name of all things reasonable, would prompt anyone to wish to hide these matters? What kind of sick mind would divert the attention of humanity away from what is evident all over the planet to those with open eyes? What kind of sick mind would also promote, so assiduously, ideas that mislead, misguide, and generally placate the populace with an assurance that, either nothing is going to happen, or if it does, it will be preceded by a long period of approach by a body that is well organized and clearly seen, so the government can probably "fix it"?

Well, the clue is right there: "placate the populace". Control.

But, Heavenly days! What kind of lunatics would want to keep everything under control in that sense if they have some idea that they, themselves, might be destroyed by the very processes they are concealing?

---

[278] http://www.cassiopaea.com/cassiopaea/adventureindex.htm

Obviously, they don't think so. Obviously, they think they have a plan. And that suggests that, obviously, they know a lot more about what's going on, what the possibilities and probabilities are than the rest of us. On August 24, 2002, when we were inquiring into the most puzzling matter of the strike against the Pentagon on the same day as the World Trade Center was hit, the C's made clear just who was in charge, what their agenda was and what they thought would be the result:

Q: Did a Boeing 757, Flight 77, crash into the Pentagon?

A: No.

Q: What did produce the damage to the pentagon?

A: It was very close to what you have surmised: a drone craft specially modified to give certain "impressions" to witnesses. Even the windows were not "real".

Q: What happened to Flight 77?

A: It was landed and now resides, in part, in fourth density.

Q: What do you mean by that?

A: As we have mentioned before, certain bases have this property due to direct interaction with denizens of that realm.

Q: What about the passengers? What happened to the humans?

A: Let us just say that the "human" part now resides at 5th density.

Q: Did they kill them and use parts of them for DNA identification?

A: "Parts" is the correct word.

Q: (Guest comments) Oh! I was hoping they were still alive somewhere!

A: Do you think that any of them could be "allowed" to survive?

Q: When you say that the plane is now partly in 4th density, do you mean it was "taken" while aloft, as happened to the military jet over Lake Michigan some years back? It was "absorbed" by a UFO?

A: It landed in the normal way.

Q: Since we know from Dolan that the real "elite" are not those who form our visible government, do any of those in the White House have awareness of the REAL reason these plans are being driven at this time?

A: The White House knows little of what transpires in any case.

Q: Well, how can it be that there is an obvious global conspiracy, with countries that appear to be in opposition that are actually working in concert? Who are the members of this global conspiracy? Who is driving them?

A: At those levels, there is only one "Master".

Q: How can they control not only America, but China, Russia, Israel, Saudi Arabia, and all the rest? What "levels" do you mean?

A: Levels that can hand down orders to bury or suppress. Those who are at that level have been bought and paid for by both giving knowledge of upcoming cataclysmic events, and promised survival and positions of power after. It is not difficult to realize that there is a body of such types in positions of power already. Power is not only attractive to such types, they are the kind most easily corrupted by it.

The conclusion that the astute reader will have drawn from my book, The Secret History of the World, is that the inner solar system experiences swarms of comets/asteroids on a fairly regular schedule. One major swarm comes at 3600 year intervals, and there are minor swarms at other intervals, and these cycles are sub-cycles of even larger swarms at hundreds of thousands of year intervals, and even million year intervals. The massive bombardment of the East Coast of the U.S. around 12,000 to 12,500 years ago resulting in the Carolina Bays is evidence of the great number, and relatively small sizes of many of these bodies, indicating that they released their energy into the air above the ground, similar to the Tunguska event. Keep in mind, of course, that *the air blast of a single small body over Tunguska resulted in the devastation of 2000 sq. km of Siberian forest.*

It now begins to make a horrible kind of sense why Hitler wasn't "taken care of" as could have so easily been done. It begins to be comprehensible why "quotas" were put on Jews who wanted to enter the U.S., why IBM created the machines to organize the killing machine, why Britain and the United States - after the war - supported the repatriation of the Jews to Israel, and why they have encouraged and supported Israeli efforts to make a "home" for themselves there. It begins to make chilling sense why the United States has done a number of things, as we will soon see.

In the end, what we finally realize is that anyone who suggested that anything in the Cassiopaean remarks about Jews was Anti-Semitic may well be serving the Nazi Aryan supremacist agenda even if they are pretending to serve the Jews. In fact, what has become increasingly clear is that the Zionist agenda is truly Anti-Semitic.

A gentleman named Joseph George Caldwell - a former contractor for a government think-tank - Lambda Corporation, has a website where he promotes the following idea:

> "What is the sustainable human population for Earth?", I propose that a
> long-term sustainable number is on the order of ten million, consisting of a
> technologically advanced population of a single nation of about five million
> people concentrated in one or a few centers, and a globally distributed
> primitive population of about five million. I arrived at this size by
> approaching the problem from the point of view of estimating the *minimum*
> number of human beings that would have a good chance of long-term
> survival, instead of approaching it from the (usual) point of view of
> attempting to estimate the *maximum* number of human beings that the planet
> might be able to support. The reason why I use the approach of minimizing
> the human population is to keep the damaging effects of human industrial
> activity on the biosphere to a minimum. Because mankind's industrial
> activity produces so much waste that cannot be metabolized by "nature," any
> attempt to maximize the size of the human population risks total destruction
> of the biosphere (such as the "sixth extinction" now in progress).

Let's stop right here and ask the question: Who said that there was such a thing as the "*Sixth Extinction*", and that it was now in progress? Is this something that is generally "known" in the circles that do this kind of research? Is this why they are doing it? What do they know that the rest of us don't? Or better, what do they think that they aren't telling us? Caldwell writes:

> "The role of the technological population is "planetary management": to ensure that the size of the primitive population does not expand. The role of the primitive population is to reduce the likelihood that a localized catastrophe might wipe out the human population altogether. The reason for choosing the number five million for the primitive population size is that this is approximately the number (an estimated 2-20 million) that Earth supported for millions of years, i.e., it is proved to be a long-term sustainable number (in mathematical terminology, a "feasible" solution to the optimization problem). The reason for choosing the number five million for the technological population size is that it is my opinion that that is about the minimum practical size for a technologically advanced population capable of managing a planet the size of Earth; also, it is my opinion that the "solar energy budget" of the planet can support a population of five million primitive people and five million "industrial" people indefinitely." [279]

Mr. Caldwell's ideas are clues to Alternative Three, a techno representation of Synarchy, a clue to the *real Stargate Conspiracy*. It seems that, there is, indeed, something very mysterious going on all over the planet in terms of shaping the thinking of humanity via books, movies, and cultural themes, but at this point, we understand that most of what is promulgated is lies and disinformation.

What seems to be true is that Organic life on Earth serves as a "transmitter station". As such a transmitter, during times of cataclysm, which are also periods of transition in terms of Time Loops, in the same manner of a quantum wave collapse, what is being "transmitted/observed" determines the "measurement". There are approximately 6 billion human beings on the planet at this moment of transition, most of them contributing to the quantitative transmission. But it is the *qualitative frequency resonance vibration* that will create the template for the New world.

The *quality* of humanity has changed little in the past many millennia. Most human beings are still ruled by fear, hunger and sex in states of misery and chaos. The disinformation machine of the Matrix has worked very hard to keep this state of affairs intact, with great success. The nonsense propagated as "ascension" is evidence of that fact. This is because the Negative hierarchy has been working for millennia to elaborate the control system in such a way that at the "ripe moment" of transition, utilizing the massive release of energy from the enormous numbers of human beings on the planet, the polarization will be induced to take place negatively.

So what does the Matrix want?

---

[279] www.foundationwebsite.org

life force.

In other words, humanity is being set up to be batteries to fuel an "event" that the STS forces hope will result in their aims of being masters of the planet in 4th Density. And this also necessitates the destruction of the Jews whose genetics both inhibit Nephilim absorption, but who also have potential abilities that might manifest upon a change in general frequency of the planet to the detriment of the STS controllers.

> C's: Groups of people represent energy portals in cosmic rather than
> global terms. Light warriors are "connectors" on a cosmic level.
> Transducers of energy of transition of your sector of space/time rather
> like capacitors!
> Now, all of you have value far beyond your own understanding to this
> point. It would be wise to remember this and be cautious. Go from this
> point with joy in this knowledge and...defend it.

We begin to understand why people with *true* Jewish genes are the enemies of the Matrix, and therefore, they are enemies also of the Global Elite.

We begin to understand why members of the "elite" on our planet, having been apprised of the secrets of cyclic cataclysm and the "eighth sphere" immediately went to work to discover the ways and means for their own escape - Alternative 3. We understand why they funded Princeton and other institutions of higher learning, and why they imported all the brains on the planet, to put them to work to devise a method that could be activated at a certain point in time to *transfer perimeters*. We also begin to understand why they have made so concerted an effort to keep the masses of humanity deaf, dumb and blind: they are the sheep who will be the "food for the Moon", the batteries to assist the "Masters of the Game" to escape.

And we see around us, every day, the events that tell us that the C's were correct when they said that the events of Nazi Germany were a "dress rehearsal" for the events prior to the Transition. In 9/11, we had the equivalent of the Reichstag Fire.

Did we learn anything?

Those STS guys are pretty desperate to make sure that *their* reality is the one that manifests at some "nexus point" in the not too distant future. However, we seek to enhance the STO option for ourselves and to make it known that there *is* an option to others who may then choose it also, and who will then assist in manifesting an STO reality at the "branching point" of our possible futures.

Even if we think there is no hope, that no small thing we do can make a difference, let us remember:

Predictions for the future have the form: if this, then this; if not, then that. If the situation, as it really is, is not known, no one will take any action and the predictions for the "future" will be "set". However, if there is a change, perhaps even so small a change as just what we are doing here in sharing this information, it can change everything in a nonlinear way.

We know what *Is*. So, let us become colinear and Act in Favor of our Destiny. It is time to defend it.

Epilogue

So where does our analysis leave us?

It is clear to us from all available evidence that the events of 9/11 were most likely organized and directed by Israeli intelligence agencies with the initial complicity, and later the forced complicity, of their "friends" in the United States, under the influence of their hyperdimensional "gods". The goal was to galvanize the American government to wage a war of aggression and conquest in the Middle East for Israel, *on Israel's terms*, and to garner the support among the American population that would make it possible. However, while some of those involved on the Israeli side believe in the conquering mission of Greater Israel, it appears that the final outcome could well be the annihilation of Israel along with its Arab neighbors. This strong possibility leads us to surmise that the real power behind 9/11, even though it may have an Israeli or Zionist face, is interested in achieving what was left undone at the end of World War Two, the killing of the Jews. Because the entire Middle East region is likely to go the way of a destroyed Israel, it appears that the destruction of the Arabs is also a priority.

We have given historical and genetic evidence that the Ashkenazi Jews are of Aryan descent; they are not Semites at all. Zionism arose among these European or Ashkenazi Jews, and the Zionists showed in their dealing with Hitler that they were quite willing to allow Hitler to cull the herd if he allowed those willing to migrate to Palestine out of Germany.

We also note that although the proclaimed goal of the establishment of Israel was to create a state where Jews would be safe, the actual situation is that there is probably nowhere on Earth where Jews are more in danger, no matter how loudly Zionists scream about anti-Semitism in the rest of the world. In fact, the repeated claims by Israeli government apologists that "a new wave of anti-Semitism is sweeping Europe", while being entirely false, is a calculated maneuver to attempt to silence any opposition to the policies of the state of Israel, policies that, due to their provocative and belligerent nature, may ultimately lead to events that decimate the Middle Eastern Jewish and Arab populations alike. It appears to us that the real goal of the invasion of Iraq, whether or not it was the intention of George Bush when he ordered the attack, was to create chaos in order to divide the country through civil war. Indeed, all the evidence from Iraq as of October 2005 suggests that Iraq is teetering on the brink of just such a civil war.

In September 2005, several media outlets reported that two members of the British covert military group, the SAS, were arrested by Iraqi police and briefly imprisoned before being "rescued" by British troops who used a tank to break into the Iraqi prison where they were being held. The men were detained after they failed to stop at an Iraqi police checkpoint in the southern Iraqi town city of Basra and they shot and killed one policeman and wounded a second when confronted.

The men were found to be wearing full traditional Arab dress. The car they were travelling in was loaded with weapons including allegedly, assault rifles, a light machine gun, an anti-tank weapon, radio gear and a medical kit ('standard' SAS issue according to the BBC). According to at least two reports, the car was also "booby-trapped" with a large quantity of explosives.

The British government quickly spun the story claiming that the men had been handed over to Iraqi "insurgents" thereby necessitating their rescue. This spin was duly parroted by the mainstream press.

What was never addressed was exactly what these men were doing dressed as Iraqis driving what was essentially a car bomb. Not one mainstream media outlet discussed the most obvious explanation: that these were British "agents provocateur" sent into the relatively peaceful town of Basra to carry out a fake Iraqi "insurgent car bombing" in order to further demonise the real Iraqi resistance, and to provide justification for the continued presence of coalition troops in Iraq to fight phantom 'terrorists'. The British government and military said that, given that the men were handed over to Iraqi resistance forces, the Iraqi police cannot be trusted.

You can see where this is going, right?

Next, we have to factor in the alarming vigor and general strangeness that we see in the world's weather and geological conditions over the past few years. Hurricanes, earthquakes, and volcanoes are all rearing their heads in unpredictable ways, increasing in number frequency and violence.

One must remember when looking at the current situation that there are many players with different, overlapping, and, sometimes, conflicting agendas. The hierarchy of power is a pyramid. Only those at the top have a complete understanding of the real plans. Those below are given only as much information as they need to do their jobs. For some, it is the excuse that "we" are running out of oil (all evidence would suggest that this is not the case). For others, it is the necessity for Israel to carve out a permanent place for itself from the shores of the Mediterranean to the banks of the Tigris in modern-day Iraq to act as a front line against "militant Islam", which by all accounts, of course, is the creation of the intelligence agencies of the U.S., Britain and Israel. For others, it is support for Israel to bring on Armageddon and the Second Coming of their Lord. For others it is knowledge of the coming cataclysmic events and a promise of safety if they cooperate. The American people are told that they need the oil to run their SUVs, while those higher up may believe they need the oil to get through the oncoming weather and geological disasters. Both are in support of doing whatever is necessary to secure oil supplies, but their justifications are different. Those wanting oil for the cataclysm believe that many of those who support the war to keep their SUVs on the road will be killed, and the others won't have any roads left on which to drive.

Indeed, it seems that, at the highest level of the pyramid, the prime motivating factor is keeping certain knowledge from humanity – the knowledge that our planet goes through cyclical catastrophes and the knowledge of the true nature of life on earth.

These conflicting agendas and goals easily add to the confusion, if one is not aware of their existence. The war in Iraq can be explained away by the need for oil, and Dick Cheney and his oil industry cronies are then given the blame. Certainly, they carry some of the blame, but when one recognizes the other agendas at play, one sees that there are other players who also have an important, and, sometimes, preponderant role.

Many analysts and commentators recognize the pyramid of power; however, they do not see that it extends into the upper mists of our hyperdimensional reality: the top of the pyramid, and the food chain, does not end with our senses and with the material world. They suffer from what we have called the third man syndrome: the inability to see the reality of the existence of our overlords, due to the social programming of modern society that states categorically and unequivocally that such things are impossible. This shapes their analysis and limits their understanding.

They tell us of a New Order and one world government that will be imposed upon the planet, particularly, the free, American people, through the auspices of the UN or the Bilderbergers, or the Council on Foreign Relations, or the Vatican, or the bankers of the City of London.

However, when one understands the true nature of our reality, it is clear to see that this one world government exists already. It is here. There is nothing left to impose; there are only the windows to be shut, the shutters pulled, and the doors permanently locked. We see this happening with greater restrictions on travel, the growing imposition of biometric identity cards and chips, and with the increased policing and monitoring of the Internet, including the use of search engines such as Google and services such as PayPal to manipulate what can and can't be found or bought and sold. What we see, are burgeoning police states in many countries that still claim to be the last line in the defence of "freedom and Democracy". It doesn't get any more devious than that.

The United States of America, far from being the beacon of freedom and liberty in the world today, is the center of a cancer that seeks to engulf us all. The myth of the free, American people dies hard. The shocks necessary to awaken Americans to their true situation will be proportional to the depth of their illusion – and the illusion is very deep indeed. The facts of the self-enslavement of the American people to the mythology of the land of the free and home of the brave are there for all to see.

As we have demonstrated, the conspiracy within which we are all experimental subjects has been unable to completely cover its tracks. Bits and pieces of the truth *do* come to the surface, only to quickly disappear beneath the flotsam of disinformation. But for the observant spectator, the signs are there.

Daily, we notice that the "Powers That Be" are circling the planet, closing off alternatives, and battening down the hatches for their own survival while they consign the majority of humanity to probable death and destruction. Georges Gurdjieff commented:

> "There are periods in the life of humanity, which generally coincide with the beginning or the fall of cultures and civilizations, when the masses irretrievably lose their reason and begin to destroy everything that has been created by centuries and millenniums of culture. Such periods of mass madness, often coinciding with geological cataclysms, climatic changes, and similar phenomena of a planetary character, release a very great quantity of the matter of knowledge. *This, in turn, necessitates the work of collecting this matter of knowledge which would otherwise be lost.* Thus the work of collecting scattered matter of knowledge frequently coincides with the beginning of the destruction and fall of cultures and civilizations."

It seems that Gurdjieff knew only too well the effect that global upheaval exerts on the illusion seeking majority of humanity. When confronted with the ever widening gap between the reality being presented to them and the facts before their eyes, and at some point unable to reconcile the two, those that attempt to cling to the lie as truth are driven mad.

Yet Gurdjieff also understood the *opportunity* that such an outpouring of fear and madness presents for those that seek the truth to finally see and know it. We cannot ignore the fact that our own civilization at present appears to be on the edge of a precipice. In a very natural way this may act as a "wake up call" to those that have an inner desire to seek and know the truth.

Gurdjieff continued:

> "This aspect of the question is clear. The crowd neither wants nor seeks knowledge, and the leaders of the crowd, in their own interests, try to strengthen its fear and dislike of everything new and unknown. The slavery in which mankind lives is based upon this fear. It is even difficult to imagine all the horror of this slavery. We do not understand what people are losing. But in order to understand the cause of this slavery it is enough to see how

people live, what constitutes the aim of their existence, the object of their desires, passions, and aspirations, of what they think, of what they talk, what they serve and what they worship. Consider what the cultured humanity of our time spends money on; even leaving the war out, what commands the highest price; where the biggest crowds are. If we think for a moment about these questions it becomes clear that humanity, as it is now, with the interests it lives by, cannot expect to have anything different from what it has."

And we see the truth of this in the current state of our planet. Yet truth was rarely, if ever, the domain of the people. Since the dawn of modern civilisation, the truth has been withheld and used to control rather than liberate.

At present, it appears that we are living at the tail end of this grand millennia-long deception. As our world stands on the brink of all out war and cataclysmic destruction, the masses continue to perform the most complex of mental gymnastics to enable the continuance of their illusions about themselves and their world. They will believe anything, as long as it is not the reality that their very existence hangs in the balance. Yet none can claim that justice is not being served, for what can be more equitable than to give that which is asked for? As a result of their insatiable appetite for illusion, it is very likely that the sleeping masses, so enamoured of illusion, will receive exactly what they have asked for - they will be the victims of the greatest deceit at the hands of those , against all logic and reason, in whom they have placed their trust..

Our published books, and the considerable body of information on our web sites, are a result of the collecting of the knowledge described by Gurdjieff and its presentation for the benefit of those that understand its application. While we attempt to facilitate an understanding of the application of this knowledge, we can only go so far. Definite and real steps must be taken by the earnest Truth Seeker in order to make clear that they understand that which they are choosing. If we choose to commit to the search for knowledge, it must be by *doing* something, not by showing a vicarious interest from the sidelines and expecting that knowledge will simply fall into our laps.

As Gurdjieff said:

"But the acquisition or transmission of true knowledge demands great labor and great effort both of him who receives and of him who gives. And those who possess this knowledge are doing everything they can to transmit and communicate it to the greatest possible number of people, to facilitate people's approach to it and enable them to prepare themselves to receive the truth.

"He who wants knowledge must himself make the initial efforts to find the source of knowledge and to approach it, taking advantage of the help and indications which are given to all, but which people, as a rule, do not want to see or recognize.

Knowledge cannot come to people without effort on their own part. And yet there are theories which affirm that knowledge can come to people without any effort on their part, that they can acquire it even in sleep. The very existence of such theories constitutes an additional explanation of why knowledge cannot come to people." [...]

Our goal is to be useful to creation, to create, to *align ourselves with that which is real*, to reject lies and deceit at every turn, both in the world "out there" and within our own beings.

People that consciously believe in and accept lies as truth are making a statement to life, to the *real objective universe*, that they do not desire to exist in such a universe where truth is valued over lies. While very often we do not get what we desire in life, we can be sure that, in the end, we will get back that which we give to life. *For those people that align themselves with illusion, with that which is not real, they will become just that - "a dream in the past".* Those who pay strict attention to objective reality right and left, become the reality of the 'Future'.

The fact is that the conditions of the present day are ideally suited to the acquisition of real knowledge. But why, you might ask, do we consider discovering the closest approximation of the truth of our past to be a worthy occupation?

It's quite simple: in a universe where the observer is as important as the observed, the closer they are in *alignment*, the more order is possible from the side of the universe which - being unimpeded by the barriers of lies - allows creation to manifest unlimited possibilities. When there is great disparity between the observer and the observed, it naturally creates disorder, chaos and destruction due to this conflict. This is why all the efforts of the New Age to have "harmonic convergence" that focus on "peace and brotherhood" - while the true foundation of our civilization is based on lies and greed - has only served to add to the chaos and disorder.

The universe - what is being observed - *is as it is* and operates based on certain principles that are little known despite millennia of claims by this or that group to "know the secrets". When you observe the universe you are, in a certain sense, observing "God". When you attempt to impose your subjective ideas, notions, beliefs, on this vast primal consciousness, you are acting "in opposition" to what IS, to "God". You are therefore, not "in alignment" with the observed, and contribute to the chaos.

It is only in purity, with the mind of the child that does not impose beliefs or subjective opinions on the cosmos, that objectivity can be achieved.

From our position of millennia of cultural and religious brainwashing, the only possibility we have of achieving the mind of the child that observes and does not judge is to strip away as many lies and illusions as possible about our reality as a whole. And the only effect we can have on the future is to "allow it to manifest" *according to our present "observational state"*. That is: objectivity does not limit creation while subjectivity attempts to limit, constrain and inhibit that which is limitless.

Our observational state determines the shape of the future! If it is in alignment with **what is**, then order results. If our "observer status" consists in a "belief" that has nothing to do with what IS, chaos results because of the conflict between what IS and what is "believed" that is not true.

It then follows that if our present observational state is based on ideas that have nothing to do with what may have objectively occurred in the past, then our "now" is delusion, and that creates a future of chaos.

The only thing we have to practice this observation on is the past! We cannot "observe the future" that has not yet manifested. What's more, we cannot observe the now objectively if our observations are based on lies of the past.

Plate 1

Plate 2

Plate 3

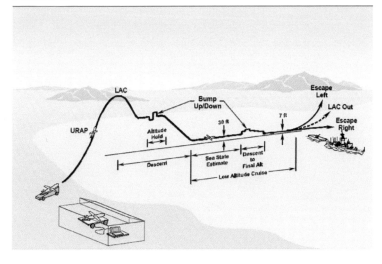

Plate 4

Plate 5

Plate 6

Plate 7

Plate 8

Plate 9

Plate 10

Plate 11

Plate 12

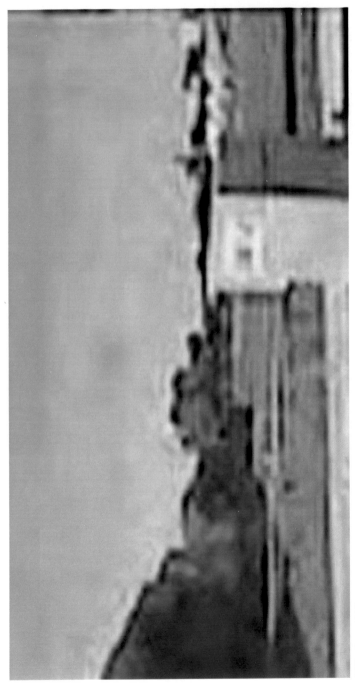

Plate 13

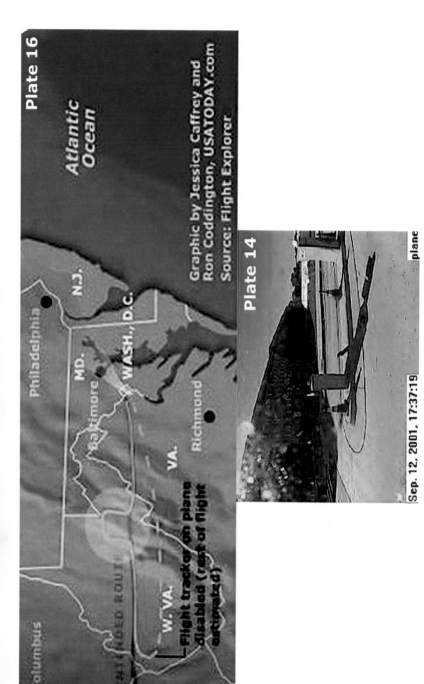

Plate 16

Atlantic
Ocean

Philadelphia

N.J.

Columbus

MD.

Baltimore

WASH., D.C.

VA.

Richmond

W. VA.

INTENDED ROUTE

Flight tracker on plane
disabled (rest of flight
estimated)

Graphic by Jessica Caffrey and
Ron Coddington, USATODAY.com
Source: Flight Explorer

Plate 14

Sep. 12, 2001, 17:37:19   plane

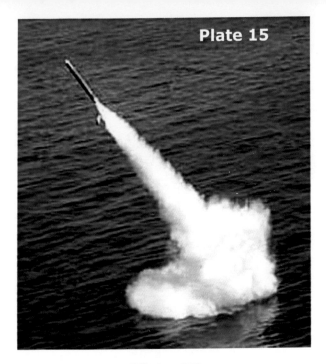

Plate 15

Plate 17

Plate 18

Plate 19

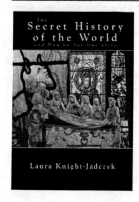

The Secret History of the World and How to Get Out Alive

If you heard the Truth, would you believe it? Ancient civilisations. Hyperdimensional realities. DNA changes. Bible conspiracies. What are the realities? What is disinformation?

The Secret History of The World and How To Get Out Alive is the definitive book of the real answers where Truth is more fantastic than fiction. Laura Knight-Jadczyk, wife of internationally known theoretical physicist, Arkadiusz Jadczyk, an expert in hyperdimensional physics, draws on science and mysticism to pierce the veil of reality. Due to the many threats on her life from agents and agencies known and unknown, Laura left the United States to live in France, where she is working closely with Patrick Rivière, student of Eugene Canseliet, the only disciple of the legendary alchemist Fulcanelli.

With sparkling humour and wisdom, she picks up where Fulcanelli left off, sharing over thirty years of research to reveal, for the first time, The Great Work and the esoteric Science of the Ancients in terms accessible to scholar and layperson alike.

Conspiracies have existed since the time of Cain and Abel. Facts of history have been altered to support the illusion. The question today is whether a sufficient number of people will see through the deceptions, thus creating a counter-force for positive change - the gold of humanity - during the upcoming times of Macro-Cosmic Quantum Shift. Laura argues convincingly, based on the revelations of the deepest of esoteric secrets, that the present is a time of potential transition, an extraordinary opportunity for individual and collective renewal: a quantum shift of awareness and perception which could see the birth of true creativity in the fields of science, art and spirituality. *The Secret History of the World* allows us to redefine our interpretation of the universe, history, and culture and to thereby navigate a path through this darkness. In this way, Laura Knight-Jadczyk shows us how we may extend the possibilities for all our different futures in literal terms.

With over 850 pages of fascinating reading, *The Secret History of The World and How to Get Out Alive* is rapidly being acknowledged as a classic with profound implications for the destiny of the human race. With painstakingly researched facts and figures, the author overturns long-held conventional ideas on religion, philosophy, Grail legends, science, and alchemy, presenting a cohesive narrative pointing to the existence of an ancient techno-spirituality of the Golden Age which included a mastery of space and time: the Holy Grail, the Philosopher's Stone, the True Process of Ascension. Laura provides the evidence for the advanced level of scientific and metaphysical wisdom possessed by the greatest of lost ancient civilizations - a culture so advanced that none of the trappings of civilization as we know it were needed, explaining why there is no "evidence" of civilization as we know it left to testify to its existence. The author's consummate synthesis reveals the *Message in a Bottle* reserved for humanity, including the Cosmology and Mysticism of mankind *Before the Fall* when, as the ancient texts tell us, man *walked and talked* with the gods. Laura shows us that the upcoming shift is that point in the vast cosmological cycle when mankind - or at least a portion of mankind - has the opportunity to regain his standing as *The Child of the King* in the Golden Age.

If ever there was a book that can answer the questions of those who are seeking Truth in the spiritual wilderness of this world, then surely *The Secret History of the World and How to Get Out Alive* is it.

Published by Red Pill Press, Preface by Patrick Rivière (867 pages).

The Wave
(4 Volume Set)

Laura Knight-Jadczyk

With a new introduction by the author and never before published, UNEDITED sessions and extensive previously unpublished details, at long last, Laura Knight-Jadczyk's vastly popular series *The Wave* is available as a Deluxe four book set. Each of the three volumes include all of the original illustrations and many NEW illustrations with each copy comprising approximately 300 pages.

The Wave is an exquisitely written first-person account of Laura's initiation at the hands of the Cassiopaeans and demonstrates the unique nature of the Cassiopaean Experiment.

Laura writes:

I began writing the Wave Series and other articles as a way of collecting excerpts together in general subjects. As I did this, a truly extraordinary thing began to happen. The Cassiopaean Experiment had resulted in transmissions from myself "in the future", and I realized that by doing the suggested research, by digging for the answers based on the clues given me, I was BECOMING myself in the future - a cosmic self. I began to see what I had been trying to convey to myself from this superconscious state. The years of experimental work had created a new circuit wherein it was possible to simply ask a question in my mind about the subject at hand, and the answer would flow through my fingers onto the keyboard. I was often as amazed at what came out as anyone.

The Wave is a term used to describe a Macro-Cosmic Quantum Wave Collapse that produces both a physical and a "metaphysical" change to the Earth and all those residing upon it. It is theorized to be statistically probable sometime in the early 21st century.

Few will deny that at present humanity appears to be perched on the edge of an ever-widening abyss. The Bush administration's "war on terror" seems set to spread further death and destruction around the planet, polarizing and entrenching humanity along religious lines as it does so. The world economy is long past its sell by date, meteorites are raining down across the globe, increasingly frequent and ferocious earthquakes and hurricanes allow no one the comfort of feeling safe. As more and more people begin to awaken to these facts, the need for the truth to be shared as widely as possible grows significantly.

The concept of *The Wave* is vital for anyone wishing to understand the deeper meaning and reality of the human experience and what our very near future may have in store for us. By skillfully collecting and arranging the pieces of the puzzle as provided by the Cassiopaean transmissions, and by coupling them with in depth research and insights from hard-won personal experiences, Laura presents the reader with a compelling and provocative picture of the cognitive, biological, historical and ontological nature of humanity. In *The Wave* books, Laura presents what the Cassiopaeans -We are YOU in the future - have to say about the eventuality of *The Wave* - FROM the future.

We all have a responsibility to equip ourselves with the necessary knowledge to weather the approaching storm – *The Wave* will provide you with that knowledge.

The High Strangeness of Dimensions, Densities and the Process of Alien Abduction

Laura Knight-Jadczyk

Anyone who wants to understand the hyperdimensional reality which is the "home" of alleged aliens, should pick up Laura Knight-Jadczyk's latest book, *The High Strangeness of Dimensions, Densities and the Process of Alien Abduction*. With diligent research and a relentless drive for the facts, Laura strips away the facade of alien abductions masquerading as mind control and mind control masquerading as alien abductions. She then goes on to show how the Evil Elite rulers of the planet have merged, at the highest levels, with the Overlords of the Matrix Control System that underlies the structure of our reality.

Now, after 9-11, the fusion of the two worlds is almost complete. We have little time left, and the Controllers know it and they have made plans...

Those who prefer the nourishment of truth over the poison of New Age myths, those who want a real peek at what is behind the Stargate Conspiracy, should get this book. Today. Read it -- and weep.

For this or other books, please visit us at
www.qfgpublishing.com